AF674773

# WARSAW INDOLOGICAL STUDIES

## VOLUME 1

*Essays in Indian Philosophy, Religion and Literature*

*Edited by*

PIOTR BALCEROWICZ

&

MAREK MEJOR

WARSAW 2002

# *Essays in*
# *Indian Philosophy, Religion and Literature*

*Edited by*

PIOTR BALCEROWICZ
&
MAREK MEJOR

*Assistant Editor*
ANNA TRYNKOWSKA

MOTILAL BANARSIDASS PUBLISHERS
PRIVATE LIMITED • DELHI

*First Indian Edition: Delhi, 2004*



Cover design and photograph: Piotr Balcerowicz
Layout design and fonts, typeset by: Piotr Balcerowicz

Devanāgarī text typeset with
Amrita © *The Amrita package — A Devanâgarî Sanskrit Keyboard Program developed by Piotr Balcerowicz*

ISBN: 81-208-1978-0

MOTILAL BANARSIDASS
41 U.A. Bungalow Road, Jawahar Nagar, Delhi 110 007
8 Mahalaxmi Chamber, 22 Bhulabhai Desai Road, Mumbai 400 026
236, 9th Main III Block, Jayanagar, Bangalore 560 011
120 Royapettah High Road, Mylapore, Chennai 600 004
Sanas Plaza, 1302 Baji Rao Road, Pune 411 002
8 Camac Street, Kolkata 700 017
Ashok Rajpath, Patna 800 004
Chowk, Varanasi 221 001

**NOTICE OF APOLOGY**

The publishers apologize for introducting, without any consultation with and against the will of the editors, significant changes in the cover slip, the layout, design, graphics and typography of the present publication that significantly lower the quality of the final printed product. Also the additional markings on pages 492-497 and 502-523 are due to the publisher's oversight.

*Printed in India*
BY JAINENDRA PRAKASH JAIN AT SHRI JAINENDRA PRESS,
A-45 NARAINA, PHASE-I, NEW DELHI 110 028
AND PUBLISHED BY NARENDRA PRAKASH JAIN FOR
MOTILAL BANARSIDASS PUBLISHERS PRIVATE LIMITED,
BUNGALOW ROAD, DELHI 110 007

# TABLE OF CONTENTS

# PREFACE

We are happy to present a collection of essays in disciplines that are vital to the understanding of the profusion of approaches to reality in India, with the hope that the contributions will deepen our knowledge of cultural heritage of the Indian Subcontinent and of the whole region inspired directly or indirectly by Indian culture, values, rational and religious concepts.

In the era of rapid globalisation, the importance of Indian as well as Oriental studies—stated jointly, in keeping with the maxim of 'the cattle and bulls': **गोबलीवर्दन्याय:** —has become more fundamental than customarily recognised. It is the competence to comprehend manifold cultural phenomena and traditions, none of which are taken to be absolute or privileged, as well as the incentive to pursue basic human cognitive instinct and interpretative faculty, that lie at the core of the humanities.

Although the title explicitly refers only to *Indian philosophy*, *religion* and *literature*, nevertheless the volume also incorporates—in accordance with the maxim: **एकसम्बन्धिदर्शनेऽन्यसम्बन्धिस्मरणम्** —the results of research in ancient and modern culture, religiosity, rationalistic attitudes, axiology, intercultural exchange of ideas, language as communicative groundwork, concepts of personality and society, the notion of freedom and liberation etc.

The issues discussed in the essays pertain to various aspects of Indian poetry and poetics, ranging from Sanskrit *kāvya* (Klaus Karttunen, Lidia Sudyka, Anna Trynkowska) to medieval and modern Hindi poetry (Renata Czekalska, Kunwar Narain, Danuta Stasik). Analysis of personalities of personages of the Vedic pantheon is juxtaposed with comparative approach to Indian mythology (Rahul Peter Das, Paolo Magnone). Examination of different historical and textual layers of Vedic exegesis (Tatiana Y. Elizarenkova, Cezary Galewicz, Joanna Jurewicz, Sven Sellmer) is enriched by reflection on Sanskrit epics and *Purāṇa*s (Horst Brinkhaus, John Brockington, Mary Brockington, Satya Vrat Shastri). Insightful pursuance of various semantic developments (Minoru Hara), combined with Bhartṛhari's philosophy of language and complexities and paradoxes embedded in phraseology (Claus Oetke, Hideyo Ogawa) are interwoven with, on the one hand, the question of rationality and philosophic discourse as reflected in Indian dialectical tradition

(Jonardon Ganeri, Shōryū Katsura, Ernst Prets) and in the Vedāntic hermeneutics (Halina Marlewicz), and with, on the other, the issue of individual freedom against the soteriological background (Marzenna Jakubczak). Historical and social considerations of the concept of democracy and the so-called 'republics' in ancient India (Albrecht Wezler) are included in the separate section of *Artha-śāstra*. A report on Giuseppe Tucci's collection of Sanskrit manuscripts (Francesco Sferra), accompanied by two facsimile manuscript samples, raises the question of the importance of the preservation of intellectual heritage of the humankind. Two papers deal with the problem of dating of Sanskrit philosophical treatises (Piotr Balcerowicz, Marek Mejor).

The essays presented in the volume are the aftermath of the International Conference on Sanskrit and Related Studies to Commemorate the Centenary of the Birth of Stanisław Schayer (8.05.1899–1.12.1941), an eminent Polish Sanskritist and Buddhologist, the founder of the Oriental Institute of Warsaw University. The Conference was held at Warsaw University, between October 7–10, 1999.

The present edition appears as Volume One of the Series *Warsaw Indological Studies* by the arrangement with Motilal Banarsidass Private Limited, Delhi. Our thanks are due to Messrs Jain, the Directors, for their kind co-operation.

We wish to extend our most sincere thanks to Mr. Vijay Tyagi (T&T Julida Co.) and M/S ALLcom Sp. z.o.o. (Gdynia) for their financial support, without which neither the International Conference on Sanskrit and Related Studies held in Warsaw nor the present publication would be possible.

Special thanks are due to our colleague Ms. Anna Trynkowska, who helped in the editorial work over the present volume.

It is our hope that the *Essays in Indian Philosophy, Religion and Literature* should one way or another contribute to a wider acknowledgement of the importance and relevance of the research on the diversity of Indian culture for the better understanding of Occidental intellectual legacy as well, and vice versa. Hopefully, also the reader will find the present volume rewarding: शास्त्रफलं प्रयोक्तरि.

The Editors

# VEDIC STUDIES

# Indra and Śiva / Rudra*

RAHUL PETER DAS

There are several aspects of ancient South Asian culture which in spite of—or maybe rather: because of—lack of clear evidence have often been the subject of speculation in the garb of authoritative pronouncements which at times remind one of theological dogmas. We find such apodictic statements with regard to, for instance, the language and religion of the culture usually known as the Indus Valley civilisation, the subject of foreign words in the Vedic texts[1] and, also, the original nature of the god Śiva.

Especially the last is extremely problematic. We may yet hope to find evidence to better tackle the other problems mentioned, but it seems a hopeless endeavour to try to find *the* nature, or even the original nature, of any of the major, and probably also most of the minor, deities of what is as a rule called Hinduism, whether they be

---

* I am indebted to Ashok Aklujkar, Willem B. Bollée, Harry Falk, Thomas Oberlies and Doris Meth Srinivasan for critical comments.

[1] Cf. DAS (1995) and the response by KUIPER (1995), which WITZEL (1999: n. 2) polemically calls not only 'rather scathing', but also 'well-deserved', without giving any further reasons. In fact, KUIPER's response is dogmatic in that it refuses to consider anything except a linear evolution from Indo-European to Vedic by means of mostly clear-cut phonetic and morphological developments, so that what does not conform to such transparent developments cannot but be 'foreign'. My contention was that it is much more probable that we are dealing with a multi-linguistic reality with different synchronic and diachronic developmental forms of Indo-Iranian and Indo-Aryan spoken side by side, as well as at different times, most probably with interferences and alterations due to varying languages not only of redactors, but also of reciters (especially before any final redaction), so that before labelling anything 'foreign' it is imperative that one first examines all such factors in detail. Since much in this realm can only be conjectured upon, this clearly may result in a situation in which one simply cannot reach any satisfactory conclusion. Of course one can brush all such considerations aside as nonsense and insist that the traditional view is the only one permissible, but that will not make the problem go away. WITZEL's own sophisticated study is heavily influenced by his teacher KUIPER's axioms, and is as such in the final analysis probably going to convince only those already convinced and leave the sceptics as sceptical as they were.

*Essays in Indian Philosophy, Religion and Literature*, pp. 3–23.

deities of the 'great tradition' such as Kṛṣṇa,[2] or of the 'little tradition' such as Dharma / Yama.[3] In some cases we can clearly see how different strands have combined to give one deity, as in the case of the agricultural Śivas of Eastern India,[4] who have little in common, apart from the name connecting them, with the Śiva of the major *Purāṇas*. But in the majority of cases we can only speculate on such processes, which are all the more difficult to analyse because of course once various deities have been identified as aspects of one certain deity a process of amalgamation and approximation is bound to take place. It is thus futile to pick out individual traits and attempt to deduce *the* nature of Śiva from them, or to attempt to arrive at this by etymological speculation on names of the deity.

But even if it does not seem possible to grasp the nature and history of the deity Śiva in its entirety, it is nevertheless possible to unravel individual strands and to follow at least some of these. One of them leads, as is well known, to the Vedic deity Rudra.[5] Now the Vedic deities too, like those of later times, more often than not have a long history, and also exhibit characteristics which justify our seeing either composite deities in them, or else deities of which various aspects have individually developed in such a manner that we cannot simply identify *the* basic nature of the individual deity, unless we have such clear cases as Agni. But even though this must make us wary in making pronouncements on *the* nature or *the* history of Rudra,[6] we can at least say, especially in the light of the studies of Doris SRINIVASAN,[7] that this deity can be followed back to pre-Vedic times, if not in all, then at least in some aspects.

SRINIVASAN has drawn attention to several traits Rudra and the Vedic deities Varuṇa and Mitra, Indra, Vāyu, Agni and Soma have in common.[8] However, it is

---

[2] See, e.g. the literature cited by DAS (1997: 92 f.).

[3] On the latter cf., e.g. DAS (1983) and (1987).

[4] See on these especially SMITH (1999a).

[5] The different names are not problematic in this context, as characterising a potentially terrible and harmful deity (in this case Rudra) as being potentially beneficial (in this case Śiva) is a known means the world over for trying to ensure that the deity does no harm; moreover, there is also surely logophobia at work here, as evinced too in the statement of *Aitareya-brāhmaṇa* 3.34.6 that it is dangerous to even utter the name of Rudra (*...brūyān na rudrêty etasyâiva nāmnaḥ parihṛtyai*).

[6] Some pronouncements of this sort have been collected by GONDA (1978: 88 f.). See also the essay 'Rudra in the Veda' in DANDEKAR (1979: 199–277) (the author of this essay has also indulged several times in speculation not supported by hard facts), as well as IVĂNESCU (1967: 90 f.).

[7] Especially SRINIVASAN (1983) and (1997: 47 ff., 52 ff.).

[8] SRINIVASAN (1983: 545 ff.) and (1997: 48 ff.).

basically particularly the ambivalent nature, both beneficial and harmful, that Rudra and most of these deities share; in some cases there are a few others of a general nature, such as omniscience, association with the North, etc. It is only with Indra that Rudra shares characteristics which are truly personal, such as being fair-lipped,[9] golden-armed and decked with bow and arrows;[10] the probably most important similarity is, however, the close association of both with the Maruts.[11] One can add more traits.[12] Thus, apart from Agni, Soma and the Maruts, all closely associated with Indra, Rudra seems to be the only deity who is characterised by the *Vajra*,[13] Indra's weapon *par excellence*.[14] Both Rudra and Indra are called *puru-rūpa-*, or multiform.[15] It is also interesting that Rudra has a special connection with healing in

---

[9] Rudra, though he can be terrible, is in fact a beautiful god (of reddish colour; cf., e.g. OBERLIES (1998: 213)), a trait which he shares with the later Śiva. The beauty of Śiva is well known even in the folklore of at least some contemporary Bengali Muslims; sẹe SEN'GUPTA (1996: 164).

[10] Note in this context also *Atharva-veda-saṁhitā* (*Paippalāda*) 2.36, which shows quite clearly that different afflictions were taken to be arrows shot at humans by non-human entities.

[11] SRINIVASAN (1983: 547); DONIGER (1993: 112 f.).

[12] See especially DONIGER (1993: 112 ff.). Attention may in this context also be drawn to NIGŪṘHĀNANDA (1996: 75 ff.), where various similarities between Indra and Rudra / Śiva in the *Veda* are discussed. Interestingly, the author holds Rudra to be the most important deity in the *Ṛg-veda-saṁhitā* (p. 75). The affinity between Rudra and Indra has also been noted by AKHOURI (1993: 19 f.).

[13] On this weapon see especially FALK (1994a), with further references.

[14] Rudra is *vajra-bāhu-* in *Ṛg-veda-saṁhitā* 2.33.3. Note also the Name 'Vajrahasta' of Śiva in the *Śiva-nāma-sahasra* according to the *Larger Petersburg Dictionary* of Otto Böhtlingk and Rudolph Roth (PW). According to *Atharva-veda-saṁhitā* (*Śaunakīya*) 4.28.6 Bhava and Śarva are characterised by a *vájra-*; in verse 2 they are called 'the best shooters of arrows among archers' (*iṣu-bhṛ́tām ásiṣṭhau*), and in verse 3 'thousand-eyed' (on thousand-eyed Rudra, Bhava and Śarva, cf. also SRINIVASAN (1997: 39)) 'slayers of Vṛtra' (*sahasrâkṣáu vṛtra-háṇā*). The characteristics are reminiscent of Indra (though not exclusively his characteristics), but Bhava and Śarva (the latter already Indo-Iranian, with an Iranian parallel; see MAYRHOFER (1996: 621)) have Śivaitic associations (cf. on this also ZEHNDER (1999: 77)), and are indeed often regarded as names of Śiva. The commentary attributed to Sāyaṇa says on 4.28.1: *bhavaty utpadyate 'smāt sarvaṁ jagad iti bhavaḥ. śṛṇāti hinasti sarvam anta-kāla iti śarvaḥ. bhavaś ca śarvaś ca bhavâśarvāv aṣṭa-mūrtīnāṁ madhye paramêśvarasya dve mūrtī* … . Note how the commentary elucidates the ambivalent nature of the deity.

[15] SRINIVASAN (1997: 28).

the Vedic texts,[16] and that according to the classical Āyurvedic tradition[17] it is Indra who divulges medical lore to humans;[18] this is apart from the fact that Indra several times is credited with individual deeds of healing in Vedic texts.[19] Moreover, some scholars maintain that the white bull, which is connected particularly with Śiva, originally was connected with Indra, this function going back to Indo-Iranian times, as Iranian parallels are taken to show.[20]

A further point of contact is the destruction of the strongholds of enemies. Indra is of course known as *purandará-* since Vedic times. In post-Vedic times, however, it is Śiva who is prominent as such a destroyer, and there is a well-known myth according to which he destroys the three strongholds of the Asuras,[21] thus gaining epithets such as *tri-purântaka-*, *tri-purâri-*, *tri-pura-ghna-* and so on. Our dictionaries list *purandara-* as one of his names too. The only other deity to whom this epithet is applied is, to my knowledge, Agni, namely in Vedic times.[22] Agni, however, shares many characteristics both with Rudra[23] and with Indra[24]; this has already been remarked upon above.

---

[16] OBERLIES (1998: 214) even writes: 'In Rudra haben wir den "Heilgott" des ṛgvedischen Pantheons vor uns.'

[17] See the first chapters of the *Suśruta-saṁhitā*, *Caraka-saṁhitā*, *Aṣṭâṅga-hṛdaya* and *Aṣṭâṅga-saṅgraha*.

[18] The chain of transmission presupposed by the medical texts cited is: Brahman—Dakṣa / Prajāpati—Aśvins—Indra—humans.

[19] Some instances are mentioned by SÖHNEN (1991: 72); add *Ṛg-veda-saṁhitā* 2.15.7.

[20] WIDENGREN (1965: 47) and (1983: 38). WIDENGREN bases his observations on Indra on CHARPENTIER (1911: 41–43). According to CHARPENTIER, the bull was not originally Śiva's beast, but has been transferred to him from Indra (p. 43).

[21] These are later transformed into a single location named Tripura. On the legend of the destruction of Tripura see also the interesting observations of DESHPANDE (1999: 114 f.).

[22] E.g. in *Ṛg-veda-saṁhitā* 1.109.8 (together with Indra: *púrandarā śíkṣataṁ vajra-hastâsmā̃ṁ indrâgnī avataṁ bháreṣu*) and 6.16.14 (*tám u tvā dadhyáṅṅ ṛ́ṣiḥ putrá īdhe átharvaṇaḥ / vṛtra-háṇaṁ purandaráṁ*; Agni is mentioned by name in verse 13: *tvā́m agne* … ).

[23] Commenting on *Vājasaneyi-saṁhitā* 11.33 of the Mādhyandina recension (= *Ṛg-veda-saṁhitā* 1.109.8ab), Mahīdhara says that Agni here refers to Rudra in his role of destroyer of the three strongholds: *purandaraṁ rudra-rūpeṇâsura-sambandhināṁ trayāṇāṁ purāṇāṁ vidārayitāram*. (He sees a reference to the same myth in his commentary on *yā́ te agne 'yaḥśayā́ tanū́r várṣiṣṭhā gahvareṣṭhā́* in 5.8, but does not mention Rudra.) In this context cf. also OBERLIES (1998: 215, n. 317): 'Bereits der ṛgvedische Rudra teilt Züge seines Wesens mit Agni. Und in nach-ṛgvedischer Zeit ist die "Identität" von Rudra und Agni gängige Vorstellung.' See too AKHOURI (1993: 20).

Moreover, though various gods are or have been associated with fertility, it is particularly these two who are thus characterised. Indra was intimately connected with fertility in ancient times, a trait still to be observed in the maypole-like Indra-pole.[25] As to the connection of Śiva with fertility, this hardly has to be drawn attention to.[26] The Indra-pole is often connected with the *axis mundi* and/or the Tree of Life.[27] Some scholars also postulate a connection between phallic symbols and the *axis mundi*,[28] which of course is interesting in connection with Śiva.

I have in previous publications already drawn attention to some of these parallels and raised the question whether such correspondences might not be signs of a more intrinsic connection between Indra and Rudra.[29] In this context I also pointed to the connections of both deities with ancient Indian sodalities;[30] this includes the special relationship not only the sodalities, but also both Rudra and Indra are said to have to dogs.[31] These sodalities also seem to have had an ambivalent nature,[32] in which

---

[24] OBERLIES (1998: 358 ff.) has developed an ingenious theory to explain the close connection of Agni with Indra on the one hand, Varuṇa on the other. This theory, which has far-reaching potential consequences for our understanding of Ṛgvedic society, will, of course, have to be examined further. See also p. 249, n. 487 and p. 439, n. 191.

[25] On this characteristic of Indra see above all the rich data in MEYER (1937). Cf. also OBERLIES (1998: 314 f.), JAIN (1995).

[26] This trait most probably greatly facilitated the amalgamation of various agricultural gods with Śiva.

[27] See on this subject e.g. BROCKINGTON (1995), GONDA (1978: 340 f. and 375), IRWIN (1990: 51, 56 and 61), TRIPATHI (1977). On the *axis mundi* see also OBERLIES (1998: 615) ('Weltenbaum'), GONDA (1966: 43 f.), WITZEL (1996: 532 ff.), DAS (1992: 410, n. 154). A critique of theories linking Aśokan pillars, the Indra-pole and the *axis mundi* is to be found in GUPTA (1980: 318–320, 341).

[28] Cf. DAS (1991: 747, n. 32).

[29] See DAS (1991: 752 f.).

[30] See on this relationship particularly the material presented by BOLLÉE (1981) and FALK (1986). Both have referred to later, even modern groups continuing the practices of the ancient sodalities; add to these the observations in DAS (1987: 248) and (1991: 757 f.) (note also—as an addendum to BOLLÉE (1981: 178 ff.)—that there was a kingdom of the Mallas in the Bengal–Bihar border region too). On some of the questions especially FALK (1986) leads to see DAS (1991: 753, n. 53).

[31] Cf. DAS (1991: 752, n. 52). Note in this connection that the epithet *śvá-pati-* 'dog-master' in the *Yajur-veda* mantra: *námaḥ śvábhyaḥ śvá-patibhyaś ca* … (*Vājasaneyi-saṁhitā* 16.28; *Taittirīya-saṁhitā* 4.5.4.2; *Maitrāyaṇī-saṁhitā* 2.9.5; *Kāṭhaka-saṁhitā* 17.13) could pertain either to Rudra or to the leader of the Vrātyas. As regards Indra, it may be brought to mind that *sārameyá-* 'descendant of [Indra's bitch] Saramā' as an

context ritual killing and cannibalism might have played a role.[33] It is especially this connection with sodalities which offers us more material for tackling the problem of the relation between Indra and Rudra.

In a recent paper[34] Thomas OBERLIES has examined the early history of the Pāśupatas and come to some most interesting conclusions. According to his analysis, various aspects in the rituals of the Pāśupatas originate in the practices of warriors, the one most striking being the provocation and insulting of enemies before giving battle.[35] OBERLIES concludes that the Pāśupatas, though intrinsically connected with Rudra / Śiva, have taken up certain traits from Indra; these also include the use of deception or illusion (*māyā-*), which is a known characteristic of Indra.[36] Indra is even portrayed as a sort of proto-Pāśupata. But OBERLIES also points to the warrior nature of Śiva, particularly in the *Mahā-bhārata*.[37] In his analysis,[38] Śiva has here usurped the

---

epithet for the dog is in the oldest texts used particularly for the two dogs of Yama; this seems an indication of Indra's connection with death too.

[32] Cf. FALK (1986: 64 f.).

[33] On the possibility of (ritual) cannibalism mentioned by DAS (1991: 753, n. 53), see also the data on cannibalism given by WEZLER (1992: 303) (cf. too DURT (1998), where the Chinese Buddhist notion of offering one's flesh as an act of filial piety is traced to Indian Buddhist notions, but also, on pp. 76–77=217–216, to the use of human flesh, especially of one's kin, as medicine in China). As regards the possible killing of the leader of the sodality, it is worth examining whether there is any relation with the supposed parallelism of leader and moon, ending with the execution of the leader, observed in some cultures (cf. LOMMEL (1978: 378 ff.)); note in this context also the connection of the *sabhā-* with death (cf. OBERLIES (1998: 424 f.)). Of special interest in this connection is the Śūlagava ritual (cf. FALK (1986: 60 ff., 136)), especially because according to GONDA (1980: 437) the bull (GONDA: 'ox') was originally Rudra, with whom, along with Indra, the leader—considered dead (see FALK (1986: 40, 70))—of the sodality seems to have been identified (cf. FALK (1986: 18, 59 f., 64)). On human sacrifice and cannibalism in the *Männerbund* cf. also AGUILAR I MATAS (1991: 94).

[34] OBERLIES (forthcoming).

[35] This practice is well known not only from ancient India, but from other cultures too. A most graphic illustration is found in the Hollywood film *Braveheart* in a scene in which the Scottish forces expose their genitals and buttocks to the opposing English army.

[36] See on Indra's *māyā-* also AGUILAR I MATAS (1991: 56 f.).

[37] On this warrior nature see SARKAR (1974: 120 ff.).

[38] In the course of this we also find interesting references to the battle as the ultimate self-sacrifice. See in this connection HEESTERMAN (1996: 133 ff.) on self-sacrifice as the consummation of the sacrifice (on HEESTERMAN's allusion, in this context, to the *tīrtha-* on pp. 137 f., see especially DAS (1997: 12–18)), also FALK (1986: 37, 43).

characteristics of Indra in the course of the supersession of the latter's cult by the former's, even to the epithet of Indra *bala-pramathana-*, 'pulveriser of Bala / Vala', being applied to Śiva in *Pāśupata-sūtra* 2.25. This is, in his opinion, because of reminiscences of ancient traits of Rudra,[39] which easily allowed such a transference. However, one could just as well argue that the similarities with Indra are due precisely to a primary, and not a secondary, identity existing between the two.[40]

In his study, OBERLIES has implicitly, if not explicitly, drawn attention to a facet of South Asian culture which is not generally taken note of in the field of Indian studies, perhaps because of their primary focus on literary documents stemming mostly from a certain group of individuals not very much involved with this facet. I am of course referring to the concept of heroism as a path for humans to follow, a path which Axel MICHAELS has labelled *vīrya-mārga-*,[41] and which may seem strange to many of us today because in modern times the concept of fighting and warfare as an intrinsic part of culture has to a large extent disappeared in the West.[42] Now fighting traditions are often, the world over, associated not only with religious concepts, but also with purity, asceticism or celibacy, which makes it *a priori* improbable that this was not the case in ancient South Asia too. Unfortunately, little is known on this subject; our information on, for instance, warrior ascetic groups is too recent to be very helpful. The matter is nevertheless important because such sodalities, too, were of course known for their violent lifestyle and unisexual organisation.

In this connection a publication by Harry FALK[43] deserves to be noticed, for in it attention is drawn to the depiction of roaming bands of aggressive armed Brahmins in later Vedic literature. According to the author, this depicts actual conditions

---

[39] One could in this connection point too to Śiva's connections with the *rudrâkṣa-* fruits, which seem to be reminiscences of the *akṣa-*s or dice used in ancient ritual dice games (cf. SYED (1998: 421–424)), also by the violent sodalities connected with both Rudra and Indra.

[40] It must be emphasised that these remarks apply only to the data on the Pāśupatas. They should not be generalised, and especially not applied to cases in which Indra's characteristics have been intentionally transferred to Śiva, an example of this being—if JAMISON (1996) is correct—the description of the burning of Kāma by Śiva in Kālidāsa's *Kumāra-sambhava*.

[41] MICHAELS (1998: 299): 'Obgleich weniger beachtet ist der Heroismus—man könnte ihn *vīryamārga* nennen—ebenso bedeutsam wie die drei anderen klassischen Heilswege (*mārga*) des Wissens, der Hingabe und der Taten.' Cf also the remarks on *vīra-bhakti* by SMITH (1999b: 395 ff.).

[42] Cf. on this subject also OBERLIES (1998: 427–429).

[43] FALK (1994b).

pertaining at the time of the supersession of the Vedic sacrificial religion by other forms of religious expression, forcing many Brahmins no longer able to earn their living as sacrificers to seek other means of livelihood.[44] At the same time the parallels to and connections with the older Vrātyas are pointed out, as also those with the Pāśupatas, including the use of stratagems of deception and illusion, which of course bring to mind the *māyā-* of Indra. Whether FALK's deductions be valid or not, they show the need for more detailed research on the connections between wandering mendicants and ascetics, and sodalities. In this context attention may be drawn to the contention of Willem B. BOLLÉE[45] that ancient Indian orders of religious mendicants were linked with the sodalities of old. What is of especial interest is BOLLÉE's contention that mendicant groups were linked with the sodalities also, and especially, in their role as representatives of the dead on earth.

This latter is, however, one of the traits that seem to mark various sodalities amongst Indo-European peoples outside India.[46] This, as well as the ubiquitous role of dogs in the context of such sodalities (and also dicing),[47] makes us take a look at

---

[44] On the upheaval FALK refers to, leading to the outer sacrifice being discarded in favour of the inner, see also HEESTERMAN (1997). However, see also the criticism levelled by FALK at the suppositions HEESTERMAN's analyses are based on, especially his remarks that HEESTERMAN looks almost solely for explanations situated in the field of the phenomenology of religion, so that his explanations of the sacrifice do not consider its practical aspects, i.e. disregard the fact that a sacrifice is also, and probably primarily, about concrete benefits, including power and might, and not only religious concepts (FALK (1986: 190 f.)). A similar criticism of HEESTERMAN's methods is to be found in LARIVIERE (1997). On FALK's own explanation of the upheaval HEESTERMAN refers to see FALK (1986: 193 ff.) (note the correction slip with text to be inserted on p. 193!).

[45] BOLLÉE (1981: 185 ff.). On the Vrātyas and their influence on Buddhism and Jainism see also BOLLÉE (forthcoming), which has, however, and unfortunately, not utilised FALK (1986).

[46] I may here remark that DE JONG (1995: 17) has commented sceptically on an Indo-Iranian *Männerbund*. However, the evidence collected by now should lay such scepticism to rest.

[47] Cf., e.g. the literature cited by FALK (1986: 18–21); see also pp. 16, 28 f., 41 f., 62, 110 and 195, and MCCONE (1987). WHITE (1988–1989: 295 ff.) draws attention to the demonic role of the dog and its connection with death, especially, but not only, with reference to ancient India, in his analysis of the significance of the killing of a dog during the horse sacrifice, the *Aśva-medha* (handily summarised on pp. 300 ff.). On the dog in Indo-European, particularly Germanic, belief see also GÜNTERT (1987), specially cols. 484 ff. on the dog as a demoniac creature, its connection with death and its role as the soul of a departed person.

non-Indian parallels to what we have so far seen.[48] In this connection particular attention must be paid to the remarkable parallels between ancient Indian and ancient Irish sodalities that the studies of Kim McCONE have unearthed.[49] The many similarities are extremely intriguing, but I shall not go into them here.[50] What

---

[48] That sodalities calling themselves 'dogs' are no purely Indo-European phenomenon is evinced by Carolyn NIETHAMMER's description of young males of the Southern Ute tribe in the USA who lived outside the camp in an aggressive band, calling themselves 'dogs', practising fighting skills and also raping women (I have access only to the German version of NIETHAMMER's *Daughters of the Earth*, namely NIETHAMMER (1992), where the passage mentioned is found on p. 306). Unfortunately, such phenomena from the non-Indo-European sphere are nearly totally *terra incognita* to me, but this one example does show clearly that we should not confine our deliberations on this matter solely to Indo-European peoples.

[49] See on the Old Irish sodalities, the *fian*, especially Chapter 9 (pp. 203–232: 'Druids and Outlaws') of McCONE (1991), and McCONE (forthcoming).

[50] Attention may be drawn to the reference by McCONE in the latter paper to the iconographic representation of the old Gallic god Cernunnos and its connection with Celtic sodalities. Now SRINIVASAN (1984: 81 f.) has concluded that the Indian *paśu-páti-* is not connected with wild animals, whereas according to HOFSTETTER (1980) he is, at least by origin, connected with them only as a cruel hunter, i.e. insofar as he hunts and kills them (pp. 139, 141). But these views are not accepted by all. In this connection we must, of course, also draw attention to theories seeing a primary connection of Rudra / Śiva with the so-called 'proto-Śiva' depictions (with wild animals) on Harappan seals. However, the 'Lord of Animals' (i.e. wild animals) is a concept found in many cultures (cf., e.g. HOFSTETTER (1980), who differentiates between him and the *paśu-páti-* on pp. 27, 139, 141), so that concrete links between known or postulated occurrences in two different cultures can only be taken to be decisively proved if more than the occurrence of this concept can be shown to be common. This would actually be the case as regards Cernunnos and Rudra / Śiva (if *paśu-páti-* be taken to refer to wild animals too) because of the connection of both with sodalities in an Indo-European context, thus serving to further substantiate the rejection of the hypothetical connection between Rudra / Śiva and the Harappan seals by SRINIVASAN (1984: 78–83) (cf. also SRINIVASAN (1983: 543)); in any case, we still have only apodictic statements, but no concrete evidence permitting us to link Harappan representations with specific later Indian deities, so that it is amazing how naïvely the labels 'proto-Śiva' and 'Yogin' continue to be used in this context. (Additional data supplementing HOFSTETTER (1980) has, incidentally, been listed by BUDDRUSS (1982).) On the *paśu-páti-* in connection with the Vrātyas cf. FALK (1986: 59 f.). Attention may in this context also be drawn to WATKINS (1999: 12 ff.), where it is argued that it is possible that there was an Indo-European Stag God, amongst whose descendants Cernunnos too would have to figure.

I would like, rather, to highlight is the important role one-eyedness plays in connection with the Celtic tradition of warriors and sodalities, and the close connections this has with cyclopean notions among other Indo-European peoples, in which connection the Germanic Oðin deserves special mention, as he is not only the leader of a fierce host, but also of ambivalent nature and often characterised as one-eyed. On the Indian side, HARRY FALK[51] has drawn attention to the connection of one-eyedness with death and destruction, and of the characterisation of Rudra as 'one-eyed' in the *Mahā-bhārata*.

But the single eye is more often than not taken to be situated in the forehead. Moreover, MCCONE[52] draws attention to the description of the first distortion that came upon Cú Chulainn, the chief hero of the Ulster cycle, in which 'he sucked one eye into his head' and 'the warrior's moon arose out of his forehead.' This, together with the proposed etymology of the Greek ὁ κύκλωψ as 'flaming-eyed' (the ancient Indian equivalent would be **śuklā́kṣ-*), cannot but remind us of the characterisation of Śiva by both a destructive eye in, and a moon on, his forehead.[53] In this connection attention may also be drawn to the often overlooked fact that already the Vedic Rudra is characterised by a knot of hair on his head,[54] this characteristic too thus not being something that need be a later development in Śiva.

In the light of all we have seen so far, especially the ambivalent character of Rudra / Śiva and his connection with the martial sodalities, I think there can be no doubt that these characteristics of Śiva are the remnants of an inheritance dating

---

[51] FALK (1986: 109).

[52] MCCONE (forthcoming).

[53] SRINIVASAN (1997: 156) sees the third eye as a symbol of supernatural power and knowledge; according to her explanation it moreover 'confers upon the possessor not only the capacity for seeing the supranormal but also a "memory" for understanding what is seen'. Cf. also pp. 173 ff., as well as her remarks on *virūpâkṣa-*, which is a known epithet of Śiva, as 'odd-eyed' (p. 208). In the later literature it is not only Śiva who has an eye on his forehead, but also other deities, especially, but not only, if associated with him. This is, of course, especially true of his consort, who also shares his ambivalent nature. Even the Bengali Snake Goddess, who like Śiva has an ambivalent character (cf. DAS (1999: 113 ff.)), and has secondarily been associated with this deity (partly in an incestuous relationship), has a third eye in the middle of her forehead (cf. DAS (1999: 117 f.)).

[54] Cf. OBERLIES (1998: 213, n. 304): 'Charakteristisch für ihn ist auch seine in Schneckenhausform gewundene Haartracht—diese hat er mit Pūṣan gemeinsam.' The illustration of the Vedic Rudra (the third illustration in the plates at the beginning of the book), drawn according to the descriptions in the relevant texts, in BHAṬṬĀCĀRYA (1984) is also very interesting in this context.

back to pre-Vedic Indo-European times, all the more so since MCCONE also points to the nakedness of warrior sodalities,[55] which must remind us of the common descriptions of Śiva. Our conclusions are also in keeping with the insight, gaining more and more ground, that much, possibly even most, of that which in so-called later Hinduism, and most probably also Buddhism and Jinism, goes back to Vedic times is not a descendant of the known Vedic sacrificial ritual, but of other Vedic sources.[56] Indeed, in a recent study Nicholas J. ALLEN expressly states that, 'as many have realised, the Vedic texts relate to only a small part of the culture of the Vedic period,'[57] without deeming it necessary to comment further upon this point, obviously regarding it as a commonplace by now.[58]

This must, of course, bring us back to the problem of the relationship between Indra and Rudra. It is, after all, Indra who is not only the warrior, but also the martial leader *par excellence*. In this he has parallels to many figures in the mythology of other Indo-European peoples, including Oðin, who, however, also has similarities with Rudra.[59] In this context mention must also be made of *Bṛhat-saṁhitā* 58.42, where Mahendra is characterised not only by a *Vajra* in his hand, but also by a third eye, placed transversely on his forehead.[60] Mahendra is usually an appellation of Indra, and here Indra is clearly meant,[61] for, even though there are

---

[55] See on nakedness also WIDENGREN (1965: 25).

[56] MICHAELS (1998) remarks succinctly: 'Das Erbe der vedischen Religion im Hinduismus wird im allgemeinen überschätzt' (p. 56). See in this regard particularly HEESTERMAN (1997), who opines that even though the sacrificial ritual 'purposely broke away from the mainstream,' which gave rise to later Hinduism (p. 49), it is this very rupture that was instrumental in shaping the latter. (I may incidentally remark that HEESTERMAN (1997) voices much admiration for and utilises several theories of Madeleine Biardeau; on these see, however, DAS (1991: 759 ff., also pp. 741 ff.).) BOLLÉE (forthcoming: 4) expressly connects worshippers of Mahādeva, an appellation also—and particularly—used for Śiva, with non-Vedic Aryans. Cf. also FALK (1986: 194 f.), ALLEN (1999: 25 f.), and—on the problem of '-isms' in the South Asian Context in general—the 'Introduction' to OBEROI (1994).

[57] ALLEN (1999: 25).

[58] FALK (1997: 70): 'We do not know exactly where Ṛgvedic religion matured before it appears in India, we do not know how far back it dates in antiquity, we do not know the extent to which it was shared by the people outside the clans of priests and kings.'

[59] Cf. GONDA (1978: 89), FALK (1986: 14 f., 18).

[60] *śuklaś catur-viṣāṇo dvipo mahêndrasya vajra-pāṇitvam /*
*tiryag lalāṭa-saṁsthaṁ tṛtīyam api locanaṁ cihnam //*

[61] As, for instance, correctly seen by DONIGER (1993: 113).

sporadic cases in which Viṣṇu and Śiva too are referred to thus, this cannot be the case here, as the verse expressly mentions the four-tusked elephant too, and this is Indra's animal. In the light of what we have seen so far, this characterisation of Indra as having three eyes is extremely intriguing.[62]

If now Rudra / Śiva exhibits ancient, pre-Indo-Aryan Indo-European characteristics, has much in common with Indra,[63] but is, in contrast to the latter, not perceptible from ancient non-Indian sources, then it must very seriously be considered whether here we might not have a development similar to that shown to have occurred in the case of Bṛhaspati by Hanns-Peter SCHMIDT,[64] i.e. that Rudra, like Bṛhaspati, represents the individual development of what was originally an aspect of Indra.[65] Perhaps an analysis of the oldest Vedic texts in this light may unearth evidence for such a development as a process still ongoing.[66]

It must, however, be pointed out that the data at our disposal, even though it strongly suggests an affirmative answer to the possibility broached, nevertheless does not allow us to make unequivocal statements on the previous identicalness of Indra and Rudra. This is not only because the pre-Vedic nature of Indra himself is not fully clear,[67] but also because some scholars are of the opinion that the early Vedic texts bear witness to a struggle between a cult centred on Indra and one centred on Varuṇa and Mitra, from which the former emerged victorious, eclipsing

---

[62] BHATT (1981–1982: 558) is so puzzled by this characterisation of Indra that he tries to explain it away by writing: 'Possibly, the transverse eye represents his thousand eyes.'

[63] It is peculiar that in the diagram on p. 242 of SÖHNEN (1997), in which the connections of Indra with other Vedic gods are shown, Rudra is absent.

[64] SCHMIDT (1968).

[65] In this context it is interesting to note that in the *Caraka-saṁhitā* (*Cikitsā-sthāna* 1.4.4) Indra is called *amara-guru-* (*tān indraḥ sahasra-dṛg amara-gurur abravīt*); *amara-guru-*, *deva-guru-*, *vibudha-guru-* and the like are usually epithets of Bṛhaspati. Is this passage a remnant of an older period? Or is *guru-* here used in the sense of 'leader'? The passage 1.4.4 could be relatively ancient, because in it we have the word *aśasta-* 'something unwished for / unwanted' (*grāmyo hi vāso mūlam aśastānāṁ*), which according to our dictionaries is otherwise found only a few times in old Vedic texts. However, this word is actually found several times in the classical medical texts, so that its evidence ultimately does not seem to count for much.

[66] Such evidence might be contained, for instance, in *Ṛg-veda-saṁhitā* 1.114 if FLOYD (forthcoming) is correct in analysing this hymn as reusing ancient Indo-European poetic elements to build up the image of Rudra in a new manner, but on ancient lines.

[67] Cf. on this, e.g. THIEME (1971: 404 ff.).

and usurping many characteristics of the latter, while at the same time there was an amalgamation of various traits of the two cults.[68] This matter will have to be discussed, especially because of the various traits Rudra shares with Varuṇa and, to a lesser extent, Mitra. What will also have to be considered are the several postulated instances of the adjectival qualification *rudrá-* being applied to various deities in the Vedic texts, all of which are according to more recent views actually to be regarded as nouns referring to the god Rudra,[69] as well as the role played by Viṣṇu, who is not an early Vedic deity, but nevertheless sporadically appears as the leader of the Vrātyas,[70] and whose problematic relationship with Indra, with whom he shares several traits,[71] is still in need of detailed study. Obviously, there is still much that needs to be done.[72]

I may here adduce my opinion that the sooner this matter becomes the subject of serious scholarly investigation, the better, for the relationship between Indra, Śiva / Rudra and Agni has already become the centrepiece of an elaborate theory by the Oriyan scholar Bansidhar BISWAL, who, in the process claiming that 'Indra had come from aboriginal stock,'[73] tries to show that the Vedic texts actually describe a pre-Aryan cult of Śiva, which we could perhaps best characterise as Yogic-Tantric, intrinsically linked with Indra.[74] We learn that 'Indra was the protector of pre-Vedic Śiva cult during the age of Vedic India,'[75] and that 'Rudra was the Power within

[68] In this context I would like to draw particular attention to AGUILAR I MATAS (1991), without commenting on the theories propounded there. More recently, OBERLIES (1998: 333–362) (see also p. 557 under 'Asuras') has developed a detailed systematic theory based on the notion of two different cults, but on lines different from AGUILAR I MATAS (1991).

[69] Cf. MAYRHOFER (1996: 453).

[70] See, e.g. FALK (1986: 18 and 55 f.).

[71] Cf. on this especially FALK (1987: 127 ff.), also SCHNEIDER (1974: 404 ff.), TRIPATHI (1977: 1008), SÖHNEN (1997: 241). According to OBERLIES (1998: 219 ff.), Viṣṇu is Indra's hunchbacked dwarfish helper and as such a parallel to similar hero's helpers in Germanic mythology. In this, OBERLIES continues the line of thought of his teacher (and my teachers' teacher) Paul THIEME; in contrast to OBERLIES, however, I do not think that we can decide the matter one way or the other without far more exhaustive research into the subject.

[72] In this connection one might also want to examine whether *-(d)ra-* of *índra-* and *rudrá-* is of any special significance.

[73] BISWAL (1988: 42).

[74] BISWAL (1988: 37 ff.).

[75] BISWAL (1988: 42).

Śiva and Indra.'[76] This theory is obviously to be seen in the context of attempts in the eastern part of the Indian subcontinent to reinterpret history on indigenous, that is non-Aryan, lines, but differently from attempts current in southern India.[77] The problem of Indra and Śiva / Rudra has, therefore, potential implications for domestic cultural conflicts and politics in India too.[78]

---

[76] BISWAL (1988: 44).

[77] On such developments see DAS (forthcoming).

[78] It was only after I had completed my investigation that the study of KERSHAW (2000) examining Oðin and the (Indo-)Germanic sodalities / *Männerbünde* appeared. It deals with much that has been mentioned above (on necrophagy and cannibalism in this context see pp. 179, 207 f.), including the connections between Oðin and Rudra. This work contains a mass of interesting and important data (much more than above) skilfully interwoven, though with such confidence that one does at times ask oneself whether this might not be too great. The one-eyedness of Rudra and Oðin was according to KERSHAW originally metaphorical: the leader of the sodality was chosen by dicing, namely by *Kali*, the worst throw appearing when the player had only one dicing-nut left. Since he becomes the leader and at the same time also Oðin or Rudra (or their homologues among other peoples), these are called 'one-eyed'. In the book it is actually stated, however, that the leader becomes the one-eyed god because he is chosen by the one-eyed throw and because the one-eyed god also enters into him (p. 253: 'The leader is chosen by the one-eyed result, and the one-eyed god enters into him: he becomes the one-eyed god'); according to this the one-eyedness of the god would have been present independently of the result of dicing. But this may be only an unfortunate choice of words. Nevertheless, I do not know whether all readers will find this explanation convincing, especially since by means of pointing out that the dots on dice are called 'eyes' in Germanic languages the throw consisting of a nut is turned into a throw consisting of one eye, which is a semantic distortion. But for our purposes the origin of the one-eyedness is ultimately of little import, since we are concerned with one-eyedness and eyes on foreheads represented as actually being there, i.e. which would (already in *ur*-Indo-European times) be secondary if KERSHAW's explanation should be correct. In this connection it would have been interesting to see what KERSHAW makes of the warriors' and cyclopean characteristics discussed above; unfortunately, he does not mention them. And even though he refers several times to the connections of Indra and Rudra with the Maruts and Vrātyas, he ultimately leaves it at that, namely with the remark that one will probably not progress further in this regard (p. 236).

## BIBLIOGRAPHY

AGUILAR I MATAS 1991 = Aguilar i Matas, Enric: *Ṛgvedic Society. Brill's Indological Library* 2, E.J. Brill, Leiden-New York-København-Köln 1991.

AKHOURI 1993 = Akhouri, Gayatri: *Śaivism in Ancient Bihar*. Bharati Prakashan, Varanasi 1993.

ALLEN 1999 = Allen, Nicholas J.: 'Hinduism as Indo-European: Cultural Comparativism and Political Sensitivities.' *Aryan and Non-Aryan in South Asia: Evidence, Interpretation and Ideology. Proceedings of the International Seminar on Aryan and Non-Aryan in South Asia, University of Michigan, Ann Arbor, 25–27 October 1996.* Edited by Johannes Bronkhorst & Madhav M. Deshpande. *Harvard Oriental Series, Opera Minora* 3, Department of Sanskrit and Indian Studies, Harvard University, Cambridge 1999. [Distributed by South Asia Books, Columbia, Missouri]: 19–32.

BHATT 1981–1982 = Bhatt, M. Ramakrishna: *Varāhamihira's Bṛhat Saṁhitā. Bṛhatsaṁhitā with English Translation, Exhaustive Notes and Literary Comments*. Vols. 1–2, Motilal Banarsidass, Delhi-Varanasi-Patna 1981–1982.

BHAṬṬĀCĀRYA 1984 = Bhaṭṭācārya, Haṁsanārāẏaṇ: *Hinduder deb'debī: udbhab o kramabikāś. Dbitīẏa parba*. Parimārjita 2ẏa saṁskaraṇ. Phirmā KeElEm, Kalikātā 1984.

BISWAL 1988 = Biswal, Bansidhar: *Cult of Śiva*. Punthi Pustak, Calcutta 1988.

BOLLÉE 1981 = Bollée, Willem B.: 'The Indo-European Sodalities in Ancient India.' *Zeitschrift der Deutschen Morgenländischen Gesellschaft* (Wiesbaden) 131 (1981) 172–191.

BOLLÉE (forthcoming) = Bollée, Willem B.: 'A Note on the Birth of the Hero in Ancient India.' *The Concept of the Hero(-ine) in Indian Culture. Papers of a Seminar Conducted by G.D. Sontheimer (Heidelberg 1990).* Edited by Heidrun Brückner, Hugh van Skyhawk, Claus Peter Zoller. Publisher not yet known, Delhi: 1–28.

BROCKINGTON 1995 = Brockington, J.L.: 'Indra and his Banner.' *Ānanda Bhāratī. Dr. K. Krishnamoorthy Felicitation Volume*. General Editors: B. Channakeshava, H.V. Nagaraja Rao. D.V.K. Murthy on behalf of Dr. K. Krishnamoorthy Felicitation Committee, Krishnamurthipuram, Mysore 1995: 109–117.

BUDDRUSS 1982 = Buddruss, Georg: Review of HOFSTETTER (1980). *Zeitschrift der Deutschen Morgenländischen Gesellschaft* 132 (1982) 228.

CHARPENTIER 1911 = Charpentier, Jarl: *Kleine Beiträge zur indoiranischen Mythologie*. Edv. Berling, Uppsala 1911.

DANDEKAR 1979 = Dandekar, R.N.: *Vedic Mythological Tracts. Select Writing 1*. Ajanta, Delhi 1979.

DAS 1983 = Das, Rahul Peter: 'Some Remarks on the Bengali Deity Dharma: Its Cult and Study.' *Anthropos* (St. Augustin) 78 (1983) 661–700.

DAS 1987 = Das, Rahul Peter: 'More Remarks on the Bengali Deity Dharma, its Cult and Study.' *Anthropos* (St. Augustin) 82 (1987) 244–251.

DAS 1991 = Das, Rahul Peter: 'On the Subtle Art of Interpreting.' *Journal of the American Oriental Society* (Ann Arbor) 111 (1991) 737–767.

DAS 1992 = Das, Rahul Peter: 'Problematic Aspects of the Sexual Rituals of the Bauls of Bengal.' *Journal of the American Oriental Society* (Ann Arbor) 112 (1992) 388–432.

DAS 1995 = Das, Rahul Peter: 'The Hunt for Foreign Words in the R̥gveda.' *Indo-Iranian Journal* (Dordrecht/Hingham, MA) 38 (1995) 207–238.

DAS 1997 = Das, Rahul Peter: *Essays on Vaiṣṇavism in Bengal*. Firma KLM, Calcutta 1997.

DAS 1999 = Das, Rahul Peter: 'The Journey to Dakṣiṇ Pāṭan and the Abode of the Snake Goddess in the *Manasāmaṅgal*.' *Essays on Middle Bengali Literature. Studies* by David L. Curley, Rahul Peter Das, Mazharul Islam, Amzad Hossain Mian, Asim Roy and William L. Smith, ed. by Rahul Peter Das. Firma KLM, Calcutta 1999: 44–129.

DAS (forthcoming) = Das, Rahul Peter: 'Bengalischer Nationalismus und die Konstruktion einer austroasiatischen Vergangenheit.' Paper read on 5.10.1999 at the conference on *'Arier' und 'Draviden'. Genese und Wechselwirkung zweier interkultureller Deutungsmuster und ihre Relevanz für die Selbst- und Fremdwahrnehmung Südasiens* in Halle. The proceedings will be published soon.

DE JONG 1995 = de Jong, Albert: 'Jeh the Primal Whore? Observations on Zoroastrian Misogyny.' *Female Stereotypes in Religious Traditions.* Edited by Ria Kloppenborg and Wouter J. Hanegraaff. *Studies in the History of Religions* (*Numen Book Series*) 66, E.J. Brill, Leiden-New York-Köln 1995: 15–41.

DESHPANDE 1999 = Deshpande, Madhav M.: 'What to do with the Anāryas? Dharmic Discourses of Inclusion and Exclusion.' *Aryan and Non-Aryan in South Asia: Evidence, Interpretation and Ideology. Proceedings of the International Seminar on Aryan and Non-Aryan in South Asia, University of Michigan, Ann Arbor, 25–27 October 1996.* Edited by Johannes Bronkhorst & Madhav. M. Deshpande. *Harvard Oriental Series, Opera Minora* 3, Department of Sanskrit and Indian Studies, Harvard University, Cambridge 1999. [Distributed by South Asia Books, Columbia, Missouri]: 19–32.

DONIGER 1993 = Doniger, Wendy: *Śiva. Érotique et ascétique.* Traduit de l'anglais par Nicole Ménant. *Bibliothèque des Sciences Humaines*, Éditions Gallimard, [Paris] 1993.

DURT 1998 = Durt, Hubert: 'Two interpretations of human-flesh offering: misdeed or supreme sacrifice.' *Journal of the International College for Advanced Buddhist Studies* (Tokyo) 1 (1998) 57–83 = 236–210.

FALK 1986 = Falk, Harry: *Bruderschaft und Würfelspiel. Untersuchungen zur Entwicklungsgeschichte des vedischen Opfers*. Hedwig Falk, Freiburg 1986.

FALK 1987 = Falk, Harry: 'Viṣṇu im Veda.' *Hinduismus und Buddhismus. Festschrift für Ulrich Schneider*. Herausgegeben von Harry Falk. Hedwig Falk, Freiburg 1987: 112–133.

FALK 1994a = Falk, Harry: 'Copper Hoard Weapons and the Vedic *vajra*.' *South Asian Archaeology 1993. Proceedings of the Twelfth International Conference of the European Association of South Asian Archaeologists held in Helsinki University 5–9 July 1993*. Edited by Asko Parpola & Petteri Koskikallio. *Volume I. Annales Academiæ Scientiarum Fennicæ* B, 271, Suomalainen Tiedeakatemia, Helsinki 1994: 193–206.

FALK 1994b = Falk, Harry: 'Von Götterfiguren und menschlichen Göttern.' *Festschrift Klaus Bruhn zur Vollendung des 65. Lebensjahres dargebracht von Schülern, Freunden und Kollegen* herausgegeben von Nalini Balbir und Joachim K. Bautze. Dr. Inge Wezler, Reinbek 1994: 313–331.

FALK 1997 = Falk, Harry: 'The Purpose of Ṛgvedic Ritual.' *Inside the Texts, Beyond the Texts. New Approaches to the Study of the Vedas. Proceedings of the International Vedic Workshop, Harvard University, June 1989*. Edited by Michael Witzel. *Harvard Oriental Series, Opera Minora* 2, Department of Sanskrit and Indian Studies, Harvard University, Cambridge 1997. [Distributed by South Asia Books, Columbia, Missouri]: 69–88.

FLOYD (forthcoming) = Floyd, Edwin D.: 'Rudra-Śiva in Ṛgveda 1.114.' Paper read on 7.1.1997 at the Xth World Sanskrit Conference in Bangalore; the publication is planned. An abstract has appeared in: *Xth World Sanskrit Conference. International Association of Sanskrit Studies January 3–9, 1997. Taralabalu Kendra Bangalore – 560 032, India. English Abstracts*. Rashtriya Sanskrit Sansthan, New Delhi 1997: 383–384.

GONDA 1966 = Gonda, Jan: *Loka. World and Heaven in the Veda. Verhandelingen der Koninklijke Nederlandse Akademie van Wetenschappen, Afd. Letterkunde Nieuwe Reeks* 73,1, N.V. Noord-Hollandsche Uitgevers Maatschappij, Amsterdam 1966.

GONDA 1978 = Gonda, Jan: *Die Religionen Indiens. I Veda und älterer Hinduismus*. Zweite, überarbeitete und ergänzte Auflage. *Die Religionen der Menschheit* 11, W. Kohlhammer, Stuttgart-Berlin-Köln-Mainz 1978.

GONDA 1980 = Gonda, Jan: *Vedic Ritual. The Non-Solemn Rites. Handbuch der Orientalistik, Zweite Abteilung Indien* 4,1, E.J. Brill, Leiden–Köln 1980.

GÜNTERT 1987 = Güntert, Hermann: 'Hund.' *Handwörterbuch des deutschen Aberglaubens*. Herausgegeben von Hanns Bächtold-Stäubli unter Mitwirkung von Eduard Hoffmann-Krayer. *Band 4. Hieb- und stichfest–Knistern*. Unveränderter photomechanischer Nachdruck. Walter de Gruyter, Berlin-New York 1987: cols. 470–490. [First edition: 1932].

GUPTA 1980 = Gupta, S.P.: *The Roots of Indian Art. (A Detailed Study of the Formative Period of Indian Art and Architecture: Third and Second Centuries B.C.—Mauryan and Late Mauryan)*. B.R. Publishing Corporation, Delhi 1980.

HEESTERMAN 1996 = Heesterman, Jan C.: 'Die Sādhyas und der Kult des Feuers.' *Studien zur Indologie und Iranistik* (Reinbek) 20 (1996) = *Veda-Vyākaraṇa-Vyākhyāna. Festschrift Paul Thieme zum 90. Geburtstag am 18. März 1995 dargebracht von Schülern, Freunden und Kollegen* herausgegeben von Hanns-Peter Schmidt und Albrecht Wezler. Dr. Inge Wezler, Reinbek 1996: 117–143.

HEESTERMAN 1997 = Heesterman, Jan C.: 'Vedism and Hinduism.' *Studies in Hinduism. Vedism and Hinduism*. Edited by Gerhard Oberhammer. *Österreichische Akademie der Wissenschaften, Philosophisch-historische Klasse, Sitzungsberichte* 642. *Beiträge zur Kultur- und Geistesgeschichte Asiens* 19, Österreichische Akademie der Wissenschaften, Wien 1997: 43–68.

HOFSTETTER 1980 = Hofstetter, Erich: *Der Herr der Tiere im alten Indien. Freiburger Beiträge zur Indologie* 14, Otto Harrassowitz, Wiesbaden 1980.

IRWIN 1990 = Irwin, John C.: 'Origins of Form and Structure in Monumental Art.' *Symbols in Art and Religion. The Indian and the Comparative Perspectives*. Edited by Karel Werner. *Durham Indological Series* 2, Curzon Press, London, and, The Riverdale Company, Glenn Dale, MD 1990: 46–67 and 219–220.

IVĂNESCU 1967 = Ivănescu, G.: 'La formation du Panthéon védique.' *Studia et Acta Orientalia* (Bucarest) 5–6 (1967) 77–91.

JAIN 1995 = Jain, Jyotindra: 'Propitiation of Babo Ind: Survival of the Ancient Cult of Indra.' *Living Traditions. Studies in the Ethnoarchaeology of South Asia*. Editor Bridget Allchin. Reprint. Oxford & IBH Publishing Co., New Delhi-Bombay-Calcutta 1995: 13–29.

JAMISON 1996 = Jamison, Stephanie W.: '*Vṛtra et Vṛθragna* and *Sur la structure du kāvya*—Some intersections: Vedic motifs in *Kumārasaṁbhava* III.' *Langue, style et structure dans le monde indien. Centenaire de Louis Renou. Actes du Colloque international (Paris, 25–27 janvier 1996)* édités par Nalini Balbir et Georges-Jean Pinault avec la collaboration de Jean Fezas. *Bibliothèque de L'École des Hautes Études, Sciences historiques et philologiques* 334, Librairie Honoré Champion, Paris 1996: 123–142.

KERSHAW 2000 = Kershaw, Kris: *The One-eyed God. Odin and the (Indo-)Germanic Männerbünde. Journal of Indo-European Studies Monograph* 36, Institute for the Study of Man, Washington, D.C. 2000.

KUIPER 1995 = Kuiper, F.B.J.: 'On a Hunt for "Possible" Objections', and, 'Foreign Words in the Rigveda.' *Indo-Iranian Journal* (Dordrecht / Hingham, MA) 38 (1995) 239–247 and 261.

LARIVIERE 1997 = Lariviere, Richard W.: 'Power and Authority: On the Interpretation of Indian Kingship from Sanskrit Sources.' *Lex et Litterae. Studies in Honour of Professor Oscar Botto*. Editors: Siegfried Lienhard and Irma Piovano. Edizioni dell'Orso, Alessandria 1997: 313–327.

LOMMEL 1978 = Lommel, Herman: *Kleine Schriften*, herausgegeben von Klaus L. Janert. *Glasenapp-Stiftung* 16, Franz Steiner, Wiesbaden 1978.

MAYRHOFER 1996 = Mayrhofer, Manfred: *Etymologisches Wörterbuch des Altindoarischen. II. Band. Indogermanische Bibliothek, 2. Reihe: Wörterbücher*, Universitätsverlag C. Winter, Heidelberg 1996.

MCCONE 1987 = McCone, Kim: 'Hund, Wolf und Krieger bei den Indogermanen.' *Studien zum indogermanischen Wortschatz.* Herausgegeben von Wolfgang Meid. *Innsbrucker Beiträge zur Sprachwissenschaft* 52, Institut für Sprachwissenschaft der Universität Innsbruck, Innsbruck 1987: 101–154.

MCCONE 1991 = McCone, Kim: *Pagan Past and Christian Present in Early Irish Literature*. Reprinted. *Maynooth Monographs* 3, An Sagart, [Maynooth] 1991.

MCCONE (forthcoming) = McCone, Kim: 'Wolfsbesessenheit, Nacktheit, Einäugigkeit und verwandte Aspekte des altkeltischen Männerbundes.' Paper read on 3.6.1998 as part of the lecture series *Geregeltes Ungestüm. Brüderschaften und Jugendbünde bei indogermanischen Völkern* organised jointly by the Institut für Indologie and the Institut für Indogermanistik, Allgemeine und Angewandte Sprachwissenschaft of the Martin-Luther-Universität Halle-Wittenberg; the publication of the collected lectures is planned.

MEYER 1937 = Meyer, J.J.: *Trilogie altindischer Mächte und Feste der Vegetation. Ein Beitrag zur vergleichenden Religions- und Kulturgeschichte, Fest- und Volkskunde.* Max Niehans, Zürich-Leipzig 1937.

MICHAELS 1998 = Michaels, Axel: *Der Hinduismus. Geschichte und Gegenwart.* Verlag C.H. Beck, München 1998.

NIETHAMMER 1992 = Niethammer, Carolyn: *Töchter der Erde. Legende und Wirklichkeit der Indianerinnen.* Aus dem Amerikanischen von Volker Bradke. 8. Auflage. *Lamuv Taschenbuch* 38, Lamuv, Göttingen 1992.

NIGŪṚHĀNANDA 1996 = Nigūṛhānanda: *Ṛgbeder debatā*. De'j Pāb'liśiṁ, Kal'kātā 1996.

OBERLIES 1998 = Oberlies, Thomas: *Die Religion des Ṛgveda. Erster Teil—Das religiöse System des Ṛgveda. Publications of the De Nobili Research Library* 26, Institut für Indologie der Universität Wien, Wien 1998. [Commission agents: Gerold, Wien; Motilal Banarsidass, Delhi].

OBERLIES (forthcoming) = Oberlies, Thomas: 'Kriegslisten und ungeziemendes Benehmen: Die Askesepraktiken des Pāśupata.' Paper read on 1.10.1998 at the *27. Deutscher Orientalistentag* in Bonn and, in a revised and expanded form, scheduled to be published in the *Studien zur Indologie und Iranistik* (Reinbek).

OBEROI 1994 = Oberoi, Harjot: *The Construction of Religious Boundaries. Culture, Identity, and Diversity in the Sikh Tradition.* Oxford University Press, Delhi-Oxford-New York 1994.

PW = Böhtlingk, Otto von; Roth, Rudolph: *Sanskrit-Wörterbuch* ('großes Petersburger Wörterbuch'), Bd. 1–7, Kaiserliche Akademie der Wissenschaften, St. Petersburg 1855–75.

SARKAR 1974 = Sarkar, A.: *Śiva in Medieval Indian Literature.* Punthi Pustak, Calcutta 1974.

SCHMIDT 1968 = Schmidt, Hanns-Peter: *Bṛhaspati und Indra. Untersuchungen zur vedischen Mythologie und Kulturgeschichte.* Otto Harrassowitz, Wiesbaden 1968.

SCHNEIDER 1974 = Schneider, Ulrich: 'Viṣṇus höchste Fußstapfe.' *XVIII. Deutscher Orientalistentag vom 1. bis 5. Oktober 1972 in Lübeck. Vorträge*, herausgegeben von Wolfgang Voigt. *Zeitschrift der Deutschen Morgenländischen Gesellschaft, Supplement* 2, Franz Steiner, Wiesbaden 1974: 390–409.

SEN'GUPTA 1996 = Sen'gupta, Mihir: *Siddhigañjer mokām.* Nayā Udyog, Kalikātā 1996.

SMITH 1999a = Smith, William L.: 'Śiva, Lord of the Plough.' *Essays on Middle Bengali Literature. Studies* by David L. Curley, Rahul Peter Das, Mazharul Islam, Amzad Hossain Mian, Asim Roy, William L. Smith edited by Rahul Peter Das. Firma KLM, Calcutta 1999: 208–228.

SMITH 1999b = Smith, William L.: 'The Jaiminibhārata and its Eastern Vernacular Versions", *Studia Orientalia* (Helsinki) 85 (1999) 389–406.

SÖHNEN 1991 = Söhnen, Renate: 'Indra and Women.' *Bulletin of the School of Oriental and African Studies, University of London* (London) 54 (1991) 68–74.

SÖHNEN 1997 = Söhnen, Renate: 'Rise and Decline of the Indra Religion in the Veda.' *Inside the Texts, Beyond the Texts. New Approaches to the Study of the Vedas. Proceedings of the International Vedic Workshop, Harvard University, June 1989.* Edited by Michael Witzel. *Harvard Oriental Series, Opera Minora* 2, Department of Sanskrit and Indian Studies, Harvard University, Cambridge 1997. [Distributed by South Asia Books, Columbia, Missouri]: 235–243.

SRINIVASAN 1983 = Srinivasan, Doris Meth: 'Vedic Rudra-Śiva.' *Journal of the American Oriental Society* (New Haven) 103 (1983) 543–556.

SRINIVASAN 1984 = Srinivasan, Doris Meth: 'Unhinging Śiva from the Indus Civilization.' *Journal of the Royal Asiatic Society of Great Britain & Ireland* (London) (1984) 77–89.

SRINIVASAN 1997 = Srinivasan, Doris Meth: *Many Heads, Arms and Eyes. Origin, Meaning and Form of Multiplicity in Indian Art. Studies in Asian Art and Archaeology* 20, Brill, Leiden-New York-Köln 1997.

SYED 1998 = Syed, Renate: 'Śiva und Pārvatī beim Spiel. Eine Untersuchung literarischer und bildlicher Quellen.' *Berliner Indologische Studien* (Reinbek) 11/12 (1998) 389–433.

THIEME 1971 = Thieme, Paul: *Kleine Schriften* [herausgegeben von Georg Buddruss]. *Teil 1. Glasenapp-Stiftung* 5,1, Franz Steiner, Wiesbaden 1971.

TRIPATHI 1977 = Tripathi, G.C.: 'Das Indradhvaja-Fest in Orissa. Die Überreste der Indra-Verehrung in Ostindien.' *XIX. Deutscher Orientalistentag vom 28. September bis 4. Oktober 1975 in Freiburg im Breisgau. Vorträge*, herausgegeben von Wolfgang Voigt. *Zeitschrift der Deutschen Morgenländischen Gesellschaft, Supplement* 3,2, Franz Steiner, Wiesbaden 1977: 1002–1014.

WATKINS 1999 = Watkins, Calvert: 'A Celtic Miscellany.' *Proceedings of the Tenth Annual UCLA Indo-European Conference, Los Angeles, May 21–23, 1998*. Edited by: Karlene Jones-Bley, Martin E. Huld, Angela Della Volpe, Miriam Robbins Dexter. *Journal of Indo-European Studies Monograph* 32, Institute for the Study of Man, Washington, D.C. 1999: 3–25.

WEZLER 1992 = Wezler, Albrecht: 'Paralipomena zum Sarvasarvātmakatvavāda II: On the Sarvasarvātmakatvavāda and its Relation to the Vṛkṣāyurveda.' *Studien zur Indologie und Iranistik* (Reinbek) 16/17 (1992) 287–315.

WHITE 1988–1989 = White, David Gordon: 'Dogs Die.' *History of Religions* (Chicago) 28 (1988–1989) 283–303.

WIDENGREN 1965 = Widengren, Geo: *Die Religionen Irans. Die Religionen der Menschheit*, W. Kohlhammer, Stuttgart 1965.

WIDENGREN 1983 = Widengren, Geo: 'Das Neujahrsfest im alten Iran.' *Iranzamin. Echo der iranischen Kultur* (Bonn) 2,1(7) (März-Mai 1983) 35–41.

WITZEL 1996 = Witzel, Michael: 'Looking for the Heavenly Casket.' *Studien zur Indologie und Iranistik* (Reinbek) 20 (1996) 531–544.

WITZEL 1999 = Witzel, Michael: 'Substrate Languages in Old Indo-Aryan (Rgvedic, Middle and Late Vedic).' *Electronic Journal Of Vedic Studies* 5,1 (September 1999) (in four parts): http://www1.shore.net/~india/ejvs/ejvs0501/ejvs0501a.txt, http://.../ejvs0501b.txt, http://.../ejvs0501c.txt, http://.../ejvs0501d.txt.

ZEHNDER 1999 = Zehnder, Thomas: *Atharvaveda-Paippalāda. Buch 2. Text, Übersetzung, Kommentar. Eine Sammlung altindischer Zaubersprüche vom Beginn des 1. Jahrtausends v. Chr. Wissenschaftliche Schriften im Schulz-Kirchner Verlag Reihe* 3, *Beiträge zur Sprach- und Literaturwissenschaft* 107, Schulz-Kirchner Verlag, Idstein 1999.

# ‘Words and things’ in the *Ṛg-veda* (field–meadow–pasture)

TATIANA Y. ELIZARENKOVA

The semantic row which can be designated as field–meadow–pasture deserves special attention, because the denotata of these words make the basis of material life of the Aryan tribes. The linguistic analysis of these words may shed more light upon the everyday life of these tribes.

It is a common opinion now that in the times of the RV (at least of the ‘family’ *Maṇḍalas*) the Aryans were semi-nomadic. Military marches (*yoga*) alternated with temporary stops (*kṣema-*) for the purpose of tilling the land, sowing, reaping crops, and the *grāma-* (kind of military detachment, and not village[1]) left its stand again, and moved on to fight the *dāsa-* / *dasyu-* and gain their land and cattle.

There is a group of words in the RV denoting field–meadow–pasture: *kṣétra-* n., *ájra-* m., *urvárā-* f., *khilyá-* m., *kṛṣí-* f., *yávasa-* n., *gáv-yūti-* f. The number of these synonyms shows that their denotata played a substantial role in the life of the speakers of the Vedic language. At the same time it should be reminded that this lexical group does not belong to the sphere of cosmogony in the RV (while cosmogony forms the ancient kernel of this text[2]), and is not strictly connected with any particular myth (which differs from the situation of mountain–rock–stone in the RV).

The dominant of this semantic row is the substantive *kṣétra-* which has the broadest meaning, is rather frequent and stylistically neutral. It is a noun derived from the verbal root *kṣi-* (*kṣéti-*, *kṣiyánti-*) ‘to live’, ‘dwell’, ‘remain’ with a connotation ‘to live in peace’, ‘to rest’[3]. It should be mentioned that there are two more homonyms of this root: *kṣi-*, *kṣáyati-* ‘to possess’, ‘to own’, ‘to govern’ and *kṣi-*, *kṣiṇā́ti-* ‘to destroy’. According to the old tradition (GRASSMANN[4], WHITNEY[5]), *kṣi-*, *kṣéti-* and *kṣi-*, *kṣáyati-* were treated as one and the same root.

---

1 RAU (1957).

2 KUIPER (1983).

3 MAYRHOFER (1986–2000: I,426–428).

4 GRASSMANN (1955: 365–367).

5 WHITNEY (1885: 29).

*Essays in Indian Philosophy, Religion and Literature*, pp. 25–34.

H. GRASSMANN in his *Wörterbuch zum Rig-Veda*[6] and O. BÖHTLINGK[7] in his *Sanskrit-Wörterbuch* treat the meaning of *kṣétra-* in the same way: 1) domain, land plot (Grundbesitz, Grundstück) and then 2) field and 3) territory, land. But M. MAYRHOFER in *EWA* does not mention this first meaning at all[8], and this seems to be the right way, as our analysis will show.

*Kṣétra-* is the dominant in this semantic row. It is frequent enough (found twenty times, *yávasa-* twenty-three times, the rest much less). Its meaning is not opposed to the meaning of any other word of this group. It is very broad, and includes in itself the meanings of all the specifications of the general notion. For instance; 6.47.20: *agavyūtí kṣétram ā́ganma devā / urvī́ satī́ bhū́mir aṁhūraṇā́bhūt*—'We have come to a place without pastures, O gods. Wide is the earth, but it became narrow for us!' This shows that *kṣétra-* may have *gáv-yūti-*, and may not. In this hymn *agavyūtí kṣétram* is used metaphorically, depicting the deplorable situation of a *Ṛṣi* who has little hope to get a reward for his work (*dákṣiṇā*). It seems to be opposed to *urú loká*—'wide space', and in this meaning *kṣétra-* is synonymous with *loká*.

The paradigm of *kṣétra-* consists almost exclusively of the sg. forms (nineteen out of twenty). So, *kṣétra-* is treated as a single notion—it is not divided or multiplied. The N. case is found only once in the late part of the text (10.33.6) in a comparison. This speaks for the fact that *kṣétra-* in the RV is not regarded as a subject of an action, and is naturally not personified.

It is an object of action, and the frequent case is the Acc. sg. It deserves attention that *kṣétram* in the Acc. sg. is never used as a direct object of *kar-* 'to do'. In Sanskrit *kṣétraṁ, kar-* is a stable phraseological combination, meaning 'to till the field'. Another combination is once found in the RV with this meaning: *kṛṣíṁ karṣ-* (10.34.13, *the Gambler's Lament*) in the direct speech of the god Savitar, who instructs the unfortunate gambler: *akṣáir mā́ dīvyaḥ kṛṣím it kṛṣasva*—'Play no longer with the dice, but till your field.'

Typical combinations with the Acc. *kṣétram* are those with the verbs meaning 'to conquer' (*ji-*), 'to gain' (*san- / sā-*), 'to get', 'to find' (*vid-*). For instance: *jáyan kṣétram abhy àrṣa jáyann apáḥ*—'Flow [for us], conquering land, conquering the waters' (an appeal to Soma); 1.100.18: *sánat kṣétram purú ścandrám vividvā́n*—'He conquered the country together with his whitish friends as the one who knows' (Indra). The god is asked to give 'wide land' (*kṣétram urú*) to his worshippers (9.91.6), which is closely synonymous with *urú lokám*. If the verb is intransitive, the Acc. *kṣétram* means usually the place of destination—'land', 'place', 'country',

[6] GRASSMANN (1955).

[7] BÖHTLINGK (1879–1886: II,130).

[8] MAYRHOFER (1986–2000: I,436).

'territory'. 6.61.14: *mā́ tvát kṣétrāṇy áraṇāni ganma*—'Let us not go away from you to distant lands!' So, being used in the Acc. constructions, *kṣétram* does not mean 'field'.

This meaning can be found mostly in the Gen. constructions, when they are represented by the proper name of a local genius *kṣétrasya páti-*, 'lord of the field', whom MACDONNELL calls 'tutelary deity'. No special hymn is dedicated to *kṣétrasya páti-*. He is invoked to grant rich crops, cattle and horses, and to fill heaven and earth, plants and waters with sweetness[9]. This name is mentioned in the text five times, out of which three times are found in 6.57—a hymn where the deified ploughshare and furrow (*śúnā-sīrā*) are invoked, and draught animals, plough and goad for driving cattle are mentioned. *Kṣétrasya páti-* can mean only 'lord of the field' in such a context. For instance, 4.57.1: *kṣétrasya pátinā vayáṁ / hiténeva jayāmasi / gā́m áśvam poṣayitnv ā́*—'Due to the Lord of the field we gain (the field) which is feeding cows and horses, as if with the help of a good friend.' Once, in the late part of the text, it is said—10.66.13: *kṣétrasya pátim prátiveśam īmahe*—'We apply to the Lord of the field who lives in the neighbourhood.' That means that he is protecting the speaker's field, his property.

The name of this mythological personage is formed according to a model which is well known in the RV: a combination of the Gen. sg. of a common noun followed by the word *páti* 'lord', like *bráhmaṇas páti-*, *vā́stoṣ páti-*.

The meaning 'domain' is clearly expressed in the text of the RV only once—7.100.4: *ví cakrame pṛthivī́m eṣá etā́ṁ* I *kṣétrāya víṣṇur mánuṣe daśasyán*—'He strode across this earth (that it should become) domain, Viṣṇu who rewards man.' This is a single example in the RV, where the primary stem *kṣétra-* has the meaning 'domain', which is characteristic of the secondary stems derived from it by means of *vṛddhi*: *kṣáitra-* (8.71.12) and the compound *kṣáitra-patya-* (1.112.13). It should be added that in 7.100.4 the meaning 'domain' of *kṣétra-* is to a certain extent influenced by the D. of aim.

There are many compounds in the RV with *kṣétra-* as a first or a second member. In the *tat-puruṣa* type *kṣétra-* occupies the place of the first member, and has usually the meaning 'land', 'territory' (and not 'field'). The second member of these compounds are, as a rule, nouns (substantives and adjectives) derived from the verbs which govern the Acc. case *kṣétram* in the syntactic constructions, that is *ji-, san- / sā-, vid-*. For instance, *kṣetra-jeṣá-* m. 'conquering of the land', *kṣetrâsā́-* adj. 'one who captures lands,' *kṣétra-sāti* f. 'capturing of lands,' *kṣetra-víd-* adj. 'knowing the locality,' '~ the territory' (epithet of gods). E.g. 10.32.7: *ákṣetra-vit kṣetra-vídaṁ hy áprāṭ / sá práiti kṣetra-vídā́nuśiṣṭaḥ*—'It was the one who did not know the territory

[9] MACDONNELL (1897: 138).

who asked the knower of the territory. He goes farther, being taught by the knower of territory' [the worshipper asked the god]. There exists only one compound word of the *tat-puruṣa* type, where *kṣétra-* means 'field', and this is *kṣetrasā́dhas-* adj. 'putting the fields in order'. It is met twice in the RV: 3.8.7 and 8.31.14 and causes various interpretations, both the compound itself, and its second member. As to its first member, there is no doubt that its meaning is 'field'.

This meaning is characteristic of *kṣétra-* when this word functions as the second member of the *bahu-vrīhi* compound *sukṣétra-* adj. 'having good fields', and an abstract noun derived from it *sukṣetriyā́-* f. 'longing for good fields.'

Drawing the conclusion one can say that there exists a certain distribution among the case grammemes and types of compounds concerning the two kinds of meaning of *kṣétra-*: the abstract one—'territory', 'locality', 'land' (*urú kṣétram* being very close to *urú lokám*) and the concrete one—'field' (it is just in this meaning that *kṣétra-* is synonymous to the other names of the field). These two semantic spheres are approximately equal in the semantic volume of *kṣétra-*.

It is known from the RV that *kṣétra-* is feeding cattle, but the shepherd is never mentioned in connection with it.

*Kṣétra-* does not reveal in the RV the metaphorical meaning 'womb' that is found in *Mānava-dharma-śāstra*—cp. the discussion: to whom the child belongs: to the owner of the *kṣétra-* or to the owner of the seed.

*Ájra-* is another name of the field in the RV. Etymologically, it is a noun derived from the verbal root *áj-* 'to drive' [a herd], though MAYRHOFER is not absolutely sure about this etymology[10]. GRASSMANN makes a historical excursion in his article about *ájra-*, saying that in the RV this word means 'field' in the broadest sense of the word, while the primary, etymological meaning was 'pasture', and only gradually, when cattle-breeding had been driven back by agriculture, the most part of *ájra-* was used as arable land[11]. In his definition of the meaning of this word GRASSMANN stresses that *ájra-* designates 'plain', 'field' covered with grass, and that its semantic volume becomes clear from the oppositions to mountains, deserts and impassable places. And that means that *ájra-* was treated as an element of landscape.

[10] MAYRHOFER (1986–2000: I,52).

[11] GRASSMANN (1955: 23). One is struck by the methodic precision with which lexical semantics is analysed in this article; it was far ahead of its time. The semantic volume of a lexeme is practically established by means of oppositions to other lexemes with the help of distinctive features.

The word *ájra-* is found in the RV nine times, out of which eight are plural forms. This contrasts sharply with the functioning of *kṣétra-*: *kṣétra-* is regarded as a single abstract notion, *ájra-* as many concrete realisations of a notion.

*Ájra-* in the RV is opposed to the other elements of landscape by means of various semantic distinctive features:

> *Ájra-* : *girí* as *flat* : *high*, e.g. 6.24.8: *ájra índrasya giráyaś cid ṛṣvā́*—'Even high mountains are plains for Indra.'
>
> The rest of the case forms are Acc. pl.
>
> *Ájra-* : *dhánvan-* as *covered with vegetation* : *dry, barren*, e.g. from the Aśvin-hymn 6.62.2: *apó dhánvāny áti yātho ájrān*—'You two move through the waters, deserts, meadows.'
>
> *Ájra-* : *durgá-* as *flat, easy to pass* : *impassable*, e.g. 5.54.4: *ví yád ájrañ ájatha nā́va īṁ yathā / ví durgā́ni maruto nā́ha riṣyatha*—'When you cross the fields, like the boats (cross) the sea, and the impassable places, O Maruts, you are not injured!'

The first of these oppositions is also represented on the level of derivation: *ajryà-* 'connected with meadows' : *parvatyà-* 'connected with mountains'. 10.69.6: *sám ajryā̀ parvatyā̀ vásūni* | *dā́sā vṛtrā́ṇy ā́ryā jigetha*—'You [have gained all] the wealth connected with meadows (and) with mountains, you have conquered [all] the *dāsa* and *ārya* enemies' (you = Indra).

In all these cases *ájra-* is opposed to lexemes that do not belong to the same semantic field, they are outside. The lack of oppositions inside its own semantic field testifies to the fact that the opposition between arable land and pasture is not relevant for *ájra-*.

This opposition models the relations between two names which are quasi-synonyms, specifications of the general notion of the field: *urvárā-* f. and *khilyá-* m. *Urvárā-* means 'fertile field', 'a field yielding rich crops', while *khilyá-* designates 'barren (or fallow) land', the distinctive feature being: *fertile* : *non-fertile*. *Urvárā-* is found in the RV eight times, *khilyá-*—two times.

There is a context where these two terms are directly opposed to each other. In 10.142.3 Agni's attacks on bushes are implicitly compared with barren patches among fertile fields: *utá khilyā́ urvárāṇām bhavanti*.

*Urvárā-* in the hymns is a symbol of fertility. As such, it functions in the Apālā-hymn 8.91 which is in its essence a fertility charm. Indra cures the girl Apālā who suffered from the absence of her pubic hair. It is imitative magic about which

Stanisław SCHAYER has written[12], and the image of a fruitful field plays a prominent part here, cp. 8.91.5:

> *imā́ni trī́ṇi viṣṭápā tā́nîndra ví rohaya /*
> *śíras tatásyôrvárām ā́d idám ma úpodáre //*
>
> 'Make these three places sprout, O Indra: my daddy's head and field and this part of me below my waist.'[13]

The most frequent case of *urvárā-* is the L. pl. (five times).

The typical context in which *urvárā-* is found in the hymns is the list, where the most precious valuables are enumerated—*urvárā-* is one of them. E.g. 4.41.6: *toké hité tánaya urvárāsu / sū́re dṛ́śīke vṛ́ṣaṇaś ca páuṁsye / índrā no átra váruṇā syātām*—'When the children and grandchildren are at stake, fertile fields, the vision of the sun, and the male power of a bull, O Indra and Varuṇa, be here with us!'

The stem *urvárā-* is used as the first member of some compound-words, the second member being derivatives of the same verbal roots or the same nouns as with *kṣétra-*: *urvarā-jít-* 'conquering arable fields', *urvarâsā́-* 'gaining ~', *urvarā-pati-* 'lord of the arable field'. Cattle is not mentioned in connection with *urvárā-*.

Another name of the arable field *kṛṣí-* (the root *kṛṣ-* 'to plough') is found only once in the RV in the late part of the text (see above).

The notion of pasture-meadow is expressed in the RV by two close synonyms: *yávasa-* n. and *gáv-yūti-* f. The two words are etymologically connected, according to MAYRHOFER (**(H)yavas-* 'meadow', **(H)yūti-* 'grazing'—cp. *yūthá-* n. 'herd').[14] *Yávasa-* is most frequent in the whole semantic field, it is found twenty-three times. The dictionaries give its meaning as 'pasture', 'a grassy meadow', 'grass [as fodder]'. There is a considerable prevalence of the sg. forms over the pl. ones in its case paradigm. The most frequent case is the L. (approximately one half of all the forms), next one in frequency is the Acc. (almost one forth of all the forms), while the N. is found only once. The rest of the case grammemes are seldom.

There is a peculiarity characteristic of *yávasa-*—this word is used mostly in comparisons (which are usually elliptic). W. P. SCHMID (1958) states it as follows: 'The image of pasture is used only in comparisons and not in metaphors with firmly established symbolics.'[15] As to comparisons, there exist certain clichés which repeat

---

[12] SCHAYER (1925).

[13] Transl. by O'FLAHERTY (1981: 257).

[14] MAYRHOFER (1986–2000: II,404).

[15] SCHMID (1958: 6).

themselves frequently in the hymns[16]. The Acc. case designates usually the place of destination: like the cow is going to the pasture; the L. case: like the cow grazing on a pasture. E.g. 4.41.5: *sā́ no duhīyad yávaseva gatvī́ / sahásra-dharā páyasā mahī́ gáuḥ*—'Let her give milk to us, as if having gone to a pasture, the great cow with thousand streams of milk!'; 5.9.4: *ágne paśúr ná yávase*—'O Agni, (you are) like cattle on the pasture'; 5.53.16: *ráṇan gā́vo ná yávase*—'Let them rejoice like cows on the pasture!' All these comparisons are characterised by a common trait: they model a real situation—it is a real pasture and a real cow. The contexts with *yávasa-* should be understood literally, they are not related either to myths, or to the ritual.

*Yávasa-* as an independent word has usually the meaning 'pasture', 'meadow' in the RV. The meaning 'grass' is found in the *tat-puruṣa* compound *yavasā́d-* adj. 'eating grass' only twice in the later parts of the text (1.94.11 and 10.27.9).

Typical of *yávasa-* are the compounds of the *bahu-vrīhi* and *karma-dhāraya* type with the adjectival prefix *su-* 'good', 'excellent', 'nice', e.g. 2.27.13: ... *apáḥ sūyávasā ádabdha / úpa kṣeti* ...—'Exempt from deception, he lives near the waters with nice meadows' (the worshipper of the Ādityas); 1.42.8: *abhí sūyávasaṁ naya*—'Lead us to a good pasture!' (to Pūṣan).

*Sūyávasa-* in its turn, is a basis of further derivation: there exist *sūyavasā́d-* adj. 'grazing on a good meadow', *sūyavasín-* 'rich of good meadows', *sūyavasyú-* 'longing for a good meadow'.

E.g. 1.164.40a: *sūyavasā́d bhagavatī́ hí bhuyā́ḥ*—'Be happy, grazing on a good meadow!' This translation is supported by the contents of *pāda* c: *addhí tṛ́ṇam aghnye viśvadā́nīm*—'O inviolable cow, eat grass for ever!'; 6.27.7: *yásya gávāv aruṣā́ sūyavasyū́ / antár ū́ ṣú cárato rérihāṇā*—'Whose pair of reddish bulls, longing for a good meadow, are moving nicely between [the sky and the earth], licking their lips all the time.'

As a member of all these compounds *yávasa-* has also the meaning 'pasture', 'meadow' (and not 'grass'). This way, one can regard *sūyávasa-* as a single notion. It is an emotional evaluation. The pasture gives joy and satisfaction to the people and the milch cows grazing (*ad-*, *riś-*) on it, it is *raṇvá-*, and everybody enjoys (*ran-*) it.

*Yávasa-* in the RV is the name of the real pasture or meadow on the earth. It belongs to the people; shepherds are mentioned in connection with it—and the enemies are compared with the cows roaming about on a meadow without a shepherd. All this testifies to the fact that cattle-breeding was still very important in the times of the RV.

[16] This was mentioned by SRINIVASAN (1979: 44–45).

The substantive *gáv-yūti-* is found in the RV twelve times. Morphologically it is a compound word: *gáv-yūti-*, meaning something like 'grazing of cows.'

The paradigm consists of eleven sg. forms and one pl. The structure of the paradigm is different from that of *yávasa-*. There are three N. forms, expressing the subject of the sentence, e.g. 9.74.3: *urvī́ gáv-yūtir áditer ṛtáṁ yaté*—'Wide is Aditi's pasture for the one who moves according to the Law.' Here *gáv-yūti-* belongs to Aditi, in two other cases to Yama (10.14.2) and to Agni (10.80.6). This way, the N. of *gáv-yūti-* does not function as an active subject of an action. All the rest are the Acc. forms, and so the paradigm consists of two cases.

There are two main types of passages with the Acc. *gáv-yūtim*. The first one is when the god is asked to sprinkle the worshippers' *gáv-yūti-* with butter, e.g. 3.62.16: *ā́ no mitrā-varuṇā / ghṛtáir gáv-yūtim ukṣatam*—'O Mitra-Varuṇa, besprinkle [our] pasture with butter.' One should be reminded that butter (*ghṛtá-*) in the RV is not only a sacrificial substance, but also a mystical focus of the vital power. Soma and the Sacred Speech are identified with *ghṛtá-*, a whole hymn 4.58 is dedicated to it. The request to besprinkle the pasture with *ghṛtá-* means in the language of the *Ṛṣis*: give us a secure life! So, these contexts with *gáv-yūti-* have always a metaphorical meaning. Such requests are addressed, as a rule, to Mitra-Varuṇa, guardians of the Cosmic Law.

The second type of contexts express practically the same thought, but by means of another formula. The god is asked to make a broad *gáv-yūti-* and absence of fear, e.g. 7.77.4: *urvī́ṁ gáv-yūtim ábhayaṁ kṛdhī naḥ*—'Create us a broad pasture, absence of fear!' (to Uṣas). *Urú- gáv-yūti-* and *ábhaya-* are semantically very close to each other, *gáv-yūti-* being used metaphorically. There is only one case out of twelve, when *gáv-yūti-* has its literal sense, and this in the late part of the text 1.25.16: *párā me yanti dhītáyo / gā́vo ná gáv-yūtīr ánu*—'My preachers go away, like cows along the pasture'—it is a single example, when *gáv-yūti-* is used like *yávasa-*.

There are a few adjectival compounds of the *bahu-vrīhi* type with *gáv-yūti-* as a second member, where this word is also used only metaphorically: *agavyūtí-*—'devoid of pastures' (unhappy), *urú-gavyūti-* 'having broad pastures' (safe) and an adverb *paro-gav-yūtí-* 'outside the pasture'.

To draw the conclusion, *gáv-yūti-* differs from *yávasa-* in many respects: in the structure of the paradigm, semantics and functioning. *Yávasa-* is referred to a real pasture, which belongs to real people and is situated on the earth, where people graze their cattle, while the denotatum of *gáv-yūti-* is an abstract notion, connected both with gods and mortals. *Gáv-yūti-* is the sphere of activity of gods (Mitra-Varuṇa, Soma, Agni), and the life of the mortals. *Yávasa-* is always used in its literal sense, mainly in comparisons. *Gáv-yūti-*, as a rule, has a metaphorical meaning, and when a god is asked to besprinkle (*ukṣ-*) the *gáv-yūti-* with butter or to create (*kṛ-*) a wide (*urú-*) *gáv-yūti-*, it means he is asked to create a safe and secure life for his worshippers.

The analysis of meaning and functioning of the names of field–meadow–pasture in the RV makes it possible to outline the contours of this semantic field at least in a preliminary way. Two fragments of it are clearly opposed to each other: the territory connected with cattle (*yávasa-*, *gáv-yūti-*)—the territory not connected with cattle (*urvárā-*, *khilyá-*). Inside the first fragment *yávasa-* is opposed to *gáv-yūti-* as a real pasture belonging to the people to an abstract notion: sphere of activity, life, referring both to gods and mortals. Stylistically they also differ: *yávasa-* has the literal meaning and is used in comparisons, *gáv-yūti-* has the metaphorical meaning. Inside the second fragment, *urvárā-* is opposed to *khilyá-* as fertile land to the infertile one.

Beyond this general opposition are the terms *kṣétra-* and *ájra-*. *Kṣétra-* has the broadest semantic volume, and is synonymous to *ájra-* only in one part of its meanings. It is more abstract in its meaning, denoting not only field, but land, or territory in general. *Ájra-* is a concrete element of landscape, opposed to mountains, deserts and impassable places. *Kṣétra-* is regarded as a single indivisible notion, while *ájra-* is treated as one of the concrete objects that are many.

Though there is direct testimony in the RV that the land was cultivated, tilled—the hymn 4.57 is dedicated to the deities of the field—the analysis of the names of the field does not give any information about how it was done. The information is of quite a different type: the fields and pastures were conquered, the gods found them for their worshippers.

The social interpretation of these linguistic data is the future task of the historians.

## BIBLIOGRAPHY


BÖHTLINGK 1879–1886 = Böhtlingk, Otto von: *Sanskrit-Wörterbuch in kürzerer Fassung*. 7 Bde., Kaiserliche Akademie der Wissenschaften, St. Petersburg 1879–1886.

GRASSMANN 1955 = Grassmann, H.: *Wörterbuch zum Rig-Veda*. 3. Aufl. Wiesbaden 1955.

KUIPER 1983 = Kuiper, F. B. J.: *Ancient Indian Cosmogony*. Essays selected and introduced by John Irwin. Delhi 1983.

MACDONNELL 1897 = Macdonnell, Arthur A.: *Vedic Mythology*. Verlag von Karl J. Trübner, Strassburg 1897.

MAYRHOFER 1986–2000 = Mayrhofer, Manfred: *Etymologisches Wörterbuch des Altindoarischen*. Heidelberg 1986–2000 (EWA).

O'FLAHERTY 1981 = O'Flaherty, W. Doniger: *The Rig Veda. An Anthology*. Penguin Books, 1981.

RAU 1957 = Rau, W.: *Staat und Gesellschaft im alten Indien nach den Brāhmaṇa-Texten dargestellt*. Wiesbaden 1957.

SCHAYER 1925 = Schayer, Stanisław: *Die Struktur der magischen Weltanschauung nach dem Atharva-Veda und den Brahmana-Texten*. Untersuchungen zur Geschichte des Buddhismus und verwandter Gebiete, XV. Oskar Schloss Verlag, München-Neubiberg, 1925. [= Offprint from: *Zeitschrift für Buddhismus und verwandte Gebiete* 6 (1925) 259–299].

SCHMID 1958 = Schmid, W. P.: 'Die Kuh auf der Weide', *Indogermanische Forschungen*, Band 64, H. 1 (1958 ) 1–12.

SRINIVASAN 1979 = Srinivasan, D.: *Concept of Cow in the Rigveda*. Delhi–Varanasi–Patna 1979.

WHITNEY 1885 = Whitney, W. D.: *The Roots, Verb-forms and Primary Derivatives of the Sanskrit Language*. Leipzig 1885.

# Changing Canons: What did Sāyaṇa think he commented upon

CEZARY GALEWICZ

It was in 1849 when the first volume of F. Max MÜLLER's critical edition of the *Ṛg-veda* came out, published with the support of the respected Court of Directors of the East India Company. It brought not only to Europe but also to India a new sense of printed canon of a Vedic text which could be a blasphemy to some and a miracle to others. The complete printed *Ṛg-veda* is said to have been a commercial success. It sold well with a second edition to follow soon, and the enlightened members of the Court being granted a 'fair return' for their kindness in the shape of 500 copies representing a sum of £ 7.500—a remarkable amount in those times[1]. The full title of this *Editio princeps* is seldom recalled today. It read as follows: *Śrīḥ Ṛg-veda-Saṁhitā Śrimat-sāyaṇâcārya-viracita-mādhavīya-vedârtha-prakāśa-sahitā*.

While the sound of the name of Sāyaṇâcārya resonates with familiar tones in the ear of those who happened to come across the *Ṛg-veda*, with that of Mādhava it is another story. The more so when a compound like the above could suggest a commentary by a Mādhava. Although MONIER-WILLIAMS, when consulted in this regard, brings some relief in assuring us that *mādhavīya-vedârtha-prakāśa* is just a title of a commentary by Sāyaṇa, our doubts resurface again with the very first lines of the commentary itself. The *Upodghāta*, or introduction to the commentary, deemed to be Sāyaṇa's, reads in line 3 that it was respected Mādhava, not Sāyaṇa, who upon instigation of Śrī Gaṇeśa was instructed by king Bukka to shed light on the *artha* of the *Veda*:

*yat-kaṭâkṣeṇa tad-rūpaṁ dadhad bukka-mahī-patiḥ /*
*ādiśan mādhavâcāryaṁ vedârthasya prakāśane //*

And in the very next line it is still the same Mādhavâcārya who, styled here as the compassionate one, endeavours to speak out the meaning of the *Veda*:

*kṛpālur mādhavâcāryo vedârthaṁ vaktum udyataḥ /*

[1] MÜLLER (1890: LII).

*Essays in Indian Philosophy, Religion and Literature*, pp. 35–44.

In the 'Introduction' to his edition of the *Ṛg-veda*, Max MÜLLER himself does not devote much time to the question of whom the ideas in the commentary really belong to. He admits only that Sāyaṇa resorts to the views of his then famous brother in some parts of the commentary. The authorship of Sāyaṇa was beyond doubt to the great scholar. So was it to most of the later Indologists. But it is a peculiar way of avoiding a more definite remark on the relation between him and Mādhava which is worth mentioning. And a history of comments on both the supposed brothers reflects to some extent division lines within the rather small Indological world itself. If we take a look at Sāyaṇa through the eyeglasses of some famous Vedic scholar we seldom find any mention of Mādhava. Nor do we find any appreciation of his exegetic ideas. And *vice versa* rarely does a *darśana* scholar mention, but in passing, the person and ideas of Sāyaṇa. It looks almost as a waste of time for a historian of *darśana* systems to read Sāyaṇa generally known somehow to belong to the old decrepit Vedic world. Thus Jan GONDA in his *Vedic Literature* includes a single short remark concerning Mādhava, while speaking about Sāyaṇa, that: 'He was a brother of the famous philosopher and author Mādhava with whom he was sometimes confounded'[2]. On the other hand E. FRAUWALLNER in his *opus magnum* mentions the author of *Sarva-darśana-saṁgraha* as 'Sāyaṇa-mādhava'[3], probably after the SDS itself which reads in 1.4: *śrīmat-sāyaṇa-mādhavaḥ prabhur upanyāsyat satāṁ prītaye*, what is rendered by E.B. Cowell and A.E. Gough in JOSHI (1986) as: '... the fortunate Sāyaṇa-Mādhava the lord has expounded them [*Śāstras*] for the delight of the good.'

FRAUWALLNER (1973: 5) adds that Sāyaṇa-Mādhava is 'a Vedānta author' who 'professes the system of Śaṅkara.' No trace of Sāyaṇa at all. Cowell and Gough refer to the problem in a way which gives impression that Sāyaṇa did not exist at all.[4]

Be it as it may, we are nonetheless lucky to be in a possession of a full scale commentary to t h e *V e d a* as it must have been initially designed. Or to a g o o d n u m b e r o f V e d i c t e x t s as we would rather put it today. If we admit the authorship of one person[5], we should think rather of the rights and royalties for the authorship than of one person's work. The sheer number of commentaries makes it rather beyond the possibilities of a single commentator's

[2] GONDA (1975: 41).

[3] FRAUWALLNER (1973: 4). The same name is given as the author of the *Ṛg-veda-bhāṣya* by an edition from the 19th century in Telugu script, according to KRIPACHARYULU (1986: 229).

[4] K.L. JOSHI (1986: 2).

[5] Cf. *Indology List April 5th 1996*, where M. Deshpande speaks of a commentary of 'so-called Sayana'.

hand. Sāyaṇa is said to have written commentaries to no less than five different *Saṁhitās*, eleven *Brāhmaṇas*, and two *Āraṇyakas* along with respective *Upaniṣads*. All are fitted with introductions or *upodghātas* which sometimes, as in the case of RV, can be studied as separate works. We know that he used to write other things as well.

Some of his commentaries characteristically display a similar preamble to the introduction part. Thus the *Upodghāta* for TS which was commented upon first, and this in Indian world does not go without meaning, features almost the same lines in the preamble as the *Upodghāta* to the RV does. The difference comes with line 4 which supplies us with what seems to be missing in the case of the *Upodghāta* to the RV. The line reads:

> *sa* [*Mādhavaḥ*] *prāha nṛpatiṁ rājan sāyaṇâryo mamânujaḥ* /
> *sarvaṁ vetty eṣa vedānāṁ vyākhyātṛtve niyujyatām* //4//
>
> 'And this [Mādhava] said to the Ruler: O King! Here is respected Sāyaṇa, —my younger brother. He knows everything of the *Vedas*— lay on him the burden of the commentary [on the *Veda*].'

And the very next line shows king Bukka bidding Sāyaṇa to shed light on the meaning of the *Veda*. It seems then that in the case of TS it is explicitly Sāyaṇa who is indicated as the commentator while it is rather Mādhava in the case of the *Ṛg-veda-bhāṣya*. Or are there just two lines missing from the text of *Ṛg-veda Upodghāta*?

The whole problem may appear to be a mere academic one if not for an opportunity it offers for reconsidering the idea of such a huge commentary: its aim, message and value. And above all for rethinking the commentator's concept of the subject of his work: a canonical *Veda* in a 14$^{th}$ century South Indian kingdom, too young to carry the burden of a Hindu empire facing rich and hungry Muslim states. For was it not an idea for a commentary to the Vedic canon that was on King Bukka's mind ?

Most probably it must have been something different in the king's mind than it eventually turned out to be in the commentator's idea. And while the former probably escapes us for good, the latter has some chances to be reconstructed.

To make use of such an opportunity one must take a step aside from most often expressed opinions on Sāyaṇa that amount to one of the field's clichés, i.e. from dismissing his ideas by way of putting them on a par with dull and worthless medieval scholastic thought. We know already that Indian medieval times did not necessarily resemble those of Europe and that the European Middle Ages were not always that scholastic as we once were prone to think of them.

Whether it was Mādhava or Sāyaṇa, or rather more than two great pandits of the time, that must have got engaged in this unique project, it was the *Veda* as a whole, i.e. the canonical one, which was at stake and it was up to the leading figure(s) among the commentatorial board to decide what it was to be. For the commentary is replete with fierce arguments concerning the probably then relevant issue of what the *Veda* really was and what its constituent elements were.

The unity of the *Veda* seems to have been quite of a problem already with the ancient commentators. The statements of the *Brāhmaṇas* concerning the elusive thing called *trayī-vidyā*[6] tell us expressly that there existed an early tendency to look at different streams of Vedic traditions as constituting one single whole. The notion of *Śruti*, only too well known today, but often misunderstood, is rather late. Yet it is most frequently taken for granted in discussion of texts that preceded it by centuries. We come across it in medieval times and it henceforth establishes itself for good both in traditional Indian as well as in Western academic discourse. It seems to roughly designate a canon of textual collections deemed to be revealed and transmitted orally through recitation and 'hearing'. It has been thus opposed to profane texts as well as to texts held as sacred but styled as being 'remembered' only, and accordingly termed *Smṛti*. The *Śruti*, as containing highly visionary lines of the *Ṛg-veda* on the one hand, and dry formulas of *yajus* type on the other, looks as if it was rifted by an inner conflict, to use HEESTERMAN's words.[7] The paradox of one *Veda* consisting somehow of many different texts and thus defying definition though held as highest authority by many traditions within Hinduism still puzzles historians of religion and literary critics.

It appears to have been a problem also in the fourteenth century emerging kingdom of Vijayanagar which desperately looked for a common ideology that could serve its imperial multinational aspirations. If Mādhavâcārya is the same person as Vidyāraṇya, the twelfth Jagadguru of a nearby important religious centre of Sringeri, then the choice of ambitious king Bukka was the right one. Being influential enough as the head of a powerful *maṭha*, Mādhava was best situated for investing the young kingdom with the religious legitimacy it needed. And the best way to build a sovereign authority was to sponsor a project on an imperial scale, which Bukka and Harihara well understood. A royal commentary, for that it was, to the one and whole *Veda* could serve that purpose among different South Hindu

---

[6] Cf. ŚB 4.6.7.1:

*trayī vai vidyā / ṛco yajūṁṣi sāmāni …*
*sāiṣā trayī vidyā saumye 'dhvare prayujyate //*

'For indeed there is a triple knowledge. There are hymns, formulas and chants … This is this threefold knowledge, my dear, which is implemented in sacrifice.'

[7] J. HEESTERMAN (1981: 3).

traditions like nothing else.[8] A legend has it that the power of Sringeri was so highly recognised that king Bukka in a symbolic gesture gave the whole of his kingdom to Vidyāraṇya Mādhava, the Jagadguru, who in a gesture of legitimation gave it back to the king[9]. The legend probably attests to a great authority and esteem of the *maṭha* and accounts for a decisive influence of Mādhava on the court of Vijayanagar. Perhaps thanks to this influence his younger brother was appointed a court supervising commentator. One of his duties must have been to preside over the work of a team of professionals gathered under royal patronage to work jointly on an unprecedented commentary. And to comment on the meaning of the *Veda* entailed drawing the limits of it first.

In the *Upodghāta* to the *R̥g-veda-bhāṣya* Sāyaṇa devotes quite a few lines to this problem, thus creating the impression that this was one of the pivotal issues of this commentary. Made in a style of medieval *vāda* tradition, Sāyaṇa's arguments are put forward in the guise of a dispute with fancy opponents whose words are fought and refuted by superior reasoning that takes advantage of the rhetoric devices used in the school of disputations he adhered to. He of course resorts to the authority of the masters he admired and followed. One of the latter was his brother Mādhava. It is the citations from his SDS which are most frequently referred to next to those of Jaimini.

One of the problems he embarks on before that of defining one unique *Veda* is the internal relation of the main Vedic traditions in terms of hierarchy. It is clear that he does not think in terms of textual collections when considering the hierarchy amongst them. Himself probably from a Yajur-vedin family of Andhra, Sāyaṇa[10] establishes the superiority of the *Yajur-veda* over the *R̥g-veda* with reference to the aim of explaining the meaning of the *Veda*. It is only a natural consequence after stating in the preamble that the meaning of the *R̥g-veda* shall be explained as concerning *hotra*, i.e. that which pertains to a *hotr̥* priest during the sacrifice. And it is also already in the preamble where Sāyaṇa gives general reason for such a hierarchy. It is because of *ādhvaryavasya yajñeṣu prādhānyāt* that YV is given preference over RV. And we have these peculiar expressions addressing domains of activity and a kind of *ethos* that we enter into by way of words like *ādhvaryava* and *hotra* here. It is clear that not bodies of text but spheres of ritual competence are

[8] Cf. KULKE (1985: 135): 'Together with his famous brother Sayana ... Vidyaranya tried to establish in an act of intentional cultural policy ... , a new system of orthodoxy in order to counteract the influence of Islamic inroads into South India.'

[9] On the history and legend concerning the kingdom of Vijayanagar see KRIPACHARYULU (1986) and KULKE (1985).

[10] Different views concerning the origin of Sāyaṇa are expressed e.g. by KULKE (1985: 124, 125), FILLIOZAT (1973: XXX) and VENKATARAMAN (1976).

referred to. The *uttara-pakṣa* argument characteristically admits some preference to the *Ṛg-veda* as a sphere of priestly competence, but eventually the *siddhânta* has it that for the very reason of knowing the *artha* of the *Veda* as the a r t h a of c a r r y i n g o u t s a c r i f i c e it is *Yajur-veda* which holds superior position as Sāyaṇa says: *artha-jñānasya tu yajñânuṣṭhānârthatvāt tatra tu yajur-vedasyâiva pradhānatvāt* ('It is indeed due to the meaning of carrying the sacrifices for the apprehension of the *artha* that we take the predominance of the *Yajur-veda*.'[11]).

What is even more peculiar for us, the final argument for the pre-eminence of YV is taken from the RV itself. In reference Sāyaṇa quotes RV 10.71.10 which he interprets rather freely though investing his comments in everything needed for a good canonical commentary: he refers to an old master Yaska, but to the words of the latter he adds his own, introducing his school's ideas under the umbrella of respected authority of the rather Ṛgvedic field. Thus he explains the above passage in a way which is far removed from RV but natural to a ritualist: he holds that by the word *pupuṣvān,* explained by Yaska as *puṣṭiṁ kurvan,* the *hotṛ* priest is meant as 'putting together parts of the remembered hymns into one proper lesson or recitation' (*bhinna-pradeśeṣu āmnātānām ṛcāṁ saṁgham ekatvaṁ saṁpādyâitāvad idaṁ śāstram*[12]). Now it is again a domain of competence named as *hautra*, not a clearly limited body of texts which is alluded to by Sāyaṇa. But it is a definition of what the *Veda* really is which was most disputed judging from the number of counter arguments from the opponents who reject any idea of the *Veda* as an entity possible to define. The *siddhânta* for this argument, recurring here and again, is that *Veda* can be defined as consisting of two parts: *mantra* and *brāhmaṇa*[13], the latter divided—as we can expect according to Mīmāṁsā—into *viddhi* and *artha-vāda.*[14] While the latter division is probably better known as widely discussed in reference to Mīmāṁsā ideas, the former draws our attention here. Obviously finding much difficulty with defining two parts of the *Veda*, the final argument of Sāyaṇa based upon Āpastamba and Jaimini states bluntly that *mantra* is nothing else than that what the priests who know the tradition call by that name. Accordingly what is not *mantra* remains to be *brāhmaṇa.*[15] Now we have again an argument which is

[11] MÜLLER (1890: 1.24).

[12] MÜLLER (1890: 1.30).

[13] MÜLLER (1890: 2.39). Another definition is put forward by Sāyaṇa in his *Upodghāta* to TS: *iṣṭa-prāpty-aniṣṭa-parihārayor alaukikam upāyaṁ yo grantho vedayati sa vedaḥ*: 'A book which informs about the divine ways to achieve the Iṣṭa (the desired) and avoid the Aniṣṭa (unwanted) is called "Veda".' (tr. by S. BALI (1999: 33)).

[14] MÜLLER (1890: 11.31).

[15] MÜLLER (1890: 12.18).

entirely extralinguistic, though it seems to be referring to, as we would rather say, types of text. As previously, Sāyaṇa thinks of the *Veda* as something to be trained and mastered in order to be put into practical ritual use by those who deem themselves to embody the orthodox tradition. Obviously the interpreting strategy adopted here by Sāyaṇa serves protecting the social status of the Brahmins. Sāyaṇa's vision of one canonical *Veda* as an almost limitless storage of detached 'sacred sayings' and authoritative explanations thereof is united by the idea of sacrifice as orchestrated by the knowing one. The unifying activity is best expressed with the verb *saṁs√kṛ*, meaning primarily 'putting together, arranging', rather than 'purifying', as rendered by PETERSON[16]. As it is not the text which is the centre of a thus conceived canon, it is no wonder that it is not the meaning of the *mantra*s that is most essential in studying one's own *Veda* but rather the perfect mastering of their sound form. What it amounts to is perhaps delimiting different kinds of performance: that of learning by *brahma-cārin*, where free interpretation should not take place from that of commenting, on the one hand, and that of experiencing the *artha*, on the other. The latter one should come out of the ritual use of carefully arranged texts and activities put into mutual relation. Reading the 'Introduction' to the *Ṛg-veda-bhāṣya* we encounter a discussion on whether the *mantra*s have meaning and, if so, whether it can be authoritative. What is rather characteristic, Sāyaṇa tends to look for the semantics of the text in relation to the situation of its performance. It seems clear to him that *mantra*s may or may not have meaning according to the extralinguistic context of the recitation. One of the examples put forward by Sāyaṇa is that of a young *brahma-cārin* reciting a 'pestle *mantra'* by the side of a girl named Pūrṇikā who happens to use her pestle in the nearby.[17] The *mantra*s here are supposed not to convey any meaning as there is no connection with the sacrifice.

Only in the situation when there is such a connection, a full meaning of the recited *mantra*s is to be grasped as coming out of the mutual relation of all elements constituting the *artha* of the *Veda* meant as carrying out the sacrifice in its complexity.

In such a model the canonical value of a text comes into play with other elements after mastering its repertoire first (*svādhyaya*), and in the situation of performance where all elements of sacrificial drama are duly applied. The text is thus rather separated from its internal meaning, though on the other hand we see Sāyaṇa

[16] PETERSON (1890: 4): 'The *brahmā*, himself alone, purifies the whole path of the sacrifice ...'—*brahmā tv eka ... yajña-mārgaṁ kṛtsnam api saṁskaroti* (MÜLLER (1890: 2.13)).

[17] MÜLLER (1890: 4.17).

commenting in principle on each word of the *Ṛg-veda*. And perhaps this idea of explaining each word in relation to the *artha* of the *Veda* rather than an autonomous message of the hymns shows Sāyaṇa's characteristic way of conceiving of a canonical text. It prevents students of the *Veda* from free interpretation of the text they strive to master over through daily study. Yet it promises the sense to emerge for the performer out of live performance in the situation that could be styled as that of insider in contradistinction to the outsider's perspective of an interpreter of the text. The former allows for manipulating the canon's powers, the latter may serve to manipulate canon in order to use its authority.[18]

Sāyaṇa, or rather the Vijayanagar kingdom's reason of state, needed an amplified image of one canonical *Veda* as a vehicle for its authority. And for Sāyaṇa (or, perhaps, Mādhava) only an idea of the aim of one whole *Veda* could give a clear rationale for the superiority of the YV over the RV which in turn was necessary to look for the meaning of *ṛc* verses as referring first and foremost to the sacrifice.

## APPENDIX

*Ṛg-veda-bhāṣyôpodghāta*:

*vāg-īśâdyāḥ sumanasaḥ sarvârthānām upakrame /*
*yaṁ natvā kṛta-kṛtyāḥ syus taṁ namāmi gajânanam //1//*
*yasya niḥśvasitaṁ vedā yo vedebhyo 'khilaṁ jagat /*
*nirmame tam ahaṁ vande vidyā-tīrtha-mahêśvaram //2//*
*yat-kaṭâkṣeṇa tad-rūpaṁ dadhad bukka-mahī-patiḥ /*
*ādiśan mādhavâcāryaṁ vedârthasya prakāśane //3//*
*ye pūrvôttara-mīmāṁse te vyākhyâtisaṁgrahāt /*
*kṛpālur mādhavâcāryo vedârthaṁ vaktum udyataḥ //4//*
*ādhvaryavasya yajñeṣu prādhānyād vyākṛtaḥ purā /*
*yajur-vedo 'tha hautrârtham ṛgvedo vyākariṣyate //5//*
*etasmin prathamo 'dhyāyaḥ saṁpradāyataḥ /*
*vyutpannas tāvatā sarvaṁ boddhuṁ śaknoti buddhimān //6//*

[18] On the role of interpretative agent in interpreting canons see PATTON (1994: 314).

'/1/ I salute the elephant-faced God, to whom the Lord of Speech and other well-disposed [gods] bow when undertaking any task (may they be successful),

/2/ Whose breath are the *Veda*s, who created the world with the help of the *Veda*s, Him I revere—*Vidyā-tīrtha* in the form of *Mahêśvara*.

/3/ At his [godly] glance king Bukka took his form and ordered Mādhavâcārya to shed light on the *artha* of the *Veda*.

/4/ After he thoroughly explained both the Pūrva and Uttara Mīmāṁsā, the compassionate Mādhavâcārya decided to speak about the *artha* of the *Veda*.

/5/ Due to the predominance of the sphere of *adhvaryu* in sacrifices it was the *Yajur-veda* which was explained first. Now the *Ṛg-veda* as the *artha* of *hotṛ*'s domain shall be explained.

/6/ In this task the first *adhyāya* [shall be presented] according to the tradition. If one manages to comprehend this one, being a *buddhiman*, he can understand all.'

*Taittirīya-saṁhitā-bhaṣyôpodghāta*:

[stanza 1–3 = *Ṛg-veda-bhaṣyôpodghāta* 1–3]

*sa prāha nṛpatiṁ rājan sāyaṇâryo mamânujaḥ /*
*sarvaṁ vetty eṣa vedānāṁ vyākhyātṛtve niyujyatām //4//*
*ity ukto mādhavâryeṇa vīra-bukka-mahī-patiḥ /*
*anvaśāt sāyaṇâcāryaṁ vedârthasya prakāśane //5//*

[stanza 6 = *Ṛg-veda-bhaṣyôpodghāta* 4]

*brāhmaṇaṁ kalpa-sūtre dve mīmāṁsāṁ vyākṛtiṁ tathā /*
*udāhṛtyâtha taiḥ sarvair mantrârthaḥ spaṣṭam īryate //7//*

/4/ And he [i.e. Mādhavâcārya] said to the Ruler: O King! Here is respected Sāyaṇa, my younger brother. He knows everything of the *Veda*s—lay on him the burden of the commentary [on the *Veda*].

/5/ Being told so by the venerable Mādhava, the brave king Bukka ordered Sāyaṇâcārya to shed light on the *artha* of the *Veda*.

/7/ With the help of explanations of both *Brāhmaṇa*s and *Kalpa-sūtra*s and two Mīmāṁsās, illustrated with examples from all of them, the *artha* of the *mantra*s is brought to light.'

## BIBLIOGRAPHY


BALI 1999 = Bali, S.: *Sāyaṇa's Upodghāta to the Taittirīya Saṁhitā and the Ṛgveda Saṁhitā*. Delhi 1999.

FILLIOZAT 1973 = Filliozat, V.: *L'Épigraphie de Vijayanagar du début à 1377*. Paris 1973.

FRAUWALLNER 1973 = Frauwallner, Erich: *History of Indian Philosophy*. Vols. 1–2, Motilal Banarsidass, Delhi 1973. [Reprinted: 1984].

GONDA 1975 = Gonda, Jan: *Vedic Literature*. Wiesbaden 1975.

HEESTERMAN 1981 = Heesterman, Jan C.: *The Inner Conflict of Tradition*, Chicago 1981.

JOSHI 1986 = Joshi, K.L.: *Sarva-Darśana-Sangraha of Mādhavācārya translated by E.B. Cowell and A.E. Gough*. 1986.

KRIPACHARYULU 1986 = Kripacharyulu, M.: *Sayana and Madhava-Vidyaranya, A Study of their Lives and Letters*. Guntur 1986.

KULKE 1985 = Kulke, H.: 'Maharajas, Mahants and Historians. Reflections on the Historiography of Early Vijayanagara and Sringeri,' in: Dallapiccola Libera (ed.): *Vijayanagara—City and Empire*. Stuttgart 1985.

MÜLLER 1890 = Müller, F. Max: *Introduction to the Second Edition of Rig-Veda, the Sacred Hymns of the Brahmanas*. London 1890. [Reprinted: Varanasi 1983].

PATTON 1994 = Patton, L.L. (ed.): *Authority, Anxiety and Canon*, Albany, SUNY 1994.

PETERSON 1890 = Peterson, P.: *Sāyaṇa's Preface to the Ṛgvedabhāṣya*. Bombay 1890. [Reprinted: Poona 1974].

SDS = *Sarva-darśana-saṁgraha*. See: JOSHI (1986).

ŚB = *The Śatapatha Brāhmaṇa*, in the Mādhyandina-Śākhā with extracts from the commentaries of Sāyaṇa, Harisvāmin and Dvivedagaṅga, ed. by Albrecht Weber, Otto Harrassowitz, Leipzig 1924.

TS = *Taittirīya-saṁhitā*.

VENKATARAMAN 1976 = Venkataraman, K.R.: *The Age of Vidyaranya*. Calcutta 1976.

# Prajāpati, the Fire and the *pañcâgni-vidyā*

JOANNA JUREWICZ

## 1. Five cosmic fires

The *pañcâgni-vidyā,* or the knowledge of the five fires, in its classical form described in the JB, ŚB, BU and CU, has already been analysed by several scholars[1]. In this paper, I would like to propose an approach that takes into consideration earlier R̥gvedic thought and a larger philosophical and ritual context of this concept. This approach reveals the meaning of the *pañcâgni-vidyā* which—as far as I know—has not been proposed yet.

*Pañcâgni-vidyā* describes the world functioning in a series of five sacrificial acts. The first sacrifice is the sacrifice of faith (*śraddhā*, ŚB, BU, CU), or of immortality and water (*amr̥tam āpas*, JB), which is poured into the heaven or the sun[2]. In this sacrifice, king Soma is born. He becomes oblation poured into the next fire, or Parjanya. Out of this sacrifice, rain comes into being as oblation for the next fire, which is the earth. Now, food is created to be oblation for Man as the next fire. Then, semen is generated and it is poured into the next fire, or the woman. Out of this sacrifice, Man is born who 'remains alive for as long as long he lives' (BU) and then dies[3].

---

[1] JB 1.45, BU 6.2.9 ff. (=ŚB 14.9.1.12 ff.), BU (*Kāṇva*) 6.2.9 ff., CU 5.4 ff. DEUSSEN (1995: 136–146, 525–529), FRAUWALLNER (1990: I, 95–97), BODEWITZ (1973: 110–149), SCHMITHAUSEN (1994), BODEWITZ (1996), KILLINGLEY (1997), OBERLIES (1998: 483–487). Since the descriptions of ŚB and BU are identical, I do not differentiate between them and when I use the term 'Upaniṣadic description' or 'the description of the BU', I also mean the description of the ŚB.

[2] For the discussion of possible reasons for the change of *amr̥tam āpas* in the JB into *śraddhā* in the *Upaniṣad*s, see BODEWITZ (1973: 113, 117), SCHMITHAUSEN (1994).

[3] Olivelle's translation in OLIVELLE (1998: 149): *sa jīvati yāvaj jīvati* / . There is a correspondence between the act of sexual union of man and woman (sacrifices 4–5) and the union between heaven and earth through the rain which inseminates the earth as

*Essays in Indian Philosophy, Religion and Literature,* pp. 45–60.

It is justified on the ground of Vedic thought to identify all the oblations which appear in the *pañcâgni-vidyā* scheme with the oblation which is the result of the first sacrifice, i.e. Soma. Already in the RV, rain, food and semen were identified with Soma.[4] Also, as early as in the RV[5], the first oblation of the JB description (*amṛtam āpas*) is identifiable with Soma. The basis for identification of *śraddhā* with Soma is not so well attested in the *Veda*. We could, however, find it in the TB 2.3.10.1–2, where Prajāpati's desire for Soma is equal to the desire for *śraddhā* (*Prajāpati ... somaṁ rājānaṁ cakame / śraddhām u sa cakame*). We can look for some possible lines of investigation in the identification of *śraddhā* with milk; milk is in turn identified with Soma very often in the *Veda*.[6] Thus, one is tempted to reduce all the sacrifices of the *pañcâgni-vidyā* to one sacrifice in which Soma is poured into fire. Understood in this way, they delimit the extent of the world, as it is put elsewhere in the BU (1.4.6): 'Food and eater—that is the extent of this whole world. Food is simply Soma, and the eater is fire' (*etāvād vā idaṁ sarvam annaṁ câivânnādaś ca / soma evânnam agnir annādaḥ /* ).[7] Ensuring the constant appearance of the new oblation of the new sacrifice, the specific structure of the five cosmic sacrifices guarantees the continuity of the whole process and, thus, the continuity of the world's existence.

---

semen inseminates a woman (sacrifices 1–3). The macrocosmic union is a two-phase process: the heaven does not inseminate the earth directly but through the embodiment of its generative power: Parjanya, who is called *reto-dhā*—'the giver of semen, the inseminator' (see MACDONELL (1897: 83–84)).

[4] In the RV, the ritual of Soma pressing is described to have also a cosmic dimension in which Soma assumed the form of rain, see e.g. RV 9.84.3, 9.39.4, 9.72.6, see also MACDONELL (1897: 107–108). The identification of Soma and food is based on the fact that Soma is a plant giving life and health (see MACDONELL (1897: 112, 154)). For the identification of Soma and semen see e.g. RV 1.164.34–35. See also ŚB 3.3.2.1., 13.5.2.21.

[5] For the identification of Soma and waters, based on its identification with rain, see above, note 4. For Soma as *amṛ́ta*, see e.g. RV 1.43.8, 8.48.12, 9.3.1 and MACDONELL (1897: 108–109).

[6] In the *Śāṅkhāyanâraṇyaka* 10, see BODEWITZ (1973: 269 ff.). The direct identification of *śraddhā* and milk can be also settled on the basis of ŚB 12.7.3.11, where *śraddhā* is called *sū́ryasya duhitṛ́*. This is the exegesis of RV 9.1.6, where *sū́ryasya duhitṛ́* can only mean the dawn (dawn is often called *sū́ryasya duhitṛ́* in the RV, e.g. 1.116.17, 1.117.13, 1.118.5). In the RV, the dawn is very often presented as a cow, which, in turn, is metonymically presented as milk, see below, note 17. For the identification of Soma and milk, see note 42.

[7] Olivelle's translation in OLIVELLE (1998: 47).

## 2. The *pitṛ-yāna* and its correspondence with the *pañcâgni-vidyā*

In the BU and the CU the description of the five sacrifices is followed by the description of the two ways a dead person may take: the way of gods (*deva-yāna*) and the way of fathers (*pitṛ-yāna*). One who follows the *deva-yāna* path finds the final release from the world and is never reborn in it, whereas one who takes the *pitṛ-yāna* comes back to the earth.

I would argue that, in its Upaniṣadic description, the *pitṛ-yāna* path refers to the same process of the world's functioning as is depicted in the *pañcâgni-vidyā* scheme. It is possible to show—as DEUSSEN already proposed—that the stages of the *pitṛ-yāna* correspond to the five successive cosmic sacrifices[8]. I would like to follow his way of investigation.

The last two sacrifices in the *pañcâgni-vidyā* scheme are explicitly enumerated in the *pitṛ-yāna* description: a dead person becomes food and he is poured into Man (the fourth *oblation* and fire), then, he becomes semen poured into the woman (the fifth *oblation* and fire). The third sacrifice in the *pitṛ-yāna* is also easy to find, for it is rain, which constitutes the final form in which a dead person descends upon the earth (rain as *oblation* is poured into the earth, which is fire).

The act of swallowing the dead by gods on the moon corresponds to the second cosmic sacrifice. The BU is more explicit about it. Assuming the form of the radiant person (*puruṣa-bhāsvara-varṇa*), a dead person goes through all the stages of the *pitṛ-yāna* and finally goes to the moon. Then, he becomes gods' food. According to the Vedic ideas, it was Soma which was gods' food.[9] The BU compares a dead person to king Soma and describes him as waxing and waning. This activity is characteristic not only of the moon, but also of Soma, which swelled before pressing and then, being pressed, lost its previous swollen form. Thus, the *oblation* of the second *pitṛ-yāna* sacrifice is the same as the *āhuti* of the second sacrifice in the *pañcâgni-vidyā*, i.e. Soma[10]. The identity of the fire of the second sacrifice at the

---

[8] DEUSSEN (1995: I,139): 'analogous with this appears also the return of man out of the yonder world as a passage of the same through five sacrificial fires, the yonder world, Parjanya (rain), earth (Bṛh 'this world'), man, woman, in which the man is sacrificed, successively as faith, Soma, rain, food, sperm (semen).'

[9] See e.g. ŚB 11.1.5.3.

[10] In the CU, it is the moon that seems to be identified with king Soma and called the food of gods eaten by gods: *eṣa somo rājā / tad devānām annam / taṁ devā bhakṣayanti /*. But KU 1.2 attests the identity of the dead with the moon: *teṣāṁ prāṇaiḥ pūrva-pakṣa āpyāyate / tān apara-pakṣeṇa prajanayati /*

*pañcâgni-vidyā* and the *pitṛ-yāna* schemes is less evident. As far as the Upaniṣadic description is concerned, we may infer it on the basis of the ŚB which identifies all the gods with Parjanya[11].

### 3. First sacrifice of the *pañcâgni-vidyā* and the *pitṛ-yāna* schemes

The first sacrifice of the *pitṛ-yāna* is constituted by the act of putting a dead person (*puruṣa*) into fire. The possible identification of heaven and the cremation fire results from the possibility of their identification with the sun.[12]

#### 3.1. Possibilities of identifying *śraddhā* with a dead person

The oblation of the first sacrifice in the *pañcâgni-vidyā* in the *Upaniṣad*s is *śraddhā*. According to DEUSSEN, *śraddhā* is identified with one's deeds and it forms an essential immortal part of a human being which remains after the death[13]. The fact that the sacrifice for the dead performed already during the cremation rite was called *śrāddha* ('that which is connected with *śraddhā*') supports DEUSSEN's thesis that it was *śraddhā* which was believed to remain after one's death and to undergo

---

[11] See ŚB 6.7.3.1: *etad vai devā akāmayanta parjanyo rūpaṁ syāmêti te etenâtmanā parjanyo rūpam abhavaṁs tathâivâitad yajamāna etenâtmanā parjanyo rūpaṁ bhavati* / . Also the conviction that plants are god's wives (ŚB 6.5.4.4) confirms the identity of gods and Parjanya, who inseminates plants (already in RV 5.83.1,7,9). In the JB, instead of Parjanya there is a thunder (*stanayitnu*); thundering is attributed to Parjanya (ŚB 14.5.5.10). BU 3.9.6 identifies *stanayitnu* with Indra who can be treated as gods' representative.

[12] In the Vedic thought the sun is not so clearly distinct from heaven, they are even named by one word *svàr*: 'heaven, sun'. The JB mentions the sun instead of heaven. Already in the RV fire was identified with the sun, see e.g. RV 1.50.1, 3.2.12, 10.88.11, see also MACDONELL (1897: 93).

[13] See DEUSSEN (1906: 333): 'As the libation poured into fire (Soma, milk etc.) [the dead person—J.J.] ascends in spiritual form to the gods, so the immortal part of man ascends to heaven from the funeral pyre.' DEUSSEN identifies it with the dead person's *karman*, and writes: 'This work—this faith—ascends to heaven as the immortal part of man and is there five times in succession offered up by the gods in the sacrificial fires of the heaven, the atmosphere, the earth, the man and the woman. By this means he is changed successively from faith to Soma etc.' BODEWITZ (1973: 113, 117) rejects the possibility of joining *śraddhā* with the dead person: 'I do not think that *śraddhā* has to be connected with the cremation and that it makes the cycle complete. This *śraddhā* starting the stream of immortal fluid from heaven does not originate from earth' (p. 117). But he does not give any convincing argument why we should not accept the identity of *śraddhā* and the dead person.

transformations during the funeral ceremony.[14] The identity of the *śraddhā* with a dead person is explicitly expressed in the JUB, according to which, after his death, Man is transformed into the *śraddhā*.[15]

### 3.2. Possibilities of identifying *amr̥tam āpas* with a dead person

In the JB description of the *pañcâgni-vidyā* scheme the first oblation is called *amr̥tam āpas*. Although this Brāhmaṇa proposes a different description of the afterlife journey as compared to that of the *Upaniṣad*s, it is worth noticing that also here it is possible to identify the first cosmic oblation with a dead person put onto a funeral pyre.

The identification of a dead person placed on a funeral pyre with immortality (*amr̥ta*) can be proved on the basis of two arguments. Firstly, this form is immortal because it is the form which somehow survives the death. Secondly, a dead person was treated as a sacrificial oblation (*āhuti*).[16] The R̥gvedic material allows us to assume that this person was identified with Soma. RV 10.16.5 describes a dead person as the oblation which is poured (*ā́huta*) into the funeral fire (see below, § 5). Further on (RV 10.16.7), it is recommended that the body of a dead person should be protected against fire by cow hide (*agner várma pári góbhir vyayasva sám prórṇuṣva pī́vasā médasā ca*). This is the only place in the RV where the word *gó* in the plural refers to cow hide. Usually, in its metaphorical sense it means the milk

---

[14] The aim of *śrāddha* performed during a funeral rite was to equip the dead person with the body enabling him to go to heaven. The aim of the first *pitr̥-yāna* sacrifice is the same. It is interesting to notice that, according to ŚB 12.8.2.4, *śraddhā* is an embodiment (*rūpa*) of *dīkṣā* (see also ŚB 12.1.2.1 and LÉVI (1898: 108)) and, according to JUB 3.11.1, the *dīkṣā* is one of the three deaths of man: the first one is the birth, when man is transformed into *prāṇa*, the second is *dīkṣā,* when man is transformed into *chandāṁsi*, and the third is the real death, when man is transformed into *śraddhā*. So, besides the explicit identification of a dead person with the *śraddhā*, we have the identification of the death and the *dīkṣā,* which is in turn identified with the *śraddhā*. This reinforces the possibility of identifying a dead person and the *śraddhā*.

[15] JUB 3.11.4,7: *athâitat tr̥tīyaṁ mriyate yan mriyate / sa śraddhām evâbhisambhavati / lokam abhijāyate … atra tr̥tīyayâvr̥tâmum eva lokaṁ jayati yad u câmuṣmiṁl loke / tad etayā câinaṁ śraddhayā samardhayati yayâivâinam etac chraddhayâgnāv abhyādadhati sam ayam ito bhaviyatîti / etaṁ câsmai lokaṁ prayacchati yam abhijāyate /*

[16] See EVISON (1989: 314, 324, 330, 331).

with which the pressed Soma is mixed[17] and association with it quite natural. The validity of this association is supported by the fact that there was a habit to cover a dead person with some milky food if the cow was not killed during the cremation rite.[18] All this shows the image of a dead person to be very close to the image of Soma covered with milk (*góbhis*) in the ritual. Soma, in turn, is called *amṛta*.[19] Thus, the identification of a dead person with *amṛta* becomes possible.

The possibility of identification of a dead person with Soma justifies identification of a dead person with water (*āpas*) because already in the RV soma is identified with water[20]. The descriptions of the cremation ceremony are also helpful in the search for the identification of the dead with waters: there we can trace the idea that a dead person was transformed into waters during the ceremony of cooling the cremation ground with water and milk. He had remained in this watery form before he acquired a new form during the bones collection rite[21]. One should notice the difference between the sequences of the funeral ceremony and the first sacrifice: in the *pañcâgni-vidyā* scheme, waters are poured into the sun, whereas in the funeral rite, the watery form of the dead person appears after he had been burnt on the funeral pyre. But what is here important is that the identification of the dead person with waters attested in the descriptions of the cremation rite. I would like to point out that correspondence can also be seen in the next step of the cremation rite,

---

[17] E.g. RV 1.134.2, 3.35.8, 9.32.3, 9.74.8, 9.103.2, *passim*. See SRINIVASAN (1979: 61 ff.).

[18] See EVISON (1989: 327).

[19] See Note 5.

[20] See its identification with rain, Note 4. See also OBERLIES (1999: 31–42).

[21] EVISON (1989: 354): 'The mantras accompanying the sprinkling of the bones as Caland points out ([*Die*] *A*[*ltindischen*] *T*[*oten- und*] *B*[*estattungsgebräuche*], p. 102—J.J.) clearly indicate that this ceremony is intended to cool and extinguish fire used during cremation ... In the ritual intended to extinguish the flame of the pyre, Agni is returned to a state of potentiality in watery womb from which he sprang. In other words, Agni is changed back into waters from which he became.' JB and BU explicitly express the identity of Agni and a dead person describing the transformation of the fire of the latter into the fire of funeral pyre (*tasyâgnir evâgnir bhavati* ...). This idea is probably based on the funeral experience: the bones of a dead person put into fire are hot. I would also like to pay attention to the JUB 3.10.9: *atha yad evâinam etad asmāl lokāt pretaṁ cityām ādadhaty atho yā evaitā avokṣaṇīyā āpas tā eva sa tato 'nusaṁbhavati prāṇam eva prāṇo hy āpaḥ* / . According to Oertel (JUB), the text only expresses the idea of being born after the waters are born. I would argue, however, that the phrase *tā eva sa tato 'nusaṁbhavati* expresses also the idea of being identified with waters and then being born out of them.

namely, in the ritual of sowing plants on the cooled cremation ground. It conveys the idea that both fertility and food are the effects of the cremation rite just as they result from the pouring of waters into the sun.

In my opinion, it is also important that the JB presents the description of the cremation rite in the middle of the description of the destiny of a dead person. Even if it was an insertion from a *sūtra* (as BODEWITZ states)[22], this insertion is significant as an expression of the compiler's / compilers' conviction that there is a link between the *pañcâgni-vidyā* and the cremation rite.

The above discussion shows the correspondence between the *pañcâgni-vidyā* and the *pitr̥-yāna* schemes. It can be discovered not only in the Upaniṣadic descriptions but also in the JB where the first sacrifice of the *pañcâgni-vidyā* corresponds to the funeral rite. In my opinion this reflects the idea that the cremation rite has its cosmic aspect and, when a dead person was put on the earthly funeral pyre, he—in the form of the heavenly oblation (*śraddhā* / *amr̥tam āpas*)—was burnt in the sun. Thus, he gained the Somic radiant (*bhāsvara-varṇa*) form. Then, according to the *Upaniṣads*, if he was destined for the *pitr̥-yāna*, instead of going higher and higher with the rising sun on its northern path, he slid down, as it were, to the moon in order to become rain and he came back to the earth. The CU 5.10.10 explicitly says: 'they do not reach the year' (*nâite saṁvatsaram abhiprāpnuvanti* / )[23]. They only catch 'the edge' of the sun, or its *dakṣiṇa-pātha*.

## 4. *Pañcâgni-vidyā, pitr̥-yāna* and the *R̥g-veda*

The idea that the dead find their final abode on the sun is an old one and appears already in the RV. The fathers (*pitáras*) are said to be in the middle of heaven (*mádhye dívaḥ*, RV 10.15.14), where also the sun is.[24] The dead are described as moving thanks to the *svadhā́* (RV 10.16.5, 1.164.30,38); the *svadhā́* is also the power that makes the sun move (RV 4.13.5, 4.14.4). They are called the heads of the sky (*divó mūrdhā́nas*, RV 9.69.8), which is the name of Agni and Soma in their solar aspects, reaching the zenith[25]. The fathers are described as joining with the

---

[22] BODEWITZ (1973: 124).

[23] Olivelle's translation in OLIVELLE (1988: 237). In the JB the dead person meets the seasons who are messengers of the sun.

[24] See first of all RV 10.139.2 and 1.108.12. Also RV 4.13.2, 5.63.4,7, 9.107.7, 10.156.4.

[25] E.g. RV 1.59.2, 9.27.3.

rays of the sun (RV 1.109.7). RV 10.15.3 describes them as being together with Agni ([*apā́m*] *nápāt*) and with the step of Viṣṇu (*vikrámaṇaṁ víṣṇoḥ*) usually interpreted as the third step of Viṣṇu identified with the sun in its highest position[26]. It can also be proven that the Yama's abode was supposed to be on the sun[27].

What is more, there are also some instances showing that already in the RV the dead were supposed to come back to the earth in the form of rain. It would go beyond the scope of this paper to consider all of them, so I will limit myself only to RV 10.16.5:

> *áva sṛja púnar agne pitṛ́bhyo yás ta ā́hutaś carati svadhā́bhiḥ /*
> *ā́yur vásāna úpa vetu śéṣaḥ sāṁ gacchatāṁ tanvā̆ jāta-vedaḥ //*

Verse b can be said to describe a sojourn of a dead person on the sun: as the Somic oblation, he is poured into the heavenly fire, or the sun with which he moves thanks to *svadhā́* (see above, p. 51). Verse a concisely expresses the return of the dead person to the earth. I would like to stress that, as far as I know, all the scholars have so far interpreted the verse as an expression of the request to Agni to send back the dead person again to the fathers[28]. But this interpretation neglects the meaning of *áva√sṛj*, which means 'releasing down' and not 'up'. The form *pitṛ́bhyas* should be interpreted not as the dative form, but as the ablative form: it denotes the starting point of a dead person's journey back to the earth. Moreover, it is important to remember that in the RV Agni had also a solar form.[29] This interpretation is confirmed by the adverb *púnas,* which expresses the repetition of the action, so it can refer only to the human return to the earth. Thus, we get a clear image: Agni, having sent the dead person to the sun to his fathers, should now release him from there and let him come back to his former home and to his offspring (*śéṣas*, see also RV 10.14.8). The rainy form of the dead person coming back to the earth can be inferred from other contexts of *áva√sṛj*. Used in the descriptions of Indra–Vṛtra fight, this verbal root expresses the act of releasing waters, meaning not only rivers

---

[26] RV 1.154.6, 1.155.5, 1.22.20–21. In RV 5.3.3, 10.1.3 it is Agni, who is present in the third step of Viṣṇu. See also MACDONELL (1917: 178). A detailed analysis of this issue is presented in JUREWICZ (2001: 313–318).

[27] First of all, see RV 9.113.7–8 and JUREWICZ (2001: 315–330).

[28] See GELDNER (1951–1957: III,148), ELIZARENKOVA (1999: 133), O'FLAHERTY (1981: 49), FINDLY (1981: 365).

[29] E.g. RV 3.2.12, 6.2.6.

flowing from pierced mountains, but also the rain coming out from the cloud[30]. So finally, I would propose a translation of the above verse:

> 'Release him down, Agni, from [his] fathers, [him] who, poured into you, wanders according to his will. Let him [who] wears life come to his offspring. Let him join with his body, Jāta-vedas!'

It is the JB that preserves the most of the Ṛgvedic ideas of the dead person's journey to the sun: it does not mention the moon at all[31]. Here, on the first path, the dead person meets one of the seasons. We could treat it as the messenger of the sun, because the sun is called the guardian of all the divisions of the year[32]. The season itself comes down along the ray of the sun (*raśminā pratyavetya*). The solar destination of the dead on the *pitṛ-yāna* path can also be traced in the *Upaniṣads*: as it has been said above (p. 51), the dead person gets in touch with the sun, although only with its southern path.

On the second path in the JB, the dead person not only meets the season, but he also finally reaches the sun (*salokatām apyeti ya eṣa tapati*). Although this path corresponds with later descriptions of the *deva-yāna*, one should notice that nothing is said here about the light of fire, which, according to the *Upaniṣads*, becomes the dead person's fate on the *deva-yāna* path[33]. Instead of this, the JB describes the principal role of the smoke in shaking off the dead person's body. This idea can also be traced back to the RV, according to which Agni carries the oblations (therefore, the dead) to the heaven with its smoke[34].

---

[30] The same meaning of 'being poured down' by Agni can be found in RV 10.16.13, where the root *nir√vap* expresses the activity of Agni towards a dead person, see JUREWICZ (2000: 332–338). The Ṛgvedic idea of the origination of rain in the sun is described in KAELBER (1990: 15 ff.).

[31] ŚB 1.9.3.15 claims that the sun is the final goal of the deceased. In AB 8.28 the dead person comes to the moon, which enters the sun, which in turn goes to the fire, which goes to the wind. The idea that the moon enters the sun preserves the Ṛgvedic idea of the sun being the final afterlife abode. However, the introduction of the moon foretells later Upaniṣadic thought. Similarly, intermediate in character is ŚB 11.6.2, where the moon, which is Soma, is the offering poured into the sun. KU 1.2 replaces the season by the moon and does not mention the sun at all. So it seems to be formulated later.

[32] JB 1.46: *tasya hâitasya devasyâho-rātre ardha-māsā māsā ṛtavaḥ saṁvatsaro goptā ya eṣa tapati* / .

[33] Also the path is different, see BODEWITZ (1973: 121, n. 22).

[34] Interesting from this point of view is the identification of Agni's smoke with the raining cloud proposed by JAMISON (1991: 272–273).

## 5. The mechanism of the world's functioning

Coming back to my main thesis, it can be assumed that the descriptions of the *pañcâgni-vidyā* and the *pitṛ-yāna* in the *Upaniṣads* refer to the same process of the functioning of the world and put it in the form of a general model. In this model, the dead are the material of the world: swallowed in the *pañcāgni-vidyā* and *pitṛ-yāna* sacrifices they condition the occurrence of the life-giving processes. The sun shines, having swallowed the dead burnt on the funeral pyre (the first sacrifice); the rain comes when gods eat the dead on the moon (the second sacrifice); the earth generates plants, having devoured the dead in the form of the rain (the third sacrifice); semen in the man appears when he eats the dead in the form of plants (the fourth sacrifice); the man is born out of a woman when she absorbs the semen which is the next form of the dead (the fifth sacrifice). It is important to notice here that all the forms of the dead clearly have a life-giving character: Soma gives health and immortality[35], rain gives water and makes the growth of plants possible, food is something that sustains life, semen is something that creates life.[36]

This idea of the cosmic and life-giving character of an individual death is also present in JB 1.46, where the acts of pouring oblation into fire in all five cosmic sacrifices and of the cremation sacrifice are described exactly in the same way[37]. Thus, the JB presents the cremation sacrifice as an activity that is performed day by day and preserves the world just as the five cosmic sacrifices.

## 6. The world functioning as the manifestation of Creator's self-devouring

The JB places the description of the *pañcâgni-vidyā* and the twofold path in the part describing the ritual of *agni-hotra*. Explaining why the ritual should be performed, ŚB 2.2.4 presents the myth of Prajāpati who, having created Agni, is in danger of being eaten by him. In order to avoid death, he has to create food for the hungry Agni, so he creates milk and performs the first act of *agni-hotra*. In the same way, the *yajamāna*, pouring the milk into fire, escapes death and preserves his own existence.

---

[35] E.g. RV 8.48.

[36] In ŚB 12.9.1.6, the seed is called *annasya rasa*.

[37] *tasmin etasminn agnau vaiśvā-nare 'har ahar devāḥ amṛtam apas / somaṁ rājānam / vṛṣṭim / annam / retas / puruṣaṁ juhvati /*.

The idea that *agni-hotra* frees the *yajamāna* from death (identified with Agni) is repeated in almost every chapter of the JB's description[38]. The JB, however, does not analyse thoroughly Prajāpati's perspective, one which gives a wider metaphysical context to the cosmic and the human processes that constitute the created world. Now, I would like to look at the *pañcâgni-vidyā* and the *pitṛ-yāna* from this point of view.

The way Agni and milk are created according to ŚB 2.2.4 entitles us to assume that in this act Prajāpati manifests his own fiery interior: by heating himself, he produces Agni out of his mouth. This act may be interpreted as the act of blowing or speaking.[39] Produced in an act of enkindling, milk appears also to be a form of fire.[40] This is to say that both fire and milk are the parts of Prajāpati that are identical with him and that manifest themselves in the creation. So, when Prajāpati gives milk to fire, he actually kills and eats himself[41].

The idea of Prajāpati dying in the creative process is most explicitly expressed in the *agni-cayana* myths of the ŚB, in which Prajāpati does not extract milk or any other food out of himself, but, having created the world, he himself becomes the food of Agni: he dies in order to be eaten by fire[42]. Here, besides the life-giving aspect of the food assuring the existence of fire, we can clearly see the aspect of food which is connected with death: in order to become food one must die, exactly as Prajāpati did.

---

[38] JB 1.2: the *yajamāna* becomes immortal when he offers *agni-hotra*. JB 1.5–6: the *agni-hotra* saves from two repeated dyings which are nights and days (day and night are embodiments of time, which is identified with Agni, the death, in JB 1.12–14). JB 1.9–10: the *agni-hotra* frees from evil (identified with the death). JB 1.11: the *agni-hotra* gives immortality and freedom. JB 1.26–38: the *agni-hotra* pacifies different parts of the world, which are identified with the death. In JB 1.7–8, the *agni-hotra* assures the existence of the world.

[39] For the identification of Agni and the breath (*prāṇa*), see ŚB 6.3.1.21. RV 1.66.1 compares Agni, identified with *ā́yus*, to the *prāṇá*. For the identification of Agni and the speech, see ŚB 3.2.2.13, 10.5.1.1 ff.

[40] In ŚB 2.5.1.3, the milk flows from the breast of the heated Prajāpati which clearly shows the fiery character of this substance and its identity with Prajāpati. In ŚB 6.1.3.1, out of heated Prajāpati, water appears, which is to be understood as sweat. The identity of milk and water is also attested by BU 1.2.1–2 in the metaphor of churning water to produce the cream that transforms itself into the earth. This metaphor goes back to the Ṛgvedic descriptions of the rain generated during Soma pressing, which is described in the metaphor of cream production, e.g. RV 9.110.8.

[41] See also ŚB 6.1.2.12, 7.1.2.1.

[42] ŚB 6.1.1 ff.

It is important to notice that ŚB 2.2.4 stresses that the death of Prajāpati should not occur too early, before he exudes his eatable part. This means that Prajāpati does not want to be the food of fire in his unmanifested form, he does not want to accept the situation when he, the Creator, is eaten by his creation, even though it is identical with him.

But having created, out of himself, the food that is adequate for his swallowing manifestation, he will be able to devour himself safely. In my opinion, the scheme of the *pañcâgni-vidyā* together with the Upaniṣadic *pitṛ-yāna* describes how the world functions ensuing this safe self-devouring of the Creator. Dead people who are the food of the world constitute the dead milky part of Prajāpati who is killed and eaten by his fiery part.

All the oblations of the *pañcâgni-vidyā* and *pitṛ-yāna* sacrifices (*amṛtam āpas* / *śraddhā* / dead person—Soma—rain—food—semen) can be identified with milk, which is the main oblation of the *agni-hotra*.[43] They can also be—as it has been said above—identified with Soma; it is worth noticing that JB 1.3–4 equates the *agni-hotra* with soma sacrifice. So the five sacrifices can be understood as the acts of the perfect *agni-hotra* in which the Creator, offering his milky / Somic part to his fiery part, saves himself from death.[44]

---

[43] For the identity of Soma and milk, see e.g. RV 9.34.3, 9.42.4, 9.91.3. The identification of milk and rain see the above, note 39. For the identification of the seed and milk, see e.g. RV 3.31.10 (here we have also identification of both substances with Soma). According to ŚB 6.5.4.15, the pouring of milk into the *ukhā* during the *agni-cayana* guarantees the presence of milk in the woman (*tasmād yoṣāyāṁ payaḥ*). Not only milk in the breasts is meant here, but also semen, because the *ukhā* also symbolises the womb, which accepts semen, see ŚB 7.1.1.41. The identification of *amṛtam āpas* with milk is based on their identification with rain (see BODEWITZ (1973: 117)) and with Soma (see above). For the identification of *śraddhā* and milk see above, note 6. The identification of a dead person with milk is based on his identity with Soma.

[44] It would be interesting to find out whether the five *prāṇa*s of the *yajamāna* created in the *agny-ādhāna* rite could correspond to the five cosmic sacrifices understood as the *agni-hotra* performed by Prajāpati and whether there is an exact correspondence between five *prāṇa*s and the five sacrifices. For sure, the fifth one, speech, is identified with Agni and the earth in the Veda. The creation of the world seen as the creation of the consecutive *prāṇa*s (seven not five) is described in the ŚB 10.5.3.1–12 (*manas—vāc—prāṇa—cakṣus—śrotra—karman—agni*). The analysis of the possible correspondence between the *pañcâgni-vidyā* and the *agni-cayana* also needs separate investigation; here I would only like to point out that the number of sacrifices corresponds to the number of layers and that every cosmic sacrifice could be treated as the creation of one layer during which Prajāpati is burnt by Agni and thus created once again.

I would like to stress the striking similarity between the ŚB's myth about Prajāpati blowing out fire which is identical with him and the JB's initial description (1.1–2) of the *yajamāna* who, in the act of enkindling fire in the *agny-ādhāna* rite, creates his own self consisting of five life breaths (*prāṇa*). In fact, it is the enkindled fire that is the *yajamāna*'s self. In this very fire-self the *yajamāna* has to perform the *agni-hotra* in order to obtain long life and immortality after the death. In the same way, Prajāpati enkindles himself as Agni and then has to redeem himself (*niṣ√krī*) from his fiery self in the repeated acts of the cosmic *agni-hotra*.[45]

I think that it is here where we should look for the reason why, in every sacrifice of the *pañcâgni-vidyā*, the creation of the oblation is described at length, whereas the existence of the succeeding fires is merely stated. Since Agni created in the first creative act constantly burns and poses a deathly threat to the Creator, who in turn has to assume the form of food satisfying the hunger of his eating part in order to avoid self-annihilation. At the same time, the aim of this self-devouring is the preservation of life within the creation, life which manifests itself in the life-giving processes of the sun's shining, of the generation of rain, food and semen, of the birth of the human being. The existence of the world thus understood becomes a kind of tight-rope act of the Creator balancing on the verge of life and death within the creation and on the verge of his total, absolute existence.

The reference to the ŚB's description enables us to discover one more semantic dimension of the *pañcâgni-vidyā* and *pitṛ-yāna* sacrifices—a cognitive one. In ŚB 2.2.4.3, it is said that the creative changes took place in Prajāpati's mind.[46] So the eating part of Prajāpati can also be interpreted as representing the subject of the cognition, the eaten one—its object. Thus, the five cosmic / afterlife sacrifices reveal the meaning of the successive subjective-objective acts undertaken by the Creator while he manifests himself in the world. They are performed only to confirm the identity of the subject and the object, as it is confirmed in the act of eating in which food becomes one with its eater.

[45] The similarities between the Prajāpati and the *yajamāna* can also be seen in the description of the last sacrifice performed by the human being, i.e. the funeral rite when a dead person becomes the food for fire. But at the same time he himself is fire, as the JB, BU and CU claim (*tasyâgnir evâgnir bhavati* … ). This is to mean that, actually, he is at the same time the devouring and the devoured entity, exactly as the Prajāpati is present both in the *agni-hotra* and the *agni-cayana* myths. Also, the bright Somic immortal form acquired by the deceased person after cremation corresponds to the immortal state obtained by the Prajāpati when he avoided death by feeding Agni with milk (the *agni-hotra* myth), and to his revival after he was burnt by Agni and then stood up full of strength (the *agni-cayana* myth, see ŚB 6.2.1, 7.1.2, 10.1.3.6.).

[46] *tad evâsya manasy āsa* /

Many issues analysed here need more investigation. I hope, though, that I have shown the importance of the metaphysical and the ritual contexts of the *pañcâgni-vidyā* and of its earlier, Ṛgvedic background, which, when taken into consideration, open new possibilities of interpretation. I would like also to draw attention to the fact that the Vedic thought resolves the problem of the Absolute and the evil differently to the Christian thought: here the most important attribute of the Absolute is its total freedom—even the freedom to be annihilated; the second one is his omnipotence to avoid the annihilation. Death in the world is just a manifestation of the Absolute's freedom and omnipotence. It is not a curse but rather a blessing: it ensures the existence not only of the world but also of its Creator.

| SACRIFICE | | FIRE | | OBLATION | |
|---|---|---|---|---|---|
| ***Pañcâgni-vidyā*** | | | | | |
| | 1. | heaven (*asau loka*) | + | faith (*śraddhā*) | |
| | | sun (*ya eṣa tapati*) | + | immortality [and] waters (*amṛtam āpas*) | → Soma |
| | 2. | Parjanya / thunder-bolt (*stanayitnu*) | + | Soma | → rain |
| | 3. | earth | + | rain | → food |
| | 4. | Man | + | food | → semen |
| | 5. | woman | + | semen | → Man |
| ***Pitṛ-yāna*** | | | | | |
| | 1. | fire | + | Man | → *puruṣa-bhāsvara-varṇa* [Soma] |
| | 2. | gods | + | *puruṣa-bhāsvara-varṇa* [Soma] | → rain |
| | 3. | earth | + | rain | → food |
| | 4. | Man | + | food | → semen |
| | 5. | woman | + | semen | → Man |
| | | PRAJĀPATI = AGNI | | PRAJĀPATI = MILK DEAD PRAJAPATI | |

## BIBLIOGRAPHY

AB = *Aitareya Brāhmaṇa*, herausgegeben von Theodor Aufrecht, Vols. 1–2, ed. by Theodor Aufrecht, Bonn 1879.

BODEWITZ 1973 = Bodewitz, Henk W.: *Jaiminīya Brāhmaṇa I, 1–65. Translation and commentary with study of agnihotra and prāṇāgnihotra*. E.J. Brill, Leiden 1973.

BODEWITZ 1996 = Bodewitz, Henk W.: 'The *Pañcāgnividyā* and the *Pitṛyāna*/*Devayāna*', *Studies on Indology (Professor Mukunda Madhava Sharma Felicitation Volume)*, ed. by Ashok Kumar Goswami, Darmeswar Chutia. Sri Satguru Publications, Delhi 1996: 51–57.

BU = *Bṛhadāraṇyaka Upaniṣad*, in OLIVELLE (1998).

CU = *Chāndogya Upaniṣad*, in OLIVELLE (1998).

DEUSSEN 1906 = Deussen, Paul: *The Philosophy of the Upaniṣads*. Tr. by A.S. Geden, Edinburg 1906.

DEUSSEN 1995 = Deussen, Paul: *Sixty Upaniṣads of the Veda*. Tr. by V.M. Bedekar and G.B. Palsule, Motilal Banarsidass, Delhi 1995. [Repr. of 1980].

ELIZARENKOVA 1999 = Елизаренкова, Татяна Я.: *Ригведа. Мандалы IX-X*. Наука, Москва 1999. [Elizarenkova, Tatiana Y.: *Rigveda. Mandalas IX–X*. Moskva 1999. In Russian].

EVISON 1989 = Evison, Gillian: *Indian Death Rituals: the Enactment of Ambivalence*. D. Phil. Thesis, University of Oxford 1989.

FINDLY 1981 = Findly, Ellison Banks: 'Jātavedas in the Ṛgveda: The God of Generations', *Zeitschrift der Deutschen Morgenländischen Gesellschaft* 131/2 (1981) 249–373.

FRAUWALLNER 1990 = Frauwallner, Erich, *Historia filozofii indyjskiej*. Vols. 1–2, Polish tr. by Leon Żylicz, Państwowe Wydawnictwo Naukowe, Warszawa 1990. [Originally publ. as *Geschichte der indischen Philosophie*, 1. und 2. Band, Salzburg 1953–1956].

GELDNER 1951–1957 = Geldner, Karl Friedrich: *Der Rig-Veda*. Aus dem Sanskrit ins Deutsche übersetzt und mit einem laufenden Kommentar versehen von Karl Friedrich Geldner, Vols. 1–3, Harvard University Press, Cambridge, Massachusetts 1951, 1957.

JAMISON 1991 = Jamison, Stephanie: *The Ravenous Hyenas and the Wounded Sun. Myth and Ritual in Ancient India*. Cornell University Press, Ithaca and London 1991.

JB = *Jaiminīya Brāhmaṇa*, critically ed. by Raghu Vira and Lokesh Candra, Motilal Banarsidass, Delhi 1996. [Second revised edition].

JUB = *Jaiminīyopaniṣad Brāhmaṇa*, ed. and tr. by H. Oertel, *Journal of Royal Asiatic Society* 16 (1986) 79–260.

JUREWICZ 2001 = Jurewicz, Joanna: *Kosmogonia Rygwedy. Myśl i metafora* [*Cosmogony of the Ṛg-veda. Thought and the Metaphor*]. Wydawnictwo Naukowe *Semper*, Warszawa 2001.

KAELBER 1990 = Kaelber, Walter O.: *Tapta Mārga. Asceticism and initiation in Vedic India*. Sri Satguru Publications, Delhi 1990.

KILLINGLEY 1997 = Killingley, Dermott: 'The Paths of the Dead and the Five fires,' in: *Indian Insights: Buddhism, Brahmanism and Bhakti*, ed. by Peter Connolly and Sue Hamilton, Luzac Oriental, London 1997.

KU = *Kauṣītaki Upaniṣad*, in OLIVELLE (1998).

LÉVI 1898 = Lévi, Sylvain: *La doctrine du sacrifice dans les Brāhmaṇas*. Ernst Leroux, Paris 1898.

MACDONELL 1897 = Macdonnel, Arthur Anthony: *Vedic Mythology*. Verlag von Karl J. Trübner, Strassburg 1897.

MACDONELL 1917 = Macdonell, Arthur Anthony: *A Vedic Reader for Students*. Clarendon Press, Oxford 1917.

OBERLIES 1998 = Oberlies, Thomas: *Die Religion des Ṛgveda. Erster Teil—Das religiöse System des Ṛgveda*. Institut für Indologie der Universität Wien, Wien 1998.

OBERLIES 1999 = Oberlies, Thomas: *Die Religion des Ṛgveda. Zweiter Teil—Kompositionsanalyse der Sama-Hymnen des Ṛgveda*. Institut für Indologie der Universität Wien, Wien 1999.

O'FLAHERTY 1981 = O'Flaherty, Wendy Doniger: *The Ṛgveda. An Anthology*. Penguin Books, London 1981.

OLIVELLE 1998 = Olivelle, Patrick: *The Early Upaniṣads*. Annotated Text and Translation, Oxford University Press, New York–Oxford 1998.

RV = *Die Hymnen des Rigveda*, herausgegeben von Theodor Aufrecht, Vols. 1–2, Adolph Marcus, Bonn 1877.

SCHMITHAUSEN 1994 = Schmithausen, Lambert: 'Zur Textgeschichte der pañcâgni-vidyā', *Wiener Zeitschrift zur Kunde des Südasiens* 34 (1994) 43–60.

SRINIVASAN 1979 = Srinivasan, Doris: *Concept of cow in the Rigveda*. Motilal Banarsidass, Delhi 1979.

ŚB = *The Śatapatha Brāhmaṇa*, in the Mādhyandina-Śākhā with extracts from the commentaries of Sāyaṇa, Harisvāmin and Dvivedagaṅga, ed. by Albrecht Weber, Otto Harrassowitz, Leipzig 1924.

TB = *The Taittirīya Brāhmaṇa of the Black Yajur Veda with the Commentary of Sāyaṇācārya*. Ed. by Rajendralal Mitra, Vols. 1–3, *Bibliotheca Indica*, Calcutta 1859–1890.

# Vedānta Exegesis of *Taittirīyôpaniṣad* 2.1

HALINA MARLEWICZ

## Part I

The purpose of this article is to give a concise exposition of chosen Vedānta approaches to the interpretation of one *śruti* from TU 2.1: *satyaṁ jñānam anantaṁ brahma*—'Brahman [is] real, knowledge, infinite.'

The exposition will be primarily based on the thirteenth century treatise *Prameya-mālā—The Garland of Objects of Knowledge*. More precisely, it is going to be confined to the sixth chapter of it, entitled *Akhaṇḍa-vākyârtha-bhaṅga—The refutation [of the view that] sentence sense/object [is] without parts.*[1] The treatise has been written by Vātsya Varadaguru (ca 1190–1275), a Viśiṣṭâdvaita writer of the post-Rāmānuja period.[2] Vātsya Varadaguru belongs to the little known period in the history of Viśiṣṭâdvaita, and his role and place in the process of adopting and precise formulating of exegetical principles and methods of his school is yet to be discovered. In the chapter Vātsya Varadaguru analyses the aforementioned *śruti* by way of polemics with the Advaita theory of *akhaṇḍa-vākyârtha*. In the course of the discussion, when introducing the ideas of the opponent (or opponents), arguing with them and then giving the exposition of his views, Varadaguru's approach to the exegesis of the TU 2.1 assumes more and more definite form. Before entering into a detailed analysis of the two approaches to the interpretation of TU 2.1, it seems necessary to introduce first the *akhaṇḍa-vākyârtha* theory, which is the pivot of the discussion.

---

[1] The *akhaṇḍa-vākyârtha* formula is, to my understanding, used to describe a certain type of *śruti* which, due to specific understanding of the functions of its constituents, is to actually convey a sense of a singular, unrelated thing as such, and to point to it as something which is without the second (*advaita*) and, consequently, without any qualification.

[2] For more information about Varadaguru's life and work see, for example: STARK (1990) and THOTTAKARA (1990).

*Essays in Indian Philosophy, Religion and Literature*, pp. 61–70.

**The *akhaṇḍa-vākyârtha* theory in Advaita**

It is rather difficult to place the notion precisely in time, though it seems that the very designation begins to be used in the post-Śaṅkara period. The first Advaita thinker to use it was, most probably, Sarvajñātman (c.a. 900 C.E.). In his SŚ he states straightforwardly:

> 'We explain: those sentences—be it Upaniṣadic or secular—[which] cannot express a thing otherwise than as [something which is] without parts (*akhaṇḍa*), they all should proclaim [something] without parts (*akhaṇḍa*).'[3]

When applying the theory to the interpretation of the TU 2.1, Sarvajñātman adopts the following schema:

> (1) The word '*brahma*', the subject-matter (*śeṣi*) of the sentence is the one and only thing to be indicated / *definiendum* (*lakṣya*), and the remaining words (*śeṣa*, i.e. *satyam, jñānam, anantam*) are its indicative terms / *definiens* (*lakṣaṇa*).[4]
>
> (2) Words indicative (*lakṣaṇa*) of Brahman join with the word which is to be indicated / defined (*lakṣya*), but not with each other.[5]
>
> (3) Words '*satya*, etc.,' have various objects as their scopes when taken in their primary senses. Therefore, in order to convey a unified sense, they adopt secondary meanings through the function of *lakṣaṇā* ('indirect indication, implication').[6]

---

[3] See, e.g. SŚ 1.148: *yad vākya-jātam atha veda-śiro-niviṣṭaṁ, yad vâpi laukikam akhaṇḍam apāsya nânyat, śaknoti vastu vadituṁ tad aśeṣam eva, brūyād akhaṇḍam iti tu pratipādayāmaḥ*.

[4] See: SŚ 1.175.1–2: *brahmêti śeṣi padam atra hi lakṣyam ekaṁ, śeṣāṇi lakṣaṇa-samarpaṇam asya kuryuḥ*.

[5] See: SŚ 1.175.3–4: *lakṣyârpaṇena saha lakṣaṇa-vāci sarvaṁ saṁgacchate*.

[6] See: SŚ 1.177.3–4: *satyâdi-śabda-viṣayāḥ śabalās ... lākṣaṇika-vṛttir apîha tulyā*. The words *satyam*... are supposed to undergo here the same process of interpretation as the words *tat* and *tvam* in *tat tvam asi* of ChU 6.7. The constituent words have to partly discard their primary meanings, which are considered to be incongruous with one another, and adopt the indirectly indicated sense, which is of course *akhaṇḍa*. This interpretative process, as explained by Sarvajñātman, is still more complicated, and the intuitive (by no way exclusively logical or linguistic) method of attaining the required *akhaṇḍa* sense / object plays here a major role. The method of interpreting ChU 6.7 and TU 2.1 in the early Advaita has been researched by e.g.: MAYEDA (1979) and MAYEDA (1980–81), as well as MAXIMILIEN (1975) and MAXIMILIEN (1975/76).

(4) The process takes place in the following manner: first there arises the knowledge of words having the same case ending (*samānâdhikaraṇa-pada*), secondly words are related as *determinandum–determinans* (*viśeṣya-viśeṣaṇa*). In the decisive step, in order to avoid incongruity arising from this relation[7], one has to adopt the indirectly indicated sense of a partless whole[8].

One cannot claim, though, that first assumptions of *akhaṇḍa-vākyârtha* theory were set forth by Sarvajñātman himself. One can notice the traces of this interpretative approach already in Śaṅkara's (c.a. 820 C.E.) exegesis of the *śruti* TU 2.1. He seems to be the thinker who first specified its crucial points, summarised below:

(1) The TU 2.1 *śruti* is meant to be a definition (indication) of Brahman[9].

(2) The three words: *satya*, etc., referring to determinants (*viśeṣaṇas*), have Brahman as something to be determined (*viśeṣya*)[10].

(3) Due to the determinants—thing to be determined relation, words *satya*, etc., having the same case ending, are co-referent (*samānâdhikaraṇa*)[11].

(4) Brahman, as something to be determined with the three determinants, i.e. *satya*, etc., is differentiated from other things to be determined[12].

(5) The purpose of the qualifications (*viśeṣaṇas*), serving primarily as defining terms (*lakṣaṇas*), is to exclude Brahman from direct expressing and define (indicate) it.[13]

---

[7] This incongruity, according to the Advaitin, arises inevitably as the consequence of different semantic scopes of words used as *determinans* (*viśeṣaṇa*) and as the *determinandum* (*viśeṣya*).

[8] See SŚ 1. 196: *sāmānâdhikaraṇyam atra bhavati prāthamya-bhāgânvayaḥ, paścād eṣa viśeṣaṇêtaratayā paścād virodhôdbhavaḥ, utpanne ca virodha eka-rasake vastuny akhaṇḍâtmake vṛttir lakṣaṇayā bhavaty ayam iha jñeyaḥ kramaḥ sūribhiḥ.*

[9] TUBh p. 443.5–6: *satyaṁ jñānam anantaṁ brahmêti brahmaṇo lakṣanârthaṁ vākyām.*

[10] TUBh p. 443.6: *satyâdīni hi trīṇi viśeṣaṇârthāni padāni viśeṣyasya brahmaṇaḥ.*

[11] TUBh p. 443.7: *viśeṣaṇa-viśeṣyatvād eva satyâdīny eka-vibhakty-antāni padāni samānâdhikaraṇāni.*

[12] TUBh p. 444.1: *satyâdibhis tribhir viśeṣaṇair viśeṣyamāṇaṁ brahma viśeṣyântarebhyo nirdhāryate.*

[13] TUBh p. 444.5: *lakṣaṇârthatvād viśeṣaṇānām* … , and p. 452.3: *evam … satyâdi-śabda-vācyāt tan nivartakā brahmaṇo lakṣaṇârthāś ca bhavanti.*

All these steps of the interpretation of TU 2.1 by Śaṅkara are present in the later development of the method, which took a definite shape in the *akhaṇḍa-vākyârtha* theory. Śaṅkara's pupil, Sureśvara (850 C.E.) follows his teacher in most of the steps enumerated above, supplying a methodological structure to Śaṅkara's interpretation[14]

The *akhaṇḍa-vākyârtha* theory as presented by Sarvajñātman contains features of Śaṅkara and Sureśvara's approach. In the *akhaṇḍa-vākyârtha* theory, words of the sentence are also to stand in the relation of *lakṣya–lakṣaṇa* (*definiendum–definiens*)[15]. For the proper interpretation of the TU 2.1, the relation of *determinandum–determinans* (*viśeṣya-viśeṣaṇa*) becomes secondary to the fundamental relation of *definiendum–definiens* (*lakṣya–lakṣaṇa*). The theory propounds, as well, the requirement of the same case ending for words related secondarily as *viśeṣaṇa* and *viśeṣya* in the sentence[16], and indicates the fact that *viśesaṇa* words have to, and do refer to one and the same object[17].

The *viśeṣaṇa*s indicate Brahman secondarily as the only object of the sentence, by excluding qualifications, contrary to those named by *viśeṣaṇa*s themselves, from Brahman's nature.

All these elements are present in Sarvajñātman's method of interpreting the *śruti* of TU 2.1. An original contribution of Sarvajñātman seems to be the introduction of a partless sense/object of the sentence (*akhaṇḍa-vākyârtha*), attained through the function of indirect indication (*lakṣaṇā*) as the conclusive step in the interpretative process.

### The *akhaṇḍa-vākyârtha* theory as introduced by Vātsya Varadaguru

Varadaguru opens the chapter stating vehemently:

> 'But if they state [that *śruti* sentences, which are aggregates] of congruent words (*samānâdhikaraṇa-pada*) communicate single, non-partial (*akhaṇḍa*) "essence" (*rasa,* here: the sentence-object) this is unwise, too, because they (= sentences) *also* like other sentences, have as their object inevitably [a thing which is] determined (*viśiṣṭa-viṣaya*).'[18]

[14] See the long exposition of it in TUBhV 2.44–107, or NS 3.3.

[15] Cf. SŚ 1.175.1–2 and TUBh p. 444.5–8.

[16] Cf. SŚ 1.196 and TUBh p. 443.6–7.

[17] SŚ 1.175 and TUBh p. 443.7.

[18] PMā p. 13.1: *yat tu samānâdhikaraṇa-pada-samudāyâtmakānām akhaṇḍâika-rasa-pratipādakatvam ācakṣate tad api mandaṁ vākyântaravat teṣām api viśiṣṭa-viṣayatvâvaśyaṁ bhāvāt.*

Varadaguru, declaring: 'like other sentences', presupposes that *śruti* can be compared to the sentences of ordinary usage, in so far as the object of words constituting a congruent sentence has to be somehow determined and because there is some kind of a dependence relation among the sentence constituents. Already in the first sentence of the chapter, we can notice an interesting feature of Varadaguru's approach to the exegesis. He correlates the language of ordinary usage with that of *śruti,* at least with regard to how they convey their sense.

This equal treatment of the praeterhuman *śruti* statement about the transempirical reality and of human sentences about the empirical reality is the foundation for Varadaguru's statement: the TU 2.1 *śruti* does teach about the qualified Brahman. It is worthwhile noticing, as well, that this co-ordinate treatment of *śruti* and human languages is in accordance with Rāmānuja's contention that ultimately *all words are Vedic.*[19]

After the introductory statement there comes the discussion about *sāmānâdhikaraṇya*, its definition(s) and its scope. Congruence is considered by both Varadaguru and his opponent as an indispensable condition for this particular *śruti* sentence to convey its meaning, which is an important aspect of the discussion. What then this congruence is?

> 'Congruence,' says Varadaguru, 'is [this particular] functioning—with regard to one object—of words which have different causes of application.'[20]

In order to explain the meaning of this terse and not very clear definition, supposedly taken from grammarians, Varadaguru introduces a classification of words dividing them into three groups:

> (1) the first group contains isolated words which, as nouns and attributive adjuncts respectively, are synonymous,
> (2) the second group contains words which, as nouns and attributive adjuncts respectively, refer to different objects,
> (3) words which, as subjects and predicates, together refer to one [and the same] object.[21]

Out of these three groups, only the last one comprises congruent words, because 'predicates (*viśeṣaṇa*s) belong to (i.e. refer to) different objects and subjects

[19] VAS § 21: *vaidikā eva sarve śabdāḥ*.

[20] PMā p. 13.5: *bhinna-pravṛtti-nimittānāṁ śabdānām ekasminn arthe vṛttis sāmānâdhikaraṇyam.*

[21] PMā p. 13.10–13.

(*viśeṣyas*) refer to one [and the same] object.'[22] Here we see that 'different causes of words' application' is to simply mean that they, as attributive adjuncts, refer to different designates. Groups 1 and 2 contain isolated words which, on the surface of it, fulfil at least one of the conditions of *sāmānâdhikaraṇya*. They have the same case ending. They either refer to one object (group 1), or to different objects (group 2), but they do not constitute a meaningful unit. Only the third group, which contains words forming a phrase or a sentence, such as *nilôtpalam*, are considered to be *samānâdhikaraṇa*.

It appears then that the above classification allows Varadaguru to modify the definition of *sāmānâdhikaraṇya* in order to give the notion a more precise sense. Therefore he says:

> 'Congruence is the functioning of words which are different determining terms (*viśeṣaṇa*) with regard to one [thing] to be determined (*viśeṣya*).'[23]

At this point there comes the objection of an Advaitin. He says:

> '[That] congruence is a oneness of object (*ekârthatva*) was not disputed before.'[24]

Having scrutinised alternative assumptions as to references of congruent words in the TU 2.1 *śruti*, the Advaitin concludes that the words '*satya*, etc.' can neither refer to attributes (*viśeṣaṇa*) nor to a thing determined by attributes, named by respective words (*tat-tad-viśeṣaṇa-viśiṣṭa*). The only acceptable position for him is that words '*satya*, etc.' refer to a proper form (*svarūpa*) of the sentence-referent. In order to do that, they neither enter into any sort of predicative relation (*viśeṣya-viśeṣaṇa*) with the thing to be determined nor into the relation among each other (*satyâdi-śabdā na parasparaṁ saṁbadhyante*, as Śaṅkara explains in TUBh, p. 446)[25].

Their aim and the reason for their usage is to exclude from Brahman's nature the attributes which are negative counterparts of attributes which they, as attributive adjuncts, actually denote. Yet it does not follow that they attribute any qualities to Brahman, whether they be the ones denoted by the used attributive adjuncts or their

---

[22] PMā p. 13.16–17: *viśeṣaṇato bhinnârthānāṁ viśeṣyataś caîkârthānām*.

[23] PMā p. 13.21: *bhinna-viśeṣaṇānāṁ śabdānām ekasmin viśeṣye vṛttis sāmānâdhikaraṇyam*.

[24] PMā p. 14.3: *sāmānâdhikaraṇyasya tāvad ekârthatvam avigītam*.

[25] PMā p. 14.5: (*samānâdhikaraṇāni satyâdi-padāni*) *na tāvad viśeṣaṇa-mātra-parāṇi, viśeṣaṇānām anekatvād ekârthatvâsiddhe*. Cf. SŚ 1.175, TUBh p. 446, and below footnotes 27, 28.

counterparts. Their aim is to exclude Brahman from everything which possesses qualities related to the material world:

> "Here the word *satya* disperses the doubt that Brahman is the seat of modification, the word *jñāna* [disperses the doubt that it] is the seat of [inanimate] matter, the word *ananta* [disperses the doubt that it] is the seat of limitation. But it does not follow, that Brahman is possessed of properties which are opposite to these very attributes, because its nature is infinitely different.'[26]

The earliest Advaita text in which one can trace this kind of an argumentation is Śaṅkara's commentary to this very *śruti*. In his analysis of TU 2.1, one can clearly discern similar phases of the argumentation. In his TUBh 2.1, he says:

> '... The purpose of attributive adjuncts is primarily the serving as definiens (*lakṣaṇa*), and, for certain, *not* primarily [the serving] as the *attributes* (*viśeṣaṇa*).'
>
> '... Words "*satya*, etc.," are *not* mutually related with one another, in accordance with the rule of referring to another.[27] Therefore each and every word [which is] an attributive adjunct, regardless of one another, is related with the word *brahman*. Thus: Brahman is real, Brahman is knowledge, Brahman is limitless.'
>
> '... Words "*satya*, etc.," have as their purport the excluding of such properties as "unreal, etc." Therefore Brahman ... is not established as the thing to be determined.'[28]

To sum up, the structure of the first part of the chapter on the refutation of the *akhaṇḍa-vākyârtha* theory shows some interesting features. Vātsya Varadaguru

---

[26] PMā p. 14.22–23: *tatra satya-padaṁ brahmaṇo vikārâspadatva-śaṅkāṁ nivartayati, jñāna-padaṁ jaḍatva-śaṅkāṁ, ananta-padañ ca paricchinnatva ... na câitāvatā brahmanas tat-tad-vyāvṛtti-rūpa-dharmavattva-prasaṅgaḥ brahma-svarūpasyâiva sakalêtara-vyāvṛtti-rūpatvāt.*

[27] Cf. MS 3.1.22: *guṇānāṁ ca parârthatvād asambandhaḥ samatvāt syāt.*—'And the qualities being subservient to others, there is no relationship between them due to equality.'

[28] TUBh p. 444.6: *lakṣanârtha-pradhānāni viśeṣaṇāni na viśeṣaṇa-pradhānāny eva. ...*, and pp. 445.1–446.1: *satyâdi-śabdā na parasparaṁ saṁbadhyante parârthatvād viśeṣyârthā hi te. ata ekâiko viśeṣaṇa-śabdaḥ parasparaṁ nirapekṣo brahma-śabdena saṁbadhyate. satyaṁ brahma jñānaṁ brahmânantaṁ brahmêti*, as well as p. 448.2–3: *... satyâdīnām anṛtâdi-dharma-nivṛtti-paratvād viśeṣyasya brahmaṇa ... aprasiddhatvāt.*

devotes relatively much attention to scrutinising and interpreting the notion of *sāmānâdhikaraṇya*. When we compare his treatment of *sāmānâdhikaraṇya* with that of the Advaitin(s) introduced in the article, or even that of Rāmānuja, we notice that the notion seemed to constitute an important part in the approach to the interpretation of the TU 2.1 by Varadaguru.

For the Advaitin, congruence means the one and only object of the sentence. He presupposes that the most important part of the grammatical definition of congruence is the requirement that any congruent sentence has one object. Overshadowing thus the other part of the congruence definition, which poses the requirement that the words used have different causes of application (which simply means that they, as isolated words, have different referents), the Advaitin shifts the centre of gravity of the sentence discussed to its subject.

Such an Advaitic 'tilt', so to say, makes it possible to interpret the *śruti*, which is obviously *saguṇa*, as the one speaking of the unqualified (*nirguṇa*) Brahman (!). The word *brahman* is considered to be the core constituent of the sentence. All the other words gain their revelatory senses inasmuch as they are related to, or rather identified in their meaning with, the word *brahman*.

Thus one can conclude that they all refer to the proper form (*svarūpa*) of Brahman, because there is no relation between them, and because they do not primarily refer to their designates (which are qualities). For the Advaitin, this is the first step to understand the function of congruent adjuncts in a congruent phrase.

The second step consists in acknowledging the fact that if the referent of all the *viśeṣaṇa*s were only the *svarūpa* of Brahman, it would be senseless to use them all—they would all be synonymous. The Advaitin finds the way out. He says that the aim of using the attributive adjuncts is to exclude Brahman's nature from everything which possesses qualities opposed to its nature.

The method of the Advaitin that is introduced by Varadaguru is a two-phase process. First, the Advaitin notices that *viśeṣaṇa*s do have their positive single referent, which is Brahman's proper form (*svarūpa*). In the second phase, he negates the attributive function of the *viśeṣaṇa*s.

Varadaguru is more straightforward in applying the definition of *sāmānâdhikaraṇya*. He understands it simply as a relation of dependence between words. They are first syntactically connected as the subject (*viśeṣya*) and its predicates (*viśeṣaṇa*s) in order to execute the requirements of congruence on the level of the sentence structure, and secondly, they refer to a determined object (*viśiṣṭa-viṣaya*). He does not stress the aspect of the same case ending for all the words. He concentrates on the fact that congruence is the functioning with regard to one thing to be determined (*viśeṣya*) in the case of words which are different determining terms (*viśeṣaṇa*). This aspect of *sāmānâdhikaraṇya* allows him to interpret the statement in agreement with the approach, represented by his school, to the nature of Brahman and its relation to the phenomenal world.

The structure of the discussion on the *akhaṇḍa-vākyârtha* theory as seen in Vātsya Varadaguru's work does not allow us to identify Varadaguru's probable opponent(s) as any of the Advaitins introduced in the first part of the article 'The *akhaṇḍa-vākyârtha* theory in Advaita' above. It seems that the discussion was developed as the continuation of the *Śrī-bhāṣya* of Rāmānuja, from which it was directly taken over.[29]

## BIBLIOGRAPHY


ChU = *Chandogyôpaniṣad. Īśādidaśopaniṣadaḥ. Ten Principal Upaniṣads with Śaṅkārabhāṣya [Works of Śaṅkarācārya in Original Sanskrit—Volume I ]*. Delhi 1992. [First edition: 1964].

MAXIMILIEN 1975 = Maximilien, Guy (intr. and trans.): *Sureśvara. La demonstration du non-agir (Naiṣkarmyasiddhi)*. Paris 1975.

MAXIMILIEN 1975, 76 = Maximilien, Guy: 'Le Langage et l'Ātman d'apres USP 188.' *Wiener Zeitschrift für die Kunde Südasiens* 19 (1975) 117–134 (Part I), 20 (1976) 125–137 (Part II).

MAYEDA 1979 = Mayeda, Sengaku: *A Thousand Teachings. The Upadeśasāhasrī of Śaṅkara*. Translated with Introduction and Notes by ..., Tokyo 1979.

MAYEDA 1980–81 = Mayeda, Sengaku: 'Śamkara and Sureśvara: Their Exegetical Method to Interpret the Great Sentence "*Tat Tvam Asi*",' *Adyar Library Bulletin* (1980–81) 147–160.

MS = *Mīmāṁsā Sūtras of Jaimini*. Translated by Mohan Lal Sandal, Vol. 1, Delhi 1980. [1st ed.: Allahabad 1923–25].

NS = Sureśvara: *Naiṣkarmya-siddhi*. (1) *The Naiṣkarmya-siddhi of Sureśvarācārya with the Candrikā of Jñānottama*. Ed. by G.A. Jacob. Revised edition by M. Hiriyanna, *Bombay Sanskrit and Prakrit Series* No XXXVIII, Bombay 1925. (2) *The Naiṣkarmyasidhi of Sureśvara*. Edited with Introduction, English Introduction, English Translation, Notes and Indexes by N. Veezhinathan. Madras 1972.


---

[29] The question who was the opponent of both Rāmānuja and Vātsya Varadaguru remains open.

PMā = *Prameyamālā by Vātsya Varadaguru.* Ed. with Transl. and Notes by R. Ramanujachari and K. Srinivasacharya. *Journal of the Annamalai University* 10, 2/3 (1940–41) 1–28.

SŚ = Sarvajñātma Muni: *Saṁkṣepa-śārīraka.* (1) *Sankshepa-Sariraka by Sarvajnatma-Muni,* with a Gloss Called Sarsangraha by Sri Madhusudan Sarasvati. Edited by Bhau Sastri Vajhe, *Kashi-Sanskrit-Series, Haridas Sanskrit Granthamālā, Vedanta Section* No. 4, Benares 1924 (Vol. 1). (2) *The Saṁkṣepaśārīraka of Sarvajñātman.* Critically edited with Translation, Annotation, and Indices by R. Balasubramanian. Madras 1988. (3) Ed. Raṅganātha Śastrī Vaidya, Vol. 1–2, *Ānandāśrama Sanskrit Series* 83, Poona 1918.

STARK 1990 = Stark, Sylvia: *Vātsya Varadagurus Tattvanirṇaya.* Teil 1: Kritische Textedition. Teil 2: Übersetzung und Anmerkungen. *Beiträge zur Kultur- und Geistesgeschichte Asiens* 4, Wien 1990.

THOTTAKARA 1990 = Thottakara, Augustine: *God, Man and Nature. A Vedantic Perspective. A Study of Varadaguru's Tattvasara.* Rome 1990.

TUBh = *Taittirīyôpaniṣad-bhāṣya.* In: *Shankarabhagavatpada's Upanishadbhasyam.* Vol. 1 [for the first eight Upaniṣads]. With the commentaries of Anandagiricharya for all, and in addition commentaries for *Kathā, Maṇḍukya* and *Taittirīya* by great Ācāryas and *Taittirīya-vārtika* of Sureśvarācārya with Commentary. Ed with notes etc. by S. Subrahmanya Shastri. *Advaita Grantha Ratna Manjusha-Ratna* 21, Varanasi 1979.

TUBhV = *The Taittirīyopaniṣad Bhāṣya-Vārtika of Sureśvara.* Edited with Introduction, English Translation, Annotation, and Indices by R. Balasubramanian. Madras 1984.

VAS = *Rāmānuja's Vedārthasaṁgraha.* Intr., crit. ed. and ann. transl. by J.A.B. van Buitenen. *Deccan College Monograph Series* 16, Poona 1956.

# The Heart in the *Ṛg-veda*

SVEN SELLMER

## 1. Introduction

Astoundingly little work has been done on what might be called 'Vedic anthropology', especially if compared with the vast amount of literature on the so-called 'Homeric man' and analogical questions in connection with Egyptian or Old Testament evidence. This is lamentable in itself, but even more so because it makes the task of comparing these, and other, 'indigenous anthropologies', difficult.[1] As an important item in such comparisons one would certainly have to choose the 'heart', for it is an obvious fact that expressions containing this word play a major role at least in the above mentioned cultures. The object of this paper is more modest, of course: it focuses on the use of heart language in the RV.[2] First, I am going to present a phenomenological notion that is of great use, I believe, not only for our problem, but for the understanding of indigenous anthropologies in general. Next, there follows a survey of the Ṛgvedic material with a view to the proposed distinctions. Finally, by way of comparison, some Greek evidence is considered.

## 2. Heart imagery: the concept of the felt body

In dealing with words like 'heart', both dictionaries and special studies mostly distinguish between 'literal' and 'figurative' or 'metaphorical' usages. References to the anatomical organ make up the first group, all the rest is gathered under the second heading. This distinction, however, is insufficient; in particular, it tends to

[1] I use this expression in analogy to 'indigenous psychologies', a term that is sometimes used with reference to psychological traditions which have developed independently of Western culture, as in HEELAS–LOCK (1981).

[2] To my mind, the best (though unfortunately quite short) study on this subject is still RENOU (1958: 60 f.).

*Essays in Indian Philosophy, Religion and Literature,* pp. 71–83.

overlook the realm of the felt body where we have to do with entities that are invisible, but at the same time very concrete.

Problems connected with the felt body have been one of the main fields of phenomenological research for a long time now, especially in France. But the most pertinent and systematic treatment of the structure of the felt body we certainly owe to the German philosopher Hermann SCHMITZ who, following Scheler, terminologically distinguishes between 'Leib' (i.e. felt body) and 'Körper' (i.e. material body)—an elegant move which we cannot, unfortunately, imitate in English.[3] The 'Leib' consists of what we feel in the area of our body. Normally, but by no means always, its extension roughly corresponds to the borders of the material body. E.g. if we hit our thumb with a hammer it may feel as big as a balloon, though the visible swelling is rather small. One result of SCHMITZ's investigations is of special interest for the present study, namely that the felt body is not uniform but possesses a structure consisting of a number of more or less stable centres (called 'Leibesinseln' by SCHMITZ), one of which is located in the central breast region. The analogy to the Tantric teachings of *cakra*s is of course quite obvious[4], and we will come to speak about it later.

We use the word 'heart' not only while referring to the material body or to the felt body, but also in a way more or less detached from these usages which, for the sake of convenience, we may call 'figurative' or 'metaphorical'. Still, to avoid intricate linguistic discussions, I would—in a common-sense manner—prefer to talk of non-concrete usages, whereas the first two are concrete in the sense that the objects they refer to can be directly touched, seen, etc., (material body), and respectively felt. In many cases, it is difficult to decide whether a given expression refers to the felt body or not. Take an adjective like 'heart-rending' for instance. I may use it in a wholly colourless way, so that 'a heart-rending story' would be equivalent to 'a very sad story' or the like; but the choice of the word may also be motivated by an actual strong, even painful sensation in the heart region. Probably, the majority of factual utterances lie somewhere in between these extremes.[5] It can even be argued that *every* conscious mental act is necessarily accompanied by some engagement on the level of the felt body—but this is a philosophical question we do not have to bother about at the moment. What is important to note is the key role of the felt body in our

[3] Cf. SCHMITZ (1965).

[4] SCHMITZ himself is well aware of this fact (1965: 298–304); he applies his theory to questions of heart imagery in (1969: 209–213) and (1996).

[5] On the process of transition from concrete to metaphorical senses cf. BUSSE (1991); the linguistically problematic distinction between literal and metaphorical meaning is defended as an element of the 'intuitives Sprachgefühl' on p. 56 f.

three-level model, for it is the level of the felt body that is linked to both of the others and therefore guarantees the unity of the system..

Although the felt body is hardly ever acknowledged as ontological region on its own right outside of a rather limited group of phenomenologists, it has not totally escaped attention in other areas of research. Scholars of early psychologies are frequently puzzled by the seemingly 'physiological' language that is used in ancient texts, and try to deal with that fact in different ways. Thus, sometimes Indian psychological theories are described as 'somatist'. The first to use this expression was probably none other than St. SCHAYER, namely in his paper 'Über den Somatismus der indischen Psychologie' (1936).[6] But it certainly would be an over-simplification, if this were understood as reducing Indian psychology to a branch of physiology. That trap is more clearly avoided by such expressions as 'psycho-physical' which one comes across quite often in Indological publications. They seem unfortunate to me as well, though, because they imply a primary division between a mental and a physical world, a view that is neither ontologically nor historically correct. Other authors are content with taking over Indian terminology, employing concepts like 'subtle' (= *sūkṣma*) and 'gross' (= *sthūla*). That solution may be accepted as a first step, still the question is asked too seldom what these words actually mean.

## 3. The Ṛgvedic evidence

Let us now, after these general considerations, turn to the RV with a view to the question if all of the three levels of meaning discussed above really occur. The main word in the RV for 'heart' is *hṛ́d* (with nom. and acc. sg. *hā́rdi*)[7]. Besides, I am going to take into account some passages containing the much less common *hṛ́daya*, though the two expressions are not exactly synonymous.[8] This slightly simplifying procedure seems to be justified considering the preliminary character of this paper.

---

[6] The same expression—in its English form 'somatism'—was used by DANDEKAR (1941), who does not mention SCHAYER, and by SCHAYER's pupil Arnold KUNST (1968).

[7] For a discussion of the declination see SZEMERÉNYI (1970: 523–526).

[8] The main difference between them is one of style. Generally speaking, *hṛ́daya* is a less poetic word that is largely confined to younger, 'Atharvanic' passages of the RV, and apparent differences in meaning are readily explained by this fact. Symptomatic for the lower status of *hṛ́daya* is the fact that it is never used in the context of Soma drinking or applied to gods—this holds true even for the AV, at least as far as anthropomorphic gods are concerned (we find a *hṛ́daya* of the Waters in AV 3.13.7, and of the Earth in AV 12.1.8, 35).

### 3.1. *hṛ́d* and *hṛ́daya* as anatomical organ

The problem of the anatomical uses of *hṛ́d* and *hṛ́daya* is not so easily settled as it might seem. The only clear reference to the anatomical organ is found in the late hymn RV 10.163.3b. Some passages point to the belief that the organ designated by the words in question is of vital importance; this can be deduced from the fact that it is depicted several times as aim of missiles, though these passages are not to be understood literally.[9] We may add some medical passages where the heart is conceived as seat of certain illnesses: *hṛd-rogá*[10] (1.50.11c), *yákṣma* (1.112.9; 10.163.3b); numerous examples of this kind, and of anatomical uses in general, can be found in the AV. More interesting in our context, however, are anatomical uses showing that functions are attributed to *hṛ́d* which are alien to our heart. In particular, it is the receptacle of the drunken Soma, a role it shares with *udára*[11] and *jaṭhára*, both commonly translated as 'belly'.[12] Probably this aspect of the Vedic heart is to be connected with the fact that the word *hṛ́d* can etymologically be traced to an Aryan blending of two words: the Indo-European expression for heart (**ker-*) and a similar word **gher-* designating something like 'bowels'[13]; at least, this is the most plausible explanation for the irregular initial sound of the Vedic word. But it also has to be remembered that a close connection between the heart and the belly, or stomach, is attested in many languages.[14] This kind of talk points to a basic level of anatomy where the interior of the human body is treated as a unity. It also seems that this conception is at least partly due to the structure of the felt body, for in normal circumstances the region of the breast and belly feels rather uniform.

---

[9] The Brahmans hit the hearts with the arrows (i.e. words) in their mouths: *āsánn-iṣūn hṛtsváso* (RV 1.84.16c). Varuṇa's words have healing powers even for a person with a pierced heart: *utā̆pavaktā́ hṛdayâvídhaś cit* (RV 1.24.8d). Agni is asked to hit the sorcerers in the heart: *vidhya hṛ́daye yātu-dhā́nān* (RV 10.87.13d).

[10] For the meaning of this term cf. FILLIOZAT (1949: 89 f.); ZYSK (1985: 29).

[11] We find *udára*, *suhā́rd* and *hṛ́d* together in hymn 8.2.1, 5, 13.

[12] Another frequent location of the drunken Soma is the *kukṣí* (mostly appearing in the dual). In spite of the fact that also this word is traditionally thought to denote the belly, I will leave it out of discussion here, for more recent investigations by JAMISON (1987: 71–81) have shown that probably the cheeks are meant. (But see the discussion in BODEWITZ (1992).)

[13] Cf. SZEMERÉNYI (1970: 519–523).

[14] E.g. in modern French ('mal au coeur' and the like). That this doctrine can also be found in classical Indian medicine is shown by DAS (forthcoming: 590–593). (My thanks are due to Professor Das for allowing me to use his yet unpublished text.)

### 3.2. The heart as part of the felt body

The clearest example for a usage of *hṛ́d* as part of the felt body can also be found in the context of Soma drinking. At RV 8.79.8c, Soma is implored not to frighten the poet, and not to 'strike my heart with violence' (*mā́ no hā́rdi tviṣā́ vadhīḥ*). The exact meaning of these words probably cannot be established. But that much seems clear that the Soma drink occasionally caused some uncomfortable sensation in the breast (or belly) region.[15] At this point, the frequent connections of heart and heat should also be mentioned that, although used in a rather figurative way, certainly go back to experiences in the felt body.[16] Also some examples of the construction *śám* + *hṛdé,* probably refer to the felt body (*vide infra*). Finally, the fact that, at two places, fear is located in the heart[17] can probably be explained by the fact that strong emotions are frequently accompanied by sensations in the area of the heart. Much more numerous than 'pure' references to the felt body are borderline cases with more or less markedly metaphorical sense.

### 3.3. Non-concrete usage

In the vast majority of occurrences, *hṛ́d* and *hṛ́daya* are used—at least partially—non-concretely, i.e. in none of the two senses discussed so far. The figurative usage of the two words cannot be analysed in detail here for that would entail a thoroughgoing interpretation of a great many single passages. Instead, I would like to present certain observations that may be helpful to future, more elaborate studies.

First, let us consider a group of passages that show particularly well that there is no clear break between the three levels of usage analysed in this paper. I am talking of the construction *śám* + *hṛdé,* that most often is found in Soma contexts. Its sense in medical hymns is easily established, when the wish is expressed that healing

---

[15] Cf. the fighting Soma juices in RV 8.2.12: *hṛtsú pītā́so yudhyante durmádāso ná súrāyām / ū́dhar ná nagnā́ jarante //*. Possibly, also the adjective *suhā́rda* (RV 8.2.5) has to be seen in this light, according to GELDNER's interpretation: 'Der 'in seinem Ḥerzen' jeden Soma gut verträgt' (1951b: 282, n. 1).

[16] Cf. RV 10.34.9d, 95.17d. BLAIR (1961: 106) points to 'a comparatively large number of passages in which an emotion of strong unhappiness is considered to be heat or flame in the body, particularly in the heart.'

[17] RV 1.32.14b; 10.84.7c.

herbs may 'do the heart good'[18]—this evidently refers to the material and probably also to the felt body of mortals. On the other hand, the same words are used when speaking of the effect successful poems and offerings are supposed to have on the hearts of the gods. Here, the anatomical organ is rather out of question, at most a reference to the felt body may be included.[19] Finally, as to the interpretation of places where S o m a is implored to be *śáṁ hṛdé*, both of these shades of meaning have to, in my opinion, be kept in mind in order not to reduce the overtones of the text.

The passages that deal with the drunken Soma in the heart seem particularly concrete, but even they display a metaphorical dimension. This is because the word *soma* denotes the drink as well as the god; one could even argue that this distinction itself is hardly feasible for the Vedic texts. In any case, it is clear that the interpretation of Soma as god in a given passage entails a less anatomical understanding of its (respectively his) abode: the heart. The two examples may suffice to highlight the puzzling questions that arise when we take a closer look at some passages. Once it is said that the Maruts dwell in the hearts just like the drunken Soma juices[20]: is the second term of the comparison really employed exclusively on the concrete level, as GELDNER (1951a: 245) would have it? At least, at RV 1.179.5, it is even the 'drunken Soma in the heart' that is addressed as a god and implored to forgive.[21] In any case, the very comparison shows that the Vedic poets do not feel any fundamental difference in meaning between the heart as the container of Soma and the other senses of the word.[22]

Beside Soma drinking, and often connected with it, another vast thematic area in which heart language is used is poetry: the heart is involved in both production and reception of poems. In the process of poetry-making, the (human) heart is depicted either as instrument (instr.) or as locus of origin (abl.). There seem to be two ways to

---

[18] RV 10.97.18, 180.1; 10.186.1a: *vā́ta ā́ vātu bheṣajáṁ śambhú mayobhú no hṛdé / prá ṇa ā́yūṁṣi tāriṣat //* . Interesting is the juxtaposition of *śáṁ hṛde* and *áraṁ kā́māya* in 10.97.18 which seems to indicate that even in medical contexts the non-concrete level is constantly present.

[19] RV 1.43.1c; 1.73.10b; 4.37.2a; 5.11.5b. In fact, we seem to have here one further example of the kind of semantic differentiation expounded by ELIZARENKOVA (1995: ch. 1).

[20] 1.168.3ab: *somā́so ná yé sutā́s tṛptā́ṁśavo hṛtsú pītā́so duváso nā́sate.*

[21] *imáṁ nú sómam ántito hṛtsú pītám úpa bruve /*
*yát sīm ā́gaś cakṛmā́ tát sú mṛḷatu pulukā́mo hí mártyaḥ //*

Cf. also 8.48.12a.

[22] This presents some difficulties to modern translators, as RENOU's rather awkward version of RV 1.168.3ab shows: 'Eux qui, tels des soma pressés aux tiges rassasiées (d'eau, une fois) bus dans les entrailles, (y) résident commes des bienfaiteurs, ...' (1962: 24).

account for this state of affairs. First, it may be seen as a normal result of the conception of the heart as the vessel in which poems are, so to speak, prepared (this function of pots and the like is normally expressed in the instrumental case). Another possible explanation would be an independent origin of both aspects of the heart: the picture of the source of hymns could be based on the function of the heart as the container of Soma while the use in the instrumental case might be associated with analogous (and much more numerous) constructions with *mánas* and other 'psychic' entities. The second solution is favoured due to the curious fact that poems are said to come forth *from* the heart, but are never located *in* it.[23]

The locative case of *hṛ́d* is used in connection with poetry, it is true, but only in contexts of its reception.[24] There, the wish is frequently expressed that the poets' works be not 'in', but 'close to' the hearts of the gods—this seems to be the sense of the locative case in such passages, insofar as the songs are also meant to 'touch' (√*spṛś*) the hearts of their addressees.[25] It has often been observed that poetry thus establishes a relation between the hearts of its creators and those of the gods.[26] Let us just add the observation that this contact is asymmetrical even on the linguistic level.

In some difficult passages the heart is the locus of experiences that go beyond normal poetry-making, and are rather associated with 'mystic' inspirations.[27] Here, the motif of light is used that plays such a truly prominent role in many traditions of mysticism. KUIPER (1960: 248–250; 1964/65: 123–126) has argued that this trait was inherited from an Aryan mystical tradition. In any case, it is the obvious historical starting point of later important developments. Some pertinent information concerning 'The sun in the heart' can be found in BODEWITZ (1991: 21-23).

Somewhat simplifying, one can say that two dimensions of interiority are expressed by the non-concrete use of the heart words in connection with events we would classify as 'mental'. Firstly, heart language is used as a signal that some process is going on 'inside' a person, i.e. that it is not outwardly observable.[28] Secondly,

---

[23] As far as I can see, the only passage where an act of productive thinking (to use our language) is said to take place 'in' the heart is the late and the unconventional hymn RV 10.129.4cd: *sató bándhum ásati nír avindan hṛdí pratī́ṣyā kaváyo manīṣā́.*

[24] See n. 19 above.

[25] RV 4.41.1c; RV 10.91.13c.

[26] Cf., e.g. DANDEKAR (1938: 61); GONDA (1963: 281 f.).

[27] E.g. RV 6.9.6; RV 10.123.6; RV 10.177.1.

[28] The term *ántar*, which is a key word denoting metaphorical inwardness in the *Upaniṣad*s, is very seldom used in a similar way in the RV, the nearest parallel being probably RV 4.58.6: *samyák sravanti sarito ná dhénā antár hṛdā́ mánasā pūyámānāḥ* / .

something done 'with the heart' or happening 'in' or 'close to' the heart may entail strong (or, as we might say, 'deep') emotional or intellectual engagement on the part of the person; in this case, what has to be taken into account is the level of the felt body.

As an instrument of 'inner' activities, the heart can be compared with several other words within the range of this semantic field, the most important ones being *mánas* and *krátu*. Of these, *mánas* deserves special interest because of its importance for later psychological theories. As I said before, *mánas* and *hṛ́d* appear together several times,[29] and in certain contexts they seem almost interchangeable.[30] A neat distinction according to which intellectual functions are attributed to the *mánas*, and emotions to the heart, as some authors have attempted to demonstrate[31], cannot be established on the basis of the RV.[32] Yet there is one trait of the heart (*hṛ́d*) that its rival does not possess and that, to a large degree, is responsible for its subsequent history. This is the fact that the heart ranges over all the three levels of reference dealt with in this paper, whereas the *mánas* is almost exclusively confined to the metaphorical one, although some traces of the felt body level may be detected.[33] As a result, it is the heart which is especially apt to express the concept of an 'inner world' in spatial terms and therefore, in the RV, it is the seat of poetical fashioning and mystical events. The mystical function of the heart is elaborated further in the AV, and leads to the well-known Upaniṣadic teachings of the cavity of the heart (*guhā*) and the heart-ether (*antar-hṛdaya ākāśaḥ*) as the seats of the key entities of Upaniṣadic speculation (*puruṣa*,

---

[29] RV 1.61.2c; RV 4.58.6b; RV 6.28.5b; RV 7.98.2c; RV 10.177.1b. In these passages both words are juxtaposed and appear in the instrumental case. The Avestan parallel *Yasna* 31.12 shows that this manner of expression belongs to the stock of Aryan poetical language.

[30] This can particularly well be shown by comparing passages where the root √*takṣ* is used in connection with poetry making. We find this kind of fashioning combined with the instrumentals *mánasā* (RV 7.64.4a), *hṛdā́* (RV 1.67.4b), both of them (RV 1.171.2b), and without any additions of this kind (RV 8.6.33c).

[31] See DANDEKAR (1938: 62) and (1950: 138), and especially VELANKAR (1966).

[32] Cf. also ELIZARENKOVA, who speaks of the 'semantic syncretism of words dealing with various emotional and intellectual phenomena' (1995:30f.), and REAT(1990:123; 129).

[33] The diachronic question whether *mánas* at one time did possess a more concrete value cannot be tackled here. It is tantamount to the problem whether *mánas* or the Homeric term μένος is closer in meaning to the Indo-European ancestor, on which some remarks can be found in SCHMITT (1967: 103–121). This author, while attempting to reconstruct elements of an Indo-European poetical language, regards the Homeric evidence to be closer to the common source in this respect.

*ātman*).[34] Later history shows that expressions of this kind do not have to be understood as purely metaphorical, for they were included in systems of meditation, which display a great awareness of the felt body. Thus, in Tantric teachings an important position is attributed to the *cakra* in the region of the heart.[35] To be sure, these two notions represent but a small part of the richness of conceptions and meanings associated with the heart in post-Vedic literature, but they may suffice to credit the thesis with some probability that it is its functioning on three levels that has made the long career of the heart possible and it is certainly one of the (so to speak) subterranean leitmotifs of its history, a history that definitely deserves to be written.

## 4. Some comparative remarks

Because it may be interesting to observe how the heart is treated in another Indo-European poetic tradition I would like to close this paper with some remarks on the heart in the Homeric poems.[36]

Homer uses three words commonly translated as 'heart': κῆρ, κραδίη, and ἦτορ. Although these are not exact synonyms, they may be treated jointly for the present purpose. In the majority of passages they are used in connection with mental events of several kinds, but most frequently with those of emotional character. As JAHN (1987) has shown in a painstaking study, in many cases the heart words are used not to convey additional infonnation, but for the sake of metre.[37] Still, there is also a considerable number of pregnant uses that can be roughly grouped in the same way as was done for the RV above. Events thus underscored are (a) private (as opposed to 'commonly observable'), and / or (b) occurring with exceptional intensity. There is, however, one fundamental difference in the way the heart is connected with

[34] Cf. GONDA (1963: 283 f.).

[35] Some information on this question is provided by KIEHNLE (1997), who furthermore discusses influences of Tantric heart language on the medieval *bhakti* literature.

[36] The first candidate for a comparison, the *Avesta*, unfortunately offers but meagre material. In the Homeric epics, on the other hand, the material is abundant, and classical scholars have been discussing questions of 'Homeric psychology' for more than 200 years now. An overview of the discussion can be found in JAHN (1987: 124–181).

[37] This holds true as regards other members of the 'Wortfeld *Seele-Geist*' as well. Nevertheless, it has to be admitted that JAHN's conclusions are somewhat overdrawn. For the critique cf. VAN DER MIJE (1991). The Ṛgvedic material is too small to venture similar contentions. The data for the root √*takṣ* (cf. n. 29 above) suggest, however, that the usage of *hṛ́d* is not a mere question of semantics.

mental events in both groups of texts. Whereas in the RV the heart features almost exclusively as instrument, object or place, the heart of the Homeric heroes plays a much more active role. It appears in the nominative case in about forty-one per cent of all occurrences and is frequently depicted not so much as an organ in the ordinary sense, but rather as a partner of the person it inhabits. Several times this independence finds its expression in uncontrollable beating—a feature that, curiously enough, is (almost?) totally missing in the RV.[38] Thus, in spite of some general structural similarities the pictures of the heart drawn by the Vedic poets and by Homer differ considerably. Nevertheless, the Greek evidence may present a background for some otherwise unparalleled Vedic passages.[39]

Deeper insights, however, would require a full-scale comparison of the respective psychological vocabularies and their usage, which would undoubtedly be a fruitful task, yet one whose realisation has to be preceded by some fundamental research on the Indological side first.

---

[38] MONTEIRO (1973: 157) claims it to be utterly absent from the RV, but the difficult passage RV 5.44.9c (*átrā ná hā́rdi kravaṇásya rejate*) most probably does refer to the trembling of the heart. Even so, the scarcity of this feature in the RV—in view of the many occurrences of heart words—is striking. An overview of expressions connected with the beating of the heart in several Indo-European languages can be found in TOPOROV (1973: 144–148).

[39] Let us take the interesting verse RV 8.100.5 as an example (Indra speaking):

*ā́ yán mā venā́ áruhann ṛtásyam̐ ékam ā́sīnaṁ haryatásya pṛṣṭhé* /
*mánaś cin me hṛdá ā́ práty avocad ácikradañ chiśumantaḥ sákhāyaḥ* //

Leaving aside several problems connected with it (e.g. does the sandhi *hṛdá* represent a dative or ablative; accordingly, does the *mánas* speaks 'to' or 'out of the heart?'), I would merely like to draw the reader's attention to the specific situation in which the speaker of this verse depicts himself: he is alone (*ékam*). And it is easy to see that on such occasions the introduction of a second (and perhaps a third) entity is a valuable literary device in order to reveal the thoughts of the person concerned by means of an artificial 'dialogue.' As regards Homer, related questions—including the special problem under which circumstances these entities are credited with the faculty of speech—have been dealt with in a brilliant study by PELLICCIA (1990). The RV will not yield much material for a comparison, however, because the above verse is, as far as I can see, the only suitable example to be found in it; but it might be interesting to have a look at the Indian epics from a similar angle.

## BIBLIOGRAPHY


AV = *Atharvaveda-saṁhitā*. Hrsg. von R. Roth und W.D. Whitney, Berlin 1856.

BLAIR 1961 = Blair, Chauncey J.: *Heat in the Rig Veda and Atharva Veda. AOS* 45, New Haven 1961.

BODEWITZ 1991 = Bodewitz, Henk W.: *Light, Soul and Visions in the Veda. Post-graduate and Research Department Series* 36—'Prof. P.D. Gune Memorial Lectures', Poona 1991.

BODEWITZ 1992 = Bodewitz, Henk W.: 'Belly, Pelvis, Buttocks or Cheeks? Vedic *kukṣí* (Dual).' *Indo-Iranian Journal* 35 (1992) 19–31.

BUSSE 1991 = Busse, Dietrich: 'Konventionalisierungsstufen des Zeichengebrauchs als Ausgangspunkt semantischen Wandels.' Idem (ed.): *Diachrone Semantik und Pragmatik: Untersuchungen zur Erklärung und Beschreibung des Sprachwandels*. Tübingen 1991: 37–65.

DANDEKAR 1938 = Dandekar, R.N.: *Der vedische Mensch. Studien zur Selbstauffassung des Inders in Ṛg- und Atharvaveda. Indogermanische Bibliothek* 16, Heidelberg 1938.

DANDEKAR 1941 = Dandekar, R.N.: 'Somatism of Vedic Psychology.' *Indian Historical Quarterly* 17 (1941) 70–76.

DANDEKAR 1950 = Dandekar, R.N.: '*Hṛd* in the Veda.' Vishva Bandhu (ed.): *Siddha-Bhāratī* [*Siddheshwar Varma Felicitation Volume*] Vol. 1, Hoshiarpur 1950: 137–142.

DAS (forthcoming) = Das, Rahul Peter: *The Origin of the Life of a Human Being*. Forthcoming.

ELIZARENKOVA 1995 = Elizarenkova, Tatyana J.: *Language and Style of the Vedic Ṛṣis*. SUNY Series in Hindu Studies, Albany 1995.

FILLIOZAT 1949 = Filliozat, Jean: *La doctrine classique de la médecine indienne*. Paris 1949.

GELDNER 1951a = Geldner, Friedrich: *Der Rig-Veda. Erster Teil. Harvard Oriental Series* 33, Cambridge, Mass. 1951.

GELDNER 1951b = Geldner, Friedrich: *Der Rig-Veda. Zweiter Teil. Harvard Oriental Series* 34, Cambridge, Mass. 1951.

GONDA 1963 = Gonda, Jan: *The Vision of the Vedic Poets. Disputationes Rheno-Trajectinae* 8, The Hague 1963.

HEELAS–LOCK 1981 = Heelas, Paul; Lock, Andrew (eds.): *Indigenous Psychologies. The Anthropology of the Self*. London etc. 1981.

JAHN 1987 = Jahn, Thomas: 'Zum Wortfeld "Seele-Geist" in der Sprache Homers.' *Zetemata* 83, München 1987.

JAMISON 1987 = Jamison, Stephanie W.: 'Linguistic and philological remarks on some Vedic body parts.' Watkins, C. (ed.): *Studies in Memory of Warren Cowgill. Untersuchungen zur Indogermanischen Sprach- und Kulturwissenschaft* 3, Berlin 1987: 66–91.

KIEHNLE 1997 = Kiehnle, Catharina: 'The Lotus of the Heart.' *Studien zur Indologie und Iranistik* 21 (1997) 91–103.

KUIPER 1960 = Kuiper, F.B.J.: 'The Ancient Aryan Verbal Contest.' *Indo-Iranian Journal* 4 (1960) 217–284.

KUIPER 1964/65 = Kuiper, F.B.J.: 'The Bliss of Aša.' *Indo-Iranian Journal* 8 (1964/65) 96–129.

KUNST 1968 = Kunst, Arnold: 'Somatism: A Basic Concept in India's Philosophical Speculations.' *Philosophy East and West* 18 (1968) 261–275.

VAN DER MIJE 1991 = van der Mije, S.R.: Review of JAHN (1987). *Mnemosyne* 44 (1991) 440–445.

MONTEIRO 1978 = Monteiro, Lino: *L'homme d'après la Ṛgveda-saṁhitā. Les sources, l'origine de l'homme, le corps et la vie. Boletim do Instituto Menezes Bragança* 119–122, Goa 1978. [= Diss. Fribourg 1973].

PELLICCIA 1990 = Pelliccia, Hayden: *Mind, Body, and Speech in Homer and Pindar. Hypomnemata* 107, Göttingen 1990.

REAT 1990 = Reat, Ross N.: *The Origins of Indian Psychology*. Berkeley 1990.

RENOU 1958 = Renou, Louis: *Études sur le vocabulaire du Ṛgveda. Publications de l'Institut Française d'Indologie* 5, Pondichéry 1958.

RENOU 1962 = Renou, Louis: *Études védiques et pāṇinéennes*. Vol. 10. *Publications de l'Institut de Civilisation Indienne* 17, Paris 1962.

RV = *Die Hymnen des Ṛigveda*. Herausgegeben von Theodor Aufrecht, Adolph Marcus; Bonn 1877.

SCHAYER 1936 = Schayer, Stanisław: 'Über den Somatismus der indischen Psychologie.' *Bulletin International de l'Academie Polonaise des Sciences et des Lettres, Classe de Philologie* (Cracow) 7–10 (1936) 159–168. [Reprinted in: Stanisław Schayer: *O filozofowaniu Hindusów. Artykuły wybrane*. Ed. by Marek Mejor. Polska Akademia Nauk, Komitet Nauk Orientalistycznych, PWN, Warszawa 1988: 495–504].

SCHMITT 1967 = Schmitt, Rüdiger: *Dichtung und Dichtersprache in indogermanischer Zeit*. Wiesbaden 1967.

SCHMITZ 1965 = Schmitz, Hermann: *Der Leib. System der Philosophie* 2.1, Bonn 1965.

SCHMITZ 1969 = Schmitz, Hermann: *Der Gefühlsraum. System der Philosophie* 3.1, Bonn 1969.

SCHMITZ 1996 = Schmitz, Hermann: 'Leibliche Quellen der Herzmetaphorik.' In: Berkemer, G.; Rappe, G. (eds.): *Das Herz im Kulturvergleich*, Lynkeus 3, Berlin 1996: 23–21.

SZEMERÉNYI 1970 = Szemerényi, Oswald: 'The Indo-European Name of the "Heart".' Rūke-Dravina, Velta (ed.): *Donum Balticum* (FS Christian S. Stang), Stockholm 1970: 515–533.

TOPOROV 1973 = Топоров, В.Н.: 'Из индоевропейской этимологии.' In: Зализняк, А.А. (ed.): *Структурно-типологические исследования в области грамматики славянских языков*. Moscow 1973: 140–154. [Toporov, V.N.: 'Some Indo-Aryan etymologies'. In Russian].

VELANKAR 1966 = Velankar, H.D.: 'Mind and Heart in *Ṛgveda*.' *Proceedings of the All-India Oriental Conference* 22.2 (1966) 1–5.

ZYSK 1985 = Zysk, Kenneth G.: *Religious Healing in the Veda. Transactions of the American Philosophical Society* 75.7, Philadelphia 1985.

# EPICS AND *PURĀṆAS*

# The Mārkaṇḍeya-Episode in the Sanskrit Epics and *Purāṇas*

HORST BRINKHAUS

Whenever the *Ṛṣi* Mārkaṇḍeya is mentioned in epic and Purāṇic literature, it is his particular longevity which is regularly emphasised. Thus he is usually characterised as *dīrghâyus*, *bahu-varṣa-sahasrâyus* and similar; and in the MBh it is even pointed out that nobody else lives longer than Mārkaṇḍeya except the god Brahmā.[1] Thus Mārkaṇḍeya was consulted as the only human being who could, as an eye-witness, report on the complete development of mankind and even on total cosmological processes in the sense of the *prabhavâpyaya*, i.e. the cyclical genesis and dissolution of the world. Mārkaṇḍeya is known as the only human being to have survived a *pralaya* process, i.e. the universal destruction by fire and water at the end of a *kalpa*; and he is the sole witness of the succeeding period of total cosmic dissolution during which he experienced a self-revelation of the supreme god.

It is this event which most clearly defines Mārkaṇḍeya's role, and his detailed report on it is known as the 'Mārkaṇḍeya episode.' It is about the development of this episode, which has been handed down to us in a number of different versions, that I am now going to present my observations.

## 1. The *Mahā-bhārata* version

The *Mahā-bhārata* has devoted to Mārkaṇḍeya a long passage within the *Āraṇyaka-parvan*, the *Mārkaṇḍeya-samāsyā-parvan*.[2] The *Ṛṣi* presents didactic

[1] In MBh 3.180.5 he is called *bahu-vatsara-jīvin*, in 180.40 *bahu-varṣa-sahasrin* and in 186.2 he is addressed by Yudhiṣṭhira with the words:

> *nâike yuga-sahasrântās tvayā dṛṣṭvā mahā-mune /*
> *na câpîha samaḥ kaścid āyuṣā tava vidyate /*
> *varjayitvā mahâtmānaṁ brahmāṇaṁ parame-ṣṭhinam //*.

[2] As a whole it comprises MBh 3.180–221, but in the present connection only the first part, i.e. *adhyāyas* 180–189, is of particular interest.

*Essays in Indian Philosophy, Religion and Literature*, pp. 87–98.

instructions there about quite a wide range of themes; among them are general topics such as questions of *karman* causality or of the greatness of Brahmins. More specifically, and with a hint at his longevity, he is requested to talk about the history of mankind and also about cosmological processes.

With regard to the anthropological question, Mārkaṇḍeya reports that originally human beings were holy and even comparable to Brahmā, but later lust and anger crept in, men were deserted by the gods and thus they degenerated and started to perpetrate evils (181.11–20). The legend of the Deluge, which is presented by Mārkaṇḍeya, not immediately, but soon afterwards (*adhyāya* 185), and in which it is reported that almost all creatures were drowned, seems to be introduced as being a consequence of that development of mankind, i.e. as a radical method of regenerating the human race simply by replacing it.

Concerning the cosmological processes, Mārkaṇḍeya explains the *yuga* and *kalpa* system as a part of the wider *prabhavâpyaya* theory (186.17–55 and 188.5–84). Out of his own experience Mārkaṇḍeya can give an account of the course of a *pralaya* in which the whole world was burnt and afterwards inundated, resulting in a sole primeval ocean (*ekârṇava*), mythologically regarded as the beginning of a 'night of Brahmā' (186.56–76). During this period of dissolution Mārkaṇḍeya had once experienced a theophany in which a divine child revealed himself as the supreme god (186.77–187.55).

As far as the theological aspect of the whole passage is concerned, it falls into two main parts.

In the first part, where Mārkaṇḍeya reports on the development of mankind as well as on the *pralaya* process, he does this with a clear and exclusive attachment to the god Brahmā. Mārkaṇḍeya is described as a devotee of Brahmā, who is explicitly defined here as the supreme deity.[3]

In the subsequent part, by distinction it is Nārāyaṇa who reveals himself as the highest god and ruler of all cosmic events (186.77–187.55). Here the episode runs as follows:

> After the *pralaya* Mārkaṇḍeya is fearfully drifting about in the empty primeval ocean, until he finally discovers a child with a *śrī-vatsa* on his breast. The child swallows Mārkaṇḍeya and shows him the whole world in his belly. Mārkaṇḍeya emerges through his mouth again, and

[3] Esp. in MBh 3.186.2–23 Brahmā is constantly named as the supreme god (*parame-ṣṭhin, loka-guru, sarva-loka-pitā-maha, svayaṁ-bhū, sarva-bhūtêśa*) and patron of Mārkaṇḍeya, and in the *pralaya* report (186.56–76) it is solely Brahmā who is involved in the cosmic event and finally retires to rest.

> this time the divine child grants him an ample self-revelation. He declares himself to be Puruṣa-Nārāyaṇa, unknown even to the gods, though identical with Viṣṇu, Brahmā, Indra, etc. As Śeṣa he supports the world, as Varāha he lifts the earth from the bottom of the ocean, and as the horse-headed ocean-fire he destroys the world. In a plain allusion to the *Bhagavad-gītā*[4] an identification with Vāsudeva-Kṛṣṇa is at least hinted at. After that the god again emphasises his identity with Brahmā as one of his manifestations in which he sleeps during the phase of dissolution and will afterwards create the world anew.

After concluding his report Mārkaṇḍeya declares to his audience, the *Mahābhārata* heroes, that it was Janārdana who had revealed himself at that time and that he is now living among them as Govinda.

The fact that Nārāyaṇa appears as a child in this self-presentation is not explained. J.W. LAINE, however, seems to be right in postulating a particular 'charm' in this 'juxtaposition of the images of the seemingly helpless child and almighty God.'[5] There is no hint whatsoever in the text that the child should be regarded here as a symbol for divine play with the universe (*līlā*). This is indirectly confirmed by the fact that immediately after his report Mārkaṇḍeya speaks of a sort of divine play which now refers to Nārāyaṇa's activities on earth as Kṛṣṇa. This observation corresponds exactly to the results of a study by Bettina BÄUMER to be found in the first part of her dissertation on the term *līlā* particularly in epic Sanskrit literature.[6]

## 2. The *Brahma-purāṇa* version

The second version of the Mārkaṇḍeya episode in the *Brahma-purāṇa* is almost a copy of that in the *Mahā-bhārata*.[7] Nevertheless there are characteristic differences. In particular, the *pralaya* report of this version has been adjusted to the subsequent

---

[4] MBh 187.26 = BhG 4.7 (the famous verse *yadā yadā hi dharmasya glānir* ..., etc.).

[5] LAINE (1989: 263).

[6] BÄUMER (1969: 53): 'Die Verbindung von *līlā* mit der Schöpfungsvorstellung scheint, was die viṣṇuitischen Quellen betrifft, sekundär zu sein: zuerst sind es die Taten Viṣṇus als *avatāra* und die Tatsache seines gnädigen Herabsteigens, die als sein Spiel empfunden werden.'

[7] BrP 52.4–56.57 agrees largely with MBh 3.186.60–187.47; for a concordance of the two versions see BrP (1987: 816).

text: on the one hand, the Brahmā of the *Mahā-bhārata* version has been explicitly replaced here by Viṣṇu, though by name only and not otherwise,[8] and an advance notice of the theophany subsequently to be narrated has been interpolated (52.11–15b). On the other hand, the designation *puruṣêśa* for the god as well as for the fig-tree in this interpolation points to a Śaiva background and thus already refers to a Śaiva addition at the end of the whole episode, where Hari (Viṣṇu) is explicitly identified with Īśvara (Śiva) and the story is related to a *Śiva-liṅga* with the name of 'Mārkaṇḍeyêśvara' in order to bestow on it its specific salutary significance (56.63–72). In fact, these two sectarian innovations may even be presumed to represent two different redactional stages of development for this passage of the *Brahma-purāṇa*.

In the report on the theophany, the Supreme Person (*puruṣôttama*), who appears as a child to Mārkaṇḍeya and only relatively late in the passage calls himself Nārāyaṇa,[9] is again identified with Viṣṇu,[10] but this time also explicitly with Kṛṣṇa (53.31), whereas he is clearly distinguished from Brahmā who is said not to understand the true nature of the supreme god.[11]

The contrast between the divine child and the old Brahmin Mārkaṇḍeya is expressly emphasised by the insertion of a small scene (53.19–24).

> Here the divine child calls Mārkaṇḍeya a tired boy[12], on top of that using his name, which again is improper according to *Dharma-śāstra* rules. Mārkaṇḍeya promptly reacts to this impoliteness with an outburst of anger; but this is simply ignored by the child.

---

[8] The MBh *śloka* 3.186.76:

> *tatas taṁ mārutaṁ ghoraṁ s v a y a ṁ - b h ū r manu-jâdhipa /*
> *ādi-padmâlayo devaḥ pītvā svapiti bhārata //*

appears in BrP 53.12c–13b as

> *tatas taṁ mārutaṁ ghoraṁ s a v i ṣ ṇ u r muni-sattamāḥ /*
> *ādi-padmâlayo devaḥ pītvā svapiti bho dvijāḥ //*.

[9] In BrP 56.48cd: *ahaṁ nārâyaṇo nāma śaṅkha-cakra-gadā-dharaḥ //*.

[10] BrP 54.23 is more important in this respect than BrP 56.14, which is taken from MBh 3.187.5 and where the god identifies himself with several gods like Viṣṇu, Brahmā, Indra, etc.

[11] In Mārkaṇḍeya's hymn to the supreme god (BrP 55.11–35), he says in 55.32c–33a:

> *yat te rūpaṁ paraṁ deva kūṭa-stham acalaṁ dhruvam //*
> *brahmâdyās tan na jānanti …*

[12] *vatsa śrānto 'si bālas tvam* (53.19a).

Finally, the question why Nārāyaṇa appears before Mārkaṇḍeya in the shape of a child, is explicitly raised by Mārkaṇḍeya in this version,[13] but in the text that follows there is no answer whatsoever to this question. In any case, there is again in the whole passage not the slightest allusion to play with the world by the divine child in the sense of *līlā*.

### 3. The version of the *Hari-vaṁśa*, *Matsya-purāṇa* and *Padma-purāṇa*

The third version of the Mārkaṇḍeya episode belongs to a longer parallel passage which is shared by three different works, the *Hari-vaṁśa*, the *Matsya-purāṇa* and the *Padma-purāṇa*.[14] These three passages correspond to each other to such an extent that we can confidently count them as slightly different variants of one single text version.

Shortly before the Mārkaṇḍeya episode of this version the parallel passage contains another *pralaya* account,[15] but this time it is completely separated from Mārkaṇḍeya: he is not the narrator here nor is there any explicit link to Mārkaṇḍeya in the text, but instead it is even stated at the end of the passage that there is nobody in the world who has seen, who can tell or who knows about the *pralaya* process with the single exception of the highest god.[16]

Thus, the Mārkaṇḍeya episode here comprises the mere report of his experience of the divine self-revelation during the cosmic dissolution. Mārkaṇḍeya twice addresses the mysterious person whom he meets alone in the ocean. The god appears before him in two different shapes: first as the sleeping 'Primeval Person' (*ādi-puruṣa*) and afterwards as a sleeping child. In order to remove his perplexity the Puruṣa first shows him the whole world in his own belly and afterwards the divine child grants him a long oral self-revelation. Right from the beginning the god

[13] BrP 56.6ab: *iha bhūtvā śiśuḥ sākṣāt kiṁ bhavān avatiṣṭhate |* .

[14] The first part of the HV passage (Appendix I.41, lines 1–574), has a parallel in MtsP 164–171 and in PdP 5.36–37. The Mārkaṇḍeya episode comprises lines 184–303 of the HV App. I.41, corresponding to MtsP 167.13–67 and PdP 5.36.88c–143.

[15] HV App. I.41, lines 96–151, corresponding to MtsP 165.19–166.21 and PdP 5.36.46–73.

[16] HV App. I.41, lines 156–157 (corresponding to MtsP 166.23c-f and PdP 5.36.75):

*na draṣṭā nâiva vaditā na jñātā nâiva pārśvataḥ |*
*na sma vijñāyate kaścid ṛte taṁ devam uttamam ||* .

introduces himself as Nārāyaṇa-Brahmā,[17] and during his long speech he describes himself as having many other different manifestations and functions as creator and destroyer of all beings, *pradhāna* and *puruṣa*, and so on. In spite of echoes of the *Bhagavad-gītā*[18] there is neither an explicit identification with Vāsudeva-Kṛṣṇa nor otherwise with Viṣṇu.

The idea of the shape of a divine child is taken up and pointedly used here in two different ways.

On the one hand, we find the same impolite addressing of the old man by the child and the same angry reaction by Mārkaṇḍeya as we have seen in the BrP version, but here this scene is even extended: the divine child again calls the old Brahmin his exhausted child and claims to be his creator, since in former times it had granted him to his real father Aṅgiras as his son.[19]

On the other hand, this is the only version known to me where the topic of playfulness seems to be traceable as the motive for the appearance as a child: in the present version the child is characterised as 'playing in the primeval ocean',[20] and the same idea of the solitary playing child is even expressed a second time in the reading of the MtsP text.[21]

Thus, for this version only, D.R. KINSLEY may be right, when he points out that the idea of playing is meant here as essentially going together with the idea of the manifestation as a child.[22]

## 4. Mārkaṇḍeya and the Flood myth

In the three versions of the Mārkaṇḍeya episode treated so far, the story referred exclusively to the *pralaya* process at the end of a *kalpa*. Apart from this traditional

---

[17] The speech starts with *ahaṁ nārâyaṇo brahmā* ... (HV App. I.41, line 258 and parallels).

[18] Thus e.g. when the god calls himself the best of different classes of beings and things: cf. particularly the HV line 261 (*aham aindre pade śakra ṛtūnām api vatsaraḥ*) with BhG 10.22b (*devānām asmi vāsavaḥ*) and 10.35d (*ṛtūnāṁ kusumâkaraḥ*) and the HV line 263 (*bhujaṁ-gānām ahaṁ śeṣas tārkṣyo 'haṁ sarva-pakṣiṇām*) with BhG 10.29a (*anantaś câsmi nāgānām*) and 10.30d (*vainateyaś ca pakṣiṇām*).

[19] HV App. I.41, lines 232–247, and parallels.

[20] HV App. I.41, line 249 (and parallels): *ekârṇava-gataṁ krīḍantam*.

[21] MtsP 167.32c: *avyagraḥ krīḍate*.

[22] KINSLEY (1979: 3).

strand, however, there was another variant in which Mārkaṇḍeya survived the transition merely from one *manv-antara* to another.

Excursus: According to a pertinent passage to be found in several *Purāṇa*s and belonging to what W. KIRFEL compiled under the title of *Purāṇa-pañca-lakṣaṇa*,[23] one *kalpa* comprises 1,000 *mahā-yuga*s and corresponds at the same time to a sequence of fourteen *manv-antara*s (of 71 *mahā-yuga*s). Particularly in the HV/BrP version of that parallel passage it is said that the transition from one Manu-era to the next is bound up with *saṁhāra* and *saṁbhava*[24] and that only gods and the Seven *Ṛṣi*s survive that inundation of the world, whereas at the end of a *kalpa* all creatures are consumed by fire and finally are absorbed by Hari-Nārāyaṇa.[25] Unfortunately, however, the passage in question does not contain any further details about the transitional process between the *manv-antara*s.

Nevertheless in a quite different Purāṇic passage, i.e. in the outer frame-story of the entire MtsP, there is a short account of a cosmological process which could be taken as intended to fulfil exactly that need.[26] In fact this text explicitly combines the *manv-antara* transition with the Flood myth, well-known from older sources,[27] though it describes the transition along the lines of the *pralaya* at the end of a *kalpa* known, e.g. from the description in the MBh (3.186.56–76) mentioned above. It is said in the MtsP passage that together with the *Veda*s and *Purāṇa*s only particular gods, the river(-goddess) Narmadā, and among human beings solely Manu, traditionally the main figure of the Flood myth, with the help of his ark, and expressly now also Mārkaṇḍeya, survive the catastrophe. Thus the clear distinction between the *pralaya* account and the Flood myth, which had been maintained in the MBh, has been obscured in the MtsP.

As a matter of fact, in the older versions of the myth of the Flood and Manu's ark, which are to be found already in the *Śata-patha-brāhmaṇa* and, as was mentioned above, in the *Mārkaṇḍeya-samāsyā-parvan* of the MBh, there was no trace at all of the concept of *manv-antara*s and their transition.[28] After, however, the Flood myth

---

[23] KIRFEL (1927), 3. Abschnitt: *manv-anṭara* (254–283).

[24] KIRFEL (1927), 272.83cd:

*manv-antareṣu saṁhārāḥ saṁhārânteṣu saṁbhavāḥ.*

[25] KIRFEL (1927) 272.85–88.

[26] MtsP 1.12–2.20.

[27] A German translation of the MtsP passage together with a collection of further important versions of the Flood myth is presented in HOHENBERGER (1930: 4–24).

[28] The Brāhmaṇa version (ŚatBr 1.8.1.1–10) tells only of an unspecified Manu who once survived the deluge; thus the whole event took place within the life-span of one

had once been conceived in the frame-story of the MtsP as a transition from one *manv-antara* to the next and also Mārkaṇḍeya had explicitly been mentioned in that context, the story was taken up and finally narrated at greater length by Kṣeméndra in his *Daśâvatāra-carita*.[29] The tale runs there as follows.

> Manu is warned by Viṣṇu in the shape of a fish that *yuga-saṁkṣaya* has already started and the *kalpa* will end soon (30–31), and in order to survive the coming *pralaya* catastrophe he is advised to construct an ark. Then there is given a proper *pralaya* account, including the universal conflagration by the *saṁvartaka* fire which is finally extinguished by the flood (34–39); yet Manu's ark wondrously remains intact and is safely drawn by the fish over the ocean.
>
> By that time Mārkaṇḍeya awakens from deep meditation and wonders where the world has gone. He is dragged away by the flood, meets Manu's ark, but cannot get hold of it and again drifts about in the water. Finally he sees a dark-skinned boy, but immediately is swallowed by the child and finds the whole world in his belly. Later on Mārkaṇḍeya is set free through the child's mouth, and now he sees Brahmā sitting on a lotus which has grown out of Viṣṇu's navel, getting ready for the next creation of the world.

Though there is no longer any mention of the transition between *manv-antaras* in this version, most of the other elements which were present in the short version of the MtsP frame-story are again combined here: there is the blending of the Flood myth with the *pralaya* concept, this time clearly and exclusively referring to the end of a *kalpa*, and there is again the involvement of Mārkaṇḍeya in this scene. The Mārkaṇḍeya episode, however, which is obviously taken up from the older tradition introduced before, appears here considerably reduced to only the first part, since the second confrontation between Mārkaṇḍeya and the divine child is omitted in this version and thus there is no longer any self-revelation of the god. Evidently the theological interest which seems to have been central in the older versions of that

---

and the same person: there was no transition from one Manu to another as different rulers of their respective eras which is the basic idea of the *manv-antara* concept. The version of the MBh (3.185) resembles the Vedic version, though Manu is here already called *vaivasvata*, but again there is no mention of a second Manu. Again it is only this Manu who with the help of an ark and together only with the Seven *Ṛṣis* survives the destruction of the worlds by inundation, 'the washing entirely away of the worlds' (*saṁprakṣālana … lokānām*, 3.185.29).

[29] DAC 1.18–59 (ed. 1891), German translation in HOHENBERGER (1930: 20–24).

episode has lost its importance in the meantime, and other aspects inspired the later author nevertheless to repeat the story. Thus, in the present version there was probably more interest in the narrative effect of a further actor illustrating the painful circumstances of the catastrophe: Mārkaṇḍeya's desperate efforts to get hold of the ark from outside until he gets water into his nose and finally has to give up his endeavours are told here in considerable detail and in quite a vivid and realistic style.

### 5. The version of the *Bhāgavata-purāṇa*

The same shortening of the Mārkaṇḍeya episode mentioned for Kṣemendra's *Daśâvatāra-carita* is to be found again in another Purāṇic version, that of the *Bhāgavata-purāṇa*. However, before I go deeper into this, I should like to say a word about the specific view of the events of the Flood in relation to the *pralaya* process presented in this *Purāṇa*. Both are described in quite different passages in the *Purāṇa*,[30] but still they belong to one and the same systematic conception: together they are said to form a scheme of two *pralaya* stages which are terminologically distinguished as *naimittika-°* and *prākṛtika-pralaya,* the former of which takes place at the end of a *kalpa*, or 'Day of Brahmā', whereas the latter denotes the end of a *para*, i.e. of Brahmā's full life-time (12.4.3–6). A detailed account of a *naimittika-pralaya* is presented in 8.24, and this process is described there in the sense of the Flood myth, i.e. as a mere inundation without any conflagration and inclusive of the motif of an ark in which king Satyavrata, explicitly said to be reborn in the present *manv-antara* as Manu Vaivasvata, survives the catastrophe. A description of the second and much more radical *pralaya* type is to be found immediately after the systematic treatment of the two in 12.4.7–22. This presentation of the *prākṛtika-pralaya* now follows exactly the lines of the older *pralaya* accounts previously conceived for the end of a *kalpa*.

Shortly after that *pralaya* treatise and obviously as a supplement to it, a sceptical question is raised by Śaunaka as to how to rate the old rumour that Mārkaṇḍeya claims to have passed through a *pralaya* process and to have witnessed a self-revelation of the supreme god during the period of dissolution (12.8.1–5). As a reply the Sūta starts to narrate Mārkaṇḍeya's biography. During the first six *manv-antaras* he lived as an ascetic and as a devotee of Viṣṇu-Nārāyaṇa. Finally in the seventh, i.e. the present *manv-antara*, Hari in his double incarnation as Nārāyaṇa and Nara

[30] The Flood myth is included in *skandha* 8 and the *pralaya* account in the concluding *skandha* 12.

paid him a visit in his *āśrama* and granted him as a favour an insight into the *viṣṇu-māyā* (12.8.6–9.9). Soon after that Mārkaṇḍeya, while meditating at his *āśrama*, had the following vision:

> A heavy rain inundates the earth and finally the whole universe. Mārkaṇḍeya floats about for huge periods of time, until he detects a child in the ocean. While curiously approaching, he is immediately drawn into the belly of the child, observes the whole world therein, and comes out again. After that he finds himself again sitting in his *āśrama* (12.9.10–34).

Thereafter the text narrates that Śiva was impressed by Mārkaṇḍeya's deep devotion to Nārāyaṇa and he granted him a lifetime and fame up to the end of the *kalpa* (12.10).

This rendering of a part of the old Mārkaṇḍeya episode is more to be judged as a rejection than as an adoption. Mārkaṇḍeya's experience of a *pralaya* process is reduced here to a mere vision, a daydream. Already from the specification of his life-span within one *kalpa* it is clear that he cannot have passed through a *pralaya* in reality, and Mārkaṇḍeya's vision is explicitly reported for the present *manv-antara*, i.e. the middle period of the present *kalpa*. Another change, however, namely that the *pralaya* process in Mārkaṇḍeya's vision corresponds to a mere deluge without any conflagration, follows logically in this work, in accordance with its specific view of a *naimittika-pralaya*. Finally, the theological message of the Mārkaṇḍeya episode is once again cut down: Mārkaṇḍeya gets the demonstration that the world is maintained in the body of Viṣṇu-Nārāyaṇa, but the whole self-explanation of the divine child is left out.

The conclusion of the story, in which Śiva comes into the picture, may perhaps have been stimulated as a reaction against the inclusivistic attempt of the *Brahma-purāṇa* to postulate the Mārkaṇḍeya episode as a sanctification story for a *Śiva-liṅga* called *mārkaṇḍeyêśvara*. In any case, here in the *Bhāgavata-purāṇa* Śiva explicitly supports Mārkaṇḍeya as an eminent devotee of Nārāyaṇa.

### 6. Two versions within the *Skanda-purāṇa*

Within the voluminous collection of disparate *Māhātmya* and other texts that goes under the title of *Skanda-purāṇa*,[31] to my knowledge, there are two quite different versions of the Mārkaṇḍeya episode presented in two separate passages. One is to be

[31] Cf. ROCHER (1986: 228–229).

found in the *Puruṣôttama-kṣetra-māhātmya* of the *Vaiṣṇava-khaṇḍa* (2.2) and the other in the *Revā-khaṇḍa* of the *Āvantya-khaṇḍa* (5.3).[32]

In the first version (in 2.2.3) it is related how Mārkaṇḍeya, who is called 'seven-*kalpa*s old' (*sapta-kalpâyuḥ*, v. 3), is floating about in the 'ocean of dissolution' (*pralayârṇave*, v. 4), until he meets Nārāyaṇa-Viṣṇu-Govinda in the shape of a child, who shows him the whole world in his belly. Again afterwards there is no self-revelation of the supreme god, and the story ends with the prophecy that Mārkaṇḍeya after the new creation of the world will stay in the Puruṣôttama-kṣetra, as a devotee of Śiva, who is identified with Nārāyaṇa. Though it is not explicitly stated in the text, the story seems to be meant to take place during the universal dissolution at the end of a *kalpa*.

In the second version (in 5.3.12–19), however, we at first get the impression that a Flood legend is again being told, though instead of the divine fish and Manu, the river-goddess Narmadā[33] is named here who offers to rescue pious Śaivas from being killed by the coming flood. One of these Śaivas is our Mārkaṇḍeya, who informs the other sages that the Narmadā was born 21 *kalpa*s back and that he himself has witnessed her for the last seven *kalpa*s (13.40–47). Afterwards Mārkaṇḍeya is said to be separately saved by the Narmadā goddess: she appears to him in the shape of a cow, and Mārkaṇḍeya, holding her tail, is drawn by her over the flood as Manu's ark previously was drawn by the divine fish. The description of the catastrophe, however, again shows many details which have definitely been taken over from older *pralaya* accounts. The process of a conflagration is again narrated at length (*adhyāya* 17) and this is finally extinguished by an inundation. Thus again a dissolution at the end of a *kalpa* seems to be meant, here combined with the Flood myth. This relatively free rendering of the Mārkaṇḍeya episode confirms once again that the originally clear difference between these two types of universal calamities had fallen into total oblivion in later times.

---

[32] I was made aware of these two versions by an article of SŪRYA KĀNTA (1949: 301–329). This article mainly contains a paraphrase of the two passages which, however, are both assigned to the *Puruṣôttama-māhātmya*. In the SkP edition at my disposal the two passages are 2.2.3 and 5.3.12–19.

[33] As was said above, the river[-goddess] Narmadā had already been mentioned in the version of the Flood myth within the frame-story of the MtsP.

## BIBLIOGRAPHY


BÄUMER 1969 = Bäumer, Bettina: *Schöpfung als Spiel. Der Begriff līlā im Hinduismus, seine philosophische und theologische Deutung*. Phil. diss., München 1969.

BhāgP = *Bhāgavata-purāṇa*, with a Hindi translation. 2nd ed., Gita Press, Gorakhpur 1951. [First edition: 1940].

BhG = *The Bhagavad-gītā*. Ed. by S.K. Belvalkar, 2nd repr., Bhandarkar Oriental Research Institute, Poona 1968.

BrP = *Sanskrit Indices and Text of the Brahma-purāṇa*, by P. Schreiner and R. Söhnen, *Purāṇa Research Publications–Tübingen* 1, Otto Harrassowitz, Wiesbaden 1987.

DAC = Kṣemendra: *Daśâvatāra-carita*. *Kāvyamālā* 26, Bombay 1891.

HOHENBERGER 1930 = Hohenberger, Adam: *Die indische Flutsage und das Matsyà-purāṇa*. Harrassowitz, Leipzig 1930.

HV = *The Hari-vaṁśa, being the Khila or Supplement to the Mahā-bhārata*. Critically ed. by P.L. Vaidya, Bhandarkar Oriental Research Institute, Poona 1969–71.

KINSLEY 1979 = Kinsley, David R.: *The Divine Player. A study of Krishna Lila*. Motilal Banarsidass, Delhi 1979.

KIRFEL 1927 = Kirfel, Willibald: *Das Purāṇa-pañca-lakṣaṇa. Versuch einer Textgeschichte*, Bonn 1927.

LAINE 1989 = Laine, James W.: *Visions of God: narratives of Theophany in the Mahā-bhārata. Publications of the De Nobili Research Library* 16. Institut für Indologie der Universität Wien, Vienna 1989.

MBh = *The Mahā-bhārata*. Critically ed. by V.S. Sukthankar and others. Bhandarkar Oriental Research Institute, Poona 1933–66.

MtsP = *Matsya-purāṇa*. *Ānandāśrama Sanskrit Series* 54, Poona 1907.

PdP = *Padma-purāṇa*. *Ānandāśrama Sanskrit Series Extra No.* 1, Poona 1893–94.

ROCHER 1986 = Rocher, Ludo: *The Purāṇas. A History of Indian Literature*, ed. by J. Gonda, II,3. Otto Harrassowitz, Wiesbaden 1986.

ŚatBr = *The Śata-patha-brāhmaṇa in the Mādhyandina-Śākhā*. Ed. by Albrecht Weber, 2nd ed., *Chowkhamba Sanskrit Series* 96, Varanasi 1964. [First edition: London 1855].

SkP = *Skanda-mahā-purāṇam*. Vols. 1–3, arranged by Nag Sharan Singh, 2nd reprint, Nag Publishers, Delhi 1984.

SŪRYA KĀNTA 1949 = Sūrya Kānta [Śāstrī]: 'Mārkaṇḍeya and the Flood Legend in the Skanda-Purāṇa', in: *Bhāratīya Vidyā* 10 (1949 = *Shri K.M. Munshi Diamond Jubilee Volume*) 301–329.

# The structure of the *Mokṣa-dharma-parvan* of the *Mahā-bhārata*

JOHN BROCKINGTON

Over the years Western scholars have put forward very different views about the nature of the *Śānti-parvan*, from Dahlmann's view that narrative and didactic elements were deliberately combined in an essentially unitary work to HOPKINS's categorisation of it as 'pseudo-epic', where however the dismissive implications of that term must be balanced by his extensive study of epic philosophy. Within the *Śānti-parvan*, the longest part and the one generally seen as most characteristic is the *Mokṣa-dharma-parvan*.[1] There is probably a broad chronological progression from the *Rāja-dharma-parvan* (12.1–128) through the *Āpad-dharma-parvan* (12.129–167) to the *Mokṣa-dharma-parvan* (12.168–353) but this need mean nothing more than that accretions were normally at the end of the then existing material. Certainly, each passage must be examined individually, since the material is often only loosely integrated into these major units. Indeed, occasionally the exceptional length of an *adhyāya* indicates that it has been incorporated at a late stage, after the division into *adhyāya*s was already established; examples in the *Mokṣa-dharma-parvan* are the *Bali-vāsava-saṁvāda* and the *Śrī-vāsava-saṁvāda* (12.220 and 221), the *Sulabhā-janaka-saṁvāda* (12.308) and the *Yāvakâdhyāya* (12.309, which also shows a late metrical pattern with its continuous iambic *anuṣṭubh* or *pramāṇikā* in verses 32–69).

As HOPKINS long ago noted about the *Mahā-bhārata*, 'its didactic parts recapitulate the later Upanishads; and it shows acquaintance with a much larger number of Vedic schools than were recognised even at a late date. Its philosophical sections … reflect varied schools and contradictory systems some of which are as late as our era.'[2] It is also wise to bear in mind HOPKINS's further point: 'No one has ever denied that there are early legends found in the late parts of the epic; but the

[1] The first draft of this paper was written before I learnt from James FITZGERALD (at the second *Dubrovnik International Conference on the Sanskrit Epics and Purāṇas*, 9–14 August 1999) about his doctoral thesis. I am most grateful to him for then sending me a copy of much of it; I have taken advantage of it to add certain points and to include reference to his work on others.

[2] HOPKINS (1901: 363).

*Essays in Indian Philosophy, Religion and Literature*, pp. 99–111.

fact that this or that legend repeated in the pseudo-epic is found in other literature, no matter how old, does nothing toward proving either the antiquity of the book as a whole, which is just what the "synthetic" method contends for, or the antiquity of the epic form of the legend.'[3]

The usual description of this material as 'encyclopaedic' carries the implications that the only ordering principle is arbitrary and that the main aim is comprehensiveness; indeed, its framework of Bhīṣma's replies to Yudhiṣṭhira's questions introducing the teachings of other individual sages suggests its episodic nature.[4] Indeed, as FITZGERALD notes, one of Yudhiṣṭhira's own questions recognises as much, referring to Bhīṣma's instruction as comprising 'many accounts of different sorts pertaining to diverse things' (*nānâśrayāś ca bahava itihâsāḥ pṛthag-vidhāḥ*, 12.189.1cd), and, although all except five of the 63 units of the *Mokṣa-dharma-parvan* are introduced by a question from Yudhiṣṭhira, these questions do not constitute an overall framework but are simply a convenient lead-in to that specific text.[5] Nevertheless, other views have been expressed by both Indian and Western scholars. I therefore plan to look in broad terms at some themes and patterns in the *Mokṣa-dharma-parvan* and to assess how far it is just a random collection and how far its growth conforms to a definite purpose or reveals a clear structure.

ZAEHNER, for example, argued for a progression, stating that 'The scheme of the twelfth book of the *Mahā-bhārata* resembles that of the *Bhagavad-gītā* in that its descriptions of liberation become increasingly theistic as the book moves towards its close.'[6] In so far as he regards the *Nārāyaṇīya* as its climax, such a view might possibly be justified, but in reality the final passage of the *Mokṣa-dharma* is the *Uñcha-vṛtty-upākhyāna*. However, in another article published in the same year, ZAEHNER was less inclined to see the *Mokṣa-dharma* as a unity: 'In the Epic rather more than half of the huge twelfth book is devoted to the subject of liberation, but much of it is inconsistent and confused because the subject always tends to get

[3] HOPKINS (1901: 381).

[4] V.M. Bedekar has expressed this view very clearly in the introduction to the *Śānti-parvan* when he says, 'These teachings can, by no means, be said to constitute any consistent, homogeneous system. ... Indeed, these teachings are, often, basically unconnected and disparate with one another' (*Mahā-bhārata* 1966: CCXXXII).

[5] FITZGERALD (1980: 170, 281, 293 and 295).

[6] ZAEHNER (1963a: 302). Earlier in this article he suggests that 'it is surely reasonable to suppose that whoever was responsible for the final redaction of the Gītā did not mix his ingredients pell-mell and in any old order, but rather arranged them in an order of increasing significance, culminating in what is stated to be the most hidden, secret, or mysterious doctrine of all' (p. 296).

mixed up with cosmogony, so inextricably interconnected are the the macrocosm and the microcosm in Hindu thought.'[7]

As a broad initial generalisation, it might be said that among the main themes of the *Mokṣa-dharma-parvan* are versions of both Sāṁkhya and Yoga, while both its title and the major part of its contents suggest that its primary theme is that of release from *saṁsāra*.[8] Descriptions of Sāṁkhya and of Yoga are indeed frequent and a regular feature of the Yoga passages is a strong emphasis on discipline and meditation.[9] While the classical schools distinguish fairly clearly between Sāṁkhya and Yoga, this is not necessarily true in the epic and the *Mokṣa-dharma* contains several assertions of their essential identity, although Sāṁkhya is typically *anīśvara*, unlike Yoga. Several teachers propound some form of Sāṁkhya, of whom some can be traced back to the older *Upaniṣad*s and many also appear later in the *Purāṇa*s, but the doctrines attributed to them vary and are not necessarily specific to Sāṁkhya. Despite its title, moreover, the *Mokṣa-dharma-parvan* contains material on topics such as the four *varṇa*s (e.g. 12.181.1–182.8, 200.31–33 and 285.1–21) which might appear more appropriate to the *Rāja-dharma-parvan*, although such passages are usually relatively brief; material on the *āśrama*s (e.g. 12.252–6 and 276) has perhaps greater relevance to *mokṣa*. More substantial are the considerable number of *adhyāya*s traditionally termed *gītā*s and *māhātmya*s, where the content frequently has little to do with *mokṣa*. These often contain appreciable narrative material and this is properly so for those passages designated *upākhyāna*; thus, for example, the legend of how Uśanas acquired his name Śukra is told at 12.278 (*Kāvyôpākhyāna*). However, even those passages termed *saṁvāda*, 'debate', with its suggestion of philosophical discourse, may well contain other material, such as the myth of Śrī deserting Bali for Indra (12.218) which concludes the first version of the *Bali-vāsava-saṁvāda* (12.216–218; expanded and separated at 12.221).

After a brief text (the *Karmâstikya*, 12.174) in which Bhīṣma replies to Yudhiṣṭhira's question himself, comes the first major block in the *Mokṣa-dharma*, the *Bhṛgu-bharadvāja-saṁvāda* (12.175–85), of which the first half forms a discourse on the origins of the world from a basically Sāṁkhya perspective; this seems to show a relatively archaic standpoint with its assignment of the *manas* to the highest place, while FRAUWALLNER saw in one *adhyāya* (12.177) some of the earliest signs of the realism and interest in natural sciences characteristic of the

[7] ZAEHNER (1963b: 220).

[8] On the proportion of the material dealing with *mokṣa* directly see FITZGERALD (1980: especially pp. 238, 246 and 249).

[9] I have examined the Sāṁkhya and Yoga passages in more detail in BROCKINGTON (1999) and BROCKINGTON (forthcoming).

Vaiśeṣika school.[10] Although this picture of a relatively early passage near the start of the *Mokṣa-dharma* may well be broadly true, we must also note that there are short prose passages in the final three *adhyāyas* of the passage (12.183–185); OLIVELLE (and earlier Deussen) suggested that the passage on the four *āśramas* is a remnant of an old *dharma-sūtra*,[11] which does point to an early date but conversely the other instances of prose in the *Mokṣa-dharma* (12.325 and 329) both occur in the clearly late *Nārāyaṇīya*, while 12.178 corresponds to 3.203.13–30. The next *adhyāya* (*Ācāra-vidhi*, 12.186) is one of the few dealing with issues of correct behaviour, *ācāra*, without any obvious reference to *mokṣa*, the others being the *Amṛta-prāśika* (12.214, also found with slight variants as 13.93) and the *Śrī-vāsava-saṁvāda* (12.221); it has no obvious links forward or back.

An early form of Sāṁkhya is found in the *Adhyātma-kathana* (12.187, repeated with some significant variations at 12.239–41[12]) in which, in the varying usage of the terms *bhāva* and *guṇa*, there are traces of a synthesis between ancient cosmological speculations and yogic theories of evolution; this is the passage which FRAUWALLNER saw as 'der epischen Grundtext des Sāṁkhya.'[13] In addition, as FRAUWALLNER indicated, besides the apparent archaism of its ideas, the fact that this text-group is textually so corrupt is another indication of an early date. Here though, instead of the pre-eminence of the *manas*, we find the *buddhi* placed above the *manas* in what is presumably a somewhat more developed version of these concepts than in the *Bhṛgu-bharadvāja-saṁvāda* (12.175–85); the same is true of the *Manu-bṛhaspati-saṁvāda* (12.194–99), where much of the dialogue is concerned to establish the existence of the *kṣetra-jña* or *śarīrin* (but which

---

[10] FRAUWALLNER (1953: 288 ff.). After these cosmogonic issues the text then moves on to a discussion of the basic constitution and functioning of the body, which leads into a debate on the existence of a *jīva*, and to statements about the nature of human action and the behaviour appropriate to each *āśrama*.

[11] See OLIVELLE (1993: 154).

[12] Such repetitions tend to reinforce the view that the material has been collected together without much plan. Another example, mentioned at the end of the previous paragraph, is 12.214, also found—where it fits better—as 13,93. In other instances, however, the borrowing is presumably from the *Śānti-parvan* by another book, as with MBh.7 App.I.8, which incorporates material both from 12.29 (the *Ṣoḍaśa-rājakīya*) and from 12.248–50, the *Mṛtyûtpatti*.

[13] FRAUWALLNER (1925: 179–80). In the Bombay edition there are three versions of this passage but its 12.286[5] is lacking in several manuscripts and its readings are given by the Critical Edition in App.II.1 as variants to 12.187; it also recurs at *Bṛhan-nāradīya-purāṇa* 44.21–82. It is translated in EDGERTON (1965: 256–60), and analysed by J.A.B. van BUITENEN (1956: 153–157); the latest study is by PETER BISSCHOP (1999).

otherwise seems closer to Advaita Vedānta views than any other text of the *Mokṣa-dharma*).

Following this Sāṁkhya passage, the next *adhyāya* is the *Dhyāna-yoga* passage (12.188) on the fourfold Yoga of meditation, which gives one of the fullest descriptions from the standpoint of suppression (*nirodha*). There then follows, however, the *Jāpakôpākhyāna* (12.189–93), where, as in some other passages, different approaches are deliberately contrasted.[14] Here the importance of *japa*, the murmuring of Vedic verses, and of the *jāpaka* is stressed; Bhīṣma declares that *japa* constitutes an independent discipline belonging to the Vedic sacrificial tradition and differing from Sāṁkhya and Yoga; from the concluding laudatory description of the *jāpaka*, the passage is obviously intended to meet the challenge of Yoga by presenting *japa* as a viable alternative, while at the same time incorporating various elements associated with Yoga. In this series of *adhyāya*s, then, we find not a sequential development but something nearer to a set of contrasts; while it is not uncommon to find passages on Sāṁkhya and on Yoga juxtaposed, the relationship is as often one of opposition as complementarity.

The *Vārṣṇeyâdhyātma* (12.203–210), although it incorporates elements of an early form of Sāṁkhya, refers instead to Yoga and operates in a basically theistic framework, the goal of release, of becoming Brahman, being to go to the unborn, divine Viṣṇu; this theistic framework—which in some ways prefigures *Viśiṣṭâdvaita* views—may well however result from later remodelling. The next passage, the *Janaka-pañcaśikha-saṁvāda* (12.211–212), might be expected to present clearly Sāṁkhya views, mentioning as it does the three teachers often referred to later as important precursors of the developed Sāṁkhya system: Kapila, Āsuri and Pañcaśikha.[15] These three are presented in that order at 211.1–16, where Pañcaśikha Kāpileya arrives at the court of Janaka of Mithilā and is described as looking like Prajāpati Kapila in form, as the first or foremost pupil of Āsuri, and as being born from Āsuri's wife, Kapilā. However, the views attributed to Pañcaśikha here in this compact text and elsewhere in the *Mokṣa-dharma* seem quite different from those that can be pieced together from the occasional quotations ascribed to him in later texts.

Soon after comes an obvious grouping of texts, at 12.215–221, which share the theme of the confrontation between Indra and a defeated Asura: the dialogues between Indra and Prahlāda, Bali, Namuci and again, in an expanded version, Bali,

[14] For a detailed study, see BEDEKAR (1963).

[15] Incidentally, several other teachers are cited in various passages as teaching some form of Sāṁkhya, some of whom can be traced back to the older *Upaniṣad*s, while many also appear in the later Purāṇic literature, but the doctrines attributed to them vary and are not necessarily specific to Sāṁkhya.

with finally (*Śrī-vāsava-saṁvāda*, 12.221) an expanded version of Śrī's dialogue with Indra.[16] The Asuras, though defeated, do not grieve and are made to propound a form of fatalistic doctrine: Prahlāda assigns everything to *sva-bhāva*, Bali to *kāla*, and Namuci more generally blames the *dhātṛ* or *dhātṛ*s. Subsequently too, in the *Nārada-devala-saṁvāda* (12.267), the first principle is *kāla*, which is impelled by its own inherent nature to create the five elements; this passage lists three psychical entities, *citta*, *manas* and *buddhi*, and adds a sixth, *bala*, to the usual five organs of action, to create a decidedly idiosyncratic scheme. On the other hand, it is less unusual than is often thought for *kāla* to be given prominence, for example *atikrāmati kāle 'smin* at 12.169.1a, almost at the start of the *Mokṣa-dharma*, besides Bali's discourse to Indra at 12.217. However, as this group of passages illustrates, there is a trend towards assigning views advocating *kāla*, *sva-bhāva* or *niyati* to Asuras, although they may still be ascribed to sages (e.g. *sva-bhāva* to Ājagara at 12.172).

The *Śukânupraśna* or *Vyāsa-śuka-saṁvāda* (12.224–247) has a supposed unity as a discourse given by Vyāsa to his son Śuka but it is in fact a very heterogeneous collection of passages, including for example both the *Veda-rahasya* (238) and an account of the Yogin's direct vision (245) and referring back at its start (224.4) to the *Bhṛgu-bharadvāja-saṁvāda* (12.175–85). The first chapter comprises a cosmogonic text which is perhaps older than the Christian era, according to HACKER:[17] a tract on the divisions of time (224.12–21) precedes one on the qualities of the *yuga*s (22–27) and one on cosmogony (31–38). FRAUWALLNER identified the *Śukânupraśna* as an example of the speculations about the ages and periods of the world as they emerge from Brahmā which gave rise to the doctrine of evolution and which form the second stage of his scheme of the evolution of Sāṁkhya. He assigns this stage to Pañcaśikha, whom he also credits with adding the notion of *ahaṁ-kāra* and standardising the *tattva*s at 25; however, a major obstacle to his interpretation is the absence of the term *ahaṁ-kāra* from any of the *Mahā-bhārata* passages linked in any way with Pañcaśikha. The main one is the *Pañcaśikha-vākya* (12.211–212), already mentioned, but another brief dialogue attributed to Pañcaśikha (12.307, *Pañcaśikha-janaka-saṁvāda*) has no obvious relevance to Sāṁkhya, although in the

[16] On this group of texts see also FITZGERALD (1980: 297–301). A similar theme occurs at 12.270, the first half of the *Vṛtra-gītā* (cf. below), which on that basis could well have been included here. Interestingly, these passages and the story of Maṅki (12.171) seem to be referred to at 12.173.3.

[17] HACKER (1961). It is worth noting that this *adhyāya* is over twice the average length at 75 verses, whereas the final *adhyāya*s of the *Śukânupraśna* (241–247) are much shorter than average. A modified version of these instructional tracts was incorporated into the opening *adhyāya* of the *Manu-smṛti*.

next *adhyāya*, the *Sulabhā-janaka-saṁvāda*, Janaka declares that he is Pañcaśikha's pupil.

Within the *Śukânupraśna* there is a marked emphasis on *dhāraṇā* in 12.228, which develops an extended metaphor identifying the parts of a warrior's chariot with the requirements of Yoga, continues by describing seven *dhāraṇā*s (12.228.13–15) and concludes with the assertion that he who has passed beyond yogic domination is released. Again, also within the *Śukânupraśna*, Vyāsa's exposition of Sāṁkhya (12.231), which implies that Sāṁkhya and Yoga are alternative ways to attain Brahman, is followed by one of Yoga (12.232), which defines the purpose of this Yoga discipline as 'unification of *buddhi* and *manas* and of the senses as a whole' (2cd).[18]

A group of passages almost immediately thereafter may well have been placed together because of their common themes of *ahiṁsā* and veneration of the cow—certainly *ahiṁsā* is not prominent elsewhere in the *Mokṣa-dharma*. Thus, the *Tulādhāra-jājali-saṁvāda* (12.253–256) narrates the encounter between a brāhman ascetic Jājali and the merchant Tulādhāra who propounds a critique of farming and insists on the abandonment of animal sacrifice.[19] Similarly the stories of Vicakhnu (*Vicakhnu-gītā* 12.257) and Satya (12.264, called *Yajña-nindā* in many manuscripts) criticise the violence done to animals in rituals, and the *Kapila-go-saṁvāda* (12.260–262) opens with the cow—actually the *ṛṣi* Syūmaraśmi—complaining about the wanton slaughter of her relatives in sacrifice, although basically Syūmaraśmi defends the system of Vedic sacrifice along traditional lines. Similarly, in the *Satyavad-dyumatsena-saṁvāda* (12.259) king Dyumatsena and his son Satyavat debate the morality of executing criminals. However, if these passages are linked by such common themes, it is less easy to see why among them is found the *Cirakārikôpākhyāna* (12.258), where Cirakārin hesitates for so long over carrying out his father's command to execute his mother, seduced by Indra, that his father has time to repent of his hasty decision. This reads more like a parody of the Rāma Jāmadagnya story than a commendation of *ahiṁsā*, although Bedekar tries to give it

---

[18] Further on in the *Śukânupraśna* the elements are listed in ascending order: *indriyas*, *indriyârthas*, *manas*, *buddhi*, *mahān ātmā*, *avyakta*, *amṛta* (12.238.3–4); here, then, *buddhi* is included in the scheme and is superior to *manas*, but *ahaṁ-kāra* is as yet absent.

[19] Chris CHAPPLE (1996) indeed suggests that the story is theologically inspired by Jainism, while Ian PROUDFOOT identifies three trends of thought: a movement away from mere detachment towards benevolent *ahiṁsā*, the growth in prominence of the cow as the object of *ahiṁsā* and sacrifice as the major interest (PROUDFOOT 1987); cf. also FITZGERALD (1980: 258–62 and 270–5).

relevance by suggesting that it reflects a new ethics in which the individual must decide his own course of action in accordance with his conscience.[20]

Another way of viewing this group of passages would be as a critique of general religious practices and ideas, especially those of the brāhmans. This is given some support by the fact that within it is also included the *Kuṇḍadhārôpākhyāna* (12.263), telling how a brāhman, frustrated by the lack of attention to his prayers for wealth from the established gods, invokes a cloud, Kuṇḍadhāra, as a deity; the satire on worshippers seeking mundane ends and on the trappings of orthodox religion is obvious, although the story has been adapted to the overall purpose of the *Mokṣa-dharma* by making the cloud show genuine concern for his worshipper and so persuade him to reject the rewards of his penances by impressing on him the doctrine of supreme desirelessness.[21]

The so-called *Vṛtra-gītā* (12.270–1), of which the second part is really a *māhātmya* of Viṣṇu by Sanatkumāra, includes a discourse by Sanatkumāra on the colours of the soul, unparalleled in any of the orthodox systems but having obvious analogies with the Jain doctrine of *leśyās*; it is hard, therefore, to see any other reason for its inclusion than a desire for comprehensiveness (which may similarly have motivated the inclusion in 12.171 of the story of Maṅki, with its Ājīvika background). However, clearly the passage as a whole is positioned just where it is because it leads into the narrative of Indra's slaying of Vṛtra (*Vṛtra-vadha*, 12.272–3). Another *gītā*, the long *Parāśara-gītā* at 12.279–87, is an interesting exhortation to pursue *mokṣa* within the context of action according to *dharma* and stresses the specific duties of the *varṇa*s; the similarity of theme to the *Bhagavad-gītā* and *Nārāyaṇīya* suggests its relative lateness, while its recognition of only three *āśrama*s (12.286.30) might point to an early date or simply to extreme conservatism.

The main text about the Yoga of heightened consciousness, *jñāna-dīpti-yoga*, the *Yoga-kathana* (12.289, in which the terms *yoga* and *yogin* occur particularly frequently), differentiates *sāṁkhya-yoga* from other kinds of Yoga and states that Sāṁkhya is non-theistic, emphasises knowledge as the only means of salvation, and relies mainly on accepted teaching as a means of knowledge, whereas Yoga is theistic, emphasises the power and strength of bodily discipline, and relies mainly on immediate perception as a means of knowledge. It contrasts this form of Yoga with the extended account of Sāṁkhya given in the next *adhyāya* (*Sāṁkhya-kathana* / *Sāṁkhya-varṇana*, 12.290); this and other features suggest that it is fairly close to Pātañjala Yoga. In the *Sāṁkhya-kathana* Bhīṣma then further elaborates on

[20] *Mahā-bhārata* (1966: CCXLVII). FITZGERALD's view is closer to mine: 'a deliberate inversion' (p. 275 n.1).

[21] There is a study of this passage by V.M. BEDEKAR (1960).

the significance of Sāṁkhya, which is the highest knowledge on which other views rely (12.290.103, cf. 95–6), in response to Yudhiṣṭhira's objection that if *mokṣa* depends on pure knowledge and has no relationship to *dharma* 'what could be more unpleasant?' (*kiṁ nu duḥkhataraṁ bhavet*, 12.290.79d).

Next, the *Vasiṣṭha-karālajanaka-saṁvāda* (12.291–6) provides a well integrated account of Sāṁkhya and gives the impression of being a late theistic reshaping of older material, of which one indicator is the occurrence of the rare technical terms *ekâgratā* and *prāṇâyāma*.[22] Another is the mythological framework where Śambhu creates *Hiraṇya-garbha* and *buddhi* or *mahad bhūta* as the first stage, and so on (291.15–28), termed a scheme of 24 *tattva*s with Viṣṇu as the 25th. As Fitzgerald suggests, the last ten units of the *Mokṣa-dharma*, from 12.291–6 onwards, 'all have a bearing on the problematic issue of defining the relative merits of the life of renunciation and *mokṣa* (*nivṛtti*) and the active life organized in terms of ritual and social *dharma* (*pravṛtti*).'[23]

Cosmological concepts typical of classical Sāṁkhya and their mirror image in the process of dissolution are both found within the *Yājñavalkya-janaka-saṁvāda* (12.298–306) but, while the passage as a whole seems relatively structured, the details of the various schemes differ. Yājñavalkya follows an exposition of Sāṁkhya with one of Yoga (12.304, which has similarities with 12.232, already mentioned), in which he views Sāṁkhya in terms of knowledge and Yoga in terms of power and, while regarding them as one, affirms that the eightfold Yoga is found in the *Veda*s. The last *adhyāya* of the passage contains a theistic version of Sāṁkhya, propounding a total of 26 *tattva*s the last a supreme being, as Yājñavalkya makes clear (12.306.27–55).[24]

[22] Teun GOUDRIAAN (1992: 140–147 and 155–160) examines this passage and interestingly suggests (p. 146) on the grounds of inconsistencies between the earlier and later parts of 12.296 that 'at least the passage from 294.1 to 296.40 is an interpolation containing a restatement of the earlier exposition' and that 'the positions taken in the latter part (294–296) seem to indicate a certain development or, perhaps better, a change of emphasis, with respect to the earlier chapters (291–293).' The term *ekâgratā* occurs only at 12.198.6c and 294.8a and *prāṇâyāma* only at 294.8bc and 304.9bc (cf. BROCKINGTON (1999)).

[23] FITZGERALD (1980: 305; cf. more generally pp. 305–339). The *pravṛtti* / *nivṛtti* opposition is also explored in other texts, including the *Amṛta-prāśika* (12.214), the *Kapila-go-saṁvāda* (12.260–2) and the *Ariṣṭanemi-sagara-saṁvāda* (12.277).

[24] This is then seen in more impersonal terms in Bhīṣma's summary of Yājñavalkya's views at 107cd; cf. also 12.187.37–39, 240.19–21, 296.22–26 and 303.13–18. Incidentally, this is the only passage apart from 211.1–16 to give any kind of list of Sāṁkhya teachers—a much longer list—but it seems to give the names in a random order (12.306.56–60).

The next *adhyāya*, the *Pañcaśikha-janaka-saṁvāda* (12.307), despite its name, contains nothing that can be linked to Pañcaśikha or even to Sāṁkhya in general; its purpose seems to be just to introduce the next *adhyāya*, the very lengthy—and so probably late—*Sulabhā-janaka-saṁvāda*, where Janaka declares that he is Pañcaśikha's pupil (12.308.24). However, this episode highlights the extent to which Sāṁkhya is oriented towards *mokṣa* when Sulabhā, a female Sāṁkhya teacher, challenges Janaka and enters his mind to test his claims to detachment; Janaka rather defensively asserts his achieving of *vairāgya* and then Sulabhā embarks on a long and elaborate refutation of his teaching, which goes unanswered and so by implication her radical asceticism is endorsed.[25] This is indeed the passage in which the tension between *pravṛtti* and *nivṛtti* is most strongly presented.

The story of Vyāsa's son, Śuka, in the *Śuka-carita* (12.310–20) also highlights the ascetic ideal but in narrative form; he is recognised as the ideal renouncer with a complete knowledge of the absolute, possessing indeed even higher sanctity than his father. If ZAEHNER's view that descriptions of liberation become more theistic towards the end of the *Śānti-parvan* is valid, one would have expected more sign of it here, in the passage immediately preceding the *Nārāyaṇīya*, which he regards as the climax of the *Mokṣa-dharma-parvan*. Instead, the main point of interest, apart from the story itself, is Nārada's statement in his dialogue with Śuka that there are seventeen constituents of a human being (12.316.45), an apparently archaic view.

The *Nārāyaṇīya* (12.321–339) is clearly a late part even of the *Śānti-parvan* and is probably no earlier than the 3rd century C.E.; its lateness is mainly shown by its contents but there are other indicators, such as the prose passages already mentioned and the fact that several of its *adhyāya*s are exceptionally long.[26] Its main purpose is to expound the Pāñca-rātra system, but in a form that gives much less emphasis to the *vyūha* doctrine than the classical school; in its devotional aspect it is close to the *Bhagavad-gītā*, though not as close doctrinally, where it assigns greater value to rites,

[25] Despite being discredited in this way by implication here, Janaka still appears as an authority in the *Śuka-carita*, since Vyāsa advises Śuka to go to Mithilā to learn everything about *mokṣa* from him (12.213.6). Incidentally, the well known line about Janaka's detachment—*mithilāyāṁ pradīptāyāṁ na me dahyati kiṁcana*—does not occur here, though found three times in all in the *Śānti-parvan* (12.17.18cd, 171.56cd and 268.4cd).

[26] For a detailed study of the *Nārāyaṇīya* see SCHREINER (1997). Although the Critical Edition divides the *Nārāyaṇīya* into 19 chapters, since it divides 329 and 330 against the majority of the manuscript evidence, the total should no doubt be 18, in view of the significance of that number within the *Mahā-bhārata* tradition later, though probably not at the earliest period.

sacrifices, *tapas* and *yoga*.[27] However, *tapas* and *yoga* are both subordinated to *bhakti*, with Nārāyaṇa identifying himself as the goal of Yoga proclaimed in Yoga texts (326.65cd, cf. 335.74c), while the juxtaposition of Sāṁkhya and Yoga has become a commonplace and so, for example, at 327.64–66 the seven mind-born sons of Brahmā—Sana, Sanatsujāta, Sanaka, Sanandana, Sanatkumāra, Kapila and Sanātana—are together described as the foremost knowers of Yoga and knowers of the Sāṁkhya *dharma*. One of its most distinctive doctrines is the fourfold nature of the Supreme Being but it gives two series of names, one (Nara, Nārāyaṇa, Hari, Kṛṣṇa) of limited significance but the other (Vāsudeva, Saṁkarṣaṇa, Pradyumna, Aniruddha) of lasting significance in the Pāñca-rātra system, and it does not clarify their relationship. The first six chapters emphasise the inaccessibility of the supreme deity, who cannot be approached by sacrifices or austerities but only by concentrating one's thought on him in single-minded devotion, presenting this around the core story of Nārada's journey to the Śvetadvīpa. This *ekânta*, worship of the One, seems to be summed up in the first six chapters, which form a complex sequence of emboxed narratives, and the subsequent chapters give the appearance of being later expansions still on the themes propounded at the beginning and of being only loosely connected. Equally, the clustering of the term *āścarya* within the *Nārāyaṇīya* may point forward to the Kṛṣṇa story in the *Hari-vaṁśa*, since some of its manuscripts call that text the *Āścarya-parvan*.[28]

If the *Nārāyaṇīya* were indeed the conclusion of the whole *Mokṣa-dharma-parvan*, then the view of it as the climax to which the rest has been building up would be attractive and perhaps justifiable. In reality the final passage is the *Uñcha-vṛtty-upākhyāna* (12.340 353), devoted to extolling the merits of living on the grain gleaned after harvest, since a brāhman who follows this way of life is described as having become a great light which was like a second sun, illuminating all the worlds with his light (350.8–15). This represents a reversion to a more traditional practice (one alluded to, indeed, in some previous passages, such as 12.264, cf. also 3.254–247), which FITZGERALD regards as a very late exaltation of brāhman poverty,[29]

---

[27] One other text, the *Sarva-bhūtôtpatti* at 12.200, presents Pāñca-rātra ideas, with an allusion to the *vyūha* theory (12.200.10), in a broader Vaiṣṇava context. This Vaiṣṇava, and specifically Kṛṣṇa-oriented, outlook is also found in the next few *adhyāyas*, the *Dik-svastika* at 12.201, the *Antar-bhūmi-krīḍana* at 12.202, and the longer *Vārṣṇeyâdhyātma* at 12.203–10, already discussed.

[28] In the *Śānti-parvan* the term *āścarya* occurs at 12.46.1a, 74.15c, 110.8a, 147.10a, 148.4c(an-), 321.22a, 326.102a, 340.7c, 350.1c[l.v.],3d,4d,5d,7d,8a (*āścaryāṇām ivâścaryam*), 351.6b and 352.1a. I owe this point to a comment by Horst Brinkhaus.

[29] Personal communication by James Fitzgerald during the second *Dubrovnik International Conference on the Sanskrit Epics and Purāṇas*, 9–14 August 1999.

while—from its size if nothing else—the passage cannot easily be explained away as a mere afterthought or appendix. Indeed, it constitutes perhaps the strongest argument against a definite structure to the *Mokṣa-dharma*.

On the other hand, it is hard to deny that there are several indicators that the sequence of material in the *Mokṣa-dharma* has been planned to a certain extent. At the lowest, the frequency with which *adhyāya*s on Sāṁkhya and on Yoga are juxtaposed suggests this. This is probably sufficient to establish the inadequacy of a view which regards it as simply built up by successive additions, but not to rebut the assumption that there is a broad chronological progression from beginning to end. It is misguided, however, to believe that our current degree of understanding of the epic is sufficient to place all these texts in a neat developmental sequence. More realistically, we should accept that the available evidence points to a number of separate and tentative beginnings along several lines of thought and to that extent it is more plausible to see the *Mokṣa-dharma* as less than fully coherent, since it attempts to bring together so many divergent views. Further analysis of terminology, especially perhaps in the passages on Sāṁkhya and Yoga, should offer clues towards the process and, with increasing understanding of the textual history of the *Mahā-bhārata*, it should become possible to give greater definition to this process. In the meantime, it is perhaps best to adopt a cautious attitude towards the issue and to affirm that there are indications of planning and organisation at various points within the *Mokṣa-dharma-parvan* but that these are not sufficient to establish that it has an overall structure.

## BIBLIOGRAPHY


BEDEKAR 1960 = Bedekar, V.M.: 'A Study of the *Mokṣadharma* Text (*Mahābhārata* XII 262): The Cloud as a Divinity', *Annals of the Bhandarkar Oriental Research Institute* 41 (1960) 73–84.

BEDEKAR 1963 = Bedekar, V.M.: 'The Place of *Japa* in the *Mokṣadharmaparvan* (MB. XII 189–193) and the *Yoga-Sūtras*', *Annals of the Bhandarkar Oriental Research Institute* 44 (1963) 63–74.

BISSCHOP 1999 = Bisschop, Peter; Bakker, Hans: '*Mokṣadharma* 187 and 239–241 reconsidered', *Asiatische Studien / Études Asiatiques* 53.3 (1999) 459–472.

BROCKINGTON 1999 = Brockington, John: 'Epic *Sāṁkhya*: texts, teachers, terminology', *Asiatische Studien / Études Asiatiques* 53.3 (1999) 473–490.

BROCKINGTON (forthcoming) = Brockington; John: 'Yoga in the *Mahābhārata*', to appear in *Yoga: its place within the traditions and its formation today*, ed. Ian Whicher, Curzon Press, Richmond.

BUITENEN 1956 = Buitenen, J.A.B. van: 'Studies in Sāṁkhya (I)', *Journal of the American Oriental Society* 76 (1956) 153–157.

CHAPPLE 1996 = Chapple, Chris: '*Ahiṁsā* in the *Mahābhārata*: a story, a philosophical perspective, and an admonishment', *Journal of Vaiṣṇava Studies* 4.3 (1996) 109–125.

EDGERTON 1965 = Edgerton, Franklin: *The Beginnings of Indian Philosophy*. George Allen & Unwin, London 1965.

FITZGERALD 1980 = Fitzgerald, James: *The Mokṣa anthology of the Great Bhārata: an initial survey of structural issues, themes, and rhetorical strategies*. University of Chicago thesis, 1980.

FRAUWALLNER 1925 = Frauwallner, Erich: 'Untersuchungen zum *Mokṣadharma*, II,' *Wiener Zeitschrift für die Kunde des Morgenlandes* 32 (1925) 179–206.

FRAUWALLNER 1953 = Frauwallner, Erich: *Geschichte der indischen Philosophie*. 1. Band, Otto Müller Verlag, Salzburg 1953.

GOUDRIAAN 1992 = Goudriaan, Teun: 'The Stages of Awakening in the *Svacchanda-Tantra*', *Ritual and Speculation in Early Tantrism: Studies in Honor of André Padoux*. Ed. Teun Goudriaan, Albany N.Y., 1992: 139–173.

HACKER 1961 = Hacker, Paul: 'The Sānkhyization of the Emanation Doctrine shown by a critical analysis of texts', *Wiener Zeitschrift für die Kunde Süd- und Ostasiens* 5 (1961) 75–112.

HOPKINS 1901 = Hopkins, E. Washburn: *The Great Epic of India*. Scribner, New York 1901.

*Mahā-bhārata* 1966 = *The Mahābhārata for the first time critically edited*, by V.S. Sukthankar et al., Vol. 16, Bhandarkar Oriental Research Institute, Poona 1966.

OLIVELLE 1993 = Olivelle, Patrick: *The Āśrama System: The History and Hermeneutics of a Religious Institution*. Oxford University Press, New York 1993.

PROUDFOOT 1987 = Proudfoot, Ian: *Ahiṁsā and a Mahābhārata Story*. Faculty of Asian Studies, Australian National University, Canberra 1987.

SCHREINER 1997 = Peter Schreiner (ed.): *Nārāyaṇīya-Studien*. *Purāṇa Research Publications, Tübingen* 6, Harrassowitz Verlag, Wiesbaden 1997.

ZAEHNER 1963a = Zaehner, R.C.: 'Utopia and Beyond: Some Indian Views', *Eranos-Jahrbuch* 32 (1963) 281–309.

ZAEHNER 1963b = Zaehner, R.C.: 'Salvation in the Mahābhārata', *The Saviour God: comparative studies in the concept of salvation presented to Edwin Oliver James*. Ed. S.G. Brandon, Manchester University Press, Manchester 1963: 218–225.

# Jarāsaṁdha and the magic mango: causes and consequences in epic and oral tales

MARY BROCKINGTON

The second book of the *Mahā-bhārata* tells us that before Yudhiṣṭhira can realise his ambition of becoming emperor (*saṁrāṭ*, a title, incidentally, which Yudhiṣṭhira has as yet done little to justify) and perform a *rāja-sūya*, he must obtain the homage of all relevant kings. Before he can do that, eighty-six kings held captive by the mighty Jarāsaṁdha must be freed and their allegiance transferred to the Pāṇḍavas. This entails eliminating Jarāsaṁdha, the present claimant of the title, who intends to sacrifice the captive kings to Rudra.[1] But before Jarāsaṁdha can become a feared and powerful ruler, he must be born, and that is a problem. His father, Bṛhadratha, king of Magadha, is barren.

This shameful situation is remedied in dramatic fashion (2.16–17). The sage Caṇḍakauśika, learning of his plight, casts a spell on a mango and gives it to the king, but Bṛhadratha gives the fruit to his two wives to share (16.31–35); inevitably, each queen gives birth to half a boy. The thoughtful author of this episode took care to prepare his audience for this complication: a few verses earlier (16.16–17) we were told that the queens were twins, and that Bṛhadratha had vowed to treat them equally. The miserable queens allow the half-boys to be exposed, but they are found by a wandering *rākṣasī*, Jarā, who picks them up meaning to devour them but fortuitously joins the pieces, whereupon they fuse and become a lusty child, named by his delighted father—consequently—Jarāsaṁdha, 'joined by Jarā'. Caṇḍakauśika returns some time later to prophesy the boy's future greatness, and Jarāsaṁdha grows up to become a particular enemy to Kṛṣṇa and his people and (not coincidentally) a rival to Yudhiṣṭhira.

This story contains a great many details familiar from later traditional tales:[2] birth to a childless king procured by a mango given by a sage, who later returns; the birth

[1] MBh 2.13.63 and 20.8; cf. 20.27. J.A.B. van Buitenen (*Sabhā-parvan* (1975: 16–17)) comments on the ambiguity of the portrayal of Jarāsaṁdha, preferring to suppose that the kings would not actually be slaughtered.

[2] The similarity in outline of the birth of Śiśupāla, whose congenitally monstrous form must be regularised before he can grow up to be an enemy of the Pāṇḍavas, is also

*Essays in Indian Philosophy, Religion and Literature*, pp. 113–122.

of half-boys, vertically divided, who nonetheless turn out to have a special power; the threat to sacrifice the hero to a form of Śiva or Kālī, and the release of captives threatened with a similar fate (or resuscitation of those who have already been decapitated). It is not always possible to determine whether the *Mahā-bhārata* tale represents the source from which later motifs were developed, or is in fact a compendium of such already-existing motifs. In the case of the birth of half-boys, however, the line of development is relatively clear: it is fundamental to this part of the plot for Jarāsaṁdha to be born in two halves; the birth-story has been contrived, in an effort to explain the name which strains the Sanskrit construction.[3] In a tale collected by R.C. TEMPLE from a boy at Firozpur in the Punjab, and another collected by LORIMER–LORIMER in south-west Iran, a single half-boy is born when his mother eats only half the fruit intended for her, and he goes through life in his original form, only mildly handicapped in his adventures: as so frequently happens in the building of a tradition, the logic of the original motif has been lost in favour of its exploitation as a fairly crude wonder.[4]

Caṇḍakauśika's mango may very well be the earliest recorded instance of use of this particular fertility-charm, though it is important to note that it is his spell which is effective, not just the fruit itself—a refinement which rarely appears in the modern tales. Mangoes have had erotic associations in Indian literature since at least the time of Kālidāsa, who relies on this symbolism when he describes Kāma's arrows as mango flowers (*Kumāra-saṁbhava* 2.64, 3.27), and attributes the erotic behaviour of cuckoos to their having eaten fermented mangoes, in a verse[5]

---

striking (MBh 2.40). Since his three eyes and four arms caricature Śiva, and are not normalised until an encounter with Kṛṣṇa, that episode can similarly be assumed to be comparatively late.

[3] I am grateful to PETER SCHREINER for pointing out to me the awkwardness of resolving this compound. Modern scholars tend to refer the first element to *jarā*, 'old age', and although the idea that Kṛṣṇa's death from Jarā's arrow (MBh 16.5) is revenge for his part in Jarāsaṁdha's death is seductive from the structural point of view, it is much more realistic to see the *Mausala-parvan* Jarā as a personified Old Age, equivalent to Kāla, distinct from the *Sabhā-parvan rākṣasī*. Some of the other speculative analyses of the name are mentioned by JOHN BROCKINGTON (1999).

[4] STEEL–TEMPLE (1881/1894) (in the original the prince is named Adhiā, 'half'); 'Tāling', LORIMER–LORIMER (1919), is a variant of the Indic form of AT 303 reflected back towards Europe (see below), in which the mango is replaced by an apple.

[5] *puṁs-kokilaś cūta-rasâsavena mattaḥ priyāṁ cumbati rāga-hṛṣṭaḥ* (*Ṛtu-saṁhāra* 6.14); I am grateful to Dr Karttunen for supplying me with this and similar references at *Kumāra-saṁbhava* 3.32, *Raghu-vaṁśa* 9.47, and Bhāravi's *Kirātârjunīya* 5.26.

mentioned by Klaus KARTTUNEN in his paper at the Warsaw conference.[6] By the time of the tales collected in the *Kathā-sarit-sāgara*, miraculous conception can be effected by a number of means—ascetic practices, offerings, and eating various kinds of special food, including fruit obtained from the gods, without any insistence that the fruit should be mangoes,[7] but the *Abbhantara-jātaka* treats a mango's supposed power to induce conception as an old wives' tale, implying that the idea is far from new: this instance is a trick by Indra to impose upon the credulity of a queen, and the mango is not effective.[8]

This association with fertility persisted to the extent that a Provincial Mughal painter working at Farrukhabad c. 1760–70 was able to make profuse use of mangoes—flowers, fruits, and leaves, amongst other erotic symbols—to indicate that his hero was about to live happily ever after with his fairy bride;[9] the exaggeration to phallic proportions of the characteristic curved point of the mango fruits leaves little to the viewer's imagination. The marriage custom of adorning doorways with mango leaves as a fertility charm, based on the traditional belief that this tree sprouts fresh green leaves at the birth of a son, and the association with fertility of the mango stone, seen among the Gadaba and Kond tribes as resembling human testicles, are reported by S.M. GUPTA (1971: 61–62).[10]

Oral tales collected during the last two centuries make frequent and increasingly fantastic use of fruit (predominantly mangoes) as a symbol of fertility or means of conception: in one, a cut mango branch is planted beside the door of a new-born baby girl, and only when it blossoms after twelve years may Rāja Rasālu consummate their union (the flowering symbolising the bride's puberty, 'How Raja Rasālu played *chaupur̥* with King Sarkap', TEMPLE (1884–1886: I,50)); in another, a mango given by Śiva is of sufficient virtue to impregnate even a male (Rāvaṇa conceives and bears Sītā in a Kannada folk *Rāmâyaṇa* sung by an Untouchable, RAMANUJAN (1991: 35–36)); in a third, a mango borne on a tree under which a king

---

[6] Klaus Karttunen: 'Sparrows in Love'—The Display and Pairing of Birds in Sanskrit Literature' (in the present volume, pp. 261-269), p. 263, n. 9.

[7] I am indebted to Lidia Sudyka for this information.

[8] SÖHNEN (1991: 71 n.14).

[9] An illustration to the romance of Saif ul-Muluk and Badi' al-Jamal, found in an album in the Bodleian Library, Oxford, MS. Pers. b1, fol.15a. The tale is of Persian origin, and one form is incorporated into the *Arabian Nights*, but it is also widely current in a variant form in Sind (LANE (1981); KINCAID (1922); ISLAM (1982: 112, 160)).

[10] Cf. the use of the banyan tree as a central instrument of sympathetic magic in the Vedic *puṁ-savana* pregnancy ritual, with the shoot between two fruits being likened to the male genitals (PARPOLA (1992)).

has urinated causes the pregnancy of a virgin (urine substituting for semen as fertilising agent, RAMANUJAN (1987: xxi)); a fourth tale is still told in a village in Maharashtra to explain a local festival (many generations of worshippers owe their origin to a couple who ate two mangoes that appeared on Mahādev's *piṇḍ* in the temple, FELDHAUS (1995: 31)); in a fifth, a murdered woman is transformed into a mango, from which she is reborn, fully grown (BECK (1987: 166)). Again, it is not always considered obligatory that the fruit should be a mango: folk tradition from the Karbi tribes of the far north-east of India preserve several variants where the magic food which engenders Daśaratha's sons can be either a mango or an orange (SINGH–DATTA (1993: 189–190, 202, 204)). In the Bengali tale of King Dalim (King Pomegranate) it is naturally a pomegranate (with no sage or divinity as intermediary, DAMANT (1872)); in a Baluchi tale it is a pair of *bers* (DAMES (1893: 285)) and in the Telugu *Palnāḍu* epic the magically endowed fruit is not further identified (BLACKBURN (1989: 24)).

A particularly relevant example of conception resulting from eating a mango has a wandering sage as donor, with the motif usually forming part of a bargain to give up to the sage one of the children so conceived. (A similar bargain is narrated as early as the story of Rohita in the *Aitareya-brāhmaṇa*.) The sage then turns out to be malicious, desiring to achieve spiritual benefit or occult knowledge by sacrificing the boy to some form of the goddess Kālī. The boy of course thwarts this scheme and kills the would-be sacrificer, thereby usurping his position and gaining the benefit of the sacrifice for himself, and bringing back to life a number of previous victims.[11] Variants of this plot have been collected as complete tales (THOMPSON–ROBERTS (1960: type TR 1121)), but it also appears as the opening episode of the distinctive Indic sub-form of a widely-dispersed international tale known as 'The Two Brothers' (AARNE–THOMPSON (1961: type AT 303)), a tale which had its origins in western Europe, where the heroes were conceived when their mother ate a magic fish, and the elder boy started his adventures by killing a marauding dragon;[12] when it was eventually transmitted to India, for a number of reasons the tale was modified and a new beginning substituted involving the mango and the malicious sage.[13] The intriguing part of this is that the Indic version then gets reflected back

[11] Stories of such malicious sages (usually identified as *kāpālikas*) were studied early in the twentieth century by Emmanuel COSQUIN (1910/1922) and Maurice BLOOMFIELD (1924).

[12] For a detailed study see RANKE (1934).

[13] I examine the reasons for the transformation of this tale in MARY BROCKINGTON (1995a), amplified in MARY BROCKINGTON (1995b). For a detailed conspectus of the Indic variants see MARY BROCKINGTON (1999). The only representative of the European

towards Europe, appearing in ever more attenuated form the further towards the Balkans it is carried; the mango, for instance, appropriately enough becomes a pomegranate, then an apple. It is noteworthy that several elements of this tale are prefigured in the Jarāsaṁdha story, though they have not at this stage been welded together to form a variant of the later tale: conception by a mango, given by a sage, to a barren king; return of the sage at a later date, when the father offers the boy to the sage (courteous hyperbole in Bṛhadratha's case rather than a genuine offer, though the verb, *nyavedayat*, 17.10d, has overtones of ritual dedication, and the sage's return, curiously, has no narrative function other than to prophesy the boy's greatness); and the threat to sacrifice the captive kings to Rudra, but made by Jarāsaṁdha himself, the hero (or hero-analogue), not by the sage, who—from Jarāsaṁdha's point of view—remains benevolent, despite his name with its Śaiva overtones. The evidence is not conclusive, but it seems likely that Jarāsamdha's birth-story has exercised a considerable influence over the development of a substantial body of subsequent oral literature, in South Asia and beyond.

Now it is obvious that the birth of a hero, villain or saint must follow his life and death, not precede it. (I am talking, of course, in terms of narrative composition.) There is no point in telling an elaborate birth-story about a child of whom we then lose sight; a miraculous birth designates future greatness—a greatness which must at the very least be in the author's mind, if not already known to the audience. Tales of birth and youthful exploits, tales of ancestors, have been a fruitful way of extending a well-received story from the time of the *Mahā-bhārata* and *Rāmâyaṇa* down to *Star Wars*, and they all presuppose the prior existence of the central narrative. This is all the more obviously true in the case of Jarāsaṁdha, where the birth-story has been devised with the specific object of explaining his name.[14] To

form collected in India which I have been able to identify (MAYEDA–BROWN (1974: 533)) nevertheless uses a mango, rather than a fish, as the medium of conception.

[14] The text of the *Sabhā-parvan* as established by the Critical Edition makes no reference back to the birth-story, but *passages inserted into 2.22, the account of Jarāsaṁdha's death, draw attention to the care taken by Bhīma to pull his enemy's body apart, splitting it into two pieces, as if in reminiscence of the birth-story (256*, 257*, 258*, App. 8; for 258* cf. *Bhāgavata-purāṇa* 10.72.44–46). Hilda DAVIDSON refers to a common folk belief, in Germanic tradition at least, that if a giant's body is severed care must be taken to prevent the pieces being rejoined (DAVIDSON–FISHER (1979–80: I,136–137)). If it could be shown that this idea was also prevalent in early Indic tradition, it would be tempting to speculate that it was that idea, reflected in the MBh *passages and the BhP, that gave rise to the explanatory story of MBh 2.16–17. Until any such evidence can be produced, it is safer to assume that these stories of Jārasaṁdha being ripped apart by Bhīma have been developed from the fuller story in MBh 2. The naming

this end, a cast of unfamiliar characters (Bṛhadratha,[15] Jarā,[16] and Caṇḍakauśika) was apparently invented *ad hoc*.

Besides these reasons of content and composition which identify the passage as late relative even to the rest of the Jarāsaṁdha story, use of the name Bṛhadratha probably indicates a date some time subsequent to the death of his namesake, the last Mauryan ruler of Magadha—a time when the name could safely be used of a king portrayed as ineffectual and indeed impotent, as well as the father of a fearsome enemy.[17] Stylistically, with its high proportion of similes, the passage is also identifiably late.

One small detail which may nonetheless be highly significant is the use to describe Jarā of the epithet *rākṣasī kāma-rūpiṇī* (17.1b), a common formulaic expression in the *Rāmâyaṇa*, but found otherwise in the *Mahā-bhārata* only in one verse (3.268.32b) of the *Rāmôpākhyāna*, which has evidently borrowed it from the *Rāmâyaṇa*; *rakṣasāṁ kāma-rūpiṇām* also occurs once (3.11.22d).[18] It seems that the poet was familiar with the diction, if not the content, of the Rāma-story, and this testifies to the general late date of the Jarāsaṁdha birth-story. It is also crucial to bear in mind that, if the poet knew the *Rāmâyaṇa* story, so would his audience; their expectations would have a considerable influence on the way the poet told his story. Can we assume that they were familiar, not only with the earlier parts of the *Rāmâyaṇa* in books 2–6, but also with the *Bāla-kāṇḍa*'s story of Rāma's miraculous birth, which, it should be noted, does not appear in the *Rāmôpākhyāna*?

---

of Jarāsaṁdha as an incarnation of the Asura Vipracitti (MBh 1.61.4) implies that an alternative birth-story was current even at the late date of the *Ādi-parvan*, suggesting the possibility of an even later date for 2.16–17 (see also 12.326.89, where the Asura is not named) although Yaroslav VASSILKOV treats these as essentially the same story and regards the whole Jarāsaṁdha episode as modelled on the ancient Indra / Vṛtra conflict (1995: 251). The enigmatic reference in 12.5.4cd to Jarāsaṁdha's death at the hands this time of Karṇa, 'pulled apart where he had been joined by Jarā' further complicates the matter. The birth-story is alluded to outside the MBh at KIRFEL (1927: 551) ('put together by Jarā', 6B verse 112).

[15] Also known as Jarāsaṁdha's father to the author of *Hari-vaṁśa* 80.3 f, although no birth-story is narrated in the HV.

[16] Jarā simply disappears at the end of the birth-story in the Critical Edition; poets of later generations expanded her role and transformed her nature in ways quite out of keeping with the original story (2.185*, 7.156.12–15; see also DANGE 1995).

[17] For possible historical references in the Jarāsaṁdha episode as a whole, and the lateness of its language by comparison with the rest of the *Sabhā-parvan*, see JOHN BROCKINGTON (1999). For the persistence in folk narrative of Jarāsaṁdha as a demonic king of Magadha, see Yaroslav VASSILKOV (1998: 145–146).

[18] JOHN BROCKINGTON (1985: 87) [repr. 2000: 350].

There is admittedly no hard evidence to support such an assumption, but let's just indulge in a little speculation based upon it, and postulate that the story of Jarāsaṁdha's birth was composed with the story of Rāma's birth in mind. What processes would be involved in the adaptation?

At first sight the two stories seem to have more differences than similarities. Why did the author of this part of the *Mahā-bhārata* feel the need to make so many changes (if indeed he did)? The most basic reason lies in the fundamental difference in purpose of the two narratives, one composed to glorify a hero, the other to glorify the enemy of a hero—both heroes by this time being well on the way to being considered *avatāras* of Viṣṇu. Rāma and his brothers are conceived, appropriately in view of their status, in the context of a major sacrifice, in an episode reworked even later to accommodate Viṣṇu's incarnation as the four brothers. Jarāsaṁdha, enemy of Kṛṣṇa and Yudhiṣṭhira, cannot be identified in this way with Viṣṇu, or with sincere religious practice. It may be going too far to suggest that the *Mahā-bhārata* author parodies the *Rāmâyaṇa* story, but he does appear to invert it. Rāma is born to Daśaratha, a mighty king from the mythical past: Jarāsaṁdha is born to the similarly-named Bṛhadratha, the defeated last ruler of a historical dynasty. Conception is procured, not in a splendid year-long public ceremony, but in a private, domestic encounter without so much as a servant mentioned as witness; the sage is not the renowned performer of the *Rāmâyaṇa* ritual, or the resplendent figure who rises from its sacrificial flames, but an unknown. The fertility-charm is no longer the divine mysterious *pāyasa*, but a single common mango, calculated to raise a snigger in the audience, especially in the banal circumstances of it suddenly dropping by chance into Caṇḍakauśika's lap, 'without parrot bites', as we are assured with mock solemnity.[19] Both kings conscientiously share the charm between their wives, but whereas Daśaratha's careful apportionment secures the birth of his four splendid sons, Bṛhadratha's hopes are at first cruelly thwarted; he is not a free agent but is bound by a vow to his twin wives (not unlike the vow which wrecks Daśaratha's hopes of installing Rāma as his heir). Instead of four whole sons comprising varying proportions of Viṣṇu, the inept Bṛhadratha is presented with two half-sons, and the creature who restores the situation is a mere wandering, predatory *rākṣasī*, also created for the purpose, and quick-witted enough to see where her advantage lies. The boy with such an inauspicious birth grows up to be a devotee, not of Viṣṇu but of Rudra, but does not fulfil Caṇḍakauśika's grandiloquent

---

[19] *avātam aśukā-daṣṭam ekam āmra-phalam* (16.28): either 'a single, fresh (*avātam*) mango fruit without parrot bites ...' or 'though there was no wind, a single mango fruit, without parrot bites ...'; van Buitenen takes *ekam* to mean 'whole', and *avātam* as 'without holes'.

prophesy that he will 'behold Rudra, who is Mahādeva, the Destroyer of the Triple City, Hara' (17.19). All in all, the poet who composed the story of Jarāsaṁdha's birth displays scant piety, an attitude consistent with later parts of both epics, and which ultimately allowed the development in literature and folk narrative of the stock figure of the comic or gullible brāhman. Are we justified in speculating that the Jarāsaṁdha birth-story represents a conscious and deliberate *reductio ad absurdum*, a parody of the story of Rāma's conception? Reading an oral narrative on the page, as we do now, inevitably distorts it, robbing it of those nuances of tone, facial expression and timing by which a skilled performer conveys its meaning; the actual words are only a part of the total performance, and we should not underestimate or ignore the role of the performer in evoking the right mood, and playing his text for laughs when required.

If there is any relationship at all between the two stories, it must be that way round: the Jarāsaṁdha story must in that case have been influenced by the *Rāmâyaṇa*, for assuredly no pious Vaiṣṇava would have chosen to base his version of the birth of his hero Rāma on such a scurrilous, light-weight anecdote. Speculative as my reconstruction is, and incapable of verification according to objective criteria, nevertheless I am strongly inclined to believe that a comparison of these two birth-stories demonstrates their closeness and reveals much about the aims, constraints and techniques of one innovative and influential *Mahā-bhārata* poet.

## BIBLIOGRAPHY

AARNE–THOMPSON 1961 = Aarne, Antti; Thompson, Stith: *The types of the folk-tale.* Second rev. edn. *Folklore Fellows' Communications* 184. Academia Scientiarum Fennica, Helsinki 1961.

BECK 1987 = Beck, Brenda E.F., and others (eds.): *Folktales of India.* University of Chicago Press, Chicago 1987.

BLACKBURN 1989 = Blackburn, Stuart H.: 'Patterns of development for Indian oral epics.' *Oral Epics in India*, ed. by Stuart H. Blackburn and others. University of California Press, Berkeley 1989: 15–32.

BLOOMFIELD 1924 = Bloomfield, Maurice: 'On false ascetics and nuns in Hindu fiction.' *Journal of the American Oriental Society* 44 (1924) 202–42.

JOHN BROCKINGTON 1985 = Brockington, John: 'Sanskrit Epic Tradition III. Fashions in Formulae.' *Proceedings of the Fifth World Sanskrit Conference, Varanasi.* Rashtriya Sanskrit Sansthan, New Delhi 1985: 77–90. [Reprinted: *Epic Threads.* Oxford University Press, New Delhi 2000: 339–352.]

JOHN BROCKINGTON 1999 = Brockington, John: 'Jarāsaṁdha's place in the history of Magadha.' To be published in: *Stages and transitions. Proceedings of the Second Dubrovnik International Conference on the Sanskrit Epics and Purāṇas.*

MARY BROCKINGTON 1995a = Brockington, Mary: 'The Rāmāyaṇa and the folk tale "The Two Brothers".' *Indian epic values: Rāmāyaṇa and its impact. Proceedings of the 8th International Rāmāyaṇa Conference, Leuven, 1991.* Ed. by Gilbert Pollet. *Orientalia Lovaniensia Analecta* 66, Peeters, Leuven 1995: 11–20.

MARY BROCKINGTON 1995b = Brockington, Mary: 'The Indic version of "The Two Brothers" and its relationship to the *Rāmāyaṇa*.' *Fabula* 36 (1995) 259–272.

MARY BROCKINGTON 1999 = Brockington, Mary: 'The relationship of the *Rāmāyaṇa* to the Indic form of "The Two Brothers" and to the Stepmother redaction.' *The Epic: oral and written.* Ed. by Lauri Honko, John Miles Foley and Jawaharlal Handoo. Central Institute of Indian Languages, Mysore 1999: 139–150.

COSQUIN 1910/1922 = Cosquin, Emmanuel: 'Le conte de "La Chaudiére bouillante et la feinte maladresse" dans l'Inde et hors de l'Inde.' *Études folkloriques.* Champion, Paris 1922: 349–399. [Reprinted from *Revue des Traditions populaires*, 1910.]

DAMANT 1872 = Damant, G.H.: 'Bengali folklore: King Dalim and the Apsarases.' *Indian Antiquary* 1 (1872) 219.

DAMES 1893 = Dames, M. Longworth: 'Balochi tales.' *Folk-Lore* 4 (1893) 285–302.

DANGE 1995 = Dange, Sindhu S.: 'The account of Jarāsandha's birth from the Mahābhārata.' *Modern evaluation of the Mahābhārata: Prof. R.K. Sharma felicitation volume.* Ed. by Satya Pal Narang. Nag, Delhi 1995: 110–112.

DAVIDSON–FISHER 1979–80 = Saxo Grammaticus: *The history of the Danes, books 1–9.* Trans. by Peter Fisher, commentary by Hilda Ellis Davidson, 2 Vols. Brewer, Cambridge, repr. in 1 Vol. 1996.

FELDHAUS 1995 = Feldhaus, Anne: *Water and womanhood: religious meanings of rivers in Maharashtra.* Oxford University Press, New York 1995.

GUPTA 1971 = Gupta, Shakti M.: *Plant myths and traditions in India.* Brill, Leiden 1971. [2nd edn. rev., Munshiram Manoharlal, New Delhi 1991.]

ISLAM 1982 = Islam, Mazharul: *A history of folktale collections in India, Bangladesh and Pakistan.* 2nd enlarged edn. Panchali Prakasan, Calcutta 1982.

KINCAID 1922 = Kincaid, C.A.: *Tales of Old Sind.* Oxford University Press, London 1922: 37–50, 'Saif-ul-Muluk'.

KIRFEL 1927 = Kirfel, Willibald: *Das Purāṇa Pañcalakṣaṇa: Versuch einer Textgeschichte.* Brill, Leiden 1927.

LANE 1981 = Lane, Edward William (trans.): *The Thousand and one nights.* 3 Vols., East-West Publications, London 1981. [Reprint of edn. 1859; first edn. 1838]: III, 283–351.

LORIMER–LORIMER 1919 = Lorimer, D.L.R.; Lorimer, E.O.: *Persian Tales*. Macmillan, London 1919: 251–255, 'The story of Tāling, the half-boy.'

*Mahā-bhārata* = *Mahābhārata*: crit. ed. by Vishnu S. Sukthankar and others, 19 Vols., Bhandarkar Oriental Research Institute, Poona 1933–66.

MAYEDA–BROWN 1974 = Mayeda, Noriko; Brown, W. Norman: *Tawi tales: folk tales from Jammu. American Oriental Series* 57. American Oriental Society, New Haven 1974: 533–535, supplementary version 2.

PARPOLA 1992 = Parpola, Asko: 'The "fig-deity seal" from Mohenjo-daro: its iconography and inscription.' *South Asian Archaeology* 1989. Ed. by C. Jarrige. *Monographs in World Archaeology* 14, Madison, Wisc. 1992: 227–236.

RAMANUJAN 1987 = Ramanujan, A.K.: 'Foreword' to BECK (1987).

RAMANUJAN 1991 = Ramanujan, A.K.: 'Three hundred *Rāmāyaṇas*: five examples and three thoughts on translation.' *Many Rāmāyaṇas: the diversity of a narrative tradition in South Asia*. Ed. by Paula Richman. University of California Press, Berkeley 1991: 22–49.

*Sabhā-parvan* 1975 = *The Mahābhārata*, II, 'The Book of the Assembly Hall', trans. by J.A.B. van Buitenen. University of Chicago Press, Chicago 1975.

RANKE 1934 = Ranke, Kurt: *Die zwei Brüder*. *FF Communications* 114, Academia Scientiarum Fennica, Helsinki 1934.

SINGH–DATTA 1993 = Singh, K.S.; Datta, Birendranath (eds.): *Rama-katha in tribal and folk traditions of India: proceedings of a seminar*. Anthropological Survey of India, Calcutta 1993.

SÖHNEN 1991 = Söhnen, Renate: 'Indra and women.' *Bulletin of the School of Oriental and African Studies, London* 54 (1991) 68–74.

STEEL–TEMPLE 1881/1894 = Steel, Flora Annie; Temple, Richard Carnac: 'Folklore in the Panjab: the mother of seven sons', *Indian Antiquary* 10 (1881) 151–152. [Rev. repr. retitled more appropriately 'Prince Half-a-son', STEEL–TEMPLE (1894: 275–283).]

STEEL–TEMPLE 1894 = Steel, Flora Annie; Temple, Richard Carnac: *Tales of the Punjab told by the people*. Macmillan, London 1894. [Reissued with different pagination by Bodley Head, London 1973.]

TEMPLE 1884–1886 = Temple, Richard Carnac: *The legends of Panjāb*. 3 Vols. Trübner, London 1884–1886.

THOMPSON–ROBERTS 1960 = Thompson, Stith; Roberts, Warren E.: *Types of Indic oral tales: India, Pakistan and Ceylon. Folklore Fellows' Communications* 180. Academia Scientiarum Fennica, Helsinki 1960.

VASSILKOV 1995 = Vassilkov, Yaroslav: 'The Mahābhārata's typological definition reconsidered.' *Indo-Iranian Journal* 38 (1995) 249–256.

VASSILKOV 1998 = Vassilkov, Yaroslav: 'An Indo-Iranian myth in Eastern India: Gayōmart and the mythology of Gayā.' *Orientalia Suecana* 47 (1998) 131–149.

# Two notes on the word *upaniṣad* in the *Mahā-bhārata*

MINORU HARA

Among his many-sided contributions to Indological studies, Professor STANISŁAW SCHAYER was noted for his illuminating study on the word *upaniṣad*. After reviewing critically the hitherto accepted translations of the word as 'sitting nearby' (Max Müller), 'Verehrung,' 'Anbetung' (H. Oldenberg), he detected with penetrating insight the meaning behind the word and advocated a unique interpretation: 'die im Akte des *upāsana* zu erfassende Äquivalenz zwischen zwei magischen Substanzen.'[1]

As is always the case with an unprecedented original exposition, his theory stimulated scholars to further detailed studies. His interpretation was basically supported by such eminent *Vedisants* as H. OERTEL[2] ('mystische Gleichsetzung [Äquivalenz] einer sinnlich unfassbaren Wesenheit mit einer sinnlich fassbaren Wortgruppe, um so einen sinnlichen Anhalt als Stützpunkt für die Versenkung [Kontemplation] zu gewinnen') and L. RENOU[3] ('connexion en védique'). It was only in 1986, sixty years after the publication of his article, that the word was taken up again by HARRY FALK (1986: 80–97), who discussed in detail the meaning of the word in a historical perspective.[4]

It is then out of great respect to the pioneer contribution of the Polish scholar that here the present writer discusses two problems relevant to the word *upaniṣad* and dedicates the discussion to his *Commemoration Volume*.

**1. *Upaniṣad*.** Those who would work on the word *upaniṣad* now must refer to the contribution of H. FALK (1986), who carefully examined the Vedic contexts in which the word occurs. According to his conclusion, the word experienced a semantic development ('Bedeutungswandel') through the Vedic literature, and thus

---

[1] SCHAYER (1927: 67) [= (1988: 358)].

[2] OERTEL (1994: 842).

[3] RENOU (1945: 55–60), RENOU (1946: 132) and RENOU (1956: 47).

[4] Other studies which have come to my attention are as follows: SCHMITHAUSEN (1971: 139): 'Grundlage od. Vorstufe: *upaniṣad-bhūtatva*,' HARTMANN (1987: 238): 'Grundlage des *Nirvāṇa*: *nirvāṇopaniṣattva*.'

*Essays in Indian Philosophy, Religion and Literature*, pp. 123–135.

we must choose different words for its translation in the respective contexts. That is to say, its meaning varies from one context to another and fluctuates from its basic meaning of 'bewirkende Macht' to 'hierarchische Beziehung' and finally to 'Voraussetzung'. Occasionally, it means the deity and text which are characterised by the 'bewirkende Macht'.

However, a similar semantic ambivalence seems to be found also in epic and classical Sanskrit literature. In the pages which follow, we shall examine the passages in which the word occurs, and discuss its relevant problems.

**1.1.** In the well-known dialogue between the virtuous hunter and a Brahmin Kauśika, in which the former explains to the latter the *śiṣṭâcāra*, we read as follows:

> *vedasyôpaniṣat satyaṁ satyasyôpaniṣad damaḥ /*
> *damasyôpaniṣat tyāgaḥ śiṣṭâcāreṣu nityadā //* (MBh.3.198.62)

J.B. VAN BUITENEN (1975) took the word in the sense of 'secret' and translated the above passage as follows,

> 'The secret of the veda is truthfulness, the secret of truthfulness is self-control, the secret of self-control is at all times relinquishment, in the deportment of the strict.'

**1.1.1.** No matter what English word one may assign to the word *upaniṣad*, the crucial point is how to relate a pair of concepts (*veda* and *satya*, etc.) which are linked by our word. Also, one wonders whether each preceding word with the genitive ending (*vedasya*, etc.) stands in a subordinate position to the following one in the nominative case (*satyam*, etc.). That is to say, in the words of H. OERTEL, which of the two is the 'sinnlich fassbar' through which one can reach the 'sinnlich unfassbar'? If the preceding one is the 'fassbar' (*veda*), then it must be subordinate to the following, which is 'unfassbar' (*satya*). In such a case, *veda* is considered as a more concrete concept than *satya*, which in its turn is less concrete, that is, more abstract. In the words of FALK, here *satya* is the 'bewirkende Macht' behind *veda*. Then a process of abstraction here starts from *veda* to *tyāga* through *satya* and *dama*.

**1.1.2.** However, there remains another possibility—to take all these four in co-ordination, instead of subordination ('Unterordnung' to 'Oberbegriff'). In order to ascertain this, it is necessary to examine the passages in the vicinity, where these concepts are enumerated in a similar way. Two passages come to our attention, which have the same refrain in *pāda* d as our verse.

> *yajño dānaṁ tapo vedāḥ satyaṁ ca dvija-sattama /*
> *pañcâitāni pavitrāṇi* ***śiṣṭâcāreṣu nityadā*** *//* (MBh.3.198.57)
>
> *guru-śuśrūṣaṇaṁ satyam akrodho dānam eva ca /*
> *etac catuṣṭayaṁ brahmañ* ***śiṣṭâcāreṣu nityadā*** *//* (MBh.3.198.60)

For clarity's sake, let us list them in a comparative table.

(62) *veda* ···················· *satya* ······· *dama*········ *tyāga* = (4)
(57) *yajña* ···················· *dāna* ······· *tapas* ········· *veda* ··· *satya* = (5 *pavitra*)
(60) *guru-śuśrūṣaṇa* ····· *satya* ······ *akrodha* ···· *dāna* = (4)

The pentad in 57, which contains *tyāga* (= *dāna*), *veda* and *satya*, constitutes *pavitra* (purification), and we discern nothing hierarchic among these five. They are enumerated in an equal position, all being subordinate to a higher concept of *pavitra*. Also the quartet (*catuṣṭaya*) in 60 is of the nature of a simple enumeration with no hint among its members of subordination ('Unterordnung') to a higher concept ('Oberbegriff'). Furnished with the same refrain *śiṣṭâcāreṣu nityadā*, what we find there is simply the co-ordination of these ethico-religious concepts. In view of the presence of a similar sort of enumeration of ethical concepts on an equal footing, we are inclined to take the word *upaniṣad* in the sense of 'equal to,' or 'equivalent with.' This is the meaning that SCHAYER advocated in 1927 ('Gleichsetzung').

**1.2.** Our passage (MBh.3.198.62) is repeated with slight variations twice later in the *Śānti-parvan*. We shall examine them in due order.

The first instance is met with in Prajāpati's discourse to the *Sādhya*s, in which the word *tyāga* in *pāda* c is replaced by *mokṣa*. Here the god, assuming the form of a Haṁsa bird, extols the practice of patience (*kṣamā*) and non-anger (*akrodha*), even when one is exposed to another's assaults, verbal as well as physical.

*vedasyôpaniṣat satyaṁ satyasyôpaniṣad damaḥ /*
*damasyôpaniṣan mokṣa etat sarvânuśāsanam //* (MBh.12.288.13)

**1.2.1.** Putting aside for a moment the translation of the passage, which has the same construction except in *pāda* d (*etat sarvânuśāsanam*), let us once again investigate other passages in the contextual vicinity, which enumerate similar ethico-religious concepts.

Here, in the opening verse of the chapter, Yudhiṣṭhira enumerates four virtues that wise men praise:

*satyaṁ kṣamāṁ damaṁ prajñāṁ praśaṁsanti pitāmaha /*
*vidvāṁso manujā-loke katham etan mataṁ tava //* (MBh.12.288.1)

'The wise men in this world praise truth, patience, self-control and intelligence. But, Grand-father, what do you think?'

Another enumeration is met in the opening verse of the Haṁsa:

*idaṁ kāryam amṛtâśāḥ śṛṇomi /*
*tapo damaḥ satyam ātmâbhiguptiḥ //* (MBh.12.288.7ab)

'Oh, you who have drunk Amṛta, I have heard that one should have recourse to asceticism, self-restraint, truth and self-denial.'

Then later, just one verse before ours, we read,

*śreṣṭhaṁ hy etat kṣamām apy āhur āryāḥ /*
*satyaṁ tathâivârjavam ānṛśaṁsyam //* (MBh.12.288.12)

'The noble-minded say that patience is the highest, so is also truth, sincerity and compassion.'

For the clarity's sake, let us again present a comparative table.

(1) ***satya*** ··········· *kṣamā* ············· ***dama*** ·············· *prajñā*
(7) *tapas* ··········· ***dama*** ·············· ***satya*** ··············· *ātmābhigupti*
(12) *kṣamā* ·········· ***satya*** ··············· *ārjava* ············· *ānṛśaṁsya*
(13) *veda* ············ ***satya*** ··············· ***dama*** ··············· *mokṣa*

Except the last verse, which is ours, the remaining three simply enumerate the ethical virtues, of which the wise (*vidvat*) or noble (*ārya*) men speak highly. We notice here in these three passages nothing hierarchical among them, as we have seen above (§ 1.1.2).

**1.2.2.** As regards the last verse, however, the situation is somewhat different from the three above. Here, in MBh.12.188.13, one gets an impression that the last word *mokṣa*, which is the highest religious ideal, distinguishes itself from the remaining three, which are ethical by nature. That is to say, here *mokṣa* seems to stand above the preceding three ethical concepts, which help one to reach the religious goal. *Mokṣa* is the 'Oberbegriff' and the remaining concepts are of the nature of 'Unterordnung'.

**1.3.** The second instance is twice as long, containing further chains, linked by the word *upaniṣad*. Its context deals with the absence of desire (*kāma*), which is characterised as *svarga* in MBh.12.243.9, or *śānti(-lakṣaṇa)* in MBh.12.243.12:

*vedasyôpaniṣat satyaṁ satyasyôpaniṣad damaḥ /*
*damasyôpaniṣad dānaṁ dānasyôpaniṣad tapaḥ //* (MBh.12.243.10)
*tapasôpaniṣat tyāgas tyāgasyôpaniṣat sukham /*
*sukhasyôpaniṣat svargaḥ svargasyôpaniṣac chamaḥ //* (MBh.12.243.11)

Here the causal chain is as follows:

*veda* ···· *satya* ···· *dama* ···· *dāna* ···· *tapas* ···· *tyāga* ···· *sukha* ···· *svarga* ···· *śama*

The words which we have met before, such as *veda*, *satya*, *dama*, *dāna* and *tyāga*, also appear here, but, as K.M. GANGULI remarks,[5] here the epic singer seems to put a special emphasis upon the last word *śama*. Here all the preceding ones, with the genitive case ending, stand in a subordinate position to the following one, the last being the ultimate goal, that is *śama*. Here we have another example of subordination.

**1.4.** Having examined these three epic passages which contain the word *upaniṣad*, let us summarise what we have discussed above and advocate an hypothesis.

First of all, we should not use any single English word for the translation of *upaniṣad*. There is a semantic ambivalence in its usage.

In the first example, there are enumerated ethical concepts of equal value with no hint of hierarchy among them. The word is used in the sense of 'Gleichsetzung'. Under such circumstances we are inclined to say that, in comparison with similar passages in the contextual vicinity, there was no absolute necessity for the epic singers to put the phrase here. One may dispense with this phrase (*vedasyôpaniṣat satyam*) in the logical sequence of the discourse.

In the last two examples, on the other hand, the religious concepts (*mokṣa* and *śama*), which come last in the causal chain linked by the word *upaniṣad*, seem to be superior to all the preceding ethical concepts. That is to say, here each preceding one with the genitive case ending (*vedasya* … , etc.) stands in a subordinate position to each following one (*satyam* … , etc.).

Reviewing these three passages, we may assume that the phrase *vedasyôpaniṣat satyam* … may have been by itself an independent authoritative set phrase, and is quoted here and there in case of need with some modifications and enlargements.

**1.5.** However, we are confronted with a further complication. In Aśvaghoṣa's *Saundarananda* 13.22, the same word *mokṣa* which comes last in the nominative case in MBh.12.288.13, as we have just seen above, appears first in the genitive case. That is to say, not only the order of appearance, but also the syntactical construction is reversed. The context demands that we take *mokṣa* as superior to the following. At any rate, let us see the passage of the *Saundarananda* 13.22–26:

/22/ *mokṣasyôpaniṣat saumya vairāgyam iti gṛhyatām /*
*vairāgyasyâpi saṁvedaḥ saṁvido jñāna-darśanam //*

/23/ *jñānasyôpaniṣac câiva samādhir upadhāryatām /*
*samādher apy upaniṣat saukhaṁ śarīra-mānasam //*

---

[5] GANGULI (1981: X,211, n. 6): 'The sense of the verse is that each of the things mentioned is useless without that which comes next; and as tranquillity (*śama*) is the ultimate end, the *Veda*s and truth, etc., are valuable only because they lead to tranquillity.'

/24/ *praśrabdhiḥ kāya-manasaḥ sukhasyôpaniṣat parā /*
*praśrabdher apy upaniṣat prītir apy avagamyatām //*
/25/ *tathā prīter upaniṣat prāmodaṁ paramaṁ matam /*
*prāmodyasyâpy ahṛl-lekhaḥ kukṛteṣv akṛteṣu vā //*
/26/ *ahṛl-lekhasya manasaḥ śīlaṁ tûpaniṣac chuci /*
*ataḥ śīlaṁ nayaty agryam iti śīlaṁ viśodhaya //*

'My friend, comprehend that salvation is based on freedom from passion ... Therefore purify your discipline (*śīla*), realizing that *śīla* goes in front as the foremost.' (JOHNSTON).

The causal chain linked by the word *upaniṣad* here is as follows,

*mokṣa* ···· *vairāgya* ···· *samvid* ···· *jñāna* ···· *samādhi* ···· *sukha* ····
···· *praśrabdhi* ··· *prīti* ···· *prāmodya* ···· *ahṛl-lekha* ···· *śīla*

Here the 'fassbar', in the words of OERTEL, starts from (the cultivation of) *śīla*, the moral concept in the nominative, and the abstraction gradually advances from 'fassbar' to 'unfassbar' connected by *upaniṣad*, and finally reaches the highest religious ideal *mokṣa*, that stands here in the genitive case. In the formula: 'A's *upaniṣad* is B,' A (*mokṣa*) naturally stands higher than B (*vairāgya*), which is a prerequisite condition to A (*mokṣa*), so to speak. Looking at all the items backwards, the last (*śīla*) is the foundation of *ahṛl-lekha*,[6] which, through the causal chain, finally leads one to *mokṣa*. If the item which comes first, that is *mokṣa*, is the ultimate ideal, and if others, starting from *śīla*, are the subordinate conditions to it, the semantic content of the word *upaniṣad* here must be 'Voraussetzung' in FALK's term (1986: 95 ff.).

This phrase is to be compared with a passage in the *Saṁhitôpaniṣad-brāhmaṇa* as quoted by FALK (1986: 96, n. 41):

*athâitā vedasyâṣṭāv upaniṣado bhavanti: vittiś côpastavaś ca damaś ca śraddhā ca saṁpraśnaś cânākāśi-karaṇaṁ ca yogaś câcārya-śuśrūṣā cêti.*

---

[6] A similar dependent relation starting from *śīla* is found in MBh.12.124 where Prahlāda's decline by trick of Indra is related:

*śīla* ···· *dharma* ···· *satya* ···· *vṛtti* ···· *bala* ···· *śrī*

Indra was successful in taking away *śīla* from Prahlāda. When *śīla* left Prahlāda for Indra, *dharma* followed *śīla*, and then *satya*, *vṛtti*, *bala*, and finally *śrī* abandoned him. Here, *śīla* is the foundation of all the virtuous activities, such as *dharma*, *satya* and *vṛtti*, as well as the items which promise secular advancement: *bala* and *śrī*.

'Eight are the premises of (or, pre-requisites for) the *Veda*: intelligence, worship, self-control, faith, inquisitiveness, non-publicity, *yoga* and obedience to one's teacher.'

Vedic study is composed of these eight items, that is to say, it cannot be accomplished without these eight. They are indispensable factors for the mastering of the *Veda*. Similar usage of 'Voraussetzung' is found in Buddhist texts, as FALK (1986) quoted in the same place (five *upaniṣads* of *dharma* in AN. 4. 351.12–22).[7]

**2. *Niṣad* and *upaniṣad*.** The word *upaniṣad* occurs in the *Śānti-parvan* once in co-ordination with *niṣad*. This co-ordination of *niṣad* and *upaniṣad*, however, appears in the *R̥g-veda Khila* 1.3.7a (*evā niṣác côpaniṣác ca*), and there they are used as appellations of the twin-deities Aśvin.[8] They appear also in a reversed order (*upaniṣan niṣat*) as the names of female seers in the *Br̥had-devatā* 2.82[9] and its related texts.[10] The epic context, however, demands that we take the words in the sense of the texts, or text groups.[11]

Now, we ask ourselves, what sort of text is meant by the word *niṣad*? FALK conjectured it to be a text of a similar nature to *upaniṣad*.[12] But let us see first the epic passage itself and how its commentary interprets it.

In a series of praises for Kr̥ṣṇa, recited by Bhīṣma on his death bed, we read:

*yaṁ vākeṣv anuvākeṣu niṣatsûpaniṣatsu ca /*
*gr̥ṇanti satya-karmāṇaṁ satyaṁ satyeṣu sāmasu //* (MBh.12.47.16)

'[You], whom people invoke in the *vāka*s, the *anuvāka*s, the *niṣad*s and *upaniṣad*s as one whose work is ever true, and in the *sāman*s as the truthful among the truthful.'

[7] FALK (1986: 96). Cf. POUSSIN (1923: 106, n. 3) and JOHNSTON (1928: 74) (AN.5.311).

[8] FALK (1986: 92), SCHEFTELOWITZ (1906: 57, 28).

[9] MACDONELL (1904: V,18):

*ghoṣā godhā viśva-vārā apālôpaniṣan niṣat /*
*brahma-jāyā juhūr nāma agasyatya svasāditiḥ //*

Cf. also, MACDONELL (1904: VI,55). In TOKUNAGA's edition (1997), it is 2.79.

[10] Cf. TOKUNAGA (1997: 31, n. *ad loc.*).

[11] Cf. FALK (1986: 92–93).

[12] FALK (1986: 93): 'mehr oder minder das selbe.'

The commentator explains,

> *niṣadaḥ, yaiḥ saṁsāro nindyate / yathā andhaṁ tamaḥ praviśanti ity-ādi / upaniṣadaḥ ātma-prakāśaka-vākyāni gītâdīni … teṣu caturbhiḥ vākânuvāka-niṣad-upaniṣadbhiḥ catur-ātmānaṁ viṣṇu-hari-nara-nārāyaṇâtmānaṁ arcayanti /*
>
> '*Niṣad*s are those [texts], by which the transmigration is condemned, such as 'they enter into blind darkness' (*Īśôpaniṣad* 9). *Upaniṣad*s are such [texts] as the *Gītā*, the sentences of which illuminate *ātman* … In these [texts]—that is, by these four [texts], *vāka*, *anuvāka*, *niṣad* and *upaniṣad*—people worship [you] in the form of four; Viṣṇu, Hari, Nara and Nārāyaṇa.'

We are somewhat puzzled by this explanation, because here the *Īśôpaniṣad* is called *niṣad*, while the *upaniṣad*s are such texts as the *Gītā* and others. But we need not be bothered by these explanations given by the commentator, and it suffices to take *niṣad* as a sort of back-formation from *upaniṣad*. As a result, we are inclined to think that no particular texts, or text group are meant here.

This formation of *niṣad* from *upaniṣad* is apparently under the influence of a similar phraseology, recurring in the Epic literature.

**2.1.** First, an example of this kind of repetition is met with in the names of a deity, such as *indra* : *upêndra*, of a demon *sunda* : *upa-sunda* and of concepts like *aṅga* : *upâṅga*, *vrata* : *upa-vrata*.[13] Here in these examples the prefix *upa-* means 'vice-' or 'acting-' as an appellation of deputy. Thus, *upendra* means Viṣṇu, and *upasunda* means a younger brother of the demon Sunda.

**2.2.** Next, we meet a similar repetition in the names of scriptures and texts, and occasionally metres. Thus, we have *veda*: *upa-veda*, *ākhyāna*: *upâkhyāna*, *purāṇa*: *upa-purāṇa*, and *śloka*: *upa-śloka*.[14] In these examples, again, the prefix *upa-* involves the idea of subordination, or inferiority. Thus, *upapurāṇa*, for example, means a group of the secondary *Purāṇa*s in contrast to the principal ones, that is, *Mahā-purāṇa*s.

**2.3.** However, these principles would not be applied in the case of the back-formation of *niṣad* from *upa-niṣad*, the former being the main and the latter the secondary. Furthermore, in the following examples, we scarcely note the hierarchical distinction between the two:

---

[13] *Baudhāyana-dharma-sūtra* 2.10.18.2–3. Cf. SCHMIDT (1968: 637, n. 1).

[14] Cf. KÖLVER (1984: 32). Cf. also VAUDEVILLE (1963: 333).

(a) *diś* : *upa-diś*:
- *diśaś côpadiśaś câiva* (MBh.2.35.25)
- *diśaś côpadiśas tathā* (MBh.3.168.5, R.1.75.22)

(b) *vana* : *upa-vana*:
- *vanāni upavanāni ca* (MBh.1.156.4, 3.145.10, 3.150.18, 14.63.6, HV. 93.68, R.3.33.22, 5.2.8, 6.30.1, 6.30.12, 6.50.14, 7.14.3)
- *vaneṣûpavaneṣu ca* (MBh.3.54.37, 5.116.18, R.6.16.11, 7.42.13).

This rhythmic repetition with the prefix *upa-* is used by the epic singers, not with the intention of allotting particular meanings to each of the words, but simply aiming at multiplying and intensifying the meaning expressed by the first word. Thus, both *diś* and *upadiś* mean simply 'various directions,' whereas *vana* and *upavana* 'various sorts of woods,' or 'woods here and there.'[15]

Under these circumstances, we should take the repetition *niṣad* ... *upaniṣad* in the sense of various sorts of philosophical treatises, not necessarily such particular texts as the *Īśôpaniṣad* or the *Gītā*.

**2.4.** Now, we may apply the same principle to *vāka* and *anu-vāka*, which appear in MBh.12.47.16 quoted above, for we have the example of *diś* and *anu-diś*, which simply mean 'various directions,' as is the case with *diś* and *upa-diś* above.

*diś* : *anu-diś*:
- *tato diśaś cânudiśaś ca pārtha* (MBh.6.55.113)
- *tato diśaś cânudiśo vivṛtya* (MBh.4.61.9).[16]

**2.5.** Further we can enumerate the same construction of *diś* with other prefixes such as *pra-*, *vi-*, and *prati-*:

(a) *diś* : *pra-diś*:
- *diśaś ca pradiśaś câiva* (MBh.8.24.69, 9.14.17)
- *diśaś ca pradiśas tathā* (MBh.9.28.12, R.3.21.25, 6.91.15)
- *diśaḥ khaṁ pradiśaś câiva* (MBh.6.89.6, 7.172.22)
- *diśaḥ pradiśa eva ca* (MBh.7.171.20)
- *diśaś ca pradiśas sarvāḥ* (R.6.94.24)
- *tato diśaś ca pradiśaś ca sarvāḥ* (MBh.8.65.24)
- *diśaḥ sa-pradiśaḥ pārtha* (MBh.7.102.62)
- *prakāśayantaṁ pradiśo diśaś ca* (MBh.5.69.1)[17]

---

[15] BROCKINGTON (1998: 132): 'forests and thickets.'

[16] STEDE (1924–1925: 91).

[17] Cf. also, MBh.3.185.41, 4.52.5, 6.112.67, 7.7.34, 7.40.21, 9.11.62, 13.145.39.

(b) *diś* : *vi-diś*:

– *diśaś ca vidiśaś câiva* (MBh.13.151.27)

– *diśaś ca vidiśas tathā* (MBh.7.81.31, R.6.66.27)

(c) *diś* : *prati-diś*:

– *diśaḥ pratidiśo vâpi* (MBh.6.53.5).

All these instances mean 'various directions,' simply multiplying the meaning of 'direction' (*diś*), as indicated by the word without prefixes.

**2.6.** We may be tempted to include in the same category such repetitive phrases as *naya* : *vi-naya* (MBh.12.223.8: *nayena vinayena ca*[18]), or *nāśa* : *vi-nāśa* (MBh.12.220.73: *nāśaṁ vināśam aiśvaryaṁ*). Though it is possible to take *vinaya* independently of *naya* in the sense of 'discipline,' we may also take it simply as 'various sorts of *naya* (the strategies).'

However, the most striking example of this sort may be that of *jñāna* and *vi-jñāna* which recurs throughout the *Mahā-bhārata*.[19] In Umā's question to Maheśvara, for example, we read:

*ime manuṣyā dṛśyante ūhâpoha-viśāradāḥ* /
*jñāna-vijñāna-saṁpannāḥ prajñāvanto 'rtha-kovidāḥ* //
*duṣprajñāś câpare deva jñāna-vijñāna-varjitāḥ* / (MBh.13.133.43)

'Some men are seen well-versed in *ūha* and *apoha*, endowed with *jñāna* and *vijñāna*. They are wise and experienced. Others are foolish and destitute of *jñāna* and *vijñāna*.'

One can take *vijñāna* in the sense of 'practical knowledge' as distinct from 'theoretical knowledge,'[20] but here it may simply mean 'various sorts of

---

[18] Cf. *Viṣṇu-purāṇa* 3.18.53, *Pratijñā-yaugandharāyaṇa* 4.6.

[19] Cf. *jñāna-vijñāna-kovida* (MBh.12.116.14, 12.118.7, 12.162.17):

*-tṛptâtmā* (MBh.6.28.8)
*-darśinaḥ* (MBh.13.132.45)
*-nāśanam* (MBh.6.25.41)
*-niṣṭhānām* (MBh.13.16.64)
*-pāraga* (MBh.13.104.17, 14.16.19, 14.20.2)
*-vat* (MBh.3.199.26, 13.131.15)
*-varjitāḥ* (MBh.13.133.43)
*-śobhitāḥ* (MBh.13.126.38)
*-saṁpanna* (MBh.12.84.39, 12.290.17, 13.131.44, 13.133.43, 13.134.27).

knowledge.' Also, here *apoha* (= *apa-ūha*) is used to intensify *ūha*[21], and we need not differentiate the two words in the technical sense[22] as they are normally used in philosophical treatises.[23]

**2.7.** All these examples testify to the fact that rhythmic repetitions—particularly employed by the epic singers—with prefixes, are not intended to assign a particular meaning to each and every repeated word, but simply have a distributive effect. The repetition of *niṣad* and *upa-niṣad* in MBh.12.47.16 also belongs to the same category.

---

[20] EDGERTON (1933) might be right in his interpretation of the following three *Gītā* passages which separate these two words (7.2: *jñānaṁ sa-vijñānam*, 9.1: *jñānaṁ vijñāna-sahitam*, 18.42: *jñānaṁ vijñānam*).

[21] For the phrase *ūhâpoha-viśārada*, cf. also MBh.12.118.17, 13.134. 27.

[22] For the meaning of *ūha*, cf. OBERHAMMER–PRETS–PRANDSTETTER (1996: 55–57) and HALBFASS (1991: 184, n. 15).

[23] We are also tempted to take the phrase *dhātā* : *vi-dhātā* (MBh.7.69.46, 9.44.4, 13.15.31, 13.145.39) in the same way, despite the ordinary translation of 'creator and distributor.'

## BIBLIOGRAPHY


AN = *Aṅguttara-nikāya*. 5 Vols., ed. R. Morris & E. Hardy, PTS, London 1985–1990.

BDhS = *Baudhāyana-dharma-sūtra*. Herausgegeben von E. Hultzsch, Leipzig 1922.

BROCKINGTON 1998 = Brockington, John: 'Formulaic Expression in the *Rāmāyaṇa*: Evidence for Oral Composition?', *The Epic, oral and written*. Ed. by L. Honko, J. Handoo and J.M. Foley, Mysore 1998: 128–139.

BUITENEN 1975 = Buitenen, J.B. van: *The Mahābhārata*. Translated and edited by ..., II: *The Book of the Assembly Hall*, III: *The Book of the Forest*, The University of Chicago Press, Chicago–London 1975.

EDGERTON 1933 = Edgerton, F.: 'Jñāna and vijñāna,' *Festschrift Moritz Winternitz*, Leipzig 1933: 217–220.

FALK 1986 = Falk, Harry: 'Vedisch upaniṣád,' *Zeitschrift der Deutschen Morgenländischen Gesellschaft* 136 (1986) 80–97.

GANGULI 1981 = Ganguli, K.M. (transl.): *The Mahabharata*, New Delhi 1981.

HALBFASS 1991 = Halbfass, Wilhelm: *Tradition and Reflection*. Albany 1991.

HARTMANN 1987 = Hartmann, Jens-Uwe: *Das Varṇārhavarṇastotra des Mātṛceṭa*. Göttingen 1987.

HV = *The Hari-vaṁśa, being the Khila or Supplement to the Mahābhārata*. Critically ed. by P.L. Vaidya, Bhandarkar Oriental Research Institute, Poona 1969–71.

JOHNSTON 1928 = Johnston, E.H. (ed.): *The Saundarananda of Aśvaghoṣa*, critically ed. with notes by .... Panjab University Oriental Publications, Oxford University Press, London 1928. [Reprinted: Kyoto 1971].

KÖLVER 1984 = Kölver, Bernard: 'Überlagerungen im *Rāmāyaṇa*: Die Legende von der Erfindung des *śloka*,' *Wiener Zeitschrift für die Kunde Südasiens* 29 (1984) 27–41.

MACDONELL 1904 = Macdonell, Arthur A.: *The Bṛhad-devatā*, attributed to Śaunaka. *Harvard Oriental Series* 5–6, Cambridge, Massachusetts 1904.

MBh = *The Mahā-bhārata*. Critically ed. by V.S. Sukthankar et al. Bhandarkar Oriental Research Institute, Poona 1933–66.

OBERHAMMER–PRETS–PRANDSTETTER 1996 = Oberhammer, Gerhard; Prets, Ernst; Prandstetter, Joachim: *Terminologie der frühen philosophischen Scholastik in Indien*. Band 2, Herausgegeben von Gerhard Oberhammer. Österreichische Akademie der Wissenschaften, Philosophisch-Historische Klasse, Denkschriften, 248. *Beiträge zur Kultur- und Geistesgeschichte* 17. Wien 1996.

OERTEL 1994 = Oertel, H.: *Kleine Schriften*. Herausgegeben von H. Hettrich und Th. Oberlies, Stuttgart 1994.

POUSSIN 1923 = Poussin, Louis de la Vallée: *L'Abhidharmakośa de Vasubandhu*. Traduction et annotations, Tome 1, Paul Geuthner, Paris–Louvain 1923. [Reprinted: Institute belge des hautes études chinoises, Bruxelles 1971; Bruxelles 1980].

PY = *Pratijñā-yaugandharāyaṇa*. In: *Bhāsa-nāṭaka-cakram. Plays ascribed to Bhāsa*. Critically edited by C.R. Devadhar. Poona Oriental Series 54, Poona 1962.

R = *The Vālmīki Rāmāyaṇa*, Critically Edited by G.H. Bhatt et al., Oriental Institute, Baroda 1960–1975.

RENOU 1945 = Renou, Louis: 'Connexion en Védique et Cause en Bouddhique,' *Kunhan Raja Volume*, Madras 1945: 55–60.

RENOU 1946 = Renou, Louis: *Litterature sanskrite*. Paris 1946.

RENOU 1956 = Renou, Louis: *Histoire de la langue sanskrite*. Paris 1956.

SCHAYER 1927 = Schayer, Stanisław: 'Über die Bedeutung des Wortes Upanisad,' *Rocznik Orientalistyczny* III (1927) 57–67. [Reprinted in: Stanisław Schayer: *O filozofowaniu Hindusów. Artykuły wybrane*. Ed. by Marek Mejor. Polska Akademia Nauk, Komitet Nauk Orientalistycznych, PWN, Warszawa 1988: 348–358].

SCHEFTELOWITZ 1906 = Scheftelowitz, I.: *Die Apokryphen des Ṛgveda*. Breslau 1906.

SCHMIDT 1968 = Schmidt, Hanns-Peter: 'The Origin of *ahiṁsā*,' *Mélanges d'Indianisme, à la mémoire de L. Renou*, Paris 1968: 625–655.

SCHMITHAUSEN 1971 = Schmithausen, Lambert: 'Philologische Bemerkungen zum Ratnagotravibhāga,' *Wiener Zeitschrift für die Kunde Südasiens* 15 (1971) 123–177.

STEDE 1924–1925 = Stede, W.: 'Reduplikationskomposita im Pali,' *Zeitschrift für Buddhismus* 6 (1924–1925) 89–94.

TOKUNAGA 1997 = Tokunaga, M.: *The Bṛhaddevatā*. Kyoto 1997.

VAUDEVILLE 1963 = Vaudeville, Charlotte: '*Rāmāyaṇa* Studies I, The *Krauñca-vadha* Episode in the Vālmīki Rāmāyaṇa,' *Journal of the American Oriental Society* 83 (1963) 327–335.

VP = *Śrī-śrī-viṣṇu-purāṇa*. Gita Press, Gorakhpur, Saṁvatsara 2033.

# Floodlighting the Deluge: Traditions in Comparison

PAOLO MAGNONE

As is well known, the deluge myth has enjoyed a wide diffusion all over the Asian subcontinent (and beyond). We shall restrict our investigation, however, to three cultures where the literary developments of the deluge myth have been particularly prominent, i.e. the Near-East, the Classical world and India[1]. Let me first of all briefly summarise the extant documents.

The Near-Eastern deluge literature is represented chiefly by a Sumerian fragment, a Paleo-Babylonian version (eighteenth century B.C.E.), and especially the renowned Neo-Assyrian version (seventh century B.C.E.) preserved in the eleventh tablet of the *Gilgameš Epos*[2]. On the Akkadian myth clearly depends the Hebrew myth of Noah, in the twofold Jahvist[3] and Elohist[4] version. The Bible myth has in turn inspired the Arab *Qur'an* versions[5].

The Classical deluge literature is found scattered in a number of rivulets[6] which it is often difficult to trace to their sources. In several cases, however, what we come across is particular accounts of local floods that scarcely have anything to do with a universal deluge. Of such deluge three possibly independent traditions seem to be attested: the Ogygian, the Dardanian and above all the story of Deucalion and Pyrrha mentioned in Pindar[7] and more diffusely Apollodorus[8], then taken over by Horace[9] and especially Ovid[10], who embellishes it with a great many details.

---

[1] For a survey cf. USENER (1899).

[2] Cf. SOLLBERGER (1962). To the aforesaid versions a more recent Hellenistic one by Berossus (*apud* Eusebius) is to be added.

[3] Gen 6.5–8; 7.1–5, 7–10, 16, 12, 17, 22–23; 8.2b–3a, 6–13, 20–22.

[4] Gen 6.9–22; 7.11, 13–16, 18–21, 24; 8.1–5, 13–19; 9.1–17.

[5] Spec. Cor 11.26–49.

[6] Cf. CADUFF (1985).

[7] PINDARUS, *Olympian*, 9.41–53.

[8] APOLLODORUS, *Bibliotheca*, 1.7.2.

[9] HORATIUS, *Odes*, 1.2.5–12.

[10] OVIDIUS, *Metamorphoses*, 1.

*Essays in Indian Philosophy, Religion and Literature,* pp. 137–148.

Lastly, the Indian tradition—to which this paper is more especially devoted—is attested in many sources, from the late Vedic to the medieval period[11]. The most ancient document is a fairly long *Śata-patha-brāhmaṇa* passage[12], already featuring Manu, the boat and the fish, whose identity, however, remains so far mysterious. Outside the Vedic literature, an intermediate link with the later Purāṇic developments is provided by a narrative in the *Vana-parvan* of the *Mahā-bhārata*[13], where the fish reveals himself as Brahmā. Only in the *Purāṇas* do we first encounter the usual story, connecting the deluge with Viṣṇu's *matsyâvatāra*. While attempts at Purāṇic chronology are admittedly aleatory, the *Matsya-purāṇa*[14] version appears to be the most ancient, together with the little known and rather anomalous *Viṣṇu-dharmôttara* one[15]. On the other hand, the extended narrative of the *Bhāgavata-purāṇa*[16] (together with two bare references elsewhere in the same book) is undoubtedly more recent, and is the basis for the abridgement in the *Agni-purāṇa*[17] *avatāra* list as well as two mentions in the *Gāruḍa-purāṇa*[18]. Other Purāṇic versions are of a more aberrant nature: the *Skanda-purāṇa*[19], for instance, has a rather singular story identifying the fish with Śiva, whereas the extensive *Kālikā-purāṇa*[20] story engrafts Tantric features on quite a traditional stock. The most outlandish version, however, is the one recounted in the *Bhaviṣya-purāṇa*[21], counterfeiting (as

[11] Cf. HOHENBERGER (1930) for a brief review of the chief sources of the deluge myth about the fish rescuing Manu on the boat (which wrongly includes, however, also the PdP version, which is really about the fish rescuing the *Vedas* stolen by the aquatic demon). Cf. also SHASTRI (1950), for an (undiscriminatingly) broader panorama, miscellaneously including: a) versions about the fish rescuing Manu on the boat; b) versions about Mārkaṇḍeya swallowed up by baby Viṣṇu; c) versions about the deluge generically as a phase of *pralaya*; d) others. Besides the ŚatBr version, which is frivolously credited with higher antiquity than the Sumero-Akkadian myths, only epic-Purāṇic sources are considered (but the important VdhP version, among others, is missing) with no attempt at thematic categorisation.

[12] ŚatBr 1.8.1–10.

[13] MBh 3.187 (ed. Bom.).

[14] MtsP 1–2.

[15] VdhP 1.75.

[16] BhāgP 8.24 (long account); 1.3, 15; 2.7, 12.

[17] AgP 2.

[18] GārP 1.23; 142.2–3.

[19] SkP 5.3.3.

[20] KālP 32–33.

[21] BhavP 3.4.1.45–60.

this *Purāṇa* is wont to do) the story of Noah under the guise of Nyūha, provided for the occasion with a Sanskrit etymology!

The deluge theme has been subsequently taken over by poets such as Kṣemendra and Jayadeva, and more recently Sūrdās, Tulsīdās and others[22]. Of particular interest among these is Kṣemendra, who deals extensively with the deluge in his *Daśâvatāra-carita*[23].

All three traditions agree on but few fundamental points: mankind is swept away by a deluge, except for one or more people surviving in a vessel, who are entrusted with the task of the renewal. However, we should hardly be justified in grounding any presumption of a common origin on the strength of similarities pertaining to such elements as could scarcely be dispensed with by any deluge myth by reason of its very internal structure. On the other hand, we sometimes do come across more particular coincidences, as in the case of the biblical and Sumero-Akkadian versions: the correspondences, e.g. in the episode of the birds sent out as scouts is too punctual to admit of an independent origin.

The relationship between the latter versions is not surprising, given their common root. It *is* more surprising, however, that many illustrious fathers of Indology—WEBER[24], MACDONELL[25], OLDENBERG[26], KEITH[27], WINTERNITZ[28]—should have subscribed to the far more demanding hypothesis of a relationship, nay, an affiliation, of the Indian to the Sumero-Akkadian versions, relying on such altogether flimsy grounds as the argument *ex silentio*, regarding the Indian myth as a late borrowing merely because it does not occur earlier than the *Śata-patha-brāhmaṇa*; and the alleged coincidence of the theme of the seeds loaded on the ship.

More of recent, other scholars have spoken in favour of the independence of the Indian myth; but, as GONDA[29] had already remarked, all the relevant points do not seem to have been adequately taken into consideration, through lack of proper contextualisation of the myth, that should in the first place be analysed and understood by itself, in its own cultural value, before positing the question of possible relationships to other cultures.

---

[22] Cf. PĀṆḌEYA (1963: 410 f).

[23] DAC 1 (spec. 18 ff.).

[24] WEBER (1850: 161 ff.).

[25] MACDONELL (1899: 218).

[26] OLDENBERG (1923: III,283).

[27] KEITH (1925: 25; 229).

[28] WINTERNITZ (1987: 194, 379).

[29] GONDA (1978: 27).

Here is, side by side, the structure of the most ancient Indian version, that of the ŚatBr (leftmost column) and the Akkadian myth (rightmost column). Shared elements are shown in the central column.

| **the *Śata-patha-brāhmaṇa*** | **Shared elements** | **the Akkadian myth** |
|---|---|---|
| A pious man (Manu) rescues a small fish | | Men incur divine displeasure |
| the fish gradually undergoes a wondrous metamorphosis into a sea monster | | the supreme god (En-lil) resolves to exterminate them |
| | the fish rewards the man by / a divine protector (Ea) aids a pious man by | |
| | warning him of the approaching deluge | |
| | the man builds a ship | |
| | | the man freights the ship with goods and beings |
| | | the man evades his neighbours' curiosity with an excuse |
| | the deluge sets in | |
| the fish comes to succour | | the minor gods are terrified and blame En-lil |
| the man fastens the ship to the horn of the fish, who tows it along | | |
| | the deluge comes to an end | |
| | the ship lands atop a mountain | |
| | | the man sends out birds as scouts |
| | the man goes ashore and offers a sacrifice | |
| the man begets offspring on the woman born from the sacrifice | | the gods gather round the sacrifice and once again censure En-lil |
| | | En-lil is incensed beholding the survivors |
| | | Ea appeases him and he bestows his blessing on the survivors |

Already this preliminary comparison is revealing. As is patent at first sight, the two structures diverge almost entirely. In the first place, the antecedent of the Semitic myth introduces an ethical motivation for the deluge as punishment of sinful mankind. Such motivation is conspicuously absent in the Indian version, which exhibits an antecedent of folkloric nature in its stead: the pious man does good to a humble creature, which ultimately turns out as powerful and repays the benefit—a well-known motif of so many folk tales.

Secondly, the Akkadian myth brings out a dissension in the divine world, between the supreme god En-lil and many other gods, and above all Ea, who decides *motu proprio* to save his *protégé*. There evidently is no room for such dissension in the monotheism of the Bible, but some interiorised traces of it might perhaps be detected in Jahve–Elohim himself, under the guise of his late repentance, betrayed by the resolve never again to send a deluge. In the Indian myth there is no trace of dissension whatsoever.

Thirdly, in the Akkadian myth the chosen one is entrusted with the task of carrying to safety exemplars of the creatures, in view of the palingenesis to-be. As I mentioned, it is indeed on account of the presumed presence of this theme in some Indian versions that some scholars have been led to postulate the dependence of the Indian myth on the Akkadian one. Actually, in the most ancient Indian version, that of the ŚatBr, this theme is absent. It does appear subsequently, but with one paramount difference: whereas in the Akkadian myth it is always the question of *couples*, or in any case complete beings, in the Indian myths it is always the question of *seeds*, the implications becoming more and more characteristically Indian as time progresses.

Last but not least, the Indian myth does not concur with the Akkadian one in any marginal particulars, whose congruence would be all the more meaningful to establish a connection, precisely because of the lack of probability of separate coincidental origination of arbitrary details. E.g. there is no trace of the episode of the birds sent out as scouts, which had on the contrary been taken over by the Jahvist version on account of its narrative efficacy.

What is, therefore, left as concordant? No more than this: a chosen pious man is warned of the impending deluge, builds a ship and sails through the cataclysm to lastly alight atop a mountain, where he celebrates a sacrifice. But even these residual concordances, generic as they are, are nevertheless more apparent than real.

For instance, the sacrifice that concludes both the Akkadian and the Indian myth has quite a different value in either context. The survivors of the Akkadian myth offer a thanksgiving sacrifice, round which the gods gather 'like flies, attracted by the pleasant smell.' The sacrifice exposes the folly of the divine resolution to send the deluge: the dissident gods had already complained in vain that the extermination of mankind would have deprived them of the sacrificial victims; now they are refreshed by the smell of the oblations, and Inanna spitefully remarks that the supreme En-lil ought not to be permitted to partake of what his improvidence had risked to annihilate. In the end En-lil himself accepts the propitiating sacrifice and welcomes the survivors among the immortals. The propagation of mankind does not constitute a problem: of course, the surviving couples will take care of it in the customary manner.

In the Indian myth, on the other hand, the procreative concern is exactly what prompts the survivor (which the myth does not credit with a wife) to sacrifice and to the typically Indian practice of *tapas*. By means of *tapas* and sacrifice Manu obtains as daughter Iḍā, the quintessence of oblation, on whom he will beget all creatures. Thus, in the Indian context sacrifice is not an instrument of reconciliation meant to appease godhead, but rather a magical procedure meant to yield fruits. The outcome of the Akkadian sacrifice is that the gods—including En-lil through Ea's intercession—bless and welcome the human couple; the outcome of the Indian sacrifice is that Manu is enabled to fulfil his creative role.

The single most prominent common feature remains, therefore, the building of the ship, which is however missing, as we are going to see, in the more recent Indian versions and is barely mentioned in the more ancient ones without elaborating on modes and dimensions, as is characteristically the case with all Near-Eastern versions[30].

The impression of reciprocal independence of the two traditions is further corroborated when we examine the subsequent developments of the Indian myth. The MBh version agrees with the one of the ŚatBr, apart from the general structure, on a couple of important points: first of all, the aforesaid theme of the building of the ship; furthermore, the MBh version declares the fish to be Brahmā Prajāpati—another trait of archaism which sets back the story to Brahmanical times (although the ŚatBr itself is silent with respect to the identity of the fish).

On the other hand, the MBh version introduces a few innovations that will later on win regular acceptance in the *Purāṇa*s. The two most important are: the cyclical frame of the *pralaya* and the motif of the 'seeds'.

As we have seen, the ŚatBr did not specify a reason for the deluge, while connecting it with the cosmogonic context, wherein Manu was confronted with the usual difficult task of peopling the world. Although not expressly mentioned, a cyclical frame *might* however seem implied, exactly in that the deluge lacked any specific motivation, as though it were but a cosmic *routine*. Be it as it may with the

---

[30] A comparable interest in modes and dimensions can be seen in some Indian versions in connection with the theme of the metamorphoses of the fish.

ŚatBr, in the MBh the cyclical frame is explicitly declared at the place[31] where the time of cosmic dissolution through a deluge is said to be at hand. By this a punitive value of the deluge is also manifestly ruled out, in case the silence of the ŚatBr might leave any doubts.

The motif of the seeds is the Indian counterpart of the Akkadian motif of the couples: but it is, indeed, unmistakably Indian in its perfect integration with the *pralaya* theme. No formed creature (save Manu and the seven *ṛṣis*) can cross the ocean of the dissolution of forms and remain whole, but everything must be resolved into rudiments, from which it shall rise again at the dawn of a new world age. Hence no couples of perfected and sexually characterised living beings, but mere seeds as yet undifferentiated are only apt to be preserved for a fresh beginning.

The Purāṇic versions, for the most part, while imitating in the main the MBh model, diverge on a single chief point: the fish has now become an *incarnation* of Viṣṇu's, in accordance with the evolution of a doctrine—the *avatāra-vāda*—which, first announced in the BhG, attains its classical perfection in the *Purāṇas*, among others with the development of different *avatāra* lists, in which the fish is reckoned as a regular member right from the outset, up to the attempted fixation of a canon with the *daśâvatāra* with the fish as first[32].

If this Purāṇic innovation is well understandable in the frame of the history of Vishnuism, another innovation is more surprising, and seemingly the sheer product of arbitrary chance—and it is this innovation that will now detain us more particularly—namely, that none of the Purāṇic versions[33] pursues the motif of the building of the ship. Some of the major versions simply skip over the question; in MtsP, however, the fish shows Manu a pre-existing ship stating that it has been fashioned by (or with) all the gods for the protection of the multitude of the creatures[34]. What is then this ship turning up all of a sudden, which Manu shall load with the four kinds of living beings—born of sweat, eggs, sprouts and placenta—which shall be tossed about by the waves of dissolution and led home through the

---

[31] MBh 3.187.28–30:

*acirād bhagavan bhaumam idaṁ sthāvara-jaṅgamam /*
*sarvam eva mahā-bhāga pralayaṁ vai gamiṣyati //*
*saṁprakṣalana-kālo 'yaṁ lokānāṁ samupasthitaḥ /*
*... tasya sarvasya saṁprāptaḥ kālaḥ parama-dāruṇaḥ //*

[32] On the *avatāra* lists see MAGNONE (: cap. I).

[33] Except for the late KālP version that besides a few noteworthy innovations follows for the rest the MBh prototype even in the detail.

[34] MtsP 1.31: *naur iyaṁ sarva-devānāṁ nikāyena vinirmitaṁ mahā-jīva-nikāyasya rakṣaṇârtham.*

firm anchorage to the fish's horn? The answer is found in the BhāgP—not however in the extended account, which just mentions the ship's being sent (again) by the fish, but in a passing hint in an *avatāra* list, where Viṣṇu is said to have assumed the form of a fish on occasion of the flood in the *cākṣuṣa manv-antara* in order to protect Manu Vaivasvata by letting him board a 'telluric ship' (*naur mahīmayī*)[35]. The identical strophe occurs in the GārP[36]. Only in the VdhP, however, is the theme articulated to some extent: when Śiva in watery form enshrouds the earth destroying all creatures, we are told, the earth personified as goddess Satī becomes a ship and carries the seeds of all things: *naur bhūtvā tu satī devi tadā ... dhārayati atha bījāni sarvāṇy eva aviśeṣataḥ*[37]. This identification is further echoed in Kṣemendra's *Daśâvatāra-carita*, where the ship fastened to the fish's horn is said to be 'as broad as the earth.'[38] Chanting the divine *līlā*, Tulsīdās will once again condense in a few essential words the *avatāra*'s deed: for his *bhakta*s' sake Rāma took on the form of a fish and made the earth into a ship[39].

Now we can see the reason why the ancient Brahmanic and epic motif of the building of the ship has been dropped in the Purāṇic versions: the ship is more than merely a produce of human craft, she is Earth herself in her 'diluvial' form. As is explicitly said in a SkP passage (pertaining to another variety of the *pralaya* myth that lies outside our present scope[40]): *ekârṇave mahā-ghore naur iva kṣetram īkṣyate*[41]. The ship is not, furthermore, an artefact, the occasional manufacturing procedures of which it makes any sense to specify (as in the Akkadian myth); she is, rather, the invariable allotrope of the Earth at the time of the deluge. The Brahmanical and epic motif of the fashioning of the ship was justified because in the original context the deluge is not yet a cyclical event (at least explicitly); whereas in the MBh it is, but the doctrine of cosmic cycles, like the *avatāra-vāda*, is still at a rudimentary stage[42], and has not yet ended up in the crystallisation of a pregnant symbolic repertoire, as in the *Purāṇa*s.

---

[35] BhāgP 1.3.15: *rūpaṁ ca jagṛhe mātsyaṁ cākṣuṣôdadhi-saṁplave nāvy āropya mahīmayyāṁ apād vaivasvataṁ manum*.

[36] GārP 1.23.

[37] VdhP 1.75.9–10.

[38] DAC 1.44: *tad-ucca-śṛṅga-saṁlagnāṁ nāvam dhṛtim ivâyatām*.

[39] Tulsīdās, *Granthâvalī*, quoted in PĀṆḌEYA (1963: 411).

[40] The myth of Mārkaṇḍeya witnessing the *pralaya* flood has been dealt with by BRINKHAUS (2002).

[41] SkP 2.2.3.9.

[42] This is evidenced, e.g. by the confusion in the usage of terms like *kalpa, mahā-yuga* and *yuga* already pointed out by BIARDEAU (1976: 121 ff.).

In the latter texts the deluge is part of the scheme of the cosmic *pralaya* brought about through fire and water, which the MtsP indeed describes contextually with the deluge: a hundred years of drought and famine, the earth scorched by a sevenfold sun and by the awakening of the submarine fire, and finally the dreadful downpour of the sevenfold cloud condensed by the smoke of the conflagration. The final picture is the *ekârṇava*, the one all embracing ocean symbolising the formless One into which all created forms have once again merged.

Still, the palingenesis of the cycle to come requires a leftover of the old world to work up afresh into a new beginning. This residue incarnates in different mythic images, among which the best known is probably Śeṣa, the serpent couch of Nārāyaṇa lying asleep on the cosmic waters: his very name betrays him as an emblem of the 'residue' of the great cosmic sacrifice[43], preserved in view of the creative awakening at the dawn of the new cycle.

Thus, the ship loaded with seeds is nothing but another emblem of the residue and its receptacle: the earth itself shrunk to the size of a ship, the only form able to withstand the triumph of the liquid element. The VdhP overloads the symbol with new values, taking advantage of the intrinsic polysemy of the symbolic function: the earth turned into a ship is at the same time Satī, the consort of Śiva, the destroyer turned into water in order to accomplish his destructive function; but in the characteristic ambivalence exemplarily expressed in the *liṅga* in its double capacity as creative phallus and destructive fire pillar, the aqueous destructive Śiva is at the same time the fecundating Śiva who embraces the Earth-ship and impregnates her with the seeds of all beings.

This symbolic identification of the earth with the ship, albeit but cursorily touched upon in the aforesaid passages, possibly by the very reason of its straightforwardness in the mythical context, is indirectly corroborated by comparison with another *avatāra* myth, which will yield to careful consideration unexpected homologies with the fish myth—namely, the boar myth as it occurs, e.g. in the MBh[44]. Viṣṇu is scouring the cosmic ocean in search of the earth. As he descries it at last at the bottom of the deep, he assumes a boar form, dives into the waters and again surfaces carrying the earth on his single tusk. In this particular instance the reading is *daṁṣṭreṇâikena*, but elsewhere[45] *śṛṅgenâikena*; and *eka-śṛṅga* is indeed one of the most common epithets of the *varāhâvatāra*.

Now precisely the horn—*śṛṅga*—is the most ubiquitous feature, occurring in almost all versions of the (diluvial) fish myth—only excepting those dispensing

[43] Cf. BIARDEAU (1981: 52 f.; 170).

[44] MBh 3.272.49–55.

[45] E.g. MBh 3.142.47.

with all details by reason of their excessive brevity. The boar myth stages a semi-aquatic animal, a fertility symbol, penetrating the womb of the waters to again emerge lifting the earth on the single ithyphallic tusk—the earth that in some variants is explicitly said to be fecundated in the process[46]. The fish myth, in much the same way, stages the aquatic animal *par excellence*, likewise a fertility symbol, as he cuts through the waves carrying something—he too—on the ithyphallic horn: the ship, whose homology with the earth in the parallel boar myth now stands out in all evidence. I mentioned before the VdhP version, which adds explicit sexual developments, as the aforesaid variant of the boar myth also does.

Incidentally, we may recall that, apart from its phallic value on the plane of sexual symbolism, the horn also has an axial value in the cosmic frame, as an image of the *axis mundi* to which the earth is anchored. The symbolism of the *axis mundi* is found in many *avatāra* myths, e.g. in the revolving mountain supported by the *kūrmâvatāra*, or in the pillar from which the *nṛsiṁhâvatāra*[47] bursts out—as well as, of course, in the *Śiva-liṅga*. As for the divine monoceros, besides the fish and the boar—in which cases, mark well, no justification is put forth for the oddity of the single horn or tusk—it is further exemplified by Gaṇeśa, also furnished with a single tusk, although in his case the myth trivially explains the mutilation as a result of the god's quarrel with Paraśurāma[48].

In the light of the above, we are now in a position to satisfactorily answer GONDA's doubt. He had remarked, noticing the twofold function of the fish—which on one hand warns Manu of the impending deluge, on the other tows the ship to safety—that the second function is superfluous from a purely rational viewpoint, as ships can move of themselves or by the aid of the winds (as usually happens in deluge myths)[49]. The answer is, that the latter function, while it has, indeed, no rational grounds, is nevertheless deeply rooted in the symbolic plexus that I have tried to sketch.

Much is left to be observed about the later developments of the myth: e.g. on the identification of the rope fastening the ship to the horn with a serpent, who is easily recognised as Śeṣa. And more unsuspected homologies between ostensibly diverse mythical representations come to the fore: Viṣṇu sleeping amidst the ocean on the serpent couch on a strip of land at the foot of a banyan—a strip of land that, as the

---

[46] Cf. VP 5.29.23–24; KālP 29; and generally, on the different versions of the *varāhâvatāra* myth, MAGNONE (1989: 14–21).

[47] In the BhāgP version 7.8.

[48] Cf. BvP 3.43; BṇP 3.42.

[49] GONDA (1978: 33).

quoted SkP passage suggests, resembles a ship—still is the fish fastened to the boat with the serpent rope—but at the same time the god upholding the Maṇḍara peak—*śṛṅga*, once again—encircled by the coils of the serpent rope and resting, at the bottom of the ocean, on the telluric turtle. But the subterranean solidarity of all these mythic representations is expressed at its best in the following rather extravagant version of the deluge myth found in the SkP[50], which I am going to summarise by way of conclusion, and without comments, leaving it to each one to pursue on his or her own the echoes resounding in the symbolic recesses of the text.

> This myth is about the arcane vision of Mārkaṇḍeya, who shares with Manu and the Seven Seers the privilege of traversing unscathed the cosmic dissolution. Mārkaṇḍeya, then, while swimming amidst the cosmic ocean, sees the primordial man (*puruṣa*) blazing like the sun, the Himālaya peak (*śṛṅga*) and Manu in filial attitude unceasingly revolving on the surface of the deep like the wheel of a potter. Then he sees a huge fish (Śiva) who swallows him up. In the interior he sees a roaring river swarming with fish, and in the river a beautiful dark-complexioned lady (Amṛtā, born of Śiva's limbs), holding a ship between her knees. This ship Manu and Mārkaṇḍeya board reaching final safety.

## BIBLIOGRAPHY


AgP = *Agni-purāṇa*. Veṅkaṭeśvara Press, Bombay: no date.

APOLLODORUS = Apollodorus: *Bibliotheca*.

BhāgP = *Bhāgavata-purāṇa*. Veṅkaṭeśvara Press, Bombay: no date.

BhavP = *Bhaviṣya-purāṇa*. Veṅkaṭeśvara Press, Bombay: no date.

BhG = *Bhagavad-gītā*.

BIARDEAU 1976 = Biardeau, Madeleine: 'Études de mythologie hindoue (iv),' *BEFEO* 63 (1976).

BIARDEAU 1981 = Biardeau, Madeleine: *Études de mythologie hindoue. Cosmogonies puraniques*. Paris 1981.

BṇP = *Brahmâṇḍa-purāṇa*. Veṅkaṭeśvara Press, Bombay: no date.

BRINKHAUS 2002 = Brinkhaus, Horst: 'The Mārkaṇḍeya-Episode in the Sanskrit Epics and *Purāṇas*.' In the present volume, pp. 87-98.

BvP = *Brahma-vaivarta-purāṇa*. Veṅkaṭeśvara Press, Bombay: no date.

CADUFF 1985 = Caduff, G.A.: *Antike Sintflutsagen*. *Hypomnemata* 82, Göttingen 1985.


[50] SkP 5.3.3.

COR = *Al-Qur'ān.*

DAC = Kṣemendra: *Daśâvatāra-carita*. *Kāvyamālā* 26, Bombay 1891.

GārP = *Gāruḍa-purāṇa*. Veṅkaṭeśvara Press, Bombay: no date.

Gen = *Genesis* of *the Bible.*

GONDA 1978 = Gonda, Jan : 'De indische zondvloed-mythe.' *Mededelingen d. Koninklijke Nederlandse Akademie van Wetenschappen*, Afd. Letterkunde, N. R., 41, 2, Amsterdam 1978.

HOHENBERGER 1930 = Hohenberger, A.: *Die Flutsage und das Matsyapurāṇa*. Leipzig 1930.

HORATIUS = Horatius: *Odes.*

KālP = *Kālikā-purāṇa*. Veṅkaṭeśvara Press, Bombay: no date.

KEITH 1925 = Keith, A.B.: *The Religion and Philosophy of the Vedas and Upanishads*. Cambridge (Mass.) 1925.

MACDONELL 1899 = Macdonell, Arthur A.: *A History of Sanskrit Literature*, 1899.

MAGNONE = Magnone, Paolo: *La teoria degli avatāra nel Viṣṇudharmottara Purāṇa con particolare riguardo alla Śaṅkara Gītā*. Tesi di Laurea—Università Cattolica di Milano, unpublished dissertation.

MAGNONE 1989 = Magnone, Paolo: 'Varāha. L'avatāra del Cinghiale.' *Abstracta* 37 (1989).

MBh = *Mahā-bhārata.*

MtsP = *Matsya-purāṇa*. Veṅkaṭeśvara Press, Bombay: no date.

OLDENBERG 1923 = Oldenberg, Hermann: *Die Religion des Veda*. Berlin 1923.

OVIDIUS = Ovidius: *Metamorphoses.*

PĀṆḌEYA 1963 = Pāṇḍeya, K.: *Madhyakālīn sāhitya mẽ avatārvād*. Vārāṇasī 1963.

PdP = *Padma-purāṇa*. Veṅkaṭeśvara Press, Bombay: no date.

PINDARUS = Pindarus: *Olympian.*

SHASTRI 1950 = Shastri, Suryakanta: *The Flood Legend in Sanskrit Literature*. Delhi 1950.

SkP = *Skanda-purāṇa*. Veṅkaṭeśvara Press, Bombay: no date.

SOLLBERGER 1962 = Sollberger, E.: *The Babylonian Legend of the Flood*. London 1962.

ŚatBr = *Śata-patha-brāhmaṇa*. The *Mādhyandina* recension.

USENER 1899 = Usener, H.: *Die Sintfluthsagen*. Bonn 1899.

VarP = *Varāha-purāṇa*. Veṅkaṭeśvara Press, Bombay: no date.

VdhP = *Viṣṇu-dharmôttara-purāṇa*. Veṅkaṭeśvara Press, Bombay: no date.

VP = *Viṣṇu-purāṇa*. Veṅkaṭeśvara Press, Bombay: no date.

WEBER 1850 = Weber, A.: *Indische Studien. I.* Berlin 1850.

WINTERNITZ 1987 = Winternitz, Moritz: *Geschichte der indischen Literatur*, Bänder 1–3, Leipzig 1909–1922. Eng. transl.: *A History of Indian Literature*, Vols. I-II, Calcutta 1927–33; Vol. III, 1–2: Calcutta 1963–1967. [Reprinted: Motilal Banarsidass, Delhi 1987].

# *Subhāṣitas* in the *Purāṇas*—a Cultural Perspective

SATYA VRAT SHASTRI

*Subhāṣitas*, or good sayings, are a characteristic feature of Sanskrit literature. They propound a fundamental truth, point towards the reality of the situation obtaining in this world of contradictions and contrarieties and draw attention to what is right and what is wrong, what one should or should not do, how one should or should not conduct oneself in life. In the texts on *nīti*, they make direct appearance but in other texts they flow out of the narrative either as illustrations or deductions. It is in the last form that they appear in the bulk of the Sanskrit literature including the vast corpus of the Purāṇic one. To point to what is right or wrong, what is acceptable or not, depends upon the values of a particular cultural milieu. The *Purāṇas*, having their origin in India, were obviously reflecting the Indian cultural milieu. When the *Purāṇas* are to be examined from the cultural perspective, it should mean on the face of it the Indian cultural perspective.

This brings us to the question as to what this Indian culture is. If it can be summarised in one sentence, it is the inculcation of *dharma*, the all-encompassing concept. It is this which sustains society: *dharmo dhārayate prajāḥ*[1]. The essence of this *dharma* is not to do unto others what one would not like to be done to oneself: *ātmanaḥ pratikūlāni pareṣāṁ na samācaret*[2]. This is the *dharma-sarvasva*. This can be achieved by following certain principles which the sage Manu has prescribed for all the four castes:

> *ahiṁsā satyam asteyaṁ śaucam indriya-nigrahaḥ* /
> *etaṁ sāmāsikaṁ dharmaṁ cāturvarṇye 'bravīn manuḥ* //[3]

The *Purāṇas* lay emphasis on each one of these.

According to the *Liṅga-purāṇa*, *ahiṁsā* is to devote oneself to the well-being of all the beings as they are one's very being. It is this which leads to the realisation of one's own self:

---

[1] *Mahā-bhārata*, *Karṇa-parvan* 69.58.

[2] *Pañca-tantra* 3.102.

[3] *Manu-smṛti* 10.63.

*Essays in Indian Philosophy, Religion and Literature*, pp. 149–157.

*ātmavat sarva-bhūtānāṁ hitāyâiva pravartatam /*
*ahiṁsâiṣā samākhyātā yā câtma-jñāna-siddhidā //*[4]

There is emphasis on *ahiṁsā* in the *Brahmâṇḍa-purāṇa* to the extent that it is proclaimed as the gateway to *dharma*:

*ahiṁsā dharmasya dvāram uktaṁ maharṣibhiḥ /*[5]

The *Padma-purāṇa* assigns higher regions to the followers of this principle and the lower ones to those who do not do so:

*ahiṁsā-nirmalaṁ dharmaṁ sevante ye vipaścitaḥ /*
*teṣām evôrddhva-gamanaṁ yānti tiryag adho 'nyathā //*[6]

*Satya*, or truth, according to the *Liṅga-purāṇa* is speaking out exactly what has been seen, heard, imagined or experienced by oneself in a manner that it does not cause pain to others:

*dṛṣṭaṁ śrutaṁ cânumitaṁ svânubhūtaṁ yathârthataḥ /*
*kathanaṁ satyam ity uktaṁ para-pīḍā-vivarjitam //*[7]

It is worthwhile to pause here and ponder over the implication of the last part of the explanation of *satya* which is to avoid *para-pīḍā*, pain or anguish to others. To reproduce exactly *yathârthataḥ*, what one has seen, heard, etc., is truth, no doubt, but not the whole truth. The more important thing about it is that it must not cause harm or unpleasantness to the listener. This is what is the import of the well-known adage: *satyaṁ brūyāt priyaṁ brūyāt, na brūyāt satyam apriyam*[8]. The *Viṣṇu-purāṇa* also says the same thing. Not only that. It goes a step further. It enjoins silence if the truth were to cause hurt to others:

*tasmāt satyaṁ vadet prājño yat para-prīti-kāraṇam /*
*satyaṁ yat para-duḥkhāya tadā mauna-paro bhavet //*[9]

The *Purāṇa* offers this injunction in view of the possibility of such occurrences where the truth may lead to violence or injury to others. According to the *Lāṭa-saṁhitā*, on such occasions truth would turn into untruth and vice versa:

---

[4] *Liṅga-purāṇa* 8.11.

[5] *Pūrvârdha* 30.35.

[6] *Padma-purāṇa* 4.41.

[7] *Liṅga-purāṇa* 8.13.

[8] *Manu-smṛti* 4.138.

[9] *Viṣṇu-purāṇa* 3.12.43.

*satyam apy asatyatāṁ yāti kvacid dhiṁsânubandhataḥ /*
*asatyaṁ satyatāṁ yāti kvacij jīvasya rakṣaṇāt //*[10]

Whatever the case, it is very difficult to keep to truth. One has to go on trying to cultivate it. The *Padma-purāṇa* declares it a *tīrtha*[11]. It is the mainstay of the world, according to it, the mainstay even of *dharma*:

*satye pratiṣṭhitā lokāḥ dharmaḥ satye pratiṣṭhitaḥ /*[12]

And then comes from it the highest praise of *satya* in a stanza which has acquired wide popularity:

*aśva-medha-sahasraṁ ca satyaṁ ca tulayā dhṛtam /*
*aśva-medha-sahasrād dhi satyam eva viśiṣyate //*[13]

'If a thousand *Aśva-medhas* and truth were to be put in a scale, truth would weigh heavier than the thousand *Aśva-medhas*.'

*Asteya* is non-stealing or non-depriving others of what rightfully belongs to them. 'Not to go in for the possessions of others in mind, action, and word even in adversity' is the elucidation of the spirit behind this provided by the *Liṅga-purāṇa*:

*anādānaṁ para-svānām āpady api vicārataḥ /*
*manasā karmaṇā vācā tad asteyaṁ samāsataḥ //*[14]

*Śauca*, purity, according to the *Bhaviṣya-purāṇa*, is avoiding the eating of prohibited articles of food, the association with the condemned people and being firm in proper conduct:

*abhakṣya-parihāraś ca saṁsargaś câpy aninditaiḥ /*
*ācāre ca vyavasthānaṁ śaucam etat prakīrtitam //*[15]

Purity does not have to concern itself with the physical aspect only. It has to have its demand on the mind and the speech as well. The physical purity is its external manifestation. Verbal purity is to devote proper thought to an activity, and the mental one is the judicious choice of non-offensive words. The *Liṅga-purāṇa* enjoins the cultivation of these after having acquired the physical purity. The

[10] *Lāṭa-saṁhitā* 6.6.7.

[11] *Padma-purāṇa* 5.11.83.

[12] *Padma-purāṇa* 5.18.396.

[13] *Padma-purāṇa* 5.18.403.

[14] *Liṅga-purāṇa* 1.12.160.

[15] *Bhaviṣya-purāṇa* 8.32.

physical purity is external, *bāhya*, the verbal and the mental purity is internal, *ābhyantara*:

*bāhya-śaucena yuktaḥ saṁs tathā câbhyantaraṁ caret* /[16]

It repeats the same idea in the verse:

*sadâvagāhya salile viśuddhāḥ kiṁ dvijôttamāḥ* /
*tasmād ābhyantaraṁ śaucaṁ sadā kāryaṁ vidhānataḥ* //[17]

'Do the Brahmins get (really) purified by bathing in water every time? So one should carry out internal purification as per the proper procedure.'

*Indriya-nigraha* is control over the senses, a recurring theme of many a Sanskrit work, including the *Purāṇas*. The *Śrīmad-bhāgavata-purāṇa* recognises the inexorability of the attraction of the senses which it terms as bondage. It is the control over them which, according to it, is deliverance:

*bandha indriya-vikṣepo mokṣa eṣāṁ ca saṁyamaḥ* /[18]

The *Bhaviṣya-purāṇa* refers to the distraction of the senses by worldly objects, which according to it are hard to resist:

*viṣayā durjayāḥ puṁbhir indriyâkarṣiṇaḥ sadā* /[19]

Indian culture has always laid the greatest emphasis on *ācāra*, good conduct, which it has regarded as *paramo dharmaḥ*[20], the quintessence of righteousness to the extent that the one who is devoid of it, even the *Vedas*, the holiest of the holy cannot redeem: *ācāra-hīnaṁ na punanti vedāḥ*[21]. *Ācāra* expressed through another word—*śīla*—is the best ornament of a person: *śīlaṁ paraṁ bhūṣaṇam*[22]. According to the *Padma-purāṇa*, one who observes *śīla*, good conduct, he alone lives: *śīlasya pālanaṁ kurvan yo jīvati sa jīvati*[23]—which means that life has meaning only if one observes *śīla*, otherwise it is mere existence, just vegetation. For a person of bad

[16] *Liṅga-purāṇa* 8.35.

[17] *Liṅga-purāṇa* 8.15.

[18] *Śrīmad-bhāgavata-purāṇa* 1.62.15.

[19] *Bhaviṣya-purāṇa* 1.18.12.

[20] *Manu-smṛti* 1.108.

[21] *Vāsiṣṭha-smṛti* 6.3.

[22] *Nīti-śataka* 83.

[23] *Padma-purāṇa* 46.95.

disposition and conduct (*kuśīla*)—the same *Purāṇa* says—the riches are a mere dirt (*mala*); for a person of good disposition and conduct (*sādhu-śīla*), even poverty is an ornament:

*kuśīlasya vibhavaḥ kevalaṁ malam /*
*janasya sādhu-śīlasya dāridryam api bhūṣaṇam //*[24]

Some of the prominent features of this *ācāra* or *śīla* are respect to parents, teachers and guests, on which Indian tradition has continued to lay great emphasis since days of yore, the Upaniṣadic commandment still ringing in the ears: *mātṛ-devo bhava, pitṛ-devo bhava ācārya-devo bhava, atithi-devo bhava.* This respect to the foursome bordering on worship, they being looked upon as *devas*, the deities, finds full echo in the *Purāṇas* as well. The *Skanda-purāṇa* declares those who serve their parents as the best of the devotees of the Lord:

*mātā-pitroś ca śuśrūṣāṁ kurvate ye narôttamāḥ,*
*te vai bhāgavatôttamāḥ /*[25]

The *Padma-purāṇa* proclaims that for a son the place where his parents live is without doubt the Gaṅgā and the holy places like Gayā and Puṣkara:

*tatra gaṅgā gayā tīrthaṁ tatra puṣkaram eva ca /*
*yatra mātā pitā tiṣṭhet putrasyâpi na saṁśayaḥ //*[26]

It further says that a son who regularly washes the feet of his parents has his daily bath in the Gaṅgā[27]. Proceeding further, it says that he who circumambulates his father and mother circumambulates the whole earth with its seven continents:

*mātaraṁ pitaraṁ câiva yas tu kuryāt pradakṣiṇam /*
*pradakṣiṇī-kṛtā tena sapta-dvīpā vasundharā //*[28]

Now, if the mother and the father bring a person into this world, it is the teacher who opens the doors of knowledge to him. It is a sin to forget him, even that one who just had taught only one syllable, just one word or the meaning of it:

*akṣarasyâpi câikasya padārthasya padasya vā /*
*dātāraṁ vismaran pāpī kiṁ punar dharma-deśinam //*[29]

---

[24] *Padma-purāṇa* 46.93.

[25] *Skanda-purāṇa*, *Vaiṣṇava-khaṇḍa*, *Veṅkaṭācala-māhātmya* 21.43.

[26] *Padma-purāṇa* 2.62.68.

[27] *Padma-purāṇa* 2.60.74.

[28] *Padma-purāṇa* 5.46.12.

According to the *Skanda-purāṇa*, if the teacher is happy, all the gods would be happy, including Indra. Reverse would be the case otherwise:

*gurau tuṣṭe ca tuṣṭāh syur devāḥ sarve savāsavāḥ* /
*gurau ruṣṭe ca ruṣṭāḥ syur devāḥ sarve savāsavāḥ* //[30]

There could be some people—indeed there are some in this strange world—who may turn to some other person and show him respect in preference to their teacher. The *Varāha-purāṇa* has a sure word of condemnation for them. They meet with misfortune, it says, and whatever they offer in charity goes in vain:

*gurau sati tu yaś cânyam āśrayet pūjayet sudhīḥ* /
*sa durgatim avāpnoti dattam asya ca niṣphalam* //[31]

The gift must be offered consciously first to one's teacher and then to someone else. The teacher may be learned or not, he is verily Janārdana (Lord Kṛṣṇa):

*prayatnena gurau pūrvaṁ paścād anyasya dāpayet* /
*avidyo vā savidyo vā gurur eva janārdanaḥ* //[32]

The *Purāṇa* is here laying down priorities for a person. When it comes to showing respect or making offerings, the first priority should be the teacher from whom one has had first lessons. Later a person may come into contact with someone more knowledgeable than his teacher. There is no reason for him to fall in for that someone else in showing his esteem over and above his teacher. Little or more knowledge has not to be the criterion in determining the order of preference for showing respect. The *Purāṇa* is very clear in this respect. It is the teacher who must have the precedence.

It is due to the pre-eminent position of the teacher that the *Skanda-purāṇa* enjoins total obedience to him. His words are only to be obeyed, and not to be ignored:

*yat kiṁcid vā samādiṣṭo guruṇā tat samācaret* /
*ājñapto guruṇā vipraḥ na tad-vākyaṁ tu laṅghayet* //[33]

According to the *Brahma-vaivarta-purāṇa*, that person is learned, is knowledgeable, is secure, is meritorious who obeys the words of his teacher. He meets with success at every step:

---

[29] *Padma-purāṇa* 21.156.

[30] *Skanda-purāṇa* (*Vaiṣṇava-khaṇḍa*, *Kārtika-māhātmya*) 2.3.

[31] *Varāha-purāṇa* 50.18.19.

[32] *Varāha-purāṇa* 50.19.20.

[33] *Skanda-purāṇa* (*Vaiṣṇava-khaṇḍa*, *Kārtika-māhātmya*) 2.5.

*sa paṇḍitaḥ sa ca jñānī sa kṣemī sa ca puṇyavān /*
*guror vacas-karo yo hi kṣemaṁ tasya pade pade //*[34]

Now, a word about *atithi*, guest. He is described in the *Skanda-puraṇa* as worthy of respect of everybody:

*agnir dvijānāṁ vipraś ca varṇānāṁ ramaṇaḥ striyām /*
*guruḥ pitā ca putrāṇāṁ sarvasyâbhyāgato guruḥ //*[35]

The belief in *karman* and reincarnation (*punar-janma*) are deeply ingrained in Indian psyche. Text after text has spoken about it, sage after sage has expounded it. Except the Cārvākas and some other thinkers, it has found general acceptance in Indian society. 'As you sow so shall you reap' is at the basis of it. One has to reap the reward of whatever actions, good or bad, one might have performed. The next birth is determined by them and the prosperity and the adversity going with it. This is the view echoed in the *Padma-purāṇa* stanza which says that it is because of the actions in the previous births that some people are born as *ārya*s and some as *mleccha*s, some with good wealth and some extremely poor:

*āryā mlecchāś ca tatrâpi jāyante pūrva-karmaṇaḥ /*
*tathā kecid dhanenâḍhyāḥ kecid atyanta-durvidhāḥ //*[36]

Actually, it is *karman*, action, which is Vedhás, Prajāpati, the Creator. It is *karman* which fashions beings, assigns them with race, colour, creed, means of subsistence, and so on. The *Mahā-purāṇa* says that Vidhi, Sraṣṭṛ, Viḍhātṛ, Daiva, Purā-kṛta, Karman and Īśvara are just different words for the same thing; they are mere synonyms:

*vidhiḥ sraṣṭā vidhātā ca daivaṁ karma purā-kṛtam /*
*īśvaraś cêti paryāyā vijñeyāḥ karma-vedhasaḥ //*[37]

People get the fruit of their actions in proportion to their—or their actions'—nature:

*karmaṇām ucitaṁ teṣāṁ prāṇināṁ jayate phalam /*[38]

---

[34] *Brahma-vaivarta-purāṇa* 1.23.7.

[35] *Skanda-puraṇa* (*Maheśvara-khaṇḍe Kaumārikā-khaṇḍa*) 10.8.

[36] *Padma-purāṇa* 14.41

[37] *Mahā-purāṇa* 4.67.

[38] *Mahā-purāṇa* 13.68.

That being the case it is in their own interest that people perform good actions. With merit earned through them, they would have happiness. With their actions earning demerit, they would opt for unhappiness. Accordingly says the *Padma-purāṇa*:

*puṇyena labhyate saukhyam apuṇyena ca duḥkhitā* /
*karmaṇām ucitaṁ lokaḥ sarvaḥ phalam upāśnute* //[39]

Death would forcibly carry away a person, says the *Agni-purāṇa*, if whatever fruit of actions one is to reap in the present birth had been reaped:

*āyuṣye karmaṇi kṣīṇe prasahya harate janam* /[40]

But if some fruit of the actions still remains to be reaped, a person would not meet with death even if pierced with hundreds of arrows: *viddhaḥ śara-śatair api*[41]. It is necessary for a person, therefore, to go in for actions with judicious application of mind. There are actions which are enjoined for certain types of people. A Brahmin is to engage himself in pursuit of learning and spiritual activities, a Kṣatriya is to apply himself to martial acts, and so on. Now, it is imperative for him to stick to those actions under all circumstances, even in adversity, says the *Brahmâṇḍa-purāṇa*:

*sadhu vâsādhu vā karma yasya yad vihitaṁ purā* /
*tad eva tena kartavyam āpady api kathañcana* //[42]

Indian culture has always aimed at producing a good and decent human being, always eager to pick up good qualities, as the *Ādi-purāṇa* says: *guṇa-gṛhyo hi saj-janaḥ*. A graphic picture of a good human being is given by this *Purāṇa* which should always remain an ideal to be achieved by all:

*sadbhāvena haren mitraṁ sambhrameṇa ca bāndhavān* /
*strī-bhṛtyān prema-dānābhyāṁ dākṣiṇyenêtaraṁ janam* //
*anindā para-kṛtyeṣu svadharma-paripālanam* /
*kṛpaṇeṣu dayālutvaṁ sarvatra madhurā giraḥ* //
*bandhubhir baddha-saṁyogaḥ svajane caturatratā* /
*ucitânuvidhāyitvam iti vṛttaṁ mahâtmanām* //[43]

---

[39] *Padma-purāṇa* 31.176.

[40] *Agni-purāṇa* 159.11–12.

[41] *Ibid.*

[42] *Brahmâṇḍa-purāṇa* 3.23.76.

[43] *Ādi-purāṇa* 238.18–22.

The conduct of the high-souled one is as follows: he should win over a friend by goodwill, the relatives by trust, the women with love, the servants with gifts, and others with politeness. He should not engage himself in finding fault with the actions of others, he should carry out his duties, be kind to the lowly and be sweet with everybody. He should maintain good relations with his kinsmen, be fair in his dealings with his kith and kin and do whatever is in order.

One who is of the type mentioned above, is a good human being. And the development of such good human being is basic to Indian culture. The *Purāṇas* being the repositories of this culture have enough statements in them, thrown in between their countless narratives which recount the imperatives, for this good human being, a cultured person, who is useful to everybody and everything around him.

# BHARTṚHARI: LANGUAGE AND TRUTH

# The Meaning of Verse 25 of the *Saṁbandha-samuddeśa* and its Context

CLAUS OETKE

## –1–

The verse 25 of the *Saṁbandha-samuddeśa* of Bhartṛhari's *Vākya-padīya* has been understood as dealing with a variant of a Liar Paradox. Apart from other scholars, this view has been advocated recently by J. HOUBEN (1995) in his book on the *Saṁbandha-samuddeśa* and Bhartṛhari's philosophy of language. I want to critically discuss this view in the light of a number of other verses belonging to the same chapter which appear to possess special relevance for the identification of the argumentative context in which *kārikā* 25 is embedded.

The crucial verse reads as follows:

> /25/ *sarvaṁ mithyā bravīmîti nâitad vākyaṁ vivakṣyate /*
> *tasya mithyâbhidhāne hi prakrānto 'rtho na gamyate //*

> /25/ '[With the expression] "Everything I say [I say] falsely," that expression is not intended to be meant, for if this is declared as [being said] false[ly] the object / meaning in question is not attained / understood.'

HOUBEN's translation of the *kārikā* runs as follows (1995: 227):

> 'With "everything I am saying is false," that statement itself is not meant. For if its own expressing is false, one does not arrive at the point in question.'

Regarding the import of the verse HOUBEN (1995: 227–228) makes the following statement:

> 'The fact that Bhartṛhari brings in the statement "everything I am saying is false" at this place shows that he was well aware of its problematic status. Therefore, if Bhartṛhari emphasizes here that the statement itself is not intended, the possibility is implied of someone proposing that such statement *did* refer to itself, with contradiction as the result. In 20 the

*Essays in Indian Philosophy, Religion and Literature*, pp. 161–201.

> same happened with the statement "[something is] unsignifiable". There, the bivalent option was between signifiable and unsignifiable; here in 25 it is between true and false. This suffices to make it a real Liar paradox, though it is only the weak paradox in which one of the two options leads inescapably to contradiction, and not an artificially strengthened one. It is the universally quantified Liar, and Bhartṛhari solves the paradox by showing that there can be no quantification over itself on the basis of the function which is usually out of the picture in Western accounts, viz. the intention of the speaker.'

Our remarks concerning the above cited passage pertain in the first place to the following ingredients:

1. '... Bhartṛhari brings in the statement "everything I am saying is false" at this place ...'
2. '... the possibility is implied of someone proposing that such statement *did* refer to itself, with contradiction as the result.'
3. '... the bivalent option ... is between true and false.'
4. 'This suffices to make it a real Liar Paradox ... and Bhartṛhari solves the paradox by showing that there can be no quantification over itself on the basis of the function which is usually out of the picture in Western accounts, viz. the intention of the speaker.'

(A) (1) The verse nowhere says or indicates 'that there can be no quantification over itself.' It contains a universal quantifier but does not employ any term that possesses the sense of 'quantification' or a similar meaning. (2) The wording of the pertinent verse does not furnish the slightest indication that it should provide us with any *solution* of a paradox or any philosophical problem at all. What the *kārikā* suggests is merely that *if* in an utterance of *sarvaṁ mithyā bravīmi* the phrase *mithyā bravīmi* were used in order to refer to this very statement itself, an unacceptable consequence would result.

(B) Not only can one not recognise any indication that it was intended that the verse should offer a solution of a problem, but one cannot even discern, how the remark of this *kārikā* should objectively contain the material for a solution of a problem, not to speak of a general solution of a philosophical paradox. For: (1) The mere *statement that* an unacceptable consequence would result, if in an utterance of *sarvaṁ mithyā bravīmi* the phrase *mithyā bravīmi* were used in order to refer to this very statement itself, provides no solution of any problem at all. At best it testifies to the fact that a possible problem has been *recognised.* (2) The utterance of the phrase *sarvaṁ mithyā bravīmi* does not by itself evoke a paradox, even if it were meant in the sense of 'Everything I am saying is false' and if the range of the universal quantification were taken as encompassing the concerned utterance or sentence or its possible content itself. If the pertinent utterer, as a matter of fact, should have said something true at any time, the utterance, sentence or its propositional content could simply be regarded as false, and this is by no means paradoxical. HOUBEN, to be sure, might have recognised this and speaks of a weak (liar) paradox in this connection. Nevertheless, a paradox emerges at best in combination with an additional premise according to which everything the concerned utterer has uttered—apart from the pertinent utterance—is, as a matter of fact, false. The possible paradox would lie in the circumstance that some statement can neither be true nor false under certain empirical circumstances which do not pertain to the statement itself. But even so the question arises as to why the writer of the verse did not indicate anything of this. To be sure, we say 'possible paradox' because it is conceivable that the concerned circumstances create a situation in which some utterance of some declarative sentence cannot possess or express a content which is able to be either true or false. Since this assumption is by no means evidently absurd, it deserves to be noted that neither the pertinent verse nor anything in the context of this *kārikā* indicates anything about such a possibility. (3) One might indeed discern an implicit suggestion to the effect that one who utters *sarvaṁ mithyā bravīmi* should not intend to refer among other things to this very phrase itself. Nevertheless, this merely shows how a particular difficulty pertaining to a *particular* expression *can* be circumvented. But even if it were supposed that a generalisation was intended—although the text does not contain any salient indicator to that effect—it remains dubious how this could be suited for the solution of any paradox. It is definitely unsuited for a solution of the problem if this should ensue from the observation that a particular phrase uttered with the intention to make a statement cannot be either true or false due to circumstances which do not relate to the concerned utterance itself. For if any paradox lies in this supposition it obviously ensues from the idea that some assertoric sentence can be neither true nor false under one of its possible readings. The mere fact that also other possible readings exist which do not involve such consequences appears entirely irrelevant in this context. Consequently, any appeal to the circumstance that the expression *sarvaṁ mithyā bravīmi* also possesses a possible reading which does not evoke any paradox and that it is possible to employ the sentence in a way that such a reading is intended is almost as immaterial for a solution of the pertinent problem as any invocation of the fact that apart from sentences involving a liar paradox also other sentences exist (which do not involve similar consequences) would be immaterial for a solution of liar paradoxes. Therefore it needs to be acknowledged that *if* HOUBEN's suggestion that Bhartṛhari in *kārikā* 25 aimed at furnishing a solution of some variety of a liar paradox by 'showing that there can be no quantification over itself on the basis of the function which is usually out of the picture in Western accounts, viz. the intention of the speaker' were true, *then* it would follow that the pertinent subject matter has been dealt with by the author of the verse in an inadequate, if not superficial, manner. Since the context does not provide more information on the topic of *sarvaṁ mithyā bravīmi* the treatment of the issue as a whole would have to be assessed as very deficient.

(C) The assumption that *kārikā* 25 refers to any truth-paradox as well as the translation of *sarvaṁ mithyā bravīmi* by 'Everything I am saying is false' is philologically questionable. The circumstance that *mithyā* is grammatically an adverb diminishes the probability that the phrase should possess the sense of 'Everything I am saying is false' as well as the probability of the supposition that *sarvaṁ mithyā bravīmi* should relate at all to the application of any predicate to the content of sentences or statements. Moreover, there are many other formulations which would express the sense of 'Everything I am saying is false' in an unambiguous manner, e.g. *sarvaṁ mayôktam asatyam, mayôktam anṛtaṁ sarvaṁ*, etc.[1] To be sure, according to some statements that are to be found in various dictionaries concerning *mithyā*, it should be legitimate to translate *sarvaṁ mithyā bravīmi* by 'Everything I am saying is a lie.' But it is possible that even this rendering would not do justice to the point. If one wants to characterise the import of *sarvaṁ mithyā bravīmi* in a manner that is sufficiently general, one should perhaps equate it with something like: 'I never (really) mean what I say.' Regarding the question as to what precisely this means one should envisage at least the following two possibilities: (a) The phrase expresses that every declarative utterance which is made by the speaker expresses something which is not considered as true by the utterer himself. (b) The phrase expresses that everything uttered by the speaker does not possess the sense which the pertinent expression should have according to the relevant linguistic rules but some other sense, possibly exactly the contrary sense. Although (a) represents the situation of a habitual liar, there is a decisive difference with respect to the situation described by 'Everything I am saying is false': The truth of the pertinent statement does not entail that everything—in fact not even anything—the speaker utters *is* false. The sentence *sarvaṁ mithyā bravīmi* refers merely to the intention of the speaker and relates to the fact that utterances of the speaker have been made with the intention of expressing untruths. The same holds true, *mutatis mutandis*, regarding alternative (b): It amounts to the claim that the meaning-intentions associated with all utterances of the speaker deviate from those which one would expect them to possess on the basis of pertinent linguistic rules. The decisive point is that the characterisation which is implicitly given by the expression *mithyā* does not pertain to any propositional content but to intentions that are connected with certain speech acts.

[1] We regard it as little promising to invoke 'metrical constraints' as an argument here.

It is not difficult to discern that an utterance of *sarvaṁ mithyā bravīmi* generates problems even under the interpretation(s) with respect to the import of *mithyā bravīmi* ('I speak falsely'), which has (have) been delineated in the preceding paragraph. If the range of the universal quantifier is not restricted, a situation ensues which involves a frustration of those communicative goals which a declarative utterance of the phrase would normally possess. Irrespective of whether we hypothesise alternative (a) or (b) above, if the utterer subsumes the very utterance of *sarvaṁ mithyā bravīmi* under the concept represented by the predicate of the sentence, i.e. 'is said falsely', any possibility of a unique determination of a proposition which the utterance should convey as true is thwarted. It should be noted that this holds good even under the supposition that *mithyā* ('falsely') possesses the precise import of referring to the fact that actual states-of-affairs or intended meanings are exactly opposite to those which the sentences uttered by the speaker should convey or express.[2] For if this were supposed, it would follow that the actual state of affairs which the utterer of *sarvaṁ mithyā bravīmi* believes to obtain corresponds to one which would be expressed by the sentence: 'Everything I say, I say truly,' or that the meaning which has to be associated with *mithyā bravīmi* corresponds to the meaning of 'I say truly.' But if the proposition which the utterer really believes is in the described manner opposite to the one which the sentence *sarvaṁ mithyā bravīmi* linguistically expresses, he is committed to believe that his utterance of *sarvaṁ mithyā bravīmi* is made with an intention of expressing something true. However, if this is the case, the utterer must intend to express something which entails that the very utterance of the pertinent sentence is made with the intention of expressing something which is not true. The identification of a proposition which the speaker of the sentence considers as true is doomed to failure for similar reasons as if someone uttered: 'I do not believe what I am saying now.' On the other hand, the supposition that the intended meaning of *mithyā bravīmi* corresponds to: 'I do not speak in accordance with valid linguistic rules,' implies both that the utterance of *sarvaṁ mithyā bravīmi* possesses its regular sense and that it does not. To be sure, if our proposed alternative interpretation is adopted the consequence that the concerned sentence or utterance cannot be true does not follow. It follows merely that either the utterance does not give any relevant information about what the utterer considers true or about what the actual (in contradistinction to the conventional) meaning of the employed expression should be. But this is no sound reason for an objection. On the contrary. The wording of the last quarter of the *kārikā*, viz. *prakrānto 'rtho na gamyate* = 'the object / goal / meaning

---

[2] *Nota bene*: We have said 'exactly opposite,' not 'contradictory'. The exact opposite of 'Everything I say is such and such' should correspond to 'Everything I say is not such and such,' and not to 'Not everything I say is such and such.'

which is undertaken / envisaged is not understood / reached', fits the above depicted alternative consequences much better. It deserves to be pointed out that even if HOUBEN's assumption regarding the import of *mithyā* were accurate, the formulation *prakrānto 'rtho na gamyate* does not support the supposition that ensuing consequences concerning the possibility of the truth of the statement and their avoidance are at stake. Let us grant—for the sake of argument—that *sarvaṁ mithyā bravīmi* means 'Everything I am saying is false.' Does not the occurrence of the phrase *prakrānto 'rtho na gamyate* make it appear more probable that under this premise Bhartṛhari had the following in mind: 'An assertoric utterance of *sarvaṁ mithyā bravīmi*—or any other sentence—is successful only if anyone who interprets this utterance can rightly assume that the utterer regards as true what the sentence must express in accordance with pertinent rules of interpreting the sentence and the statement made by it; but the realisation of this aim is prevented if the expressed proposition entails that the statement cannot be true'? If our interpretation is correct, the point is not that the content of some (uttered) sentence involves a semantic anomaly under one of its possible readings but that the *utterance* of the phrase *sarvaṁ mithyā bravīmi* is infelicitous because the goals which should be hypothesised as existing would be necessarily thwarted, if it were intended to make a statement involving a universal quantification whose domain includes the pertinent utterance, statement or sentence itself.[3] I assume that this difference is highly important for the interpretation of the entire textual passage which constitutes the context of verse 25 of the *Saṁbandha-samuddeśa*, but for the time being I put this topic aside.

Since according to our interpretation the restriction of the range of the quantifier that might be considered as being proposed in verse 25[4] does not relate to the solution of a paradox but to the avoidance of a frustration of communicative goals, we are confronted with a problem which does not affect the alternative interpretation in the same way. For whereas the idea of the solution of a paradox at once bestows plausibility on the occurrence of the pertinent remark, it is not immediately intelligible why the topic of stratagems for the removal of obstacles for the realisation of certain communicative goals should have been brought up in the present textual passage. We

[3] It needs to be noticed that the expression *na gamyate* does not even suggest the existence of a contradiction and that the employment of other expressions, in particular *virudhyate*, which do involve such a suggestion, would have been excellently suitable if the idea of any kind of contradiction should be conveyed.

[4] The reason why I am using the clumsy formulation 'might be considered as being proposed' is that, if one looks at the matter more closely, it turns out to be doubtful whether the writer of verse 25 really intended to advocate a quantifier-restriction as a solution to some problem. But we will discuss this issue only at the end of the paper.

claim, however, that in view of the context this fact can be made perfectly comprehensible. In order to demonstrate this, I will give an outline of the way in which the verse 25 is embedded in the argumentative context. This entails an explication of the import of a number of verses that precede *kārikā* 25 in the chapter which bears the name *Saṁbandha-samuddeśa*. It needs to be said in advance, however, that we will not undertake here a detailed investigation of all the interpretative possibilities with respect to every verse and do not offer a fully explicit justification for the proposed reconstruction, since I intend to discuss these issues in another paper. Nevertheless, our account will present a highly plausible train of thought, and at least in this regard our proposal appears superior to previous interpretations.

## –2–

We assume that the following *kārikās* represent the key positions with respect to the argumentation in which the statement of verse 25 is embedded:

/1/ *jñānaṁ prayoktur bāhyo 'rthaḥ svarūpaṁ ca pratīyate /*
*śabdair uccaritais teṣāṁ saṁbandhaḥ samavasthitaḥ //*

/3/ *asyâyaṁ vācako vācya iti ṣaṣṭhyā pratīyate /*
*yogaḥ śabdârthayos tattvam apy ato vyapadiśyate*[5] //

/4/ *nâbhidhānaṁ sva-dharmeṇa saṁbandhasyâsti vācakam /*
*atyanta-para-tantratvād rūpaṁ nâsyâpadiśyate //*

/20/ *avācyam iti yad vācyaṁ tad avācyatayā yadā /*
*vācyam ity avasīyeta vācyam eva tadā bhavet //*

/21/ *athâpy avācyam ity evaṁ na tad vācyaṁ pratīyate /*
*vivakṣitâsya yâvasthā sâiva nādhyavasīyate //*

/22/ *tathânyathā*[6] *sarvathā ca yasyâvācyatvam ucyate /*
*tatrâpi nâiva sâvasthā*[7] *taiḥ śabdaiḥ pratiṣidhyate //*

/23/ *na hi saṁśaya-rūpe 'rthe śeṣatvena vyavasthite /*
*avyudāse svarūpasya saṁśayo 'nyaḥ pravartate*[8] //

/24/ *yadā ca nirṇaya-jñāne nirṇayatvena nirṇayaḥ /*
*prakramyate tadā jñānaṁ sva-dharme nâvatiṣṭhate*[9] //

---

[5] The variants: *ity ato*, *athato*, instead of *apy ato*, are potentially relevant.

[6] Variant: *athânyathā*.

[7] Variant: *sâiva nâvasthā*.

[8] Relevant variant: *pratīyate*.

[9] Variant: *sva-dharmeṇâvatiṣṭhate*.

These verses can be translated as follows:

/1/ 'Through words which are uttered the cognition of the one who employs [them], the external object and their own form are discerned; their relation is [already] established.'

/3/ '[In the expressions:] "This is a / the signifier of this" [and "This] is the *significandum* of this" the link between word and meaning is known / understood by the sixth nominal ending (i.e. the genitive ending). Also the being-that is conveyed on that account.'

/4/ 'There is no expression which is a signifier of the relation (*saṁbandha*) according to / on account of its own *dharma* (property, nature). Because of [its] being absolutely dependent, its nature is not pointed out.'

/20/ [Objection:] 'If it were ascertained that what is to be said (= characterised) [by the words:] "[it is] not to be said (= characterised)"[10], were to be said (= characterised) by [the property of] being something which is not to be said (= characterised), then it would be [something which] *is* to be said (= characterised).'[11]

/21/ 'If, however, it is not recognised as [being something which] is to be said (= characterised) in that way by "[it is] not to be said = characterised)," [then] the very situation which is wanted to be expressed is not ascertained.'

---

[10] I.e. '[it] should not be said (= characterised)' or '[it] can not be said (= characterised)'. Although the existence of the same ambiguity must be kept in mind even with respect to the other occurrences of *(a)vācya-*, we attempt to propose interpretations which do not crucially depend on particular decisions in this regard.

[11] Or alternatively: 'If that which is to be said (= characterised) [by the words:] "[it is] not to be said (= characterised)" were ascertained as [something which is] to be said (= characterised) by [the property of] being something which is not to be said (= characterised), then it would be [something which] *is* to be said (= characterised).' This possibility exists because the formulation of the verse does not contain sufficiently specific indications regarding the intended scope of the occurrence of *iti* after *vācyam*. For the general interpretation of the textual interpretation which we propose, this difference seems to be irrelevant, however. This holds equally good with respect to the question as to whether the instrumental case of *avācyatayā* should be interpreted as expressing a 'genuine' instrumental meaning or rather as possessing a 'modal' sense such that *avācyatayā* … *vācyam* should be rendered by 'is to be said (= characterised) as [something which is] not to be said (= characterised).'

/22/ 'It is not so that even with regard to that whose unsignifiability in this, in another or in every manner is said / asserted, this situation is prevented by those words.'

/23/ [Reply:] '[This objection is not valid.] For with regard to an entity possessing the nature of a doubt, which is determined as something subsidiary, another doubt does not become operative as long as its own nature is not thrown off.'

/24/ 'And when with regard to an ascertainment-cognition, an ascertainment as an ascertainment is undertaken, then the cognition does not persist in its own character.'[12]

What train of thoughts does this represent? I propose the following account:

---

[12] HOUBEN (1995: 145 ff.) gives the following rendering:

'/1/ The cognition of the speaker, the external thing meant and the own form [of the word] are understood through words which are uttered. The relation of these (namely, the cognition, external thing meant and own form) [with the words which are uttered] is well-established.

/3/ "This is the signifier of this, [and this] is the signified [of this]," thus the connection of word and thing-meant is known through the sixth nominal ending (genitive). On this ground, the real nature (*tattvam*, sc. of word and thing-meant) is also indicated.

/4/ There is no word that signifies the relation according to its specific property. Because it is extremely dependent, its form cannot be pointed out.

/20/ If it is ascertained that what is to be signified by "unsignifiable" is signifiable as being unsignifiable, then it would become signifiable.

/21/ But if it is understood that it cannot be signified this way by "unsignifiable", that very situation of its which one wants to signify is not apprehended.

/22/ If something is signified as unsignifiable, in this way, in another way or in all ways, then with regard to that thing this situation (*avasthā*, sc. being unsignifiable) is certainly not (*na eva*) also denied by those [very] words [that signify its being unsignifiable].

/23/ No other $doubt_2$ is operative with regard to an object which is [itself] a $doubt_1$ and is [as such] subordinate, if [$doubt_1$] does not lose its own character [of a doubt or, more generally, of a cognition which functions towards and is subordinate to some object].

/24/ And when an $ascertainment_2$ is undertaken, with the characteristics of an ascertainment, concerning [another] ascertaining $cognition_1$, then that [other] $cognition_1$ does not remain in its own nature.'

The first *kārikā* formulates a general theorem which says that the utterance of linguistic expressions conveys three things, namely (a) a cognitive or, more generally, a psychological state of the utterer[13], (b) an 'external'—i.e. probably a non-linguistic and non-mental—object[14], and (c) the 'own form' of the concerned linguistic expression[15]. The relation of the expressions, i.e. obviously their meaning relation, is however fixed beforehand. This last statement possesses utmost significance in the present context. It appears that Bhartṛhari intends to say here that meaning relations are not something which is imparted as new information by linguistic expressions and, accordingly, not something which is recognised on the part of a hearer *by* the utterance of linguistic expressions, but something which is established in advance. This suggests the following picture: On account of utterances of linguistic expressions, a hearer *recognises* only (a) the existence of certain psychological states of the speaker, (b) what the expressions signify or express and (c) linguistic types corresponding to the uttered tokens. But once these components are identified there is nothing additional which needs to be recognised or which is imparted as new information, and this holds true in particular of the semantic relations which are associated with the pertinent linguistic types. *Prima facie* at least this appears quite plausible.[16]

But now, in the *kārikā*s 3–4, a difficulty for the view presented in verse 1 is implicitly recognised and accounted for. The tenet that semantic relations are *never* imparted by utterances of linguistic expressions appears to be untenable in view of the fact that *sometimes* utterances occur which aim at giving information about semantic relations, in particular (utterances of) expressions of the form: 'A is the signifier of B,' 'B is the *significandum* of A,' or similar ones. Verses 3 and 4 represent nothing but an answer to this difficulty. The essence of the reply appears

[13] This might be identified with the utterer's 'propositional attitudes' of beliefs, desires, etc., inasmuch as their existence can be inferred from the very fact that certain expressions have been uttered.

[14] This might be identified with an expressed proposition or a state of affairs or, in case of naming expressions, a particular object.

[15] Perhaps this should be identified with the corresponding type of a token-expression or anything which comes quite close to the notion of a type.

[16] In the subsequent *kārikā* 2, Bhartṛhari makes the additional point that uncertainties or doubts pertain merely to the cognitive states of the utterer as well as to the 'external objects', but never to the 'own forms'. On the background of the suggested identification of 'own forms' (*svarūpa*) with types this assertion might appear doubtful. But possibly, this is due to the fact that the notion of a type represents only an approximation to the concept of 'own form' which might come close to that of a pattern which is exemplified by some sequence (of sounds or phonemes).

to be the following: It is acknowledged that statements specifying semantic relations occur, and it is even admitted that expressions performing such a function might contain linguistic elements—in particular the genitive morpheme—which relate to semantic relations. But this does not refute the original thesis that linguistic expressions generally do not specify their own semantic relations. The reason is the following: Linguistic elements such as genitive morphemes relate to semantic relations at best in a general way, but they can never perform the function of fixing the semantic relations of the expressions in which they occur or impart any information about them. This is so because the semantic relations which are at stake in the theorem formulated in verse 1 are not semantic relations in general but the particular semantic relations of uttered expression-tokens or their corresponding types (or patterns). They are essentially or constantly dependent at least in the following regards: 1. being individual relations, their identity depends on the identity of their *relata* in a similar manner in which the identity of 'quality-individuals' (*guṇa*) depends on the identity of the substances in which they inhere; 2. being something which linguistic expressions exhibit or possess, such that the knowledge of the fact that linguistic expressions exhibit them makes it possible that utterances of them convey information, in particular the kind of information that has been specified in verse 1, they can at best be *exploited* for the purpose of deriving information from the expressions exhibiting them whenever they are uttered, but it is not possible that the very same expressions which exhibit them fix or specify those semantic relations. Such specifications could at best be achieved by the employment of *different* expressions which refer to the former ones and characterise them with respect to their meaning relations.[17] This tenet is objectively plausible if it is taken in a specific way: Linguistic expressions cannot specify their semantic relations in the manner of providing characterisations or descriptions of them such

[17] In this connection it might be appropriate to point out that the interpretation of *atyanta-para-tantratvā[t]* in verse 4, according to which the expression is meant to relate to the meaning relation, represents merely one possible alternative. It would be by no means outlandish to interpret it as referring to the act which is described by the words *rūpam ... asyâpadiśyate* that follow immediately. This means that *atyanta-para-tantratvā[t]* could equally be used in order to convey that the (own) nature of any individual meaning relation cannot be imparted (by expressions which themselves exhibit that meaning relation), because any act of doing this necessarily—this might be the import of *atyanta-* in this particular context—depends on something else (*para*), namely other means of conveying a meaning apart from the concerned expression(s). To be sure, it seems rather improbable that this should be the only intended sense of *atyanta-para-tantratvā[t]*. But it is by no means unlikely that the author of the verse intended that the formulation should be understood in both senses.

that the content of the descriptions is determined by nothing else than the meaning of linguistic expressions. To be sure, Bhartṛhari nowhere makes this restraint explicit. But this does not refute that it harmonises with his intentions. Probably the author was not aware of the fact that a specification of this sort might be objectively required. Anyhow, if one looks at the situation under this aspect, the tenet appears highly plausible: Linguistic expressions, in particular sentences, never fix their meaning relations by giving true descriptions or characterisations of them inasmuch as the content of those descriptions is determined by the meaning relations of expressions containing them. They cannot objectively specify their meaning relations in this manner at least under certain assumptions of the dependence of sentence-meaning on meanings of their constituent parts. On the other hand, and this was possibly more what Bhartṛhari had in view, they cannot impart in this manner complete knowledge about their meaning to a hearer of utterances, because in order to grasp the content of the pertinent descriptions he must exploit previously existing knowledge concerning meaning relations of expressions that belong to the sentence in question. If such knowledge should be imparted at all by description, it is not the concerned expression itself but other expressions that must be invoked, more precisely the expressions whose understanding does not require a complete understanding of the concerned expression.

Although the possible objection on account of metalinguistic uses of expressions can be, as it seems, satisfactorily answered in this manner, the reply is threatened by the danger of self-inconsistency, and we suppose that this topic is dealt with in the textual passage which begins with *kārikā* 20.

## –3–

A component of the crucial theorem of *kārikā* 1 can be expressed as follows: No linguistic expression gives a true description of its meaning relation and thereby fixes its meaning. Although this is, strictly speaking, not tantamount to the thesis that no linguistic expression *can* fix its meaning by giving a true description of its meaning relation, it is not improbable that Bhartṛhari's position embraced also the thesis which is formulated by the preceding sentence. The crucial point is, however, that this holds good under a particular reading of 'No linguistic expression gives a true description of its meaning relation.' The idea that meaning relations are fixed beforehand and are exploited in order to identify the 'external' objects corresponding as meanings to linguistic expressions in situations of their utterance makes it natural to suppose that no sentence can be used in such a manner that it expresses a true characterisation of its own meaning relation because the identification of this particular meaning relation depends—apart from the sentence itself—on its meaning, or in Bhartṛhari's terms, on the external object which it means. Accordingly, what the sentence which should say something about its meaning relation means must be considered as determining what it is about. But since it is natural to suppose that, the other way round, what a sentence means is determined by what it is about, in the case of descriptive sentences the object of predication, a mutual dependency—that which Indian philosophers designate by the technical term *parasparâśraya*—threatens to emerge from the supposition. The relevant sense of 'No linguistic expression gives a true description of its meaning relation' is accordingly that no linguistic expression can be employed in a way that it both is true and expresses the subsumption of its own meaning relation under some concept. An 'epistemic' correlate of this position would be that it is impossible for a speaker to convey to somebody else what the meaning relation, or let us say the sense[18], of any linguistic expression he utters is like, merely by formulating a true (and sufficiently exhaustive) description of this meaning relation (sense) by the very same expression which is uttered. The relevant consideration is that the addressee, in order to identify what the description is about, must have identified the meaning relation (sense) of the pertinent expression, which requires that he knows beforehand what it is. If it is really true that such knowledge has to rely on a prior identification of what the characterisation given by the expression is about as well as of the meaning relation of all the predicates occurring in the expression, there is little hope to get rid of the circularity.

In view of the occurrence of the expression *sva-dharmeṇa* in *kārikā* 4, it is not unreasonable to assume that the thesis is even a bit more specific than it has been depicted above: It might not concern characterisations or descriptions of meaning relations in general but specifically such characterisations which provide essential descriptions in the sense that if one knows that the description applies to something, one is also equipped with knowledge which puts one in a position to identify the particular meaning relation, i.e. one knows *which* meaning relation is concerned. We leave it to the reader's discretion to take the pertinent theorems in the broader or the narrower sense.

In the present context we need not discuss the question as to whether the considerations suggested above are in fact objectively cogent. It matters however

---

[18] I use the word 'sense' here and at some other places mainly as an abbreviation and stylistic variant of the expression 'meaning relation'. But it will also be used in order to suggest that in certain regards the difference between Bhartṛhari's concept of 'meaning relation' and other notions of 'meaning' or 'sense' is not relevant.

that an inconsistency is imminent here which can be best depicted on the background of a less specific example.

Let us suppose that someone makes the assertion:

(S) Nothing true has ever been said about Socrates.

Let us further assume that (S) has been used in order to express that nothing true has ever been said about Socrates. The following objection imposes itself: Granted that, apart from (S), nothing true has ever been said about Socrates. Even then there is the following dilemma, namely

(A) (S) should say about Socrates that nothing true has ever been said about him.

or

(B) (S) should not say about Socrates that nothing true has ever been said about him.

In the case of (A) the assertion of (S) becomes self-refuting. This results from the circumstance that the very act of making the assertion of (S) creates a situation which falsifies the statement. For by making this assertion a situation has been created in which *something* has been said about Socrates, namely that nothing true has ever been said about him. Therefore, if (S) should say about Socrates that absolutely nothing true has ever been said about him, it is impossible that the assertion be true. In the case of (B), on the other hand, the assertion of (S) would not express what it should express because one of the assumptions was that (S) has been used in order to express that nothing has ever been said about Socrates. But now it might appear that this reasoning could be assailed on account of the following consideration:

(C) The presented reasoning does not entail a refutation of the tenet. It merely demonstrates that the range of the quantification should be taken in an absolutely unrestricted manner so that it relates also to the predicate of (S). In other words, (S) should be understood as saying that absolutely nothing true has ever been said about Socrates, including this that nothing true has ever been said about him. Under these premises, the circumstance that the assertion of (S)—both under supposition (A) and (B)—cannot be true is welcome. For it is precisely this fact which entails that, under the given premise that nothing true has been said about Socrates elsewhere, absolutely nothing true has ever been said about him. But this is precisely what is asserted by (S) under supposition (A) and this confirms the assertion of (S).

This might appear baffling at first glance, but it needs to be accounted for. What could one say about that move? If one wants to give a concise description of the bizarreness of the situation which is envisaged in (C) one might say that it is absurd to suppose that nothing else but the self-refuting character of some sentence or statement should constitute a basis for its truth. But one might put the point also differently:

> 'If one asserts about something that nothing can be said about it in one way or the other or in no way at all, one states that a certain situation obtains, namely the situation that the concerned entity is such that nothing can be said about it in one way or the other or in no way at all. But the "verification" that has been proposed in (C) relies on the premise that precisely the situation which must be expressed—under the pertinent supposition (A)—cannot obtain, because it has been derived among others from the assumption that (S) should not even correctly say that about the pertinent subject which it should say that nothing true has ever been said about it. By resorting to the idea that one's statement should be verified by denying with respect to some entity the state which it should ascribe to it one becomes even more entangled in self-inconsistency. Therefore the rejoinder which is envisaged in (C) deserves to be rejected.'

A different, but parallel objection could run as follows: The following alternative is exhaustive, namely

> (A)* Socrates is in fact such as he is claimed to be by the assertion of (S).

or

> (B)* Socrates is in fact not such as he is claimed to be by the assertion of (S).

In case of (A)* the assertion of (S) is self-refuting for analogous reasons as above. In case of (B)* the situation whose existence is claimed by the assertion, whatever this might be, cannot be ascertained as obtaining. Accordingly, it is impossible that the assertion of (S) is true. The continuation would correspond to (C) and its dismissal.

I want to suggest that the reasoning represented in the *kārikā*s 20–22 parallels the one depicted above. It is not difficult to discern, how the analogy might look like. But since the wording leaves room for different readings, we prefer to proceed slowly and carefully. On one of the readings, the role of the assertion of (S) would be played by (a statement of) a theorem which can be formulated as follows:

(T) E cannot be truly described in any manner.[19]

What 'E' refers to is immaterial. What matters is only that—by hypothesis—the term has been employed in (the claim made by) (T) in such a way that it refers to something in particular.[20] The two alternatives corresponding to (A) and (B) above are:

(1) E can be truly described in the manner in which it is described in (T).

or

(2) E cannot be truly described in the manner in which it is described in (T).

Evidently, if (1) were assumed, (T) cannot be regarded as true. It would be impossible to maintain the claim in its generality. If (2) were supposed, the possibility is precluded that (T) might give a true description of E, and since it appears that (T) can only be true if what it says about E holds true of E, the possibility of the truth of (T) would be ruled out under this hypothesis too. Moreover, if it is supposed that (T) is used with the intention of making a true statement or of conveying some correct information, the relevant (communicative) goal is frustrated. As before, the issue is not yet completely settled, because it could be retorted that precisely the inconsistencies which are invoked by the opponent give room for the possibility that the statement made by (T) represents the situation as it is. But again the price is high because this idea exploits the consideration that (T) *cannot* provide a true description of E. Admittedly, I have attributed to the remark represented by verse 22 an argumentative role which is not necessitated by the wording. Perhaps it appears more natural to read *kārikā* 22 as stating merely that, if something is asserted to be indescribable in some way or the other, the proponent cannot simply accept the fact that the utterance of his words creates a situation which militates against his thesis of indescribability, in other words, he cannot acquiesce in granting that his assertion entails the consequence mentioned in verse 20. One should note, however, that both interpretations are not so different:

[19] This is in fact only a variant formulation of 'Nothing true can be said about E,' which we employ here in order to make the affinity to the original wording of the text more obvious.

[20] This is, by the way, a plausible explanation as to why *kārikās* 20–22 do not offer any specification of the relevant subject that is described as *avācya* ('unsignifiable'). It should also be mentioned that the omission of a term designating the logical subject of predication might in this context perform exactly the same function as the employment of 'arbitrary names' in modern logic.

Whereas on the alternative reading verse 22 expresses that the proponent cannot be satisfied with the consequence that is pointed out in *kārikā* 20 it conveys according to the reading envisaged here that the proponent cannot use that consequence and transform it to a positive argument for his contention. My inclination to favour the latter interpretation stems from the fact that it enables us to avoid the conclusion that verse 22 merely explicates what has been implicitly conveyed before so that it could even engender an impression of repetitiousness.

But we must envisage another equally possible reading because of the fact that the expression *vācya*, in particular *vācya* in certain syntagmata with constituents in the instrumental, can be understood *both* in the sense of 'can be said / expressed / characterised as,' which might amount to something like 'is correctly / truly described / describable as,' *and* in the sense of 'is to be said / expressed / characterised as' = 'should be said / expressed / characterised as' = 'is such that someone intends to say of it that it is such and such / describe it as such and such ...'. The same holds good *mutatis mutandis* for *avācya* and all related expressions. Thus, if everything were made fully explicit, the pertinent theorem would amount to something which could be formulated as follows:

(T)* There is no true statement by which it has been intended to say anything true about E.

The dilemma is:

(1)* (T)* should truly say about E that there is no true statement by which it has been intended to say anything true about it.

or

(2)* (T)* should not truly say about E that there is no true statement by which it has been intended to say anything true about it.[21]

In an analogous manner as before, under the first alternative the assertive utterance of (T)* engenders a situation which prevents the truth of (the statement made by) (T)*. For *if* its truth *were* supposed, it would follow that the statement of (T)* itself fulfils the descriptive content of the predicate of (T)*, viz. 'is a true

[21] In a more pedantic manner one might describe the relevant alternatives as follows: 'In the statement made by (T), it has been intended that it be truly said about E that there is no true statement by which it has been intended to say anything true about it,' and 'In the statement made by (T), it has not been intended that it be truly said about E that there is no true statement by which it has been intended to say anything true about it.' We presume that the relevant points can be successfully conveyed even by formulations which might be a little less precise, but are less cumbersome.

statement by which it has been intended to say anything true about E,' and accordingly constitutes an exception to the generality claim of (T)*. The second alternative, on the other hand, would amount to an inconsistency of the speaker's behaviour, if he did not possess an intention to the effect that something true should be claimed by his assertion, because his act of making his assertion would lose its point and accordingly one could not decide which communicative goals he intended to achieve by his utterance. Against this it might be retorted that it is *in fact* the speaker's intention to say something true by (his assertion of) (T)*. It was, however, *not* the intention to say about E that there is no statement by which it has been intended to say anything true about it, but it was rather intended to deny exactly this with respect to E because, as it had been demonstrated in the first step, this must be denied in order to create room for the possibility that the assertion which is made by (the utterance of) (T)* turns out to be true. This attempt to escape from the difficulty is not acceptable for similar reasons as before: It cannot be tolerated that a sentence which expresses that a certain entity possesses a certain property should be used in order to deny exactly that property with respect to exactly that entity.

One might point out that the wording of the *kārikā*s 20–22 is too ambiguous in order to rule out other readings and interpretations. In particular, opinions differ regarding the question as to whether *kārikā* 22 represents a continuation of the objection or the beginning of its refutation. Nevertheless, our presentation which has been given above suffices for a definite rebuttal of the claim made by HOUBEN (1995: 221) that this verse must be placed 'unmistakably on the side of the solution of the paradox' and that any understanding which considers it as representing a continuation and elaboration of the objection is forced to hypothesise artificial readings.[22] It is therefore quite possible

[22] One might be puzzled by the fact that according to our interpretation the proposition expressed in verse 22 represents nothing more than a denial of a premise of the counter-argument. Two things deserve to be noted in this connection: (1) If we hypothesise the above presented explanation of the verses 20–22, we must of course supplement the conclusion of the implicit meta-reasoning so that an explicit account of the argumentative import of verse 22 should be described as follows: '[But it is] not [possible that, on the one hand,] something is [correctly] described as being indescribable in some way or another and that, on the other hand, those words [which describe it as such] exclude [exactly that] situation [which the words according to the hypothesis correctly ascribe to some entity from obtaining] with respect to the pertinent object.' Only constituents which have not been put in brackets possess explicit correlates in the verse. Given that the whole 'meta-reasoning' has been hypothesised in an implicit manner, it is not at all mysterious that some of its ingredients have not been made fully explicit by the wording of the verse. It deserves to be noted in addition that the import of *api* occurring in the second half of the verse could be taken as being identical to that of

to follow Helārāja with respect to the assignment of the verse to the objection even if one should not accept all the details of his explanation.[23]

It goes without saying that also the claim that *kārikā* 22 must be understood as offering a solution of a paradox or a part of such a solution is unfounded. *Pace* HOUBEN and other scholars, it is not even certain that the whole passage of verses 20–22 is meant to deal with a paradox at all—if one does not employ the expression 'paradox' in a sense which is so liberal that any sort of inconsistency can be subsumed under that concept. The objection formulated in those *kārikā*s demonstrates with respect to certain statements that if they were assumed as being true, it would follow that they must be false or cannot be true, but no clue is given how one should, the

---

the expression 'on the other hand' in the above presented description of the argumentative import. This means that *api* possesses a whole sentence as its focus. Nevertheless, our interpretation concerning the import of *kārikā* 22 is equally compatible with an analysis which assumes that *tatra* constitutes the focus of the particle. The rendering of the verse which had been previously given by us was based on this supposition.—If this analysis is preferred, the expression 'on the other hand' should be taken as if it were put in brackets. (2) We could equally accept the view that appears to be advocated by Helārāja concerning *kārikā* 21, according to which this verse represents the beginning of the 'meta-argument' which is continued in verse 22. We refrain from going into the details of the alternative possibility and comment only in passing that HOUBEN has probably not grasped the essential point of Helārāja's explanation of *kārikā* 21 (cp. HOUBEN (1995: 220)).

[23] It might be worth pointing out that if one did not interpret verse 22 as representing a continuation of the objection, it would be conceivable that the proposition to which the objection implicitly refers does not correspond to (T) or (T)* or similar ones, but to something like

(T)+ E is such that nobody has ever intended to say anything about E.

or even

(T)++ E is such that I never intend to say anything about E.

Here the situation is that—given a wide range of application of the implicit quantifiers—the statement is self-refuting. A reasoning which corresponds to the discussion of the alternatives (A)* and (B)* or (1)* and (2)* would be sufficient to demonstrate this and the argument could end at this point. The situation that this very refutation opens a way for a conceivable vindication of the relevant theorem arises only if we take it in the sense of (T) or (T)* or similar ways which are characterised by the fact that they contain implicit references to truth. In such cases the argument is not complete with a demonstration of the fact that the theorem cannot be true and only then a plausible motive for a continuation of the objection exists. In view of the linguistic meaning of *avācya* it is, however, not at all outlandish to hypothesise a reference to truth.

other way round, derive their truth from the supposition of the falsity or non-truth.[24] Not only this, the second step within the objection formulated by the (fictitious) opponent which relates to the 'meta-reflexion' suggests even the idea that any attempt to deduce truth from the supposition of falsity leads to absurd consequences. Accordingly a paradox-structure exhibited by the derivability of falseness from the supposition of truth and of truth from the supposition of falseness cannot be detected from the wording of the text, at least as far as *kārikās* 20–22 are concerned.

To be sure, this circumstance does not refute the possibility that the writer of the text might have brought up a topic that *objectively* involves a paradox. If this were the case, it would be worth noting that fact. It would be an interesting result not merely from the standpoint of philosophical analysis but also under the historical aspect and the perspective of comparative philosophy. For it would be remarkable if some writer belonging to some different cultural milieu had neglected certain objective consequences which appear highly important in our eyes, possibly because he looked upon the subject matter from a different angle. But is it really true that the phenomenon mentioned in the verses 20–22 is paradoxical. One might be inclined to think so, because of the possibility of making the above depicted 'baffling' rejoinder to the first part of the objection. But it is imperative to look at the matter more carefully. To be sure, if we consider the sentences

(I) Nothing true can be said about E.

(II) It cannot be truly said about E that nothing true can be said about it.

(III) Nothing true can be said about E by any sentence different from (I).

(I) could be considered as confirmed, if (II) and (III) were assumed as true. Nonetheless, (III) is not only doubtful in itself, but generates even an inconsistency on account of its difference from (I): If (III) were assumed to be true, there would be something which can be truly said about E by some sentence that differs from (I), and accordingly (III) should not be true. The possibility of deriving inconsistencies from inconsistencies is not surprising, however. It is natural to derive from all this that there can be no entity about which absolutely nothing true *can* be said. Accordingly, either (II) or (III) must be repudiated. On the other hand, as regards the sentences

[24] It must be observed that if 'Nothing true can be said about E' is supposed to be not true, the immediate consequence is merely that something true can be said about E. But this is not equivalent to 'Something true can be said about E, namely that nothing true can be said about it' or 'It can be truly said about E that nothing true can be said about it'.—The same holds good *mutatis mutandis* for other similar sentences.

(I)* Nothing true has ever been said about E.[25]
(II)* It has never been truly said about E that nothing true has ever been said about it.
(III)* Nothing true has been ever said about E by any sentence different from (I)*.

the circumstance that (I)* might be vindicated by the conjunction of (II)* and (III)* is irrelevant for the generation of a paradox. The conjunction consisting of (I)*, (II)* and (III)* would be true, if no statement had been made about E at any time. In particular the supposition that (I)* or the proposition expressed by it might be true if (I)* had never been uttered is not blatantly absurd. Consequently the group of (I)*–(III)* does not confront us with a situation in which we possess *prima facie* good reasons to accept a number of sentences / propositions which turn out to involve inconsistencies. One should not say that the objection formulated in the *kārikās* 20–22 has implicitly shown that (the statement made by) the sentence 'Nothing true has ever been said about E' would be true, if by the pertinent statement absolutely nothing had been said about E, not even that nothing has ever been said about E, and that this is paradoxical. For this would rest on a confusion. The situation is rather as follows: If it were true that absolutely nothing has ever been said about E, a state of affairs would obtain in which what the sentence 'Nothing true has ever been said about E' in fact expresses were the case. But in this hypothetical situation the sentence 'Nothing true has ever been said about E' *would* not express that nothing true has ever been said about E, and accordingly there is no situation in which the relevant sentence would ascribe absolutely nothing to E and would nevertheless be true. One might formulate the same fact also in the following manner: There might be a 'possible world' *w* in which absolutely nothing is ascribed to E by (some assertive use of) the sentence in question—perhaps because the words occurring in the sentence possess a different meaning in *w* or for other reasons—and in which nothing is ascribed to E on any other occasion by any sentence. In this 'world' *w* a state of affairs obtains which is expressed by the sentence 'Nothing true has ever been said about E' in any 'world' *w** in which this sentence is used in order to assert that absolutely nothing has ever been said about E. But in any such world *w** the sentence is never true. Accordingly there is no such thing like a derivation of truth from the supposition of falseness. A similar phenomenon can be observed if one considers the sentence: 'This sentence does not possess any meaning,' if 'this' is used in a token-reflexive manner. It might follow that anything which a sentence expresses can be the case, even if that has never been asserted by any sentence. But is this paradoxical?

[25] We hypothesise an atemporal reading for the phrase 'has ever (been)' so that 'ever' can be understood as equivalent to 'at any time during the entire history of the universe.'

Something which seems puzzling becomes apparent at best if we consider a situation in which (I)* has been in fact used in order to make a statement about E and no other statement has been ever made concerning E (by any other sentence). It is hardly possible to deny that such a situation can be easily imagined. If the quantifier represented by 'nothing' is taken in an unrestricted manner, the statement made by (I)* is self-refuting and cannot be true. But if we assume that it is not true, we feel inclined to accept as a consequence that something true has been said about E at some time. Since, however, by hypothesis nothing true has ever been said about E on any other occasion (by any other sentence), it seems that something true must have been said about E by (I)* on the pertinent occasion and that accordingly the statement should be considered as true.

It might be instructive to point out that even the last sketched reasoning is not absolutely water-tight. The crucial step lies in the derivation of the proposition that something true has ever been said about E from the supposition that (I)* is not true. The inference is not conclusive because it overlooks an alternative possibility: That (I)* is not true might not result from the fact that something true has been said about E at some time but is due to the circumstance that nothing has been said at all about E at any time. This means that the speaker of (I)* has not succeeded in making any statement at all under the described circumstances. *A fortiori* (I)* has not been successfully used in order to make any *true* statement *about E* or to say something true about E, notwithstanding the fact that the utterer might have *intended* to do this. If the concerned predicate-expressions do not express any concept and are not associated with any descriptive content, there remains no room for the supposition that sentences like (I)*, if they are employed in the envisaged manner and under the hypothesised circumstances, describe any entity E in one way or the other. The objection that the supposition of lack of content appears counterintuitive is hardly probative. For it is by no means improbable that intuitions of this sort rely on the fact that the expressions occurring in sentences like (I)* possess something which one could call 'linguistic meaning' even in the crucial circumstances. But possession of linguistic meaning is not automatically tantamount to possession of conceptual content. Whether some expressions, in particular predicate expressions, express a conceptual content in specific situations as well as what content (and how many contents) they represent might depend both on linguistic meaning and the circumstances of their employment.[26] (Similar things could be said concerning

[26] The idea of circumstances of employment should be taken in a very comprehensive manner which involves much more than situational features of particular utterances. If we imagine that some astronaut lands for the first time on a certain planet which is not inhabited by rational beings, utters the sentence

sentences and propositional contents). In the present context it would be inappropriate to go into further details of these questions. Only one point has to be noted: Deeper investigations into the topic are not only reasonable but even relevant to issues of the philosophy of language. But Bhartṛhari is commonly considered as a philosopher of language. Why did he not scrutinise the consequences ensuing from assertive utterances of (I)* under the described circumstances or from similar situations in more detail? I think the answer is that the author of the *Saṁbandha-samuddeśa* was not at all concerned about paradoxes resulting from certain ways of using sentences. But he was apprehensive about the threat that his own semantic tenet and its statement might turn out to be self-contradictory.[27] In this connection the following two points attain importance: (1) The proposition that is brought up for discussion in the objection formulated in the verses 20–22 does not exhibit the form of (I)*, but corresponds rather to (I) or some proposition containing some other modal component. (2) The form of the crucial semantic principle is not exactly equivalent to the form of the proposition which is mentioned in the objection, and

---

(U) Nothing true is ever said on this planet.

re-enters his spaceship without saying anything more and never visits the planet again, the decision about whether or not (U) possesses descriptive content and whether or not the predicate-expression it contains represents a concept depends on the subsequent history of the universe. If in fact nobody visits the concerned planet again, (U) is without conceptual content. It fails to be a representation of how things are in the world. There are no other conditions of its truth except its own non-truth. On the other hand, if it should happen that later other astronauts land on the same planet and make (among others) some true statements, there is no reason to dispute (U)'s conceptual content.—In this case the statement made by (U) is false.—Those who find this implausible are probably beset by the idea that concepts *must* be something mental, something which merely resides 'in the heads' of persons or other rational beings. But internalism about concepts represents at best one possible position among others. Why not be an externalist *both* with respect to linguistic meaning *and* to concepts?

[27] Ironically, it is specifically our interpretation of the verses 20–22, and in particular of *kārikā* 22, which establishes at least an indirect link to some paradox. Those, however, who—like HOUBEN—do not even offer the idea of the 'meta-reflection' but, nevertheless, claim that the pertinent textual passage is meant to discuss—and solve—a philosophical paradox are probably bound to be unfair to Bhartṛhari. They represent him as a thinker who treated the very topic, which supposedly was his concern, in quite a superficial manner. We, on the other hand, explain the lack of deeper and more elaborate investigations of the topic in a different manner: A paradoxical phenomenon was simply not Bhartṛhari's concern and it was not his main concern because it is pretty irrelevant for the pertinent argumentative context.

this holds true irrespective of the details of its interpretation. The semantic thesis is at any rate more specific. It cannot be equated with a statement of the form: 'Nothing true can be said about E,' but corresponds to something like: 'Nothing true can be said by F about G,' and is obtainable by replacing 'F' by 'any expression' and 'G' by 'its own meaning relation,' or more explicitly: 'that meaning relation which exists between the concerned expression and its meaning as relata.' In a similar manner as we have adduced the example (S) above merely in order to demonstrate some relevant features by a partial analogy, it was not Bhartṛhari's intention that the objection formulated in the passage of *kārikās* 20–22 should be directed against a proposition which exactly coincides with the pertinent tenet, but the decisive point was to bring into play a statement which exhibits precisely those features on account of which the statement of the relevant semantic thesis is endangered by inconsistency. The subsequent verses show this with even more clarity.[28]

## –4–

At the beginning of the preceding chapter it has been stated that the assertion expressed in *kārikās* 1 and 4 involves theorems which could be expressed either as:

(P) No expression says anything true of/about its own MR (= meaning relation).[29]

---

[28] It might be apropos to remark that HOUBEN himself obviously does not believe that *kārikā* 22 offers anything like a convincing solution of a paradox. He says (1995: 221): 'The most important point is however that kārikā 22 is in itself no doubt very insufficient either to convince a 'believer' in the paradox, or to persuade a tenacious opponent who is making use of the paradox,' and 'If the kārikā would not have emphasised that the words do *not* deny that X is unsignifiable, it would have been a part of the statement of the paradox. How can this ever result in its solution?'. Since HOUBEN supposes that 'what 22 says amounts to the following:

Suppose: words signify → X is unsignifiable.

Then: the words signifying that X is unsignifiable do *not* deny that X is unsignifiable.'

I find it difficult to see, how this could represent even the beginning of a solution.

[29] This is only a variant formulation of 'No expression expresses a true description of its own MR'. The expression 'MR' is an abbreviation of 'meaning relation', but in the subsequent paragraphs it could equally be replaced by 'sense' or other related semantic terms.

or as

(Q) For every expression it holds good that one cannot impart to a hearer something about its MR by giving a true description of it (i.e. its MR) by the concerned expression itself.[30]

First of all one must note that (P)—or one should perhaps better say, the formulations in the original text, which (P) attempts to reflect—possesses a reading which exposes the thesis to the danger of a devastating refutation. The phrase 'A does not say anything true of/about B' could be understood as being equivalent to 'A does not say anything which is true of B' and if it is supposed that the term 'A' refers to a predicate-expression it is natural to read this in the sense of 'A is not true of B'. By resorting merely to the premises that components of sentences, however complex, and in particular predicate-expressions are meaningful units and that to every meaningful expression belongs at least one MR, an opponent could easily refute the thesis by invoking only principles which harmonise with 'standard logic' or intuition.

—Let '$xRy$' be an abbreviation for '$y$ is a linguistic expression and $x$ is a meaning relation such that $y$ is related by $x$ to something which is $y$'s meaning (= the thing meant = the *artha* of $y$),' in other words, let '$R$' be a symbol for a relation which holds good between any expression and any meaning relation if the meaning relation 'belongs' to that expression.

1 (1) There is no MR of which any linguistic expression which is a relatum of that MR says anything true (= There is no MR, such that any linguistic expression which is a relatum of that MR says anything true of it)

$-(\exists x)(\exists y)(xRy$ & $y$ says anything true of $x)$ A(ssumption)

*Because of the proponent's thesis under the assumed reading*

---

One must not be misled by the fact that—as it has been indicated earlier—the theorem could be also expressed by the formulation: 'No expression can say anything true about its own meaning relation'. In this case the modal word 'can' functions as a 'sentence-operator' and the formulation amounts to nothing else but 'It holds good with necessity that no expression says anything true about its own meaning relation.'

[30] As a matter of fact, the subsequent remarks do not crucially depend on the supposition that the pertinent thesis has to be exactly equivalent to the formulations exhibited by (P) or (Q). It is only essential that the relevant tenet exhibits all the relevant logical properties which (P) exemplifies. Therefore the following remarks could comply even with certain views according to which the thesis advocated in the passage of the verses 1 + 4 differs from the one represented by (P) and (Q).

2 (2) (The predicate) 'to be a MR of which no linguistic expression which is a relatum of that MR says anything true'[31] is a meaningful expression—and the same holds true for any expression which is obtained if one substitutes 'to be' by any finite verb form, in particular by 'is'

'$-(\exists y)(xRy$ & $y$ says anything true of $x$)' is a meaningful expression A

2,3 (3) There is a MR of which 'to be a MR of which no linguistic expression which is a relatum of that MR says anything true' is a relatum = There is a MR which belongs to 'to be a MR of which no linguistic expression which is a relatum of that MR says anything true'

$(\exists x)(xR$ '$-(\exists y)(xRy$ & $y$ says anything true of $x$)') A *Motivated by the circumstance that the pertinent predicate-expressions are meaningful*

4 (4) Let $m$ be a MR which belongs to 'to be a MR of which no linguistic expression which is a relatum of that MR says anything true'

$mR$ '$-(\exists y)(xRy$ & $y$ says anything true of $x$)' A

1,4 (5) 'to be a MR of which no linguistic expression which is a relatum of that MR says anything true' does not say anything true of $m$

'$-(\exists y)(xRy$ & $y$ says anything true of $x$)' does not say anything true of $m$

1,4 UE + MPP [*Since '$-(\exists x)(\exists y)(xRy$ & $y$ says anything true of $x$)' is equivalent to '$(x)(y)(xRy \rightarrow -y$ says anything true of $x$']*

1,4 (6) $m$ is not a MR of which no linguistic expression which is a relatum of that MR says anything true

$- -(\exists y)(mRy$ & $y$ says anything of $m$) *From 5 on the assumption that if some predicate is not true of something (which exists) the corresponding negated predicate holds true of it and that to say of any arbitrary e that 'F' is not true of e amounts to the same as saying 'not Fe'*

1,4 (7) $m$ is a MR of which some linguistic expression which is a relatum of that MR says something true

$(\exists y)(mRy$ & $y$ says anything true of $m$) 6 DN

1,4 (8) There is some MR of which some linguistic expression which is a relatum of that MR says something true

$(\exists x)$ $(\exists y)(xRy$ & $y$ says anything true of $x$) 7 EI

---

[31] Or a bit simpler: 'to be a meaning relation of which no linguistic expression to which it belongs says anything true.'

1,2,3 (9) There is some MR of which some linguistic expression which is a relatum of that MR says something true

$(\exists x)\,(\exists y)(xRy$ & $y$ says anything true of $x)$ 3,4,7 EE

1,2,3 (10) There is no MR of which any linguistic expression which is a relatum of that MR says anything true and there is some MR of which some linguistic expression which is a relatum of that MR says something true

$(\exists x)\,(\exists y)(xRy$ & $y$ says anything true of $x)$ &
$-(\exists x)(\exists y)(xRy$ & $y$ says anything true of $x)$ 1,9 & I

2,3 (11) It is not the case that there is no MR of which any linguistic expression which is a relatum of that MR says anything true. In other words, the thesis is false

$- -(\exists x)(\exists y)(xRy$ & $y$ says anything true of $x)$ 1,10 RAA.

To be sure, only a refutation, but no paradox is derivable because the negated counterpart of (1), namely

> There is some MR of which some linguistic expression which is a relatum of that MR says something true
>
> $(\exists x)\,(\exists y)(xRy$ & $y$ says anything true of $x)$,

does not imply that being a MR of which no linguistic expression which is a relatum of that MR says something true must be the only thing which can be said about MRs and about the MR that is associated with s in particular. One must not be misled by the fact that for somebody who *asserts* that there is no MR of which any linguistic expression which is a relatum of that MR says anything true (= 1 above) it might be *natural* to suppose that if there should be anything at all which could be correctly ascribed to a MR by any expression to which it belongs then it should be at best this that there is no linguistic expression which is a relatum of it and which says something true of it. Moreover, as it is made explicit by the above presented derivation—and this is sometimes an important yield of the employment of formal logic—the conclusion rests on the assumptions of the lines 2 and 3 and, accordingly, on the supposition that there is a MR associated with the pertinent expression. The underlying assumption that every meaningful expression possesses a 'meaning relation' is, however, far from evident, and thus there is no basis for the supposition that a contradiction is derivable only from *prima facie* evident assumptions.[32]

[32] The same holds good with respect to propositions such as: 'Nothing can be said (by any linguistic expression) which is true of MRs,' 'MRs are indescribable' or even

Nevertheless, as no intuitively implausible principles are employed in the refutation, it is desirable to reject such a reading for the pertinent thesis.

But one can understand the position as it is reflected by (P) also in another way so that no denial is implied to the effect that it is impossible that any description which any expression involves could be true of the MR of that expression. (P) must not say that no expression *contains* a true description of its MR, but it can be interpreted as saying that there is no expression which both says something that *could* be correctly said about its own MR and which expresses that such a description holds good with respect to its own MR. It might occur that the descriptive component of a sentence expresses a property that some object in fact possesses. Nevertheless, the sentence or what is stated by employing the sentence might not at all refer to that object. Evidently, the above presented 'refutation' can not be employed in order to disprove the thesis in the variant reading and which could be explicated as follows:

> No expression says anything which is true of its MR about it.

---

'inherence is inexpressible' (the thesis that is ascribed to Bhartṛhari by Helārāja), etc. In all these cases, one can retort: 'Well, if these entities are indescribable, inexpressible etc., then one should give up the assumption that there are such entities.' One must not confuse the above argument with a different reasoning that does not start from (1) but from the supposition that every meaningful expression must possess some MR and poses the question whether the predicate 'is a MR such that no linguistic expression to which it belongs says anything which is true of it' is or is not true of the MR associated with that expression. First of all, that is not a question with which the pertinent textual passage of the *Saṁbandha-samuddeśa* is concerned; at least this is highly improbable both in view of the verses 23–24, which we will consider shortly, and in view of the preceding context. Moreover, as regards the connection of this problem to the issue of paradox one should be cautious when the question is at stake what really follows from the supposition that such a predicate is not true of its MR. Especially two points need not be overlooked: (1) Must one take for granted that at most one linguistic expression possesses some MR? This hangs together with the topic of the criteria of the individuation of MRs. Perhaps such a supposition harmonises with Bhartṛhari's view, but nevertheless one must ask whether it is mandatory. (2) Is it really imperative to assume that a predicate like 'is a MR of which no linguistic expression to which it belongs says anything true' (or synonymous ones) says exactly one thing about any entity of which it is predicated? Moreover, is it actually absurd to suppose that it could depend on context, especially on the question to what particular entity one ascribes such a predicate, whether it says exactly one thing or nothing or perhaps several things of it, some of which are false and some of which are true of that entity? The last considerations are similar to ones which had been delineated in the preceding chapter.

Let us henceforward suppose that only this is the relevant reading of (P) and that it should be appropriately formulated thus:

(P) No expression says anything true about its own MR.

Using '*s*' as an abbreviation designating any expression which is used in order to formulate the thesis asserted in (P) we can ascertain that, since (P) represents a universal statement, it entails

($P_i$) *s* does not say anything true about its own MR.

and this could be explicated as being equivalent to:

*s* does not say anything which is true of *s*'s MR about *s*'s MR.

Nevertheless, it is not easy to see any more why the objection which had been formulated in the verses 20–22 should endanger the thesis. To be sure, if ($P_i$) holds true, one must also acknowledge the truth of

($P_k$) It is true of *s*'s MR that s does not say anything true about it.

But this is insufficient for a refutation. That which is stated by ($P_k$) could be the case if nothing had ever been said about *s*'s MR, and accordingly it appears mysterious why such a fact should disprove the thesis on account of the circumstance that *s* says something true about its own MR so that, as the objection in the *kārikās* 20–22 suggested, the proponent's statement itself creates the basis for a falsification of its truth:

Only if one were entitled to assert not only ($P_i$) but also

($P_s$) *s* says that *s* does not say anything true about its own MR,

the situation would be different. Now, one could argue that *s* must say something both about itself and about its own MR. If the sentence

Kepler said that Galileo did not say anything true about Socrates

is uttered, it can be read as saying that Kepler said something about Galileo, namely that he did not say anything true about Socrates, and also as saying that Kepler said something about Socrates, namely that Galileo did not say anything true about him. If Galileo did in fact not say anything true about Socrates, Kepler would have said something true about Galileo and/or Socrates. In an analogous manner, on certain readings at least, it can be derived from ($P_s$) that *s* says something about its own MR, namely that *s* does not say anything true about it. But the fact that (P) entails ($P_i$) and ($P_k$) guarantees that if the proponent's thesis were true and ($P_s$) on the relevant reading were also true, then *s* would say something true about its own MR, namely that *s* does not say anything true about it. Thus the proponent's thesis could indeed be refuted if ($P_s$)—on the relevant reading—were acknowledged as true. But why should one accept ($P_s$)?

Since (P) entails ($P_i$) and given that there is a MR which belongs to *s*, it can be maintained that if (P) is true *s* and *s*'s MR must be related in some manner, in particular they are related in the way that the former does not say anything true about the latter. One might say that it is an objective fact about both *s* and its MR. Accordingly, if one hypothesises the following principle

($P_H$) For every linguistic expression *e*, if *e* is objectively related in some way to some *f*, then it says about itself (i.e. *e*) and about *f* that it is related in that manner.

there would exist a support for ($P_s$) (in the required reading). On the other hand, as long as one considers ($P_H$) in isolation, one wonders why this should be accepted. A basis for the acceptance of this theorem could lie in the more general principle that all linguistic expressions convey about themselves all properties—including relational ones—which they objectively possess. At this place it becomes mandatory to take the historical context of the *Saṁbandha-samuddeśa* into account. For as long as this is not done, the citation of ($P_H$) and the more general principle of some sort of self-reflexivity of linguistic expressions must appear capricious. However, the situation changes dramatically as soon as one takes into consideration the fact that theorems of self-reflexivity have been propounded with respect to mental states, or 'cognitions' as one uses to say. The doctrine that cognitions possess the double aspect of cognising both objects and themselves represents a prominent tenet of the Buddhist school of epistemology, in particular of Dignāga. One needs merely a transference of the theorem that cognitions cognise themselves all features which they objectively possess to the realm of linguistic expressions in order to obtain a basis on which ($P_H$) could be put and which is suited to make ($P_S$) intelligible.

Seen against this background, the remarks of the *kārikā*s 23–24 can be excellently understood. The assertions to the effect that if there is a doubt pertaining to some object that is external to itself (i.e. that pertains to some other object than itself) no other doubt pertains to that doubt itself—and if this occurred it would assume a different character than before—and that even in such cases in which the ascertainment of something is ascertained as an ascertainment the cognitive state undergoes a change can now be interpreted as aiming at a rejection of the idea that linguistic expressions might exhibit a self-reflexive nature which entails that if any linguistic expression objectively possesses some property it also conveys this fact about itself. The argumentative relevance of these statements stems from the fact that they undermine the basis for such a theorem by attacking the assumption that an analogous case in the realm of mental states—or rather mental episodes—exists.

This makes all at once comprehensible, why the theme shifts to the sphere of cognitions in the verses 23–24.

If this is true, it could have historical relevance. We know that the theory of 'self-cognition' (*sva-saṁvitti*) has been elaborated by the Buddhist 'logician and epistemologist' Dignāga. It has been equally suggested that the lifetimes of Bhartṛhari and Dignāga were close to each other, but the evidence points to a somewhat earlier date for Bhartṛhari. On this background the question arises as to whether Bhartṛhari's remarks in the verses 23–24 were motivated by an acquaintance with Dignāga's views.[33]

However this might be, something else is important too: On the one hand the *kārikā*s 23–24 suggest that it is in principle possible to make linguistic expressions and together with this MRs objects of (true) descriptions, but on the other hand, they insinuate the thought that *if* this happens, the concerned MRs must assume an entirely different role. In this way the remarks intimate the view that MRs cannot fulfil both roles simultaneously.[34]

The upshot of the preceding discussion is first that the 'strong' reading of the thesis in the sense of 'No expression says anything which is true of its own MR' is implicitly repudiated as irrelevant by the verses 23–24. More important is, however, the following: On the one hand, it is shown that even in the realm of 'cognitions' it

---

[33] In this connection one must not forget, however, that the theory of *sva-saṁvitti* is not the only conceivable starting point that could have triggered the writer of the *Saṁbandha-samuddeśa* to take into account the theorem that linguistic expressions convey all objective facts concerning their own MRs as a possibility. In the first *kārikā* of the *Saṁbandha-samuddeśa* it was stated that linguistic expressions convey, apart from the mental state of its user and the 'external object' (the thing meant), also their 'own form', whereas the MR is independently established. On this background it could be natural to entertain the thought that the realm of 'own form' might be extended so that it comprises MRs too, or to consider the possibility that the exceptional status which is attributed to MRs might be revoked with the result that a theory is embraced which assumes that linguistic expressions convey all semantic facts that pertain to them. To be sure, this by itself would not automatically furnish a sound basis for the adoption of ($P_H$) or ($P_s$) because it is natural to retort that different senses of 'convey' need to be distinguished and that the sense in which information is conveyed about MRs might be very different from the sense of 'say (about)' employed in (P). More important is, however, the fact that these considerations pertaining to immanent features of Bhartṛhari's theory do not furnish a similarly striking explanation for the circumstance that the theme of the *kārikā*s shifts to that of mental episodes.

[34] This is probably the point that the verses 26–27—which we do not discuss here—were meant to substantiate.

holds good that something can be objectively true of a cognition, although there might not exist a cognition which cognises about that cognition that this is true of it. Accordingly there is no basis for the assumption that in the realm of linguistic expressions something's being objectively true of an expression requires that this fact is said with respect to that expression. Therefore one does not *need* to say about linguistic expressions and about their MRs that they are related in some manner in order to guarantee that they are in fact related in this way.[35]—I regard this as the import of *kārikā* 23.—On the other hand, in view of the situation that exists in the field of cognitions it should be even impossible that any linguistic expression says anything true about its own MR. For this would require that a MR simultaneously assumes the two roles of being a means and of being an object, of being exploited for expressing something and of being mentioned. Therefore it holds even good that one *cannot* say anything (be it true or false) about the MR of an expression which one is just uttering. The fear that the very statement of the thesis could create a situation that engenders a sufficient condition for its falseness on account of the 'self-reflexive' nature of linguistic expressions is therefore unfounded.—I consider this to be the import of *kārikā* 24.—Since no linguistic expression can be utilised in such a manner that it both 'uses' its own MR, in order to express some characterisation of something, and 'mentions' it, in order to identify the subject of predication, one can conclude that any attempt to achieve such an aim must be doomed to failure—if Bhartṛhari is right.

As it is thus possible to attribute a clear argumentative import to the *kārikā*s 23–24 there is no need to adopt the view that they are mysterious. We are not merely in a position to explain why the remarks expressed by the two verses are made at all but can make it even intelligible why they occur at exactly the place in the text at which they in fact occur.

## –5–

Now we are sufficiently equipped for an answer to the question of the contextual function of verse 25. If we consider the reply which has been given so far, we can discern that it is still incomplete in a crucial respect. The incompleteness of the

---

[35] It is only because the underlying principle that something could be the case although this has never been said appears like a truism that a reference to the theory of *sva-saṁvitti* could be called for in order to make understandable why the author of the *Saṁbandha-samuddeśa* felt the need to make this point plain concerning linguistic expressions.

defence of the thesis results from the generality of the claim embodied in (P) or (Q). Let us begin with (P). In the light of the clarification which has been implicitly provided by the verses 23–24, it says that no expression can be used in such a manner that it conveys a true statement about its own MR. In so far as it merely refers to the way in which people are able to use linguistic expressions it appears less probable that its content is self-inconsistent. But since (P) has been claimed without any explicit restriction it is natural to assume that the proponent *intended* to say also about the expression by which the thesis is formulated that it does not express a true description of its MR. However, such an intention militates against what is claimed in (P), which, if it is correct, makes it imperative to assume that any intention to that effect is doomed to failure. If, on the other hand, such an intention does not exist, must one not say that it is inappropriate to make such a general claim? The same holds true *mutatis mutandis* for (Q). It expresses that for every expression it holds good that one cannot impart to a hearer something about its MR by giving a true description of it (i.e. its MR) by the concerned expression itself. Again it is natural to suppose that it has been intended to convey by (Q) also information about the MR of (Q), which should be impossible in the light of (Q)'s propositional content. How should we solve the pragmatic inconsistency of someone's pursuing communicative goals which can by no means be successfully achieved in the attempted manner in view of the content of the pertinent communicative act?

*Kārikā* 25 gives the answer: There is no such inconsistency because the supposition that utterances of (P) or (Q) pursue the communicative goal of giving characterisations of their MRs and to impart to the hearers or readers any new knowledge about the MRs associated with the expressions of (P) or (Q) is simply incorrect. *Kārikā* 25 tells us moreover, why any charge of inappropriateness of linguistic behaviour on the part of an utterer of (P), (Q) or similar sentences is unjustified: It is also possible to utter sentences such as 'Everything I say I say falsely'—or 'I never mean what I say'—etc., without any intention to thwart one's communicative goals by including this very statement in the range of the quantification. This is not only possible, but one can even say that *if* such things are uttered it is rather normal that such intentions do not exist and, accordingly, anyone who makes such utterances possesses a right to expect that his addressees do not hypothesise such goals and interpret his utterance in this manner. The difficulty which affected the interpretation of *kārikā* 25 as a solution of a paradox, which resulted from the circumstance that merely showing how one might avoid a problem by intending to employ certain linguistic expressions in some manner is quite a poor solution of a philosophical paradox, vanishes in this way. For, on our preferred interpretation the verse aims only at refuting a possible accusation of having inappropriate intentions. On this background it is entirely appropriate to retort that (a) the relevant statements do not oblige one to have such intentions and (b) one does not in fact possess such intentions. After all, if some linguistic expression can be legitimately employed in different ways, a speaker of a language can freely decide which alternative he wants to choose, but he cannot arbitrarily lay down which meanings linguistic expressions *can* possess or even capriciously deny that a certain (use of some) expression exists which involves a paradox, provided his concern does not pertain to a language which he himself creates.

To be sure, *kārikā* 25, as interpreted in the preceding paragraph, does not represent the only possible answer to the charge of pragmatic inconsistency. It could be also retorted that universal claims do not necessarily amount to the same as making claims about every single object which is within the range of the quantification. The truth of a universal proposition surely involves that *if* somebody makes corresponding singular statements about individual objects (of some relevant domain) he will say something true no matter which object he chooses. But this is something different. There is evidence that at the time and in the milieu in which Bhartṛhari wrote universal propositions tended to be viewed as something which concerned a plurality of objects and involved statements about them, so that expectations to find ways of reacting to the problem that rely on finer-grained distinctions could appear anachronistic. Moreover, one should not forget that even in modern times it has been envisaged to 'reduce' universal propositions to conjunctions of (possibly infinite) propositions containing terms denoting individual objects so that it should not surprise us if the writer of the *Saṁbandha-samuddeśa* had solved the problems under the presupposition that general statements are statements about several individuals without investigating other alternatives. Nevertheless, the basis for the supposition that Bhartṛhari really viewed universally quantified statements as statements about each particular object of a group might be unsound. In that case there is not even sufficient reason to assume that the solution offered in the verse 25 amounts to a restriction of the quantifier. Neither the formulation exhibited by verse 25 nor the argumentative situation make this interpretation mandatory. The need to meet the difficulties which are raised by the objection of the *kārikā*s 20–22 requires merely the postulates (a) that it is not intended by the advocator of the semantic principle that by uttering it he should refer to the MR belonging to any expression used for stating the principle and say something true about it and (b) that by asserting the principle something is said which is in fact true of the semantic relation associated with its expression. As soon as the supposition is given up that every universally quantified statement must say something about each single object in a domain, in the strong sense of 'say about', a non-restriction of the range of the quantifier is compatible with compliance with the postulates. As regards the formulation of *kārikā* 25 one can easily convince oneself that it does not contain a clear indication of the demand of a quantifier-restriction. The mere wording of the verse allows us to derive at the most that it is not or should not be intended to say anything about a certain universally quantified statement or sentence. But this leaves room for two possibilities: (1) The concerned statement or linguistic expression does not belong to the realm of entities to which the statement pertains, (2) the concerned statement or linguistic expression belongs to the realm of entities to which the statement pertains but is not something to which one refers or intends to refer by making the statement. One can make statements pertaining among others to future objects (e.g. persons living in the future or future events) without possessing even requirements for any individuating reference to those entities. However, even if the first alternative is at stake, one might distinguish between (at least) two possibilities: (a) the quantification is restricted, e.g. by attributing to the expression 'every A' a 'contextual meaning' equivalent to 'every A except B' or (b) it is assumed that the expression containing a universal quantification *as a whole* is used in order to express a proposition that could be equally expressed by a restricted quantifier. What feature of *kārikā* 25 or the context should force us to prefer (1a) to the remaining alternatives? To be sure, it could be retorted that no indications exist which rule out (1a) as a possibility and that the author of the pertinent textual passage did not make a clear distinction between the alternatives. But if there is indeterminateness or vagueness in this regard, what gives us the right to impose a one-sided determination? Possibly HOUBEN's contention that the 'solution' embodied in verse 25 of the *Saṁbandha-samuddeśa* exhibits features that are 'usually out of the picture in Western accounts', in particular features which relate to the intention of a speaker, can be vindicated though in a manner which is quite different from the one which HOUBEN had in mind. But let us leave this issue for the time being.

It should be noticed that there are other uncertainties concerning interpretation which would remain, even if one settled the question of the decision between the alternatives mentioned in the preceding paragraph, in particular even if one adopts the view that Bhartṛhari wanted to advocate a quantifier-restriction by the remark of *kārikā* 25. The theorem

> No expression says anything true about its own MR.

involves not only two but even three universal quantifiers, if one interprets it as equivalent to

> No expression says anything true about any MR of which it is one of its (i.e. the MR's) relata.

Given that verse 25 proposes a restriction of a universal quantifier, the question arises which of the quantifiers should be restricted. Although the most natural answer seems to be that the quantification should not include the MR which belongs to any expression used to formulate the thesis, it deserves to be noted that the difficulties formulated in the verses 21–22/23 could be equally circumvented, if a restriction pertaining to 'anything' in 'anything true' were hypothesised. At least it appears to be so. Therefore the question as to whether Bhartṛhari wanted to suggest that the restriction should be exclusively associated with the first or the last quantifier or not cannot be derived from the formulation of the text with absolute certainty. Anyhow, the considerations as to why the example referred to in verse 25 can perform the function of defending the thesis are not affected by this ambiguity.[36]

If the interpretation that has been suggested above is correct, Bhartṛhari's defence of his thesis represented by the verses 23–25 primarily pertains to an explication and clarification of his own intentions underlying his statement of the theorem. In this way he tries to disclose how his statement of the thesis should be understood. In the concerned textual passage the author makes it plain that, on the one hand, he intends to state something which holds good and is true of absolutely all linguistic expressions and their MRs, including the expressions which are used in order to

---

[36] If one considers the thesis

> No linguistic expression says anything correct about any meaning relation which belongs to it (= of which it is one of its relata),

one can easily construct a dilemma in the following way:

> '*s*' = 'No linguistic expression says anything correct about any meaning relation which belongs to it.'
>
> (1) There is something which is a meaning relation which belongs to *s*.
>
> (2) Let *m* be a meaning relation which belongs to *s*.
>
> (3) *s* does not say anything correct about *m*.
>
> (4) *s* does not correctly say about *m* that no linguistic expression to which it belongs says anything correct about it.
>
> (5) If *s* says about *m* that no linguistic expression to which it belongs says anything correct about it, then this is not correct.
>
> (6) Either *s* does not say about *m* that no linguistic expression to which it belongs says anything correct about it or it is not true that no linguistic expression to which *m* belongs says anything correct about *m*.

Bhartṛhari accepts the first proposition of the disjunction and is thus free to reject the second alternative.

formulate the theorem, but on the other hand, he does not intend to say *that* (the MRs of) the expression(s) by which the thesis is expressed exhibit(s) the feature which (all MRs of) all linguistic expressions should exhibit according to the thesis; the (MRs of the) expression(s) employed for the formulation of the thesis are exempt from the range about which the author intends to say anything in his thesis. It is the function of the verses 23 and 24 and the reference to first and second order mental states to make the first point, viz. the intention of stating something which holds true of all linguistic expressions and all MRs, clear whereas verse 25 is meant to clarify the second point, viz. the intention not to say anything about the (MRs of) linguistic expression(s) employed in order to state the thesis. If this is correct it is remarkable that the author of the *Saṁbandha-samuddeśa* would *not* solve his problem by advocating a hierarchy of types or levels, in particular with respect to predicates. It is Bhartṛhari's intention that any predicate occurring in the thesis should be true both with respect to other expressions or their MRs and with respect to themselves or their own MR or the expressions and their MRs of which they are constituents; the predicates are the same in all cases. Or, to put it more cautiously, the preferred interpretation suggests the ascription of such a view.

One might ask whether the outlook depicted above is inconsistent and whether the detection of an inconsistency would refute the interpretation. I am inclined to say 'No' to both questions. First of all, the occurrence of inconsistent views is not an impossibility, and the demand to accept only interpretations which entail consistent opinions on the part of the writer of a text is exceedingly strong. One should rather confine the postulate of avoiding inconsistency in text-interpretation to the postulate that one should attempt to avoid the ascription of views which are obviously inconsistent. Second, I consider the intentions which the interpreted author ascribes to himself according to our interpretation as consistent. Perhaps the plausibility of this view can be enhanced by considering an example which is not in all, but in certain important respects similar. Let us assume, somebody intends to make a statement by uttering the sentence:

> Leaving my own statement which I am making now out of consideration—all statements which are made today in this room in which we are presently sitting are true.

By saying *expressis verbis* that the speaker's own present statement should be kept apart the speaker indicates his intention not to say anything about his own statement. Nevertheless, it might be, and probably is, his intention to make a *true* statement by the words he utters. The predicate 'if *x* is a statement which is made today in this room in which we are presently sitting then it is true' (and even '*x* is a true statement which is made today in this room in which we are presently sitting') should be true of the speaker's own statement according to the speaker's intentions. Both intentions, not to say anything about the own present statement and to produce something of which the predicate of the presently uttered sentence is true, coexist without inconsistency. Moreover, in the case under consideration the circumstance, that the predicate 'if *x* is a statement which is made today in this room in which we are presently sitting then it is true' holds true for all statements except the one which the speaker presently makes, would ensure the fulfilment of the latter intention. In some sense of 'convey', a speaker of the above mentioned sentences can convey that all pertinent statements, including his own present statement, are true.

Ironically, the fact that our interpretation implies that Bhartṛhari's defence of the thesis aims at a clarification of his underlying intentions, assigns to speaker-intentions a much more prominent place than HOUBEN's proposal. But HOUBEN's remark that Bhartṛhari brings the intention of a speaker into play might stem from a good intuition. However, our tenet is more radical than HOUBEN's. Not the solution of a paradox, but the entire defence of Bhartṛhari's principal theorem advocated in the pertinent section of the *Saṁbandha-samuddeśa* relates to intention, but not to the intention of any arbitrary utterer of certain types of sentences, but to Bhartṛhari's own intentions which underlie the statement of his thesis.

Bhartṛhari's reply implicitly refers to a 'use–mention' distinction with respect to MRs. The central ingredient of his tenet can be also formulated thus:

> (TH) There is no MR which is mentioned by any expression which functions as a relatum of that relation = If anything is a MR of which some linguistic expression is a relatum, then that MR is not mentioned by that expression.

Alternatively one might say that no linguistic expression mentions its own MR. The situation is also here analogous to the one depicted above: On the one hand, it is intended to say something which holds good for all MRs and all linguistic expressions without exception, but on the other hand, there are reasons to fear the objection that because of the universality of the thesis the MR associated with the expression by which the thesis is formulated must be mentioned by it. Therefore the fundamental features of averting the danger of refutation by an opponent could also be made intelligible if one supposed that Bhartṛhari's defence refers to (a) 'cannot be mentioned' and (b) 'is inexpressible' = 'is such that nothing true can be said about it,' as two possible readings of *avācya* occurring in the verses 20–22.

It appears that specific features of Bhartṛhari's conception of MRs is not essential for the argument and that the tenet could and should be defended in an analogous manner if it related not to MRs (in Bhartṛhari's sense) but to meanings or senses, however they are conceived. It is only required that those meanings or senses are something which every meaningful linguistic expression possesses, or more precisely, that an existential claim can be made with respect to those entities concerning every linguistic expression, in particular the expression(s) which is (are) used in order to formulate the relevant theorem. We are also able to see now that our reconstruction of the argument allows for the possibility of understanding *sarvaṁ mithyā bravīmi* in the sense of 'Everything I say is false'. The decisive point is, however, that we are not *forced* to rule out other equally possible, if not more natural readings of this phrase, and this I consider as a remarkable advantage.

Since it appears that the subsequent verses do not throw any new light on the issue which would necessitate major revisions of the proposed interpretation, we abstain from investigating them here.

## –6–

In contradistinction to some other interpreters, I suppose that the entire textual segment of *kārikā* 1–29 of the *Saṁbandha-samuddeśa* is devoted to only one main theme, namely the fixity of the relation between expressions and their meanings, such that all other topics are subordinate to that. This explains why the issue of a paradox does not play a prominent role. The central topic is a certain semantic theorem which is endangered by self-inconsistency. Only by considering the global structure of the investigated textual passage we obtain a realistic assessment of the way in which the remarks made in *kārikā* 25 and other verses are related to the topic of philosophical paradoxes. This could appear self-evident, but perhaps it should be stated nonetheless.

The circumstance that paradox is not the vital issue in any segment of the examined textual passage must not mean that it cannot embody tenets which are philosophically significant. That it would be illegitimate to draw such a conclusion can be gathered from the circumstance that the semantic theorem, as we have interpreted it, intimates a consequence which is by no means trivial: If the tenet that no expression specifies its own MR (or sense) were true, one could derive that at any time there must be some facts which are not stated at that time. In other words, at no time can everything be stated which is the case at that time. (This must not be confused with the tenet that there are facts which cannot be stated at any time!). To be sure, a number of additional premises might be needed in order to justify the derivation, for example that there are semantic facts. But one can hardly assert that the proposition is trivial. Perhaps it is not even true.

It is not my intention to contend that deviant interpretations of particular verses could not be equally legitimate. I am rather inclined to believe that with respect to the interpretation of individual *kārikā*s several alternatives exist which would not affect the principal results. On the other hand, it is certain that interpretations have been advocated which could not be made compatible with my claims.[37] In view of the fact that it might not be realistic to expect unanimity concerning all details of interpretation with respect to the *Saṁbandha-samuddeśa* in the near future, a more general point should be stressed: Interpretations of the section of *kārikās* 20–25 should not disregard the circumstance that—given the undisputed assumption that the verses 22 or 23–25 represent a reply to some objection or objections—the answer comprises not only the declaration formulated in the last *kārikā* but also the statements of the two preceding verses 23 and 24. The question as to why Bhartṛhari did not directly remove the difficulties by advancing the remark made in verse 25 but offers a more complex reply should be accounted for. Obviously we have taken this fact more seriously than previous interpreters.

---

[37] In order to convey a clearer picture of the extent to which the interpretations which have been presented above deviate from others we cite the sketch of the train of thought represented by the discussed *kārikās* which has been presented by Ashok Aklujkar in EIPHIL V (: 157–158):

> '/1–2/ (*E*68; *T*66–77). From linguistic forms that are uttered three entities can be known: the speaker's awareness (what he is thinking of), the external object, and the linguistic form's own nature. A hearer may fail to cognize the first two, but not the third.
>
> /3–28/ (*E*68–70; *T*79–92). The relation between word and meaning is indicated by the use of the genitive case ("*y* is the meaning of *x*"). There is no expression that designates this relation as a relation, for expressions reify—turn dependent entities like relation into independent, apparently substantive entities. …
>
> *Objection*: You say that inherence is inexpressible; but because you have just expressed it, it has become expressible! Or if you say even the word 'inexpressible' does not express it, we would not understand what your claim means.
>
> *Prima facie reply*: What we mean is that inherence's dependent nature cannot be expressed.
>
> *Objector's reply*: Then inherence itself cannot be expressed, and your words do not convey anything.
>
> *Siddhāntin's answer:* A doubt cannot itself be doubted. Again, a belief cannot itself come to be the thing it itself believes. To take another case: in saying "all that I am saying is false" (*sarvaṁ mithyā bravīmi*) one does not intend to include that very sentence in the scope of its meaning, for then, as what one is saying would be implicitly false, the intended meaning would not be conveyed.'

## BIBLIOGRAPHY

EIPHIL V = *Encyclopedia of Indian Philosophies.* (General editor: Karl H. Potter.)—Vol. V: Coward, H.G.; Raja, K. Kunjunni (eds.): *The Philosophy of the Grammarians.* Princeton University Press, Princeton–New Jersey 1990. [Indian edition: Motilal Banarsidass, Delhi 1990].

HOUBEN 1995 = Houben, J.E.M.: *The Saṁbandha-samuddeśa (Chapter on Relations) and Bhartṛhari's Philosophy of Language.* Gonda Indological Studies, Groningen 1995.

# Bhartṛhari on *pravṛtti* as the First *kāraka* *

HIDEYO OGAWA

A deep analysis of the problem of what ultimately brings about an action (*kriyā*) leads Bhartṛhari to posit the notion of *pravṛtti* ('activity'). *Pravṛtti*, according to Bhartṛhari, is that which incites an agent (*kartṛ*) of an action (*kriyā*) to undertake it. *Pravṛtti* is, properly speaking, the first *kāraka* (*prathamaṁ kārakam*), and the agent the second *kāraka*. He characterises *pravṛtti* as substrateless (*anapāśrita*), imperishable (*anapāyin*) and universal (*sāmānya-bhūta*) and he argues that *pravṛtti* serves to draw out an agent's capacity to function as an agent.

Interestingly, Bhartṛhari states *pravṛtti* is nothing but what some theorists have called *apūrva*. Commenting on this statement by Bhartṛhari, HALBFASS (1991: 302) observed that *apūrva* has something to do with 'an old Mīmāṁsā theory of *apūrva* which is conspicuously different from its explication in Kumārila Bhaṭṭa school, and which is in general not well documented in the extant Mīmāṁsā literature.' He goes on to say that '*apūrva* is a synonym of *dharma* itself, and it is an impersonal and substrateless (*anāśrita*) potentiality, a kind of cosmic principle or power to be manifested or actualized by the ritual acts (*kriyāvyaṅgya*; *yāgādikarmanirvartya*).'

It seems to me, however, that he has given insufficient attention to the question of what *pravṛtti*, also described as *apūrva*, might be.[1] The crucial point he missed is that the *pravṛtti* has a universal character. Two kinds of *apūrva* are found in Mīmāṁsā literature: epistemic *apūrva* (the Newly Known *apūrva*) and ontic *apūrva* (the Newly Born *apūrva*). The *apūrva* referred to by Bhartṛhari corresponds exactly to the former and this is quite different from what is described by HALBFASS as *apūrva*. The *apūrva* HALBFASS noted, being epistemic, or newly known, *apūrva* and

---

* Thanks are due to Professor Brendan S. Gillon for reading the manuscript and making a number of helpful suggestions. But responsibility for the text with any surviving errors rests entirely upon the author.

[1] Recently his line of thinking has been developed by KATAOKA (2000), who tries to reconstruct the Mīmāṁsā *apūrva*-theory (in his terminology, **dharmâbhivyakti-vāda*, or the theory of *dharma*-manifestation) HALBFASS has noticed, dealing with such a theory as discussed by Bhartṛhari. But the question of what is the *pravṛtti* which is identified with *apūrva* is outside his scope of consideration.

*Essays in Indian Philosophy, Religion and Literature*, pp. 203–228.

further identified with *pravṛtti*, is the universal *dharma* which is understood from the injunctive statement of the *Veda*, or a kind of ideal activity to be realised.

Thus the aim of this paper is, first of all, to investigate the question of what *pravṛtti* is, and then, to show that Mīmāṁsā linguistic theory justifies *pravṛtti*'s being treated as epistemic, or newly known, *apūrva*.

## –1–

Bhartṛhari introduces the notion of *apūrva* in the *Sādhana-samuddeśa* chapter of his *Vākya-padīya*. As his readers know, Bhartṛhari sets out to explain Pāṇini's *kāraka* theory. According to Pāṇini, a simple sentence expresses a *kriyā* (action). Each *kriyā* comes about as a result of the operation of a number of factors, called *kāraka* by Pāṇini and called in this chapter by Bhartṛhari *sādhana*.[2] Thus, for example, the simple sentence *devadatta odanaṁ pacati* ('Devadatta is cooking rice-gruel') expresses an action, namely cooking, whose realisation results from the operation of two factors, or *sādhana*s—namely, Devadatta, the agent of the action, and rice-gruel, its patient. In general, it is the *sādhana* of an action which brings it about. This relation of bringing about is referred to as *sādhya-sādhana-bhāva*, or the relation of what is to be accomplished and what does the accomplishing.

The starting point of Bhartṛhari's chapter is a question initially raised by Patañjali: is a *sādhana* a quality (*guṇa*) or a quality bearing substance (*dravya*). Bhartṛhari defends the view that *sādhana*s are *guṇa*s, or more specifically, that they are capacities (*sāmarthya*; *śakti*).[3] Beginning with VP 3.7.32, Bhartṛhari deepens his inquiry into *sādhana*s. There, he notes that there are three views regarding these

[2] Pāṇini's use of the superlative *sādhakatama* in defining *karaṇa* ('instrument') in Pāṇ 1.4.42 says that any *kāraka* is properly termed *sādhaka* ('that which accomplishes') or *sādhana* ('that by which something is accomplished').

[3] Bhartṛhari states that what is called *sādhana* is the capacity of bringing to accomplishment the action which inheres in the same substratum as the capacity and the action as well which inheres in the one different from the capacity's. See VP 3.7.1: *svâśraye samavetānāṁ tadvad evâśrayântare / kriyāṇām abhiniṣpattau sāmarthyaṁ sādhanaṁ viduḥ //* For each *kāraka* there is a separate action, which is called a subsidiary action (*guṇa-kriyā*) in comparison with the principal action (*pradhāna-kriyā*) that is to be brought to accomplishment by them. With respect to the subordinate action, the action and the capacity of bringing it to accomplishment are said to inhere in the same substratum; with respect to the principal action, they are said to inhere in the same substratum for an agent (*kartṛ*) and an object (*karman*), and not for other *kāraka*s.

capacities. The first is that the capacities of the things that bring about an action are brought about by other causes existing previous to the action. The second is that the capacities are brought about simultaneously with the coming into being of the action. The third is that there is some further, previously existing action, which brings about the capacities which bring about the action:

VP 3.7.32: *prāṅ nimittântarôdbhūtaṁ kriyāyāḥ kaiś cid iṣyate /*
*sādhanaṁ sahajaṁ kaiś cit kriyânyaiḥ pūrvam iṣyate //*

'Some admit that a *sādhana* [as a capacity] has been produced through causes other than [what produces its substratum] before an action [is brought to accomplishment]; some that it is born together [with an action]; others that there has already been an action before [the *sādhana*s exist].'

In the next verse, Bhartṛhari elaborates on what the further action posited on the third view might be:

**VP 3.7.33:** ***pravṛttir eva prathamaṁ kva cid apy anapāśritā /***
***śaktīr[4] ekâdhikaraṇe srotovad apakarṣati //***

'[The action in precedence to *sādhana*s] is precisely what is called *pravṛtti*. In the initial stage it does not abide anywhere. But in the next stage [where it abides in a particular substance as the *sādhana*], it draws out the capacities in the same substratum where it abides, like a stream.'

Bhartṛhari refers to this further action as *pravṛtti*. The idea is that *pravṛtti* is initially substrateless and then, when it comes to abide in a particular substratum, it draws out from the substratum its capacity to operate, together with the other *sādhana*s, to bring out the relevant action (*kriyā*). Thus, in the case of Devadatta cooking rice-gruel, *pravṛtti* draws out from Devadatta his capacity to operate as the agent of the action of cooking and from the rice-gruel its capacity to operate as the patient of the same action. In short, Bhartṛhari holds that *pravṛtti* is that which draws out from each substance, which operates to bring about an action its capacity to bring it about, and in that way, *pravṛtti* is the activator of each substance.

---

[4] Both Wilhelm RAU and SUBRAMANIA IYER give the reading *śaktir* instead of *śaktīr*. I have adopted RAGHUNĀTHA ŚARMĀ's suggestion.

## –2–

Indeed, this view of *pravṛtti* is further developed by Bhartṛhari in his next chapter, the *Kriyā-samuddeśa*.[5] He says:

VP 3.8.37: *kriyām anye tu manyante kva cid apy anapāśritām /*
*sādhanâikârtha-kāritve pravṛttim anapāyinīm //*

'Others, on the other hand, consider that the *pravṛtti*, which does not abide anywhere and is imperishable, is an action (*kriyā*) when it brings about a single result together with *sādhana*s.'

VP 3.8.38: *sāmānya-bhūtā sā pūrvaṁ bhāgaśaḥ pravibhajyate /*
*tato vyāpāra-rūpeṇa sādhyeva vyavatiṣṭhate //*

---

[5] It is noteworthy that Helārāja's commentary on VP 3.7.34 is regrettably not available except an introductory statement. The lacuna is supplied by Phullarāja, who introduces the present *kārikā* by saying that Bhartṛhari 'states [the *kārikā*] in order to describe the essence of the *sādhana* according to other views' (*idānīṁ matântarânusāreṇa sādhana-svarūpaṁ varṇayitum āha*). If we follow Phullarāja, what is meant by this *kārikā* is: 'There is also a difference of views concerning what it is that brings about the action and bestows the status of means on entities—some of the candidates include karmic force (*apūrva*), time (*kāla*), the power of time, and action itself,' as is summarised by Ashok Aklujkar (in EIPHIL V (: 162)). However, Helārāja properly introduces the *kārikā* in question by saying that Bhartṛhari continues to state what is the *pravṛtti* which is substrateless and eternal (*kêyaṁ pravṛttir anapāśrayā nityêty āha*). In the *Kriyā-samuddeśa* he is consistent in interpreting that the *kārikā* in question discusses the *pravṛtti*. There he states:

Helārāja on VP 3.8.37: *pravṛtti-lakṣaṇêyaṁ kriyā nityânāśritā apūrvaṁ kāla-śaktiṁ vā ityâdinā pūrvam eva vyākhyātā ... /* ('The Action characterised as the *pravṛtti*, eternal and substrateless, has been explained by VP 3.7.34.')

Helārāja on VP 3.8.38: *prathamâvasthāyām apūrvâdi-rūpatayā sā pravṛttiḥ sāmānyenâbhidhīyate /* ('The *pravṛtti* as *apūrva* and others in the initial stage is designated as the universal.')

Helārāja on VP 3.8.39: *apūrvādi-svabhāvâsau sāmānya-bhūtā pravṛttir ... /* ('the *pravṛtti* which is something universal and which is essentially *apūrva* and the like.')

From these it will be clear that Helārāja understands that Bhartṛhari in VP 3.7.34 clarifies the essence of the *pravṛtti* which precedes the *sādhana*s.

> 'In the first stage, the [*pravṛtti*] is something general. In the subsequent stage, becoming the activities [of *sādhanas*,] it is divided into parts [i.e. particular acts such as cooking and cutting] and appears as if it were something to be brought about.'
>
> VP 3.8.39: *prakṛtiḥ sādhanānāṁ sā prathamaṁ tac ca kārakam /*
> *vyāpārāṇāṁ tato 'nyatvam aparair upavarṇyate //*
>
> 'The [*pravṛtti*] is the original source of *sādhanas*; and it is the first *kāraka*. Others, however, declare that the activities [of *sādhanas*] are different from it.'

According to Bhartṛhari, the *pravṛtti* identified with the Action has the following characteristics:

1. It is substrateless (*kvacid apy anapāśritā*). Considering what is stated in VP 3.7.33, it is so before it inheres in a particular substance-*sādhana*.

2. It is imperishable (*anapāyinī*).

3. It brings about a single result together with *sādhanas* (*sādhanâikârtha-kāritva*), which means in the light of VP 3.7.33 that it draws out from substance-*sādhanas* their capacities of functioning as *kārakas* for the accomplishment of an action.

4. It is something general (*sāmānya-bhūtā*) in the initial stage, which is differentiated (*bhāgaśaḥ pravibhajyate*) in the later stage.

5. It appears as if it were something to be brought to accomplishment (*sādhyeva vyavatiṣṭhate*). According to Bhartṛhari, an action, by definition, has the property of being to be brought to accomplishment (*sādhya*).[6] In reality, however, it cannot be something brought to accomplishment because of its eternity.

---

[6] According to Bhartṛhari, the essential feature of what is understood to be an action is that it has sequence (*krama*) and is accordingly spoken of as something that is brought to accomplishment (*sādhyatvenâbhidhīyate*), whether it has or has not been brought to accomplishment:

> VP 3.8.1: *yāvat siddham asiddhaṁ vā sādhyatvenâbhidhīyate /*
> *āśrita-krama-rūpatvāt tat kriyêti pratīyate //*

For the idea that the *pravṛtti* appears as if it were something to be brought to accomplishment, it will be useful to adduce the following *kārikā*:

> VP 3.8.21: *jātim anye kriyām āhur aneka-vyakti-vartinīm /*
> *asādhyā vyakti-rūpeṇa sā sādhyenôpalabhyate //*
>
> 'Others have declared that universal which inheres in many individual action-moments to be action. [Being eternal,] it is not something that is brought to accomplishment, but in terms of its [inhering in] an individual

6. It is the original source of *sādhanas* (*prakṛtiḥ sādhanānām*) in that it bestows the status of *sādhana* on entities by drawing out the capacities from them.

7. It is the first *kāraka* in that it is not brought to accomplishment by any other things.

8. It is distinct from particular actions (*vyāpārāṇāṁ tato 'nyatvam*) from the viewpoint that the universal and the particular are mutually distinct from each other.

The important point to note is that the *pravṛtti* which is considered to be that which draws out the capacity is said to be something general that is yet to be differentiated and eternal; the differentiation of the *pravṛtti* takes place in the same substratum where the capacity to be drawn out abides (*ekâdhikaraṇa*), as is suggested by VP 3.7.33. This implies that the *pravṛtti* and a particular activity Devadatta has are viewed as being in the relation of the universal and the particular (*sāmānya-viśeṣa-bhāva*), irrespective of their ontological status. Therefore, it is proper to say that when inhering in the particular substance-*sādhana*, the *pravṛtti*, exciting a substance-*sādhana*'s capacity of functioning as *kāraka*, raises or becomes the particular activity of the substance-*sādhana*.[7] And the reason that the *pravṛtti* is

---

action-moment, it appears as though something to be brought to accomplishment.'

[7] We can distinguish between two stages: the one in which the *pravṛtti* is of the nature of the universal (*sāmānya-bhūta*) and hence yet to be differentiated (*anudbhinna-viśeṣa-daśā*) and the one in which there takes place its differentiation. Helārāja pictures it in each stage as follows:

Undifferentiated stage:

Helārāja on VP 3.7.38: *kāraka-śaktīnāṁ pravartikā* / ('[The *pravṛtti*] excites the capacities of functioning as what brings about an action (*kāraka-śakti*).')

Helārāja on VP 3.7.39: *dravyāṇāṁ kāraka-śaktīr ādadhānā* / ('[The *pravṛtti*] arouses the *kāraka-śakti*s of substances.')

Helārāja on VP 3.7.39: *pravartakatvāt srotasā tulyā kathitā* / ('[The *pravṛtti*] is said to be comparable to the stream because of exciting one to take action.')

Helārāja on VP 3.7.39: *kārakāṇām api sādhakam* / ('[The *pravṛtti*] is what brings to accomplishment even *kāraka*s.')

Differentiated stage:

Helārāja on VP 3.7.38: *sādhana-vyāpārôpapādita-pravibhāgā* / ('The division of [the *pravṛtti*] is justified in terms of the activities of *sādhana*s.')

what draws out the capacity, as a matter of fact, lies in its being something universal and eternal in a stream, on account of which it will also be explained why the *pravṛtti* is conceived of as the original source (*prakṛti*) of all *sādhana*s or the first *kāraka* (*prathamaṁ kārakam*).[8]

---

Helārāja on VP 3.7.38: *sādhana-samavāyinī* / ('[The *pravṛtti*] inheres in *sādhana*s.')

Helārāja on VP 3.7.39: *sādhana-bhedeṣu pravibhakta-śarīraṁ viśiṣṭa-kriyā-svabhāvam* / ('[The *pravṛtti*] is differentiated according to different *sādhana*s and becomes a particular action.')

Helārāja on VP 3.7.39: *sādhana-bheda-samavetānāṁ viśiṣṭa-kriyā-svabhāvānāṁ vyāpārāṇām* / ('[The *pravṛtti*] becomes that activity inhering in a particular *sādhana* which is nothing but a particular action (*viśiṣṭa-kriyā*).')

It is to be noted in passing that Helārāja bases his argument on Patañjali's statement: *kārakāṇāṁ pravṛtti-viśeṣaḥ kriyā*, which has to be interpreted as 'the Action becomes a particular act of *kāraka*s,' though Patañjali himself suggests a different interpretation of it. In MBhā *ad* Pāṇ 1.3.1 Patañjali states that the action consists in the difference of the manners in which *kāraka*s function towards different actions.

[8] It is interesting to note here that the idea of the precedence of the Action or *pravṛtti* over *sādhana*s is invoked in order to explain the correlativity of what brings an action to accomplishment and what is to be brought to accomplishment. With reference to Patañjali's interpretation of the word *dhātv-artha* in Pāṇ 5.1.118 *upasargāc chandasi dhātv-arthe*, Bhartṛhari states as follows:

VP 3.14.582: *dhātv-arthenôpajanitaṁ sādhanatvena sādhanam* /
*dhātunā kṛtam ity evam asmin sūtre pratīyate* //

'The meaning of the verb root [i.e. the action] makes a candidate for the *sādhana* the *sādhana*. [The word *dhātv-artha*] in this *sūtra* is understood as signifying that which is brought about by [the action that is the meaning] of the verb root.'

An entity cannot be the *sādhana* in itself. It is regarded as a *sādhana* in correlation to it when involved in the accomplishment of a particular action. Thus the action is something that gives an entity the status of being a *sādhana*. For the state of being a *sādhana* is in correlation to what is to be brought to accomplishment (*sādhyâpekṣatvāt sādhana-bhāvasya*). Helārāja argues that this is established by VP 3.7.33.

This precedence of the Action is more typically found in the situation where one is involved in the accomplishment of a certain action with using its means. With an action to be brought to accomplishment in mind, one sets to use entities capable of bringing it about. The pre-existing action is called *sambhāvita-kriyā* ('the action in mind'). According to Helārāja on VP 3.14.582, the precedence of the Action to *sādhana*s shows

## –3–

Bhartṛhari's claim that *pravṛtti* is a first *kāraka* requires some explanation. Among the six *kārakas*, an agent (*kartṛ*) is the principal one. In this sense we may call the agent the second *kāraka*. Let us consider the following remark made by Patañjali in answer to the question why an agent is looked upon as the principal *kāraka* of the action (MBhā on Pāṇ 1.4.23):

> *yat sarveṣu sādhaneṣu sannihiteṣu kartā pravartayitā bhavati* /
>
> 'Because the agent, when all other *sādhanas* are present, sets them into play (*pravartayitṛ*).'

An agent is that *kāraka* which sets all other substance-*sādhanas* into play, while the latter are those whose activities take place in dependence upon the former (*tad-adhīna-pravṛttitvāt*).[9] For example, if Devadatta is cooking rice in a pot with firewood (*devadattas taṇḍulān edhaiḥ sthālyāṁ pacati*), it is he who puts the pot on the stove, fills it, etc.; the activities of the firewood (*edha*), pot (*sthālī*), and rice grains (*taṇḍula*) that function respectively as instrument (*karaṇa*), locus (*adhikaraṇa*), and object (*karman*) depend upon Devadatta. We cannot say, however, that the agent is brought into play by other substance-*sādhanas*. In giving in VP 3.7.101–102 the properties which characterise an agent, Bhartṛhari states as follows:

> VP 3.7.101a: *prāg anyataḥ śakti-lābhāt* /
>
> '[An agent is called independent] because [the agent] acquires the capacity [to bring an action to accomplishment] from things other [than what are to be set into play by that agent] prior to [other participants].'[10]

---

that an action activates an entity by urging it to get involved in the accomplishment of an action (*kriyā hi sādhanāni pravartayati*).

[9] VP 3.7.101c.

[10] In VP 3.7.101–2 Bhartṛhari explains Pāṇ 1.4.54 *sva-tantraḥ kartā*, which provides that that *kāraka* be called *kartṛ* which is spoken of as an independent (*sva-tantraḥ*) participant in comparison with other participants in an act. The capacity of an agent is, according to Vṛṣabha, independency (*svātantrya*) and the independency consists in having other *sādhanas* play their roles in the accomplishment of an action. See PDh on VP 1.3: *svātantryaṁ kartṛ-śaktiḥ*; Helārāja on VP 3.7.122–3: *sādhanântara-viniyoga-lakṣaṇaṁ svātantryam*.

The other participants in the act serve no function in making a substance-*sādhana* an agent. What bestows the capacity of functioning as agent upon the substance-*sādhana*, to put it another way, what makes it an agent, is an external factor (*anyataḥ*). Therefore, with respect to the accomplishment of an action, the external factor should come first in that without that the agent who is the principal *kāraka* of the action does not take action. Thus the prompting of the agent into action by the external factor turns out to be essential for the accomplishment of the action. When Bhartṛhari calls the *pravṛtti* the first *kāraka*, he obviously regards it as the external factor which sets the agent, the second *kāraka*, into play and thereby brings a particular action to accomplishment. It is precisely because of its being what prompts the second *kāraka*, an agent, into action, that the *pravṛtti* is called the first *kāraka*.

**–4–**

The *pravṛtti* as the first *kāraka* is the incitor of the agent as the second *kāraka*. Then how does the prompting of the agent into action by the *pravṛtti* occur?

**–4.1–**

Consider the following remark:

VP 3.7.122–3: *saṁbhāvanāt kriyā-siddhau kartṛtvena samāśritaḥ /*
*kriyāyām ātma-sādhyāyāṁ sādhanānāṁ prayojakaḥ //*
*prayoga-mātre nyagbhāvaṁ svātantryād eva niśritaḥ /*
*aviśiṣṭo bhavaty anyaiḥ sva-tantrair mukta-saṁśayaiḥ //*

> 'One who has been chosen as agent with respect to the accomplishment of an action on the supposition [that he has the capacity of bringing the action to accomplishment] and one who is the incitor of other *sādhana*s in relation to the action which is to be brought to accomplishment by himself—they become subordinate to the causation in general (*prayoga-mātra*) [which others perform] precisely because of their independence; they are not distinguished from the other independent [agents] as to whose [independence] there is no doubt.'

Here is given the situation in which an agent functions. An agent functions independently (*sva-tantra*) in some cases and dependently (*para-tantra*) in others. The dependent functioning of the agent is raised by causation or prompting (*prayoga*); and the agent who is prompted into action is either one who is supposed to have the capacity of functioning as agent or one who is in action, activating other *sādhanas* for the accomplishment of an action.[11]

Bhartṛhari mentions two sorts of prompters: One who gives a command (*preṣaṇa*) or makes an entreaty (*adhyeṣaṇa*), in short, one who performs the activity which serves to incite one to actions (*tat-samartha-caraṇa*);[12] and an object (*karman*) itself as one of the six *kārakas*. What we have to note here is his characterisation of the object as a prompter, which seems to be contradictory to his statement in VP 3.7.101a that what calls an agent into play is something different from other *sādhanas*.

> VP 3.7.128: *kriyāyāḥ prerakaṁ karma hetuḥ kartuḥ prayojakaḥ /*
> *karmârthā ca kriyôtpatti-saṁskāra-pratipattibhiḥ //*
>
> 'An object prompts (*preraka*) an action and a causal agent (*hetu*) [defined by Pāṇ 1.4.55[13]] is an incitor of an [independent] agent. The action serves the object by way of *niṣpatti* ("bringing into existence"), *saṁskāra* ("adding new qualities"), or *pratipatti* ("arriving at").'

The object is the prompter of the action (*kriyāyāḥ prerakaṁ karma*). Having taken into consideration Pāṇ 1.4.49: *kartur īpsitatamaṁ karma*, which provides that that is *kāraka* which an agent most wishes to reach or obtain (*īpsitatamam*) through the act in which it participates,[14] it is entirely fair to say that an object prompts the action, which is the means through which an agent desires to obtain the object. But, while,

---

[11] The two cases in which an agent is prompted into action are explained in VP 3.7.126.

[12] VP 3.7.125:

> *preṣaṇâdhyeṣaṇe kurvaṁs tat-samarthāni cācaran /*
> *kartâiva vihitāṁ śāstre hetu-saṁjñāṁ prapadyate //*

[13] Pāṇ 1.4.55 *tat-prayojako hetuś ca* provides that a *kāraka* that plays the role of causing an independent agent to participate in an act is called *hetu* as well as *kartṛ*.

[14] According to Bhartṛhari, an object participates in an action in the following manner:

> VP 3.7.54: *nirvartyâdiṣu tat pūrvam anubhūya sva-tantratām /*
> *kartr-antarāṇāṁ vyapāre karma saṁpadyate tataḥ //*
>
> 'In the case of a thing to be made (*nirvartya*) and others, after having enjoyed independence at first [in regard to actions like coming into being (*nirvṛtti*)], they become the object in regard to the actions of other agents.'

In the situation expressed by *ghaṭaṁ karoti*, the pot is an agent with reference to its own activity, i.e. coming into existence (*nirvṛtti*), as in *ghaṭaṁ nirvartate* ('the pot is coming into existence'), and becomes the object in regard to the prompting activity of the principal agent (*kartṛ-praiṣa*), i.e. the action of calling the object into existence (*nirvartanā*).

as in *yajñadatto devadattenâudanaṁ pācayati* ('Yajñadatta has Devadatta cook rice-gruel'), the causal agent causes one who participates in an action to do the action, the object causes the action, directly in the sense that there is no intervention by another agent. As is suggested by VP 3.7.122–3, the causation takes place in two ways: with reference to an agent who is active, an actual agent, and the one who is inactive but capable of functioning as agent, a possible agent. Then, in the case of the causation of the action by the object, how is the agent involved in that causation? Consider the following *Bhāṣya*:

> MBhā on Pāṇ 3.1.26: *iha kaścit kaṁcid āha—pṛcchatu mā bhavān, anuyuṅktāṁ mā bhavān iti, atra ṇic kasmān na bhavati / akartṛtvāt / na hy asau saṁprati pṛcchati, tūṣṇīm āste / kiṁ ca bho vartamāna-kālāyā eva kriyāyāḥ kartrā bhavitavyaṁ na bhūta-bhaviṣyat-kālāyāḥ / bhūta-bhaviṣyat-kālāyā api bhavitavyam / abhisambandhas tatra kriyate—imāṁ kriyām akārṣīd imāṁ kriyāṁ kariṣyatîti / iha punar na kaścid abhisambandhaḥ kriyate na câsau saṁprati pṛcchati, tūṣṇīm āste / yadi tarhi kartā nâsti kathaṁ tarhi kartṛ-pratyayena loṭâbhidhīyate / atha katham asminn apṛcchaty ayaṁ pracchir vartate / abhisambandhas tatra kriyate—imāṁ kriyāṁ kurv iti / kartrâpi tarhy abhisambandhaḥ kriyate / katham / kartā câsyāḥ kriyāyā bhavêti /*
>
> 'Here someone asks someone, "You ask me (*pṛcchatu mā bhavān*)," "You question me (*anuyuṅktāṁ mā bhavān*)." Why does the causative affix ṆiC not occur in this case? Because [one who is urged to ask or question] has no quality of being an agent (*akartṛtvāt*). Indeed, he does not currently ask; he keeps silent. But, sir, should there be an agent only in relation to the action referred to the present and not in relation to the action referred to the past or the future? There should be an agent in relation to the action referred to the past or the future also. In that case the connection is formed [between an agent and the action referred to the past or the future] as in *imāṁ kriyām akārṣīt* ("he took this action") or *imāṁ kriyāṁ kariṣyati* ("he will take this action"). In the present case, however, no connection is formed [between the agent and the action of asking]. For he does not currently ask; he keeps silent. Then if there is no agent [in relation to the action of asking], how then will [the agent] be denoted by the imperative affix LOṬ which is used to convey an agent and how will the verb root *pracch* occur when he does not ask? In that case, the connection [of the agent with the action] is formed, so that we have the utterance *imāṁ kriyāṁ kuru* ("Take this action"). The connection [of the action] with the

agent also, in that case, is formed. How? In such a way that we have the utterance *kartā asyāḥ kriyāyā bhava* ("Become the agent of this action").'

When an imperative sentence such as *pṛcchatu mā bhavān* is used, one who utters the sentence causes to take action a hearer who is not currently taking the action in question, and hence cannot be regarded as the agent in relation to that action. Therefore, in the injunctive causation of the action, as is importantly pointed out by Patañjali, the quality of being an agent (*kartṛtva*), to use Bhartṛhari's term, the capacity of functioning as agent (*kartṛ-śakti*), is brought out from one who is inactive. Bhartṛhari states:

VP 3.7.126: *dravya-mātrasya tu praiṣe pṛcchyāder loḍ vidhīyate /*
*sakriyasya prayogas tu yadā sa viṣayo ṇicaḥ //*

'The imperative affix (LOṬ) is used after verb roots like *pracch* when the bare substance is prompted. When the already active object is prompted, it comes within the scope of the use of the causative affix (ṆiC).'

Accordingly, with reference to the bare substance (*dravya-mātra*) that is without any activity, saying that its action is prompted amounts to saying that the capacity of functioning as agent in relation to that action is drawn out from it.

Then what is the case with the object? The same observation applies to the causation of the action by the object. For both an object and a speaker who utters an imperative sentence equally cause one in whom an action has not yet occurred (*apravṛtta-kriyā*) to take action, unlike the causal agent who prompts the active agent (*pravṛtta-kriyā*). Thus it follows that, in the case of the causation of the action by the object also, there occurs the causation of the action through drawing out from a substance-*sādhana* the property of being an agent in regard to the action. A substance-*sādhana* from which the capacity of functioning as agent is drawn out by the object is precisely the possible agent.

## –4.2–

According to Pāṇinīyas, an object defined by Pāṇ 1.4.49 has three subtypes: a thing which is made (*nirvartya*), modified (*vikārya*), and reached (*prāpya*). In the case of an object of *nirvartya*-type, a difficulty arises. In the situation expressed by utterances like *ghaṭaṁ karoti* ('He is making a pot'), the object which is characterised as something brought into being cannot play a role of causing the action of making, since it is not existent until the act of bringing it into existence is completed and what has not been brought about cannot function as the causer of an action.[15] Then what can function as the prompter of the action in the case of the *nirvartya*-object? Take into account the following statement in the *Pada-mañjarī*:

> PM on Pāṇ 1.4.49: *tatra nirvartyam—ghaṭaṁ karotîti, vyakty-abhiprāyeṇa janma sāmānyâbhiprāyeṇa prakāśanam* /
>
> 'Of these, the *nirvartya* [is a pot] as in *ghaṭaṁ karoti*. [If the word *ghaṭa* is used] with the intention of conveying the particular pot, its birth (*janman*) is said of it; [if it is used] with the intention of conveying the universal [potness (*ghaṭatva*)], its manifestation is said of it.'

In *ghaṭaṁ karoti* the pot as a particular is something brought into existence and the universal potness is something manifested with the realisation of the particular pot. Where does the universal potness come in? It takes part in the act of making the pot in such a way that it causes the action of bringing the particular pot into existence precisely because of its eternity. The role of the universal here is nothing but to set an agent into play for the sake of bringing the particular into being. In the case of the object of *nirvartya*-type, thus, what functions as the prompter of the action is the universal to be manifested.

**–4.3–**

The idea that the universal (*jāti*) prompts the action is set forth by Bhartṛhari in the context where he argues that the word denotes the universal (*jāti-padârtha-pakṣa*).

> VP 3.1.25: *na tad utpadyate kiṁ cid yasya jātir na vidyate* /
> *ātmâbhivyaktaye jātiḥ kāraṇānāṁ prayojikā* //
>
> 'Whatever does not have its universal is not produced. For the sake of its own manifestation, the universal incites the causes [of producing the particular that is its own substratum] to take action.'
>
> VP 3.1.26: *kāraṇeṣu padaṁ kṛtvā nityânityeṣu jātayaḥ* /
> *kva cit kāryeṣv abhivyaktim upayānti punaḥ punaḥ* //
>
> 'In some effects [i.e. in perceptible effects], the universals, after having obtained a footing among the eternal and non-eternal causes [on account of its omnipresence], manifest themselves again and again.'

---

[15] Helārāja on VP 3.1.27: *ghaṭaṁ karotîti katham asato nirvartyamānasya kriyāyāṁ sādhana-bhāvaḥ karmaṇaḥ* ... /

VP 3.1.27: *nirvartyamānaṁ yat karma jātis tatrâpi sādhanam /*
*svâśrayasyâbhiniṣpattyai sā kriyāyāḥ prayojikā //*

'The universal is the cause even of that object which is newly produced. In order that its substratum might be produced, it prompts the actions [of the *kāraka*s] to come to be.'

The point made is as follows: In the case of the situation conveyed by *ghaṭaṁ karoti*, the universal potness, being eternal, is pre-existent in relation to a particular pot that is to be brought about. When one makes a pot, one first brings it to mind on the basis of its universal and then takes action toward the causes capable of producing it.[16] But for that, he would not act. Therefore, of the two elements, the universal and the particular, which are involved in the act of bringing the particular into existence, the universal which is directly denoted is what brings the act to accomplishment (*sādhana*) and the particular which is to be brought about is an object (*karman*) in the sense that it is something which an agent wishes to obtain.[17] Here in this situation, the universal functions as what prompts the causes of its substratum to produce its substratum for the sake of its own manifestation (*ātmâbhivyaktaye*) or what prompts one to take action for the sake of the realisation of its own substratum (*svâśrayasyâbhiniṣpattyai*). And this amounts to saying that the universal is the first *kāraka*.

## –4.4–

All these things make it clear that the *pravṛtti* as the first *kāraka* is the incitor of the agent as the second *kāraka*. The *pravṛtti* has been characterised as the activity in general which is to be differentiated into particulars and which is eternal. If the universal, as the first *kāraka*, can function as the prompter of the action, then we may assume that the *pravṛtti* also causes entities to take action and prompts one to take activity precisely because it is of a generic nature; that is, led by the universal action, one exerts oneself to realise a particular action through which the universal action manifests itself. Given a sentence such as *devadattaḥ pākaṁ karoti* ('Devadatta is doing the cooking'), it is proper to say that the universal property of

---

[16] Helārāja on VP 3.1.27: *jāty-ātmanā ca nirūpya vastu kāraṇeṣu yogyeṣu pravartante tad-arthinaḥ /*

[17] Helārāja on VP 3.1.27: *jāti-rūpâśrayeṇa ca sādhanatā, vyakti-rūpâśrayeṇa ca karmatā /*

being the cooking sets Devadatta into play for the sake of the realisation of the particular action of cooking.[18]

–5–

With this background, we are now in a position to inquire into what Bhartṛhari means by the term *apūrva*. *Apūrva* enters the picture in the *kārikā* following the one where Bhartṛhari introduced *pravṛtti*.

VP 3.7.34: *apūrvaṁ kāla-śaktiṁ vā kriyāṁ vā kālam eva vā /*
*tam evaṁ-lakṣaṇaṁ bhāvaṁ ke cid āhuḥ kathaṁ cana //*

'From different points of view, of the very entity (*bhāva*) characterised as such, some say that it is *apūrva* itself; some that it is Time-capacity itself; some that it is Action itself; others that it is Time itself.'

Here Bhartṛhari reports that *pravṛtti* can be viewed in any of four ways: as *apūrva*, as Time-capacity (*kālà-śakti*), as Action (*kriyā*) and as Time (*kāla*).[19] What could be meant by the term *apūrva* here?

---

[18] From the viewpoint that the word denotes the particular (*vyakti*), too, Bhartṛhari gives the interpretation of sentences such as *ghaṭaṁ karoti*, in which objects of actions are of the *nirvartya*-type:

VP 3.7.7: *vyaktau padârthe śabdâder janyamānasya karmaṇaḥ /*
*sādhanatvaṁ tathā siddhaṁ buddhi-rūpa-prakalpitam //*

'In like manner, in the view that a word-meaning is an individual, it is established that an object like the sound [in *śabdaṁ karoti* ('... is making a sound')], which is something brought into being, is assumed to be a *sādhana* on the basis of its representation appearing to mind.'

In this view what has the mental existence (*upacāra-sattā*) is the prompter of the action of externally realising it.

[19] Of the Time-capacity and Time, we have the following statements made by Bhartṛhari himself.

VP 1.3: *adhyāhitakalāṁ yasya kāla-śaktim upāśritāḥ /*
*janmādayo vikārāḥ ṣaḍ bhāva-bhedasya yonayaḥ //*

'In dependence upon whose [i.e. Brahman's] Time-capacity, upon which its divisions are superimposed, there appear the six modes of modifications such as birth, which are the womb of particular existences [like the act of cooking].'

VP 3.9.3: *utpattau ca sthitau câiva vināśe câpi tadvatām /*
*nimittaṁ kālam evâhur vibhaktenâtmanā sthitam //*

**–5.1–**

Now Bhartṛhari uses the term *apūrva* in two other *kārikās*: VP 2.1.119 and VP 3.1.69. We now turn to these two *kārikās*. We start with the second *kārikā*. Bhartṛhari is discussing the interpretation of the Vedic sentence *grahaṁ saṁmārṣṭi* ('One should cleanse the cup'),[20] Bhartṛhari states as follows:

VP 3.1.69: *apūrvasya vidheyatvāt prādhānyam avasīyate /*
*vihitasya parârthatvāc cheṣa-bhāvaḥ pratīyate //*

'[In interpreting a Vedic sentence] what has not been known (*apūrva*) is determined to be the principal because of being what is to be enjoined; what has already been enjoined by [another sentence] (*vihita*) is understood to be a subsidiary since it serves something else.'

To Bhartṛhari as a grammarian, the notion of *apūrva* as the Newly Known *apūrva* is familiar since it is applied to determine whether the character of Pāṇini's rule is *apūrva-vidhi* ('statement of something new') or *niyama* ('restriction').[21] What Bhartṛhari states here, however, is less than specific to him. Mīmāṁsakas admit that the injunction (*vidhi*) consists in making known what is not otherwise established, commonly referred to by the term *apūrva-vidhi*: what the term *apūrva* signifies is, according to Kumārila, what is not known before hearing a Vedic sentence,[22] and according to Śālikanātha, what is not cognisable by any of the ordinary means of knowledge (*mānântarâpūrva*).[23] Viewed in this light, we may say that the notion of the Newly Known *apūrva* is commonly accepted as utilised for the sentence-analysis.

---

'They consider Time, which itself is differentiated, to be the cause of being born, stay and destruction of objects which go through these states.'

According to Bhartṛhari, the six modes of modifications (*ṣaḍ-bhāva-vikāra*), that is, origin, being, transformation, growth, decay and destruction, are the womb of all particular actions. In the same line of thought Helārāja (on VP 3.9.3) properly points out that all sorts of actions are included by the triplet, being born, being and destruction. Thus Time-capacity and Time can be regarded as the cause of the action.

[20] This is an objective sentence (*viṣaya-vākya*) discussed in *Grahâikatvâdhikaraṇa* (JS 3.1.7.13–15).

[21] For example, MBhā *ad* Pāṇ 1.4.3: *tatra apurvo vidhir astu niyamo 'stv iti apūrva eva vidhir bhaviṣyati na niyamaḥ /*

[22] TV on JS 1.2.4.34: *tatra yaḥ atyantam aprāptaḥ na ca prāpsyati prāg vacanād ity avagamyate /*

[23] VAM 2 k.25cd: *ato mānântarâpūrvam apūrvam iti gīyate //*

We now turn to the second of the two *kārikā*s mentioned earlier.

> VP 2.119: *asty arthaḥ sarva-śabdānām iti pratyāyya-lakṣaṇam /*
> *apūrva-devatā-svargaiḥ samam āhur gavâdiṣu //*
>
> 'Whatever word is uttered, one understands that what is conveyed by it exists (*asti*). This is the characteristic of what is conveyed by the word. In the case of words like *go*, they say, it is similar to what is denoted by such words as *apūrva*, *devatā* and *svarga*.'

It is obvious that *apūrva* is treated as something transcendental side by side with *svarga* and *devatā*. From the word *apūrva* one understands, Bhartṛhari argues, that it exists.

Taking the present *kārikā* as asserting that all words denote *sattā* ('being'), Kumārila argues that the words like *apūrva* cannot be considered to denote *sattā*, showing what the term *apūrva* is to be taken to signify. He states:

> TV on JS 1.3.9.30–35 (*Ākṛty-adhikaraṇa*): *sarva-padârthānām eva kāryârthâpatti-gamyāni sāmarthyāni santi, yāgâdi-janitaṁ ca puṁsāṁ phala-prāpti-sāmarthyam apūrva-śabda-vācyaṁ yāgânuṣṭhānāt pūrvam abhūtam, anuṣṭhānôttara-kālaṁ câpūrvaṁ jāyata iti yaugikatvād evâpūrva-śabdâbhidhānaṁ sarvatra labhyate /*
>
> 'All entities indeed have the capacities (*sāmarthya*) which are to be known through the assumption on the basis of their effects (*kāryârthâpatti*). And human beings have the capacity, produced by the sacrifice, of attaining its result. [The word *apūrva*] is the term which retains its etymological sense (*yaugika*): to show its etymology, [*apūrva* is] something which has not arisen before the performance of the sacrifice and which is newly born after it. Precisely for this reason, the word *apūrva* is found to denote whatever is of such a nature.'

The term *apūrva* here, as interpreted by Kumārila, means something which has not arisen before the performance of the sacrifice and which is newly born after it, the capacity (*sāmarthya*) to produce the sacrificial result. Of course, we cannot arrive at the certainty that Bhartṛhari also uses the term *apūrva* in this sense in VP 2.119 because Kumārila interprets it in that way.

According to CLOONEY (1990: 221–253) who examined a historical development of the concept of *apūrva* in Mīmāṁsā literature, the term *apūrva* is used within the Mīmāṁsā in two senses: in the sense of that which has not been known through any means other than the injunction in question (i.e. epistemic *apūrva* or the Newly Known *apūrva*); in the sense of that which is newly born by the performance of ritual acts and which functions as linkage between them and their results (i.e. ontic *apūrva* or the Newly Born *apūrva*); the former use of the term *apūrva* is found in Jaimini and the latter in Śabara and Kumārila; Prabhākara returns to Jaimini's understanding of *apūrva*, his position being closer to that of Jaimini. Here I will introduce Jayanta's following remark, which is good evidence to show that in the Mīmāṁsā the term *apūrva* is used in two senses:

> NM 1.255: *vṛddha-mīmāṁsakāḥ yāgâdi-karma-nirvartyam apūrvaṁ nāma dharmam abhivadanti, yāgâdi-karmâiva śābarā bruvate, vākyârtha eva niyogâtmâpūrva-śabda-vācyo dharma-śabdena sa evôcyate iti prābhākarāḥ kathayanti* /
>
> 'The older Mīmāṁsakas declare *dharma* to be something which is to be brought about by ritual acts such as the sacrifice and which is called *apūrva*.[24] The followers of Śabara say that the ritual acts like the sacrifice themselves are [the *dharma*]. The followers of Prabhākara say that it is something which is precisely the meaning of [an injunctive] sentence, which is in essence obligation (*niyoga*) and which is denoted by the term *apūrva* that is spoken of by the word *dharma*.'

Thus in the Mīmāṁsā we have the two types of *apūrva*: ontic *apūrva*, or the Newly Born *apūrva*, and epistemic *apūrva*, or the Newly Known *apūrva*. Of these, the former cannot be the *apūrva* which is identified with the *pravṛtti*. For the *pravṛtti* is said to be the first *kāraka* and hence to be eternal. Accordingly there is much possibility of the latter being the *apūrva* at issue.

## –5.2–

From Mīmāṁsakas' point of view, the *pravṛtti* in question is explained by Helārāja:

> Helārāja on VP 3.7.33: *satata-vyāpāra-pravahad-rūpā nadī-pravāha iva tṛṇa-parṇa-latâdīn sādhana-śaktīḥ*[25] *pravṛtti-lakṣaṇā kriyā karṣati vahatîti keṣāṁcij jaran-mīmāṁsakānām āgamaḥ* /[26]

---

[24] In his MŚV, *Codanā*, k. 195, Kumārila criticises the identification of the *apūrva* of this sort with *dharma*.

[25] I have adopted the reading *sādhana-śaktīḥ* suggested by RAGHUNĀTHA ŚARMĀ, instead of *sādhana-śaktiḥ*.

[26] It is important to note that Bhartṛhari uses the simile of *srotovat* ('like a stream'), which reminds us of *Triṁśikā* 4d: *tac ca vartate srotasâughavat*, stated with reference to

'According to the tradition handed down by some old Mimāṁsakas, just as a river-stream takes away things such as blades of grass, leaves and creepers [from the plants growing in banks], so does the Action characterised as the *pravṛtti*, in the form of a continuously flowing stream of activities, take away the capacities of *sādhanas*.'

According to the tradition of some old Mimāṁsakas, behind actions, transient in essence, there is something continuing as a flow, which causes entities to take activity for the accomplishment of an action by way of drawing out their capacities. What is permanent in the form of a continuous flow is the Action characterised as the *pravṛtti* (*pravṛtti-lakṣaṇā kriyā*), which is what is called *apūrva*.

Now let us consider Bhartṛhari's statement in his *Mahā-bhāṣya-dīpikā* on *Paspaśâhnika*. With regard to the third interpretation of the word *dharma-niyama* that is taken to mean 'the restriction motivated by *dharma*' (*dharma-prayojano niyamaḥ*), Bhartṛhari states as follows:

---

*ālaya-vijñāna*, which produces a 'forthcoming' mind (*pravṛtti-vijñāna*) and a defiled *manas*. Helārāja uses a strikingly similar expression to Sthiramati on *Triṁśikā* 4d:

> *yathā hy oghas tṛṇa-kāṣṭha-gomayâdīn ākarṣayan gacchati evam ālaya-vijñānam api puṇyâpuṇyâneñjaya-karma-vāsanânugataṁ sparśa-manas-kārâdīn ākarṣayat srotasā saṁsāram avyuparataṁ pravartata iti /*
>
> 'Just as a stream flows taking away blades of grass, pieces of wood and pieces of cow dung [from banks]', in the similar manner *ālaya-vijñāna*, which is followed by impressions implanted by meritorious-demeritorious-immoral *karmans*, also is in activity, takes away—in a stream—touch, mental reflection and others, insofar as the transmigration does not end.'

The interpretation from a Sāṁkhya viewpoint is also given, which will not be taken into account here; Helārāja on VP 3.7.33:

> *rajo-lakṣaṇā vā pravṛttir nityā sarva-bhāveṣv anuyāyinī sva-kārya-prasava-samarthā kāryāṇi janayatîti sāṁkhya-nayaḥ / vyāpārâviṣṭasya sarvasya kārya-janakatvād vyāpāraḥ pūrva-bhāvī samavasthitaḥ tena ca śakty-ākṣepaḥ iti yuktam /*
>
> 'Or according to the Sāṁkhya view, the *pravṛtti* is something characterised by *rajas*. It is eternal. When it follows a thing, whatever the thing may be, it becomes capable of producing its own effect and then produces the effect. Whatever is endowed with the activity (*vyāpārâviṣṭa*) produces its effect. Consequently, it is determined that the activity exists prior to [the *sādhana* as substance]. And, for this reason, it is proper that the capacity is drawn out [from the substance by the *pravṛtti*] (*śakty-ākṣepa*).'

In this interpretation also the *pravṛtti* is equally regarded as the drawer of the capacity.

MBhāD I [25: 24–27]: *dharma-prayojano vā iti mīmāṁsaka-darśanam / avasthita eva dharmaḥ / sa tv agni-hotrâdibhir abhivyajyate / tat-preritas tu phalado bhavati / yathā svāmī bhṛtyaiḥ sevāyāṁ preryate phalaṁ praty evam ayaṁ niyamo dharmasya phala-nirvṛttiṁ prati prayojaka iti /*

'The alternative interpretation *dharma-prayojano vā* [*niyamaḥ*] represents the Mīmāṁsaka view. *Dharma* is something fixed (*avasthita*). It is however manifested (*abhivyajyate*) by [acts] like *Agni-hotra*. On the other hand, it is when [the *dharma*] is prompted by virtue of those [acts manifesting it] that it becomes fruit-bearing. Just as a lord is prompted to giving the benefit [to servants] when they are actually in his service; in the same way, this restriction is the prompter of *dharma* to giving the benefit.'[27]

A lord is to pay wages to his servants in reward for their services. The servants demand that the lord should pay wages when they are in his service. Similarly the *dharma* is to bring forth its fruit. The *Agni-hotra* oblation demands that the *dharma* should bear its fruit when the former manifests the latter.

In the Vedic injunction *agni-hotraṁ juhuyāt svarga-kāmaḥ* ('Let one who desires heaven have the *Agni-hotra* oblation performed'), it is stated that there is the relationship of the accomplisher and the accomplished between the *Agni-hotra* oblation and its fruit, heaven. When does the *Agni-hotra* oblation bring forth its fruit? Obviously at the time when it is actually performed. Let the *Agni-hotra* oblation as understood from its direct statement in the injunction in question be the *dharma*. And recall that in *ghaṭaṁ karoti* the universal potness prompts an agent to take action toward making a particular pot for the sake of its own manifestation. Here in the present *Mahā-bhāṣya-dīpikā*, the *dharma* is characterised as something manifested by the *Agni-hotra* oblation. Therefore we may say in a similar manner

---

[27] JOSHI–ROODBERGEN (1986: 119, fn. 486), BRONKHORST (1987: 85), and KATAOKA give different interpretations of the lord-servant example cited here in order to illustrate how *dharma* becomes fruit-bearing. JOSHI–ROODBERGEN: 'Just as a lord, with a view to the benefit (arising from it) is prompted by the service (rendered) by his servants (to employ servants), ...' BRONKHORST: 'Just as a lord is brought closer to his desired end by servants when they are in his service; ...' KATAOKA: 'For example, a master is urged to [give] fruit by servants when they serve.' In my opinion, KATAOKA's interpretation can best explain the very heart of the problem. The lord makes it a rule to pay wages to his servants in reward to the service they render. What motivates him to pay wages is their being in his service. Similarly what incites *dharma* to bring forth its fruit is the manifestation of the *dharma* by the *Agni-hotra* oblation.

that the *dharma* prompts one who desires heaven to perform the *Agni-hotra* oblation for the sake of its own manifestation. As in the case of the pot the manifestation of the universal potness means the realisation of a particular pot, so in the present case also the manifestation of the *dharma* means the realisation of the *Agni-hotra* oblation.

In this connection, it is interesting to note the view which in his *Nyāyâgamânusāriṇī* Siṁhasūri refers to as that of some Mīmāṁsakas and which was first noticed by KATAOKA. It says:

> NĀA 1.141: *agni-hotram iti dharmaḥ kriyā-vyaṅgya ucyate kārye kāraṇôpacārād agni-hotrâbhivyaṅgyo 'gni-hotram iti / tataḥ agni-hotraṁ dharmaṁ juhuyād bhāvayet svarga-kāmaḥ ity eṣa vākyârtho nirdoṣaḥ* ... /
>
> 'What is meant by the word "*agni-hotra*" is the *dharma* which is to be manifested by the action [of performing the *Agni-hotra* oblation]. On account of the extended application of the word whose proper referent is the cause to the effect, what is to be manifested by the *Agni-hotra* oblation is referred to by the word "*agni-hotra*". Therefore the sentence in question can be without fault paraphrased as follows: *agni-hotraṁ dharmaṁ juhuyāt bhāvayet svarga-kāmaḥ* ("Let one who desires heaven have *dharma* (*agni-hotra*) brought into being (*juhuyāt bhāvayet*")).'

If *agni-hotraṁ juhuyāt* can be interpreted as *dharmaṁ bhāvayet*, we will easily see that the universal *dharma* prompts the action of realising the particular *dharma* so that the universal *dharma* may be manifested through that action. In this respect, what Pārthasārathi states in his *Śāstra-dīpikā* is especially significant. Concerning the question of what is the means of knowing *dharma*, he says:

> ŚD on JS 1.1.2: *jagad-vaicitryârthâpattyā kim apy adṛṣṭam astîti sāmānyena prasiddho dharmaś codanayâgni-hotrâdi-viśeṣa-rūpeṇa gamyate tasmāt samuccaya iti pakṣântaram* /
>
> 'The different view is set forth: *Dharma* is established in a general form by means of assuming, on the basis of the variety of the world, that there is something transcendental (*kim apy adṛṣṭam*). The *dharma* is understood as a particular [act] like *Agni-hotra* through *codanā* ("injunction"). Therefore, [the means for knowing *dharma* is] the combination [of empirical means of knowledge and *codanā*].'

Although this view is a prima facie view since the final view is that for knowing *dharma codanā* alone is the sole means, it is interestingly stated that there is the *dharma* in general, in relation to which *Agni-hotra* is a specific *dharma*. This clearly shows that there is the universal *dharma* to be differentiated to the end of the particular.

Thus if we put the *pravṛtti* into the Mīmāṁsā frame of reference, it is likely that the Action characterised as the *pravṛtti*, permanent in a stream, is the *dharma* which Bhartṛhari considers to be assumed by Mīmāṁsakas. For the *dharma*, which is something fixed or eternal, is said to be manifested (*abhivyajyate*) by individual and concrete sacrificial acts and hence considered to be what prompts one to perform them for the sake of its own manifestation.

It is quite natural for Mīmāṁsakas to postulate the universal *dharma* according to their linguistic theory that the word (*śabda*) denotes the universal.[28] For *codanā* ('injunction'), by which alone *dharma* is made known, is essentially the injunctive statement (*vacana*).[29] Insofar as *dharma* is what is conveyed by the injunctive statement, the *dharma* has to be the universal *dharma*. Consequently, if the *pravṛtti* is identified with the universal *dharma*, it can properly be called the Newly Known *apūrva*.[30]

---

[28] JS 1.3.33: *ākṛtis tu kriyârthatvāt* ('But a generic form (*ākṛti*) is the meaning of the word. For it serves the ritual act'). According to Śabara, the generic form is the universal property (*sāmānya*), which substances, qualities, and actions may have. ŚBh on JS 1.3.9.30: *ākṛtir dravya-guṇa-karmaṇāṁ sāmānya-mātram*.

[29] JS 1.1.2: *codanā-lakṣaṇo 'rtho dharmaḥ* ('*dharma* is something profitable, which is made known by the injunction'). *Codanā*, Śabara says, is a statement that urges one to take action (*kriyāyāḥ pravartakaṁ vacanam*).

[30] It should also be added that, with reference to the interpretation of the word *dharma-niyama* as *dharma-prayojano niyamaḥ*, Kaiyaṭa and Nāgeśa understand that this interpretation has been given according to the view adopted by Prabhākara. Nāgeśa states:

> *Uddyota*: *prabhākarâṅgī-kṛta-matenêdam / tan-mate hi liṅ-ādīnām apūrva-sañjñakaṁ kāryaṁ vācyam / tad eva ca svasmin puruṣaṁ prayuñjānaṁ niyoga ity ucyate / sa eva dharmaḥ /*
>
> 'This [has been stated] according to the view adopted by Prabhākara. Because, in his view, the meaning of [the verbal endings like] LIṄ is *kārya* ("what one should do"), which is called *apūrva*. And the very [*kārya*], which prompts a man to fulfil itself is called *niyoga* ("obligation"). That [*niyoga*] itself is *dharma*.'

What is important to note here is that Kaiyaṭa and Nāgeśa regard the *dharma* as what is called *apūrva* from the viewpoint of Prabhākara. As has been pointed out by CLOONEY, Prabhākara's understanding of *apūrva* is closer to Jaimini's.

## Conclusion

The *pravṛtti*, as the first *kāraka*, sets the agent, as the second *kāraka*, into play. The most significant characteristic of the *pravṛtti* lies in its universality, from which stems its being a prompter, or a causer of particular actions. Therefore, it constitutes the essential feature of the causation of the action by the *pravṛtti* that the *pravṛtti* which has no substratum (*anapāśrita*) seeks for its substratum for the sake of its own manifestation (*ātmâbhivyakti*), whereby the action of realising the substratum of the *pravṛtti* (*svâśrayâbhiniṣpatti*) takes place.

Assuming the activity in general, which is existent in precedence to candidates for the *sādhana* as well as particular and concrete actions, and which is eternal, Bhartṛhari explains how those particular actions, which are ephemeral, are actualised, in terms of his view of *sādhana* as the capacity. As in the case of *ghaṭaṁ karoti*, the universal potness is regarded as the prompter of the action of bringing the particular pot into existence from the viewpoint that the universal is the meaning of the word; in the same way, the activity in general is considered to prompt the action of realising the particular activity. The point is that the universal activity is what draws out the capacity of functioning as agent from the bare substance.

A semantic approach to the Vedic injunction on Mīmāṁsakas' part will have to lead to the conclusion that the universal *dharma* is the prompter of the action of realising a particular *dharma*. For the sole source for knowing *dharma* is the *Veda*, the word in essence, and what is directly understood from the injunctive statement in the *Veda* should be the universal *dharma*, and not a particular *dharma*. Suppose that the sentence *dharmaṁ bhāvayet* ('Let one have *dharma* brought into existence') were given in the *Veda*, the universal *dharma* as understood from that sentence would prompt the action of bringing a particular *dharma* to accomplishment for the sake of its own manifestation or for the sake of the realisation of its own substratum, by way of drawing out the capacity of functioning as agent in regard to that action. Therefore, when such a universal *dharma* is meant by the *pravṛtti*, it is proper to identify the latter with the Newly Known *apūrva*.

It is true that what Bhartṛhari means by the word *apūrva* is not the Newly Born *apūrva*, as is pointed out by HALBFASS. But, what Bhartṛhari calls *apūrva*, being the *pravṛtti* as the first *kāraka* or the universal *dharma*, is far from being a cosmic principle or power. It is a kind of 'ideal' activity to be realised.

## BIBLIOGRAPHY


ABHYANKAR–JOŚI 1970–1976 = Abhyankar, Kashinath Vasudev; Jośi, G.A. (eds.): *Mīmāṁsā-darśanam*. 7 Vols., *Ānandâśrama-saṁskṛta-granthâvaliḥ* 17, Ānandāśrama, Pune 1970–1976.

BRONKHORST 1987 = Bronkhorst, Johannes: *Mahābhāṣyadīpikā of Bhartṛhari, Fascicule* IV: *Āhnika* I. *Post-Graduate and Research Department Series* 28, Bhandarkar Oriental Research Institute, Poona 1987.

CLOONEY 1990 = Clooney, Francis X, S.J.: *Thinking Ritually: Rediscovering the Pūrva Mīmāṁsā of Jaimini. Publications of the De Nobili Research Library*, Vienna 1990.

DHARMADATTA JHA 1988 = Dharmadatta Jha (Baccha Jha), Srī: *Shāstradīpikā of Parthasarathi Mishra, with the Commentary Mayukhamalika (from Second Pada of First Chapter to the end) by Somanātha and with the Commentary Yuktisnehaprapurani (for the First Tarkapada) by Rāmakrishṇa. Krishnadas Sanskrit Series* 103. Krishnadas Academy, Varanasi 1988.

DVĀRIKĀDĀSA ŚĀSTRĪ 1978 = Dvārikādāsa Śāstrī, Svāmī: *Ślokavārttika of Śrī Kumārila Bhaṭṭa, with the commentary Nyāyaratnākara of Śrī Pārthasārathi Miśra. Prāchyabhārati Series* 10. Tara Publications, Varanasi 1978.

EIPHIL V = *Encyclopedia of Indian Philosophies*. (General editor: Karl H. Potter.)—Vol. V: Coward, H.G.; Raja, K. Kunjunni (eds.): *The Philosophy of the Grammarians*. Princeton University Press, Princeton–New Jersey 1990. [Indian edition: Motilal Banarsidass, Delhi 1990].

HALBFASS 1991 = Halbfass, Wilhelm: *Tradition and Reflection: Exploration in Indian Thought*. State University of New York Press, Albany 1991.

Helārāja = See: SUBRAMANIA IYER (1963, 1966).

JAMBŪVIJAYAJĪ 1966 = Jambūvijayajī, Muni: *Dvādaśāraṁ Nayacakraṁ of Ācārya Śrī Māllavādi Kṣamāśramaṇa, with the commentary Nyāyāgamānusāriṇī of Śrī Siṁhasūri Gaṇi Vādi Kṣamāśramaṇa*: Part I (1–4 *Aras*); edited with critical notes. *Śrī Ātmānand Jain Granthamālā Series* 92, Khimchand Champshi Shah, Bhavanagar 1966.

JOSHI–ROODBERGEN 1986 = Joshi, S.D.; Roodbergen, J.A.F.: *Patañjali's Vyākaraṇa-Mahābhāṣya: Paspaśāhnika; Introduction, Text, Translation and Notes*. Publications of the Centre of Advanced Study in Sanskrit, Class C 15, University of Poona, Pune 1986.

JS = *Jaimini-sūtra*, in: *Mīmāṁsā-darśana*. See ABHYANKAR–JOŚI (1970–1976).

KATAOKA 2000 = Kataoka, Kei: 'Reconstructing the '*Dharma-abhivyakti-vāda*.' In *Japanese Studies on South Asia* 5 (2000): *The Way to Liberation—Indological Studies in Japan*. Ed. S. Mayeda, Y. Matsunami, M. Tokunaga, and H. Marui.

LÉVI 1925 = Lévi, Sylvain: *Vijñaptimātratāsiddhi: Deux Traités de Vasubandhu; Viṁśatikā (la Vingtaine) accompagnée d'une Explication en Prose et Triṁśikā (la Trentaine) avec la commentaire de Sthiramati*. Bibliothèque de l'École des Hautes Études 245, Paris 1925. [Reprinted: Sankibo, Tokyo: no date].

MBhā = Patañjali's *Vyākaraṇa-mahā-bhāṣya*. See VEDAVRATA (1962–63).

MBhāD = Bhartṛhari's *Mahā-bhāṣya-dīpikā*. See BRONKHORST (1987).

MISRA 1985 = Misra, Srīnārāyaṇa: *Kāśikavṛtti of Jayāditya-Vāmana, along with Commentaries Vivaraṇapañcikā-Nyāsa of Jinendrabuddhi and Padamañjarī of Haradatta Miśra*. 6 volumes. *Ratnabharati Series* 5–10, Ratna Publications, Varanasi 1985.

MŚV = Kumārila Bhaṭṭa: *Mīmāṁsā-śloka-vārttika*. See DVĀRIKĀDĀSA ŚĀSTRĪ (1978).

NĀA = Siṁhasūri: *Nyāyâgamânusāriṇī*. See JAMBŪVIJAYAJĪ (1966).

NM = Jayanta Bhaṭṭa: *Nyāya-mañjarī*. See ŚUKLA (1971).

Pāṇ = Pāṇini: *Aṣṭâdhyāyī*.

PDh = Vṛṣabhadeva: *Pad-dhati*. See SUBRAMANIA IYER (1966).

PM = Haradatta: *Pada-mañjarī*. See MISRA (1985).

RAGHUNĀTHA ŚARMĀ 1974, 1991[2] = Raghunātha Śarmā: *Vākyapadīyam*, Part III (*Pada-kāṇḍa, Jāti, Dravya and Sambandha Samuddeśa*) *with the Commentaries 'Prakāśa' by Śrī Helārāja and 'Ambākartrī' by 'Padmaśrī' Pt. Raghunātha Śarmā. Sarasvatī Bhavana Grantha-mālā* 91. Sampurnanand Sanskrit University, Varanasi 1974, 1991[2].

RAGHUNĀTHA ŚARMĀ 1979 = Raghunātha Śarmā: Vākyapadīyam, Part III, Vol. II (*Bhūyodravya, Guṇa, Dik, Sādhana, Kriyā, Kāla, Puruṣa, Saṅkhyā, Upagraha* and *Liṅga Samuddeśa*) *with the Commentary 'Prakāśa' by Helārāja and Ambākartrī by Pt. Raghunātha Śarmā. Sarasvatī Bhavana Grantha-mālā* 91. Sampurnanand Sanskrit Vishvavidyalaya, Vāraṇasī 1979.

RAU 1977 = Rau, Wilhelm: *Bhartṛharis Vākyapadīya: Die Mūlakārikās nach den Handschriften herausgegeben und mit einem Pāda-Index versehen von ....* Abhandlungen für die Kunde des Morgenlandes XLII, 4. Franz Steiner Verlag, Wiesbaden 1977.

ŚBh = Śabarasvāmin: *Mīmāṁsā-śābara-bhāṣya*; in: *Mīmāṁsā-darśana*. See ABHYANKAR–JOŚI (1970–1976).

ŚD = Pārthasārathi Miśra: *Śāstra-dīpikā*. See DHARMADATTA JHA (1988).

SUBRAMANIA IYER 1963 = Subramania Iyer, K.A.: *Vākyapadīya of Bhartṛhari with the Commentary of Helārāja, Kāṇḍa* III, Part 1. *Deccan College Monograph Series* 21. Deccan College, Poona 1963.

SUBRAMANIA IYER 1966 = Subramania Iyer, K.A.: *Vākyapadīya of Bhartṛhari with the Commentaries Vṛtti and Paddhati of Vṛṣabhadeva. Deccan College Monograph Series* 32. Deccan College, Poona 1966.

SUBRAHMANYA SASTRI 1961 = Subrahmanya Sastri, A. (ed.): *Prakaraṇa Pañcikā of Śālikanātha Miśra, with the Nyāya-siddhi of Jaipuri Nārāyaṇa Bhatta*; edited with Introduction and Notes. *Banaras Hindu University Darśana Series* 4, Banaras Hindu University, Vārāṇasī 1961.

ŚUKLA 1971 = Śukla, Pt. Surya Nārāyaṇa: *Nyāyamañjarī of Jayanta Bhaṭṭa*. Part 1. *Kashi Sanskrit Series* 106, Chowkhamba Sanskrit Series Office, Varanasi 1971.

*Triṁśikā* = Vasubandhu: *Triṁśikā*. See LÉVI (1925).

TV = Kumārila Bhaṭṭa: *Tantra-vārttika*, in: *Mīmāṁsā-darśana*. See ABHYANKAR–JOŚI (1970–1976).

*Uddyota* = Nāgeśa: *Uddyota*. See VEDAVRATA (1962–63).

VAM = *Vākyârtha-mātṛkā*, in: *Prakaraṇa-pañcikā*. See SUBRAHMANYA SASTRI (1961).

VEDAVRATA 1962–63 = Vedavrata: *Śrī-bhagavat-patañjali-viracitaṁ Vyākaraṇa-mahābhāṣyam* (*Śrī-kaiyyaṭa-kṛta-pradīpena-nāgojībhaṭṭa-kṛtena-bhāṣya-pradīpôdyotena ca vibhūṣitam*). 5 volumes. Hairyāṇā-Sāhitya-Saṁsthānam, Gurukul Jhajjar (Rohatak) 1962–63.

VP = Bhartṛhari: *Vākya-padīya*. See RAU, SUBRAMANIA IYER. [*Kārikā* numbers are given according to RAU's edition.]

# HINDI LITERATURE

# Between Myth and Mystique: Thematic Spheres Shared by Modern Hindi Poetry and Polish Avant-garde Poetry

RENATA CZEKALSKA

Hugo FRIEDRICH, while analysing the attitude towards literary tradition and modernity shared by European poets, stated that a deep interest in all the literatures and religions of the world goes against the evident breaking away from tradition, as does the inclination to dive into the deep world of the human psyche, where Europe and Asia, magical and mythical primary images meet together.[1] This 'diving' can be observed through a figure of speech fundamental for avant-garde poetry, in other words—through metaphor.

The following metaphors are most often used by avant-garde poets: metaphor of a road or a path, a bridge, a light, and, above all, the metaphor of the horizon. They lead a reader into a circle of questions directly or indirectly connected with three themes:

(1) mythology,
(2) philosophical threads common to Hinduism and Christianity,
(3) sensuality and mystique.

Elements of these three themes are present in the poetry of *Tār Saptak*[2] as well as in the Polish poetry of the avant-garde period. The two above-mentioned poetic currents could be understood and interpreted as historical parallels.

---

[1] FRIEDRICH (1978: 231–232): 'Temu jawnemu zerwaniu z tradycją przeciwstawia się wielkie zainteresowanie wszystkimi literaturami i religiami świata, a także chęć zanurzenia się w głębinowy świat ludzkiej psychiki, gdzie spotykają się Europa i Azja, magiczne i mityczne praobrazy.'

[2] The first anthology of modern Hindi poetry, ed. by Ajñey and originally published in 1943, contained poems by seven young poets: Gajānan Mādhav Muktibodh, Nemicandr Jain, Bhāratbhūṣan Agravāl, Prabhākar Mācve, Girijākumār Māthur, Rāmvilās Śarmā, Ajñey.

*Essays in Indian Philosophy, Religion and Literature*, pp. 231–240.

**–1–**

From the mythical elements I will briefly comment on three: the myth of the moon, of dance and of the Absolute.

(a) The moon appears frequently in the poems of the analysed collection. It is seen and described in different ways. It could be treated anthropomorphically, as in Śarmā's poem, where 'the yellow moon shrinks from the cold,'[3] in Ajñey's poem: 'who saw the moon had to have seen the smiling face'[4]; or comparatively, as in Nemicandr's poem: 'like the moonlight tender memory of your beauty,'[5] as well as in Māthur's work: 'the moonlight is reminiscent of flowers.'[6]

In Indian mythology the moon possesses feminine qualities. The colour and the perfect shape of a full moon are the paradigms of beauty. The moon is also believed to be the master of plants, the guardian of farming, the shelter and the source of life. A bright moon can also depict a bright mind.

(b) Dance is a common theme in this poetry. In India dance can be understood as a creative act, as a form of magic, which causes trance and ecstasy. Śiva, the cosmic dancer, symbolises cosmic energy. Dance is reminiscent of life as much as it is also a mixture of cruelty, gentleness, destruction, creation, death and triumph of life. Only through interpreting dance in such a way is it possible to find the sense of a line from Śarmā's poem, 'the nymphs are not dancing,'[7] or of the following words of Nemicandr: 'the heart of a poet dances in the silver moonlight.'[8] Both the myths, of dance and of the moon, have been metaphorically employed in these lines.

(c) In the poems of *Tār Saptak*, the Absolute appears directly several times, yet in most cases, it is represented through the agrarian symbols such as ploughing the earth, or sewing seeds. Orthodox Hinduism and Hindu philosophy share a common

---

[3] *ṭhiṭhuran se choṭā ho pīlā candrmā*; from: *Pratyūṣ ke pūrv* [*Before dawn*]. All the English translations of the quoted Hindi and Polish verses—apart from the MIŁOSZ's *Love*—come from the author of the article.

[4] *kis ne dekhā cāṅd- ... / ek mātr voh smit-mukh ...* ; from: *Kis ne dekhā cāṅd* [*Who saw the moon*].

[5] *... junhāī-sā hī / terī chavī kā sudhi-sammohan ...* ; from: *Anajāne cupcāp* [*Unknowingly silent*].

[6] *... phūloṁ kī yād banī cāṅdnī*; from: *Chāyā mat chūnā* [*Do not touch the shadow*].

[7] *nahīṁ kintu sur-sundariyoṁ kā nartan*; from: *Keral: ek haśya* [*Kerala: one episode*].

[8] *dekh cāṅdnī rāteṅ kavi kā nāc uṭhā ur*; from: *Kavi gātā hai* [*A poet sings*].

principle: they are monistic and monotheistic. People ('guests' of gods) are only the aspect of energy. They are ever-changing and phenomenal manifestations of the one God, one Substance. The echo of this fundamental belief can be found in a line from Śarmā's poetry: 'There are imprints of dead shadows on the face of the earth, of some traditions, some laws, / some unclear thoughts'[9]. Muktibodh, on the other hand, asks directly: 'Does the Absolute exist? Does it experience pleasures, / Like summer, or sentiments like spring?'[10] And this is a question about a personified Absolute, similar to the one present in Christianity.

Identical mythical elements operate quite univocally in Polish avant-garde poetry. The moon, however, serves a different purpose. It is treated as a witness of night. That is why BRZĘKOWSKI writes about 'children greyed by the moon,'[11] and CZECHOWICZ describes the moonlight as 'moon glaze.'[12] The meaning of dance is a little closer to Indian tradition. In the stereotyped way of understanding, it depicts joy, but its origins reach deep into the human psyche, into rites and archetypes. In CZYŻEWSKI's poetry it appears as 'laughter-sound', 'bliss-madness' and 'circles-fiery-rainbows / Radiance.'[13] God, or Absolute, from time to time appears in images only through allusions, as in BRZĘKOWSKI's poem: 'Sunrise, a purple bishop,'[14] or in STERN's poem, as 'zeppelin R III', which 'hangs' as a 'great round / god's spirit.'[15]

## –2–

From the philosophical threads common in Hinduism and Christianity I would like to outline one, which seems to me the most important: the place of the human being in the universe.

---

[9] *rūṛhiyoṁ kī, niyamoṁ kī, aspaṣt vicāroṁ kī, / sadiyom ke purātan mṛt sanskāroṁ kī, / cihrit heṁ pretarūp chāyāeṅ maṭīle muṅh par* ; from: *Kārya-kṣetr* [*A working field*].

[10] *Kyā pūrṇ hai? Kyā tṛpti pātā śīgr hai, / Voh grīṣm-sā hai yā madir madhumās-sā?*; from: *Aśakt* [*Powerless*].

[11] *dzieci siwe od księżyca*; from: *Księżyc nad Olchawą* [*Moon over Olchawa*].

[12] *księżycowe szkliwo*; from: *Kościół Św. Trójcy…* [*Holy Trinity Church…*].

[13] *śmiech–dźwięk, rozkosz–szał, koła–ogniste–tęcze / Blask*; from: *Taniec* [*Dance*].

[14] *Wschód, fioletowy biskup*; from: *Wschód słońca w górach* [*Sunrise in the mountains*].

[15] *wielki okrągły / duch boży / wisi / zeppelin R III*; from: *Drogą wysokiego zwycięstwa* [*On the path of high victory*].

Let me start with the words of Ajñey, who wrote: 'I am the two planets / Joined by destiny, which have constant radiance, always the same speed / And are trespassing the blue desert courtyard of the sky.'[16] A lot of matters divide Hinduism and Christianity, but there are similar or common elements in the domains of both religions. The meaning of these elements goes far beyond the strictly religious sense. They are the components of the cultural heritage of human civilisation. The attitude towards understanding the *logos* is the main difference between both religions. Christianity seeks transcendency beyond the earthly reality, in the Absolute, while the followers of Hinduism try to find within themselves the realisation of the principle of being one with the universe. This is why the Absolute, portrayed as a Person, the primary cause of existence, of the heavens, the planets and man, could be employed as the common quality which allows us to see and to point out the similarities of both religions. In this context, Ajñey's self-identification gains its proper proportion and meaning. Through this identification the existence of man and the existence of his language obtain a metaphysical sense. The Revd. Stanisław PASIERB, influenced by Dante, stated that 'Christ was a poet.'[17] Therefore, it is possible to assert that the central problem of both religions evolves around human existence, the place of man in the world, in culture, in the universe. Myths are also the components of human consciousness and they keep being re-discovered and prophetically brought back to life by the poets.[18] Anatol STERN wrote:

> you
> who sniff against the wind
> searching for a man
> just look around—
> the entire universe
> is dripping a living man![19]

And then, he formulated a philosophical postulate:

> one should sing together with the centuries
> one should note
> all the explosions of
> atoms
> to bare

---

[16] *Maiṁ voh tārak-yugm, / apalak-dyuti, anathak-gati, baddh-niyati / jo pār kiye jā rahā nīl maru-prāṅgaṇ nabh kā*; from: *Uṣaḥkāl kā bhavya śānti* [*The peace of daybreak*].

[17] PASIERB (1983: 214).

[18] JUNG (1993: 333): '[mity] wciąż od nowa odkrywają i proroczo ożywiają poeci.'

[19] *ty / który węszysz pod wiatr / szukając człowieka / spójrz tylko rozejrzyj się wokół – / to kosmos cały / żywym człowiekiem ocieka!*; from: *Anielski cham* [*Angelic churl*].

the seismograph of
sub-consciousness[20]

Similarly, Muktibodh wrote:

I want to trust in every son of Manu[21]

and added:

His path is guided by the great Christ with all his love[22]

The motif of Christ in Polish avant-garde poetry appeared quite frequently, although in different connotations, for example in JASIEŃSKI's poem:

from a black mad town
hiding his face in the tail of his coat
was running away christ,
when suddenly in the market the crowd
got hold of him.[23]

Julian PRZYBOŚ presented quite a contradictory vision of the tragedy of the Man–God. He came up with his own idea on how to overcome and convert the Christian tradition into a new intellectual value:

Crosses burdened with Jesuses
need to be sharpened into the perpendiculars of the building-site ladders[24]

And these are of course only a few poetic implications of the philosophical problem, central for both traditions and for both avant-garde movements.

–3–

As regards the motives of sensuality and mystique, I will treat them only typologically, as the subject is far too vast to be covered in this paper in detail. A

---

[20] *trzeba śpiewać wiekami, / trzeba odnotować / wszystkie eksplozje / atomów / obnażyć / sejsmograf / podświadomości*; from: *Europa* [*Europe*].

[21] *Is lie pratyek Manu ke putr viśvās karnā cāhtā hūṁ*; from: *Dūr tārā* [*A distant star*].

[22] *Us ke path par pahrā dete Isā mahān ve snehvān*; from *Mere antar* [*My inner self*].

[23] *z czarnego oszalałego miasta / w pole płaszcza kryjąc twarz / uciekał chrystus / gdy nagle tłum go na placu / dopadł*; from: *Pieśń o głodzie* [*The hunger song*].

[24] *Obciążone Jezusami krzyże / trzeba wyostrzyć w piony budowniczych drabin*; from: *Notre Dame*.

common tendency, however, was present in both avant-garde movements: a process from detail to generalisation.

Sensualistic elements in comprehending the world are present in works of the Hindi poets. For example, what we come across in Muktibodh's poems are 'burning rays of a delicate space,'[25] 'blue, jasmine, red day'[26] and a statement that 'in the senses the meaning is invented'[27]; Agravāl's poems bring 'jingle of bangles,'[28] 'the water of a river / breaking obstacles / goes forward'[29]; Mācve speaks of 'lightning in a deep forest,'[30] 'active bird,'[31] 'hazy evening'[32]; Śarmā declares that 'the dawn is hiding in the sky,'[33] 'wintry frost is covering fields,'[34] 'the rain is falling on some parts of the ocean.'[35]

A similar way of sensual perception of the world can be noticed in Polish avant-garde poetry. JASIEŃSKI wrote: 'dressing her silently, they stopped the clock'[36]; CZYŻEWSKI described the 'Screaming of the white wings of the clouds'[37]; WAT remembered when 'On the seas of greenery we sailed softly'[38]; CZUCHNOWSKI drew a drastic picture: 'spitting out the soul: a blue sack filled with eternity'[39]; PEIPER was lost 'among the words of a hue of laughter'[40]; STERN imagined how 'a brown

[25] *Un sablatam, tīvr, komal deś kī cingāriyoṁ ...*; from: *Khol āṅkheṅ* [*Open eyes*].

[26] *... nīlā, jāmunī, ati lāl, ... divas*; from: *Khol āṅkheṅ* [*Open eyes*].

[27] *Arth-khojī praṇ ye uddhām hai*; from: *Aśakt* [*Powerless*].

[28] *valay kī khankār, / dīp bālo rī suhāgini ...*; from: *Jāgte raho* [*Be alert*].

[29] *Jaise nadī kā jal / ḍhūhoṁ ko toṛ kar / choṛ calā jātā hai, ...*; from: *Dūngā maiṁ* [*I will give*].

[30] *... ālok-saśay ke saghnāndhakār meṁ vidyunmālā*; from: *Soneṭ* [*A sonnet*].

[31] *capal vihanhini*; from: *Soneṭ* [*A sonnet*].

[32] *sanjhā hai dhuṁdhalī ...*; from: *Rekha-citr* [*A sketch*].

[33] *... chipā hai bhoṛ abhī ākāś meṁ, ...*; from: *Pratyūṣ ke pūrv* [*Before dawn*].

[34] *Baras rahā khetoṁ par him-himant hai*; from: *Pratyūṣ ke pūrv* [*Before dawn*].

[35] *Hariyālī kā-sā sāgar ... / ... par utarā varṣā kā dal, ...*; from: *Keral: ek haśya* [*Kerala: one episode*].

[36] *Ubierali ją po cichu, zatrzymali zegar*; from: *Pogrzeb Reni* [*Renia's funeral*].

[37] *Krzyk białych skrzydeł obłoków*; from: *Skrzydła nad Cagnes* [*Wings over Cagnes*].

[38] *Po morzach zieleni płynęliśmy miękko*; from: 'Po morzach zieleni ...' ['over the sees of the green ...'—No title].

[39] *wypluwając duszę: błekitny worek z wiecznością*; from: *Kraków 1931*.

[40] *wśród słów o barwie śmiechu*; from: *Wśród* [*Among*].

fig—the earth / falls straight into your mouth'[41]; and in WAŻYK's poem, 'a spark shone on the lyre-like tram'[42]; in CZECHOWICZ's poem, 'the hay smells of sleep'[43]; and KUREK pictured 'A shiny engine of events'[44]; and finally ZAGÓRSKI confessed that 'With an angel of humility / I walked through a valley filled with evening.'[45]

Asceticism and mysticism can be understood as the opposites of sensuality. In the Polish avant-garde movement, asceticism referred mainly to the discipline of structure or the discipline of expressing feelings, and even so it was only noticeable in works of some poets, mostly those, who followed the slogan: 'maximum contents in minimum words.'[46] Mysticism itself was almost systematically condemned. But what did it really mean when STERN wrote about the 'metaphysics of the process of building'[47]? If we take a closer look at some of the works of PRZYBOŚ, not only from the point of view of the text, but also trying to see the whole image they create, we will notice that, for instance, a poem *Nike* is like a moving structure constructed from memory and sensitivity, fastened to scaffolding-like words. Accordingly, we have to deal with the whole psychological process, in which apologetic attitude towards city-planning, directions and blocks has been transferred into a similar attitude towards poetry, and has been employed to the structure of a poem. In this way, what has been created is a well-nigh mystic sphere. This is why some deep relationship between the sensual perception of reality and the sacred treatment of poetic vision can legitimately be argued to exist in Polish avant-garde poetry. Apart from the oeuvre of PRZYBOŚ and PEIPER, examples can be found in KUREK, CZECHOWICZ and WAŻYK.

The elements of mysticism in the work of Hindi poets appear equally frequently. They might be consciously employed or may also be a result of some experiments with language. In Śarmā's work one can find 'merged rays of consciousness,'[48]

---

[41] *brunatna figa ziemi / spada ci prosto do ust*; from: *Śmierć 30-letniego mężczyzny* [*Thirty-years-old man's death*].

[42] *iskra zaświeciła na lirze tramwaju*; from: *Tramwaj* [*A tram*].

[43] *siano pachnie snem*; from: *Na wsi* [*In the countryside*].

[44] *Błyszcząca lokomotywa zdarzeń*; from: *Liryka* [*Lyrics*].

[45] *Z aniołem pokory / szedłem doliną pełną wieczoru*; from: 'wiersze powstają z ognia ... ' ['poems rise from fire'—No title].

[46] A slogan of the group of poets called *Awangarda Krakowska* [*The Cracow Avant-garde*] (T. PEIPER, J. PRZYBOŚ, J. BRZĘKOWSKI, J. KUREK, 1922–1933).

[47] *metafizyka budowania*; from: *Drogą wysokiego zwycięstwa* [*On the path of high victory*].

[48] *Cetnā kī kiraṇoṁ ...*; from: *Kaliyug*.

Nemicandr 'sees the past, the future and the present,'[49] for Agravāl there exists a 'fire whose flames cannot burn,'[50] Muktibodh declares: 'the knowledge is in my senses'[51]. But most traces of mysticism are hidden deeper in images and in symbols, or between the lines.

Having this in view, it is worth comparing two poems about love, *Love: a definition* by Prabhākar Mācve[52] and *Love* by Czesław MIŁOSZ[53]. MIŁOSZ's poem was published in 1943, and it is a part of a longer work *Świat* [*The World*]. Both poems are closely related. They depict the simplest things that can be understood as elementary philosophical questions and, at the same time, as the most common experiences intrinsic to human existence.

Mācve asks a rhetorical question whether love is the desire for a warm touch? In this way he opens the sphere of everyday experiences analogical to those of

---

[49] *Bhūt-bhaviṣyat-vartman ko dekh rahā …*; from: *Kavi gātā hai* [*A poet sings*].

[50] *Yeh āg / jis kī cinagī meṁ jalan to kyā / tāp bhī nahīṁ*; from: *Dūngā maiṁ* [*I will give*].

[51] *… Jñan mere prāṇ meṁ …*; from: *Aśakt* [*Powerless*].

[52]

| *Prem: ek paribhāṣā* | *Love: a definition* |
|---|---|
| *Prem kyā kisī mṛdūṣṇ sparś kā bhikhārī?* | *Is love a desire for that delicate warm touch?* |
| *Prem vo prapāt* | *Love is that falling stream-song* |
| *Gīt divārāt* | *Sung day and night* |
| *Gā rahā aśānt* | *In despair* |
| *Prem ātmā – vismṛt par lakṣy-cyut śikārī.* | *Love is a forgetting soul of a defeated hunter* |
| *Prem vo prasann* | *Love is so happy* |
| *Khet meṃ nirann* | *A field without grain* |
| *Durbhikṣāvasann* | *Hurt by famine* |
| *Sṛjak kṛṣak khaṛā dīn annādhikārī* | *The Creator Farmer is standing as a poor grain collector.* |

[53]

| *Miłość* | *Love* |
|---|---|
| *Miłość to znaczy popatrzeć na siebie,* | *Love means to learn to look at yourself* |
| *Tak jak się patrzy na obce nam twarze,* | *The way one looks at distant things* |
| *Bo jesteś tylko jedną z rzeczy wielu.* | *For you are only one thing among many.* |
| *A kto tak patrzy, choć sam o tym nie wie* | *And whoever sees that way heals his heart,* |
| *Ze zmartwień różnych swoje serce leczy,* | *Without knowing it from various ills —* |
| *Ptak mu i drzewo mówią: przyjacielu.* | *A bird and a tree say to him: Friend.* |
| *Wtedy i siebie i rzeczy chce użyć,* | *Then he wants to use himself and things* |
| *Żeby stanęły w wypełnienia łunie.* | *So that they stand in the glow of ripeness.* |
| *To nic, że czasem nie wie czemu służyć:* | *It doesn't matter whether he knows what he serves:* |
| *Nie ten najlepiej służy, kto rozumie.* | *Who serves best doesn't always understand.* |

[Transl. by Cz. MIŁOSZ (1996)]

MIŁOSZ's poem. These parts of Mācve's poem which situate love close to desire, or even describe it as desire itself, are quite intriguing. Thus, love is described as a 'stream-song' and 'field without grain / hurt by famine,' as 'a forgetting soul of a defeated hunter.' These concise images refer to the simplest reality, but are at the same time filled with the metaphysics that is difficult to define.

Similarly in MIŁOSZ's poem, 'love means to learn to look at yourself / the way one looks at distant things,' 'and whoever sees that way heals his heart, / (...) from various ills,' and further, 'a bird and a tree say to him: Friend'. MIŁOSZ himself wrote about his poem: 'The stanzas, "as if from the alphabet," describe the beauty of the simplest things,'[54] but they are also a 'metaphysical treatise.'

Both poems are the artistic attempt to seize the triumph of life over despair. MĀCVE writes directly: 'love is the falling stream song / sung day and night / in despair.' Bożena CHRZĄSTOWSKA, interpreting MIŁOSZ's poetry states that, through his long poem *The World*, he opposes the temptation of despair in the years of the Second World War nightmare.[55] In this way, she refers to a concrete historical context. And precisely here would lie the difference in the attitudes of both poets. MĀCVE is more abstract, his lyrical reflection is inscribed within the human fate in general, in the meaning of life. Maybe this is why one can sense a small dose of melancholy in the poem. MĀCVE writes about the everyday world, about a common psychological experience. MIŁOSZ writes about the world he would like to meet, about the world which would be the opposite to the terror of the historical reality. However, we cannot fail to notice one and the same artistic tendency in both poems: a process from a detail to generalisation, a shift from a 'warm touch' to a 'forgetting soul of a defeated hunter' in MĀCVE's poem, and a progression from 'seeing yourself' to the situation when the man 'wants to use himself and things / so that they stand in the glow of ripeness' in MIŁOSZ's *Love*.

Both poets, in spite of the artistic differences, decipher this universal human experience in the context of an individual involved simultaneously in everyday life and metaphysics. With the contents of their metaphors and with various ways of employing them, they create a great circle of universal parallels which are also referred to as 'non-contact comparative studies' in the terminology of the theory of literature.

---

[54] MIŁOSZ (1959: 206): 'Jego strofy "jak z abecadła" opisują piękno najprostszych rzeczy.'

[55] CHRZĄSTOWSKA (1982: 107): 'Poematem "Świat" przeciwstawia się Miłosz "pokusie rozpaczy" w latach okupacyjnego koszmaru.'

## BIBLIOGRAPHY

BRZĘKOWSKI 1981 = Brzękowski, Jan: *Wiersze awangardowe*. Wydawnictwo Literackie, Kraków 1981.

CHRZĄSTOWSKA 1982 = Chrząstowska, Bożena: *Poezje Czesława Miłosza*. Wydawnictwa Szkolne i Pedagogiczne, Warszawa 1982.

CZECHOWICZ 1988 = Czechowicz, Józef: *Poezje*. Wydawnictwo Lubelskie, Lublin 1988.

CZUCHNOWSKI = Czuchnowski, Marian; see: WAŻYK (1976: 156).

CZYŻEWSKI = Czyżewski, Tytus; see: WAŻYK (1976: 105).

FRIEDRICH 1978 = Friedrich, H.: *Struktura nowoczesnej liryki*. PIW, Warszawa 1978.

JASIEŃSKI 1972 = Jasieński, Bruno: *Utwory poetyckie, manifesty, szkice*. Oprac. E. Balceman. Ossolineum, Warszawa—Wrocław—Kraków—Gdańsk 1972.

JUNG 1993 = Jung, Carl Gustav: *Wspomnienia, sny, myśli*. Wrota, Warszawa 1993.

KUREK = Kurek, Jalu; see: WAŻYK (1976: 142).

MIŁOSZ 1959 = Miłosz, Czesław: *Rodzinna Europa*. Paryż 1959.

MIŁOSZ 1996 = Miłosz, Czesław: *Selected Poems*. Wydawnictwo Literackie, Kraków 1996.

PASIERB 1983 = Pasierb, Janusz Stanisław: *Światło i sól*. Paryż 1983.

PEIPER 1979 = Peiper, Tadeusz: *Poematy i utwory teatralne*. Wydawnictwo Literackie, Kraków 1979.

PRZYBOŚ 1975 = Przyboś, Julian: *Utwory poetyckie*. Ludowa Spółdzielnia Wydawnicza, Warszawa 1975.

STERN 1964 = Stern, Anatol: *Poezja zbuntowana*. PIW, Warszawa 1964.

STERN 1985 = Stern, Anatol: *Wiersze zebrane*. Oprac. A.K. Waśkiewicz, Wydawnictwo literackie, Kraków 1985.

*Tār Saptak* = Ajñey (ed.): *Tār Saptak*. 4th ed., New Delhi 1972.

WAT = Wat, Aleksander: *po morzach zieleni …* ; see: WAŻYK (1976: 109).

WAŻYK 1976 = Ważyk, A.: *Dziwna historia awangardy*, Czytelnik, Warszawa 1976.

ZAGÓRSKI = Zagórski, Jerzy: *wiersze powstają z ognia …* ; see: WAŻYK (1976: 170).

# Modern Hindi Poetry: a Look at its Medieval Past

KUNWAR NARAIN

An immense body of good research material is available on medieval Hindi literature. A close familiarity with this period of Indian history and of poetry (about the eighth to eighteenth centuries) can be illuminating in many ways. Using some of this material I have tried to touch upon a few points which seem to be of special interest in relation to modern Hindi poetry.

Modernity, it seems, has been more at ease with antiquity than with its medieval past. A look at medieval India is necessary to realise the crucial role of poetry in a people's social, personal and religious life and its intimate relationship with other arts like music, dance and painting. Poetry was not confined to a select few but was one of the most important vehicles of a message of love and peace across a politically turbulent and instable India, giving it a unique cultural and emotional unity. To dismissively call it a simple religious movement would be to miss in sweeping generalisation its real power and reach which lay not in the conflicts that various ethnic groups faced when they came to India, but in the human necessity to find common bonds that could make it possible for them to live together amicably as human beings, despite ethnic and religious differences. It was poetry of the people and for the people in the best sense of the term.

One striking feature of medieval Hindi poetry, specifically devotional poetry (*bhakti kāvya*), is how it has been an integral part of a socio-cultural movement more than of politics. There used to be an influential and highly respected body of saint-poets who determinedly avoided kings and royal favours, and insisted on a modest life-style that could easily be supported by the simple patronage of the people. The attitude is strongly expressed in the lines of Kumbhandās (1468–1582)[1]:

भक्तन को क्या सीकरी सों काम।
आवत जात पन्हैयाँ टूटी बिसरि गयो हरिनाम।
जाको मुख देखी अघ लाघे ताको करन परी परनाम।
कुंभनदास लाल गिरधर बिन यह सब झूठो धाम॥ [2]

---

[1] VARMĀ (1986: 92).

[2] HSBI (1974: 75).

*Essays in Indian Philosophy, Religion and Literature*, pp. 241–250.

'Why should a devotee go to Sikri?
Why wear out his shoes
Coming and going there
Forgetting the name of Hari?
Why bend to salute them
Whose very facé spells calamity?
Kumbhandas has his Lord Girdhar,
Without Him the world is empty.'[3]

We have to locate the source of this courage not in the defensive pride of a poor man, but in the moral stature of an honest and upright man. We see this spirit at work in the late nineteenth century Hindu reformist movement and, more effectively, in Gandhi's moral stand against imperialism in Africa and India.

The Gandhian ethics, more pronounced in the Hindi nationalist poetry of the 20s and 30s, never lost its hold on Indian intelligentsia, nor on the masses. Even Premcand remained as much a Gandhian as a progressive in his convictions. It will not be far-fetched to infer that the mass response to Gandhian ways had a pre-existing base in the psyche of the Indian people. His favourite song: **वैष्णव जन तो तेने कहिए, जे पीर पराई जाणे रे**... ('Call them the real people of [God] Viṣṇu who can feel the pain of others ...')[4] extols the virtue of compassion. The extreme mystical and metaphysical elements in devotional poetry have often been criticised for being life-negating, escapist and other-worldly, but when we focus on the human values it sought to inculcate—universal love, compassion, humility, etc.—its aesthetics of the 'other world' seems only a device to stimulate that *other side* of human nature which is not all physical.

The Western influence on Indian writing has been much talked about, but the core of Indian sensibilities can perhaps be better understood by a reference to the old Middle Eastern intellectual legacy which, unlike the European 'Dark Ages' was replete with a high degree of Renaissance-like intellectual activity. After the death of Alexander of Macedonia, the city of Alexandria (founded by him in 332 B.C.E.) had slowly become the meeting ground of Hellenistic and Eastern scholars and thinkers. It has been pointed out that Alexander's eastern campaign was also a prelude to the Greek thought moving eastwards and coming in close contact with eastern philosophies and literatures through Arabian, Persian and Buddhist thinkers. The Ptolemies of Egypt were great patrons of learning and the Alexandrian Library

[3] Where it is not otherwise stated the translations are by the author of the present paper.

[4] These are the opening lines of Mahatma Gandhi's favourite Vaiṣṇava song regularly sung at his prayer-meetings.

established by them was a store-house of rare world classics which attracted scholars from all over the civilised world. It is about this time that a number of Greek, Persian and Sanskrit classics were translated into Arabic. The process did not stop at Alexandria, but continued long after Alexandria lost its importance, and Constantinople, Baghdad, Basra, etc., became the centres of intellectual activities. Despite their theological reservations, the Arab scholars, and later Islamic thinkers, were generous towards other philosophies, and had it not been for their relentless zeal to translate classics into Arabic and Persian, a good deal of Greek philosophy would perhaps have been lost. Given the eclectic propensities of Islamic thinkers it is not unlikely that Sufism, before it came to India, had already absorbed some of the Buddhist and Vedāntic traits in its living and thinking. Prof. A.L. BASHAM observes:

> '... similarities between the teachings of western philosophers and mystics from Pythagoras to Plotinus and those of the Upaniṣads have frequently been noticed. (...) We can only say that there was always some contact between the Hellenic world and India, mediated first by the Achaemenid Empire, then by that of the Seleucids, and finally, under the Romans, by the traders of the Indian ocean. Christianity began to spread at the time when this contact was closest. We know that Indian aṣcetics occasionally visited the West, and that there was a colony of Indian merchants at Alexandria. The possibility of Indian influence on Neo-platonism and early Christianity cannot be ruled out.'[5]

Where Vedānta and Sufism met was also the point where the Hindu and non-Hindu sensibilities could find a common meeting ground for what was universal in their social and spiritual thinking. Modern Hindi poetry still derives a good deal of its moral and aesthetic reflexes from this long and persistent tradition of devotional poetry which dominated the Indian literary scene for more than a thousand years, and is still very much alive in the Indian psyche. The linguistic, ethical and esthetical challenges faced by Hindi devotional poetry in the Middle ages, if studied conjointly as different facets of a single problem, tend to make better sense in the context of modern Hindi poetry (and even poetry in general) than if they are treated as isolated problems far removed in time. Sometimes a syncretic approach provides a better insight into how art functions and affects human consciousness. Art tries to unify, balance and harmonise diverse, even discordant, elements in nature and human nature. Devotional poetry at its best seems to be a sustained effort to achieve that ideal, aspiring to cut across difficult political, religious and racial differences. It has left behind a strong legacy of humanism and, in the arts at least, a remarkably united India.

---

[5] BASHAM (1985: 486).

In our times the influence of Kabīr on Rabindranath Tagore and on *chāyāvād* poetry (1920–1940) was crucial in inspiring that mystico-romantic strain in Hindi poetry which should be distinguished from English Romanticism. Indirectly, it had more in common with Vedāntic, Sufi and neo-Platonic sensibilities, which survived in devotional poetry and osmosed into modern Hindi poetry, than with English romantic poetry even when directly inspired by the latter. No doubt the roots are in Vedānta, Buddhism and Jainism, but in modern Hindi poetry it is more to be located in the Advaita or Sufi 'moods' than in actual philosophies connected with the two. Remote affinities between Vedāntic and existential thinking are also not to be missed. We can see, for instance, in Śamśer Bahādur SIṀH (1911–1992) how even contemporary ideas are put on a Vedāntic base:

जो मैं हूँ -
मैं कि जिसमें सब कुछ है...

क्रांतियाँ, कम्यून,
कम्यूनिस्ट समाज के
नाना कला विज्ञान और दर्शन के
जीवंत वैभव से समन्वित
व्यक्ति मैं

मैं, जो वह हरेक हूँ
जो, तुझसे, ओ काल, परे है[6]

'That which is me
Is the "I" that contains all …

The revolutions, the communes
The communist societies
The different arts, sciences and philosophies
Imbued with a living richness
All by the subjective "I"

"I" that means all of us
Which is stronger than thou, O time!'

It is interesting to note how the old ideas assimilate new ones and give it a typically Indian identity. Likewise, in the poem *Lakṛī kā Rāvaṇ* (*The Wooden*

[6] SIṀH (nd: 172).

*Ravana*) by MUKTIBODH (1917–1964), the evil capitalist system is identified with the mythical villain Rāvaṇa in the *Rāmâyaṇa*.[7] The process is ages old and the tendency can easily be recognised in modern poetry. It is also reflected in the way a composite Indian culture has taken shape through the ages.

Three distinct categories of poets, whose activities lead to the development of modern Hindi language and poetry can distinctly be located in medieval India, viz.: 1. the peripatetic saint-poets; 2. the regional poets who wrote in their own regional languages like Avadhī or Brajbhāṣā, and 3. the court poets who were attached to some king or his influential vassal.

The way modern Khaṛī bolī has come into being owes a good deal to the travelling life-style of the saint-poets familiar since the days of the Buddha in the sixth century B.C.E. The Buddha's teachings had a strictly philosophical and ethical content but later we see poetry slowly becoming the vehicle of conveying philosophical and ethical ideas, with music joining hands. An early example is that of Śaṅkara (?788–820 C.E.)[8] who was no less a poet than a philosopher, and a little later in Saraha (tenth century), the Indian master of Tantric Buddhism whose *Doha-kośa* is as much poetry as philosophy. We see this tendency to poeticise philosophy, or vice versa, reaching its high watermark in Kabīr (*fl.* fifteenth century) where Vedāntic and Sufi elements intermixed in his poetry. Kabīr is an important example of a saint-poet who helped create a powerful language defying all rules of grammar and conventions of purity of diction. It is not without reason that modern Hindi poetry feels strongly drawn towards Kabīr's example, not only in matters of what he did to and for Hindi, but also how he succeeded in creating a poetic idiom which defied all barriers. An experimentalist par excellence, his poetry if at one extreme is wholly down-to-earth in drawing precepts from common everyday life for his teachings, at the other extreme it touches mystical and metaphysical heights rare in poetry. He was as unorthodox in his poetic and linguistic methods as he was bold in his religious convictions. The forms and idiom of Kabīr's poetry owe a good deal to Buddhist *sahajiyas* and Śivaite *nāth-panthīs*, whose influence is apparent not only in his '*ulaṭ-bāṁsī*'[9] but also in the *dohā*, or the couplet form he favoured.

In practice, a medieval saint-poet's dire need to communicate prompted not only linguistic innovations, but also, more importantly, inventing unique poetic devices that put maximum stress on the medium of expression. The near total breakdown of the language under extreme creative pressure is that point where the poet also seeks to establish a new relationship with the language. The familiar is de-familiarised,

[7] See: MUKTIBODH (1997: 172–177).

[8] Comp. BASHAM (1985: 328).

[9] Topsy-turvy juxtapositions in poetry.

and the world as we know it in day-to-day language dematerialises into 'airy nothings' only to be re-born as a new construct or concept. The ethical and esthetical become the higher realities that guide the vision of the saint as that of the poet. It reminds us of Wittgenstein and the Vienna Circle to whom Iris MURDOCH refers:

> 'This running up against the limits of language is ethics … In ethics we are always making the attempt to say something that cannot be said, something that does not and never will touch the essence of the matter. (…) But the inclination, the running up against something, indicates something.'[10]

No one, perhaps, knew it better than Kabīr that 'this running up against language' is not only ethics but also poetry. He knew that the ethical, like the mystical experience, could not be expressed in words; at best it could only be indicated negatively against the 'absurd'—the absurd backdrop of life. He says in one of his *śabda*s in *Bījak*:

बेद कितेब दीन औ दोजक, को पुरुषा को नारी।
माटी के घट साज बनाया, नादे बिंदु समाना।
घट बिनसे का नाम धरहुगे, अहमक खोज( त ) भुलाना।
एकै तुचा हाड़ मल मूत्रा, एक रुधिर एक गूदा।
एक बूँद सों सिस्ट कियो है, को ब्राह्मन को सूद्रा।
रजगुन ब्रह्मा, तमगुन संकर, सत्तगुना हरि सोई।
कहँहिं कबीर राम रहिये रमि, हिन्दू तुरुक न कोई॥ ७५॥

'It's a heavy confusion.
Veda, Koran, holiness, hell, woman, man,
a clay pot shot with air and sperm …
When the pot falls apart, what do you call it?
Numskull: You've missed the point.
It's all one skin and bone, one piss and shit,
One blood, one meat.
From one drop, a universe.
Who's Brahmin? Who's Shudra?
Brahma *rajas*, Shiva *tamas*, Vishnu *sattva* …
Kabir says, plunge into Rama!
There: No Hindu. No Turk. [75]'[11]

---

[10] MURDOCH (1992: 43).

[11] *Bījak* (1986: 78).

The reference to Rāma and the castes (Brahmin, Śūdra) is significant in this poem and reveals the deep-rooted Vaiṣṇava and Sufi sensibilities in Kabīr. They also remind us of Gandhi—his last words 'He Rām!' and the name 'Harijan' (God's people) he gave to the underprivileged. It is also easy to see in his (and his follower Vinoba Bhave's) *pad-yātrā*s reminiscences of wandering saint-poets.

In the second category, there are such poets like Vidyāpati (late fourteenth – early fifteenth century), who wrote in Maithilī on the Rādhā-Kṛṣṇa themes; Malik Muhammad Jāyasī (?1475–1542)[12] and Tulsīdās (1532–1623), who wrote in Avadhī and are best known for their epics *Padmāvat* and *Rām-carit-mānas* respectively; and Sūrdās (?1483–1563)[13], the blind poet, whose lyrics on the Kṛṣṇa-theme are collected in his *Sūr-sāgar*. They all preferred to stay mostly at one place and wrote in their regional languages. The power and appeal of their poetry lies in its deep-rootedness in local traditions, beliefs and mythology. It was more of their poetic, rather than linguistic, influence on later Hindi poetry that mattered. If Avadhī had a powerful epic tradition, Brajbhāṣā had an equally strong lyric base. In Maithilīśaraṇ Gupta's (1886–1964) *Sāket* and Nirālā's (1896–1961) *Rām kī Śakti pūjā* the epic narrative style is easily identifiable, so is a clear *śakta* influence on the latter. In Jayaśaṇkar Prasād's (1889–1937) *Kāmāyanī* both the epic narrative of Avadhī and the lyric sensibilities of Brajbhāṣā blend. Later, it is easy to recognise in MUKTIBODH's diction and poetic syntax, as well as in his *Brahma-rākṣas*, undertones of this past. The Rāma theme recurs in Nareś Mehta's (1922–2000) *Saṁśay kī ek rāt*. The *Mahā-bhārata* and Rādhā-Kṛṣṇa love theme provide the source material for Dharmavīr Bhāratī's (1926–1997) *Andhā yug* and *Kanupriyā* respectively. In passing it may be mentioned that Khaṛī bolī, long considered to be unfit for poetry because it lacked the tender charm of Brajbhāṣā and Avadhī, had to take up the challenge and prove that anything Brajbhāṣā or Avadhī could do, Khaṛī bolī could do as well. Prasād's language, as that of nearly all the *chāyāvādī* poets, seems to be obsessed with this challenge. It is with the advent of *pragativād* (the Progressive Movement), inspired by Marxism, that social, political and economic concerns became more important in Hindi poetry. However, the poetic sentiments nurtured by earlier poetry, it seems, have left too deep an emotional impact on the poetic diction and syntax of Hindi poetry and still continue despite more realistic attitudes. Sometimes, as if to break away from the insistence of that tradition, the new poets chose themes from contemporary realities, or else preferred to go back to

[12] Comp., e.g. VARMĀ (1986: 429–432) and MCGREGOR (1984: 67–71).

[13] Comp., e.g. VARMĀ (1986: 642–644), MCGREGOR (1984: 76) and LORENZEN (1996: 269).

an ancient or mythological past for lesser used episodes. New kinds of creative insights in modern art and literature were being prompted following researches in psychology and anthropology.

The court-poets of the third category have left an influence on subsequent Hindi poetry no less important than that of the saint-poets. In devotional poetry the 'content', i.e. the Rāma or Kṛṣṇa themes, seldom change. It is in Amīr Khusro (1253–1325)[14], attached to the kings of the Delhi Sultanate, that we notice a definite shift and a lively interest in day-to-day life, enriched by his strong Sufi background. His experiments included a very conscious and skilful effort to create a new language he called Hindavī, or Hindī, by combining local dialects with alien Persian.[15] A genius born much ahead of his times, Amīr Khusro's zeal to integrate diverse cultural elements has been as revolutionary in language and poetry, as in the development of Hindustani classical music. His total awareness of 'form-and-content', while experimenting with both, prefigures an approach very much significant in poetry even today.

Classifying some of the best-known poets of medieval times and post-medieval period (known as the *rīti-kāl*, c. 1650–1850) as 'court-poets', is not at all meant to denigrate their achievements. They worked with consummate skill within the classical and traditional moulds, but this did not hamper their innovative and imaginative talents. For instance, the Hindi *dohā* or couplet form is centuries old, but in Bihārīlāl's (?1595–1663)[16] *Satsaī* we see it acquire a new lustre and finesse. It shows no signs of fatigue; on the contrary, like a timeless form of a familiar *rāga*, it prompts rather than inhibits creative originality. That poetic 'experimentation' need not necessarily mean a simplistic rejection of all meters is well-proved by an earlier poet Keśavdās (?1555–1621)[17], who is at times loosely rated next to Sūrdās and Tulsīdās, in his short epic *Rām-candrikā*, based on the Rāma-story. It is a veritable museum of metrical compositions, and quite an achievement. Often decried as a difficult and obscure poet (somewhat like the English Metaphysicals of seventeenth century) he does, however, set a convincing example that experimenting *with* metres can be as important as experimenting *without* them.

To conclude, a few observations about the Hindi poetic mood today may be pertinent. The general modernist prejudice against medieval devotional poetry is due to an over-concentration on the terms 'medieval' and 'devotional' rather than on

---

[14] Comp. McGregor (1984: 24).

[15] See his 'Fārsī-hindī miśrit chand' in: Tivārī (1992: 117–118).

[16] Comp. Varmā (1986: 384–385).

[17] Comp., e.g. Varmā (1986: 107) and McGregor (1984: 126–129).

'poetry'. A shift of emphasis on poetry could perhaps yield a very different kind of insight into what poetry could achieve in unusually difficult times. This, perhaps, has implications for even today. The mystical and metaphysical bents of Hindi poetry have not always been easy to reconcile with a scientific and rational temperament. The Western model of technological and material progress has its own irresistible attraction. Visionary thinking may often blur, even cheat, a clear perception of the realities of life being faced by a majority of Indians; it may be more so where a mass of population may have been conditioned to accept deprivation as a pseudo-religious attitude towards a life that ought to change. But things change as they move, and problems of practical nature are best solved in a practical way. Science has solved many mysteries, but there are psychic dimensions of life which cannot be explained rationally, nor in physical terms, and poetry itself may be one of those mysteries born out of man's consistent need for beauty, moral order and an abiding faith in life ...

Poetry has survived hard times. Social, political and economic conditions in India are hard enough even today. Sometimes in utter despair a poet may feel about poetry the way, for example, Tadeusz RÓŻEWICZ felt in Poland at the end of World War II: 'What I revolted against was that it had survived the end of the world, as though nothing had happened.'[18] Yet, one cannot help admiring his intense faith both in life and in poetry as if the two were one:

'After the end of the world
after death
I found myself in the midst of life
creating myself
building life
people animals landscapes'[19]

---

[18] WEISSBORT (1993: 262).

[19] RÓŻEWICZ (1994: 51).

## BIBLIOGRAPHY


BASHAM 1985 = Basham, A.L.: *The Wonder That Was India*. Sidgwick & Jackson, London 1985.

*Bījak* 1986 = Kabīr: *The Bījak of Kabir*. Transl. by Linda Hess and Shukdev Singh. Motilal Banarsidass, Delhi 1986. [First edition: 1983].

HSBI 1974 = *Hindī sāhitya kā bṛhat itihās*. Ed. by Devendranāth Śarmā and Vijayendra Snātak. Vol. V. Nāgarī pracāriṇī sabhā, Vārāṇasī 1974.

LORENZEN 1996 = Lorenzen, David N.: *Praises to a Formless God*. SUNY Press, Albany 1996.

MCGREGOR 1984 = McGregor, R.S.: *Hindi Literature From Its Beginnings to the Nineteenth Century*. Otto Harrassowitz, Wiesbaden 1984.

MUKTIBODH 1997 = Muktibodh, Gajānan Mādhav: *Pratinidhi kavitāẽ*. Rājkamal prakāśan, Naī Dillī 1997.

MURDOCH 1992 = Murdoch, Iris: *Metaphysics as a Guide to Morals*. Penguin Books 1992.

RÓŻEWICZ 1994 = Różewicz, Tadeusz: *Poezje wybrane—Selected Poems*. Transl. by Adam Czerniawski, Wydawnictwo Literackie, Kraków 1994.

SIṀH nd = Siṁh, Śamśer Bahādur: *Pratinidhi kavitāẽ*. Rājkamal prakāśan, Naī Dillī—no date.

TIVĀRĪ 1992 = Tivārī, Bholānāth: *Amīr Khūsro aur unkī hindī racnāẽ*. Prabhāt prakāśan, Dillī 1992.

VARMĀ 1986 = Varmā, Dhīrendra (ed.): *Hindī sāhitya koś*. Vol. II, Jñānmaṇḍal limiṭeḍ, Vārāṇasī 1986. [2nd ed.].

WEISSBORT 1993 = Weissbort, Daniel (ed.): *The Poetry of Survival*. Penguin Books 1993.

# *Sāket*: Maithilīśaraṇ Gupta's* Version of *Rām-kathā*

DANUTA STASIK

Although on the title page of GUPTA's poem we find a couplet saying:

> राम तुम्हारा वृत्त स्वयं ही काव्य है,
> कोई कवि बन जाय, सहज सम्भाव्य है।[1]
>
> 'Rām, the tale of your life is a poem in itself,
> that someone becomes a poet is only natural.'

an investigation into the circumstances of *Sāket*'s genesis reveals that the poem was being born in a very long process which was neither simple nor spontaneous. It seems, however, that the responsibility for it rests not with Rām as such, or rather not with the account of his life, but with Ūrmilā[2]—Lakṣmaṇ's wife, a minor character in *rām-kathā*—who, for many years, attracted GUPTA's attention.

In this paper I would like to deal with *Sāket*, one of modern retellings of the *Rāmâyaṇa*, the *magnum opus* of the *rāṣṭra-kavi* (national poet) Maithilīśaraṇ GUPTA (1886–1964). I will try to show that in fact it consists of two vividly distinct parts, quite evidently not as a result of the poet's design; they are so distinct that it even seems justified to view *Sāket* not as one poem but as two poems within one. I must admit that this study has resulted from a kind of personal discomfort I felt every time while reading Canto 9 of the poem, and to a somewhat lesser degree Canto 10 as well—they seemed not to belong to the rest of the work! I even had an impression of having missed something important for a proper understanding of

---

* Note on transliteration: throughout the study I follow a commonly accepted convention of transliterating Hindi words without final 'a'; the only exception are the words which end with consonant clusters.

[1] Vālmīki addressed these words to Rām when they met in Citrakūṭ (Canto 5); GUPTA (1961: 156).

[2] In some authors' works this name is spelt Urmilā, but throughout this paper the form Ūrmilā is used, wherever it refers to *Sāket*, as this is the spelling employed in GUPTA's poem.

*Essays in Indian Philosophy, Religion and Literature*, pp. 251–257.

GUPTA's poem. However, after becoming familiar with some of Indian reactions to *Sāket*[3], I felt relieved—my reaction was not isolated.

But before we deal with this issue in greater detail, let us first dwell upon other related questions—the sources of inspiration for GUPTA's poem and the process of its creation.

## 1. How *Sāket* was written

In 1908, in a Hindi journal *Sarasvatī* Mahavīrprasād Dvivedī published an essay entitled 'Poets' Indifference to Ūrmilā.'[4] Drawing inspiration from an article by Ravīndranāth Ṭhākur, he concerned himself with Ūrmilā as an exemplification of female characters neglected by Indian authors of all epochs. Dvivedī wrote: 'What a pity that till the present day poets have kept concealing such a radiant character portrait as that of Ūrmilā in this way.'[5] And he held that such a situation should change.

Twenty-two year old GUPTA, who especially at that time, was under a great influence of Dvivedī, felt it his natural obligation to try to satisfy his guru's wish and started writing a poem entitled *Ūrmilā*.[6] Apart from Dvivedī's encouragement he was also, at a somewhat later period, stimulated by Choṭelāl Bārhaspatya, an erudite contributor to *Sarasvatī*.[7] From the correspondence between GUPTA and Bārhaspatya we know that between 1909–1910 GUPTA managed to complete a little bit more than two cantos (out of intended four) and left the work unfinished.[8]

---

[3] See, e.g. one of the most telling of them, i.e. Gāndhī's letter to GUPTA, dated 5 April 1932, in: BARUĀ (1959: 198–199); comp. also PĀṬHAK (1960: 32–33, 398–400).

[4] 'Kaviyõ kī Ūrmilā-viṣayak udāsīntā', written under a pen name Bhujaṅgbhūṣan Bhaṭṭācārya, appeared in the July issue of *Sarasvatī*, one of the most—if not the most—influential (Hindi) journalş of that time. It was edited by Dvivedī and GUPTA was then emerging as the main poet contributing to *Sarasvatī*; comp. BARUĀ (1959: 49–50, 86–87) and PĀṬHAK (1960: 393).

[5] Cited in BARUĀ (1959: 88); comp. also PĀṬHAK (1960: 393).

[6] Not only GUPTA responded to Dvivedī's essay. In June 1914 (in *Sarasvatī*) Ayodhyāsiṁh Upādhyāy 'Hariaudh' published a poem *Urmilā*, and much later, in 1936, (in an annual issue of *Pratāp*) Bālkṛṣṇ Śarmā 'Navīn' published the opening section of Canto 3 of his poem *Urmilā* under the title *Van-gaman*; BARUĀ (1959: 86).

[7] Bārhaspatya advised also GUPTA on how the poem should be written. See his letter to GUPTA, dated 1 January 1911, in: BARUĀ (1959: 86–87).

[8] GUPTA's letter to Bārhaspatya, dated 4 January 1911, in: BARUĀ (1959: 88, 89, 194) and PĀṬHAK (1960: 394).

Though in September 1915 he attempted to resume writing, until November the work was not really proceeding. He complained: 'I'm feeling sad and ashamed not being able now to write anything about Devī Ūrmilā.'[9] Finally, in the beginning of 1916 GUPTA overcame that creative impasse; he also started to refer to his work as *Sāket*, though he continued to use the older title as well. All that time he kept on consulting, among others, Dvivedī and Bārhaspatya and discussing the form of his work with them. In a few months the beginning cantos were ready and the first of them came out in the June issue of *Sarasvatī* under the title *Sāket* and was soon followed by four other cantos.[10]

Yet, the work on the poem took still sixteen years more before it was finally published in 1932. In his preface to *Sāket*, GUPTA admitted that the poem had been ready two years earlier[11] but he had not been satisfied with its Canto 9: '... at that time something was unfinished in Canto 9 and, according to my perception, even today it is still incomplete.'[12]

## 2. How *Sāket* is written

*Sāket* is a full-length poem (often termed by Hindi critics as a *mahā-kāvya*[13] and, e.g. by Peter GAEFFKE as 'a huge epic on the Rāma story'[14]) divided into twelve cantos (*sarga*). It is written in a generally not too heavily sanskritised Hindi (esp. from the point of view of syntax[15]), mostly in couplets arranged in over sixty different meters.[16]

Canto 1 opens up with clarifying the reasons of Rām's *avatār* in this world; Rām has been born: **पथ दिखाने के लिए संसार को, दूर करने लिए भू-भार को, सफल करने के**

[9] Cited in: BARUĀ (1959: 194).

[10] Canto 2 in July 1916, Canto 3 in January 1917, Canto 4 in May 1917, and Canto 5 in July 1918; BARUĀ (1959: 194–195) and PĀṬHAK (1960: 177–178, 395).

[11] The date given at the end of *Sāket* (p. 253) is: *Dīpāvalī* 1986 (i.e. November 1929).

[12] GUPTA (1961: III).

[13] E.g. PĀṬHAK (1960); see esp. pp. 510–519, where also the discussion of different authors' opinions is included on pp. 517–519.

[14] GAEFFKE (1978: 81).

[15] E.g. long nominal appositions, so typical of Hindi of the *chāyāvādī* poetry of that time, are relatively rare.

[16] The figure calculated on the basis of the listing of *Sāket* metres made by PĀṬHAK (1960: 695–696).

लिए जन-दृष्टियाँ ('to show the way to the world; to deliver the earth from the burden of [sin]; to fulfil the expectations of the people').[17] After a very brief introduction to Rām's family, GUPTA proceeds to describe the prosperity of Sāket-Ayodhyā[18] and then concentrates on a lively dialogue between Lakṣmaṇ and Ūrmilā which is first and foremost expressive of their happy married life; it also refers to the investiture of Rām as Crown Prince[19] and Bharat's absence from Ayodhyā[20] (Canto 1). Then up to Canto 8, we witness the events from the well-known *Rāmâyaṇa* tradition which cover roughly the story of Book 2. the *Ayodhyā-kāṇḍa*, as presented, e.g. by Vālmīki and Tulsīdās.

In Canto 9 the narrative comes to a standstill; this section is entirely devoted to the description of Ūrmilā as a *virahiṇī*, i.e. suffering the pangs of separation from her beloved Lakṣmaṇ. With Canto 10 Ūrmilā's thoughts flash back to her own and her sisters' childhood and adolescence, and to the bow tournament followed with her and her sisters' marriage with Daśarath's sons. She confides all her memories to the river Sarayū.

Two last cantos, 11 and 12, cover the rest of the story, as it is contained in the traditional Books 3 to 6, though most of the events are narrated in an unconventional manner. The beginning of Canto 11 introduces us to Bharat's hermitage, in the vicinity of the royal palace, where he leads a renouncer's life worshipping Rām's sandals enthroned in a golden temple.[21] Māṇḍavī, Bharat's wife, is accompanying him and when, after a while, Śatrughna joins them, they listen to what he heard about Rām from one merchant visiting their city.[22] He narrates to them the events which followed Rām's departure from Citrakūṭ for the Daṇḍak forest where the incident of severing of Śūrpaṇakhā's ears and nose took place and was followed up with the battle in which Rām killed the demons Khar and Dūṣaṇ. Still wondering about Rām's victory, Bharat aims an arrow at a dark object he has noticed in the sky; considering it a demon, he actually wounds Hanumān flying for a life-giving herb, *sañjīvanī*, for Lakṣmaṇ. Luckily, Hanumān recovers very quickly, thanks to some amount of *sañjīvanī* which Bharat was given earlier by one *yogī*[23],

---

[17] GUPTA (1961: 18).

[18] Although the name *Sāket* is more often used, at some places GUPTA uses them interchangeably; see e.g. GUPTA (1961: 19–20).

[19] GUPTA (1961: 33).

[20] GUPTA (1961: 37).

[21] GUPTA (1961: 389).

[22] GUPTA (1961: 410 ff.).

[23] GUPTA (1961: 409).

and then narrates how Śūrpaṇakhā persuaded his brother Rāvaṇ to take revenge on Rām and kidnap his wife Sītā. He tells also how finally Rām invaded Laṅkā to fight Sītā back. Many brave warriors on both sides were killed during that war and Lakṣmaṇ, seriously wounded, was waiting for *sañjīvanī* that could save his life. Therefore Hanumāṇ—eager to fulfil his mission—takes the herb and leaves Sāket (Canto 11).

In the last, twelfth, canto Bharat—at the instigation of Māṇḍavī—orders Śatrughna to get the troops ready for the attack on Laṅkā. Almost all the citizens of Ayodhyā, and among them also Kaikeyī and Ūrmilā, deeply moved by the news about wounded Lakṣmaṇ are prepared for the battle. But then Vasiṣṭh intervenes and persuades them to calm down and to look onto the sky where, thanks to his inner powers, they can see what is happening in Laṅkā (one would like to call it 'a live broadcast from Laṅkā'!).[24] And thus they learn about the fate of Lakṣmaṇ, the final victory of Rām over Rāvaṇ, and the release of Sītā. After Rām's return to Sāket everyone rejoices, especially Ūrmilā reunited with Lakṣmaṇ is unable to contain her happiness.

## 3. Ūrmilā, *Sāket* and *rām-kathā*

As we have seen in the foregoing discussion, the work on the poem took GUPTA more than twenty years from its inception, or sixteen years from the publication of its first canto in *Sarasvatī*. It is worth noting in this context, however, that this was not just that single work to engage his attention—during all those years GUPTA was very active and published a lot.[25] But as far as *Sāket* is concerned, GUPTA kept postponing its writing, then he had problems while working on it and yet, after all those years—as we know from his preface, and what does not look like a token expression of poet's modesty—he was not satisfied with the final effect (i.e. with its Canto 9). Although GUPTA did not give the actual reasons of his dissatisfaction, the analysis of *Sāket*'s contents indicates that Canto 9 and 10[26] are a distortion of an otherwise traditional narrative, which is not only an integral part of *Sāket*'s retelling but forms also its core—these two cantos, 9 and 10, disrupt the poem's natural flow.

[24] GUPTA (1961: 476 ff.).

[25] E.g. *Raṅg mẽ bhaṅg* (1910), *Jayadrath-vadh* (1910), *Bhārat-bhāratī* (1914), *Pañcavaṭī* (1925) or *Jhaṅkār* (1929), to name the most important works.

[26] It may be interesting to note here that while Canto 9 constitutes about 20 per cent of the poem and Canto 10 about 10 per cent, Cantos 1–8 constitute about 50 per cent and Cantos 11–12 about 20 per cent.

What more, whereas the major focus of the poem are Rām and Sītā[27], Canto 9 and, to a lesser degree, also Canto 10 are monopolised by Ūrmilā, otherwise not of such significance in the rest of the poem, although—it must be acknowledged—treated with much attention and more sympathy than ever before. As a result, the overall impression of *Sāket* can be that we deal with two autonomous works. And such an attitude is corroborated in the tradition of *Sāket*'s criticism where, very often, authors either concentrate on the story of Rām with its leading characters Rām and Sītā or view it as a poem of which Ūrmilā is the heroine.[28] It is also not uncommon to view *Sāket* as a *virah-kāvya* (a poem of separation [from the beloved]),[29] which is a telling example of Canto 9, together with Canto 10, being a poem within a poem; it does originate from *Sāket*'s main narrative but neither develops it nor enriches it, living its own life washed down with Ūrmilā's tears.

Let us consider the reasons of such a form of GUPTA's work.

We have already mentioned that in the beginning GUPTA had intended to write a poem concerned with Ūrmilā but after some time changed his initial idea and began to conceive it on a wider scale; the first result of such an attitude were the first cantos published in *Sarasvatī* under the title *Sāket*, and eventually in 1932 a finished poem in a book form.

The time GUPTA began his work was witnessing the rising tide of Indian national movement. Hindi poetry of the first decades of this century served the cause of that movement by drawing inspiration from the lost ideal of the traditions of India's past (in order to promote the pride in it—*atīt gaurav*) and interpreting it anew. For example, poets were looking for the characters and motifs known from the tradition, but neglected by it, as was in the case of Ūrmilā. In their reinterpretations, they were willing to enhance the awareness of Indian society (*jan-jāgraṇ*), to educate it, and to evoke national feelings. Here arises a very important question—was the potential of Ūrmilā's character powerful enough to meet such a challenge? The evidence we find in the present form of *Sāket* itself, as well as in GUPTA's correspondence of that time, suggests a negative answer to this question and to indicate the reason why GUPTA decided to narrate the story of Ūrmilā against the background of the story of

[27] Or even more accurately—Sītā-Rām, as Gupta put it in his letter to Gāndhī: 'In *Sāket*, Sītā-Rām are celebrated as the leaders of the leaders and the teachers or the rulers of all.' ('सीता-राम 'साकेत' में नायकों के नायक और सबके शिक्षक अथवा शासक के रूप में प्रतिष्ठित हैं।'); BARUĀ (1959: 200). It should be noted here that the word *nāyak* used by GUPTA (which we translate as 'leader') can also mean 'leading character, hero.'

[28] E.g. PĀṬHAK (1960: 444).

[29] E.g. DHAM (1971) or BHĀṬĪ (1971).

Rām.[30] But composing a retelling conceived in such a way took him many years and it seems that this long haul should be seen first of all in terms of an, as it seems, insoluble dilemma—how to reconcile the status of Ūrmilā as a *nāyikā* (heroine) with *rām-kathā*?

It may be mentioned here that, according to some critics, GUPTA's problems were caused by the fact that the idea to write about Ūrmilā was imposed on him by his *kāvya-guru*, Dvivedī, and GUPTA actually never made this conception his own.[31]

In conclusion I would like to quote GUPTA's answer to the question about the reasons for writing *Sāket*. After many years from its publication, he said in one interview: 'I had to write about my favoured deity. I wrote *Sāket*.'[32] No mention of Ūrmilā.

> 'Rām, the tale of your life is a poem in itself,
> that someone becomes a poet is only natural.'

## BIBLIOGRAPHY


BARUĀ 1959 = 'Baruā', Ṛṣi Jaiminī Kauśik (ed.): *Rāṣṭrakavi Maithilīśaraṇ Gupta abhinandan-granth*. Jaiminī-prakāśan, Kalkattā 1959.

BHĀṬĪ 1971 = Bhāṭī, Deśrājsiṁh: *Sāket kā navam sarg*. Aśok prakāśan, Dillī 1971.

DHAM 1971 = Dham, Vinod: *Maithilīśaraṇ Gupta ke virah-kāvya*. Sanmarg prakaśan, Dillī 1971.

GAEFFKE 1978 = Gaeffke, Peter: *Hindi Literature in the Twentieth Century*. Otto Harrassowitz, Wiesbaden 1978.

GUPTA 1961 = Gupta, Maithilīśaraṇ: *Sāket*. Sāhitya-sadan, Cirgā̃v (Jhā̃sī) 1961.

NAGENDRA 1960 = Nagendra: *Sāket: ek adhayan*. Sāhitya-ratna bhaṇḍār: Āgrā 1960.

PĀṬHAK 1960 = Pāṭhak, Kamlākānt: *Maithilīśaraṇ Gupta: vyakti aur kāvya*. Raṇjīt priṇṭars eṇḍ pabliśars: Dillī 1960.

SAKSENĀ 1961 = Saksenā, Dvārikāprasād: *Sāket mẽ kāvya, saṁskṛti aur darśan*. Vinod pustak mandir: Āgrā 1961.


[30] Comp. NAGENDRA (1960: 13).

[31] NAGENDRA (1960: 2) and SAKSENĀ (1961: 50).

[32] 'इष्टदेव के विषय में कुछ लिखना ही था। 'साकेत' लिख गया'; cited in: BHĀṬĪ (1971: 5).

# *KĀVYA*

# 'Sparrows in Love'
# The Display and Pairing of Birds in Sanskrit Literature*

KLAUS KARTTUNEN

Some time ago I saw a reference to the rut of elephants as the most important sexual image in Sanskrit literature. This is certainly true. Everyone familiar with classical Sanskrit literature easily recalls many passages describing elephants in musth. Think about the mighty bull elephants with their temples moist with ichor, surrounded by swarming bees, and frightening everybody in their uncontrolled rage.[1]

But at the same time it also reminded me of a passage in Varāhamihira's *Bṛhat-saṁhitā* where the special virility of the sparrow (*caṭaka*)[2] is mentioned. It is a recipe for an aphrodisiac preparation and it is guaranteed that with this preparation one is even able to cut out a sparrow.[3] The sexual ability more or less rightly

---

* I would like to express here my thanks to Professor Rahul Peter Das, who sent me both a copy of MONGA (1999) and some textual material. Margot Stout Whiting has kindly checked and corrected my English.

[1] See e.g. the *Ṛtu-saṁhāra* 2.15; *Avi-māraka* 1.5 f.; *Kādambarī* p. 57. For the present purpose, it is not important that the biologists are in fact uncertain of the real connection between musth and rut.

[2] The house sparrow (*Passer domesticus* Linn., ALI (1977: n. 257)) is common in most parts of South Asia. However, it must be pointed out that the three names commonly used for the sparrow, viz. *caṭaka*, *kuliṅga* and *kalaviṅka*, are also used for many other kinds of small birds, especially buntings and finches, but also swallows, etc. Occasionally the house sparrow is specified as *gṛha-kuliṅga* or *grāma-caṭaka*. DAVE (1985: 92 f.) is useful, although his conclusions must always be taken with care. DAVE (1985), HENSGEN (1958), RAU (1986), and THAKER (1972), have been much used as sources of text references, but all are checked from the original.

[3] *Bṛhat-saṁhitā* 76.7:

*kṣīreṇa bastâṇḍa-yujā śṛtena samplāvya kāmī bahuśas tilān yaḥ /*
*suśoṣitān atti payaḥ pibec ca tasyâgrataḥ kiṁ caṭakaḥ karoti //*

Bhat: 'A lustful man should boil milk with goat's testicles and sesamum several (seven) times and thus concentrate it. He should eat and drink milk

*Essays in Indian Philosophy, Religion and Literature*, pp. 261–269.

ascribed to the sparrow is also the reason for names such as *kāmuka, kāmin, kāma-cārin,* given to the sparrow by lexicographers and noted as such in MONIER-WILLIAMS' dictionary. Śrīharṣa, in the rather detailed description of Nala's and Damayantī's lovemaking in the eighteenth canto of the *Naiṣadhīya-carita*, remarks that the loving couple, observed by a *sārikā* from its perch, was imitating the sport of heated sparrows.[4] Actually there lies good observation behind this; although it is common to think of the sparrow as a modest grey thing, whoever has observed a displaying sparrow cock remembers its strikingly black and brown plumage (cf. *nīla-kaṇṭha* as a name of the sparrow) and the strong sexuality of its behaviour.[5]

These amorous sparrows gave me the idea of examining the display and pairing of other birds, too, in Sanskrit literature. It is common knowledge that song birds (and many other birds as well) sing in order to entice a female or to secure a territory. The song of the koel (*kokila*)[6] heard in springtime is one of the most powerful symbols of love, again and again referred to in classical literature.[7] Often the koel is mentioned together with another symbol of spring and love, the humming bees. The

---

> after that. He will then be able to put even the sparrow to shame by his exuberant virility.'

The sense is further explained by Bhaṭṭotpala in his commentary: *bahu-strī-gamanam atīva strīṣu bahu-vāraṁ śīghra-gāmī bhavatîty arthaḥ.*

[4] *Naiṣadhīya-carita* 18.15 f.:

> *yatra puṣpa-śara-śāstra-kārikā-sārikâdhyuṣita-nāga-dantikā* /
> *bhīmajā-niṣadha-sārva-bhaumayoḥ pratyavaikṣata rate kṛtâkṛte* // 15 //
> *yatra matta-kalaviṅka-śīlitâślīla-keli-punar-uktavat tayoḥ* /
> *kvâpi dṛṣṭibhir avāpi vāpikôttaṁsa-haṁsa-mithuna-smarôtsavaḥ* // 16 //

Though so translated by Handiqui, the *sārikā* on its ivory perch in 15 does not refer to a sparrow, but to a myna, while *kalaviṅka*, occasionally used for other birds, too, is defined as *gṛha-caṭika* by the commentator Nārāyaṇa.

[5] In addition to my own observations of our northern sparrows (which belong to the same species, *Passer domesticus* Linn., ALI (1977: n. 257)), I can refer to the lively description of Indian sparrows in MONGA (1999).

[6] The koel (*Eudynamus scolopacea* Linn., ALI (1977: n. 115)) is common everywhere in South Asia. It should not be called the Indian cuckoo as this name is used for another species of parasitic cuckoos, the short-winged *Cuculus micropterus* (ALI (1977: n.117)).

[7] E.g. *Vikramôrvaśīya* 4.12; 4.25 (*tvāṁ kāmino madana-dūtam udāharanti*); 4.56; *Kumāra-saṁbhava* 4.16; 6.2; *Raghu-vaṁśa* 9.34; *Ṛtu-saṁhāra* 6.20–22, 24 f., 27 f.; *Ratnâvalī* 1.16 f.; *Kādambarī* p. 305.

bird himself is intoxicated by spring and life and is therefore called *matta-kokila*.[8] In one case, at least, the intoxication is clearly associated with sexual behaviour.[9] The cuckoo's way of living was well known, too, and the she-cuckoo, as *para-bhṛtā*, leaving other birds to raise its offspring, was presented as an example of female deviousness.[10] The cuckoo belongs to spring; when its voice is heard at the onset of winter, it is inauspicious (*Bṛhat-saṁhitā* 46.69).

There are other sounds of birds mentioned in literature, but while the voice of geese (*haṁsa*) is considered erotic, it has, in fact, nothing to do with the pairing of these birds, which takes place in their northern nesting areas, not in their wintering places in India. The female ospreys (*kurarī*) are rather crying from fear. I have found only one passage where the cooing of nesting pigeons is specifically mentioned, which is answered by wild cocks from below.[11]

The gallinaceous birds are famous of their display, involving dance, song and fight. In India, as in the ancient West, too, the fighting instincts of cocks and quails were used for entertainment, but the history of cock-fights deserves a separate treatment. The quail (*cakora*) is better known for its red eyes and its supposed habit of feeding on moonbeams, though even pairing is occasionally mentioned.[12] But here I would rather concentrate on the peacock and its dance.[13]

The peacocks' dance belongs to the rainy season, during the summer they are quiet and exhausted.[14] Their eager anticipating of and welcome to the rain clouds is

[8] E.g. *Artha-śāstra* 2.26.5 (*matta-kokila* among protected birds); *Mālavikâgnimitra* 3.4; *Raghu-vaṁśa* 9.47; *Kādambarī* p. 42.

[9] *Ṛtu-saṁhāra* 6.14: *puṁs-kokilaś cūta-rasâsavena mattaḥ priyāṁ cumbati rāga-hṛṣṭaḥ*. Here *cūta-rasâsava* seems to refer to fermented mango juice. In several other passages, however, fresh sprouts are the origin of the bird's intoxication. See e.g. *Śakuntalā* 6.2 f. (on female koel seeing young mango sprouts); *Kumāra-saṁbhava* 3.32 (*cūtâṅkurâsvāda-kaṣāya-kaṇṭhaḥ puṁs-kokilaḥ*); *Kirātârjunīya* 5.26 (*apanidra-cūta-gandhair … madayati kokilān*).

[10] E.g. *Śakuntalā* 5.22; *Kuṇāla-jātaka* (*Jātaka* 536).

[11] *Mālatī-mādhava* 9.7: *virunnīḍa-kapota-kūjitaṁ krandanty adhaḥ kukkubhāḥ*.

[12] *Mālatī-mādhava* 9.30: *kāntām antaḥ-pramodād abhisarati mada-bhrānta-tāraś cakoraḥ*.

[13] The peacock (*Pavo cristatus* Linn., ALI (1977: n. 71)) is found practically everywhere in South Asia, in the Himalayas up to the altitude of more that 1500 metres.

[14] *Ṛtu-saṁhāra* 1.16 (*hutâgni-kalpaiḥ savitur gabhastibhiḥ kalāpinaḥ klānta-śarīra-cetasaḥ*); cf. *Śakuntalā* 3.23 f.; *Mālatī-mādhava* 3.4.

often mentioned in literature as a sign of the imminent rains,[15] and their wild dance is one of the characteristics of the rainy season.[16] Usually this behaviour is not directly connected with mating and the dance is thought to be a direct response to thunder. Therefore, the peacocks were often induced to dance by other kinds of noise.[17] The sexual significance of the dance is clearly seen in the famous *Jātaka* story of the peacock, who, overjoyed from being chosen as the bridegroom of the goose princess, indecently exposed himself and was dismissed.[18] When the rains stop and the autumn begins, the dance is stopped.[19] The dancing peacock is often depicted in Indian art.[20]

The golden peacocks which live the life of ascetic recluses in mountains and are caught only when yielding to the temptation of mating seem to me to be pheasants rather than peacocks.[21]

The art of reading omens from birds' and animals' cries (*śakuna*) does not help us much further here. According to the *Bṛhat-saṁhitā*, animals seen as couples (*dvandva*) or in rut (*matta*) are not accepted as omens (86.25). This applies, for instance, to crows and cuckoos in spring (86.26) and to geese and cranes in autumn (86.27).[22] At the same time, animals mating with animals of another species (86.66:

---

[15] *Megha-dūta* 22 (seeing the rain cloud the peacocks shed tears of joy), 32 (Ray's 34); *Raghu-vaṁśa* 16.64; *Ṛtu-saṁhāra* 2.6; *Mālatī-mādhava* 9.42; see further *Kirātârjunīya* 4.16; 7.22, 39; 10.23.

[16] *Vikramôrvaśīya* 4.17 f., 18.21 f.; *Megha-dūta* 44 (Ray 46); *Raghu-vaṁśa* 6.51; *Ṛtu-saṁhāra* 2.6, 16 (rainy mountains are *pravṛtta-nṛtyaiḥ śikhibhiḥ samākulāḥ*); *Mālatī-mādhava* 9.15, 18; *Śyainika-śāstra* 5.33: *śikhaṇḍi-kṛta-tāṇḍave*. In the *Kādambarī* p. 40, too, they dance like Śiva.

[17] *Mālavikâgnimitra* 1.21 (by a drum); *Mālatī-mādhava* 1.1 (by a drum); *Kādambarī* p. 55 (by flapping of wild elephants' ears), 104 (by drums), 171 (by the noise of stumbling feet).

[18] *Nacca-jātaka* (*Jātaka* 32); the idea of the indecency of the peacock's dance is also disclosed in the *Vikramôrvaśīya* 4.22 and in the *Pañca-tantra* of Pūrṇabhadra 1.26, last verse. In the famous Greek parallel to the story (Herodotus 6.129), the actors are humans, Cleisthenes of Corinth, his daughter Agariste, and the young Hippocleides (see LURIA (1930)).

[19] *Ṛtu-saṁhāra* 3.13: *nṛtya-prayoga-rahitāñ śikhino*; cf. *Kirātârjunīya* 4.25, and *Mudrā-rākṣasa* 3.8.

[20] See the summary in KADGAONKAR (1993).

[21] See *Mora-jātaka* (*Jātaka* 159) and *Mahā-mora-jātaka* (*Jātaka* 491).

[22] Nevertheless, in various passages of the *Bṛhat-saṁhitā*, bird pairs are mentioned as omens. Thus the simultaneous cry of a pair of cranes (*sārasa*) is favourable, but one responding to the other after an interval is inauspicious (88.37). Two crows, the male

*para-yoniṣu gacchanto maithunaṁ*) are mentioned as a particularly dark omen. A special point used in divination is the time of the building of a crows' nest and its location on a tree or elsewhere and the number and appearance of their chicks (*Bṛhat-saṁhitā* 95).

Though cross-breeding between different species was deemed inauspicious (with the single exception of producing mules), there are some cases of curious marriages in literature. Repeatedly, the parrot and the myna are represented as a couple.[23] This may not necessarily mean much more than that the two talking birds were often kept together in a cage, and there is at least one passage where it is plainly stated that in reality a parrot weds a parrot and a myna a myna.[24] In the *Jātaka* Commentary there are also other cases of supposed cross-marriages. In the *Kukkuṭa-jātaka* (*Jātaka* 383), the clever cat makes a proposal of marriage to a cock (who is wise enough not to accept it). In the *Vinīlaka-jātaka* (*Jātaka* 160) we meet the arrogant offspring of an union between the King Goose and a she-crow. It seems clear that the idea of the possibilities of cross-breeding was as much exaggerated in ancient India as in the Hellenistic West.[25]

Related to the belief in curious cross-breeding is the belief in the propagation without a male. Several texts ascribe this to female egrets (*balākā*), who are impregnated by the thunder of rain clouds.[26] This is also indicated in two passages of Śaṅkara's *Brahma-sūtra* commentary.[27]

---

and the female, putting food into the mouth of each other and cawing simultaneously are considered auspicious (95.43).

[23] E.g. *Śuka-saptati*, frame-story, where the couple is explained as a Gandharva and an Apsaras reborn as birds. Note that in the parallel stories of the *Jātaka* Commentary there are two parrots instead of a parrot and a myna (the two *Rādha-jātaka*s, n. 145 and 198). Further e.g. in the *Kādambarī* p. 568.

[24] *Mahā-ummaga-jātaka* (*Jātaka* 546), p. 421 Fausbøll:

*suvo va suviṁ kāmeyya sālikā pana sāḷikāṁ* /
*suvassa sāḷḷikāya ca saṁbhāvo hoti kīdiso* // —

—"Parrot should love parrot, and maynah maynah; how can there be union between parrot and maynah?".

[25] On these western ideas see GRMEK (1988).

[26] *Megha-dūta* 9 (Ray's 10); *Lola-jātaka* (*Jātaka* 274), first verse; and *Milinda-pañha* 4.1.49. Cf. THIEME (1975, 15 f.).

[27] Śaṅkara on the *Brahma-sūtra* 2.1.25 (*SBE* 34, p. 348) and 3.1.19 (*SBE* 38, p. 126). Thibaut translated the bird as crane, but the word used in the text is *balākā* (*balākā cântareṇâiva śukraṁ garbhaṁ dhatte* and *balākâpy antareṇâiva retaḥ-sekaṁ garbhaṁ dhatta iti loka-rūḍhiḥ*).

This short presentation started with the amorous promiscuity of the sparrow and now I am concluding it with the classical example of marital love, the *cakra-vāka* duck.[28] Actually, it was founded on an accurate observation: The ducks are monogamous and have a very close relationship. As a symbol of marital love, they are already mentioned in the *Veda* and in Pāli sources.[29] To this observation was then added the poetical embellishment that the *cakra-vāka* pair must, on account of a curse, separate over the night.[30] Bāṇa elaborates the theme: Ujjayinī is so brightly illuminated (not by lamps, but by the self-illuminating jewels of women) that even the night brings no separation for the ducks.[31] A more overwhelming grief of separation is naturally felt when one mate is slain.[32] In this connection, I would also mention the introductory passage of the *Rāmâyaṇa*, with the famous passage about the courtship of cranes (*krauñca*).[33] In addition to the brahminy ducks, the relation of a pair of geese is often described as a close one,[34] and the voice of a goose heard in autumn is deemed as erotic.[35]

---

[28] The ruddy sheldrake (or shelduck, *Tadorna ferruginea* Pallas, the name *Anas casarca* is completely antiquated), also known as the brahminy duck (ALI (1977: n. 29)). It is a common winter visitor in South Asia. See also DAVE (1985: 450 ff.).

[29] In the *Veda*: *Atharva-veda-saṁhitā* 14.2.64; in Pāli: *Cakkavāka-jātaka* (*Jātaka* 434) and *Milinda-pañha* 7.5.8 (p. 401 Trenckner).

[30] *Mālavikâgnimitra* 5.9; *Kumāra-saṁbhava* 5.25; 8.32, 51; *Megha-dūta* 80 (2.20); *Raghu-vaṁśa* 8.56; *Svapna-vāsavadattā* 1.13, 3.0; *Mālatī-mādhava* 2.12; *Kirātârjunīya* 8.56; 9.4, 13, 30; *Śiśupāla-vadha* 9.15; 11.26, 64; *Naiṣadhīya-carita* 7.77; 21.162; *Kādambarī* p. 110, 171, 196, 299, 322, 350, 391.

[31] *Kādambarī* p. 109.

[32] *Bhūridatta-jātaka* (*Jātaka* 543), p. 189 Fausbøll; *Vessantara-jātaka* (*Jātaka* 547), p. 501 Fausbøll.

[33] The sarus crane (*Grus antigone* Linn., ALI (1977: n. 73)). See THIEME (1975: 11 f.), further BUCK (1971) and RONEY (1983).

[34] *Vikramôrvaśīya* 4.2–4.6; *R̥tu-saṁhāra* 3.11.

[35] *R̥tu-saṁhāra* 3.25 (*kāmyaṁ haṁsa-vacanaṁ*); *Kirātârjunīya* 4.25 (*unmada-haṁsa-nisvanaṁ*). On goose in Indian tradition see VOGEL (1962).

## BIBLIOGRAPHY

Texts:

*Artha-śāstra* = *The Kauṭilīya Artha-śāstra*. Edited & transl. R.P. Kangle, Vols. 1–2, 2nd ed., Bombay 1969–72. [Reprinted: Motilal Banarsidass, Delhi 1986].

*Avi-māraka* = *Avi-māraka* of Bhāsa: (1) *Plays ascribed to Bhāsa*. Crit. edited by C.R. Devadhar. Poona 1962. [Reprinted: Motilal Banarsidass, Delhi 1987]. (2) *Thirteen Plays of Bhāsa*. Translated into English by A.C. Woolner and Lakshman Sarup, Lahore 1930. [Reprinted: Motilal Banarsidass, Delhi 1985].

*Bṛhat-saṁhitā* = *Varāhamihira's Bṛhat Saṁhitā*. Ed. with English translation by M. Ramakrishna Bhat, Vols. 1–2, Motilal Banarsidass, Delhi 1981–82.

*Jātaka* = (1) *The Jātaka together with its commentary being Tales of the anterior births of Gotama Buddha*. For the first time edited in the original Pāli by V. Fausbøll, Vols. 1–6. London 1877–96. [Vol. 7] *Index to the Jātaka and its Commentary* by Dines Andersen. London 1897. (2) *The Jātaka or stories of the Buddha's Former Births*. Transl. from the Pāli by various hands under the editorship of E.B. Cowell, Vols. 1–6. Cambridge 1895–1907 and Index-Vol. 1913. [Reprinted: London 1969].

*Kādambarī* = *Kādambarī* of Bāṇa: (1) *Śrīmad-vāṇa-bhaṭṭa-praṇītā Kādambarī (kathā-mukha-paryantā). Śrī Bhānucandra-Siddhacandra Gaṇi-viracitayā saṁskṛta-ṭīkayā saṁvalitā hindī-bhāṣânuvādena câlaṅkṛtā*. Anuvādakaḥ Ratinātha Jhā. Motīlāl Banārasīdās, Dillī 1967. [but passages are given according to the pages of the old NSP edition, as given by Ridding]. (2) *The Kādambarī of Bāṇa*. Translated by C.M. Ridding, Royal Asiatic Society, London 1895. [Reprinted: Oriental Books Reprint Corporation, New Delhi 1974].

*Kirātârjunīya* = *Kirātârjunīya* of Bhāravi: *Kirātârjunīyam (3–6 sargaḥ)*. Sampādakaḥ anuvādakaḥ Janārdana Śāstrī Pāṇḍeya. Motīlāl Banārasīdās, Vārāṇasī 1976.

*Kumāra-saṁbhava* = *Kumāra-sambhava of Kālidāsa. Cantos I–VIII*. Ed. by M.R. Kale, Seventh edition, Motilal Banarsidass, Delhi 1981. [1st ed.: 1923].

*Mālatī-mādhava* = *Mālatī-mādhava* of Bhavabhūti: *Mālatī-mādhava with the Commentary of Jagaddhara*. Ed. with a literal English Translation, Notes and Introduction by Moreshwar Ramchandra Kale, 3rd ed., Motilal Banarsidass, Delhi 1967. [First edition: 1913].

*Mālavikâgnimitra* = *Mālavikâgnimitra* of Kālidāsa: *Works of Kālidāsa*. Edited with an exhaustive introduction, translation and critical and explanatory notes by C.R. Devadhar. Vol. I. *Dramas*. Motilal Banarsidass, Delhi 1966. [Reprinted: 1977].

*Megha-dūta* = *Kālidāsa's Megha-dūta*. With some notes of Saradaranjan Ray, ed. by Kumudranjan Ray. 6th ed. rev. and enlarged. Kumudranjan Ray, Calcutta 1968. [1st ed. 1928]. [The numbers of De's edition are also given].

*Milinda-pañha* = *Milinda-pañha (Questions of Milinda)*. Ed. by Swami Dwarikadas Shastri. *Bauddha Bharati Series* 13, Bauddha Bharati, Varanasi 1979.

*Mudrā-rākṣasa* = *Mudrā-rākṣasa* of Viśākhadatta: *The Mudra-Rakshasa. A Sanskrit Drama by Bisakhadutta*. Ed. with tr. into English and Bengali, a commentary in Sanskrit and annotations in English and Sanskrit by Srish Chandra Chakravarti. 2nd ed., Bhattacharyya & Son, Mymensingh–Calcutta 1919.

*Naiṣadhīya-carita* = (1) *Śrīharṣa-viracitaṁ Naiṣadhīya-caritam. Śrīman-nārāyaṇa-viracitayā Naiṣadhīya-prakāśâkhya-vyākhyayā ... samullasitam.* Nārāyaṇa Rāma Ācārya 'Kāvyatīrtha.' 9th ed., Nirṇaya Sāgar Pres, Mumbaī 1952. (2) *For the first time translated into English with critical Notes* by Krishna Kanta Handiqui. *Deccan College Building Centenary and Silver Jubilee Series* 33, Deccan College, Poona 1965.

*Pañca-tantra* = *Pañca-tantra* of Pūrṇabhadra: *The Panchatantra. A Collection of Ancient Hindu Tales, in the Recension, called Panchakhyanaka, and dated 1199 A. D., of the Jaina Monk Pūrṇabhadra*. Critically edited in the original Sanskrit by Johannes Hertel. *Harvard Oriental Series* 11, Cambridge, Massachusetts 1908.

*Raghu-vaṁśa* = *The Raghu-vaṁśa of Kālidāsa with the Commentary (the Sañjīvinī) of Mallinātha*. Edited by Kāśīnath Pāṇḍurang Parab and Wāsudev Laxmaṇ Śāstrī Paṇśīkar. 10th edition, Nirnaya Sagar Press, Bombay 1932.

*Ratnâvalī* = *Ratnāvalī of Harṣa*. Edited by C. Cappeller in O. Böhtlingk, *Sanskrit-Chrestomathie*. 3. Auflage hrsg. von R. Garbe. Leipzig 1909: 326–382. [Reprinted: Wissenschaftliche Buchgesellschaft, Darmstadt 1967].

*Ṛtu-saṁhāra* = *The Seasons. Kālidāsa's Ṛtu-saṁhāra*. A translation with introduction [and text] by John T. Roberts. Center for Asian Studies, Arizona State University, Tempel, Arizona 1990.

*Śakuntalā* = *Śakuntalā* of Kālidāsa. See: *Mālavikâgnimitra*.

*Śaṅkara* = *Śrī-śaṁkarâcārya-granthâvalī. Tṛtīyo bhāgaḥ. Brahma-sūtra Śāṁkara-bhāṣya sametāḥ*. Motīlāl Banārasīdās, Dillī 1964.

*Śiśupāla-vadha* = *The Śiśupāla-vadha of Māgha with the Commentary of Mallinātha*. Ed. by Pt. Durgāprasād and Pt. Śivadatta of Jaypore. Rev. 11th ed. Nirnaya Sagar Press, Bombay 1940.

*Svapna-vāsavadattā* = *Svapna-vāsavadattā* of Bhāsa. See: *Avi-māraka*.

| | |
|---|---|
| *Śyainika-śāstra* | = *Śyainika-śāstram. The Art of Hunting in Ancient India of Rājā Rudradeva of Kumaon* [Ed. &] transl. into English by M.M. Haraprasad Shastri, ed. with a critical introduction by Mohan Chand. Eastern Book Linkers, Delhi 1982. |
| *Vikramôrvaśīya* | = *The Vikramorvaśīya of Kālidāsa.* Critically edited by H.D. Velankar. Sahitya Akademi, Delhi 1961. |

Secondary Sources:

| | |
|---|---|
| ALI 1977 | = Ali, Sálim: *The Book of Indian Birds.* 10th revised and enlarged ed., Bombay Natural History Society, Bombay 1977. [Originally publ.: 1941]. |
| BUCK 1971 | = Buck, Harry M.: 'Two Krauñca Birds. A Phenomenological and Form-Critical Study of the Opening Ślokas of the *Vālmīki-rāmāyaṇa.*' in: *Professor K. A. Nilakanta Śastri Felicitation Volume.* Madras 1971: 368–380. |
| DAVE 1985 | = Dave, K.N.: *Birds in Sanskrit Literature.* Motilal Banarsidass, Delhi 1985. |
| GRMEK 1988 | = Grmek, Mirko D.: 'Antiikki ja perinnöllisyys.' *Hippokrates. Suomen Lääketieteen Historian Seuran vuosikirja* 5 (1988) 42–57. [With English summary: 'Ideas on heredity in Greek and Roman antiquity']. |
| HENSGEN 1958 | = Hensgen, Hans: 'Die Fauna bei Kālidāsa.' *Indo-Iranian Journal* 2 (1958) 33–53 and 128–148. |
| KADGAONKAR 1993 | = Kadgaonkar, Shivendra B.: 'The Peacock in ancient Indian Art and Literature.' *Bulletin of the Deccan College Research Institute* 53 (1993) 95–115. |
| LURIA 1930 | = Luria, S.: 'Der Affe des Archilochus und die Brautwerbung des Hippokleides.' *Philologus* 85 (1930) 1–22. |
| MONGA 1999 | = Monga, Sunjoy: 'The ubiquitous house sparrow.' *New India Digest* No. 72 Vol. 4/5 (1999) 39–42. |
| MONIER-WILLIAMS 1899 | = Monier-Williams, Monier: *A Sanskrit–English Dictionary.* New edition, greatly enlarged and improved. Oxford 1899. [Reprinted: Motilal Banarsidass, Delhi 1984]. |
| RAU 1986 | = Rau, Wilhelm: 'Poetical conventions in Indian Kāvya literature.' *Adyar Library Bulletin* 50 (1986) 191–197. |
| RONEY 1983 | = Roney, Stephen: 'Vālmīki's bird story: the art behind the epic.' *Journal of the Oriental Institute* (Baroda) 32/3–4 (1983) 216–229. |
| THAKER 1972 | = Thaker, J.P.: 'Fauna in Bhāravi.' *Journal of the Oriental Institute* (Baroda) 21/3–4 (1972) 228–239. |
| THIEME 1975 | = Thieme, Paul: 'Kranich und Reiher im Sanskrit.' *Studien zur Indologie und Iranistik* 1 (1975) 3–36. |
| VOGEL 1962 | = Vogel, J.-Ph.: *The Goose in Indian Literature and Art.* Leiden 1962. |

# What does the *Bhaṭṭi-kāvya* teach?

LIDIA SUDYKA

Bhaṭṭi, the author of the *mahā-kāvya* called *Bhaṭṭi-kāvya* after its creator, or—according to its subject matter—*Rāvaṇa-vadha* or *Rāma-carita*, lived probably in the seventh century C.E. His work belongs at the same time to the *śāstra-kāvya* genre, which means that the work describes not only the life of the hero, in our case Rāma, but simultaneously deals with some scientific problems. Bhaṭṭi's poem used to be described as giving examples from two fields of science: grammar and poetics.

In his *Kāvya-praśasti*[1], Bhaṭṭi writes that his work was meant only for intelligent people and all those who know the science of grammar:

/33/ *dīpa-tulyaḥ prabandho 'yaṁ śabda-lakṣaṇa-cakṣuṣām /*
*hastâmarṣam ivândhānāṁ bhaved vyākaraṇād ṛte //*

/34/ *vyākhyā-gamyam idaṁ kāvyam utsavaḥ sudhiyām alam /*
*hatā durmedhasaś câsmin vidvat-priyatayā mayā //*

'/33/ This composition is like a lamp for those whose eyes are grammar. Without grammar it would be like touching with the hand for the blind.

/34/ If this poem, understandable only with the help of commentary, is a feast for the wise, [it is] enough. The unintelligent are knocked down by me because of [my] fondness for the learned.'[2]

However, in the first *śloka* of his *Kāvya-praśasti* Bhaṭṭi assures us that the work, if properly studied, can be a good weapon for all who want to win in discussion:

/32/ *idam adhigatam ukti-mārga-citraṁ vivadiṣatāṁ vadatāṁ ca sannibandhāt /*
[opt.: *idam adhigata-mukti-mārga-citraṁ vivadiṣatāṁ vadatāṁ ca sannibandhāt /* ]
*janayati vijayaṁ sadā janānāṁ yudhi susamāhitam aiśvaraṁ yathâstram //*

'/32/ Striking through the way of expression and beautifully adorned, [when] studied, because of [its] excellent composition, it [i.e. the poem] brings success to those people who desire to debate and are speakers; just as a powerful missile, well levelled, marvellous with its

---

[1] RV-Bh 22.32–35.

[2] All translations from Sanskrit are my own unless otherwise stated.

*Essays in Indian Philosophy, Religion and Literature*, pp. 271–282.

> accomplished ways of discharging due to its construction, produces victory in a battle for those who fight and wish to be triumphant.'

Despite such a clear statement the work has never been treated as a kind of manual for speakers. A. WARDER writes about the *Bhaṭṭi-kāvya*:

> 'Its purpose is to work systematically through categories of grammar and also the figures of speech (following Bhāmaha).'[3]

Apart from the fact that Bhaṭṭi's analysis is not systematic and he does not follow Bhāmaha, this fusion of grammar and poetics was something rare. 'No grammarian includes rhetoric in his treatment of grammar,' wonder M.A. Karandikar and S. Karandikar in their 'Introduction' to the translation of the *Bhaṭṭi-kāvya*[4]. S.P. NARANG (1987), the author of a monograph on the *Bhaṭṭi-kāvya*, sees the reason for this in Bhaṭṭi's attempt to demonstrate his learning and scholarship[5].

Surprisingly enough nobody paid attention to the words of Bhaṭṭi himself. Why is it strange or unusual to treat his words seriously? The art of debating was a basic skill for exponents of different theories, perhaps for literary critics, too.

It is widely known that the exponents of the Advaita-vedānta thought developed certain dialectic methods. The discussion should be carried on according to a fourfold scheme called *anubandha-catuṣṭaya.* These four points should consider the following problems:

1. Who is entitled to deal with the subject—*adhikārin*,
2. What is the subject-matter—*viṣaya*,
3. What is the relationship between the *adhikārin* and *viṣaya*, and what are its benefits,
4. What is the purpose or the acquired result—*prayojana*.

The answers to these four questions can be found in many writings on Sanskrit poetics. It means that Indian literary criticism applied this scientific methodology like many other disciplines.

The impact of the *Mīmāṁsaka* dialectic on the structure of certain *alaṁkāra-śāstra*s is also visible. In the opinion of the Mīmāṁsakas the subject should be discussed in five stages:

1. the subject-matter (*viṣaya*),
2. a doubt (*viśaya*),

---

[3] WARDER (1983: 118, 119).

[4] RV-Bh(4), 'Introduction', p. XXX.

[5] NARANG (1987: 33).

3. an opponent (*pūrva-pakṣa*),
4. a rejoinder of the exponent (*uttara-pakṣa*),
5. the conclusion (*nirṇaya*).

Needless to say this is the way of presenting some problems of the theory of literature.

Indian logic supplied the tools not only to the authors of scholarly treatises but also to disputants. Each discipline using the particular device had to adjust it to its own purposes and to show how it works in the new surroundings. Thus Caraka, the famous physician and the supposed author or redactor of the *Caraka-saṁhitā*[6], in his own way defined the methods of debate (*vāda-mārga-pada*). Here the opponents in the discussion are, of course, physicians (*bhiṣak bhiṣajā saha saṁbhāṣeta*[7]). Caraka names forty four means which the physicians can apply in discussion. Among them there are twelve devices which are described as the figures of speech in the treatises on poetics. These are as follows: *anumāna*, *arthâpatti*, *ahetu*, *uttara*, *aupamya*, *dṛṣṭânta*, *pratyakṣa*, *viśeṣa*, *śabda*, *saṁśaya*, *sāmānya* and *hetu*[8].

Of course, in most cases both theoreticians of literature and representatives of other disciplines had to redefine the ideas offered to them by other branches of knowledge.

The art of debating was very important for the Buddhists and Jainas who also developed their own dialectic methods which are explained in numerous works. Their systems influenced the development of poetics, too. In the fifth chapter of his *Kāvyâlaṅkāra*, Bhāmaha (ca. 7th century C.E.) applied Buddhist logic to *kāvya*, following Vasubandhu (5th C.E.) and Diṅnāga (ca. 480—540 C.E.)[9]. As A.K. WARDER writes:

> 'Bhāmaha on the other hand proposes to compose *kāvya* in the guise of logic propositions and arguments based on experience. … The omissions of these logical members of discourse (proposition, reason and example) is listed among the faults in *kāvya* given by Bhāmaha, which otherwise are generally similar to those described in the *Nāṭyaśāstra*.'[10]

---

[6] The text comes from ca. 2nd–9th century C.E., see: OBERHAMMER–PRETS–PRANDSTETTER (1991: 142).

[7] CS 8.25 (p. 264).

[8] One can find the meaning of these terms in logic in the OBERHAMMER–PRETS–PRANDSTETTER (1991, 1996), while their description as figures of speech is given in GEROW (1971).

[9] WARDER (1989: 84).

[10] WARDER (1989: 85, 86).

One can look at the problem from another point of view and pose a question: Could the art of carrying on the debate profit from the knowledge of problems described by poeticians?

It is obvious that figures of speech and other stylistic devices were commonly used by the speakers. According to Ānandavardhana (9th century C.E.):

> *aśabdam arthaṁ ramaṇīyaṁ hi sūcayanto vyavahārās tathā vyāpārā nibaddhāś ca anibaddhāś ca vidagdha-pariṣatsu vividhā vibhāvyante / tān upahāsyatām ātmanaḥ pariharan ko 'tisandadhīte sacetāḥ /*
>
> 'Various turns of speech both in verse and prose which are suggestive of non-denoted beautiful meanings are commonly met with in the gatherings of wits. Which man of taste can be deaf to their implications without becoming a butt of ridicule?'[11]

The habit of holding public debates was part and parcel of intellectual life of India starting from Vedic times. One can indicate a great number of proofs. Such scenes have been depicted throughout the centuries in Indian literature. The popularity of the custom is even attested to by its existence as a tale motif. There are stories in which the hero's aim is to become invincible in the discussions. Of course, the way of achieving this goal is often very unusual.[12]

Really, it would be difficult to believe that the theoreticians of literature, often poets themselves, were an exception from the rule. And they were not. The *kavi-samāja*s or *kāvya-goṣṭhi*s were the occasions not only to read poems and point out their *doṣa*s and *guṇa*s, but to exchange the views on more complicated theoretical problems.

Rājaśekhara (10th century C.E.) says that the poetical contests were often accompanied by readings from scholarly treatises and discussions, or discussions were organised separately. According to Rājaśekhara, in Pāṭaliputra mainly the grammarians were the disputants. Ujjayinī was the place where the poets and poeticians held their meetings[13].

Interestingly enough, H. TIEKEN (1992), the author of the article dealing with the *Kāvya-mīmāṁsā*, ends his reflections with such a statement:

[11] DhĀ 3.33, p. 216.

[12] There is a story in the KSS 10.10 in which a mendicant who wants to be invincible in the discussion obtains this gift from a certain Yakṣa.

[13] KM, the last passages from chapter X '*Kavi-caryā rāja-caryā ca*': *mahā-nagareṣu ca kāvya-śāstra-parīkṣârthaṁ brahma-sabhāḥ kārayet / ... śrūyate côjjayinyāṁ kāvya-kāra-parīkṣā ... śrūyate ca pāṭaliputre śāstra-kāra-parīkṣā ... .*

'One may therefore ask if the rambling style of the text with its abrupt changes of topics, its unmotivated turns, its associative transitions does not itself serve some definite purpose, for instance, as a didactive device, providing points of discussion between teacher and pupil.'[14]

In this connection it is also worth remembering L. RENOU's analysis of the *Kirātârjunīya*[15]. He noticed the presence of two styles in *mahā-kāvyas*: descriptive and discursive.

While examining the discursive passages one can notice without any difficulty that Bhāravi (ca. 6th century C.E.) also teaches the way of discussing! We learn what a good speech should look like. It is endowed with such qualities as lucidity (*prasāda*), floridity (*ojas*), etc. Arguments are put in conformity with logic (*nyāya-nirṇīta*). Its meaning should be beautiful (*rucirârtha*). It is full of good reasoning (*upapattimat*) and possesses lofty purposes (*urjitâśraya*), to mention only a few features named in chapters two and eleven of the *Kirātârjunīya*[16].

Taking all this into consideration my proposal is to look at the *Rāvaṇa-vadha* as a kind of handbook for all those 'who desire to debate and are speakers' in accordance with Bhaṭṭi's clearly expressed will.

In this case nobody can be surprised that there is a grammar section in the *Bhaṭṭi-kāvya*. The speaker should know grammar excellently. Perhaps it is also not fortuitous that Bhaṭṭi omits certain *sūtras* from Pāṇini's *Aṣṭādhyāyī*, including only the most important ones. He did not illustrate Vedic *sūtras* for example. Definitely they were interesting for a grammarian but not for someone who wanted to be an orator, as the Vedic forms were not in use in the epoch of classical Sanskrit. Giving examples of a particular suffix, Bhaṭṭi excludes the roots which are too rare and obsolete.

The *Prasanna-kāṇḍa* of *Bhaṭṭi-kāvya* deals with figures of speech (tenth canto), the *mādhurya guṇa*, or the quality of 'sweetness' (eleventh canto), the *bhāvikatva*, or the quality of 'realism' (twelfth canto), and the *bhāṣā-sāma*, a paronomasia with regard to two different languages (thirteenth canto).

Why does Bhaṭṭi, as a poetician, chooses these particular devices from the wide realm of poetics? As a matter of fact, it is not really possible to find the answer to this question. Even early poeticians consider some clues more vital for the understanding the phenomenon of literature and its creation. Would it not be easier to find an answer to it, if we took Bhaṭṭi to be a teacher of rhetoric? Figures of speech were important for both poets and orators, as was mentioned above. It means

[14] TIEKEN (1992: 373).

[15] RENOU (1959).

[16] KA-Bh 2.1; 2.5; 11.38,39.

that the presence of the chapter depicting figures of speech cannot be a decisive proof in our case. However, we have another three chapters to analyse.

The eleventh canto is entirely devoted to the *mādhurya guṇa*. What can one learn from early poeticians about this *guṇa*?

The *Nāṭya-śāstra*, dating back to the beginning of our era, names ten *guṇas* among which one can also find *mādhurya*:

> *śleṣaḥ prasādaḥ samatā samādhir mādhuryam ojaḥ pada-saukumāryam / arthasya ca vyaktir udāratā ca kāntiś ca kāvya bhakti kāvya sya guṇā daśâite //* [17]
>
> 'There are ten qualities in *kāvya*, namely coherence (union), lucidity (perspicuity), evenness (uniformity), smoothness, sweetness, strength (floridity), delicacy or softness of words, manifestation of meaning, magnificence (exaltedness) and grace (brightness).'

The *mādhurya guṇa* is defined as follows (NŚ 16.104):

> *bahuśo yac chrutaṁ vākyam uktaṁ vâpi punaḥ punaḥ /*
> *nôdvejayati tasmād dhi tan mādhuryam iti smṛtam //*
>
> 'That is known as sweetness, by virtue of which an utterance, even though heard or spoken many times, causes no distress.' [18]

It seems that Bharata unites the *mādhurya guṇa* with the euphonic qualities of the poetic utterance: the utterance 'though heard or spoken many times' sounds equally pleasant and sweet to the ear. However, Abhinavagupta comments this statement as follows:

> *mādhuryam āha—bahuśo yac chrutam ityâdi. yad iti yasmād dhetor vākyaṁ śrutaṁ saṁśaya-viparyayayor āspadaṁ na bhavatîti tan mādhuryam. drāghīyasi samāse tāv avaśyaṁ bhavata iti tad-viraha eva mādhuryaṁ śabda-guṇa ity uktaṁ bhavati.*
>
> 'He defines sweetness—*bahuśo yac chrutam*, etc. That is sweetness, because of which an utterance that is heard does not become an occasion of doubt or of misunderstanding. What he is saying is that these two will certainly arise when there is a very long compound, so that the *śabdaguṇa* of sweetness is simply the avoidance of that [lengthiness of compounds].' [19]

---

[17] NŚ(4) 17.96.

[18] The translation based on the Baroda edition given in Tubb (1985: 572).

[19] After Tubb (1985: 572).

Bhāmaha (ca. 7th century C.E.) accepts only three of the *guṇa*s. These are *ojas*, *prasāda* and *mādhurya*. The rest, according to Bhāmaha, can be classified as certain figures of speech (for instance *śleṣa*) or the absence of the faults (*doṣa*).

Bhāmaha notes twice (KAl 2.2–3) that the composition endowed with the *mādhurya guṇa* does not have too many compounds. It must also be pleasant to the ear (*śravya*)[20].

Daṇḍin (late 7th century C.E.) discusses the *guṇa*s as qualities connected with the poetic mode of expression (*mārga*). He considers all the ten *guṇa*s as characteristics of *vaidarbha-mārga*.[21] As regards *mādhurya*, it is depicted as excellence of both sense and sound.[22] According to Daṇḍin the proper choice of sound elements, namely the alliterations, evokes the *rasa* which is the basis of *mādhurya*.[23]

---

[20] KAl 2.1, 3ab:

*mādhuryam abhivāñchantaḥ prasādaṁ ca sumedhasaḥ* /
*samāsavanti bhūyāṁsi na padāni prayuñjate* //1//
*śravyaṁ nâtisamastârthaṁ kāvyaṁ madhuram iṣyate* /

'/1/ The knowledgeable ones longing for sweetness and perspicuity [in composition] do not employ many compound words. ...
/3/ *Kāvya* agreeable to ear on account of not having too many compounds is regarded as sweet ... .'

[21] KĀd 1.41–42:

*śleṣaḥ prasādaḥ samatā mādhuryaṁ sukumāratā* /
*artha-vyaktir udāratvam ojaḥ kānti-samādhayaḥ* // 41 //
*iti vaidarbha-mārgasya prāṇā daśa guṇāḥ smṛtāḥ* /
*eṣāṁ viparyayaḥ prāyo dṛśyate gauḍa-vartmani* // 42 //

'41.42. Schmiegsamkeit (43), Klarheit (45), Gleichmässigkeit (47), süsser Klang (51), Zartheit (69), Deutlichkeit des Sinnes (73), Bedeutsamkeit (76), Kraftfülle (80), Anmuth (85) und Uebertragung (93). Diese zehn Vorzüge gelten für die Seele des Stils der Vidarbha, im Stile der Gauḍa trift meistentheils das Gegentheil von jenen zu Tage.' (BÖHTLINGK (1890: 8)).

[22] RAGHAVAN (1963: 274, 275).

[23] KĀd 1.51–52:

*madhuraṁ rasavad vāci vastuny api rasa-sthitiḥ* /
*yena mādyanti dhīmanto madhunêva madhu-vratāḥ* // 51 //
*yayā kayā cic chrutyā yat samānam anubhūyate* /
*tad-rūpā hi padâsattiḥ sânuprāsā rasâvahā* // 52 //

'51. Süss klingend (41) ist das, was geschmackvoll ist, eine Beständigkeit des Geschmacks im Ausdruck und in der Sache, an dem Verständige sich berauschen wie Bienen am Honig.

However, the presence of even the sweetest sounding alliterations is not enough to create the *mādhurya*, if the sense is too ordinary or vulgar, and—as regards vulgarity—'That is vulgar which gives rise to a nasty apprehension, either by means of the juncture of words or by the sense of the sentence, as for example [by juncture of words] in *yā bhavataḥ priyā* ("she who is your beloved") [which may be understood as *yābhavataḥ priyā* ("the beloved of a man addicted to sexual intercourse")].'[24]

In the eleventh canto of the *Bhaṭṭi-kāvya*, one can notice an absence of long compounds, but alliterations are also almost absent there. The whole chapter is mainly pervaded with *śṛṅgāra rasa*. Is this because of the poetic convention of the description of the dawn or does it result from the connection between the *mādhurya guṇa* and *śṛṅgāra rasa* underlined by Ānandavardhana? Or more generally: *mādhurya guṇa*, the *guṇa* of sweetness, requires an equally pleasant subject.

This question cannot be answered decisively. What is clear and undeniable is the fact that the *mādhurya guṇa* was mentioned by all theoreticians, independently of the number of *guṇa*s enumerated by them. It was also present among the qualities of the royal order (*śāsana*) enlisted by Kauṭilya[25], and in the inscription of Rudradāman (150 C.E.).

If one looks from the point of view of the orator who wants to win the debate, mastering such a way of expression which is pervaded by *mādhurya* would be highly recommended. The sweetness of sounds, harmony, the absence of long compounds is desirable.

Another *guṇa* which is indispensable in a well prepared speech is definitely clarity—the *prasāda guṇa*. The title of the chapter, the *Prasanna-kāṇḍa*, points out what Bhaṭṭi's opinion in this matter was: the *prasāda guṇa* is a basic *guṇa* for the whole of the utterance.

The twelfth canto is devoted to the *bhāvikatva*. The *bhāvikatva* was understood by some poeticians as a figure of speech, a figure of 'realism', as A.K. WARDER calls

---

52. Ein Nebeneinanderstehen von Worten mit organisch verwandten Consonanten in der Weise, daß man bei jedem beliebigen Klange (er komme aus diesem oder jenem Organ) Gleichartiges vernimmt, bereitet Genuss.' (BÖHTLINGK (1890: 10)).

[24] KĀd 1.66:

*pada-saṁdhāna-vṛttyā vā vākyârthatvena vā punaḥ /*
*duṣpratīti-karaṁ grāmyaṁ yathā yā bhavataḥ priyā // 66 //*

The translation of KĀd 1.66 is given in TUBB (1985: 569).

[25] Kauṭilya mentions six *guṇa*s of a royal order (*śāsana*) in the AŚ 2.9. These qualities are: *artha-krama*, *sambandha*, *paripūrṇatā*, *mādhurya*, *audārya* and *spaṣṭā*.

it[26]. Bhāmaha also discusses it in chapter III, but he introduces the *bhāvikatva* as the *guṇa* of the entire work which causes the past or future objects to be seen as if present before one's eyes[27]. Daṇḍin starts with almost the same statement, but his explanation goes further[28] and the definition of the *bhāvikatva* given by E. GEROW (1971: 220) agrees with it:

> 'the relevance of the various parts of the story to one another, the clarification of difficult contexts by an emphasis on a chain of events, the suitability of the story to be represented in the form chosen, clarity of language, and so on.'

In my opinion, Bhaṭṭi's standpoint is close to that expressed by Bhāmaha and Daṇḍin and the choice of the *bhāvikatva* as the leading subject of the whole chapter was not fortuitous, inasmuch as it also makes Bhaṭṭi's intention, namely the

---

[26] WARDER (1989: 85).

[27] KAl 3.53–54:

*bhāvikatvam iti prāhuḥ prabandha-viṣayaṁ guṇam /*
*pratyākṣā iva dṛśyante yatrârthā bhūta-bhāvinaḥ //53//*
*citrôdāttâdbhutârthatvaṁ kathāyāḥ svabhinītatā /*
*śabdânākulatā cêti tasya hetuṁ pracakṣate //54//*

'The *bhāvikatva* is called the quality of the whole composition. In it the things of the past and future are seen as if taking place before one's eyes. The beauty, exaltedness and marvellousness of the idea of the story, good presentation and easy language—these are considered as its causes.'

[28] KĀd 2.364–366:

*tad bhāvikam iti prāhuḥ prabandha-viṣayaṁ guṇam /*
*bhāvaḥ kaver abhiprāyaḥ kāvyeṣv āsiddhi saṁsthitaḥ //364//*
*parasparôpakāritvaṁ sarveṣāṁ vastu-parvaṇām /*
*viśeṣaṇānāṁ vyarthānām akriyā sthāna-varṇanā //365//*
*vyaktir ukti-krama-balād gambhīrasyâpi vastunaḥ /*
*bhāvâyattam idaṁ sarvam iti tad bhāvikaṁ viduḥ //366//*

'364. Das Vortreffliche, das in den literarischen Erzeugnissen zu Tag tritt, nennt man Bhâvika (7) d.i. die gute Absicht. Bhâva (wovon Bhâvika abgeleitet ist) ist des Dichters Absicht, die in Kunstgedichten von Anfang bis zu Ende besteht.

365 fg. Dass alle Glieder des behandelten Gegenstandes einander unterstützen, das Vermeiden unnützer Beiwörter, Beschreibung eines Ortes, das Klarwerden auch eines dunklen Gegenstandes dadurch, dass in der Rede eine richtige Folge beobachtet wird, alles dieses beruht auf der Absicht. Daher nennt man dieses Bhâvika.' (BÖHTLINGK (1890: 84, 85)).

education of the speaker, clearly visible. A good speaker has to remember about such things as those contained in the term *bhāvikatva*.

The last chapter of the *Prasanna-kāṇḍa* is based on the *bhāṣā-śleṣa* or *bhāṣā-sama*. According to G. Leonardi: 'This sarga is in any case not conspicuous for the excellency of its artistic achievement: on the contrary, it is twisted and tautological.'[29]

Bhāmaha and Daṇḍin do not name the *bhāṣā-śleṣa* as a poetic figure. It is Rudraṭa (9th century C.E.) who for the first time describes such a figure. It seems that neither does Bhaṭṭi treat the *bhāṣā-śleṣa* as a figure, because it is not enumerated among other figures of speech in the tenth chapter of his work. Why does Bhaṭṭi choose such a peculiar stylistic device? It was never very much in fashion among poets. If we think about Bhaṭṭi as the orator, the question still remains difficult to solve. Does it mean that the speaker should consider the word as a carrier of numerous meanings and make use of this feature? Or is it just the curiosity of Bhaṭṭi, the grammarian, which leads him to experiment with the language? There was no place for this 'play on words' in the section on grammar, so it is added to the *Prasanna-kāṇḍa*.

Strangely enough the *śloka* 32 belonging to the *Kāvya-praśasti*, in which Bhaṭṭi assures us that his poem aims at those people who want to practice the art of discussion, is also based on paronomasia, viz. the figure called *śleṣa* is present here.

To sum up: No one can doubt that the arrangement of Bhaṭṭi's work was carefully planned and words were carefully chosen. It seems to me also that nothing can be found to prevent us from trusting Bhaṭṭi's words and treating his work as a manual for speakers. Perhaps Bhaṭṭi was a grammarian, for he emphasised the importance of grammar. The middle part of his work is constituted by the *Prasanna-kāṇḍa*, the section on stylistic devices, which is surrounded by grammar sections. As far as this section is concerned, it must be pointed out that he lived in the epoch of the development of the Alaṁkāra school and, in agreement with the interests of his contemporaries, he discussed the adornments of speech. However, his choice was made to achieve a certain purpose: prepare an orator. He illustrated the figures of speech, and what he selected from the *guṇa*s was the *prasāda* (perspicuity) and *mādhurya*, which was mainly understood as the absence of long compounds. He paid attention to such stylistic device as the *bhāvikatva*, i.e. the quality which causes that the past or future objects are seen as if present before one's eyes. He also highlighted the power of word to carry more than one meaning. One has to admit that these points are of great importance for the speaker. Had he intended to give advice to writers, he would definitely have selected those problems that seem more vital for the writer's creativity (*kāvya-kriyā*), or the theory of literature in general.

---

[29] RV-Bh(5), p. 130.

He did not concentrate on the structure of debate based on logic but he explored the sphere which in Europe was called by the ancients *elocutio* in Latin, or λέξις in Greek, and was one of the five domains of rhetoric. It was to become the main field of research and interest for theoreticians of literature as well as for poets and writers themselves. No one denies that the connections between rhetoric, on the one hand, and literature and poetics, on the other, existed in Europe. Perhaps such 'natural' links were present also in India, and Bhaṭṭi's *Kāvya-praśasti* proves the fact. As Bhaṭṭi's work was written in the form of an epic poem (*mahā-kāvya*), it was the subject of analysis for literary critics and accordingly exercised its influence on the development of poetics and on other authors' writings.

## BIBLIOGRAPHY

Texts:

AŚ = *Artha-śāstra*. Kangle, R.P.: *The Kauṭilīya Arthaśāstra*. Part I: *A Critical Edition with a Glossary*. Part II: *An English Translation with Critical and Explanatory Notes*. Part III: *A Study*. University of Bombay, Bombay 1960, 1963, 1965. [Reprinted: Delhi 1986–88].

CS = *Caraka-saṁhitā. The Charaka saṁhitā of Agniveśa*. Revised by Charaka and Dṛdhabala with the Āyurveda-dīpikā Commentary of Charakapāṇidatta, ed. by Vaidya Jādavaji Trikamji Āchārya, 4[th] ed., Bombay 1981.

DhĀ = Ānandavardhana: *Dhvanyâloka*. Critically ed. with Introduction, Translation & Notes by K. Krishnamurthy, 2.ed., Delhi 1982.

KA-Bh = Bhāravi: *Kirātârjunīya*. *The Kirātārjunīya of Bhāravi*, with the commentary (*Ghaṇṭāpatha*) of Mallinātha and various readings, ed. by Mahāmahopādhyāya Paṇḍit Durgāprasād and Kāśīnāth Pāṇḍurang Parab, 'Nirṇaya-sāgara' Press, Bombay 1903.

KĀd = Daṇḍin: *Kāvyâdarśa. Sanskrit und Deutsch*. Hrsg. von O. Böhtlingk, Leipzig 1890.

KAl = Bhāmaha: *Kāvyâlaṅkāra*. Ed. with English translation and notes by P.V. Naganatha Sastry, reprinted: Delhi 1991.

KM = Rājaśekhara: *Kāvya-mīmāṁsā*. Ed. with 'Prakāśa' Hindi Commentary by Ganga Sagar Rai, the Vidyabhawan Sanskrit Series 121, Varanasi 1964.

KSS = Somadeva: *Kathā-sarit-sāgara*. Ed. by Paṇḍit Durgāprasād and Kāśīnāth Pāṇḍurang Parab, Bombay 1889.

NŚ = Bharata: *Nāṭya-śāstra*. (1) *The Nāṭyaśāstra* by Śri Bharatamuni. Ed. Pt. Kedarnath, Delhi-Varanasi 1983. (2) *Nāṭyaśāstra* of Bharatamuni, with the commentary *Abhinavabhāratī* by Abhinavagupta. Ed. by K.I. Joshi, Vol. 2, second ed., Delhi 1988. (3) *Nāṭyaśāstra*. Ed. M.M. Ghosh, Calcutta 1967. (4) *Nāṭyaśāstra*. *Kashi Sanskrit Series*, Benares 1929.

RV-Bh = Bhaṭṭi: *Rāvaṇa-vadha* (*Bhaṭṭi-kāvya*). (1) *Bhatti Kavya. A Poem on the Actions of Rama*, with the commentaries of Jayamangala and Bharatamallika, Calcutta 1828. (2) *Bhaṭṭikāvyam* of Mahakavi Bhatti. Ed. with the *Chandrakala-Vidyotini* Sanskrit-Hindi Commentaries by Shesaraj Sharma Shastri. *Haridas Sanskrit Series* 136, Varanasi 1983. (3) *The Bhaṭṭi-Kâvya or Râvaṇavadha composed by Śri Bhaṭṭi*. Vol. I, cantos I–IX, ed. with the commentary of Mallinâtha and with critical and explanatory notes by Kamalâśaṅkara Prâṇaśaṅkara Trivedî, *Bombay Sanskrit Series* LVI, Bombay 1898. (4) *Bhaṭṭi-kāvyam*, ed. with an English transl. by M.A. Karandikar and S. Karandikar, Delhi 1982. (5) *Bhaṭṭikāvyam*, transl. and notes by G.G. Leonardi, Leiden 1972.

Secondary Sources:

BÖHTLINGK 1890 = See: KĀd.

GEROW 1971 = Gerow, E.: *A Glossary of Indian Figures of Speech*. The Hague–Paris 1971.

NARANG 1987 = Narang, Satya Pal: *Bhaṭṭi-Kāvya. A Study*. Delhi 1987.

OBERHAMMER–PRETS–PRANDSTETTER 1991, 1996 = Oberhammer, Gerhard; Prets, Ernst; Prandstetter, Joachim: *Terminologie der frühen philosophischen Scholastik in Indien. Ein Begriffswörterbuch zur altindischen Dialektik, Erkenntnislehre und Methodologie*. Herausgegeben von Gerhard Oberhammer. Österreichische Akademie der Wissenschaften, Philosophisch-Historische Klasse, Denkschriften, 248. *Beiträge zur Kultur- und Geistesgeschichte* 17. Band 1: A–I (1991), Band 2: U–Pū (1996), Wien.

RAGHAVAN 1963 = Raghavan, V.: *Bhoja's Śṛṅgāra Prakāśa*. Madras 1963.

RENOU 1959 = Renou, Louis: 'Sur la structure du kāvya', *Journal Asiatique* 247 (1959) 1–113.

TIEKEN 1992 = Tieken, H.: 'Style and Structure of Rajaśekhara's Kāvyamīmāṁsā,' *Ritual, State and History in South Asia. Essays in Honour of J.C. Heesterman*. Ed. by A.W. Van Den Hoek, D.H.A. Kolff, MS. Oort, Leiden 1992.

TUBB 1985 = Tubb, G.: 'Abhinavagupta on Phonetic Texture,' *Journal of the American Oriental Society* 105/3 (1985) 567–578.

WARDER 1989, 1983 = Warder, A.K.: *Indian Kāvya Literature*. Motilal Banarsidass, Delhi–Varanasi–Patna: Vol. I: 1989 (revised ed.); Vol. IV: 1983.

# The Structure and Function of the First *Sarga* of Māgha's *Śiśupāla-vadha*

ANNA TRYNKOWSKA

How does the *sarga-bandha* begin? Or rather, passing over the issue of homage-, benediction- and other introductory stanzas, in what way does the story of the Sanskrit *mahā-kāvya* start? Is the author of a Sanskrit court epic poem free to compose the beginning of its story as he chooses, or are there any pertinent rules which he is supposed to follow?

An examination of all the extant early *sarga-bandha*s[1] leads to the conclusion that there exists a traditional model of starting the story of a Sanskrit court epic poem, which was created by generations of authors of literary compositions belonging to the above-mentioned genre, and which was evidently deeply rooted in the minds of *mahā-kavi*s and hearers or readers of their works as early as in the times of Aśvaghoṣa.

The first stanza of the story of a *sarga-bandha* composed in accordance with that model begins with *asti* ('there is') or *āsīt* / *babhūva* / *abhūt* ('there was'), which is followed by a description of a flourishing city and praise of its king: the future father of the hero or the hero himself.[2]

Later the above-mentioned model of starting the story of a Sanskrit *mahā-kāvya* is partly included in the descriptive-normative definition (*lakṣaṇa*) of the Sanskrit court epic poem advanced by Rudraṭa in his treatise on literary theory *Kāvyâlaṅkāra* (the third quarter of the ninth century C.E.[3]):

---

[1] I.e. all the extant Sanskrit *mahā-kāvya*s earlier than or contemporary with Māgha's *Śiśupāla-vadha* (the third quarter of the seventh century C.E.—according to WARDER (1983: 133)), viz. BC (1.1–8ab as restored by E.H. Johnston; see also HAHN (1975: 77–84)) and S (the first half of the first century C.E.—according to WARDER (1990a: 144)), RV-K and KS (the second and the third quarter of the fifth century C.E.—according to WARDER (1990b: 123)), KA-Bh (the second quarter of the sixth century C.E.—according to WARDER (1990b: 199)), RV-Bh (the second and the third quarter of the seventh century C.E.—according to WARDER (1983: 118)), and JH (the second half of the seventh century C.E.—according to WARDER (1983: 254)).

[2] Cf. HUECKSTEDT (1985: 23–32, esp. 25–27).

[3] According to GEROW (1977: 239).

*Essays in Indian Philosophy, Religion and Literature*, pp. 283–291.

*... pūrvaṁ san-nagarī-varṇanaṁ mahā-kāvye /*
*kurvīta tad-anu tasyāṁ nāyaka-vaṁśa-praśaṁsāṁ ca //*
*tatra tri-varga-saktaṁ samiddha-śakti-trayaṁ ca sarva-guṇam /*
*rakta-samasta-prakṛtiṁ vijigīṣuṁ nāyakaṁ nyasyet //*
*vidhivat paripālayataḥ sakalaṁ rājyaṁ ca rāja-vṛttaṁ ca /*
*tasya ... //* [4]

'... in the ... *mahā-kāvya* [the author] should first place a description of a beautiful city and after that a passage praising the dynasty [ruling] over it, to which the hero belongs. Next, he should present the hero, who is intent on [pursuit of] the three aims of human life, possessed of all the three royal powers[5], possessed of all virtues, loved by all the subjects and desirous of victories, and the whole kingdom of the hero, who rules over it in accordance with the law, and his royal occupations ....'

What is the artistic function of beginning the story of the *sarga-bandha* in the above-mentioned way? The initial *asti / āsīt / babhūva / abhūt*, being typical of Sanskrit narratives, signals that a story starts.[6] Next, the hearer or reader is shown the setting for the first phase of the action of the poem, as well as the ideals of its world: a perfect monarch, with whom the person of the villain is going to contrast sharply, and a perfect state, to which the villain's deeds are going to pose a threat.

The above model, constructed by generalising from the selected empirical material, presents the typical way of starting the story of a Sanskrit *mahā-kāvya*. The beginnings of the stories of real Sanskrit court epic poems may to a certain extent differ from that ideal type. Thus, some of its elements may be omitted or modified: the verbal forms *asti*, *āsīt*, *babhūva* and *abhūt* may figure at the beginning of the second verse (as in Aśvaghoṣa's *Saundarananda*[7] and Kālidāsa's *Raghu-vaṁśa*[8]) or in another position in the first stanza of the story (as in E.H. Johnston's restoration of the first stanza of Aśvaghoṣa's *Buddha-carita*[9]); a city may be replaced with a hermitage (as in Aśvaghoṣa's *Saundarananda*[10]) or a mountain

[4] KA-R 16.7–9, p. 168.

[5] *Śakti-traya*, viz. *mantra-śakti*, *prabhu-śakti* (*prabhutva-śakti*, *prabhāva-śakti*) and *utsāha-śakti*. For a long list of definitions of those terms and examples of their use quoted from Sanskrit literature see HARA (1981: 19–24). See also ŚV 2.26, p. 37 and SK on ŚV 2.26, p. 37.

[6] Cf. HUECKSTEDT (1985: 24–25).

[7] S 1.1, p. 1.

[8] RV-K 1.11, p. 4.

[9] BC (2), p. 1.

[10] S 1.5–17, pp. 1–3.

range (as in Kālidāsa's *Kumāra-saṁbhava*[11]), a king with a hermit (as in Aśvaghoṣa's *Saundarananda*[12]), the hero with the villain (as in Meṇṭha's *Hayagrīva-vadha*[13]). Two especially witty modifications can be seen in the above-mentioned part of the *Kumāra-saṁbhava* and in Bhāravi's *Kirātârjunīya*[14]. Kālidāsa starts his poem with a description of the Himalayas: the mountainous setting for the first phase of the action, as well as the king of all mountains and the future father of the heroine. At the beginning of the *Kirātârjunīya* a perfect monarch ruling over the kingdom of the heroes, the Pāṇḍavas, is praised. However, that passage does not eulogise the eldest of the five brothers, Yudhiṣṭhira; it praises Suyodhana, the eldest of their enemies, the Kauravas, who have won the realm in a dice game.[15]

This paper deals with a case where all the above-mentioned traditional rules for starting the stories of *sarga-bandhas* are broken, i.e. with the first canto (*sarga*) of Māgha's *Śiśupāla-vadha* ('The Slaying of Śiśupāla'), one of the best and most famous Sanskrit *mahā-kāvyas*, based on the episode of the *Mahā-bhārata*[16] in which Kṛṣṇa kills wicked Śiśupāla, King of the Cedis, during Yudhiṣṭhira's *rāja-sūya* sacrifice.

The first stanza of that poem:

> *śriyaḥ patiḥ śrīmati śāsituṁ jagaj jagan-nivāso vasudeva-sadmani /*
> *vasan dadarśâvatarantam ambarād dhiraṇya-garbhâṅga-bhuvaṁ munim hariḥ //* [17]
>
> 'Hari, the husband of Śrī, the abode of the world, dwelling in the fortunate house of Vasudeva in order to control the world, saw the sage born of Brahmā's body descending from the sky.'

begins with the auspicious word *śriyaḥ* (the genitive singular of the noun *śrī*)[18] and does not contain any of the above-mentioned forms of the verbs √*as* and √*bhū*. The

---

[11] KS 1.1–17, pp. 1–7.

[12] S 1.1–4, p. 1.

[13] The first quarter of the fifth century C.E.—according to WARDER (1990b: 93). That *sarga-bandha* has been lost. However, its first stanza is preserved, quoted, among others, by Bhoja in his ŚP 11 (p. 472). Meṇṭha starts it with *āsīd daityo hayagrīvaḥ* ('There was a *daitya* [named] Hayagrīva'), which is followed by praise of the demon.

[14] KA-Bh 1.7–22, pp. 5–11.

[15] Cf. SMITH (1985: 30).

[16] MBh 2.30–42, pp. 154–209.

[17] ŚV 1.1, p. 2.

[18] In imitation of KA-Bh 1.1 (p. 2). The first stanza of the *Hayagrīva-vadha* ends with *śriyaḥ* (the nominative plural of *śrī*)—see ŚP 9, p. 472.

place of the initial phase of the action of Māgha's *sarga-bandha*, the house of Vasudeva, though pointed out here, is not described; the *avatāra* of the god Viṣṇu dwelling there, though introduced as the hero, is not properly eulogised. The stanza immediately tells the hearer or reader of an incident in Kṛṣṇa's life and thus, without any preliminary description and / or eulogy, the action of the *Śiśupāla-vadha* starts. One more person, the sage Nārada, is introduced here as a participant in its first event.

The following nine stanzas (2–10) contain a more and more detailed description of Nārada descending from the sky, being observed by people and Kṛṣṇa. With the eleventh stanza, where the sage arrives at the hero's house, a narrative-descriptive part begins. Its remaining thirteen stanzas (12–24) speak about the welcome which the guest is given by his host, reveal the feelings of Kṛṣṇa, who is full of joy because of Nārada's visit, as well as portray the contrasting appearance of the two characters. The twenty-fifth stanza announces Kṛṣṇa's address to Nārada, which comprises the following five stanzas (26–30): in the first four the hero praises the sage; in the fifth one the host enquires of the guest the purpose of his visit. The first quarter (*pāda*) of the thirty-first stanza announces Nārada's address to Kṛṣṇa; in the remaining three *pāda*s the speech begins: the sage denies that his arrival has any purpose other than seeing the hero. The guest thus introduces the next nine stanzas (32–40), where he praises his host, mostly as the god who descends from heaven to earth in order to kill wicked human kings such as Kaṁsa and *asura*s such as Hiraṇyākṣa. However, in the forty-first stanza Nārada reveals that he has brought a message from Indra and announces that he is going to convey it to Kṛṣṇa. The first six stanzas of the message (42–47) remind the hero of the fate of Hiraṇyakaśipu, the wicked *daitya*, more powerful than Indra and other gods, who was killed by Viṣṇu's Nṛsiṁha *avatāra*. Significantly, Māgha starts that story with *abhūt*[19], followed by praise of the demon's might. By thus reminding the hearer or reader of the traditional rules which govern the beginning of the story of the Sanskrit *mahā-kāvya*, he makes it clear that the breach of them in the *Śiśupāla-vadha* has not been caused by his unforgivable ignorance but is the result of a conscious artistic decision. In the forty-eighth stanza Indra reminds Kṛṣṇa that later Hiraṇyakaśipu was reborn as the terrifying *rakṣas* Rāvaṇa. The story of that demon's war with the gods for the mastery over the three worlds and his slaying by Viṣṇu's Rāma *avatāra* comprises the next twenty stanzas (49–68). The sixty-ninth stanza calls the hero's attention to the fact that Rāvaṇa has at present been reborn as Śiśupāla. The following three stanzas (70–72) praise the power of the king of the Cedis, which surpasses the might of other human rulers, gods and demons, as well as lament over the sufferings of the world caused by that villain. In the seventy-third stanza the king of gods asks Kṛṣṇa to kill Śiśupāla and thus ends his message. There

[19] ŚV 1.42, p. 17.

follows the last stanza of Nārada's speech (74), where he appeals to the hero to fulfil Indra's request. The canto ends with the seventy-fifth stanza, in which the sage leaves and Kṛṣṇa, angry with the king of the Cedis, agrees to slay him, while a frown on the hero's face, like a comet in the sky, portends the villain's death. It should be added that the event which the canto narrates is not present in the thirteen *adhyāya*s of the *Mahā-bhārata* which form the basis of Māgha's poem.

What artistic aims does the author of the *Śiśupāla-vadha* seek to achieve by starting his *sarga-bandha* in that way?

The answer to this question has to be looked for in the text of Māgha's *mahā-kāvya*.[20] In my opinion, the key to the understanding of the structure and function of the first *sarga* of the *Śiśupāla-vadha* is found, perhaps not by pure chance, at its very beginning, i.e. in the second and third stanzas:

> *gataṁ tiraścīnam anūru-sāratheḥ prasiddham ūrdhva-jvalanaṁ havir-bhujaḥ /*
> *pataty adho dhāma visāri sarvataḥ kim etad ity ākulam īkṣitaṁ janaiḥ //*
> *cayas tviṣām ity avadhāritaṁ purā tataḥ śarîrîti vibhāvitâkṛtim /*
> *vibhur vibhaktâvayavaṁ pumān iti kramād amuṁ nārada ity abodhi saḥ //* [21]
>
> '"It is well known that the sun moves horizontally [and] fire burns upwards. [Then] what is this light, [which] is moving downwards, spreading in all directions?" So thinking people looked [at him] with confusion. At first he was considered to be a mass of light; afterwards, when his form could be seen, he was ascertained to be a living creature, [and] when his limbs could be distinguished, a man; the Lord gradually recognised him as Nārada.'

When a mass of light first appears in the sky, the people who notice that phenomenon are unable to identify it. They begin to conjecture but, while the light remains distant, it is impossible for them to ascertain the truth. Their confusion is increased by the fact that what they look at does not seem to be anything they have seen before. Curiosity makes them continue the observation. As the mysterious object approaches, the observers can see it more and more distinctly. That gradually

---

[20] Despite the well-known fact that Māgha has based the general structure and a considerable number of individual stanzas of his poem on KA-Bh (see JACOBI (1889)) ŚV is, I think, a *sarga-bandha* of great originality, differing from its model in many respects; cf. SMITH (1985: 7–13) on Ratnākara's *Hara-vijaya* and ŚV. Although I am aware of the similarities between the first canto of Māgha's *mahā-kāvya* and KA-Bh 2.54–59, 3.1–29, it seems to me that the detailed structures and artistic purposes of those two passages are widely different. However, a comparative study of their texts is beyond the scope of this paper.

[21] ŚV 1.2–3, pp. 2–3.

enables them to determine the category and subcategory to which it belongs. At last the identity of the man descending from the sky is established and the initial uncertainty of the people resolved.

In my opinion, the whole of the first canto of Māgha's poem is structured by the author with a view to initiating and sustaining a similar process in the hearer's or reader's mind. A person who hears or reads the first stanza of the *Śiśupāla-vadha* learns that the author has chosen an episode from the life of Kṛṣṇa as the theme for his *sarga-bandha*. However, the hearer or reader is unable to identify the episode, which reduces him to conjectures. Moreover, since the original episode of the slaying of Śiśupāla, as narrated in the *Mahā-bhārata*, does not include the incident mentioned in the first stanza of Māgha's *mahā-kāvya*, all the hearer's or reader's surmises must be wrong. Unless he hears or reads more, it is not possible for him to establish the truth. Curiosity adds to his willingness to continue the listening or reading. As the hearer or reader becomes acquainted with the text of the *sarga*, he comes across hints dropped by the author. In the ten stanzas describing the sage Nārada descending from the sky and his arrival at Kṛṣṇa's house (2–11), the word *indra* occurs as many as five times: the clouds above Nārada's head resemble the skin of 'an excellent elephant' (*gajêndra*)[22]; the sage looks like 'the king of mountains' (*dharā-dharêndra*)[23] and 'the excellent elephant' (*nāgêndra*) which is 'Indra's mount' (*indra-vāhana*)[24]; the house of Kṛṣṇa—when approached by Nārada—appears as beautiful as 'the abode of great Indra' (*mahêndrâlaya*)[25]. It may indicate that the king of gods has something to do with the story of Māgha's poem, perhaps with the sage himself. A person who hears or reads the stanzas which follow the above-mentioned description of Nārada and precede the mention of Śiśupāla (11–68) is repeatedly reminded of previous heroic deeds of Kṛṣṇa, of other *avatāra*s of Viṣṇu and of Viṣṇu himself: first the hero is called 'the destroyer of the good fortune of *daityas*' (*sādita-daitya-saṁpad*)[26], 'he who defeated Kaṁsa' (*kaṁsa-kṛṣ*)[27] and 'the enemy of Kaiṭabha' (*kaiṭabha-dviṣ*)[28]; next, the sage praises Viṣṇu as the god whose *avatāra*s slay villainous human monarchs such as Kaṁsa and demons such as Hiraṇyākṣa (36–40); lastly Indra draws attention to the fate of two incarnations of a mighty wicked demon: Hiraṇyakaśipu and Rāvaṇa,

---

[22] ŚV 1.4, p. 3.
[23] ŚV 1.5, p. 4.
[24] ŚV 1.8, p. 5.
[25] ŚV 1.11, p. 6.
[26] ŚV 1.11, p. 6.
[27] ŚV 1.16, p. 8.
[28] ŚV 1.23, p. 10.

who were killed by two *avatāras* of Viṣṇu: Nṛsiṁha and Rāma respectively (42–68). It may mean that what the author has chosen to retell in his *sarga-bandha* is a heroic story where Kṛṣṇa slays a powerful villain, possibly a human ruler or a demon. This supposition is supported by the fact that, in the same part of the canto, one of Viṣṇu's weapons, his discus, is mentioned no less than three times: first the hero is called 'the owner of a discus' (*cakrin*)[29] and 'having a discus in his hand' (*rathâṅga-pāṇi*)[30]; later the hearer or reader is reminded that Viṣṇu used the discus (*cakra*)[31] in the war of the gods against Rāvaṇa. As no other weapon of Viṣṇu is mentioned in any of those fifty-eight stanzas, the above fact may also suggest that in the story retold by Māgha in his *mahā-kāvya* Viṣṇu's discus plays a role; perhaps it is the weapon with which the hero kills his opponent. While hearing or reading the *sarga*, one is also given pieces of information, which confirm some of his conjectures and serve as the basis for further surmises: the eleventh stanza divulges that Nārada descends from the sky to visit Kṛṣṇa; the forty-first stanza reveals that the sage has brought the hero a message from Indra. Each of those clues slightly relieves the tension produced by the initial uncertainty of the hearer or reader about the story selected by the author for his poem, which, if unduly prolonged, might eventually become unbearable. However, before the sixty-ninth stanza the tension never diminishes considerably, because its occasional easing is balanced with sustaining: each of the useful pieces of information is withheld for a long time (Nārada's destination and the purpose of his descent from the sky, which one starts to speculate about immediately after hearing or reading the first stanza of the canto, are not disclosed until after nine more stanzas and thirty-nine more stanzas respectively); moreover, they do not suffice. To determine which episode from the life of Kṛṣṇa Māgha has chosen as the theme for his *mahā-kāvya*, one has to hear or read the last seven stanzas of the *sarga* (69–75), where the introduction of the hero's contemporary, Śiśupāla, another incarnation of the demon who previously lived as Hiraṇyakaśipu and Rāvaṇa (69), Indra's appeal to Kṛṣṇa for slaying the villain (73) and the hero's promise to fulfil that request (75) leave no doubt as to the answer to this question and the tension created by the initial uncertainty of the hearer or reader is finally completely relieved.

By then the author of the *Śiśupāla-vadha* has demonstrated his narrative skill as well as a great talent for composing descriptions and speeches. The first canto of Māgha's *sarga-bandha* thus gives its hearer or reader an appetite for the rest of the poem.

---

[29] ŚV 1.11, p. 6.

[30] ŚV 1.21, p. 9.

[31] ŚV 1.54, p. 21.

## BIBLIOGRAPHY

BC = Aśvaghoṣa: *Buddha-carita. The Buddhacarita: Or, Acts of the Buddha.* (1) Part I—Sanskrit text. Ed. by E.H. Johnston, *Panjab University Oriental Publications* 31, Calcutta 1935. (2) Part II: Cantos i to xiv translated from the original Sanskrit supplemented by the Tibetan version together with an introduction and notes by E.H. Johnston, *Panjab University Oriental Publications* 32, Calcutta 1936.

GEROW 1977 = Gerow, E.: *Indian Poetics. A History of Indian Literature*, ed. by Jan Gonda. Vol. V, fasc. 3, Otto Harrassowitz, Wiesbaden 1977.

HAHN 1975 = Hahn, Michael: 'Buddhacarita I, 1–7 und 25–0,' *Indo-Iranian Journal* XVII 1–2 (April-May 1975) 77–96.

HARA 1981 = Hara, Minoru: 'Utsāha,' *The Journal of Oriental Research, The Kuppuswami Sastri Research Institute Silver Jubilee Volume*, ed. by S.S. Janaki, The Kuppuswami Sastri Research Institute, Madras 1981: 15–30.

HUECKSTEDT 1985 = Hueckstedt, Robert A.: *The Style of Bāṇa: An Introduction to Sanskrit Prose Poetry*. Lanham–New York–London 1985.

JACOBI 1889 = Jacobi, Hermann: 'On Bhâravi and Mâgha,' *Wiener Zeitschrift für die Kunde des Morgenlandes* 3 (1889) 121–145.

JH = Kumāradāsa: *Jānakī-haraṇa. The Jànakìharaṇam of Kumàradàsa* (I–X). Ed. by Gopal Raghunath Nandargikar, Bombay 1907.

KA-Bh = Bhāravi: *Kirātârjunīya. The Kirâtârjunîya of Bhâravi*, with the commentary (*Ghaṇtâpatha*) of Mallinâtha and various readings, ed. by Durgâprasâd and Kâśînâth Pâṇdurang Parab, fourth rev. edition, 'Nirṇaya-sâgara' Press, Bombay 1902.

KA-R = Rudraṭa: *Kāvyâlaṁkāra. The Kâvyâlankâra (A Treatise on Rhetoric) of Rudrata*, with the commentary of Namisâdhu, ed. by Durgâprasâd and Wâsudev Laxmaṇ Śâstrî Paṇśîkar, third edition, Kâvyamâlâ 2, 'Nirṇaya Sâgar' Press, Bombay 1928.

KS = Kālidāsa: *Kumāra-saṁbhava. The Kumârasambhava of Kâlidâsa*, with the commentary (the *Sanjîvinî*) of Mallinâth, ed. by Vâsudev Laxman Shâstrî Fansikar, fourth edition, 'Nirṇaya-sâgara' Press, Bombay 1906.

MBh = *Mahā-bhārata. The Mahābhārata*, for the first time critically ed. by Vishnu S. Sukthankar and S.K. Belvalkar, *The Sabhāparvan*, for the first time critically ed. by Franklin Edgerton. Bhandarkar Oriental Research Institute, Poona 1944.

RV-Bh = Bhaṭṭi: *Rāvaṇa-vadha. The Bhaṭṭi-Kâvya or Râvaṇavadha composed by Śri Bhaṭṭi.* Vol. I., cantos I.–IX., ed. with the commentary of Mallinâtha and with critical and explanatory notes by Kamalâśaṅkara Prâṇaśaṅkara Trivedî, *Bombay Sanskrit Series* LVI, Bombay 1898.

RV-K = Kālidāsa: *Raghu-vaṁśa. The Raghuvamśa of Kâlidâsa*, with the commentary (the *Sanjîvinî*) of Mallinâth, ed. by Kâśînâth Pâṇḍurang Parab. Fifth rev. edition, 'Nirnaya-sagara' Press, Bombay 1904.

S = Aśvaghoṣa: *Saundarananda. The Saundarananda of Aśvaghoṣa*, critically ed. with notes by E.H. Johnston. Panjab University Oriental Publications, Oxford University Press, London 1928.

SK = Mallinātha: *Sarvaṁ-kaṣā*. See ŚV.

SMITH 1985 = Smith, David: *Ratnākara's Haravijaya. An Introduction to the Sanskrit Court Epic*. Oxford University South Asian Studies Series, Oxford University Press, Delhi–Bombay–Calcutta–Madras 1985.

ŚP = Bhoja: *Śṛṅgāra-prakāśa. Maharaja Bhojaraja's Sringara Prakasha,. The Great tenth century work on Samskrit and Prakrit Rhetoric*. Second Vol., Prakashas 9 to 14, ed. by G.R. Josyer, Mysore 1963.

ŚV = Māgha: *Śiśupāla-vadha. The Śiśupâlavadha of Mâgha*, with the commentary (*Sarvankashâ*) of Mallinâtha, ed. by Durgâprasâda and Śivadatta. Eighth edition, rev. by T. Śrinivâsa Venkatrâma Śarmâ, 'Nirnaya-sagar' Press, Bombay 1923.

WARDER 1983 = Warder, A.K.: *Indian Kāvya Literature*. Vol. IV: *The Ways of Originality (Bāṇa to Dāmodaragupta)*, Motilal Banarsidass, Delhi–Varanasi–Patna 1983.

WARDER 1990a = Warder, A.K.: *Indian Kāvya Literature*. Vol. II: *The Origins and Formation of Classical Kāvya*. Second rev. edition, Motilal Banarsidass, Delhi 1990. [First edition: Delhi–Varanasi–Patna 1974].

WARDER 1990b = Warder, A.K.: *Indian Kāvya Literature*. Vol. III: *The Early Medieval Period (Śūdraka to Viśākhadatta)*. Second rev. edition, Motilal Banarsidass, Delhi 1990. [First edition: Delhi 1977].

# ARTHA-ŚĀSTRA

# Some Remarks on the 135th *Adhikaraṇa* of the 'Kauṭilīya' *Artha-śāstra* entitled 'Policy towards *saṁghas*'

ALBRECHT WEZLER

## –1–

Two years ago I was asked by my students to read with them part of the 'Kauṭilīya' *Artha-śāstra*. I readily agreed, but wanted to select a part which would meet two conditions, viz. be not yet known to myself and of such a size that we would be able to cope with it in its entirety, even when scrutinising each and every word of it. The part finally chosen was *Adhikaraṇa* 135 (= AŚ 11.1) named *Saṁgha-vṛttam*.[1] This choice was mainly determined by my personal interest in the problem of the so-called 'republics' in ancient India. Accordingly, apart from introducing the students to the AŚ as such, I drew their attention first of all to J.P. SHARMA's well-known book of 1968 (SHARMA (1968)), which bears this very title, viz. 'Republics in Ancient India'.

Now, this book is a highly impressive and indeed thorough attempt to get even with the earlier Indian nationalistic historians who, significantly enough, claimed to have discovered that democracy is not an achievement of the British culture, but in fact existed already in early times in India—so that India after independence can pride herself on being not only the largest, but also the oldest democracy of the world.[2] SHARMA most plausibly, though always in a fair manner, unmasks his predecessors, and exposes their heavy biases, and the ideological determination of their work.

Yet I find this critical part of his exposition much more convincing than his own attempt to draw a new, and truer picture of the historical situation at the time of the Buddha, it's later development, and the Vedic period. He does not, unfortunately, define the conceptual categories he uses, and his manner of dealing with the textual sources is not at all reliable, in any case not acceptable, and this to such an extent that I have come to the conclusion that all of his sources have to be carefully re-

[1] Cf. SCHARFE (1968: 47) (= 1993: 40 f.) on the names of the *Adhikaraṇas*.

[2] Cf. also Basham's 'Foreword' in SHARMA (1968).

*Essays in Indian Philosophy, Religion and Literature*, pp. 295–309.

examined. Another fundamental shortcoming of SHARMA's work is that German studies on Vedic society, first of all the fundamental work of RAU (1957), have not been taken into account, and it is hardly a consolation to note that this is a weakness which SHARMA shares with most of his Indian colleagues, also younger ones—who quite often give descriptions of Indian society in middle-Vedic or later-Vedic times, not to mention the Saṁhitā period, which can only be styled as bizarre.

I am afraid that somebody will have to sit down to do all the work of examining and historically interpreting the relevant source material again, and that this person will then have to come to terms not only with more recent secondary literature on the topic, but also with the new source material primarily made available by archaeology over the last 30 years, that concerning coins above all.[3]

I need hardly state explicitly that this is not what I have set as my task for today. All I am in fact able to present here are some remarks or suggestions or proposals for solutions of problems posed by just one out of the many textual sources, viz. AŚ 11.1,[4] and even with regard to it I shall have to focus on a selection of problems, because I am still chewing on some of them, and time and space are limited.

### –2.1–

Already the very first paragraph (i.e. AŚ 11.1.1) confronts us with a problem. For it reads *saṁgha-lābho daṇḍa-mitra-lābhānām uttamaḥ*, and this is translated by KANGLE (1963: 526): '[t]he gain of an oligarchy is best among gains of an army and an ally,' to which he adds, in a footnote, the remark: 'the use of the comparative would have been better. Having a *saṁgha* under you and loyal to you is preferable to having an army of one's own or an ally.' One is tempted to react by saying: 'Perhaps it would have been better to have taken the wording of this sentence more seriously,' although KANGLE admittedly translates the genitive plural as a *genitivus partitivus*;[5] this function of the genitive is indeed common with superlatives.[6] And the compounds *daṇḍa-lābha* or *mitra-lābha* are not attested anywhere in the AŚ.[7] It is hence more likely that *daṇḍa-mitra-lābhānām* represents a three-membered

[3] E.g. K.M. SHRIMALI (1983).

[4] The edition used is KANGLE (1960).

[5] Cf. SPEIJER (1886: 86, § 116).

[6] Cf. VON HINÜBER (1968: 231, § 224).

[7] The name of the corresponding 'book' of the *Pañca-tantra* is *Mitra-prāpti*.

*dvandva* compound, and the posterior member is an abbreviation[8] of *saṁgha-lābha*. A correct translation of this paragraph, i.e. one that removes all grammatical and logical unevenness, is therefore: 'The best among the [three factors of power, viz.] [one's own] army, an ally / allies and the gaining [of a *saṁgha*], is the gaining of a *saṁgha*.'

This is, of course, a statement made from the point of view of a *vijigīṣu*, a monarch who wants to extend the territory ruled by him and thus to be victorious, albeit not necessarily by waging war, as is shown particularly clearly by this *Adhikaraṇa* of the AŚ. That this is indeed the viewpoint and, grammatically speaking, that the *vijigīṣu* is the subject of most of the finite verbs in this *Adhikaraṇa* is confirmed—if confirmation is at all necessary in view of the wider context of this 'book'[9]—[10]by paragraphs 54 and 55 where, however, the expression *eka-rāja* is used, and quite clearly in order to bring into proper relief the essential difference between the 'single king', i.e. a single monarch who has sovereign power over a territory whatever its size, and the 'leaders', or 'headmen', (*mukhya*) of a *saṁgha* who in one way or another share such power with others.

GAṆAPATI ŚASTRI, in his *Śrīmūla* commentary, voices the opinion that members of a *saṁgha* referred to here are those who live either within the *vijigīṣu*'s own territory or in a neighbouring country (*vijigīṣu-bhūmau tad-antara-bhūmau vā vāstavyānām* ...); but I believe that the explanations of the *Naya-candrikā*[11] are—as in fact quite often—to be preferred, provided some emendations[12] are made and the text

[8] Cf. GONDA (1968).

[9] *Adhikaraṇa* 7 deals with the 'Six Measures of Foreign Policy' (*ṣāḍguṇyam*), no. 8 is entitled 'Concerning the Topic of Calamities' (*vyasanâdhikārikam*), no. 9 is devoted to 'The Activity of the King about to March' (*abhiyāsyat-karma*) and no. 10 bears the title 'Concerning War' (*sāṁgrāmikam*). *Adhikaraṇa* 12, on the other hand, is named 'Concerning the Weaker King' (*ā-balīyasam*). Particularly close are the relations between *Adhikaraṇa*s 11 and 12.

[10] Cf. e.g. the names of *Adhikaraṇa*s 9 and 10.

[11] Already GAṆAPATI ŚASTRI (1924/25) knew and used this commentary (cf. *Naya-candrikā*, *Upodghāta* of the editor, Udayavira Śāstrin, p. 2) in addition to the Malayalam commentary. In fact his own *Śrīmūla* can be regarded as a tool for deciphering, emending and interpreting the *Naya-candrikā*.

[12] The emendations of the editor given in footnotes are in most cases convincing; but it is often possible to go beyond his reconstruction and to propose many more conjectures or corrections.

> *sāmâdīn saṅgrāma-paryāya-daṇḍântān uktvā* (viz. in preceding chapters[13]) *ye bhūmy-ānantaryeṇa sva-bhūmāv eva apy ekâikaśaḥ kṣudrā-varttāḥ* (recte: *kṣudrā vārttā-*) *śatrûpajīvina-* (recte: *śastrôpajīvinaḥ*) *kṣatriyâdīnāṁ saṅghī-bhāvâikabalāḥ saṅghāḥ saṅghātena nityam ajayyāḥ*, ...

correctly understood is to mean that 'the *saṁgha*s reside in the neighbourhood of the territory [of the *vijigīṣu*] on their own territory (*eva*)...'.

As for the source of their extraordinary military strength, and hence their clear superiority over other factors of power, the second paragraph of AŚ 11.1 provides the necessary information: *saṁghā hi saṁhatatvād*[14] *adhṛṣyāḥ pareṣām*—'for *saṁghas* are unassailable[15] by enemies because they are closely and firmly knit together.' I do not know whether *saṁ√han* implicitly, i.e. by way of association refers to a concrete object serving as a model, like, e.g. a chariot (*ratha*); but it is in any case clear, and nicely explained by Mādhava Yajvan, the author of the *Naya-candrikā*,[16] that the type of *saṁghāta* referred to here is entirely different from, and much superior to, an alliance voluntarily formed by kings each ruling his own territory, who on the basis of a mutual treaty live in peace with each other, that is, an alliance which serves a particular common purpose; the *saṁghāta* of the *saṁgha*s, on the other hand, consists in a *samavāya*, 'an inseparable union' between several small groups which have one common aim and reside in one and the same territory, on the basis of a shared economical vocation. This is one of the reasons for rendering *saṁgha* rather by 'confederacy' than 'republic', etc.

---

[13] What the commentator refers to are the '[four] means' (*upāya*) which are introduced and defined at AŚ 2.10.47–56, and are dealt with again at 9.5.9 ff. and 9.6.20 ff.; cf. also 11.1.3.

[14] This is the reading put into the constituted text by KANGLE. The *Naya-candrikā*, however, clearly reads *saṁghātāt*, which it explains by *saṁhatatvāt*, and I think its reading should be preferred.

[15] This statement can be taken as the justification for the means recommended in this *Adhikaraṇa* for 'gaining a *saṁgha*.' Direct military actions against *saṁgha*s are too risky, to put it mildly.

[16] Cf. *Naya-candrikā* (205.14 ff.): *nanu sambhūya-prayāṇam evâitat, tac ca prāg evôktam* (cf. 7.4.19 ff.) *iti cen na / tad-dhi svātantryeṇa eka-deśâ-°* (recte: *aneka-deśâ-*) *dhipatīnāṁ rājñāṁ mithaḥ paṇâdi-kṛta-saṁdhīnām eka-kārya-karaṇa-rūpaḥ* (recte: *rūpaṁ*), *na tv etat tathā, api tv ekasminn eva deśa-°* (recte: *deśe*) *vārttâdi-jīvinām ekeṣāṁ kṣudrāṇām ekârthatayā samavāya-rūpam, ato 'tyantaṁ bhīmam ity alam /* .

## –2.2–

The expression *vārttâdijīvin* in the *Naya-candrikā* stands for *vārttā-śastrôpajīvin*, and thus is nothing but a repetition of the predicate used in AŚ 11.1.3 with reference to the subject *kāmboja-surāṣṭra-kṣatriya-śreṇyâdayo*, the interpretation of which is controversial.[17] The exact meaning of this predicate (*vārttā-śastrôpajīvinaḥ*) is, to all appearances, another of the problems[18] the AŚ almost continuously confronts its readers with; this is true also of the expression *rāja-śabdôpajīvin*, i.e. the predicate of the next paragraph. KANGLE (1963: 327) renders it by 'make use of the title of king,' and explains, in a footnote, 'that this simply means that the chiefs who formed the ruling council of the *saṁgha* styled themselves "*rājan*".' This is a fact confirmed by the *Jātaka*s as also by the *Lalita-vistara* (1: p. 21),[19] as is also noted by SHARMA (1968: 58.98 ff., and 100 n. 6). Yet, more has to be said about the expression *rāja-śabdôpajīvin*. The prior member is not a *dvandva*, as it is in the case of the compound *jāti-mātrôpajīvin* used by Haradatta in commenting on GautDhS 3.2 (= 20)1.[20] The posterior member also has to be taken seriously in terms of semantics. The groups of people mentioned at the beginning of this paragraph are hence characterised as 'earning their living by the word (i.e. title) "king".' That is to say, the author or redactor of the AŚ[21] recognises that the tribes in question, i.e. their 'headmen' do not do any work other, for their subsistence, than that of a king, i.e.

---

[17] See e.g. KANGLE (1963: 526 fn. 4), but see also the explanation in the *Naya-candrikā*: *kāmboja-surāṣṭrayoḥ kṣatriyāḥ śreṇībhūtāḥ* ('having become a bond / federation') *ekâikacāriṇo atikṣūdrāḥ kṛṣi-śāstrâ-°* (recte: *kṛṣi-śastrâ)dibhir jīvanti / ādi-śabdād varṇântarīyā* ('members of other *varṇa*s') *api grāhyāḥ /*.

[18] As is well-known, *vārttā* is defined in AŚ 1.4.1 to comprise 'agriculture, cattle-rearing and trade' (*kṛṣi-pāśu-pālye vaṇijyā ca vārttā*); nevertheless the author of the *Naya-candrikā* thinks of *kṛṣi* only (cf. n. 12). And what exactly is meant by the characterisation of a person as 'earning his living by (a) weapon(s)'? Bravados like the *tīkṣṇa* (on whom cf. SCHARFE (1968: 251 ff., 265–273) = (1993: 215 ff., 230–236)), or mercenaries or just soldiers / warriors?

[19] The passage could, however, also be taken to mean that all the members of the *saṁgha* want to become a *rājan* and compete with each other in this regard. If this interpretation is correct, the passage could only be classed as a late reflection of the original situation, the distortion of a—once different—information.

[20] ***Rājā*** *atrâbhiṣikto, na jāti-mātrôpajīvī / (taṁ hatavān rāja-ghātakaḥ / )* …

[21] Cf. my forthcoming paper 'On the Problem of the Authorship and Structure of the "Kauṭilīya" *Arthaśāstra*'.

(most probably) ruling over the community, administering the law and perhaps also levying taxes in recompensation for the protection of their subjects, etc., but at the same time he denies them the rank of a real king: They use the title 'king', are addressed as 'kings', but they are no real kings, and this, of course, means that they cannot be compared to the *vijigīṣu*, the *eka-rāja* as regards the latter's religious[22] and 'constitutional' rank, his position in society, his power, etc. According to the author, the title *rājan* is misused in the case of the 'headmen' of the *saṁghas*, but this is clearly said from a standpoint which derives its conception of a 'king' exclusively from the single absolute ruler, i.e. that type of ruler who forms both the object and the audience of the 'Kauṭilīya' AŚ. As the *Larger Petersburg Dictionary* (PW) shows, the word *eka-rāja* is attested since the RV, but it need hardly be stressed that its meaning, or rather that which it refers to, considerably changed in the course of the centuries in accordance with the tremendous social and political development of Northern India. The essential step in the semantic development of the word *eka-rāja* must have taken place—and this is something we already know from other sources—prior to Kātyāyana, the author of the *Vārttika* on the *Aṣṭâdhyāyī*; for *vārttika* 1 on Pāṇ 4.1.168[23]—discussed also by SHARMA (1968)—quite clearly testifies to the existence of an opposition between an *eka-rāja*-member of the second order and the *saṁghas*.

The grammatical interpretation of the prior member of the compound *rāja-śabdôpajīvin* mentioned just now is confirmed by the secondary noun *rāja-śabdin* used in AŚ 11.1.20: *rāja-śabdibhir avaruddham avakṣiptaṁ vā kulyam abhijātaṁ rāja-putratve sthāpayet*—'he (i.e. the *vijigīṣu* who wants "to gain a *saṁgha*") should confer the rank of "*rāja-putra*" to a nobly born member of the [ruling] families who is in disfavour (or: kept in prison?) or has been discarded (or: divested of his privileges?) by those who use the title "king".' In this particular context, all that counts is clear reference to those responsible for the predicament of the young man, not the manner of their earning their living.

[22] Viz. brought about by the *abhiṣeka* (cf. also n. 20). In the *Naya-candrikā* the persons 'who only bear the title "king"' (*rāja-śabda-mātra-dhāriṇo*) are said to be *niṣparikarāḥ* 'having no retinue'!

[23] It reads (*Mahā-bhāṣya* ed. KIELHORN (1897: II,268.20)): *kṣatriyād eka-rājāt saṁgha-pratiṣedhârtham*—'[instead of *kṣatriyāt* alone, in Pāṇ 4.1.168,] it should be read *kṣatriyād eka-rājāt* ("after the name of a member of the second order who is a single monarch") [the affix *añ* is added], in order to prevent that it is added to [the name of] a *saṁgha*.'

## –2.3–

The passage quoted just now (AŚ 11.1.20) forms part of the main body of this *Adhikaraṇa* which, in accordance with the introductory portion, deals with various means, tricks and crimes of secret agents, all of which aim at what nowadays would be called the 'destabilisation' of a *saṁgha* and finally, with the 'gaining' of it. That is to say, it does not offer anything essentially new, but is rather an application of central elements of the 'foreign policy'[24] recommended by the AŚ, although it, too, deserves the full attention of all those interested in the history, and antiquity, of human meanness, political unscrupulousness and readiness to mercilessly take advantage not only of the weakness, but also of the moral strength of other human beings for one's own benefit and success. It is, of course, possible to keep one's distance from the text, to refrain from jumping to premature conclusions and feeling moral indignation, and to study without passion, e.g. the—in fact—remarkable knowledge of human psychology,[25] and this is, in my view, a particularly significant, albeit so far sadly neglected aspect of the AŚ's 'secret service', the basis itself and the heart (if this is the right word) of it, and it is in this regard that the AŚ almost reads like a textbook of the fundamental principles of this type of—obviously—perennial governmental activity. It is rather cold comfort that the author / redactor of the *Adhikaraṇa* almost at its very end, viz. immediately before the concluding verse,[26] advises the *saṁghas* on their part to guard themselves similarly against these deceitful tricks of the single monarch (*saṁghāś câpy evam*[27] *eka-rājād etebhyo 'tisaṁdhānebhyo rakṣeyuḥ*, AŚ 11.1.55); for it cannot simply be assumed that this testifies to the author's sense of fairness, love of justice, his impartiality[28] or even secret sympathy for the *saṁghas*. At least the explanation given by the author of the *Naya-candrikā*: *rājñi saṁghānām api vṛttaṁ lāghavenôdīrayati* ...—'[the author] briefly states the policy [to be followed] by the *saṁghas* on their part with regard to the king (i.e. the single monarch),' would not support such a view. It

[24] On which see, e.g. RUBEN (1955).

[25] Cf. in this particular regard MEYER (1926: 'Einleitung', LIII).

[26] On the relation in which these verses stand, in general, to the (preceding) prose see SCHARFE 1968: 48–75 (= 1993: 42–66).

[27] The *evam* is left out in KANGLE's translation, in spite of the fact that it is also used in, e.g. 11.1.54.

[28] KANGLE (1963: 532 n.) speaks of the 'usual impartiality' with which 'the text offers advice to both sides'. One or two references, at least, would have been in order here.

is true this is nothing but the statement of a fact, but is the lack of any attempt to explain the motive of the AŚ's 'impartiality' not amazing in itself?

## –2.4–

The passage which I should like to discuss now equally forms part of the main body of 135th *Adhikaraṇa*; and in this case I believe KANGLE is even farther off the mark. It reads as follows (11.1.28–29): *saṁghānāṁ vā vāhana-hiraṇye kālike gr̥hītvā saṁgha-mukhyāya prakhyātaṁ dravyaṁ prayacchet // tad eṣāṁ yācite 'dattaṁ amuṣmai mukhyāya' iti brūyāt //*. According to KANGLE (1963: 529) this means: 'Or, borrowing for temporary use vehicles or money from members of the oligarchy, he should give a well-known article to a chief of the oligarchy. When it is demanded back by them, he should say: "It has been given to such and such a chief!"'

The decisive expression of this paragraph, viz. *prakhyātaṁ dravyam*, has not been correctly understood by KANGLE. The solution which I want to propose is based on the assumption—originally suggested by one of my students[29]—that it refers to the rent and the interest to be paid for the vehicles and / or the loan by the *eka-rāja*, as to be distinguished from statued labour. The word *dravya* does not really pose a problem, for the 'material' referred to here could well be a 'material possession', some 'goods' or even 'money' itself; or it is possible that the word is used in the sense of 'transaction', noted by KANGLE himself (1963: Glossary 40), and that 'the profit to be gained from a transaction' is what is meant here. It is rather the attribute *prakhyāta* which calls for a more circumstantial investigation. KANGLE himself (1963: 529 f.) refers to AŚ 9.6.31, a passage which is, however, also not entirely free of problems: *śatru-prakhyātaṁ vā paṇyam avijñātaṁ vijigīṣuṁ gacchet* rendered by KANGLE (1963: 491): '[o]r an article, well-known as belonging to the enemy, should go unknown to the conqueror.' In a footnote he says of *śatru-prakhyātaṁ paṇyam* that it 'is curious' and that '*śatroḥ prakhyātaṁ* would be better.'

He could have referred to at least one more occurrence of the expression *prakhyāta*, viz. AŚ 5.2.49 (the other[30] having been put by him into the critical apparatus) where the compound *prakhyāta-vyavahāra* is met with, used with

---

[29] Viz. Mrs. Monika Martin.

[30] Viz. 1.20.10; on which see KANGLE (1960: 28 App.) and (1963: 56 and n.); the reading °-*pratyākhyāta*-° is obviously due to a misunderstanding or mistake made by a copyist.

reference to 'an agent appearing as a trader' (*vaidehakạ-vyañjana*)[31] and translated by KANGLE (1963: 347) as 'with well-known dealings.'

The word *prakhyāta* is another[32] of those instances which show how important and fruitful it can be to compare the AŚ with other textual traditions, especially with *Dharma-śāstra* literature. By way of *the Smaller Petersburg Dictionary* (BÖHTLINGK 1879–1886), as also of course *the Sanskrit-English Dictionary* (MONIER-WILLIAMS (1899)), we are led to verse 8.399 of the *Manu-smṛti*:

> *rājñaḥ prakhyāta-bhāṇḍāni pratiṣiddhāni yāni ca /*
> *tāni nirharato lobhāt sarva-hāraṁ haren nṛpaḥ //* ,

in which we are told that 'the king should confiscate the whole property of [anyone] who through greed exports articles which are *prakhyāta* by the king and / or those that are forbidden [by him]'.

The second predicate of the relative clause (*pratiṣiddhāni*) is interpreted by the commentators (i.e. those who explain it at all, viz. Medhātithi, Govindarāja and Kullūka, except for Bhāruci) as referring to a temporary export prohibition like e.g. of food grains during a famine. This explanation is not only plausible in itself, but also suggests that the articles which are *prakhyāta* are also in some way or other of vital importance to the king, and also to the subjects, yet the export prohibition is in their case rather a principal one. Indeed Medhātithi says (JHA (1992: II 233.15 ff.)):

> *rājñaḥ sambandhitayā prakhyātāni yāni bhāṇḍāni rājôpayogitayā— yathā hastinaḥ, kāśmīreṣu kuṅkumaṁ, prācyeṣu paṭṭôrṇâdīni, pratīcyeṣv aśvāḥ, dākṣinātyeṣu maṇi-muktâdīni / yad yasya rājño viṣaye sulabham anyatra durlabhaṁ tatra tasya prakhyāpanaṁ bhavati / tena hi rājāna itarêtaraṁ saṁdadhate /* —

—'those commodities that have been "proclaimed" to belong to the king's monopoly", translates JHA (1992: 420), opting for too free a rendering of the expression 'state of being useful to the king,' and continues his translation: 'e.g. elephants in the eastern countries, saffron, silks and woolens in Kashmir, ... ,' thereby clearly indicating that he thought that the text should be emended. And indeed the parallelism of locatives denoting a region and nominatives of commodities typical of it, in the subsequent part of the *yathā*-sentence, is such that one is tempted to supplement the name of a region at the beginning, too; yet the

[31] On compounds ending in *-vyañjana* cf. SCHARFE (1968: 239–242), on the *vaidehaka-vyañjana* also 246 and 273 (= 1993: 209–212, 213–215 and 236). Some of SCHARFE's conclusions, however, call for a critical re-examination.

[32] Cf., e.g. KÖLVER (1985) and WEZLER (2000).

region missing is the north. Are elephants associated with this region, or were they at least during the time of the AŚ, or are they rather not connected with any particular region at all? In the latter case, *hastinaḥ* would have to be taken as exemplifying the very concept of possible export commodities which are useful to the king, by mentioning the most important arms—which are often also the most decisive for combat. Therefore I should like to propose the following translation:

> 'e.g. elephants [in any region], in Kashmir saffron, in the eastern countries silks, woolens,[33] etc., in the western countries horses, in the southern countries precious stones, pearls, etc.; such articles which are easily obtainable in the dominion / territory of a king but difficult to obtain elsewhere, they are proclaimed there (i.e. in that king's dominion). For by this (i.e. by presenting such commodities directly to each other), kings come to a mutual understanding among themselves (i.e. a state of *sandhi*, peace and co-operation).'

If one looks into Bhāruci's *Manu-śāstra-vivaraṇa*, it becomes immediately clear that Medhātithi owes much to him, but it is rather in the light of the latter that the text of the former can be improved upon, beyond the stage reached by DERRETT (1975: 152).[34] Not, however, already found in Bhāruci's commentary on M.8.399 is the expression *rājôpayogin* which, although evidently not meant to semantically explain *prakhyāta*, is of no little use also in that it leads us to the parallel verse 2.261 in the *Yājñavalkya-smṛti*[35]—where it is, however, replaced by *rāja-yogya*—, etc., but it is not possible to follow this trail here further.

JHA's association of a monopoly is certainly not entirely wrong, because *prakhyāta-bhāṇḍa* is, if I am not mistaken, the term used, at least in relatively late texts and perhaps not fully understood any longer by later commentators, to

---

[33] Woolens, so one could think, are rather associated with the North, viz. Nepal. See, however, RITSCHL–SCHETELICH (1973: 243).

[34] The text as reconstructed by DERRETT (1975) reads: *yad yatra pracuraṁ yatra ca* (read: *anyatra ca*) *durabhaṁ tat tasya rājñaḥ prakhyātaṁ bhavati. tathôdīcyeṣv ājāneyā aśvāḥ* (the meaning 'of good breed' is confirmed by MONIER-WILLIAMS) *kuṅkumaṁ kāśmīreṣu, prācyeṣv agaru-karpūrâdi tad-anyatra* (read: *tad anyatra*) *na nirhāryam. anirhṛtaṁ hi durlabhatvād.* (the point should be removed, and the whole phrase taken as part of the subsequent sentence) *itarêtaraṁ rājñāṁ kārya-pratibandhād upāyanaṁ bhavati …*

[35] The verse reads as follows:

> *ardha-prakṣepaṇaṁ dviṁśaṁ bhāgaṁ śulkaṁ nṛpo haret /*
> *vyāsiddhaṁ rāja-yogyaṁ ca vikrītaṁ rāja-gāmi tat //.*

characterise certain regionally produced, or easily available commodities, as exclusively reserved for the king, first of all for political, but probably also for economical and military reasons. They seem to form one of the *regalia* of the ancient Indian kings, if this term is taken to include, as it is indeed by German scholars of mediaeval history and history of law,[36] also particular rights and prerogatives of the king. On the other hand, these special commodities are certainly to be subsumed under the class of the *rāja-paṇya*, the 'royal commodities',[37] a term used several times, but significantly not defined in the AŚ, yet among these latter they no doubt form a distinct subgroup.

In view of the literal meaning of *pra√khyā*, and the expression *prakhyāpana* of the meaning of which Medhātithi[38] seems to have a clear idea, it is nothing but natural, when trying to understand the attribute *prakhyāta*, to start from 'proclaiming'. To proclaim means to announce or declare in an official manner. Though the precise manner of public announcement is anybody's guess—a public notice would not have been sufficient in those days, given that only a few people were able to read, and thus announcement via somebody like a town crier seems much more probable—in the case of the special commodities it would have basically consisted in forming the declaration that they are under no condition to be exported. 'Publicly announced' is almost tantamount to 'officially determined', and from this, in its turn, it is but a very short step to 'officially fixed', and for that very reason 'well-known'.[39]

And this is the meaning the expression has at AŚ 11.1.28, if I may return now to this passage. The rent for the vehicles, and the interest for the loan, are not a matter of individual negotiations, but 'officially fixed'; they are at least 'fixed' when the deal is made. The deceitful trick taught in this passage hence consists in paying the rent or interest 'fixed', or agreed upon, to somebody else and frankly stating this fact when the owner comes in order to ask for it; for the logical subject of *yācite*[40] is, and to be sure not only because of the number, the *prakhyāta-dravya*, and not the

---

[36] Cf., e.g. ERLER–KAUFMANN (1990: 472–478). (My thanks are due to my colleague Franz-Reiner Erkens from the university of Leipzig for coming to my help in this matter.) SCHARFE (1989: 86–92) does not mention this type of *regalia*.

[37] Cf. also RITSCHL–SCHETELICH (1973: 244 ff.).

[38] Cf. Rāmacandra on M 8.399: *prakhyāta-bhāṇḍāni bahu-mūlyatve sati rāja-yogyāni* ...

[39] Cf. above p. 303.

[40] Note that JOLLY (1896: 141) adds *yācita* within brackets (due to an oversight it is spelt *yāëita*) after the expression 'geborgter Gebrauchsgegenstand' ('borrowed utensil').

vehicles and the money.[41] The fun of this paragraph, if fun is the right word, is—not that the vehicles or the loan are not returned in the end, i.e. not just plain fraud, but rather—that everything is done according to law and decency, but the rent / interest due to the owner is given to the or a 'headman' of the *saṁgha*—the only too patent ultimate intention of course being to set (the) members of the *saṁgha* against the *mukhya*, to sow distrust and to create quarrels, or even feuds.

As for the variant *vaidyaka-prakhyāta*,[42] which indeed looks very much like a secondary explanatory addition to the text, it could well mean '[an establishment for maternity and sickness] recommended (lit. officially proclaimed) by the / a physician(s).' And AŚ 9.6.31, which is anyway a close parallel to our passage, can naturally be taken to refer to commodities which are proclaimed by the enemy, i.e. the export of which is not allowed by the enemy, or a hostile king. And a similar interpretation suggests itself for AŚ 5.2.49: The 'agent appearing as a trader' is a man 'whose dealings [with goods] are publicly announced.' But in this particular case I agree with KANGLE that *prakhyāta* is perhaps already hollowed out semantically to such an extent that it may better be rendered by 'well-known'. And this holds good, as far as I can see, for a singular case where the expression is used by one of the commentators of the AŚ, viz. Bhikṣu Prabhamati. Explaining the first words of AŚ 2.12.2, he says (HARIHARA ŚASTRI (1957–61: 149.19 f.)): *yasmāt sarvatra bhūmiḥ vasumatī viśeṣeṇa parvatānāṁ bilâdiṣu śāstrāl loka-prasiddher vā prakhyātôddeśānām*—'[those liquids are gold-bearing that flow] inside a hole, etc.,[43] particularly of the mountains, because[44] the earth is everywhere richly bearing goods, [of the mountains] whose regions / places are known [to contain gold] because of the *śāstra* or of general knowledge of the people.'[45] The commentator has simply replaced *abhijātôddeśānām* of the original by *prakhyātôddeśānām*, and as is quite clearly shown by the ablatives preceding it, the

---

[41] Cf. the *Naya-candrikā* (JOLLY–SCHMIDT (1924: 207.14 f.)): *atha saṁghātais tad dravyaṁ yācito vijigīṣur amuṣmai mukhyāya dattam iti brūyāt* / …

[42] See above n. 30. AŚ 1.20.10 as reconstructed by KANGLE reads thus: *pṛṣṭhataḥ kakṣyā-vibhāge strī-niveśā garbha-vyādhi-saṁsthā vṛkṣôdaka-sthānaṁ ca* / , the variant under discussion being °-*vyādhi-vaidya-prakhyāta-saṁsthā*-°.

[43] The *ādi* of *bilâdiṣu* is an abbreviation used by the commentator for *bila-guhôpatyakālayana-gūḍha-khāteṣu* of the AŚ itself.

[44] Or is the text corrupt here, and has to be emended to *yady api*?

[45] What is 'made known' becomes eventually 'known' or even 'well-known'; *prasiddhe* is used to explain, or in the place of, *prakhyāta*, e.g. in the *Naya-candrikā* (JOLLY–SCHMIDT (1924: 207.12)) and by Sarvajñanārāyaṇa in his *Commentary* on M. 8.399.

word is used by him in the sense of 'well-known', but, and this should certainly be noted, 'known' for a particular quality, and this aspect could be done justice by saying 'named / mentioned as promising with regard to … '.

**–3–**

By way of summary let me just emphasise that the AŚ is beset with problems of this type, and that we can only hope to surpass the degree of understanding reached by earlier research on this highly important text if we confront all of them one after the other, step by step, with untiring persistency, although the assistance of luck is of course welcome too. And only by a fresh survey of this type will it be possible to sift out in an reliable manner whatever historical information this *Adhikaraṇa* contains about the so-called 'republics in ancient India'.

## BIBLIOGRAPHY

AŚ = *Artha-śāstra*. See: KANGLE (1960).

BÖHTLINGK 1879–1886 = Böhtlingk, Otto von: *Sanskrit-Wörterbuch in kürzerer Fassung*, 7 Bde., Kaiserliche Akademie der Wissenschaften, St. Petersburg 1879–1886.

DERRETT 1975 = *Bhāruci's Commentary on the Manusmṛti (The Manu-śāstra-Vivaraṇa, Books 6–12)*. Text, Translation and Notes, ed. by J. Duncan M. Derrett, 2 Vols., F. Steiner Verlag GmbH, Wiesbaden 1975.

ERLER–KAUFMANN 1990 = *Handwörterbuch zur Deutschen Rechtsgeschichte (HRG)*. Herausgegeben von Adalbert Erler und Ekkehard Kaufmann unter philologischer Mitarbeit von Ruth Schmidt-Wiegand. Mitbegründet von Wolfgang Stammler. Redaktion: Dieter Werkmüller. IV. Bd., E. Schmidt, Berlin 1990.

GautDhS = *Gautama-Dharma-Sūtra with the Commentary of Haradatta*. Ed. by Dr. Ramesh Chandra Pandey, *the Kashi Sanskrit Series* 172, Chowkhamba S.S.O., Varanasi 1966.

GONDA 1968 = Gonda, Jan: 'Abbreviated and Inverted Nominal Compounds in Sanskrit.' In: *Pratidānam. Indian, Iranian and Indo-European Studies Presented to F.B.J. Kuijper on his Sixtieth Birthday*. Mouton, The Hague 1968: 221–246.

VON HINÜBER 1968 = Hinüber, Oskar von: *Studien zur Kasussyntax des Pāli, besonders des Vinaya-Piṭaka. MSS, Beihefte, Neue Folge* 2, J. Kitzinger, München 1968.

JHA 1992 = *Manu-smṛti with the 'Manubhāṣya' of Medhātithi*. Ed. with the Help of Several Manuscripts, by Mahāmahopādhyāya Gaṅgānātha Jhā, 2 Vols. [Reprinted: Delhi Parimal Publications 1992].

JOLLY 1896 = Jolly, Julius: *Recht und Sitte (einschliesslich der einheimischen Literatur). Grundriss der Indo-Arischen Philologie und Altertumskunde* II Bd., 8. Heft, J. Trübner, Strassburg 1896.

JOLLY–SCHMIDT 1924 = *Arthaśāstra of Kauṭalya*. A New Edition by J. Jolly and Dr. R. Schmidt. Vol. II: *Notes, with the commentary Naya Candrikā of Mahāmahopādhyaya Yajva*. Motilal Banarsidass, Lahore 1924.

KANGLE 1960 = Kangle, R.P.: *The Kauṭilīya Arthaśāstra*. Part I: *A Critical Edition with a Glossary*. University of Bombay, 1960.

KANGLE 1963 = Kangle, R.P.: *The Kauṭilīya Arthaśāstra*. Part II: *An English Translation with Critical and Explanatory Notes*. University of Bombay, 1963.

KIELHORN 1897 = Kielhorn, F.: *The Vyākaraṇa-Mahābhāṣya of Patañjali*. Ed. by F. Kielhorn, 3 Vols., The Department of Public Instruction, Bombay 1891–1909.

KÖLVER 1895 = Kölver, Bernard: 'Kauṭalyas Stadt als Handelszentrum: der Terminus *puṭabhedana-*,' *Zeitschrift der Deutschen Morgenländischen Gesellschaft* 135 (1985) 299–311.

*Lalita-vistara* = *Lalita-vistara*. Ed. by S. Lefmann. Erster Teil: Text. Verlag der Buchhandlung des Weisenhauses, Halle 1902.

M = *Manu-smṛti*. See DERRETT (1975) and MANDLIK (1886).

MANDLIK 1886 = *Mānava-Dharma Śāstra*. [Institutes of Manu] with the Commentaries of Medhātithi, Sarvajñanārāyana, Kullūka, Rāghavānanda, Nandana and Rāmachandra, and an Appendix by Vishvanāth Nārāyan Mandlik. 2 Vols., Bombay 1886. [Reprinted: Munshiram Manoharlal, Delhi 1992].

MEYER 1926 = Meyer, Johann Jakob: *Das altindische Buch vom Recht- und Staatsleben. Das Arthaśāstra des Kauṭilya*. O. Harrassowitz, Leipzig 1926.

MONIER-WILLIAMS 1899 = Monier-Williams, Monier: *A Sanskrit-English Dictionary*. Oxford University Press, Oxford 1899. [originally].

*Naya-candrikā* = Yajvan: *Naya-candrikā*. See: JOLLY–SCHMIDT 1924.

Pāṇ = Pāṇini: *Aṣṭâdhyāyī. Pāṇini's Grammatik* herausgegeben, übersetzt, erläutert und mit verschiedenen Indices versehen von Otto Böhtlingk. Haessel, Leipzig 1887. [Reprinted: (1) Georg Olms Verlag, Hildesheim–New York 1964, 1971, 1977. (2) Motilal Banarsidass, Delhi 1998].

| | |
|---|---|
| PW | = Böhtlingk, Otto von; Roth, Rudolph: *Sanskrit-Wörterbuch* ('großes Petersburger Wörterbuch'). Bd. 1–7, Kaiserliche Akademie der Wissenschaften, St. Petersburg 1855–75. [1: 1855 (Die Vocale); 2: 1858 (k-ch); 3: 1861 (j-dh); 4: 1865 (n-ph); 5: 1868 (b-m und Verbesserungen von a-m); 6: 1871 (y-v); 7: 1875 (ś-h nebst den Verbesserungen und Nachträgen zum ganzen Werke)]. |
| RAU 1957 | = Rau, Wilhelm: *Staat und Gesellschaft im Alten Indien nach den Brāhmaṇa-Texten dargestellt.* O. Harrassowitz, Wiesbaden 1957. |
| RITSCHL–SCHETELICH 1973 | = Ritschl, Eva; Schetelich, Maria: *Studien zum Kauṭilīya Arthaśāstra* (Schriften zur Geschichte und Kultur des Alten Orients 9), Akademie-Verlag, Berlin 1973. |
| RUBEN 1955 | = Ruben, Walter: 'Inter-State Relations in Ancient India and Kauṭalya's Arthaśāstra.' In: *Indian Yearbook of International Affairs*, Madras 1995. |
| GAṆAPATI ŚASTRI 1924/25 | = *The Arthaśāstra of Kauṭalya with the Commentary 'Śrīmūla' of Mahāmahopādhyāya T. Gaṇapati Śāstri.* (Triv. S. S. 79, 80 and 82), Trivandrum 1924/25. [Reprinted with an elaborate Introduction by N.J. Unni, Bharatiya Vidya Prakashan, Delhi–Varanasi 1984]. |
| HARIHARA ŚASTRI 1957–61 | = Bhikṣu Prabhamati: *Cāṇakya-Ṭīkā.* Ed. by Harihara Śāstri, *JOR* (Madras) XXVI–XXX (1957/58–1960/61). |
| SCHARFE 1968 | = Scharfe, Hartmut: *Untersuchungen zur Staatsrechtslehre des Kauṭalya.* O. Harrassowitz, Wiesbaden 1968. |
| SCHARFE 1989 | = Scharfe, Hartmut: *The State in Indian Tradition. HdO* II, III,2, E.J. Brill, Leiden (etc.)1989. |
| SCHARFE 1993 | = Scharfe, Hartmut: *Investigations in Kauṭalya's Manual of Political Science.* O. Harrassowitz, Wiesbaden 1993. |
| SHARMA 1968 | = Sharma, J.P.: *Republics in Ancient India c. 1500 B.C.—500 B.C.* with a Foreword by Professor A. C. Basham. E.J. Brill, Leiden 1968. |
| SHRIMALI 1983 | = Shrimali, Krishna Mohan: *History of the Pañcāla to c. AD 55.* 2 Vols., Munshiram Manoharlal, Delhi 1983. |
| SPEIJER 1886 | = Speijer, J.S.: *Sanskrit Syntax* by Dr. J.S. Speijer with an Introduction by Dr. H. Kern, E.J. Brill, Leiden 1886. [Reprinted: Kyoto 1968]. |
| *Yājñavalkya-smṛti* | = *Yājñavalkyasmṛti of Yogīśvara Yājñavalkya with the Commentary Mitākṣarā of Vijñāneśvara.* 5th ed. by Nayayan Ram Acharya. Nirnaya Sagar Press, Bombay 1949. |
| WEZLER 2000 | = Wezler, Albrecht: 'A Note on the expression *saṁpad* in the Bhagavadgītā' [to be published in the Felicitation Volume for Prof. Minoru Hara]. |
| WEZLER (forthcoming) | = Wezler, Albrecht: 'On the Problem of the Authorship and Structure of the "Kauṭilīya" *Arthaśāstra'.* |

# PHILOSOPHY

# On the Date of the *Nyāyâvatāra*

PIOTR BALCEROWICZ

The *Nyāyâvatāra* (NA.), a work in thirty-two verses—and hence also called *Dvātriṁśikā*—erroneously ascribed by tradition to Siddhasena Divākara, is deemed to open a new era in the history of Jaina epistemology. It is mostly in the realm of Jaina epistemic pursuits that the *Dvātriṁśikā* might claim the status of an innovative or prototypical work. When we, however, consider the development of logic and epistemology in India on a larger scale, the work seems to lose its flavour of originality and novelty.

The problem of the exact dating of the *Nyāyâvatāra*[1] should be solved independently, irrespective of whether Siddhasena Mahāmati, the author of the *Nyāyâvatāra*, can be accurately identified with a Siddhasena (Divākara?), the celebrated author of a series of *Dvātriṁśikā*s, or— inaccurately—with Siddhasena Divākara, the author of the *Saṁmati-tarka-prakaraṇa*.[2] The earliest indication of the

[1] The most comprehensive bibliographic survey of publicatio..s on Siddhasena Divākara is furnished by UPADHYE (1971) in his 'Introduction' (pp. xi-xxvii) and 'Bibliographic Survey' (pp. *3–*72). A few more publications have been published since the review: MOOKERJEE (1971), DHAKY (1981–82), GRANOFF (1989–1990), DHAKY (1990), DHAKY (1995) and WAYMAN (1996).

[2] The question has been discussed at length in BALCEROWICZ (2001) and BALCEROWICZ (forthcoming). A number of features found in the *Nyāyâvatāra* and the *Saṁmati-tarka-prakaraṇa* evince a discrepant attitude towards the Jaina Canon and tradition of both works, different choice of vocabulary, which was not necessitated by the use of different languages (Sanskrit and Prakrit), and the notions and ideas they use are likewise at variance. A detailed comparison of the contents, style and philosophical background of Siddhasena Mahāmati's *Nyāyâvatāra* and Siddhasena Divākara's *Saṁmati-tarka-prakaraṇa* (*vide infra* p. 343 f.), brings me to the conclusion that these two works were written by two different persons. Following the findings, esp. in view of the lack of any hint that the author of STP. knew of Diṅnāga, I would maintain that STP. must have been composed slightly before or circa 500 C.E. Comp. also MUKTHAR (1948): 'The following points are clear: (1) The *Dvā.s* were not composed in the present order; (2) they are not of one and the same Siddhasena; (3) the *Nyāyāvatāra* is one of them; (4)... No indisputable evidence is brought forth for the common authorship of the *Dvā.s*, *Nyāyāvatāra* and *Sanmati*. ... There were thus three clear

*Essays in Indian Philosophy, Religion and Literature*, pp. 313–352.

name of the author of NA. is, it seems, Haribhadrasūri who makes mention of him under the appellation 'Mahāmati' (*vide infra* p. 343). The subsequent source from which we learn that NA. was composed by a Siddhasena is NAVV. of Śāntisūri. The author of NA. is explicitly identified there in at least four places[3]. In the last reference Śāntisūri is even more specific to give the full name of the author as well: Siddhasenārka[4]. All other references we encounter in the Jaina literature of this period are to Siddhasena Divākara as the author of other works, but none to him as the author of NA.[5] Strangely enough, the available colophons of NA. and NAV.

and distinct Siddhasenas: (1) the author of *Sanmati*; (2) the author of *Nyāyāvatāra*; (3) and another, the author of some *Dvā.s.*' [according to UPADHYE (1971:*28)].

[3] [1] NAVV.36§ 7 (p. 95.8): *śrīsiddhasena-ghaṭita-sphuṭa-gīḥśalākāṁ śuddhām avāpya vimalaṁ vihitaṁ mayâitat //*, [2] NAVV.21.§ 2 (p. 78.9–10): *evaṁ-rūpasya vadhaḥ tyāgaḥ siddhasenārkasyêty arthaḥ.*, [3] NAVV.53.§ 2 (p. 107.18): *siddhasenasya sūtra-kartuḥ...*, [4] NAVV.1.§ 11 (p. 13.14–15): *tat kiṁ svātantryeṇa? na ity āha—siddhasenārka-sūtritam iti. siddhasena eva jagaj-jantu-mano-moha-saṁtatitām asītamaḥ samūhâpoha-kāritvāt arka iva arkaḥ, tena sūtritam.*

[4] Indeed, Śāntisūri speaks of Siddhasenārka, not of Siddhasena Divākara, as UPADHYE (1971: xxiv) would like to have it: 'iii) ... The earliest author, as far as I know, who specifies the name of Siddhasena Divākara as the author of the *Nyāyāvatāra* is Śāntisūri of the 11th century A.D. or so.' Nevertheless, I would side with UPADHYE in asserting that 'Arka' is just another name for 'Divākara'. Thus, I see absolutely no justification for the contention of DHAKY (1995: 49, n. 9), who—commenting on the clause: *siddhasena eva jagaj-jantu-mano-moha-saṁtati-tāmasītamaḥ-samūhâpoha-kāritvāt arka iva arkaḥ, tena sūtritam*—maintains that '"Arka" here is not in the sense of "Divākara" but "essence".' Clearly, *arka* here is an epithet of Siddhasena, who is compared to the sun (*arka iva*; *arka=divā-kara*), and by him (*tena*) the idea discussed before is composed in a *sūtra* form (*sūtritam*). If we took *arka* as DHAKY would like it, the whole clause could hardly be construable.

[5] Cf., e.g. [1] UPADHYE (1971: xiii): 'Haribhadra is one of the earlier authors to mention Siddhasena Divākara and his *Sanmati.* First, he calls him Śrutakevalin; and secondly, he tells us that his name was Divākara (p. *1). Then he has a pun on the name that he was like *Divākara*, sun, to the darkness of Duḥṣama-kāla.' [2] UPADHYE (1971: xvii): '...Pūjyapāda ...quotes Siddhasena's Stuti III.16 in his *Sarvārthasiddhi* (II.10; VII.13).' [3] H.R. Kāpadīā (AJP., 'Introduction', Vol. II, pp. 98 ff.): 'Haribhadra refers to Siddhasena in his *Sammaipayaraṇa*, in his *Anekāntajayapatākā* as well as in his *Paṁcavatthuya* (vv.1047–8), calling him Suyakevali. Jinadāsagaṇi (c. 676 A.D.) refers to him thrice in his *Niśīhavisehacuṇṇī*.' [4] DAVE (1962): 'So Siddhasena is earlier than Mallavādi and the tradition puts him as a contemporary of Vikramāditya who flourished in 57 B.C.' [according to UPADHYE (1971:*53)] and 'Akalaṅka and Vidyānanda quote the *Sanmati*.' [according to UPADHYE (1971:*59)].

contain no reference to the name of the author of NA. Therefore, for the sake of convenience, I tentatively call the author of the *Nyāyâvatāra* Siddhasena Mahāmati.[6]

On subsequent pages I shall try to establish the chronology of the *Nyāyâvatāra* and its correlation to other, mostly Buddhist, works.

There is a variance of opinions regarding the date of Siddhasena as the author of the *Nyāyâvatāra* and the date of the *Nyāyâvatāra*, and these fall in four groups: (1) Siddhasena was pre-Diṅnāgan[7], (2) Siddhasena flourished soon after Diṅnāga and before Dharmakīrti[8], (3) Siddhasena belongs to a post-Dharmakīrtian tradition[9], whereas (4) some hold that his date is still an open question[10].

The first to notice some chronological dependence of NA was JACOBI (1926: iii), who observed that 'To about the same time [i.e. Śaka-year 598 = 677 C.E.—P.B.] belongs Siddhasenadivākara whom Haribhadra quotes; for he uses, no doubt Dharmakīrti[1], though he does not name him.' There are two points, according to him, that justify such a conclusion: (1) Siddhasena (NA.5) applies the term *abhrānta*—and Dharmakīrti was the first to use it in his definition of *pratyakṣa*, thus improving upon Diṅnāga's definition[11]—to both *pratyakṣa* and *anumāna*; (2) Siddhasena (NA.11[12]) 'extends the distinction of *svārtha* and *parārtha*, which properly applies to *anumāna* only, to *pratyakṣa* also, ibidem 12 f. Apparently, he thought to improve on Dharmakīrti by a wholesome generalisation of nice distinctions!' (JACOBI (1926: iii, n. 1)). VAIDYA (1928: xviii-xx) elaborates upon JACOBI's laconic remarks. (3) He further brings up one more important point:

> '...verses 6 and 7 above of Nyāyāvatāra unmistakably presuppose Dharmakīrti and the later phase of the Yogācāra school, as, without them, it is difficult for us to explain why Siddhasena Divākara is required to these views and emphatically declare:

[6] See BALCEROWICZ (2001) and BALCEROWICZ (forthcoming).

[7] E.g. SUKHLAL (1945/a) and SUKHLAL (1945/b), H.R. Kāpadīā (AJP., 'Introduction', Vol. II, pp. 98 ff.), KRAUSE (1948), DAVE (1962), SUKHLAL–DOSHI (1928), WILLIAMS (1963: 19), MATILAL (1985: 241).

[8] E.g. Malvania (NASV., 'Introduction', pp. 141 f.) and QVARNSTRÖM (1999: 178).

[9] E.g. JACOBI (1926), VAIDYA (1928), MUKTHAR (1948), V.P. Johrapurkar ('Introduction' to VTP., pp. 41 ff.).

[10] UPADHYE (1971: xxv).

[11] PS.1.C,k3c-d: *pratyakṣaṁ kalpanâpoḍhaṁ nāma-jāty-ādy-asaṁyuktam*, and NB.1.4: *tatra pratyakṣaṁ kalpanâpoḍham abhrāntam*, respectively.

[12] Not NA.12, as VAIDYA (1928: xviii, line 16) has it.

सकलप्रतिभासस्य भ्रान्तत्वासिद्धितः स्फुटम् ।
प्रमाणं स्वान्यनिश्चायि द्वयसिद्धौ प्रसिध्यति ॥ ७ ॥ ' (p. xx).

On my part, I would only add that also NA.31 (*pramātā svânya-nirbhāsī*) must have been inspired by similar thoughts as NA.7.

The first argument is sound. Admittedly, the idea of *abhrāntatva* of perception was latent in pre-Dharmakīrti's literature[13], but Dharmakīrti was the first to use the term.[14]

---

[13] The term *bhrānta* (*bhrānti*) itself is attested in the pre-Dharmakīrtian literature, for instance in MAVBh.1.4; SacAcBh.(2).2 and in several places of MSA. and Comm. thereon (11.13a, 11.15, 11.17, 11.24–26, Comm. *ad* 10.2 and *ad* 11.27). In all such passages, however, the term *bhrānti* does not occur in the context of *pramāṇa*, still less of valid perception (*pratyakṣa*), in the first place. The term refers either to a general error based on the perceiving of subject–object duality in the world (*dvaya-bhrānti*), and is synonymous to *māyā* (in MSA.), or to the nature of the cognised object (MAVBh.1.4). The latter rests on a rather subtle difference: erroneous is not the cognition as such (the emphasis on the inner, cognitive aspect, viz. erroneous correspondence of an act of cognition), but the way an object is constituted in the cognition (the emphasis on the 'outer', 'objective' side). In none of these texts where we come across the term *bhrānti* is the idea of cognitively valid procedures (*pramāṇa*) discussed; at the most, it points to an antithesis of a general, soteriologically relevant outlook of a person, viz. *citta-bhrānti / bhrāntaṁ cittaṁ / kṣipta-cittaṁ* (SacAcBh.(2).2). This is confirmed by the application of the past passive participle to people MSA.11.18 (*loko hy abhrāntaḥ*), as loci of *bhrānta-citta*. To sum up, none of the occurrences of the term *(a)bhrānta* in Yogācāra works seems to have been an inspiration for Siddhasena.

[14] An interpretation of non-erroneousness (*abhrāntatva*) is offered by Dharmottara in NBṬ.3.2: *abhrāntam artha-kriyā-kṣame vastu-rūpe 'viparyastam ucyate. artha-kriyā-kṣamaṁ ca vastu-rūpaṁ sanniveśôpādhi-varṇâtmakam. tatra yan na bhrāmyati tad abhrāntam.* Thus, there are two pivotal aspects of *abhrāntatva*, the lack of contrariety (*aviparyastatva*) and its reference to a thing capable of efficient action (*artha-kriyā-kṣama-vastu*). The first element, viz. the lack of contrariety, or correspondence to facts, may be taken to have been preconceived in the idea of *avyabhicāritva* in the non-Buddhist literature as early as NS.1.1.4 (*indriyârtha-sannikarṣôtpannaṁ jñānam avyapadeśyam avyabhicāri vyavasāyâtmakaṁ pratyakṣam*) and NBh. *ad loc.* (*yad atasmin tad iti tad vyabhicāri, yat tu tasmin tad iti tad avyabhicāri pratyakṣam iti*). This tendency can be also observed in Jaina sources, e.g. in TBh.1.32 (p. 30.6, p. 31.1–2): *jñāna-viparyayo 'jñānam iti ... mithyā-darśana-parigrahād viparīta-grāhakatvam eteṣāṁ* (= *viparyayāṇām*). *tasmād ajñānāni bhavanti.* See also PVin.I(1).4 (p. 40, n. 1).
However, the second element *artha-kriyā-samartha*, the capability to execute efficient action, is Dharmakīrti's innovation, see PV.1.3: *pramāṇam avisaṁvādi jñānam artha-kriyā-sthitiḥ / avisaṁvādanam śābde 'py abhiprāya-nivedanāt //*, as well as PV.2.3:

If we were to take this latency of *abhrāntatva* as a serious counter-argument—which seems totally unconvincing to me—it would imply that Siddhasena chose the term *abhrānta* intuitively and applied it indiscriminately to both *pratyakṣa* and *anumāna*, as if he had adumbrated that Dharmakīrti would once qualify perception as a non-erroneous cognition and inference as erroneous. Coincidentally, his way of expression would tally with the actual term used by Dharmakīrti, who would follow him!

Whereas I completely agree with JACOBI–VAIDYA's first argument, their second argument is not entirely convincing to me. Indeed, we cannot understand the idea of *svârtha-vākya* and *parârtha-vākya* (NA.10) as well as *svârtha-pratyakṣa* and *parârtha-pratyakṣa* (NA.11) without Diṅnāga's and Dharmakīrti's well-known division of *svârthânumāna* and *parârthânumāna*. It should suffice to remind the reader of NB.2.1–2: /1/ *anumānaṁ dvividhā.* /2/ *svârthaṁ parârthaṁ ca.* and of NB.3.1–2: /1/ *tri-rūpa-liṅgâkhyānaṁ parârthânumānam.* /2/ *kāraṇe kāryôpacārāt.*

There can be no doubt, in my opinion, that the idea of *vākyasya parârthatvaṁ* necessarily presupposes the idea of *vākyasya svârthatvaṁ*, and that both these concepts—expressed in NA.10 ff.: *parârthaṁ mānam ākhyātaṁ vākyaṁ*—could only have been developed in the context of *svârtha-°* and *parârthânumāna*.

However, the idea of *svârtha-pratyakṣa* and *svârthânumāna* / *parârthânumāna*—central for JACOBI–VAIDYA's reasoning—which is a prerequisite for Siddhasena to establish the thesis of *parârtha-pratyakṣa*, predates Dharmakīrti and is found also in the *saṅgraha-śloka* (*iti śāstrârtha-saṅgrahaḥ*) of *Nyāya-praveśa* of Diṅnāga's disciple, Śaṅkarasvāmin[15].

---

*artha-kriyā-samarthaṁ yat tad atra paramārtha-sat / anyat saṁvṛti-sat proktaṁ te sva-sāmānya-lakṣaṇe //*. Cf. also HATTORI (1968: 14): 'The concept of "*artha-kriyā*" is unfamiliar to Dignāga, but it is an important criterion for the distinguishing of "*sva-lakṣaṇa*" from "*sāmānya-lakṣaṇa*" in Dharmakīrti's system of thought.', HATTORI (1968: 79 § 1.14) and FRANCO (1987: 445 n. 203), esp.: 'the concept of *arthakriyā* does not appear anywhere in Dignāga's writings.'

On the other hand, Dharmakīrti's definition does go back to the usage of the term *bhrānta* in the Yogācāra school; his novelty was to mould it to the demands of his *pramāṇa* theory. We should remember about his idea that *anumāna* is *bhrānta* (cf. PVin.II(1).2.6–7, p. 24.6–7: *de ma yin la der ḥdzin phyir || ḥkhrul kyaṅ ḥbrel phyir tshad ma ñid || = atasmiṁs tad-graho bhrāntir api sambandhataḥ pramā //* ), which is a proper point of reference here, not the nature of *citta* / *vijñāna*.

[15] *sādhanaṁ dūṣaṇaṁ câva sâbhāsaṁ para-saṁvide / pratyakṣam anumānaṁ ca sâbhāsaṁ tv ātma-saṁvide //*. As for a possible objection that the verse might be later, at least the commentator Haribhadra takes it to be a genuine part of the original work (NP.(1). p. 9.12 ff.): *...ity ādāv eva ślokaḥ*, etc.

Certainly it is not Śaṅkarasvāmin who developed the concept of *svârtha-*° and *parârthânumāna*. It was probably fathomed by Vasubandhu[16], but terminologically conceived and worked out by Diṅnāga[17].

There are, however, two other traits to be noticed in the aphorisms NA.10–11 that point, in my opinion, to Dharmakīrti as their source. The first of them is the idea of metaphorical transference (*upacāra*) used in a very similar context. Siddhasena speaks of the term 'inference for others' (*parârthaṁ mānam*)—which denotes, to be precise, the inferential cognition arisen in another person as a result of an argumentative procedure and/or debate—which is applied through metaphorical transference (*upacāra*) to a 'syllogistic' sentence (*vākyaṁ*), that is, as a matter of fact, merely a cause of such a cognition in another person. We come across the same idea in NB.3.1–2, and even the wording is to a certain extent similar (one should here take into account stylistic differences necessitated by the succint *sūtra* style and versified *kārikās*). Below, both passages in question are given for the sake of convenience, relevant expressions being underlined: [18]

/NA.10/ *sva-niścayavad anyeṣāṁ niścayôtpādanaṁ budhaiḥ /*
*parârthaṁ mānam ākhyātaṁ vākyaṁ tad-upacārataḥ //*

NB.3.1–2: *tri-rūpa-liṅgâkhyānaṁ parârthânumānam. kāraṇe kāryôpacārāt.*

Dharmottara's gloss confirms the interpretation: *kāraṇa* = *vacana* = *vākya*; *kārya* = *[parârtha] anumāna* = *parârtha-māna*.[19] Siddharṣigaṇi, whose comments are in a similar spirit, even quotes a verse, that establishes the relation between speech (*kāraṇa*) and resulting cognition (*kārya*)[20]. Another striking feature is that the

---

[16] Cf. FRAUWALLNER (1933: 476–477 [297–298]) and HATTORI (1968: 12, n. 60).

[17] E.g.: PS.2.1ab: *anumānaṁ dvividhā svârthaṁ tri-rūpāl liṅgato parârthânumānaṁ tu sva-dṛṣṭârtha-prakāśanam*; also PS.3.1ab, and PSV.2, K 109a.2–3 = V 27a.5 (*svârthânumāna*): *tshul gsum paḥi rtags las rjes su dpag paḥi don* (V: *rjes su dpag par bya baḥi don*) *mthoṅ ba gaṅ yin pa de ni raṅ gi don gyi rjes su dpag paḥo*. Cf. RANDLE (1926: 28–9), HATTORI (1968: 78, n. I.11) and Steinkellner's note 1, p. 21 in PVin.II(2).

[18] In my analysis throughout I shall use, for the sake of brevity, underlining to mark corresponding phrases in NA. and works of Dharmakīrti or of other authors.

[19] NBṬ.3.2, p. 150.12–151.1: *tasmin kāraṇe vacane kāryasyânumānasyôpacāraḥ samāropaḥ kriyate. tataḥ samāropāt kāraṇaṁ vacanam anumāna-śabdenôcyate. aupacārikaṁ vacanam anumānaṁ, na mukhyam ity-arthaḥ.*

[20] *vikalpa-yonayaḥ śabdā vikalpāḥ śabda-yonayaḥ /*
*kārya-kāraṇatā teṣāṁ nârthaṁ śabdāḥ spṛśanty api //*

The verse is so far untraced, but it refers most probably to another verse by Dharmakīrti, and—at any rate—to an idea expressed in PV.1.286.

reference to the idea of the metaphorical transference (*upacāra*) occurs in both works (NA. and NB.) precisely at the moment of introducing the discussion of *parârtha-anumāna* and that this is the only occurrence of this idea in both works. Neither the term nor the idea as such is encountered at any other point.

Further, VAIDYA's third point is rather weak, as well. He says: 'These verses [NA.6–7—P.B.] contain the favourite view of the Yogācāra School on the subject and the object (grāhya and grāhaka), which both they declare illusory. This view is dependent on the definition of pratyakṣa, and though its origin must be sought in Diṅnāga's works [emphasis—P.B.], the scholars who brought the idea to perfection are Dharmapāla and his pupil Dharmakīrti.' (p. xix). Indeed, we find the idea referred to by VAIDYA in Diṅnāga's works, e.g. in his PS.1.10[21] (cf. n. 67):

| Vasudhararakṣita/Seṅ-rgyal 15b.4: | Kanakavarman/Dad-paḥi śes-rab 96a.4–5: |
|---|---|
| *gaṅ tshe snaṅ ba de gṣal bya* \| | *gaṅ ltar snaṅ ba de gṣal bya* \| |
| *tshad ma daṅ deḥi ḥbras bu ni* \| | *tshad ma daṅ deḥi ḥbras bu ni* \| |
| *ḥdsin rnam rig pa de yi phyir* \| | *ḥdsin rnam rig paḥo de yi phyir* \| |
| *de gsum tha dad du ma byas* \|\| | *de gsum tha dad du ma byas* \|\| |

However, we do not find anything in NA.7[22] that would allude to either Diṅnāga's specific theory of triple division of *vijñāna* or to Dharmakīrti's ideas[23]. What we do find instead is the realist's position that, at least: (1) acts of cognition are real, (2) acts of cognition happen to be true and accurate, (3) acts of cognition are self-validatory, (4) acts of cognition are accurate representations of external world, (5) the external world is real.

To have Diṅnāga's or Dharmakīrti's views criticised here we would need an explicit element of *sva-saṁvitti* (*sva-saṁvedana*) or *phala*. There are three possible expressions in NA.7 that might refer to *sva-saṁvitti* (and none to refer to *phala*): (A) *sphuṭaṁ*, (B) *svânya-niścāyi*, (C) *dvaya-siddhau*. (Ad A) The first of the list is highly improbable, for it never—to my knowledge—is used in Buddhist sources to refer to the idea of self-revelatory character of cognition (*sva-saṁvitti*). It is generally used to describe either the veracious, direct, non-inferrential or the

[21] See HATTORI (1968: 107, n. 1.67):

*yad-ābhāsaṁ prameyaṁ tat pramāṇa-phalate punaḥ /*
*grāhakâkāra-saṁvittī trayaṁ nâtaḥ pṛthak-kṛtam //*

[22] *sakala-pratibhāsasya bhrāntatvâsiddhitaḥ sphuṭaṁ /*
*pramāṇaṁ svânya-niścāyi dvaya-siddhau prasidhyati //*

[23] On the triple and fourfold division of *vijñāna* in the Yogācāra school see HATTORI (1968: 107, n. 1.67).

indubitable, etc., character of acts of cognition. It is explained by Siddharṣigaṇi accordingly by *suniścitatayā*. (Ad B) The second of these expressions (as a similar one in NA.31: *svânya-nirbhāsī*) mentions in fact only two aspects: the cognition (*sva*) and its counterpart—the object (*anya*). If *sva* were to mean *sva-saṁvitti*, the primary act of cognition would not be mentioned; if *anya* were taken to be *sva-saṁvitti*, the *bahyârtha*, so fundamental for the realist, would not be mentioned. The expression is explained in NAV. as *sva-para-prakāśakaṁ*, which does not bring anything new to our analysis. However, it is coupled in the NAV. with the third expression. (Ad C) The third expression refers to duality, in the first place, and—like in the preceding case—it is highly problematic to take it to allude to Diṅnāga's theory of triple division of *vijñāna*. However, it is Siddharṣigaṇi's gloss on *dvaya-siddhau*: *svarūpârtha-lakṣaṇa-yugma-niṣpattau* that could be implicative of *sva-saṁvitti*: in it, *svarūpa* might refer to the self-revelatory character of cognition. It is especially suggestive in view of his statement in NAV.1 quoted in n. 24. But even then, the third aspect of an act of cognition (apart from the act as such, an object), its self-revelatory character, is not explicitely mentioned here. As a matter of fact, Siddharṣigaṇi, so well conversant with Buddhist ideas, would not have wasted the availing opportunity to indicate the idea of *sva-saṁvitti* and to utilise it[24], if he had noticed any allusion to the Buddhist theories of triple or fourfold division of *vijñāna* in the aphorism of Siddhasena. In other words, there is nothing in Siddharṣigaṇi's gloss that might suggest that Siddharṣigaṇi had seen any point of convergence between the ideas expressed in NA.7 and certain concepts ascribable to Diṅnāga, as VAIDYA would like it. To expell our doubts, he concludes, as a matter of fact, with *anyathā prameyâbhāve pramāṇâbhāvāt*, to show that no third element is implied.

In my opinion, NA.7 can be safely taken to disprove the doctrine of illusory character of worldly appearance propounded by the Buddhist idealist (*Vijñāna-vādin*), whose ideas directly influenced Diṅnāga and Dharmakīrti[25]. The aphorism is

---

[24] As he does in several places, for instance in NAV.1 (the section beginning with: *ayam atrâbhiprāyaḥ: sva-saṁvedanaṁ prati nikhila-jñānānām eka-rūpatayā sākṣāt-karaṇa-caturatvān nâsty eva bhedaḥ...*), NAV.29 (the section beginning with: *tathôrarī-kṛta-yogâcāra-matam api balād anekânta-prakāśa-rajjur āveṣṭayaty, ekasyâpi jñānasyâneka-vedya-vedakâkāratayā prathanôpagateḥ...*, and the section beginning with: *atha jñāna-vādy advaita-prakāśam alakṣitam abhyupetya tena bāhuvidhyaṁ dadhāno bodho bādhyamānatvād bhrānta ity abhidadhyāt, tad ayuktam ...* ), NAV.31, etc.

[25] Cf. HATTORI (1968: 106, n. 1.65).

clearly evocative of such ideas as those expressed, e.g. in MAV.1.1,3[26], Triṁś.1, 29[27] or Viṁś.1ab[28], 16[29]. As Siddharṣigaṇi expresses himself, if there is nothing to be cognised, there can be no cognition. Therefore, to establish the thesis of the existence of the external world is essential for the realist. Similarly, *mutatis mutandis*, it is crucial for the Buddhist idealist to deny the existence of external object. Furthermore, NA.7 fits quite well into the line of critics of the so-called 'Dreaming Argument'[30], that was commonly ascribed to the Buddhist and refuted, for instance, by Kumārila (MŚV.4.(*Nirālambana-vāda*).23, p. 159.7–8), Uddyotakara (NV. on NBh.4.2.33), Śaṅkara (BSŚBh.2.2.5.29, p. 476.2–3) and by Siddharṣigaṇi (NAV.29, the *Śūnya-vāda* section).

Therefore, NA.7 is not a very useful indication to establish the date of the *Nyāyâvatāra*. However, there is a number of other conspicuous traits, that are instrumental in establishing the time of composition of the treatise quite convincingly as posterior to Dharmakīrti. To achieve this, I shall analyse several aphorisms of NA. step by step in order to show Siddhasena's indebtedness to Dharmakīrti (especially to NB.) in respect not only of certain 'loan' ideas but also, partially, of the dialectical structure of the text. Some of the following points are not entirely convincing, when taken singly. Their high number, on the other hand, could not have been a matter of mere coincidence.

[1] The opening line of NA.0 (*pramāṇa-vyutpādanârtham idam ārabhyate*) closely resembles the formulations of HB. p. 1*.5–6: *parokṣârtha-pratipatter anumānâśrayatvāt tat-vyutpādanârthaṁ saṅkṣepata idam ārabhyate*.

[2] Practically, the very first ideas expressed in the opening lines of NA. and NB. are very similar and have similar wording:

---

[26] *abhūta-parikalpo 'sti dvayaṁ tatra na vidyate / śūnyatā vidyate tv atra tasyām api sa vidyate // artha-sattvâtma-vijñāpti-pratibhāsaṁ prajāyate / vijñānaṁ nâsti câsyârthas tad-abhāvāt tad apy sat //*

[27] *ātma-dharmôpacāro hi vividho yaḥ pravartate / vijñāna-pariṇāme 'sau pariṇāmaḥ sa trividhā // acitto 'nupalambho 'sau jñānaṁ lokôttaraṁ ca tat / āśrayâsya parāvṛttir dvidhā dauṣṭhulya-hānitaḥ //*

[28] *vijñāpti-mātram evâitad asad-arthâvabhāsanāt /*

[29] *pratyakṣa-buddhiḥ svapnâdau yathā sā ca yadā tadā / na so 'rtho dṛśyate tasya pratyakṣatvaṁ kathaṁ matam //* (to be coupled with NA.6–7).

[30] In a typical formulation: 'The sensation in the waking state is erroneous, because it is a cognition, like the sensation in a dream' (*jāgrat-saṁvedanaṁ bhrāntaṁ, pratyayatvāt, svapna-saṁvedanavat*). See TABER (1994).

NA.1: *pramāṇaṁ* [...] *pratyakṣaṁ ca parokṣaṁ ca dvidhā.*

NB.1.1.2–3: *dvividham samyag-jñānam. pratyakṣam anumānaṁ ca.*

The differences are that (1) Siddhasena does not have *samyag-jñānam* (this expression is completely absent from NA.), and (2) he has *parokṣa* instead of *anumāna*. The second difference is dictated by the Jaina demand to incorporate *śābda* / *āgama* (testimony, verbal cognition) in the *pramāṇa*s (as a quasi-separate category, one of the two—alongside *anumāna*—primary sub-divisions of *parokṣa*). However, Siddhasena marks an important, widely known shift in Jaina epistemology, to interpret the directness of *pratyakṣa* in terms of sensory organs (*akṣa* = *indriya*), not—as it was customary—in terms of the cognitive subject (*akṣa* = *jīva* / *ātman*). The commentators are quite explicit about the interpretational shift, which diverts from the *Āgamic* tradition advocated, e.g. by Akalaṅka among many others.[31]

The question is what prompted Siddhasena to introduce this shift? Obviously, these were the demands of the general philosophic discourse in India to be up-to-date with and understood by such schools as Nyāya or Sāṁkhya. But I am deeply convinced that what was responsible for that shift to take the senses as the criterion of directness of *pratyakṣa* was, to a larger degree, Dharmakīrti's inspiration and his works (predominantly the *Nyāya-bindu*) as a groundwork for the *Nyāyâvatāra*. For what other reason would Siddhasena speak of the two-fold division of valid cognition and justify it by referring to Dharmakīrtian ideas? And thereby we come to another element of NA.1 that resembles Dharmakīrti's formulations.

According to Siddhasena, the factor responsible for the division of cognitive acts into *pratyakṣa* and *parokṣa* is not the character of the 'cognising organ' (*akṣa*), either the sense organs (*indriya*) or the cognitive subject (*jīva, ātman*) as such. In his opinion, what is crucial in the categorisation of *pramāṇa*s is the character of the object of cognition that determines the way the object of cognition is determined, or cognised. Clearly, in this revolutionary rearrangement he goes against the whole Jaina tradition. The expression he uses: *meya-viniścayāt* (NA.1d), can hardly be explicated without Dharmakīrti's formulations: *tasya viṣayaḥ svalakṣaṇam* (NB.1.1.12), *so 'numānasya viṣayaḥ* (NB.1.1.17) and *mānaṁ dvividhaṁ viṣaya-*

[31] See, e.g. NAV.1: ***pratyakṣaṁ*** *cêty-ādi; tatra siddhânta-prasiddha-pāramārthika-pratyakṣâpekṣayâkṣa-śabdo jīva-paryāyatayā prasiddhaḥ. iha tu vyāvahārika-pratyakṣa-prastāvād akṣa-dhvanir indriya-vacano gṛhyate. tataś câkṣaṁ pratigataṁ pratyakṣaṁ. yad indriyam āśrityôjjihīte 'rtha-sākṣāt-kāri jñānaṁ tat pratyakṣam ity arthaḥ. ... akṣebhyaḥ parato vartata iti parokṣam. akṣa-vyāpāra-nirapekṣaṁ mano-vyāpāreṇâsākṣād-artha-paricchedakaṁ yaj jñānaṁ tat parokṣam iti bhāvaḥ.*

*dvaividhyāt* (PV.2.1ab)[32]. Even Siddharṣigaṇi[33] confirms that what is pivotal for the distinction is, in the first place, the character of extrinsic data apprehended by the cognitive subject, that determines the way of apprehension, irrespective of whether the 'cognising organ' are the senses or the soul. It is only in NA.4d that Siddhasena emphasises the way of cognising, or '[the manner of] grasping [an object]', for the first time: *grahaṇêkṣayā*. But even then, the tradition in the person of the commentator Siddharṣigaṇi takes the locution to refer to the existence and the nature of the cognoscible (see his detailed discussion in NAV.4 apropos of *grahaṇêkṣayā*).

Truly, a formulation similar to NA.1 is found also in PS.(1).1.2ab[34], so Dharmakīrti is not the only potential source. However, if we compare what Diṅnāga has further to say on the two-fold division of *pramāṇa*, we discover that he does not mention the reason for the division explicitly, as Dharmakīrti and Siddhasena do, but he merely points to the parallelism of the two-fold *prameya*[35]. Clearly, one can easily understand the statement *lakṣaṇa-dvayaṁ prameyam* to be a reason adduced by the author for *pratyakṣam anumānaṁ ca pramāṇe* ('there are two cognitive criteria: perception and inference, [because] the cognoscible has two characteristics'), as the commentator himself does[36]. However, neither the word 'because' (*yasmāt* / °-*tvāt*) nor any direct explanation why *pramāṇa* is twofold is mentioned by Diṅnāga explicitly, as it is by Dharmakīrti in PV.2.1bc (*viṣaya-dvaividhyāt śakty-aśaktitaḥ / artha-kriyāyām* ... ). Moreover, Diṅnāga's elucidation

[32] Cf. also PV.2.63 (*anumāna-vicāraḥ*): *na pratyakṣa-parokṣābhyāṁ meyasyânyasya sambhavaḥ / tasmāt prameya-dvitvena pramāṇa-dvitvam iṣyate //*

[33] NAV.1 *ad loc.* (on *meya-viniścayād*): *bahir-arthaṁ punar apekṣya kaścic cakṣurâdi-sāmagrī-bala-labdha-sattākaḥ svâvayava-vyāpinaṁ kālântara-sañcariṣṇuṁ sthagita-kṣaṇa-vivartam alakṣita-paramâṇu-pārimāṇḍalyaṁ sannihitaṁ viśada-nirbhāsaṁ sāmānyam ākāraṁ sākṣāt-kurvāṇaḥ prakāśaḥ prathate, tatra pratyakṣa-vyavahāraḥ pravartate. yaḥ punar liṅga-śabdâdi-dvāreṇa niyatâniyata-sāmānyâkārâvalokī parisphuṭatā-rahitaḥ khalv ātmano 'rtha-grahaṇa-pariṇāmaḥ samullasati sa parokṣatāṁ svī-karoti.*

[34] *pratyakṣam anumānaṁ ca pramāṇe* (Vasudhararakṣita/Seṅ-rgyal 13b.6: *mṅon sum daṅ ni rjes su dpag tshad ma*; Kanakavarman/Dad-paḥi śes-rab 94a.4: *mṅon sum daṅ ni rjes su dpag tshad ma dag ni*); here, the difference is the absence of the explicit (*sc.* with a numeral, not with the dual form °-*e* / *dag*) mention of 'twofold' (*dvividham* / *dvidhā* / *rnam pa gñis*).

[35] PS.(1).1.2bc: *lakṣaṇa-dvayam / prameyam* ... (Vasudhararakṣita/Seṅ-rgyal 13b.6 = Kanakavarman/Dad-paḥi śes-rab 94a.5: *mtshan ñid gñis gṣal bya*).

[36] *yasmāt* = Vasudhararakṣita/Seṅ-rgyal: ...*phyir ṣe na*; Kanakavarman/Dad-paḥi śes-rab: ... *gaṅ gi phyir*.

of the two-fold character of *pramāṇa* (*lakṣaṇa-dvayaṁ prameyam*) differs completely in character from Siddhasena's explanation (*meya-viniścayāt*) and Dharmakīrti's (*viṣaya-dvaividhyāt śakty-aśaktitaḥ artha-kriyāyām* ... ), insofar as it is 'static' or 'taxonomic', viz. plainly juxtaposes two cases of double division (*pramāṇa—prameya*), whereas Siddhasena and Dharmakīrti offer 'intentional', i.e. actively directed to an object of cognition either by way of determining it (*viniścaya*, cognitive activity) or by any sort of efficient action (*artha-kriyā*).

[3] Apart from the noticeable similarity in wording between NA.1 and NB.1.1.2–3, there is another striking correspondence to be observed in the ideas expressed by Dharmakīrti and Siddhasena. Siddharṣigaṇi introduces NA.1 in the following way: *tatra tāval lakṣaṇa-saṁkhyā-vipratipattī nirācikīrṣur āha*. There is no doubt that Siddharṣigaṇi regarded NA.1 to aim at—beside enumerating subdivisions of *pramāṇa* (*pratyakṣaṁ ca parokṣaṁ ca dvidhā* ... )—formulating its definition (*pramāṇaṁ sva-parâbhāsi jñānaṁ bādha-vivarjitam*). And, further, there can hardly be any doubt that a descriptive definition of *pramāṇa* is precisely what Siddhasena in NA.1ab does. In the aphorism, he does not only group all cognitively valid procedures under respective categories of 'direct' and 'indirect', which is a case of a typological definition that demarcates a notion by mentioning specimens to which the definition is applicable (ὁ διὰ τῶν γενῶν ὁρισμὸς), but he also attempts a real definition that describes the character and essential aspects or intrinsic characteristics of a thing (ὁ λέγων ἐξ ὧν ἔστιν ἐνυπαρχόντων [ὁρισμὸς]).[37] Clearly, these two definitions represent two diverse approaches and the latter is intellectually more sublime. Whereas we quite frequently find typological definitions of *pramāṇa* (viz. statements of its divisions) in Jaina literature, we do not, as a matter of fact, come across any attempt at a descriptive definition of *pramāṇa* of the second type in any works, both Jaina and non-Jaina, prior NA. Thus, the formulation of a descriptive definition of cognitive criterion seems definitely to be an advancement. And it would perhaps be surprising to find such an innovation in a work of generally secondary character that repeatedly borrows from other works (it relies, for the most part, on the Buddhist legacy and has very little new ideas, genuinely of its own, to offer), if NA. had no predecessor. However, it is Dharmakīrti who must have inspired Siddhasena's descriptive definition. The opening verse (if we skip the first two introductory verses of obeisant nature) of the *Pramāṇa-siddhi* chapter, i.e. PV.1.3 and PV.1.7cd present such a descriptive definition of *pramāṇa* that specifies its character and individual features. This

[37] Cf. Aristotelian twofold division in *Met.*998b (p. 47.12–14): ἕτερος δ' ἔδται ὁ διὰ τῶν γενῶν ὁρισμὸς καὶ ὁ λέγων ἐξ ὧν ἔστιν ἐνυπαρχόντων.

section of PV. is traditionally[38] assumed to offer the first comprehensive definition of *pramāṇa*. Clearly, for both Manorathanandin and Siddharṣigaṇi the passages of NA.1ab and PV.1.3/7cd respectively are cases of a *pramāṇa-lakṣaṇa*. Occasionally[39], a doubt is raised whether Dharmakīrti's design was indeed a descriptive definition and that actually it was the subsequent Buddhist tradition of commentators where the idea of a comprehensive descriptive definition developed. Irrespective of whether one assumes that the formulation of PV.1.3 was a genuine descriptive definition or that an idea of such a definition first originated with post-Dharmakīrtian commentators, both sides agree that such a descriptive definition did not exist before Dharmakīrti (*ergo* it is altogether absent from Diṅnāga, Śaṅkarasvāmin, etc.). Accordingly, since NA. appears to present such a definition of a descriptive character, it must have been composed after Dharmakīrti and PV.[40]

[4] Late Buddhist sources allegedly refer to NA.2.[41] Surprisingly, NA.2, being a statement of *pūrva-pakṣa*, is the least suitable verse of the whole *Dvātriṁśikā* to serve as an object of anybody's critique. Thus, anyone referring to the verse with the purpose to refute it would have to be highly incompetent and incapable of noticing that the very verse is refuted by Siddhasena himself in NA.3! Therefore it could

---

[38] See: FRANCO (1997: 59–61), esp.: 'Therefore, we can safely conclude that the definition of *pramāṇa* in general, unlike the definition of each *pramāṇa* in particular, was not undertaken by any Indian philosopher before Dharmakīrti's time. Consequently, there is no reason why one should expect Dharmakīrti to do so. During the time that separates Dharmakīrti from his commentators, some change in the philosophical requirements must have occurred that produced the expectation of a general definition of *pramāṇas*.' [p. 60]. Cf. also STEINKELLNER–KRASSER (1989: 3–5). Cf., e.g. PVV.1.3 (1: 2.17 ff.; 3: 3.17 ff.): *ayam ācāryo bṛhad-ācāryīya-pramāṇa-samuccaya-śāstre vārttikaṁ cikīrṣuḥ svataḥ-kṛta-bhagavan-namaskāraḥ tac-chāstrârambha-samaye tad-ācārya-kṛta-bhagavan-namaskāra-ślokaṁ vyākhyātu-kāmaḥ prathamaṁ pramāṇa-sāmānya-lakṣaṇam āha* ... and PVV.1.7–8 (1: 4.36 ff.; 3: 8.6 ff.): *tad evam avisaṁvādanaṁ pramāṇa-lakṣaṇam uktam. idānīm anyad āha* ...

[39] See: FRANCO (1997: 54–62), e.g.: '...Dharmakīrti did not attempt a general definition of the *pramāṇas*, but only wanted to prove that the Buddha is a *pramāṇa* ... ' [p. 61].

[40] I am indebted to Claus Oetke for drawing my attention to the above issue of PV.1.3–7 and its relevance to the problem of dating of NA.

[41] QVARNSTRÖM (1999: 178): 'In the eighth-century commentary on Dharmakīrti's *Pramāṇavārttika* (II.5), Śākyabuddhi (or Śākyamati) quotes the second verse of *Nyāyāvatāra* and claims that this verse is the object of Dharmakīrti's critique', and refers to p. 163, n. 38 of Chr. LINDTNER's 'Marginalia to Dharmakīrti's Pramāṇaviniścaya.' *Wiener Zeitschrift für die Kunde Südasiens* 28 (1984) 149–175.

hardly be an 'object of Dharmakīrti's critique.' Furthermore, any reference to allegedly such a state of affairs would prove the source of such an information to be a highly unreliable one. Consequently, either Śākyabuddhi cannot have referred to NA.2 or his acquaintance with Jaina tradition would be liable to doubt.

As a matter of fact, NA.2 may plausibly be taken as a *prima facie* objection ('no purpose is known for stating the definition of cognitive criterion') against formulating a comprehensive definition of *pramāṇa* of descriptive character, inasmuch as '*cognitive criteria* (mind the plural!—P.B.) are well-known and everyday practice is accomplished by them.' Siddharṣigaṇi takes 'the definition of cognitive criterion' to be '[a statement] consisting in mentioning specific properties of cognitive criterion that are capable of distinguishing [it from that which has] another form,'[42] which is a very accurate explanation of a descriptive definition. Interestingly enough, the reason adduced why such a definition is not necessary in case of *pramāṇa* is *prasiddhāni pramāṇāni*, where the plural is expressly used. This would point to the more archaic kind of definition based on classification, that would define the notion of *pramāṇa* merely by specifying the *pramāṇa* 'inventory'. Thereby NA.2 supports our supposition that what Siddhasena really does is a descriptive definition of *pramāṇa*. Accordingly, NA.2 would rather be a record of the historical change and certain resistance against a new approach towards defining *pramāṇa*. This would also explain the role of the verse, that might seem unnecessary at first glance, in such a succinct work as NA. is.

[5] The *pāda* c (*tad-vyāmoha-nivṛttiḥ*) of NA.3[43]—which is a rejoinder to the doubt raised in NA.2 whether it is 'purposeful to state the definition of cognitive criterion' (viz. whether the treatise, *śāstra* = NA., has a purpose), since 'cognitive criteria are well-known and everyday practice is accomplished by them'—recalls Dharmakīrti's statement found in PV.1.7:

> ***prāmāṇyaṁ vyavahāreṇa śāstraṁ moha-nivartanam /***
> ***ajñātârtha-prakāśo vā svarūpâdhigateḥ param //***

A statement expressing a similar idea seems to be absent from PS.

[6] Corresponding to the sequence of topics discussed in NB. (truly, it is a typical sequence not restricted to NB.), as a next step, Siddhasena in NA.5 makes his polemical statement and declares also inference to be 'non-erroneous because it is a

[42] NAV.2 *ad loc.*: ***pramāṇa-lakṣaṇasyôktau*** *para-rūpa-vyāvartana-kṣamâsādhāraṇa-pramāṇa-dharma-kathana-rūpāyāṁ*.

[43] *prasiddhānāṁ pramāṇānāṁ lakṣaṇôktau prayojanam /*
*tad-vyāmoha-nivṛttiḥ syād vyāmūḍha-manasām iha //*

cognitive criterion, just like perception.' (… *anumānaṁ, tad abhrāntaṁ pramāṇatvāt samakṣavat* …). The use of the term *abhrānta* as well as the polemical character directly points to NB.(1).1.4: *tatra pratyakṣaṁ kalpanâpoḍham abhrāntam*. This issue, that was taken up by JACOBI and VAIDYA, has been already discussed above p. 315 ff. Dharmakīrti expressed such ideas that could have served both as a target and inspiration for Siddhasena also in PV.2.45–46 (*anumāna-vicāraḥ*)[44].

But this is not the only Dharmakīrtian trace to be found in NA.5. Inference is defined by Siddhasena to 'determine the *sādhya* on account of *liṅga*; *liṅga* (the inferential sign) is, in its turn, inseparably connected with the *sādhya*; the determining factor is here the relation of *avinā-bhāva*: NA.5ac: *sādhyâvinā-bhuno liṅgāt sādhya-niścāyakaṁ smṛtam / anumānaṁ*. This definition follows, in most—if not all—details, the ideas expressed by Dharmakīrti in PV.1.287:

> *anumānâśrayo liṅgam avinā-bhāva-lakṣaṇam /*
> *vyāpti-pradarśanād dhetoḥ sādhyenôktañ ca tat sphuṭam //*

This striking correspondence does not only concern central elements in inference and their character as well as their mutual connection, but even the choice of vocabulary. The inseparable connection with the probandum as the defining characteristic of the probans reoccurs in NA.13: *sādhyâvinā-bhuvo hetor*.[45]

[7] NA.8 may have been influenced by Diṅnāga both in terms of vocabulary and notions. Its *pāda* d (*mānaṁ śābdaṁ prakīrtitam*) reminds of PS.(2).5.1 (esp. *śābda*, *sgra las byuṅ ba*):

> *na pramāṇântaraṁ śābdam anumānāt tathā hi tat /*
> *kṛtakatvâdivat svârtham anyâpohena bhāṣate //* [46]

[8] In NA.13 Siddhasena takes a closer look at *parârthânumāna* and the conditions of its validity: *sādhyâvinā-bhuvo hetor vaco yat pratipādakam / parârtham anumānaṁ tat pakṣâdi-vacanâtmakam //* The phrasing is reminiscent of NB.3.1: *tri-rūpa-liṅgâkhyānaṁ parârthânumānam*. Clearly, the element of *tri-rūpa*—a criterion of validity of *anumāna* for the Dharmakīrtian tradition—is absent in NA., for this idea was not recognised by the Jainas. Instead, syntactically and semantically in the same

---

[44] *ayathâbhiniveśena dvitīyā bhrāntir iṣyate / gatiś cet para-rūpeṇa na ca bhrānteḥ pramāṇātā // abhiprāyâvisaṁvādād api bhrānteḥ pramāṇatā / gatir apy anyathā dṛṣṭā, pakṣaś câyaṁ kṛtôttaraḥ //*

[45] Cf. also PV.3.31: *kārya-kāraṇa-bhāvād vā svabhāvād vā niyāmakāt / avinā-bhāva-niyamo 'darśanān na na darśanāt //* , etc.

[46] *sgra las byuṅ ba rjes dpag las | tshad ma gźan min de ltar de | byas sogs pa bźin du raṅ don la | gźan sel bas ni rjod par byed |* The verse is quoted in TSaP. *ad* TSa.1514 (p. 441.6–7), with a minor alteration (*anumānāt tathā hi saḥ* (*tat*) / ).

position, we have the Jaina criterion of validity, viz. *sādhyâvinā-bhuvaḥ*. Thus, NA.13 may be taken as Siddhasena's polemical reply to the Buddhist doctrine of *trairūpya*.

On the other hand, *pādas* c-d of NA.13 (*...anumānaṁ tat pakṣâdi-vacanâtmakam*) bear close resemblance to (1) NP.(2).2 (= NP.(1), p. 1.4–5): *tatra pakṣâdi-vacanāni sādhanam. pakṣa-hetu-dṛṣṭânta-vacanair hi prāśnikānām apratīto 'rthaḥ pratipādyata iti //* as well as to (2) the verse of NM.1: **pakṣâdi-vacanānîti sādhanam; tatra hi svayaṁ / sādhyatvenêpsitaḥ pakṣo viruddhârthânirākṛtaḥ //* . However, this similarity is not decisive at all, inasmuch as all the quotations merely describe the widely known structure of any 'syllogistic' reasoning, that is composed of respective links, viz. members of 'syllogism'.

[9] In the definition of *pakṣa*, NA.14ab: *sādhyâbhyupagamaḥ pakṣaḥ* ***pratyakṣâdy-****anirākṛtaḥ* / , we come across other formulations that bear obvious similarity especially to NB.(2).3.37: *svarūpeṇâiva svayam iṣṭo 'nirākṛtaḥ pakṣa iti* (but also to NB.(2).3.49–53). Dharmakīrti's *svarūpeṇa* stands for *sādhyatvena*, which is confirmed both by Dharmakīrti himself in the next two *sūtras* (NB.(2).3.39–40: *svarūpeṇêti sādhyatvenêṣṭaḥ. svarūpeṇâivêti sādhyatvenâivêṣṭo na sādhyatvenâpi.*) as well as by Dharmottara (NBṬ.(2).3.37 *ad loc.*: *svarūpeṇâivêti sādhyatvenâiva.*). Dharmottara explains *anirākṛtaḥ* as *pratyakṣâdy-anirākṛtaḥ* (NBṬ.(2).3.37 *ad loc.*: *evaṁ-bhūtaḥ san pratyakṣâdy-anirākṛto yo 'rthaḥ sa pakṣa ity ucyate.*), and—if we suppose that he expressed original ideas of Dharmakīrti (and I believe he did in this regard)—Siddhasena's formulations express almost the same idea as Dharmakīrti did in NB., barring Dharmakīrti's specific delimiting use of *eva* as well as *svayam*.

However, there can hardly be any doubt that the formulations of NA.14ab: *sādhyâbhyupagamaḥ pakṣaḥ* ***pratyakṣâdy****-anirākṛtaḥ* / , go back to PV.4.86 (1: p. 378, 3: p. 390):

> *sādhyâbhyupagamaḥ pakṣa-lakṣaṇaṁ teṣv apakṣatā /*
> *nirākṛte*[47] *bādhanataḥ śeṣe 'lakṣaṇa-vṛttitaḥ //*

The idea itself goes back to Diṅnāga and NM. (**svayaṁ sādhyatvenêpsitaḥ pakṣo viruddhârthânirākṛtaḥ*), as it was pointed out by Manorathanandin in PVV., p. 378.26. Another plausible source for NA.14 might be PS.3.2:

> *svarupeṇâiva nirdeśyaḥ svayam iṣṭo 'nirākṛtaḥ /*
> ***pratyakṣ****ârthânumānâpta-prasiddhena svadharmiṇi //* [48]

---

[47] Cf. Manorathanandin's *Vṛtti ad loc.*: *tathā ca teṣu śāstrêṣṭâdiṣu pañcasu vyāvartyeṣu mādhye nirākṛte pratyākṣâdi-bādhite bādhanato 'pakṣatā viruddhârthā.*

[48] The above Sanskrit reconstruction of PS.3.2 follows FRAUWALLNER (1957/b: 885) and TILLEMANS (1997: 178, n. 2). Tibetan text reads as follows: *raṅ gi ṅo bo kho na*[a]

Clearly, the word *ādi* of the phrase *pratyakṣâdi* of NA.14b might allude to the categories [*pratyakṣârtha*?], *anumāna*, *āpta*, *prasiddha* enumerated in Diṅnāga's *anirākṛtaḥ pratyakṣârthânumānâpta-prasiddhena*, but it does not necessarily have to, since Siddharṣigaṇi (NAV.14 *ad loc.*: ***ādi***-*śabdād anumāna-sva-vacana-lokā gṛhyante*) takes *ādi* to stand for *anumāna-sva-vacana-loka*. Another predecessor of Dharmakīrti in this regard was Śaṅkarasvāmin[49].

Out of all these possible sources, NA.14 has most in common with Dharmakīrti in terms of (1) exact wording (*sādhyâbhyupagamaḥ pakṣa* … ), (2) replacement of Diṅnāgan *iṣṭa* with *abhyupagama*, (3) affinity in the explicit correlative *sādhya* (instead of Diṅnāgan *svarupeṇâiva nirdeśya*) to *abhyupagama* / *iṣṭa*.

[10] The description of *hetu* and its role in the inference for others (*parârthânumāna*) in NA.17 is not so conspicuously similar to NB. in phrasing. Nevertheless, semantically both expositions are quite akin to each other. That in NA.17 we still deal with *parârthânumāna* is clear from the context itself, but also Siddharṣigaṇi leaves not doubt (NAV.17 *ad loc.*: ***parârthânumānasya*** *vacana-rūpatvād* … ). Thus, in both cases we have 'the pronouncement of the logical reason' (*hetos* … *prayogo,* NA.) or 'the announcement of the inferential sign' (*liṅgâkhyānaṁ,* NB.) as the principal element of the inference for others (*parârthânumāna*) and the idea that there is no difference in 'demonstrative force' between the two formulations of the logical reason:

NA.17: *hetos tathôpapattyā vā syāt prayogo 'nyathâpi vā /*
*dvi-vidho 'nyatareṇâpi sādhya-siddhir bhaved iti //*

NB.3.1,3–7: */1/ tri-rūpa-liṅgâkhyānaṁ* ***parârthânumānam****. /3/ tad dvi-vidham. /4/ prayoga-bhedāt. /5/ sādharmya-vaidharmyavac cêti. /6/ nânayor arthataḥ kaścid bhedaḥ. /7/ anyatra prayoga-bhedāt.*

The idea expressed by Dharmakīrti goes back to his PV.3.16 and PVSV. *ad loc.*[50]

---

*bstan* | *bdag 'dod raṅ gi chos can la* | *mṅon sum don daṅ rjes dpag daṅ* | *yid ches grags pas ma bsal ba'o* || [[a] TILLEMANS 1997 reads *nar.*] PS.3.2 must have been in its turn the source for NB.(2).3.37.

[49] NP.(2).2.1: *tatra pakṣaḥ prasiddho dharmī prasiddha-viśeṣaṇa-viśiṣṭatayā svayaṁ sādhyatvenêpsitaḥ.* ***pratyakṣâdy***-*viruddha iti vākya-śeṣaḥ.*

[50] In PV.3.15 [p. 180] Dharmakīrti first recalls the triple character of *hetu* defined by Diṅnāga in *Nyāya-mukha*: *hetos triṣv api rūpeṣu niścayas tena varṇitaḥ / asiddha-viparītârtha-vyabhicāri-vipakṣataḥ //*. Then (PV.3.16ab) he states the reason for expressing the concomitance by way of dissimilarity (*vaidharmya-vacana*): *vyabhicāri-vipakṣeṇa vaidharmya-vacanaṁ ca yat /*, only to quote Diṅnāga in PVSV.(1).3.16ab: *yad*

[11] In NA.20 Siddhasena maintains that *dṛṣṭânta* is not an essential part of 'syllogistic' reasoning, inasmuch as the relation of invariable concomitance (*vyāpti*) suffices to prove the thesis. This is a continuation of the 'economical' trend in Indian logic—that starts with Vasubandhu and his *Vāda-vidhāna* and *Vāda-vidhi*[51]—to limit the number of necessary 'syllogistic' members, to simplify the reasoning procedures and to make such procedures universally binding, without any need for further empirical justification than the premises themselves:

NA.20: *antar-vyāptyâiva sādhyasya siddher bahir-udāhṛtiḥ /*
*vyarthā syāt tad-asadbhāve 'py evaṁ nyāya-vido viduḥ //*

NB.(2).3.121: *tri-rūpo hetur uktaḥ. tāvatā cârtha-pratītir iti na pṛthag dṛṣṭânto nāma sādhanâvayavaḥ kaścit. tena nâsya lakṣaṇaṁ pṛthag ucyate gatârthatvāt.*

Siddhasena was not so much innovative as it might seem at first glance, inasmuch as it is Dharmakīrti (NB.(2).3.121) who had intuitively foreshadowed such an idea before him, when he had claimed that the example (*dṛṣṭânta*) is not a separate member of the proof (*sādhanâvayava*). It is much more natural and less surprising to find the direct continuation of the 'economical' trend, that had started with Vasubandhu, in the Yogâcāra tradition and Dharmakīrti's works, rather than in the Jaina tradition in the person of Siddhasena, where we do not find such an 'economic' tendency before Siddhasena. In my opinion, Siddhasena verbalised what had already been latent in Dharmakīrti's statement, even though Dharmakīrti himself had not been able to do without the example, which he had considered an integral part of the logical reason (*hetu*), indispensable to authenticate the general principle by taking recourse to its instantiations (relevant portions underlined): NB.(2).3.122: *hetoḥ sapakṣa eva sattvam asapakṣāc ca sarvato vyāvartī rūpam uktam abhedena. punar viśeṣeṇa kārya-svabhāvayor ukta-lakṣaṇayor janma-tan-mātrânubandhau darśanīyāv uktau. tac ca darśayatā—yatra dhūmas tatrâgnir, asaty agnau na kvacid dhūmo yathā mahānasêtarayor, yatra kṛtakatvaṁ tatrânityatvam, anityatvâbhāvo kṛtakatvâsambhavo yathā ghaṭâkāśayor—iti*

*āha—eṣa tāvan nyāyo yad ubhayaṁ vaktavyaṁ viruddhânaikāntika-pratipakṣeṇa iti.* The rule is further explained by Dharmakīrti in PVSV. as follows: *sādharmya-vācanaṁ viruddha-pratipakṣeṇa, vaidharmya-vācanam anaikāntika-pratipakṣeṇa.* Thereupon, in PV.3.16cd and PVSV. *ad loc.*, he adds that: *yady adṛṣṭi-phalaṁ tac ca yadi tena vipakṣe 'darśanaṁ khyāpyate tad anukte 'pi gamyate //*. Cf. also PVSV.(1).3.24–25 [p. 185]: *tasmāt svabhāva-pratibandhād eva hetuḥ sādhyaṁ gamayati. sa ca tad-bhāva-lakṣaṇas tad-utpatti-lakṣaṇo vā. sa evâvinā-bhāvo dṛṣṭântābhyāṁ pradarśyate.*

[51] Cf. FRAUWALLNER (1933) and FRAUWALLNER (1957/a).

*darśanīyam. na hy anyathā sapakṣa-vipakṣayoḥ sad-asattve yathôkta-prakāre śakye darśayitum. tat-kāryatā-niyamaḥ kārya-liṅgasya, svabhāva-liṅgasya ca svabhāvena vyāptiḥ. asmiṁś cârthe darśite eva dṛṣṭânto bhavati. etāvan-mātra-rūpatvāt tasyêti.* Dharmakīrti expressed a similar idea already in his PV.3.27: *tad-bhāva-hetu-bhāvau hi dṛṣṭânte tad-avedinaḥ / khyāpyete, viduṣāṁ vācyo hetur eva hi kevalaḥ //*. Siddhasena, however, has to his credit that he clearly states the conditions of internal formal validity of the proof and dismisses the need to quote any instantiation: the proof is valid because the premisses are valid and the relation between them is universally binding.

[12] Siddhasena states explicitly five conditions that invalidate *pakṣa*—and adds that there are, in fact, several varieties of *pakṣâbhāsa*—in NA.21:

> *pratipādyasya yaḥ siddhaḥ pakṣâbhāso 'kṣa-liṅgataḥ /*
> *loka-sva-vacanābhyāṁ ca bādhito 'nekadhā mataḥ //*

These five *pakṣâbhāsas* are in concord with the list exemplified by Siddharṣigaṇi in NAV.: (1) *pratipādya-siddha*, (2) *pratyakṣa-bādhita*, (3) *anumāna-bādhita*, (4) *loka-bādhita*, (5) *sva-vacana-bādhita*. Having enumerated five varieties of *pakṣâbhāsa*, it would be redundant and pointless on Siddhasena's part to say by way of recapitulation in a succinct *kārikā* that these varieties are numerous: *anekadhā mataḥ*, unless he had other varieties, not mentioned already by name, in mind. That being the case, he probably referred to other enumerations well-known from other sources.

In fact, Siddhasena's enumeration overlaps with Dharmakīrti's list of fallacies of the thesis, enumerated in NB.(2).49–53[52]. Interestingly, Dharmakīrti subsequently (NB.(2).3.54[53]) adds a few more conditions and the failure to meet them would render the *pakṣa* defective as well. Thus, Siddhasena—by *anekadhā mataḥ*—may have referred to Dharmakīrti's catalogue of defective *pakṣas*. But not necessarily to Dharmakīrti's. He may have as well referred, e.g. to NP.(2).3.1[54].

---

[52] /49/ (2) *tatra pratyakṣa-nirākṛto yathā: aśrāvaṇaḥ śabda iti.* /50/ (3) *anumāna-nirākṛto yathā: nityaḥ śabda iti.* /51/ (4?) *pratīti-nirākṛto yathā: acandraḥ śaśîti.* /52/ (5) *sva-vacana-nirākṛto yathā: nânumānaṁ pramāṇam.* /53/ *iti catvāraḥ pakṣâbhāsā nirākṛtā bhavanti.*

[53] *evaṁ siddhasya, asiddhasyâpi sādhanatvenâbhimatasya, svayaṁ vādinā tadā sādhayitum aniṣṭasya, ukta-mātrasya nirākṛtasya ca viparyayeṇa sādhyaḥ. tenâiva svarūpeṇâbhimato vādina iṣṭo 'nirākṛtaḥ pakṣa iti pakṣa-lakṣaṇam anavadyaṁ darśitaṁ bhavati.*

[54] *sādhayitum iṣṭo 'pi pratyakṣâdi-viruddhaḥ pakṣâbhāsaḥ, tad yathā:* (1) *pratyakṣa-viruddhaḥ*, (2) *anumāna-viruddhaḥ*, (3) *āgama-viruddhaḥ*, (4) *loka-viruddhaḥ*, (5) *sva-*

In any case, NA.21 can in no way attest that Siddhasena was posterior or prior to Dharmakīrti. It merely points to certain similarities between Siddhasena's list and the Buddhist tradition. Probably, it was the tradition of Śaṅkarasvāmin and Dharmakīrti that Siddhasena alluded to by *anekadhā mataḥ*.

[13] In Siddhasena's subsequent aphorism, we find further similarities with NB., though they are less of linguistic nature (similarities in formulations) but rather of methodological character. Analogously to the structure of NB, Siddhasena—after describing fallacious theses—proceeds to discuss fallacious logical reasons (*hetv-ābhāsa*). However, both the authors first look back to their previous definitions of a correct, not defective *hetu*:

NA.22: *anyathânupapannatvaṁ hetor lakṣaṇam īritam*[55] /
*tad-apratīti-sandeha-viparyāsais tad-ābhatā* //

NB.(2).3.55–56: *tri-rūpa-liṅgâkhyānaṁ parârthânumānam ity uktam*[56]. *tatra trayāṇāṁ rūpāṇām ekasyâpi rūpasyânuktau sādhanâbhāsaḥ. uktāv apy asiddhau sandehe vā pratipādya-pratipādakayoḥ.*

Incidentally, it is the only case in both works that the authors first remind the reader/hearer of the definition of a correct 'syllogistic' member/term, and only then deal with its particular fallacies.

Likewise incidentally, both the authors first state general factors that invalidate a correct *hetu*, either singly or jointly, and subsequently enumerate resulting fallacies one by one. There are two such general invalidating factors for Dharmakīrti, viz. *asiddhi* and *sandeha* (NB.3.56,109): various combinations (with regard to *trairūpya*) are responsible for particular varieties of *hetv-ābhāsa*. For Siddhasena, however, there are three—polemically, as it were—such factors: *tad-apratīti*, *sandeha* and *viparyāsa*; thus Dharmakīrti's *asiddhi* factor would seem to bifurcate into Siddhasena's *tad-apratīti* and *viparyāsa*. For instance, for Siddhasena the fallacies of NB.3.58 and 59[57] would be probably a case of *viparyāsa*, whereas the

*vacana-viruddhaḥ*, (6) *aprasiddha-viśeṣaṇaḥ*, (7) *aprasiddha-viśeṣyaḥ*, (8) *aprasiddhôbhayaḥ*, (9) *prasiddha-sambandhaś cêti // tatra …*

[55] Either in NA.5 (according to Siddharṣi) or in NA.17 (*hetos tathôpapattyā vā syāt prayogo 'nyathâpi vā*, see NAV. *ad loc.*: ***anyathâpi vêty*** *anenâvayave samudāyôpacārād anyathânupapattiṁ lakṣayati*).

[56] NB.3.1: *tri-rūpa-liṅgâkhyānaṁ parârthânumānam*; cf. also NB.(2).2.5,11–12.

[57] NB.(2).3.57–9: /57/ *ekasya rūpasya dharmi-sambandhasyâsiddhau sandehe vâsiddho hetv-ābhāsaḥ.* /58/ *yathā: anityaḥ śabda iti sādhye cākṣuṣatvam ubhayâsiddham* [not proved for both parties]. /59/ *cetanās tarava iti sādhye sarva-tvag-*

fallacy of NB.3.60[58] should rather be considered a case of *tad-apratīti*. One could analyse all the remaining cases of fallacious *hetu*s (ensuing from the combination of the factors *asiddhi* and *sandeha*) found in NB. and map them onto the triple classification of Siddhasena in the same manner. Practically, it would mean to decide which of the *asiddhi* cases of Dharmakīrti would correspond to *tad-apratīti* cases of Siddhasena, and which to his *viparyāsa* cases. However, we do not have any explicit statement in the far too succinct NA., nor in NAV., that would provide us any algorithm of such a mapping, and the issue is open to our conjectures only.

Interestingly, in NP., for instance, to which NA. might be thought to have occasionally referred to, we do not find any trait of such invalidating factors as *asiddhi* and *sandeha*, or anything similar.

[14] Also NA.23 and the classification of particular varieties of *hetv-ābhāsa*s points to secondary sources of Siddhasena's ideas. There seem to be only two such potential sources, i.e. NB. and NP.:

NA.23: *asiddhas tv apratīto yo yo 'nyathâivôpapadyate* /
*viruddho yo 'nyathâpy atra yukto 'naikāntikaḥ sa tu* //

NB.(2).3.109: *evam eṣāṁ trayāṇāṁ rūpāṇām ekâikasya dvayor dvayor vā rūpayor asiddhau sandehe vā yathā-yogam asiddha-viruddhânaikāntikās trayo hetv-ābhāsāḥ.*

NP.(2).3.2. *asiddhânaikāntika-viruddhā hetv-ābhāsāḥ* //

However, NB. is a more probable source, inasmuch as the sequence of fallacies (*asiddha, viruddha, anaikāntika*) listed in NA. is exactly the same as that of NB., not of NP., where the two last varieties are interchanged (*asiddha, anaikāntika, viruddha*). Diṅnāga has the *aniścita* (or *sandigdha*) variety, istead of *anaikāntika*.

What is striking is that Siddhasena has only three varieties of *hetv-ābhāsa*, like Dharmakīrti and Śaṅkarasvāmin, unlike Diṅnāga. Moreover, Dharmakīrti outspokenly rejects Diṅnāga's subvariety, i.e. *viruddhâvyabhicārin*[59]: NB.(2).3.110: *viruddhâvyabhicāry api saṁśaya-hetur uktaḥ. sa iha kasmān nôktaḥ.* We do not find any polemical trait in NA., which could even suggest that Siddhasena adopted

---

*apaharaṇe maraṇaṁ prativādy-asiddham, vijñānêndriyâyur-nirodha-lakṣaṇasya maraṇasyânenâbhyupagamāt, tasya ca taruṣv asambhavāt* [not proved for the opponent].

[58] NB.(2).3.60: *acetanāḥ sukhâdaya iti sādhya utpattimattvam anityatvaṁ vā sāṁkhyasya svayaṁ vādino 'siddham* [not proved for the proponent himself].

[59] Cf. also RANDLE (1926: 68–69, 79).

Dharmakīrti's criticism of *viruddhâvyabhicārin*. Apparently he subscribed to the criticism unhesitatingly.

It is worth noticing that NA. diverges also from the tradition of Kumārila, whose triple classification—into *asiddha, sandigdha, viruddha* in MŚV.—is more akin to Diṅnāga's: MŚV.5.4.75 p. 264 mentions the classification (*saṁśayâdī-viparyāyāḥ*); subsequently (1) the threefold *asiddha* fallacious reason is mentioned in MŚV.5.4.76–83ab; (2) *sandigdha* and (3) *viruddha* occur in MŚV.5.4.83cd–107 (e.g. in MŚV.5.4.83cd: *sandeha-viparītatva-hetū câtra nirākṛtau*); besides, (2) *sandigdha* is further found in MŚV.5.4.84b–96b, whereas (3) *viruddha* is mentioned in MŚV.5.4.96cd–107ab. Kumārila nowhere in the *Anumāna-pariccheda* section uses the term *anaikāntika* as a *hetv-ābhāsa*, he has *sandigdha* instead, like Diṅnāga, unlike Dharmakīrti, Śaṅkarasvāmin and Siddhasena. However, Pārthasārathi Miśra follows the general post-Dharmakīrtian typology in his classification, while commenting on Kumārila (p. 264.11 *ad* MŚV.5.4.75): *samprati hetv-ābhāsān asiddhânaikāntika-viruddhān prapañcayan* ...

[15] NA.24–25 reveal further similarities pointing to NB. as its possible inspiration. One of them is the phraseological affinity as regards the use of *dṛṣṭânta-doṣa*, instead of *dṛṣṭântâbhāsa*, in both works. Both Siddhasena and Dharmakīrti use the expression *pakṣâbhāsa* as well as similarly *tad-ābha* and *hetv-ābhāsa*. However, both of them deviate from the general use of derivatives of *ā√bhās* to technically denote logical fallacies, when they refer to *dṛṣṭânta* by the term *doṣa*, and to *dṛṣṭânta* only:

> NA.24: *sādharmyeṇâtra dṛṣṭânta-doṣā* ... ,
> NA.25: *vaidharmyeṇâtra dṛṣṭânta-doṣā* ... ,
>
> NB.(2).3.123, 128–129: /123/ *etenâiva dṛṣṭânta-doṣā api nirastā bhavanti.* /128/ *sādharmyeṇa dṛṣṭânta-doṣāḥ.* /129/ *vaidharmyeṇâpi: paramāṇuvat karmavad ākāśavad iti sādhyâdy-vyatirekiṇaḥ.*

Indeed, also Śaṅkarasvāmin has *dṛṣṭânta-doṣa* twice, but in a slightly different context, viz. that of refutation. Generally, when he discusses fallacious examples, he uses the standard term *dṛṣṭântâbhāsa*, e.g. NP.3.3: *dṛṣṭântâbhāso dvividhaḥ: sādharmyeṇa vaidharmyeṇa ca* // The only two occurences of *dṛṣṭânta-doṣa* are found in NP.(2).6,7[60].

[60] (6) *sādhana-doṣôdbhāvanāni dūṣaṇāni* // *sādhana-doṣo nyūnatvam. pakṣa-doṣaḥ pratyakṣâdi-viruddhatvam. hetu-doṣo 'siddhânaikāntika-viruddhatvam. dṛṣṭânta-doṣaḥ sādhana-dharmâdy-asiddhatvam. tasyôdbhāvanaṁ prāśnika-pratyāyanaṁ dūṣaṇam* // (7) *abhūta-sādhana-doṣôdbhāvanāni dūṣaṇâbhāsāni* // *saṁpūrṇe sādhane nyūnatva-*

Conspicuously, *dṛṣṭânta-doṣa* occurs as exemplification of *dūṣaṇāni*, in the series of *sādhana-doṣa*, *pakṣa-doṣa*, *hetu-doṣa* and *dṛṣṭânta-doṣa*.[61] Another occurrence of *doṣa* (however, *pratijñā-doṣa*, not *dṛṣṭânta-doṣa*) in NP. is attested in the concluding lines of NP.(2).3.1, that summarise the discussion on *pakṣâbhāsa*[62]. Also here, the term *doṣa* has a more general meaning than the technical term *ābhāsa*, and the peculiarity of the usage of *pratijñā-doṣa* is confirmed by the closing *uktāḥ pakṣâbhāsāḥ*. The usage of *doṣa* in NP. confirms the fact that in works preceding Diṅnāga, Dharmakīrti or Śaṅkarasvāmin—e.g. in NS., VS., NBh., PBh., etc.—*doṣa* is employed to denote general defects and is not used specifically as a *terminus technicus* in the sense of *ābhāsa*.

[16] There is a structural similarity to be observed: both Siddhasena (NA.24) and Dharmakīrti (NB.(2).3.122–3) explicitly define fallacious examples by referring to the definition of a correct *hetu*. Accordingly, NB.3.122 recapitulates the definition of correct *hetu* as well as conditions of its validity. The successive statement of NB.3.123 (*etenâiva dṛṣṭânta-doṣā api nirastā bhavanti*; *vide supra* p. 334) shows that fallacious examples are refuted by referring to the correct definition of *hetu*, and all fallacies of the example share the same characteristic. Similarly, Siddhasena relates the deficiency of *dṛṣṭântâbhāsa*s to deficient logical reasons and, with *apalakṣaṇa-hetûtthāḥ*, he expresses the idea known from the work of Dharmakīrti.

[17] Strangely, in NA.24–25 Siddhasena refers to some tradition by *nyāya-vid-īritāḥ* as regards the classification of fallacious examples. However, there seems to have been no earlier (or contemporary) Jaina source he could have referred to. Thus, in default of any extant evidence attesting to a Jaina tradition which offered a typology of fallacious examples, one is prone to assume—unless we find any indication to the contrary—that, apparently, he must have referred to a general Indian tradition, where we do find such a typology of *sādharmya-°* and *vaidharmya-dṛṣṭântâbhāsa*s.

Besides, he also seems to have taken it for granted that the reader/hearer could easily determine what is meant by *sādhyâdi-vikalâdayaḥ* in NA.24. This task would

---

*vacanam. aduṣṭa-pakṣe pakṣa-doṣa-vacanam. siddha-hetuke 'siddha-hetukaṁ vacanam. ekânta-hetuke 'nekânta-hetukaṁ vacanam. aviruddha-hetuke viruddha-hetukaṁ vacanam. aduṣṭa-dṛṣṭânte duṣṭa-dṛṣṭânta-doṣa-vacanam. etāni dūṣaṇâbhāsāni. na hy ebhiḥ para-pakṣo dūṣyate, niravadyatvāt tasya // ity uparamyate //*.

[61] NP.6: *sādhana-doṣôdbhāvanāni dūṣaṇāni // sādhana-doṣo nyūnatvam. pakṣa-doṣaḥ pratyakṣâdi-viruddhatvam. hetu-doṣo 'siddhânaikāntika-viruddhatvam. dṛṣṭânta-doṣaḥ sādhana-dharmâdy-asiddhatvam. tasyôdbhāvanaṁ prāśnika-pratyāyanaṁ dūṣaṇam //*.

[62] *eṣāṁ vacanāni dharma-svarūpa-nirākaraṇa-mukhena pratipādanâsaṁbhavataḥ sādhana-vaiphalyataś cêti pratijñā-doṣāḥ // uktāḥ pakṣâbhāsāḥ //*

naturally be quite easy for anyone who was acquainted with NB.(2).3.124–125. At the same time, however, his elliptical formulation *sādhyâdi-vikalâdayaḥ* was, polemically as it were, unequivocal enough to rule out the three remaining varieties, viz. (A7) *ananvaya*, (A8) *apradarśitânvaya* and (A9) *viparītânvaya*, formulated by Dharmakīrti (NB.(2).3.126–127), which could by no means have been hinted at by the formulations of NA.24.

Similarly, the sixfold classification of dissimilar *dṛṣṭântâbhāsa*s systematised in NA.25 (*sādhya-sādhana-yugmānām anivṛtteś ca saṁśayāt*) closely corresponds to the first six fallacious examples of NB.(2).3.129–132: (V1) *sādhyâvyatirekin*, (V2) *sādhanâvyatirekin*, (V3) *sādhya-sādhanâvyatirekin*, (V4) *sandigdha-sādhya-vyatireka*, (V5) *sandigdha-sādhana-vyatireka*, (V6) *sandigdha-sādhya-sādhana-vyatireka*. Seemingly, NA. and NB. are at variance as regards terminology, for Siddhasena's formulation: *sādhya-sādhana-yugmānām anivṛtteś ca saṁśayāt*, differs from Dharmakīrti's (V1)–(V6). In my opinion, however, *anivṛtteś* and *saṁśayāt* of NA.25 indicate rather plainly °-*vyāvṛtta* and *sandigdha*-° as the last and first elements of the compounds (V1)–(V3) and (V4)–(V6), respectively. Optionally, we could have (V1) **sādhyânivṛtta*, (V2) **sādhanânivṛtta*, (V3) **sādhya-sādhanânivṛtta*, (V4) **saṁśayita-sādhya*, (V5) **saṁśayita-sādhana*, (V6) **saṁśayita-sādhya-sādhana*, which is not different at all from the idea expressed in NB.(2).3.129–132.[63]

[63] True, theoretically speaking, one could also interpret NA.25 to enforce the acceptance of only (1) *sādhyâvyatirekin*, (2) *sādhanâvyatirekin*, (3) *sādhya-sādhanâvyatirekin*—to use Dharmakīrti's terminology—and only one or more varieties out of (4) *sandigdha-sādhya-vyatireka*, (5) *sandigdha-sādhana-vyatireka*, (6) *sandigdha-sādhya-sādhana-vyatireka*, but not necessarily all of them. While *anivṛtteḥ* is unquestionably construed with *sādhya-sādhana-yugmānām*, the expression *saṁśayāt* might be conjectured to be taken separately, without any dependence on all elements of *sādhya-sādhana-yugmānām*. In this respect, attention should be drawn to an instance of different conceivable ways of construing an aphorism of NA. by commentators which we encounter in the case of NA.8: *dṛṣṭêṣṭâvyāhatād vākyāt paramârthâbhidhāyinaḥ / tattva-grāhitayôtpannaṁ mānaṁ śābdaṁ prakīrtitam //* The aphorism is explained differently by the commentators, viz. (1) NAV. *ad loc.*: ***dṛṣṭena*** *pramāṇâvalokitenê**ṣṭaḥ*** *pratipādayiṣito* **'*vyāhato*** *'nirākṛtaḥ sāmarthyād artho yasmin vākye tat-tathā*; and (2) NAṬ. ad loc.: ***dṛṣṭenêty-ādi***. *ayaṁ bhinnâdhikaraṇas tri-pado bahu-vrīhiḥ yadi vā iṣṭo 'vyāhato 'rtho yatra tad iṣṭâvyāhataṁ vākyam, tadanu dṛṣṭena pramāṇa-nirṇītena iṣṭâvyāhatam iti tat-puruṣaḥ* (cf. BALCEROWICZ (1999: 4, n. 8)). Definitely, such an unnatural interpretation—i.e. to take *anivṛtteś* to refer to all elements of the triad *sādhya-sādhana-yugmānām*, while limiting the scope of *saṁśayāt* to selected element(s) of the compound *sādhya-sādhana-yugmānām*—would be a mere

As for another possible source of insipration, also NP.(2).3.3 distinguished—in accord with the prevalent tradition of those days—two general categories: similar and dissimilar fallacious examples (*dṛṣṭântâbhāso dvividhaḥ: sādharmyeṇa vaidharmyeṇa ca //* ). However, a closer look at Śaṅkarasvāmin's varieties reveals essential differences, apart from the terminological ones. Accordingly, I see no way how the formulations of fallacies of examples based on similarity found in *Nyāya-praveśa*[64] could be interpreted to have influenced Siddhasena's *sādhyâdi-vikalâdayaḥ*. As regards *Nyāya-praveśa* on fallacies of examples based on dissimilarity[65], the influence might have been restricted to (V1), (V2) and (V3) only.

[18] Also NA.26, where criticism / refutation (*dūṣaṇa*) and its fallacy (*dūṣaṇâbhāsa*) are discussed, might have partly been inspired by Dharmakīrti's NB.(2).3.137–140. Thus, NA.26a-c: *vādy-ukte sādhane prokta-doṣāṇām udbhāvanam / dūṣaṇaṁ*, reveals a certain similarity—in terms of both formulations and ideas—to the *dūṣaṇa*-section of NB.(2).3.137–8: */137/ dūṣaṇā nyūnatâdy-uktiḥ. /138/ ye pūrvaṁ nyūnatâdayaḥ sādhana-doṣā uktās teṣām udbhāvanaṁ dūṣaṇaṁ. tena parêṣṭârtha-siddhi-pratibandhāt.* Less conspicuous, though, is the remaining portion of the second hemistich of NA.26: *niravadye tu dūṣaṇâbhāsa-nāmakam //* The corresponding *dūṣaṇâbhāsa*-section of NB.(2).3.139–140 reads: */139/ dūṣaṇâbhāsās tu jātayaḥ. /140/ abhūta-doṣôdbhāvanāni jāty-uttarāṇîti.* The reoccurring element *dūṣaṇâbhāsa* is not decisive at all, whereas Siddhasena's *niravadye* could be a vague echo of Dharmakīrti's *abhūta-doṣa*.

As a matter of fact, NA.26c-d (*niravadye tu dūṣaṇâbhāsa-nāmakam*) betrays more affinity to the closing section of NP.(2).7: *abhūta-sādhana-doṣôdbhāvanāni dūṣaṇâbhāsāni // ... etāni dūṣaṇâbhāsāni. na hy ebhiḥ para-pakṣo dūṣyate, niravadyatvāt tasya // ity uparamyate //* It is this section, in all probability, that

guesswork, and one would rather, as a rule, construe *sādhya-sādhana-yugmānām* with both *anivṛtteś* and *saṁśayāt*, and obtain six varieties of dissimilar *dṛṣṭântâbhāsas*. One would not, in any case, obtain any further varieties mentioned by Dharmakīrti in NB.(2).3.133–135: (V7) *avyatireka*, (V8) *apradarśita-vyatireka* and (V9) *viparīta-vyatireka*. Thus, Siddhasena apparently does not accept without reservation the Buddhist typology by rejecting (V7), (V8) and (V9).

[64] NP.(2).3.3.1: *tatra sādharmyeṇa tāvad dṛṣṭântâbhāsaḥ pañca-prakāraḥ, tad yathā:* (1) *sādhana-dharmâsiddhaḥ,* (2) *sādhya-dharmâsiddhaḥ,* (3) *ubhaya-dharmâsiddhaḥ,* (4) *ananvayaḥ,* (5) *viparītânvayaś cêti // tatra ...*

[65] NP.(2).3.3.2. *vaidharmyeṇâpi dṛṣṭântâbhāsaḥ pañca-prakāraḥ, tad yathā:* (1) *sādhyâvyāvṛttaḥ,* (2) *sādhanâvyāvṛttaḥ,* (3) *ubhayâvyāvṛttaḥ,* (4) *avyatirekaḥ,* (5) *viparīta-vyatirekaś cêti // tatra ...*

influenced both Dharmakīrti's NB.(2).3.139–140 (*dūṣaṇâbhāsās tu jātayaḥ. abhūta-doṣôdbhāvanāni jāty-uttarāṇîti.*) and the portion of NA.26c-d in question.

[19] The twenty-sixth aphorism (the exposition of *dūṣaṇa*) is the last section of the *Nyāyâvatāra*, where possible influences from Dharmakīrti's side—in terms of Siddhasena's direct use of Dharmakīrti vocabulary or his response to Dharmakīrti's ideas—are easily detectable. Strangely enough, the topic dealt with in NA.26 closely corresponds to the final issue discussed by Dharmakīrti in NB. Thus, the conspicuous absence of further possible Dharmakīrtian traces in NA.—theoretically derivable from other works of Dharmakīrti—points, in my opinion, to the fact that Siddhasena—while composing NA.—closely followed the structure and the contents of NB., up to NA.26.

In the remaining aphorisms (28–32) Siddhasena discusses issues peculiar to Jainism (viz. corollaries of *kevala-jñāna* and *syād-vāda*) and there could hardly have been any Buddhist influence to be noticed in any case: [27] the character of absolute cognition (*kevala-jñāna*); [28] the result of valid cognition in general; the results of absolute cognition (*kevala-jñāna*); the results of valid cognitive procedures other than *kevala-jñāna*; [29] the multiplex character of reality; the domain of cognitive acts; the domain of viewpoints (*naya*); [30] the character of viewpoints (*naya*); the description of the doctrine of seven-fold modal description (*syād-vāda*); [31] the character of the cognitive subject, the soul (*jīva*); [32] the eternal character of Jaina epistemology.

[20] The phrase *pramāṇa-phala* occurring in NA.28 is occasionally taken to be a proof of its dependence on Diṅnāga.[66] It is commonly assumed that the phrase in question goes back to Diṅnāga, e.g. PS.(1).1.8cd–10[67]. In these verses Diṅnāga

[66] Cf., e.g. QVARNSTRÖM (1999: 178): 'Furthermore, the *Nyāyāvatāra* (28) uses the signature element of Dignāga, namely "pramāṇaphala"[61];' in his note 61, he further draws the reader's attention to the work of G. Dreyfus and Chr. Lindtner: 'The Yogācāra Philosophy of Dignāga and Dharmakīrti". *Studies in Central & East Asian Religions*. Vol. 2, Ed. by Per K. Sørensen et al. Copenhagen 1989: 27–52.

[67] *savyāpāra-pratītitvāt pramāṇaṁ phalam eva sat // sva-saṁvittiḥ phalaṁ vâtra tad-rūpo hy artha-niścayaḥ / viṣayâkāratâivâsya pramāṇam tena mīyate // yad-ābhāsaṁ prameyaṁ tat pramāṇa-phalate punaḥ / grāhakâkāra-saṁvittī trayaṁ nâtaḥ pṛthak-kṛtam //* . For the Sanskrit text, see HATTORI (1968: 97, n. 1.55—107, n. 1.67). Tibetan text reads as follows:

| Vasudhararakṣita/Seṅ-rgyal 15a.5–15b.4: | Kanakavarman/Dad-paḥi śes-rab 95b.5–96a.5: |
|---|---|
| *bya daṅ bcas par rtogs paḥi phyir \|* | *bya daṅ bcas par rtogs paḥi phyir \|* |
| *tshad maḥi ḥbras bu ñid du ḥdod \|\|* | *ḥbras bu ñid du yod tshad ma \|\|* |

asserts that the result of *pramāṇa* is *pramāṇa* itself, or introspective cognition which consists in the determining of an object (*sva-saṁvitti, artha-niścaya*). Precisely the same idea (*ātmânubhāva, artha-viniścaya*) is echoed in PV.2.306–307ab, 339[68]. Generally, the idea is discussed at length by Dharmakīrti both in his PVin.I(1).78.12–100.26 and in PV.2.301–366, 388–391. Accordingly, NA.28 might be taken to be a rejoinder of both Diṅnāga and Dharmakīrti, and there seems to nothing decisive to be found in NA.28 that would exclude any of the two authors.

On the other hand, any attempt to look for inspiration of NA.28 in works of either Diṅnāga or Dharmakīrti seems to me to be a result of misapprehension of the true import of the aphorism. In it, Siddhasena does not discuss the problem whether *pramāṇa-phala* can or cannot be equated with *pramāṇa* itself, which is the major concern of Diṅnāga and Dharmakīrti. What is intended in the verse are rather extra-epistemological issues of both soteriological (*kevala*) and mundane (*śeṣa*) character, viz. the result of *pramāṇa* is 'the cessation of nescience' (*ajñāna-vinivartana*), whereas the result of specific kinds of cognition is two-fold. The first category subsumes happiness and indifference (*sukhôpekṣe*) in case of the perfect knowledge (*kevala*), being a prerequisite of liberation (*mokṣa*) and commonly taken by the Jainas to be tantamount to the destruction of nescience. Since it results from the destruction of *karman*[69] it is necessarily associated with innate happiness, etc.[70] that are inhibited by *karman*. The other—pragmatic, as it were—category of results refers to 'the faculty of appropriation and avoidance' (*ādāna-hāna-dhī*) in case all the remaining kinds of (mundane) cognition.[71] Consequently, what really the verse is reminiscent of is rather

---

*raṅ rig la yaṅ ḥdir ḥbras bu |*
*de yi ṅo bo las don ṅes |*
*yul gyi snaṅ ba ḥdi ñid ḥdi |*
*tshad ma de yis ḥjal bar byed ||*
*gaṅ tshe snaṅ ba de gṣal bya |*
*tshad ma daṅ deḥi ḥbras bu ni |*
*ḥdsin rnam rig pa de yi phyir |*
*de gsum tha dad du ma byas ||*

*yaṅ na raṅ rig ḥdir ḥbras bu |*
*de yi ṅo bo las don ṅes |*
*yul gyi snaṅ ba ñid de ḥdiḥi |*
*tshad ma de yis ḥjal bar bya ||*
*gaṅ ltar snaṅ ba de gṣal bya |*
*tshad ma daṅ deḥi ḥbras bu ni |*
*ḥdsin rnam rig paḥo de yi phyir |*
*de gsum tha dad du ma byas | |*

[68] *tasmāt prameyâdhigateḥ sādhanaṁ meya-rūpatā / sādhane 'nyatra tat-karma-sambandho na prasiddhyati // sā ca tasyâtma-bhūtâiva tena nârthântaraṁ phalam / yadā saviṣayaṁ jñānaṁ jñānâṁśe 'rtha-vyavasthiteḥ / tadā ya ātmânubhāvaḥ sa evârtha-viniścayaḥ //*

[69] Cf. TS.10.1: *moha-kṣayāj jñāna-darśanâvaraṇântarāya-kṣayāc ca kevalam.*

[70] Cf., e.g. TBh.10.7 (p. 231 f.) v.23 ff. (*saṁsāra-viṣayâtītaṁ muktānām avyayaṁ sukham*).

[71] Cf. also FRANCO (1997: 65).

NBh.1.1.3: *yadā jñānaṁ tadā hānôpādānôpekṣā-buddhayaḥ phalam*, with all the three elements of *hāna*, *upādana* / *ādāna* and *āpekṣā*, as a result (*phala*) of cognition (*jñāna*).

What is important to remember is that there are numerous similarities, more and less conspicuous, and not all of them are decisive when taken alone. Some of these similarities indicated on the preceding pages may equally well point to a tradition or author prior to Dharmakīrti, viz. to Diṅnāga or Śaṅkarasvāmin. Some of such similarities may be due to the general style of writing, of arranging a philosophical treatise, of structuring a philosophical discourse, etc. We should remember that both the *Nyāya-bindu* and the *Nyāyâvatāra* were primarily handbooks of logic and their purpose was predominantly didactic. Nonetheless, the accumulation of evidence only enforces those of them that are quite conclusive and convincing. To sum up, my impression is that in all dubious cases, when both NP. and NB. seem relevant as possible sources of Siddhasena's ideas, Siddhasena probably took recourse to Dharmakīrti rather than to Śaṅkarasvāmin, inasmuch as in all those rare cases when there are clear similarities to be found between NA. and NP., they are also traceable in NB. However, not all cases of similarities between NA. and NB. can be shown with regard to NA. and NP. In other words, the development of certain ideas that had taken place in the period connecting Śaṅkarasvāmin and Dharmakīrti, was reflected in the contents of NA. and some ideas still absent from NP., that were later either introduced or modified by Dharmakīrti, found their way into NA. Similarly, certain influences to be found in NA. point both to Diṅnāga and to Dharmakīrti. However, Siddhasena seems to be acquainted with certain new developments or ideas that first developed with Dharmakīrti (not necessarily only in NB.) and are not found in Diṅnāga's works.

Paradoxically as it were, would it not be thinkable to claim that it was Siddhasena who influenced Dharmakīrti and who was the intermediary stage between Diṅnāga and Dharmakīrti? For at least three reasons we should dismiss such a possibility. There is, in the first place, a continuous tradition in epistemic concepts referred to by both Dharmakīrti and Siddhasena that go back to Diṅnāga. Dharmakīrti himself refers to Diṅnāga so explicitly that would seem highly implausible to believe that he had availed himself of the Jaina epistemological tradition with respect to the number of points mentioned above in §§ 1–20, without even a single mention of it: one would expect Dharmakīrti embarking on at least an accidental discussion of a few issues he had supposedly taken over from the Jainas. Secondly, Satkari MOOKERJEE, who believed Siddhasena to flourish in the sixth century and to precede Dharmakīrti,[72] puzzled over what was in his opinion Dharmakīrti's lack of reaction as regards Siddhasena's interpretation of the intrinsic invariable concomitance (*antar-vyāpti*) and the superfluous character of the example as an exemplification (*bahir-udāhṛti*) external to the most elementary constituents of the proof formula, as

[72] See: MOOKERJEE (1935: 398).

well as the definition of the logical reason as 'inexplicability otherwise'.[73] This becomes no longer a query when we assume that Siddhasena was post-Dharmakīrtian. Moreover, it is for precisely the same reason that also Pātrasvāmin should be taken to flourish after Dharmakīrti. Thirdly, the concepts of *svârtha-vākya* and *parârtha-vākya* (NA.10) as well as *svârtha-pratyakṣa* and *parârtha-pratyakṣa* (NA.11) would have with certainty evoked a refutal from the side of Dharmakīrti, had he known about it. Likewise, Dharmakīrti would have certainly commented upon the idea of non-erroneousness of inference (*anumānaṁ ... abhrāntaṁ*) proven by its being a cognitive criterion alone (*pramāṇatvāt*), found in NA.5. The same holds true for the idea of 'inexplicability otherwise' (*anyathânupapannatva*). Thus, any supposition that Siddhasena preceded Dharmakīrti can safely be dismissed.

Accordingly, depending on whether we follow the widely accepted dating of Dharmakīrti, viz. c. 600–660[74] or the results of latest research by KIMURA (1999) who assigns the years 550–620 for Dharmakīrti, we would have for the *terminus post quem* Siddhasena as the author of the *Nyāyâvatāra* circa 620 or 660, respectively.

There is still another factor to be taken account of, viz. the question of the defining characteristic of the logical reason (*hetu*) characterised as 'the fact of being otherwise inexplicable', or 'inexplicability otherwise' (*anyathânupapannatva, anyathânupapatti*) in NA.22: *anyathânupapannatvaṁ hetor lakṣaṇam īritam*. The author clearly refers to an earlier source and the idea did not originate with him in his NA. Independently, we find the idea reported and criticised by Śāntarakṣita in TSa.(1).1364 ff. (p. 405 f.) in the context of the validity of inference (*anumāna*).[75] The most famous and relatively often quoted verse is TSa.1369:

> *anyathânupapannatvaṁ yatra tatra trayeṇa kim /*
> *nânyathânupapannatvaṁ yatra tatra trayeṇa kim //* [76].

---

[73] See: MOOKERJEE (1935: 4–5): 'What however strikes us is the intriguing situation created by Siddhasena's reference to *antarvyāpti* and the definition of *hetu* (probans) as *anyathānupapanna* in the verse 20 and 22 respectively. It is nothing short of enigma that this innovation of the Jaina logicians did not evoke a reply from Dharmakīrti.'

[74] See: FRAUWALLNER (1961). Cf. also STEINKELLNER–MUCH (1995: 23).

[75] The relevant section is edited and translated in KUNST (1939: 11–53). See also PATHAK (1930–31) 71–83.

[76] Strangely enough, Śāntarakṣita in TSa. interchanges the *pādas* ab with cd. The verse is also found in (1) TŚVA. p. 203 [the discussion of *anyathânupapatti* and the refutation of *tri-lakṣaṇa* is found there on pp. 198–217], (2) TBV. Vol. II, p. 569.28–29, (3) PMī.2.1.9 § 33 (p. 45.17–18). Hemacandra's criticism against the Buddhist idea of *trairūpya* in PMī.2.1.9 § 33 (p. 45.1–16) closely follows the exposition of Pātrasvāmin's aphorisms quoted in TSa. attesting to the authenticity of the quotation. Hemacandra, instead of the terms *anyathânupapatti*, uses the expression *avinā-bhāva*, cf. PMī.2.1.9 (p. 43.34–35):

Significantly enough, Śāntarakṣita TSa.(1).1364, p. 405.1) mentions Pātrasvāmin as the source of the idea: *anyathêty-ādinā pātrasvāmi-matam āśaṅkate* ..., and the treatise in question is the lost *Tri-lakṣaṇa-kadarthana*[77] by Pātrasvāmin, identified occasionally with Pātrakesarin / Pātrakesarisvāmin = Vidyānanda. For obvious reasons this Pātrasvāmin cannot be Vidyānanda (*c.* 850), the author of the *Śloka-vārttika* on Umāsvāti's *Tattvârtha-sūtra*—as SUKHLAL–DOSHI (1928)[78] and CHATTERJEE (1978: 331) would have it—but some else who preceded Śāntarakṣita (*c.* 725–788)[79], the teacher of Kamalaśīla.[80] Since the author of NA. alludes to his predecessors and Śāntarakṣita mentions only Pātrasvāmin, it must have been the latter who was responsible for the idea of *anyathânupapannatva*.[81] Had it been Siddhasena who introduced the idea, Śāntarakṣita would not, in all probability, have missed the opportunity to mention this. Certainly Pātrasvāmin is post-Diṅnāgan, for his *Tri-lakṣaṇa-kadarthana* was conceived to refute the latter, but his dating is quite uncertain. It is surprising, nonetheless, that Śāntarakṣita seems nowhere to allude to

---

*svârthaṁ sva-niścita-sādhyâvinā-bhāvâika-lakṣaṇāt sādhanāt sādhya-jñānam.* The formulation *sādhyâvinā-bhāvâika-lakṣaṇāt* resembles both Pātrasvāmin's *Tri-lakṣaṇa-kadarthana* (*tenâika-lakṣaṇo hetuḥ prādhānyād gamako 'stu naḥ* / = TSa.1379) as well as NA.5ac: *sādhyâvinā-bhuno liṅgāt sādhya-niścāyakaṁ smṛtam / anumānaṁ.*

[77] A reference to the work is found in DHAKY (1995: 43), who refers to Jugal Kishor Mukhtar: 'Saṁmatisūtra aur Siddhasena' (Hindi), *Jaina Sāhitya aur Itihāsa par Viśada Prakāśa*, Calcutta 1956: 538–543 [the work was not available to me].

[78] Cf. UPADHYE (1971: *14–15), PATHAK (1930: *passim*) and PATHAK (1930–31: *passim*), who refers to him as Pātrakesari Vidyānanda or as Pātrakesarisvāmi.

[79] Cf. STEINKELLNER–MUCH (1995: 56).

[80] Cf. BHATTACHARYYA (1926: ixvi-ixvii): 'In that case Pātrasvāmin must be an earlier author than both Śāntarakṣita and Vidyānanda, and he must have first propounded the theory that valid reason is that the existence of which cannot be maintained unless it is invariably concomitant with the major term ... *cir.* 700 A.D.'.

[81] Cf. MUKTHAR (1948) [according to UPADHYE (1971:*30)]: '7) The *Nyāyāvatāra* is composed centuries later than the *Sanmati-sūtra*, because it shows the influence of Pātrasvāmi (later than Samantabhadra) as well as Dharmakīrti and Dharmottara'; and V.P. Johrapurkar ('Introduction' to VTP., pp. 41 ff.) quoted in n. 9 above. See also DHAKY (1995: 42–3): '...the first foot of the *kārikā* 22 concerning the *hetu-lakṣaṇa* (character of probans) reflects sense-agreement, even partial verbal concordance with the verses from Pātrasvāmi's (Pātrakesari's) *Trilakṣaṇakadarthana* cited by the Buddhist scholiast Śāntarakṣita in his *Tattvasaṅgraha* (*c.* 2nd quarter of the 8th century A. D.)[32].' SHASTRI (1990: 31) is a bit more reserved and does not take for granted that Pātrasvāmin was anterior to Siddhasena: 'Nyāyāvatāra also defines hetu in the same manner.'

the NA. or its author. Consequently, the widespread opinion assuming that NA. is the first Jaina treatise on epistemology per se loses its weight, inasmuch we can safely assume that Siddhasena had his predecessor in the person of Pātrasvāmin.

As regards the *terminus ante quem*, in view of the fact that the verse no. 4 of the *Nyāyâvatāra* is incorporated into ṢDSa. as verse no. 56, it should be assigned to the date of Haribhadrasūri. A supposition that it is ṢDSa.56 that was the source which NA.4 was borrowed from and that NA.4 is merely an interpolation seems inadmissible to me. NA.4 fits ideally the argumentative structure of the text: (1) NA.1 states the definition of *pramāṇa*, as well as the types and a general criterion of such a division, (2) NA.2 is polemical concerning the meaninglessness of formulating a definition for a well-known term/idea of *pramāṇa*, (3) NA.3 is a rejoinder to the objection, (4) NA.4 defines the two main divisions of *pramāṇa* along with a specific reason for such a division,[82] (5) NA.5 opens a section dealing with erroneousness of *pramāṇa*s, etc. The use of vocabulary in NA.4 is not unusual for NA. Coincidentally, two adjacent verses, viz. NA.4 and NA.5, are stylistically and structurally quite akin: *pāda* a–b: ⌜reason⌝ (*aparokṣatayā*, *sādhyâvinā-bhuno liṅgāt*) + ⌜object + verbal derivative in the meaning of a present participle⌝ (*arthasya grāhakaṁ*, *sādhya-niścāyakaṁ*) + ... + *pāda* c: ⌜subject⌝ (*pratyakṣam*, *anumānaṁ*) ... Admittedly, the similarity is not a crucial argument in favour of the same authorship of the two verses, however, there is nothing that could speak against a common authorship. The argument gains on strength in view of the fact that Haribhadrasūri quotes the verse no. 2 of NA. in his *Aṣṭaka*[83] and refers to its author as Mahāmati[84].

---

[82] Both NA.1 and 4 go against the prevalent Jaina tradition to subsume cases of sensory cognition, inference and verbal testimony under *parokṣa*, whereas *pratyakṣa* was taken to denote extra-sensory and extra-mental acts of cognition (viz. *avadhi*, *manaḥ-paryāya* and *kevala*). For Siddhasena the criterion of directness (*akṣa*) was not the cognising subject, or the soul (*akṣa*=*jīva*=*ātman*), but—like in the general *pramāṇa* tradition—the senses (*akṣa*=*indriya*).

[83] The work is not available to me. I am forced to rely here on Pt. Dalsukhbhai MALVANIA (1979: 287–288). Cf. also UPADHYE (1971: xxiv) and DHAKY (1995: 44).

[84] UPADHYE (1971: xxiv) is right to point out 'that Haribhadra, in his *Aṣṭaka*, quotes the *Nyāyāvatāra* 2, by referring to its author as Mahāmati. Elsewhere, however Haribhadra speaks plainly about the author of the *Sanmati* as Divākara and Śrutakevalin.'

In view of the above, DHAKY's (1995: 44) claim[85]—to handle the discomfort that Haribhadra himself ascribes one of the verses to a Mahāmati—that both NA.2 and 4 were taken from lost *dvātriṁśikā*s of Siddhasena Divākara is highly debatable to me. Not only NA.4 seems to represent an original *kārikā* of NA., but the same holds good in the case of *kārikā* 2. We could not make head or tail of NA.2 (the objection) if we did not have NA.1. Moreover, NA.3 (the rejoinder) would be pointless without NA.2. All the lost *dvātriṁśikā*s of Siddhasena Divākara as a reference source in argumentation resemble rather a kind of *śaśa-viṣāṇa*. Naturally, as long as we do not have all *dvātriṁśikā*s written by Siddhasena Divākara, we cannot, theoretically speaking, preclude the possibility that the verses indeed were taken from some lost *dvātriṁśikā*. But such an argumentation is not very constructive. I see no reason to doubt the authenticity of *kārikā*s 2 and 4 as long as they form a consistent logical part of the *Nyāyâvatāra* as a whole and bear stylistic similarities to adjacent *kārikā*s,[86] especially when the counter-arguments begin with 'perhaps' and are of merely could-or-may-have-been nature.

Further, the identification of Siddharṣigaṇi as the author of both NA. and NAV., postulated by DHAKY, has very weak foundations. In the first place, there is ample evidence that Siddharṣigaṇi (the author of NAV.) is not Siddhasena (the author of

[85] 'A formidable objection, however, to the above-postulated identification (Siddharṣi was the author of both NA. and NAV.—P.B.) as well as the period determination (ninth/tenth century for NA.—P.B.) can be raised on the grounds of the ascription of a verse, which appears as the *kārikā* 2 of the *Nyāyāvatāra*, to Mahāmati (=Siddhasena Divākara) by Yākinisūnu Haribhadra sūri (active c. A. D. 745–785) in his *Aṣṭaka*[38]. And the *kārikā* 4 figures as a part of the *Ṣaḍdarśana-samuccaya* of the same Haribhadra sūri[39]. Since Haribhadra sūri ascribed the particular verse (*kārikā* 2) to Siddhasena Divākara, it must be so. However, this *kārikā* could be originally from some *dvātriṁśikā*, one of the lost 11 of Siddhasena Divākara, perhaps the *Pramāṇa-dvātriṁśikā*, from which Gandhahasti Siddhasena quotes in his *sa-bhāṣya-Tattvārthādhigama-sūtra-vṛtti*[40]. The *kārikā* 4 in the *Ṣaḍ-darśana-samuccaya* may likewise have been taken from one of the unavailable *dvātriṁśikā* of Siddhasena Divākara. Alternatively, if that verse is Haribhadra's own, Siddharṣi must have borrowed it from the *Ṣaḍdarśana*. In any case, Haribhadra and Siddharṣi could have common sources from which they apparently may have drawn.'

[86] I have dealt briefly with the style of NA.4 above. The same is even more true for NA.2 that is closely followed by NA.3 (the most conspicuous similarities underlined):

/2/ *prasiddhāni pramāṇāni vyavahāraś ca tat-kṛtaḥ* /
*pramāṇa-lakṣaṇasyôktau jñāyate na prayojanam* //
/3/ *prasiddhānāṁ pramāṇānāṁ lakṣaṇôktau prayojanam* /
*tad-vyāmoha-nivṛttiḥ syād vyāmūḍha-manasām iha* //

NA.) and that the two texts were written by different authors, inasmuch as Siddharṣigaṇi refers to the author of NA. explicitly, although not by name, but by the term *ācārya* or *sūtra-kṛt*, to cite a few cases only:[87] [1] Introductory lines of NAV.3: /3/ *adhunâcāryo gṛhītas tāvakīno 'bhiprāyo 'smābhir iti paraṁ pratyāyayaṁs tan-matam anudrāvya tad evânumanyamānas tathâpi lakṣaṇôkteḥ sāphalyam āvedayann āha:* ...; [2] the final sentence of NAV.3: *tad evaṁ pramāṇa-lakṣaṇaṁ sāmānyena pratipādya tad-gataṁ kucodyaṁ paryahāry ācāryeṇa*; [3] NAV.13: *yad vâtyantâbhyāsena parikarmita-matitvāt tāvatâiva prastuta-prameyam avabudhyate, tadā hetu-pratipādanam eva kriyate, śeṣâbhidhānasya śrotṛ-saṁskārâkāritayā nairarthakyād ity-ādau hetu-pratipādanaṁ sūtra-kṛtā parârtham anumānam uktam*; [4] NAV.29: *ata evâcāryasya na tal-lakṣaṇâdi-svarūpa-kathane 'pi mahânādaraḥ*. Additionally, in some cases (e.g. on NA.8), Siddharṣigaṇi does offer at least two different interpretations of a *kārikā*, or diverges from the contents of NA., e.g. in the case of NA.4d[88].

Thus, we can safely take the date-brackets for the *Nyāyâvatāra* to be firmly fixed after 620 C.E. (Dharmakīrti) and Pātrasvāmin and before *c.* 800 C.E. (Haribhadrasūri).[89] As for the date of Haribhadrasūri, JACOBI (1926: *Introduction*) assigns Haribhadra to *c.* 750, whereas UPADHYE (1971: xxv) to *c.* 750–800 C.E. and DHAKY (1995: 44) to *c.* 745–785. However, the *terminus post quem* for Haribhadra is Arcaṭa, since the latter is quoted in Haribhadrasūri's NPV.9.15–19[90]. Arcaṭa, the teacher of Dharmottara, can be assigned to *c.* 730–790 or 720–780.[91]

[87] DHAKY (1995: 43) is so far right that indeed Siddharṣi nowhere mentions the author of *Nyāyâvatāra* by name: 'As noted in the beginning, Siddharṣi does not ascribe the *Nyāyāvatāra* to Siddhasena Divākara or to a different Siddhasena or for that matter to any other author.' However, he clearly misses the point when he further claims: 'Nor does he mention it as a composition of a *pūrvācārya*, *vṛddhācārya*, or some *cirantanācārya*. Also, in his verse by verse exposition, he nowhere uses qualificatory phrases such as *śāstrakāra*, *sūtrakāra*, *kārikākāra*, *ācārya*, etc. which may have denoted a second, an earlier revered personage, as the *kārikās'* author.'

[88] Siddhasena emphasises the way of cognising, or '[the manner of] grasping [an object]', whereas Siddharṣi takes the expression to refer to the existence and the nature of the cognoscible. See p. 323 above.

[89] Thus, I cannot but side with the opinion already expressed in VAIDYA (1928: xx): 'The *terminus a quo* would be the date of Dharmakīrti and the *terminus ad quem* that of Haribhadra.'

[90] Acc. to STEINKELLNER–MUCH (1995: 119) the original title found to the colophon is *Nyāya-praveśa-ṭīkā śiṣya-hitā*.

[91] See: STEINKELLNER–MUCH (1995: 64) and FRAUWALLNER (1961: 148).

## BIBLIOGRAPHY


AJP. = Haribhadra Sūri: *Anekānta-jaya-patākā*. Ed. *with his own commentary and Municandra Sūri's supercommentary*. Vol. 1 & 2, Ed. H.R. Kāpadīā, *Gaekwad's Oriental Series* 88, 105, Oriental Institute, Baroda 1940, 1947.

BALCEROWICZ 1995 = Balcerowicz, Piotr: 'Śaṅkarasvāmin: *Nyāya-praveśa*—"Wprowadzenie w logikę" ("Introduction to Logic").' Part One: *I. Polish Translation, II. Sanskrit Text, III. Notes § 1, Abbreviations and Bibliography*. *Studia Indologiczne* (Warsaw) 2 (1995) 39–87.

BALCEROWICZ 1999 = Balcerowicz, Piotr: 'Taxonomic approach to *dṛṣṭântâbhāsa* in *Nyāya-bindu* and in Siddharṣigaṇi's *Nyāyâvatāra-vivṛti*—Dharmakīrti's typology and the Jaina criticism thereof.' In: *Dharmakīrti's Thought and Its Impact on Indian and Tibetan Philosophy (Proceedings of the Third International Dharmakīrti Conference—Hiroshima, November 4–6, 1997)*. Ed. Shoryu Katsura, Verlag der Österreichischen Akademie der Wissenschaften: *Beiträge zur Kultur- und Geistesgeschichte Asiens* Nr. 32, Wien 1999: 1–16.

BALCEROWICZ 2001 = Balcerowicz, Piotr: 'Two Siddhasenas and the Authorship of the *Nyāyâvatāra* and the *Saṁmati-tarka-prakaraṇa*'. *Journal of Indian Philosophy* 29/3 (2001) 351–578.

BALCEROWICZ (forthcoming) = Balcerowicz, Piotr: 'On the Relationship of the *Nyāyâvatāra* and the *Saṁmati-tarka-prakaraṇa*.' Presented at *the XIth World Sanskrit Conference*, Turin, April 3rd–8th, 2000; forthcoming.

BHATTACHARYYA 1926 = Bhattacharyya, B.: 'Foreword' to TSa.(1).i-cxvii.

BSŚBh. = Śaṅkara: *Brahma-sūtra-śāṅkara-bhāṣya*. Ed. with the commentaries: *Bhāṣya-ratna-prabha* of Govindānanda, *Bhāmatī* of Vācaspatimiśra, *Nyāya-nirṇaya* of Ānandagiri; ed. by J.L. Shastri, Motilal Banarsidass, Delhi 1980. [Reprinted: Delhi 1988].

CHATTERJEE 1978 = Chatterjee, Asim Kumar: *A Comprehensive History of Jainism (up to 1000 A.D.)*, Firma KLM Private Ltd., Calcutta 1978.

DAVE 1962 = Dave, P.N.: *Siddhasena Divākara: A Study*. A Thesis submitted to the University of Bombay for the Ph.D. degree, September 1962. [After UPADHYE (1971:*51)].

DHAKY 1981–82 = Dhaky, M.A.: 'Some less known verses of Siddhasena Divākara.' *Sambodhi* 10 (1981–82) 169–173.

DHAKY 1990 = Dhaky, M.A.: 'The Date and Authorship of Nyāyāvatāra.' A typescript of a paper—presented to me by the author in 1990—prepared for publication in *B.K. Thapar Felicitation Volume* [the edition was not available to me].

DHAKY 1995 = Dhaky, M.A.: 'The Date and Authorship of Nyāyāvatāra.' *Nirgrantha* (Ahmedabad, eds. M.A. Dhaky, Jitendra Shah) 1 (1995) 39–49.

DhPr. = *Paṇḍita Durveka Miśra*'s *Dharmottara-pradīpa* [*being a subcommentary on Dharmottara's Nyāya-bindu-ṭīkā, a commentary on Dharmakīrti's Nyāya-bindu*], Ed. by Pt. Dalsukhbhai Malvania, Kashi Prasad Jayaswal, Research Institute, Patna 1971.

FRANCO 1987 = Franco, Eli: *Perception, knowledge and disbelief: a study of Jayarāśi's scepticism. Alt- und Neu-Indische Studien* 35, Franz Steiner Verlag, Stuttgart 1987. [Reprinted: Motilal Banarsidass, Delhi 1994].

FRANCO 1997 = Franco, Eli: *Dharmakīrti on Compassion and Rebirth. Wiener Studien zur Tibetologie und Buddhismuskunde* 38, Wien 1997.

FRAUWALLNER 1933 = Frauwallner, Erich: 'Zu den Fragmenten buddhistischer Logiker im Nyāyavārttikam.' *Wiener Zeitschrift für die Kunde Morgenlandes* 40 (1933) 300–304. [Reprinted: FRAUWALLNER (1982: 479–483)].

FRAUWALLNER 1957/a = Frauwallner, Erich: 'Vasubandhu's Vādaviddhi.' *Wiener Zeitschrift für die Kunde Morgenlandes* (1957) 104–146. [Reprinted: FRAUWALLNER (1982: 716–758)].

FRAUWALLNER 1957/b = Frauwallner, Erich: 'Review of R. Sāṅkṛtyāyana's Edition of the *Pramāṇavārtikabhāṣya*.' *Journal of the American Oriental Society* (1957) 58–60. [Reprinted: FRAUWALLNER (1982: 883–885)].

FRAUWALLNER 1961 = Frauwallner, Erich: 'Landmarks in the History of Indian Logic.' *Wiener Zeitschrift für die Kunde Süd- und Ostasiens* 5 (1961) 125–148.

FRAUWALLNER 1982 = Frauwallner, Erich: *Kleine Schriften*. Hrsg. von Gerhard Oberhammer und Ernst Steinkellner, Glassenapp-Stiftung 22, Franz Steiner Verlag, Wiesbaden 1982.

GRANOFF 1989–1990 = Granoff, Phyllis: 'The Bibliographies of Siddhasena—A Study in the Texture of Allusion and the Weaving of a Group Image.' Part I: *Journal of Indian Philosophy* 17 (1989) 329–384. Part II: *Journal of Indian Philosophy* 18 (1990) 261–304.

HATTORI 1968 = Hattori, Masaaki: *Dignāga, On Perception, being the Pratyakṣa-pariccheda of Dignāga's Pramāṇa-samuccaya*, edition of Tibetan translations and the Sanskrit text as well as the English translation of the Chapter I. Harvard University Press 1968.

HB. = Steinkellner, Ernst: *Dharmakīrti's Hetubinduḥ. Teil I: Tibetischer Text und rekonstruierter Sanskrit-Text; Teil II: Übersetzung und Anmerkungen. Veröffentlichungen der Kommission für Sprachen und Kulturen Süd- und Ostasiens* 4, 5; Wien 1967.

JACOBI 1926 = Jacobi, Hermann: 'Introduction and Contents' to *Haribhadra: Samarāïcca-kahā—A Jaina Prakṛta Work*. Volume I: Text and Introduction, *Bibliotheca Indica*, Calcutta 1926: i-cxxx.

KIMURA 1997 = Kimura, Toshihiko: 'New Chronology of Dharmakīrti', in: In: *Dharmakīrti's Thought and Its Impact on Indian and Tibetan Philosophy (Proceedings of the Third International Dharmakīrti Conference—Hiroshima, November 4–6, 1997)*. Ed. by Shoryu

Katsura, Verlag der Österreichischen Akademie der Wissenschaften: *Beiträge zur Kultur- und Geistesgeschichte Asiens* Nr. 32, Wien 1999: 209–214.

KRAUSE 1948 = Krause, Charlotte: 'Siddhasena and Vikramāditya.' *Vikrama Volume*, Scindia Oriental Institute, Ujjain 1948: 213–280.

KUNST 1939 = Kunst, Arnold: *Probleme der buddhistischen Logik in der Darstellung des Tattvasaṅgraha* (*Zagadnienia logiki buddyjskiej według Tattvasangrahy Siantarakszity*). Polska Akademia Umiejętności, *Mémoires de la Commission Orientaliste* 33, Kraków 1939.

MALVANIA 1979 = Pt. Dalsukhbhai Malvania: 'Pariśiṣṭa 1, *Nyāyāvatara kī Tulanā*'. 1979.

MATILAL 1985 = Matilal, Bimal Krishna: *Logic, Language and Reality: Indian Philosophy and Contemporary Issues*. Motilal Banarsidass, Delhi 1985.

MAV. = Asaṅga (Maitreyanātha?): *Madhyânta-vibhāga[-sūtra]*; ed. by Nathmal Tatia and Anantalal Thakur with Vasubandhu's *Bhāṣya*, *Tibetan Sanskrit Works Series* 10, K.P. Jayaswal Research Institute, Patna 1967.

MAVBh. = Vasubandhu: *Madhyânta-vibhāga-bhāṣya*. See: MAV.

Met. = *Aristotelis Metaphysica*. Ed. W. Jaeger, *Scriptorum Classicorum, Bibliotheca Oxoniensis*, Oxford University Press, London 1957.

MOOKERJEE 1935 = Mookerjee, Satkari: *The Buddhist Philosophy of Universal Flux – An Exposition of the Philosophy of Critical Realism as Expounded by the School of Dignāga*. Motilal Banarsidass, Delhi 1993. [First edition: University of Calcutta, 1935].

MOOKERJEE 1971 = Mookerjee, Satkari: 'A critical and comparative study of Jain Logic and Epistemology on the basis of the *Nyāyâvatāra* of Siddhasena Divākara.' *Vaishali Institute Research Bulletin* 1, Vaishali 1971.

MSA. = Asaṅga (Maitreyanātha?): *Mahāyāna-sūtrâlaṅkāra*. (1) Ed. Sylvain Lévi, Paris 1907. (2) Ed. and transl. Surekha Vijay Limaye, *BIBS* 94, Sri Satguru Publications / Indian Books Centre, Delhi 1992.

MŚV. = Kumārila Bhaṭṭa: *Mīmāṁsā-śloka-vārttika*. *Ślokavārttika of Śrī Kumārila Bhaṭṭa with the Commentary Nyāya-ratnâkara of Śrī Pārthasārathi Miśra*. Ed. Dvārikādāsa Śāstrī, *Ratnabharati Series* 3, Tārā Publications, Varanasi 1978.

MUKTHAR 1948 = Mukthar, Jugalkishore: 'Sanmati Siddhasenāṅka.' *Anekānta*, IX.11–2, December 1948; reprinted in the Introduction of the *Purātana-Jaina-Vākya-sūcī*, Delhi 1950. Included in his *Jaina Sāhitya aura Itihāsapara Viśada-prakāśa*, Part I, Delhi 1956; its English Translation (by A.N. Upadhye): *Sanmati-sūtra and Siddhasena*, Virasewamandira Trust, Delhi 1965. [After UPADHYE (1971:*25)].

NA. = Siddhasena Divākara: *Nyāyâvatāra*. (1) Ed. with Siddharṣigaṇi's *Vivṛti* and Devabhadra's *Ṭippana*, by Bhagavandas Harakhchand; Ahmedabad–Patan 1917. (2) Ed. with Siddharṣigaṇi's *Vivṛti* and Devabhadra's *Ṭippana*, by P.L. Vaidya, Shri Jain Shwetamber Conference, Bombay 1928. [Reprinted in *Vaishali Institute Research Bulletin* 1, Vaishali 1971: 1–95].

NASV. = *Nyāyâvatāra-sūtra-vārttika of Śrī Śānti Sūri critically edited in Sanskrit with notes, indices etc. in Hindi* [with the *Vṛtti*] by Dalsukh Malvania, published by Singhi Jain Śastra Śikshapitha, Bharatiya Vidya Bhavan, Bombay 1949.

NAṬ. = Devabhadra's *Nyāyâvatāra-ṭippana*. See: NA.

NAV. = Siddharṣigaṇi: *Nyāyâvatāra-vivṛti*. See: NA.

NAVV. = Śrī Śānti Sūri: *Nyāyâvatāra-vārttika-vṛtti*. See: NASV.

NB. = Dharmakīrti: *Nyāya-bindu*. See: DhPr.

NBh. = Vātsyāyana Pakṣilasvāmin: *Nyāya-bhāṣya*. See: NS.

NBṬ. = Dharmottara: *Nyāya-bindu-ṭīkā*. See: DhPr.

NM. = *Nyāya-mukha* of Dignāga. Ed. Giuseppe Tucci, Heidelberg 1930.

NP. = Śaṅkarasvāmin: *Nyāya-praveśa*. (1) [Part One:] *Nyāya-praveśa* of Diṅnāga with Commentaries of Haribhadra Suri & Parsavadeva' ed. by A.B. Dhruva, Oriental Institute, Baroda 1930. (2) See: BALCEROWICZ (1995: 72–77).

NPV. = Haribhadrasūri: *Nyāya-praveśa-vṛtti*. See: NP.(1).

NS. = Akṣapāda Gautama: *Nyāya-sūtra*. *Mahāmuni Vātsyāyan's Nyāya-bhāṣya on Gautama-Nyāya-sutras . With Prasannapadā Commentary of Pt. Sudarśanācārya Shastrī*. Ed. Dvārikādāsa Śāstrī, *SS* 10, Sudhī Prakāśanam, Vārāṇasī 1986.

NV. = Uddyotakara: *Nyāya-vārttika*. *Nyāya-darśana (= Nyāya-sūtra) with Vātsyāyana's Bhāṣya, Uddyotakara's Vārttika, Vācaspati Miśra's Tātparyaṭīkā and Viśvanātha's Vṛtti*. ed. by Taranatha Nyaya-Tarkatirtha and Amarendramohan Tarkatirtha, *Kalikātā-saṁskṛta-grantha-mālā* 18, Calcutta 1936.

PATHAK 1930 = K.B. Pathak: 'Śāntarakṣita's reference to Kumārila's Attacks on Samantabhadra and Akalaṅkadeva.' *Annals of the Bhandarkar Oriental Research Institute* 11 (1930) 155–164.

PATHAK 1930–31 = K.B. Pathak: 'Dharmakīrti's Trilakṣaṇahetu attacked by Pātrakesari and defended by Śāntarakṣita.' *Annals of the Bhandarkar Oriental Research Institute* 12 (1930–31) 71–83.

PBh. = Praśastapāda: *Praśastapāda-bhāṣya*. Bronkhorst, Johannes and Ramseier, Yves: *Word index to the Praśastapādabhāṣya: a complete word index to the printed editions of the Praśastapādabhāṣya*; Motilal Banarsidass, Delhi 1994.

PMī. = Hemacandra: *Pramāṇa-mīmāṁsā*. Ed. and trans. by Satkari Mookerjee and Nathmal Tatia, Tārā Publications, Varanasi 1970.

PS. = Diṅnāga: *Pramāṇa-samuccaya*. (1) Chapter I, see: HATTORI (1968). (2) *The Tibetan Tripitaka—Peking Edition*, ed. Daisetz T. Suzuki, Tibetan Tripitaka Research Institute, Tokyo—Kyoto 1957—*Bstan-ḥgyur, Mdo-ḥgrel, Gtan-Tshogs Rig-pa* I, Vol. 130, No.5700.

PV. = *The Pramāṇa-vārttikam of Ācārya Dharmakīrti with Sub-commentaries: Svôpajña-vṛtti of the Author and Pramāṇa-vārttika-vṛtti of Manorathanandin*. Ed. by Prof. Dr. Ram Chandra Pandeya, Motilal Banarsidass, Delhi 1989.

PVin.I(1) = *Dharmakīrti's Pramāṇaviniścayaḥ, 1. Kapitel: pratyakṣaṁ*. Hrsg. und übers. von T. Vetter. *Veröffentlichungen der Kommission für Sprachen und Kulturen Süd- und Ostasiens* Heft 3, Österreichische Akademie der Wissenschaften, Wien 1966.

PVin.II(1) = *Dharmakīrti's Pramāṇāviniścayaḥ, 2. Kapitel: Svārthānumānaṁ*. Tib. Text und Sanskrittexte von Ernst Steinkellner. *Veröffentlichungen der Kommission für Sprachen und Kulturen Süd- und Ostasiens* 12, Österreichische Akademie der Wissenschaften, Wien 1973.

PVin.II(2) = *Dharmakīrti's Pramāṇāviniścayaḥ, 2. Kapitel: Svārthānumānaṁ*. übers. von Ernst Steinkellner. *Veröffentlichungen der Kommission für Sprachen und Kulturen Süd- und Ostasiens* 15, Österreichische Akademie der Wissenschaften, Wien 1979.

PVSV. = Dharmakīrti: *Pramāṇa-vārttika-svôpajña-vṛtti*. See: PV.

PVV. = Manorathanandin: *Pramāṇa-vārttika-vṛtti*. See: PV.

QVARNSTRÖM 1999 = Qvarnström, Olle: 'Haribhadra and the Beginnings of Doxography in India.' In: *Approaches to Jaina Studies: Philosophy, Logic, Rituals and Symbols* [Proceedings of the International Conference on Approaches to Jaina Studies: Philosophy, Logic, Rituals and Symbols, 31.03–2.04.1995 Toronto]. Ed. by N.K. Wagle and Olle Qvarnström, *South Asian Studies Papers* 11, University of Toronto: Centre for South Asian Studies, Toronto 1999: 169–210.

RANDLE 1926 = Randle, H.N.: *Fragments from Dignāga*. Prize Publication Fund, Royal Asiatic Society, London 1926. [Reprinted: Motilal Banarsidass, Delhi 1981].

SacAcBh. = Asaṅga: *Sacittikā Acittikā ca Bhūmiḥ* [A Section of *Yogācāra-bhūmi*]. (1) Wayman, Alex (Ed.): 'The *Saccittikā* And *Acittikā Bhūmi*—Text and Translation.' In: *Buddhist Insight—Essays by Alex Wayman*. Ed. with an Introduction by George Elder, *Buddhist Tradition Series* VII, Delhi 1984. [Reprinted Motilal Banarsidass, Delhi 1990; 1st ed.: *Journal of Indian and Buddhist Studies* (Tokyo) 7/1 (1960) 375–379]. (2) See: SCHMITHAUSEN (1987: 220–2, 'Appendix I').

SCHMITHAUSEN 1987 = Schmithausen, Lambert: *Ālayavijñāna—On the Origin and the Early Development of a Central Concept of Yogācāra Philosophy.* Part I: Text, Part II: Notes, Bibliography and Indices. *Studia Philologica Buddhica, Tokyo* IVa/IVb, The International Institute for Buddhist Studies, Tokyo 1987.

ṢDSa. = Haribhadrasūri: *Ṣaḍ-darśana-samuccaya.* Ed. with the Commentaries of *Tarka-rahasya-dipikā* of Guṇaratnasūri and *Laghuvṛtti* of Somatilaka Sūri and an *Avacūrṇi*; by Mahendra Kumar Jain, with the Introduction of Pt. Dalsukh Malvania, JMJG-SG 36, Benares 1981.

SHASTRI 1990 = Shastri, Indra Chandra: *Jaina Epistemology. P. V. Research Series* No. 50, P. V. Research Institute, Varanasi 1990.

STEINKELLNER–KRASSER 1989 = Steinkellner, Ernst; Krasser, Helmut: *Dharmottaras Exkurs zur Definition gültiger Erkenntnis im Pramāṇa-viniścaya. Beiträge zur Kultur- und Geistesgeschichte Asiens* No.2, Österreichische Akademie der Wissenschaften, Wien 1989.

STEINKELLNER–MUCH 1995 = Steinkellner, Ernst; Much, Michael Torsten: *Texte der erkenntnistheoretischen Schule des Buddhismus—Systematische Übersicht über die buddhistische Sanskrit-Literatur II. Abh. der Akad. der Wissenschaften in Göttingen, Philologisch-Historische Klasse*, Dritte Folge 214, Vandenhoeck & Ruprecht, Göttingen 1995.

SUKHLAL 1945/a = Pt. Sukhlalji Sanghavi: 'Pratibhāmūrti Siddhasena Divākara.' *Bhāratīya Vidyā*, III.i, Bombay 1945: 9–20 (in Hindi) [See: UPADHYE (1971:*18)].

SUKHLAL 1945/b = Pt. Sukhlalji Sanghavi: 'Śrī Siddhasena Divākarano Samayano Praśna.' *Bhāratīya Vidyā*, III, Bombay 1945: 152 f. (in Gujarati) [See: UPADHYE (1971:*21)].

SUKHLAL–DOSHI 1928 = Pt. Sukhlalji Sanghavi; Bechardas Doshi: '*Sanmati-tarka* and its Importance.' *Jaina Silver Jubilee Number*, Bhavnagar 1928 (Saṁ. 1985): 109–121 (in Gujarati) [After UPADHYE (1971:*12)].

TABER 1994 = Taber, A. John: 'Kumārila's Refutation of the Dreaming Argument: the *Nirālambanavāda-adhikaraṇa.*' In: *Studies in Mīmāṁsā—Dr. Mandan Mishra Felicitation Volume.* Ed. R.C. Dwivedi, Motilal Banarsidass, Delhi 1994: 27–52.

TBh. = Umāsvāti: *Tattvârthâdhigama-bhāṣya.* See TS.

TBV. = Abhayadevasūri's *Tattva-bodha-vidhāyinī* on Siddhasena Divākara's *Saṁmati-tarka-prakaraṇa.* Ed. by Sukhlāl Saṅghavi and Becardās Dośi; Vol. I & II, *Rinsen Buddhist Text Series* VI 1,2; Kyoto 1984. [Reprinted from the original edition published in 5 Vols., *Gujarāt-purā-tattva-mandir-granthāvalī* 10, 16, 18, 19, 21, Gujarāt-purā-tattva-mandir, Amdāvād, 1924–1931].

TILLEMANS 1997 = Tillemans, Tom J.F.: 'Dharmakīrti on *prasiddha* and *yogyatā*.' In: *Aspects of Buddhism: Proceedings of the International Seminar on Buddhist Studies, Liw, 25 June 1994*, eds.: Agata Bareja Starzyńska, Marek Mejor = *Studia Indologiczne* (Warszawa) 4 (1997) 177–194.

Triṁś. = Vasubandhu: *Triṁśikā-vijñapti-kārikā*. See: VMS.

TS. = Umāsvāmin: *Tattvârtha-sūtra*. Ed. together with *Tattvârthâdhigama-bhāṣya* by M.K. Mody, *BI* No.1044, Calcutta 1903–5.

TSa. = Śāntarakṣita's *Tattva-saṅgraha* together with Kamalaśīla's *Pañjikā*. Ed. by Embar Krishnamacharya with a Foreword by B. Bhattacharyya, 2 Vols., *Gaekwad's Oriental Series* 30–31, Baroda 1926. [Reprinted: 1984].

TSaP. = Kamalaśīla: *Tattva-saṅgraha-pañjikā*. See: TSa.

TŚVA. = Vidyānanda Pātrakesarisvāmin: *Tattvârtha-śloka-vārtikâlaṁkara*. Ed. by Manoharalāl, Ramacandra Nātha Raṅgaji, Bombay 1918.

UPADHYE 1971 = Upadhye, A.N.: *Siddhasena Divākara's Nyāyāvatāra (edited by the late S.C. Vidyabhusan with English Translation, Notes etc.) and with the Vivṛti of Siddharṣi as well as The Text of 21 Dvātriṁśikās and the Sammaï-suttam; Vinayavijaya's Nayakarṇikā edited by … with an Introduction, Bibliographic Review, Indices etc.*; Jaina Sāhitya Vikāsa Maṇḍala, Bombay 1971.

VAIDYA 1928 = Vaidya, P.L.: 'Introduction' to *Nyāyâvatāra*. See: NA (2): vii-xliii.

Viṁś. = Vasubandhu: *Viṁśatikā*. See: VMS.

VMS. = Vasubandhu: *Vijñapti-mātratā-siddhi* (*Viṁśatikā* and *Triṁsikā*). *Deux traités de* Vasubandhu, *Viṁśatikā et Triṁśikā, 1 Partie—Texte, Sthiramati's Bhāṣya*. Ed. by Sylvain Lévi, *Bibliothèque de l'École des Hautes Études*, Paris 1925.

VS. = *The Vaiśeṣika-sūtra of Kaṇāda with the Commentary of Candrānanda*. Ed. Muni Jambūvijayaji, *GOS* 136, Baroda 1961.

VTP. = Bhāvasena: *Viśva-tattva-prakāśa*. Ed. by Vidyadhara Pasusa Johrapurkar, *Jīvarāja Jaina Granthamālā*, Sholapur 1964.

WAYMAN 1996 = Wayman, Alex: 'The Nyāyāvatāra and Buddhist Logical Works by Dignāga and Ratnākaraśānti.' *Nirgrantha* 2 (1996) 1–8, eds. M.A. Dhaky, Jitendra Shah, Ahmedabad.

WILLIAMS 1963 = Williams, Richard: *Jaina Yoga*. *London Oriental Series* 14, New York–Toronto 1963.

# Rationality as a Method of Research into the Nyāya System

JONARDON GANERI

One of the many enduring achievements of STANISŁAW SCHAYER was his introduction of the methods of contemporary logical theory into the study of Indian logic. In his celebrated paper of 1933, 'Über die Methode der Nyāya-Forschung', SCHAYER recognised that philological and historical methods for investigating the Nyāya system have to be supplemented with techniques of analysis drawn from logic. His source for new instruments of theoretical analysis came from the example provided by Łukasiewicz, who had already reinterpreted the Aristotelian syllogistic as a system of formal deduction. SCHAYER consequently attempted to study the Nyāya system as if it were a formal logic. Since SCHAYER, the potentialities as well as the limits of this approach have gradually become clear. What I would like to suggest in this paper is that formal validity is too restricted a concept to do justice to the nature of the Naiyāyikas' philosophical project. I want to suggest that we might do better if we take as our operative concept the concept of rationality, and interpret the Nyāya system as if it were a theory of what constitutes rational belief. I will illustrate my point by examining the model of rationality that is implicit in the concept of an 'example' (*udāharaṇa*) in early Nyāya logical theory.

## 1. Rationality and extrapolation

The capacity to extrapolate from what one has perceived to what one has not is a core function of reason. That extrapolation is a key concept in the early history of Indian logic is clear from some of the examples Vātsyāyana gives under NS 1.1.5 (*Nyāya-bhāṣya* 12.7–16[1]). Seeing a rising cloud, one infers that it will rain; or the variant: seeing the ants carrying their eggs, one infers that it will rain. Seeing a full and swiftly flowing river, one infers that it has been raining. Seeing a cloud of smoke, one infers the existence of an unseen fire. Hearing a cry, one infers that a peacock is nearby. Seeing the moon at one place at one time and at another place at

[1] References are to page and line numbers in THAKUR (1997).

*Essays in Indian Philosophy, Religion and Literature*, pp. 353–361.

another time, one infers that it is moving (even though one cannot *see* it move). Caraka (*Caraka-saṁhitā*: *Sūtra-sthāna* 11.13–14) has some other examples: inferring impregnation from pregnancy; inferring the future appearance of fruit from the presence of seeds. In the *Upāya-hṛdaya*[2], we also find: inferring from a child's special mark that this person is that child, now grown up; inferring from the salty taste of one drop of sea water that the whole sea is salty. The *Ts'ing-mu* (TUCCI (1929: xvii–xviii)) has a similar example: inferring that all the rice is cooked on tasting one grain. And the *Vaiśeṣika-sūtra*[3] mentions another sort of extrapolation—the inference of an entire cow from the perception only of its horns.

Extrapolation from the seen to the unseen can take place in any of the three dimensions of time—past, present and future. Our interest is in the Indian theory of rationality, and for this we want to look at answers given to the question: on what basis, if any, ought the extrapolation be made? For while dice-throwing, guesswork and divination are ways of extrapolating, they are not rational ones. Extrapolation must be done 'on the basis of reasons,' and a theory of 'reasons' is a theory of what makes an extrapolation warranted. So we discover the Indian theories of rationality in their explanations of why the extrapolations in the examples mentioned above are warranted. Rationality here is the search for extrapolative license.

Vātsyāyana says only that there should be a *connection* between what is seen and what is inferred (*Nyāya-bhāṣya* 12.4). Certainly, many of the early writers have a definite interest in prediction and scientific explanation, and assume that extrapolation is warranted when underwritten by a causal relation. On the other hand, it is clearly recognised that not all warranted extrapolation is causal. The *Vaiśeṣika-sūtra* lists, in addition, the relations of contact, inherence, coinherence in a third, and being contrary [3.1.8, 9.18], while the *Ṣaṣṭi-tantra*, an early Sāṁkhya text, has a partially overlapping list of seven relations.[4] Take the inference from a drop of salty sea water to the conclusion that the whole sea is salty. This is not an inference based on any causal relation between the drop of sea water and the sea as a whole; rather, the relation between them is mereological. I shall claim that it is what would now be called an inference from sampling, where a 'typical' member of a group is taken to have properties representative of the rest. This is a very common

---

[2] *Upāya-hṛdaya* or *Prayoga-sāra*, see TUCCI (1929).

[3] *Vaiśeṣika-sūtra* 2.1.8: 'It has horns, a hump, a tail hairy at the extreme and a dewlap—such is the perceived mark of cowness.'

[4] The relations of master to property, matter to its altered condition, cause to effect, efficient cause to caused, matter to form, concurrent occurrence, and hindering to hindered. E. FRAUWALLNER (1958: 84–139, esp. 123, 126–7). See also Nancy SCHUSTER (1972: 341–395).

and useful form of reasoning—witness the example of checking that all the rice is cooked by tasting a single grain! It is not formally valid, but it is a pervasive and powerful species of informal reasoning. An 'example' is now to be thought of as a typical sample, a thing whose properties can be taken as a guide to the properties of every other thing of the same kind. It has other functions too, as we will now see.

## 2. Rationality and debate

H.N. RANDLE (1930: 148) observed a long time ago that 'the Naiyāyika was from first to last a *tārkika*, a disputant.' More recently, B. K. MATILAL (1998: 32) has called debate the 'preferred form of rationality' in classical India. There is a good deal of truth in these observations. A sophisticated theory of rationality evolved in the debating arenas. Kauṭilya had already observed that rationality is about the best means to an end, and the end of the debater is to win. But what counts as winning a debate? If the debate is the victory-at-any-cost sort (*jalpa*), and a debater wins when his opponent is lost for words or confused or hesitant, then the best and so most rational way to proceed would be to employ such tricks as play on the opponent's weaknesses: speaking very quickly or using convoluted examples or referring to doctrines of which one suspects one's opponent is ignorant. In the other sort of debate, the truth-directed sort (*vāda*), 'winning' is a matter of persuading one's opponent and also an impartial audience that one's thesis is true, and the rational debater must find some other methods. The debating room is a theatre for the art of persuasion. It is a metaphor for any situation in which one wants to persuade others of the correctness of one's point of view. It will include by extension both the mundane situation of persuading one's walking companion that something is about to happen, and the refined situation of convincing a scientific community that one's hypothesis is true. The model of rationality which comes out of the theory of debate is that of persuasion in accordance with public norms of correctness. Nothing is more persuasive than an argument backed up by well-chosen examples and illustrations. And so, when the Naiyāyikas came to codify the form of rational debating demonstration, the citation of examples was given at least as much prominence as the citation of reasons, and what constitutes an example came to be a matter of what was adduced by publicly acceptable criteria to be a representative sample of its kind.

The proper way to formulate one's position is in accordance with a 'five-limbed' schema: tentative statement of the thesis to be proved; citation of a reason; mention of an example; application of reason and example to the case in hand; final assertion of the thesis [1.1.32]. Suppose I want to persuade my companion that it is about to rain. I might reason as follows: 'Look, it is going to rain. For see that large black cloud. Last time you saw a large black cloud like that one, what happened? Well, its the same now. It is definitely going to rain.' In order to be able to generalise the structure of such patterns of reasoning, the Naiyāyikas make an important simplifying assumption. They assume that the underlying pattern is one of property-substitution. The claim is that all such patterns exemplify the same canonical form: *Fa* because *Ka*. An object (the *pakṣa*, or locus of the inference) is inferred to have a property (the *sādhya*, or to-be-proved) on the grounds that it has some other property (the *hetu*, or reason). The simplification, then, is to think of reasoning as taking us from an object's having one property to that same object's having another.

This simplification scarcely seems justified. A cursory inspection of the cases mentioned at the beginning of the last section shows that only about half fit such a pattern. The cases of the swollen river, the ants, the peacock's cry, the fruit and the salty sea do not seem to fit at all. The canonical schema seems to fit the case of the moon, the pregnancy, and the child's special mark, but it is only at a stretch that one can force the case of smoke and fire into the pattern (an irony as this is a hackneyed example which all the logical texts quote). Bearing in mind the ways in which Indian logic was later to develop, one can be forgiven for feeling that this adoption of a property-substitution model at an early stage, while perhaps a helpful and necessary simplification for the sake of initial progress, eventually came to be more of a straight-jacket, and to some degree stifled the study of other patterns of inferential reasoning.

What licences an inference? The *Nyāya-sūtra* answer is given in five brief and controversial aphorisms [1.1.34–38]:

> *udāharaṇa-sādharmyāt sādhya-sādhanaṁ hetuḥ.*
> *tathā vaidharmyāt.*
> *sādhya-sādharmyāt tad-dharma-bhāvī dṛṣṭânta udāharaṇam.*
> *tad-viparyayād vā viparītam.*
> *udāharaṇâpekṣas tathêty upasaṁhāro na tathêti vā sādhyasyôpanayaḥ.*

> 'A reason is that which proves what is to be proved through [its] being like an example.
> Again, through being unalike.
> An example is an observed instance which, being like what is to be proved, possesses its property.
> Or else, being opposite, is opposite.
> The application is an assimilation to what is to be proved "this is thus" or "this is not thus" depending on the example.'

Likeness is property-relative. Something is 'like' another thing if both share a property. They are unalike if they do not both share it. Now arguably the natural way to interpret these *sūtra*s is as follows. Either the locus of the inference is like the example (in that both possess the reason property) and, since the example has the to-be-proved property, so does the locus. Or else the locus of the inference is unlike the example (it possesses the reason-property but the example does not), and since the example *does not* have the to-be-proved property, the locus *does* have it. If we let '*b*' stand for the example, then we seem to have:

| | |
|---|---|
| $a$ is like$_K$ $b$ | $a$ is unlike$_K$ $b$ |
| $Fb$ | $\sim Fb$ |
| $\therefore Fa$ | $\therefore Fa$ |

This formulation actually makes the inference a generalisation of the inference from sampling we have already seen. The example is a typical member of the class of things having the reason-property. And it has this other property, the to-be-inferred property. But the locus of the inference is also a member of the class of things having the reason-property. So it too has the to-be-inferred property (the negative formulation is similar). This is a powerful form of reasoning, one which we engage in all the time. It is not formally valid, but it is a pervasive type of informal reasoning. We employ it whenever we infer that an object has a property on the grounds that it belongs to a type the typical members of which have that property. Compare: this grain of rice is typical of the whole pan of rice, and it is cooked. So any other grain will be cooked as well. This drop of water is typical of the entire sea, and it is salty. So this other drop must be salty as well.

We said that in the debating model, rationality is subject to public norms of correctness. In arguments of the kind being considered, public norms do indeed have a role to play, for they determine whether the object adduced by the debater as an 'example' is adequate. For something to be capable of playing the role of example, it must be generally and uncontroversially accepted as a member of $K$ and as an $F$. The debater must, when he chooses an example, be careful to select one that will fit public criteria of acceptability. If the example is to fulfil its role as a representative of its kind, then it must be certified as such by common assent. It is for this reason that the pattern of reasoning here is neither formally valid nor in any way reducible to an Aristotelian syllogism.

### 3. The deductive-nomological model

There is a strong pressure, nevertheless, to fit such arguments into a deductive-nomological model. These arguments, the thought goes, rest on an underlying lawlike universal generalisation—that all the members of kind *K* are *F*s. The argument is then enthymematic for a deductively valid one: *Ka*, all *K* are *F* ∴ *Fa*. The role of the example would, it is alleged, be to provide empirical support for the universal rule, either by being something which is both *K* and *F* or by being something which is neither *K* nor *F*. SCHAYER had a different idea (SCHAYER (1933: 247–257)). He read the step labelled 'example' in the five-step proof as an application of a logical rule, the one we would now call 'universal instantiation'. This is the rule that permits one to infer from '$(\forall x)(Kx \rightarrow Fx)$' to '$(Ka \rightarrow Fa)$'. But he still sees the overall inference as a formally valid one whose validity is a consequence of the fact that there is a hidden premise '$(\forall x)(Kx \rightarrow Fx)$'.

More light can be thrown on this point if we examine the early Nyāya account of a pair of debating moves called the 'likeness-based rejoinder' (*sādharmya-sama*) and 'unlikeness-based rejoinder' (*vaidharmya-sama*). A sophistical rejoinder (*jāti*) is a debating tactic in which the opponent tries unsuccessfully to produce a counter-argument, an argument designed to prove the opposite thesis. It is sophistical because the counter-argument is based on a false or superficial analogy. *Nyāya-sūtra* 5.1.2–3 state:

> *sādharmya-vaidharmyābhyām upasaṁhāre tad-dharma-viparyayôpapatteḥ sādharmya-vaidharmya-samau.*
>
> *gotvād go-siddhivat tat-siddhiḥ.*
>
> 'When there is assimilation through likeness or unlikeness, the likeness-based and unlikeness-based rejoinders lead to the opposite property.
>
> [The reply is:] the proof of [the thesis] is just like the proof of a cow from cowness.'

One debater, debating properly, tries to prove that a certain object has a certain property by pointing out that it is like another object which does have that property. (The black cloud overhead now is like the cloud we saw yesterday—both are black. But that cloud caused it to rain, so this one will too.) The opponent now tries to counter by pointing out that the object is also similar to an object which does not have the property. (The black cloud overhead is like the white cloud we saw the day before yesterday—both are clouds. But that cloud did not cause rain, so this one won't either.) As an argument, the rejoinder seems to follow the very same pattern as the original one, so why is it false? The existence of such rejoinders shows that mere likeness is not sufficient for good argument. The likeness has to be of the right type.

| | |
|---|---|
| $a$ is like$_{K1}$ $b$ | $a$ is like$_{K2}$ $c$ |
| $Fb$ | $\sim Fc$ |
| $\therefore Fa$ | $\therefore \sim Fa$ |

When is the likeness of the 'right type'? The *Nyāya-sūtra*'s very cryptic comment is that the 'right type' is the type displayed by the relationship between a cow and its genus cowness. Vātsyāyana, the commentator, is unclear and confused on this point. He does, however, make one important observation:

> 'If one proceeds to establish the required inferable property on the basis simply of likeness or unlikeness then there will be lack of regularity (*vyavasthā*). Irregularity does not arise with respect to some special property. For something is a cow because of its likeness with another cow, which likeness is actually cowhood, not the cow's having dewlap, etc. It is because of cowhood that a cow is unlike a horse, etc., not because of a difference of particular qualities. This has been explained in the section on the limbs of a demonstration. In a demonstration, each limb serves a single purpose because they are connected with means of knowing. The irregularity rests only on a bogus-reason.' [*Nyāya-bhāṣya* 285.4–8; below 5.1.3].

If the likeness must be of the right type, then the reason-property, as determiner of the likeness relation, must also be of the right type. The object under investigation must be like objects which belong to a group the typical members of which have the to-be-inferred property. Vātsyāyana implies that if the property in question is a property shared by typical members of the class of cows, then the reason-property must be the class-essence cowness.

What we are asking for are the conditions under which it is admissible to extrapolate a property from one object to another. It appears to be admissible to extrapolate the property 'rain-maker' from one black cloud to another black cloud, but not from a black cloud to a white cloud. It appears to be admissible to extrapolate the property 'has a dewlap' from one cow to another cow, but not from one four-legged animal (a cow) to another (a horse). There seems to be an order in the world of objects, a structure which licenses the extrapolation of properties in some directions but not others. Objects are grouped together on the basis of their likenesses and unlikenesses to one another. The possibility of likeness- and unlikeness-based rejoinders shows, however, that there are many different ways of making these groupings, many different metrics of likeness. So the problem is this: given some arbitrary property we wish to extrapolate from one object to another, how do we decide which such metric determines a standard for proper and warranted extrapolation? For an extrapolation may be warranted under one likeness relation but not another. So not every inference of the standard pattern is valid:

$$a \text{ is like}_K\, b$$
$$Fb$$
$$\therefore Fa$$

The response in the tradition to this problem is to impose further constraints on the relation of likeness. Relevant or extrapolation-warranting likeness is said to consist in the sharing of a property at least as narrow in extension as the property to be extrapolated. The important point is that this not the introduction of a new *premise* into the inference pattern, but rather it is a condition on when an inference is admissible. The constraint is of the form: it is valid to infer $Fa$ from $Fb$ if $a$ is like$_K$ $b$ when $b$, the example is relevantly like $a$ (i.e. when the property it shares with $a$ is narrower in extension than the property being extrapolated). An inference rule is not another premise in the inference, but rather that in virtue of which the inference is valid or invalid. And the treatment of the early Nyāya theory as a theory of inference from sampling shows how the rule that there be a 'universal connection' (*vyāpti*) of this kind between the properties is not an enthymematic premise but a genuine inference rule of an informal logic.

SCHAYER concludes his article 'Über die Methode der Nyāya-Forschung' with an interesting remark. He says that 'we do not compare Indian and modern logic in order to find individual differences along with similarities. Instead, we judge Indian logic from the standpoint of modern scientific logic in order to find out why it is logical in our sense.' That is why the comparison of Nyāya logic with the Aristotelian syllogistic theory was pointless for SCHAYER; he was more interested in seeing whether there are any anticipations of the propositional and predicate calculus in the Indian theories. Modern logic, he thinks, broadens the horizon, explaining as it does many new kinds of formal validity that traditional Aristotelian logic cannot recognise. My argument has been that the horizon needs to be broadened further still. For there are many ways to arrive rationally at belief other than that of formal deduction. Informal argument schemes, such as the inference from sampling, are just as much ways of reaching beliefs it is rational for someone to hold, and it is with this wider concept of rational belief that we can make better sense of the Nyāya philosophical enterprise. Studying the Indian philosophers we hope to find new forms of rationality and new philosophical paradigms, and this is one way for the discoveries made by the classical Indian investigators into the possibilities of human reason to be of interest and relevance to us today.

## BIBLIOGRAPHY


FRAUWALLNER 1958 = Frauwallner, Erich: 'Die Erkenntnislehre des klassischen Sāṁkhya-Systems,' *Wiener Zeitschrift für die Kunde Süd- und Ost-Asiens* 2 (1958) 84–139.

MATILAL 1998 = Matilal, Bimal Krishna: *The Character of Logic in India*. State University of New York, Albany 1998.

RANDLE 1930 = Randle, H.N.: *Indian Logic in the Early Schools*. Oxford University Press, Oxford 1930.

SCHAYER 1933 = Schayer, Stanisław: 'Über die Methode der Nyāya-Forschung,' in O. Stein and W. Gambert (eds.): *Festschrift für Moritz Winternitz*. Leipzig 1933: 247–257. [Reprinted in: Stanisław Schayer: *O filozofowaniu Hindusów. Artykuły wybrane*. Ed. by Marek Mejor. Polska Akademia Nauk, Komitet Nauk Orientalistycznych, PWN, Warszawa 1988: 422–432].

SCHUSTER 1972 = Schuster, Nancy: 'Inference in the Vaiśeṣikasūtras,' *Journal of Indian Philosophy*, 1 (1972) 341–395.

THAKUR 1997 = Thakur, Anantal: *Gautamyanyāyadarśana with Bhaṣya of Vātsyāyana*. Critically edited by .... Indian Council of Philosophical Research, Delhi 1997.

TUCCI 1929 = Tucci, Giuseppe: *Pre-Diṅnāga Buddhist Texts on Logic from Chinese Sources*. Oriental Institute, *Gaekwad's Oriental Series* 49, Baroda 1929.

## BIBLIOGRAPHY

# Living Liberation (*jīvan-mukti*) in Sāṁkhya and Yoga

MARZENNA JAKUBCZAK

Among the natural needs of each and every individual, one is to attain the perfect condition of human existence, which is commonly called happiness. Various definitions of such a perfect state can be found in many cultures and religions, present and past. Generally, the concept of ideal happiness, or bliss, is directly derived from a definition of human nature. The endeavour to reach full happiness means a striving to actualise one's own true nature.

A search for 'the European way of being a man,' to cite Edmund Husserl, was undertaken from two different perspectives: from the view-point of Athens, where the unlimited aspiration of reason (*ratio*) predominated, and from the view-point of Jerusalem, delimited by inexhaustible need for faith. The philosophers sharing the first perspective tried to define the most desirable state of worldly happiness—*eudaemonia*[1]—which can be achieved through applying rationally motivated advice or precepts. An equally important stream in European culture flowed from the Judeo-Christian conception of salvation, reached after death and only partly dependent on the individual's endeavour and deeds.

In the majority of Indian philosophical schools, both in the orthodox Brahmanical systems and in the Buddhist or Jaina tradition, every kind of eudaemonism was subordinated to soteriology. The only exception is the hedonist Cārvāka school which encourages people to seek for every pleasure, and claims that 'it's foolish to give up eating rice simply because the grains come enfolded with husk.' Generally, worldly happiness (*bhadra, sukha, śrī*) is regarded in India as temporal and delusive by nature and always lesser than eternal bliss (*ānanda*), which accompanies the realisation of the ultimate religious aim—deliverance from the cycle of suffering

[1] The Greek term εὐδαιμονία (lit. 'having a good δαιμόνιον,' that is happiness, prosperity or success) was first used in a technical meaning by Aristotle in his *Nichomachean Ethics*. He characterises happiness as the best, the noblest and the most pleasant thing under the sun, which we can achieve through the activity of virtuous psychic powers consistent with reason. The concept of *eudaemonia* was also applied by Pre-Socratic philosophers such as Democritus (ευθυμία = εὐδαιμονία) and Heraclitus (ἔθος = δαιμόνιον), but Aristotle's definition is commonly referred to as the classical one.

*Essays in Indian Philosophy, Religion and Literature*, pp. 363–371.

and rebirth (*saṁsāra*). However, unlike religious thinkers in many other cultures, who focus on salvation after death, many Hindu and Buddhist philosophers maintain that embodied liberation (*jīvan-mukti*) is possible. This unique conception of liberation while living seems to combine the human desire of perfection with the longing for undisturbed bliss reached within a life-time.

In Indian philosophy, we can find many diverse expressions of this highly problematic conception,[2] as it provoked vivid disputes among Indian authors themselves, even within one and the same school. The germ of the idea of *jīvan-mukti* can be traced in some *Upaniṣads* ($8^{th}$–$6^{th}$ centuries B.C.E.)[3], but the first person to clearly articulate the view that the release from *karman* in a living state (*nirvāṇa*) is possible was the Buddha ($6^{th}$–$5^{th}$ century B.C.E.). An interesting explanation of this question is found in epic and the Purāṇic literature. It was also frequently undertaken in Vedānta, Sāṁkhya and Yoga schools as well as in the Śaiva tradition.

In the present paper I am going to investigate the question how the idea of living liberation is expressed in the oldest texts of two Brahmanical schools, Sāṁkhya and Yoga. In doing that, I focus on two crucial questions: (1) who is the actual subject of the act of discriminative cognition (*viveka-khyāti*)? and (2) how does the cognition of a *jīvan-mukta* work?

## The concept of *jīvan-mukta* in Sāṁkhya

Īśvarakṛṣṇa, the author of the *Sāṁkhya-kārikā* (c. fifth century C.E.), argues that the reason for suffering, inseparable from every existence, lies in the contact or union (*saṁyoga*) of two opposed domains of reality: the three-*guṇa* Nature (*prakṛti*) and the transcendent Self (*puruṣa*) (SK 2, 20). The first is characterised as unconscious, objective, active and manifested (*vyakta*), while the other one is conscious, subjective and separate from the *guṇas* (*sattva, rajas* and *tamas*). Because of this contact, the unconscious (*acetana*) apparently shows the feature of the conscious (*cetana*), and the non-active *puruṣa* seems to take on the characteristic

---

[2] The individual who has managed to overcome all saṁsāric limitations of the human condition is in various traditions also called *jīvan-mukta*, *kevalin*, *buddha*, *arhat*, *jina*, etc.

[3] Despite the fact that the term '*jīvan-mukti*' itself does not appear in the *Upaniṣads*, some phrases seem to clearly confirm the possibility of achieving the state of living liberation, e.g. *Bṛhad-āraṇyaka* 4.4.7 and 4.4.14; *Kena* 2.5; *Muṇḍaka* 3.2.9; *Maitrī* 6.20; cf. RADHAKRISHNAN (1953: 273, 587, 692, 831–832, etc.).

of the three *guṇa*s (SK 20). The only efficient remedy for suffering caused by the contact of *puruṣa* and *prakṛti*, who are compared by Īśvarakṛṣṇa to the blind and the lame condemned to each other (SK 21), is valid cognition (*pramāṇa*). One can attain it through knowledge from reliable authority (*āpta-vacana*) or by inference (*anumāna*) or, best of all, through direct perception (*dṛṣṭa*), when the *puruṣa* and the *prakṛti* are recognised and discriminated (*viveka*) (SK 4–6).

The author of the *Sāṁkhya-kārikā* explicitly maintains in SK 67 the possibility of living one's life after the liberating knowledge has been achieved. From this pivotal *kārikā* we learn that due to the attainment of knowledge we are released from the influence of the predispositions (*bhāva*s) that are immanent in the empirical consciousness (*buddhi*). According to SK 23 and 63, the only predisposition, out of eight, that leads to liberation is cognition (*jñāna*), while the remaining ones—viz. the three positive predispositions such as virtue (*dharma*), non-attachment (*virāga*) and power (*aiśvarya*), as well as the four negative ones: vice (*adharma*), ignorance (*ajñāna*), attachment (*rāga*) and impotence (*anaiśvarya*)—lead to continued living and suffering. The positive predispositions, although they contribute to spiritual progress, are not direct causes of liberation. Since empirical consciousness (*buddhi*) is not any longer influenced by desire and ignorance (which normally are the reason for committing either wrong or virtuous deeds), the *karman* deposit loses its footing. Yet, in *kārikā* 67 we read that the *jīvan-mukta* continues his life due to the imprints of past deeds recorded in the form of *saṁskāra*s. To illustrate this relationship, Īśvarakṛṣṇa uses the well known metaphor of the potter's wheel which keeps turning for some time after the potter's last movement.

Now, let us consider the question: how, according to Sāṁkhya, does the cognition of the *jīvan-mukta* work? The answer is offered in *kārikā*s 64–66:

/64/ *evaṁ tattvâbhyāsān nâsmi na me nâham ity apariśeṣam /*
*aviparyayād viśuddhaṁ kevalam utpadyate jñānam //*

/65/ *tena nivṛtta-prasavām artha-vaśāt sapta-rūpa-vinivṛttām /*
*prakṛtiṁ paśyati puruṣaḥ prekṣakavad avasthitaḥ svasthaḥ //*

/66/ *dṛṣṭā mayêty upekṣaka eko dṛṣṭâham ity uparamaty anyā /*
*sati saṁyoge 'pi tayoḥ prayojanaṁ nâsti sargasya //*

In SK 64, we find out what the cognition of the *jīvan-mukta* precisely consists in: as a result of concentration on the twenty-five principles (*tattva*s), the *jīvan-mukta* gets rid of delusive identity; namely, he rejects the identity of *puruṣa* and *prakṛti*, ascertaining: *nâsmi, na me, nâham*. To interpret this crucial phrase, one must, first of all, define the subject of the sentence. Who states: *nâsmi, na me, nâham*? This is either the empirical consciousness (*buddhi*) that still operates and discriminates, or the Self (*puruṣa*), who distinguishes himself from the *prakṛti*, regaining thus his true self-identity. In both cases there are several alternative translations that could be proffered. I present just two proposals within each perspective. If we assumed that the *buddhi* is the subject, the translation could be as follows:

> 1.1. 'I am not [the Self], [liberation is] not mine, [there is] no me (*ego*)';

or

> 1.2. 'I am not [conscious], [the conscious is] not mine, "I" is not [conscious].'[4]

But if we assume the *puruṣa* to be the subject, the translation runs:

> 2.1. 'I am not [any of the 24 *tattvas* of *prakṛti*], [suffering is] not mine, not me [is who transmigrates in *saṁsāra*]';

or

> 2.2. 'I am not [of three-*guṇa* nature], nothing, [especially my body, is] mine, no [object of cognition is] me.'

The first two translations present a description of the last all-important act of knowledge performed by the empirical consciousness (*buddhi*), considered as a relative subject. In the act of discrimination (*viveka*), the *buddhi* recognises its own subjectivity as something relative, subordinated to and of instrumental character in relation to the Self. The *buddhi* operates—for the sake of the *puruṣa's* release—'as unconscious milk which functions for the sake of nourishment of the calf' (SK 57). And now, it realises that liberation of the *puruṣa* means the end, or its cessation, because attaining the state of 'perfection', or 'oneness' (*kaivalya*) excludes the coexistence of the empirical subject.

Translation 1.2. emphasises, as LARSON (1979: 205) notes, that discrimination separates out pure consciousness from everything which is not conscious. As a result of this intuitive discrimination which occurs in the *buddhi*, consciousness emptied of all content (SK 37) becomes a kind of translucent emptiness or nothingness, which is a condition of absolute freedom and liberation from all suffering. The empirical *ego* that distinguishes *prakṛti* from *puruṣa* simply 'disidentifies' himself from the absolute subject, saying: 'the Self is not me.'

According to the third and fourth versions, the state of living liberation is a result of 'becoming oneself', which means identification with the real Self, not with his empirical counterpart. The phrase under discussion appears to be an expression of

---

[4] *Kārikā* 64 is translated in this manner by Gerald J. LARSON (1979: 274): 'Thus, from the study (or analysis) of the principles (*tattvas*), the "knowledge" (or salvation-knowledge) arises, I am not (conscious); (consciousness) does not belong to me; the "I" is not (conscious) ...'

the view-point of the absolute subject. Now, the *puruṣa* seems to 'disidentify' himself from everything that could be an object of his cognition. Both translations 2.1. and 2.2., which accept this perspective, reflect the exhaustive gradual elimination of alternatives that demonstrates the impossibility of identifying the Self with anything empirical, and thereby indicates his transcendence.

Regardless of which point of view—the *buddhi*'s or the *puruṣa*'s—we assume the knowledge of the *jīvan-mukta* to be, according to Sāṁkhya, it has purely negative character. This is a well-known pattern of reasoning employed in early *Upaniṣad*s in the discussion of the identity of the Self, who is *nêti nêti* ('not this, not this').[5] We can ask, however, which of these two—either the relative or the absolute subject-oriented—perspectives is more compatible with the whole doctrine of Sāṁkhya. Since the functioning of the *buddhi* enables all cognitive processes to go on, it seems natural to admit that the act of discrimination occurs within the empirical consciousness. But the knowledge achieved by the *buddhi* is confined to the discovery: 'I am not the Self,' which still is not the same as the regaining of Self-identity. The above limitation seems to be easily avoided if instead we assume the *puruṣa* to be the subject of discrimination. However, that being the case, we are confronted with another problem, namely with the non-intentional character of the *puruṣa* consciousness. How can the transcendent being, which is a non-active subject, not involved in any empirical activity, make any discrimination, even the liberating one? Despite this doctrinal difficulty, the denial that every object of cognition has the nature of the Self seems to be the logical and pervasive procedure for the direct attainment of the ultimate liberation.

It is proper to point out here that the *buddhi*-oriented perspective predominates in contemporary interpretations of Sāṁkhya, probably due to the uncritical reliance on Gauḍapāda and other later commentators. Gauḍapāda in his *Bhāṣya* interprets the sentence 'I am not' in the sense of 'I do not exist' (*nâham eva bhavāmi*); 'naught is mine' to mean 'this body is not mine since I am one thing and the body another' (*na me mama śarīraṁ tat, yato 'ham anyaḥ śarīram anyat*). 'There is no I (*ego*),' he tends to understand as 'I am free from ego' (*ahaṁ-kāra-rahitam apariśeṣam*) (MAINKAR (1972: 197)). The phrase under discussion has invariably been translated thus since Thomas COLEBROOKE's (1837) first rendering of SK.[6] DEUSSEN (1908: 462) and LARSON (1979: 274) clearly follow him. Among the supporters of the

[5] *Bṛhad-āraṇyaka* 2.3.6.

[6] In COLEBROOKE's (1887: 240) translation the *kārikā* runs as follows: 'So, through study of principles, the conclusive, incontrovertible, one only knowledge is attained, that neither I AM, nor is aught mine, nor do I exist.' And in DEUSSEN's (1920: 462): 'Das bin ich nicht! das ist nicht mein! ich bin nicht!'

*puruṣa*-oriented perspective are Tuvia GELBLUM (1970: 75–82), the author of a critical review of LARSON's *Classical Sāṁkhya*, and W.T. DE BARRY (1958: 309), who considers the eighth *bhāva*, knowledge, the cause of release, not as a form of *prakṛti* but as a reflection of the spirit (*puruṣa*). The other seven dispositions of mind, viz. virtue, vice, etc., which constitute bondage, both good and bad, are understood as those from which the *buddhi* now withdraws.

Now, let us consider SK 65 and 66, where the state of *jīvan-mukta* is defined in positive terms. The author of the *Sāṁkhya-kārikā*, this time using a metaphorical language, compares the liberated *puruṣa* to a passive, indifferent witness or spectator who, comfortably situated, watches a performance of the active and unconscious *prakṛti*. She, like a mysterious dancer (SK 59), having shown all her beauty and having been seen through, finishes her play and ceases her activity. Expanding this metaphor, one can say that the *jīvan-mukta* is the one who applauds the *prakṛti*, the applause which is the inseparable part of the performance and which announces its definite and inevitable end.

Īśvarakṛṣṇa makes an important remark regarding this final stage of the show of Nature (*prakṛti*) in SK 68.[7] In this *kārikā*, the state of isolation (*kaivalya*) and final cessation of *prakṛti* is considered not to be accomplished sooner than the *puruṣa* attains separation from the body. Thus, it turns out that the completion of full liberation needs the deposit of *karman* to be totally exhausted, which implies the death of the physical body of the knower. The state of being liberated while living is not, therefore, according to Sāṁkhya, equal to the state of ultimate bliss and *kaivalya*. It refers to the period of life between the attainment of the discriminative knowledge and the end of embodiment. The *jīvan-mukta* plays a pedagogical role of an ideal spiritual master who, with his own presence, proves the efficiency of the Sāṁkhya method.

## Liberated while living in Yoga

In the *Yoga-sūtras* by Patañjali the term *jīvan-mukta* does not appear even once. Nevertheless, Vyāsa in his commentary (the seventh century C.E.) *Yoga-sūtra-bhāṣya* notes the possibility of continuing one's life after the abolishment of the afflicted fluctuations in mind (*kliṣṭa*) and of the deposit of *karman*. He twice uses the phrase: 'having body for the last time' (*carama-deha*), which is the synonym of the *jīvan-mukta* (YBH 2.4, 4.7).

[7] SK 68: *prāpte śarīra-bhede caritârthatvāt pradhāna-vinivṛttau, aikāntikam ātyantikam ubhayaṁ kaivalyam āpnoti.*

While analysing the question of living liberation in the system of Patañjali, the conception of Īśvara cannot be omitted. Īśvara is regarded by the commentators as a prototype of the *jīvan-mukta*. He possesses all the essential properties of the liberated while living, and the only difference is that he has never ever been involved in *karman*. Īśvara, as the inner guru and the ideal of sage, seems to fill up the same place as *jīvan-mukta* in Sāṁkhya.

In order to examine Patañjali's views on living liberation, we should read carefully his description of the final stages of meditative practice. In *sūtra* 4.29, we find an interesting expression that may help us in grasping the uniqueness of the Yoga attitude towards that question. Indeed, says YS 4.29, in the state of reflection (*prasaṁkhyāna*), for the one who has discriminative discernment and always takes no interest, there is the cloud of *dharma samādhi*.[8]

The key term of this *sūtra* is 'the cloud of *dharma*' (*dharma-megha*). Several possible meanings of this phrase emerge according to the reading of the term '*dharma*' as 'feature', 'property', 'duty' or 'virtue'. As a result of comparison of these meanings, two alternative interpretations can be suggested:

1. Achieving the *samādhi* of the '*dharma-megha*' type (with the meaning of 'cloud of virtue')[9], which follows discriminative knowledge (*viveka-khyāti*), means that from that moment all deeds of the knower— in Sāṁkhya terms called the living liberated—are 'soaked through' with virtue and can be classified only as good and virtuous. In other words, the liberated (*esp.* sage or saint) is not able to commit any wrong deed which is opposed to his own moral duty,[10] and the *karman* produced by such a person is neither white nor black (*aśuklâkṛṣṇa*, YS 4.7).[11]

---

[8] I cite here CHAPPLE's rendering (1990: 119–120).

[9] This interpretation is supported by, among others, Vācaspati Miśra (ninth century C.E.), the author of a commentary on the *Yoga-sūtra* and Vyāsa's *Bhāṣya*, and by Vijñāna Bhikṣu, who commented on the *Yoga-sūtra* in the sixteenth century C.E. Vācaspati Miśra claims: 'Hence because by its light it rains [that is] pours down all kinds of knowable things, it is called the Rain-cloud of [knowable] things' (*Tattva-vaiśāradī* 4.31); cf. WOODS (1988: 342–343). Vijñāna Bhikṣu maintains that the man who does not desire anything, even the state of 'elevation', is able to stay at all times in the state of discriminate-discernment, and due to the dwindling away of the seeds of subliminal impressions, other thoughts do not arise. Then he attains the '*dharma-megha*' *samādhi* which is the furthest limit of *saṁprajñāta-yoga*. It is called '*dharma-megha*' because it rains '*dharma*' which totally uproots or destroys afflictions (*kleśa*s) and deeds (*karman*); cf. RUKMANI (1989: 121–122).

[10] 'Duty', which is understood here in the same way as in the *Bhagavad-gītā*, refers mainly to what is mentioned by Patañjali as the five fundamental ethical precepts, or restraints (*yama*): non-violence, trustfulness, non-stealing, sexual restraint, and non-

2. In the course of '*dharma-megha*' concentration, with the meaning of 'rinsing out the properties,'[12] all latent traces of the past activities, accumulated in the form of *vyutthāna saṁskāra*, are totally abolished, or rinsed out. Among the *saṁskāras* which are cleared out, there are both imprints of true knowledge, which is non-afflicted (*akliṣṭa*), and all the *vāsanas* that determinate the category of embodiment, the length of life and the type of dominant experience (*sukha–duḥkha*) that is a reward for our past deeds. According to this interpretation, there is an essential difference between the state of knowledge reached in the *saṁprajñāta-samādhi*, or even the state of *asaṁprajñāta-samādhi*, and the state of full liberation of *kaivalya* achieved only after death. The knower who recognises his own true nature (*svarūpa*, YS 4.34)[13] should neither rely solely on the natural course of life, nor await passively and patiently the extinction of the rest of the *karman* traces. The path of Yoga, in contradistinction to the Sāṁkhya teachings, recommends the active approach. There is another act of concentration which is to be realised, namely *dharma-megha-samādhi*. As if a rain cloud, this concentration is able to rinse out the last, deepest germs of empirical consciousness. The ultimate liberation of the Self is not, according to Patañjali, a mere product of the *jīvan-mukta*'s death, but rather a result of concentration completed by the last act of will.

---

possession; and five observances (*niyama*): purity, contentment, austerity, self-study, and dedication to Īśvara (YS 2.30–32). Both the restraints and observances combine to form the famous eight limbs of yoga (*yogâṅga*).

[11] Vyāsa in his commentary on YS 4.7 explains that there are four kinds of *karman*: (a) the black *karman* produced by mean, wicked people; (b) the white-and-black *karman* is produced by people applying outer means-of-attainment; (c) the white *karman* belongs to those who practice austerity, self-study and who cultivate contemplation; (d) the neither-white-nor-black *karman* is found in the saints (*sannyāsin*), whose hindrances have dwindled away and whose actual bodies are their last; cf. WOODS (1988: 305).

[12] Such an alternative rendering of this term was suggested by the late Polish translator of YS, Leon CYBORAN (1986: 236) who, however, did not give any broader interpretation of this *sūtra*.

[13] YS IV.34: *puruṣârtha-śūnyānāṁ guṇānāṁ pratiprasavaḥ kaivalyaṁ svarūpa-pratiṣṭhā vā citi-śaktir iti*; CHAPPLE (1990: 122): 'The return to the origin of the *guṇas* (*pratiprasava*), emptied of their purpose for *puruṣa*, is *kaivalyam*, the steadfastness in own form, and power of higher awareness.'

## BIBLIOGRAPHY


DE BARRY 1958 = Barry, W.T. de (trans. and comm.): *Sources of Indian Tradition*. Vol. I. Cambridge University Press, New York–London 1958: 303–310.

CHAPPLE 1990 = Chapple, Christopher K. (trans.): *The Yoga Sūtras of Patañjali*. Sri Satguru Publications, Delhi 1990.

COLEBROOKE 1887 = Colebrooke, Henry Thomas: *The Sānkhya Kārikā*. Subodha-Prakash Press, Bombay 1887. [First edition: Oxford 1837].

CYBORAN 1986 = Cyboran, Leon (trans. and comm.): *Klasyczna joga indyjska* [Polish translation of YS and YBh]. PWN, Warszawa 1986.

DEUSSEN 1908 = Deussen, Paul: *Allgemeine Geschichte der Philosophie*. Vol. 1, pt. 3, Leipzig 1920. [First edition: Leipzig 1908].

GELBLUM 1970 = Gelblum, Tuvia: 'Sāṁkhya and Sartre.' *Journal of Indian Philosophy* 1 (1970) 75–82.

LARSON 1979 = Larson, Gerald J.: *Classical Sāṁkhya – An Interpretation of its History and Meaning with The Sāṁkhya-kārikā of Īśvarakṛṣṇa (romanized text with translation)*. Second revised ed., Motilal Banarsidass, Delhi–Varanasi–Patna 1979.

MAINKAR 1972 = Mainkar, T.G. (ed. and trans.): *Sāṁkhyakārikā of Īśvarakṛṣṇa with Gauḍapādabhāṣya. Poona Oriental Series* 9, Poona 1972. [First edition: 1964].

RADHAKRISHNAN 1953 = Radhakrishnan, Servepalli (ed. and trans.): *The Principal Upaniṣads*. George Allen & Unwin Ltd., London 1953.

RUKMANI 1989 = Rukmani, T.S. (trans. and comm.): *Yogavārttika of Vijñānabhikṣu: Text along with English Translation and Critical Notes along with the Text and English Translation of the Pātañjala Yogasūtras and Vyāsabhāṣya*. Vol. 4: *Kaivalyapāda*, Munshiram Manoharlal, New Delhi 1989.

SK = Īśvarakṛṣṇa: *Sāṁkhya-kārikā*. See: COLEBROOKE (1887).

WOODS 1988 = Woods, James H. (trans.): *The Yoga-System of Patañjali or The Ancient Hindu Doctrine of Concentration of Mind, Embracing Yoga-Sūtras, Yoga-Bhāṣya and Tattva-Vaiśaradi*. Motilal Banarsidass, Delhi 1988. [First edition: Cambridge (Mass.) 1914].

YBh = Vyāsa: *Yoga-sūtra-bhāṣya*. See: RUKMANI (1989).

YS = Patañjali: *Yoga-sūtra*. See: RUKMANI (1989).

# Nāgārjuna and the Trilemma or *traikālyâsiddhi* *

SHŌRYŪ KATSURA

The aim of this paper is to discuss the nature of Nāgārjuna's destructive Trilemma argument from the point of view of a historian of Indian logic. In another paper[1] I have analysed the destructive Tetralemma (*catuṣ-koṭi*) used in the *Mūla-madhyamaka-kārikā* (= MMK). Here I would like to present the basic structure of his Trilemma, examine its applications in the debate between Nāgārjuna and the Naiyāyika, and finally evaluate it against the background of the Indian debate tradition.

## 1. The Trilemma Arguments in MMK Chapter 2 (*gatâgata-parīkṣā*)

In MMK Chapter 2 Nāgārjuna analyses the notions of 'going' (*gamana / gati*), 'goer' (*gantṛ*), and 'path to be gone over' (*gantavya*) in relation to the three times, viz. past, present, and future. Those notions respectively correspond to those of 'action' (*kriyā*), 'agent' (*kartṛ*), and 'object' (*karman*) used by Indian grammarians. After having applied various arguments in the forms of Trilemma and Dilemma to those notions, he concludes that there is no act of going, no goer and no path to be gone over.[2]

Now does he really deny our act of going over a certain path? I do not think so. As I understand him, Nāgārjuna admits our everyday activity of going and coming at least on the level of our common sense (*saṁvṛti*). He would even admit that we can talk about it in our ordinary language. However, he refuses to admit that it can be described precisely and ultimately (*paramârthataḥ*) in any language, whether it is the technical language of Indian grammarians or that of Buddhist Abhidharma philosophers. It is to be noted that he is denying those notions as held by the Realist

---

* I would like to thank Prof. Mark Siderits for kindly going through this paper and correcting my English.

[1] KATSURA (2000).

[2] MMK 2.25cd: *tasmād gatiś ca gantā ca gantavyaṁ ca na vidyate* // For MMK I shall follow DE JONG (1977).

*Essays in Indian Philosophy, Religion and Literature*, pp. 373–397.

who, he thinks, posits an intrinsic nature for each of them (*svabhāva-vādin*). Therefore, I am inclined to believe that he does not really deny our act of going but he denies the 'ultimate' one-to-one correspondence between our conceptual notions or verbal expressions, such as 'going', 'goer' and 'path to be gone over', and the real and complex state of affairs, i.e. our act of going.

Nāgārjuna presents six Trilemmas in MMK Chapter 2. The first Trilemma argument runs as follows:

Trilemma 1

'(1) In the first place the [path] already gone over (*gata*) is not [now] being gone over (*na gamyate*);

(2) nor indeed is the [path] not yet gone over (*agata*) being gone over.

(3) The [path] presently being gone over (*gamyamāna*) that is distinct from the [portions of path] already gone over and not yet gone over is not being gone over.'[3]

Here Nāgārjuna assumes for purposes of *reductio* each of the following propositions in order to deny all of them:

(1) 'The path already gone over is being gone over' (*gataṁ gamyate*),

(2) 'The path not yet gone over is being gone over' (*agataṁ gamyate*),

(3) 'The path presently being gone over is being gone over' (*gamyamānaṁ gamyate*).

Since '*gata*', '*agata*' and '*gamyamāna*' respectively correspond to the past, the future and the present, the subjects of the three propositions are mutually exclusive and exhaust the universe of discourse consisting of portions of the path. Thus, by denying all the three propositions, Nāgārjuna can conclude that no path whatsoever is possibly being gone over, which implies that no act of going is possible in any portion of the path or in the three times.

The first two propositions are easily dismissed because the present act of going cannot be said to belong to the path gone over (i.e. the past) or not yet gone over (i.e. the future). They simply deviate from our verbal conventions. Therefore,

[3] MMK 2.1:

*gataṁ na gamyate tāvad agataṁ nâiva gamyate /*
*gatâgata-vinirmuktaṁ gamyamānaṁ na gamyate //*

The translations of MMK chap. 2 is a result of the joint work with Mark Siderits. We are planning to publish a new English translation of MMK. It is to be noted that we have different interpretations of Nāgārjuna's philosophy.

Nāgārjuna does not make any effort to discuss and deny them in the subsequent verses. However, the third proposition, which attributes the present act of going to the path presently being gone over, seems to make sense and it is not very apparent how Nāgārjuna can deny it. So he assumes the following objection:

> '[The opponent:] Where there is movement (*ceṣṭā*) there is the act of going (*gati*). And since movement occurs in the [path] presently being gone over, the act of going occurs in the [path] presently being gone over, not in the [path] already gone over and not yet gone over.'[4]

The opponent is clearly supporting the third proposition, by saying that the act of going occurs in the path being gone over (*gamyamāne gatiḥ*). In order to refute the above objection, Nāgārjuna gives the following counter-argument:

> 'How could it be right (*upapatsyate*) to say that the act of going is in the [path] being gone over (*gamyamānasya gamanam*) when it is not at all right (*upapadyate*) to say that there is the [path] presently being gone over without the act of going?'[5]

Here Nāgārjuna is concerned with the expression 'The act of going is in the path being gone over' (*gamyamāne gatiḥ* or *gamyamānasya gamanam*). In this connection it is to be noted that when two linguistic items (*śabda*) are put in different cases in Sanskrit, they refer to two different objects or loci (*vyadhikaraṇa*). In the particular expression under consideration 'the act of going' (*gati* or *gamana*) is in the nominative case, while 'the path being gone over' (*gamyamāna*) is in the locative or genitive case. Therefore they must refer to two different things. However, Nāgārjuna points out that the very concept of 'the path being gone over' is impossible without the act of going; in other words, they cannot be two separate things. Thus, he denies that the act of going is in the path presently being gone over.

Now, just for the sake of argument, Nāgārjuna accepts that the act of going is in the path being presently gone over, then he points out a couple of undesirable consequences (*prasaṅga*) in the following manner:

---

[4] MMK 2.2:

> *ceṣṭā yatra gatis tatra gamyamāne ca sā yataḥ /*
> *na gate nâgate ceṣṭā gamyamāne gatis tataḥ //*

[5] MMK 2.3:

> *gamyamānasya gamanaṁ kathaṁ nām ôpapatsyate /*
> *gamyamāne vigamanaṁ yadā nâivôpapadyate //*

DE LA VALLÉE POUSSIN reads '*dvigamanam*' (1970: 94) instead of '*vigamanam*' of DE JONG's edition (1977: 2). The latter reading is supported by Tibetan translation.

> 'If [you say] the act of going is in the [path] presently being gone over, it follows (*prasajyate*) that the [path] being gone over is without the act of going, since [for you] the [path] presently being gone over is being gone over (*gamyamānaṁ gamyate*).'[6]
>
> 'If the act of going is in the [path] presently being gone over, then two acts of going will follow (*prasakta*): that by which the [path] presently being gone over [is said to be such], and moreover that which [supposedly exists] in the act of going.'[7]

If we accept that the act of going and the path being gone over are the two different things (with their own intrinsic nature or *svabhāva*), then the path presently being gone over is separated from the actual act of going, which is absurd. Now if we deny that undesirable consequence and admit that the path being gone over is endowed with the act of going, then we must admit that there are two acts of going, viz. one in the path being gone over and the other, i.e. the act of going itself, which is absurd, too.

According to Indian grammarian's analysis accepted by majority of Indian philosophers, the act of going demands the presence of a goer. Nāgārjuna is thereby able to point out further undesirable consequences.

> 'If two acts of going follow, then it will follow (*prasajyate*) that there are two goers (*gantṛ*), for it is not right to say that there is an act of going without a goer.[8]
>
> If it is not right to say that there is an act of going without a goer, how will there be a goer when the act of going does not [yet] exist?'[9]

---

[6] MMK 2.4:

*gamyamānasya gamanaṁ yasya tasya prasajyate /*
*ṛte gater gamyamānaṁ gamyamānaṁ hi gamyate //*

[7] MMK 2.5:

*gamyamānasya gamane prasaktaṁ gamana-dvayam /*
*yena tad gamyamānaṁ ca yac câtra gamanaṁ punaḥ //*

[8] MMK 2.6:

*dvau gantārau prasajyete prasakte gamana-dvaye /*
*gantāraṁ hi tiras-kṛtya gamanaṁ nôpapadyate //*

[9] MMK 2.7:

*gantāraṁ cet tiras-kṛtya gamanaṁ nôpapadyate /*
*gamane 'sati gantâtha kuta eva bhaviṣyati //*

If the act of going is in the path presently being gone over, there will be two acts of going; if there are two acts of going, there will be two goers, which is absurd. Furthermore, if there is no act of going without a goer, there will be no goer without the act of going. By pointing out the absurd consequences of the opponent's position that the act of going is in the path being gone over, Nāgārjuna denies the third proposition mentioned above. He also indicates that the notion of going and that of goer are mutually dependent, hence without intrinsic nature.

Let me now describe the standard process of Nāgārjuna's Trilemma argument.

(1) First, he assumes the three possible propositions the subjects of which are mutually exclusive and exhaust the universe of discourse.

(2) Then he denies all three propositions, often by means of *reductio ad absurdum* (*prasaṅga*).

(3) Finally he concludes that there are no entities which are to be expressed by the subjects or the predicates of those propositions; those notions are empty of their intrinsic nature.

In Trilemma 1 the act of going is denied with reference to the path gone over, not yet gone over, and presently being gone over; in other words, the act of going is denied in the three times. Similarly the act of beginning to go (*gamanârambha* or *saṁpravṛtti*) and that of stopping (*sthiti* or *nivṛtti*) are denied with reference to the three kinds of path in the following Trilemmas:

Trilemma 2

'(1) [A goer] does not begin to go in [the path] gone over,
(2) neither does [a goer] begin to go in [the path] not yet gone over.
(3) [A goer] does not begin to go in [the path] presently being gone over.
— Then where does [a goer] begin to go?'[10]

Trilemma 3

'(1) [The goer] does not stop in the [path] presently being gone over,
(2) neither in the [path] already gone over,
(3) nor in the [path] not yet gone over.'[11]

[10] MMK 2.12:
*gate nârabhyate gantuṁ gantuṁ nârabhyate 'gate /*
*nârabhyate gamyamāne gantum ārabhyate kuha //*

[11] MMK 2.17ab: *na tiṣṭhati gamyamānān na gatān nâgatād api /*

Furthermore, Nāgārjuna presents another type of Trilemma with reference to the act of going and its agent. Namely,

Trilemma 4 (= Dilemma 1)

'(1) In the first place a goer (*gantṛ*) does not go;
(2) nor indeed does a non-goer (*agantṛ*) go.
(3) And who could be the third person distinct from goer and non-goer who goes?'[12]

Since 'goer' and 'non-goer' are taken to be complementary to each other, there is no third person who is either both-goer-and-non-goer or neither-goer-nor-non-goer. Thus the third lemma is simply rejected and Trilemma 4 is actually reduced to Dilemma. In this connection it is to be noted that the negative particle *nañ* of *'a-gantṛ'* ('non-goer') should be interpreted as *paryudāsa* (negation of the complementary), while the negative particle of '*a-gata*' ('not yet gone over') in Trilemma 1 should be interpreted as *prasajya-pratiṣedha* (simple negation) which allows the third possibility of 'both-*gata*-and-*agata*', i.e. '*gamyamāna*' ('presently being gone over').

Here Nāgārjuna presupposes the following two propositions:

(1) 'A goer goes' (*gantā gacchati*),
(2) 'A non-goer goes' (*agantā gacchati*).

Since the second proposition expresses a sheer nonsense, Nāgārjuna does not bother to reject it. Regarding the first proposition he denies it by pointing out a few undesirable consequences (*prasaṅga*) similar to those of the third proposition of Trilemma 1.[13] In this way, the act of going is denied with reference to the agent of going. Similarly, Nāgārjuna denies the act of stopping with reference to the agent of going in the following Trilemma:

Trilemma 5 (= Dilemma 2)

'(1) In the first place a goer does not stop,
(2) nor indeed does a non-goer stop.
(3) And who could be the third person distinct from goer and non-goer who stops?'[14]

---

[12] MMK 2.8:
*gantā na gacchati tāvad agantā nâiva gacchati /*
*anyo gantur agantuś ca kas tṛtīyo 'tha gacchati //*

[13] See MMK 2.9–11.

[14] MMK 2.15:
*gantā na tiṣṭhati tāvad agantā nâiva tiṣṭhati /*
*anyo gantur agantuś ca kas tṛtīyo 'tha tiṣṭhati //*

Nāgārjuna applies Dilemma of identity and difference to the act of going and the goer. Namely,

Dilemma 3

'(1) It is not right to say that the act of going is identical with the goer.

(2) Nor, again, is it right to say that the goer is distinct from the act of going.'[15]

In order to justify the above Dilemma, Nāgārjuna points out a few undesirable consequences (*prasaṅga*) just as before.[16] Thus, the act of going is neither identical with nor different from the goer; hence, both the act of going and the goer cannot be said to exist independently with their own intrinsic nature.

In conclusion, Nāgārjuna offers the following complex Trilemma:

Trilemma 6

'(1) One who is [already] a real (*sad-bhūta*) goer does not perform an act of going [of any] of the three kinds,[17] [i.e. past, future, or present].

(2) Neither does one who is not [yet] a real (*asad-bhūta*) goer perform an act of going [of any] of the three kinds.

(3) One who is a both-real-and-unreal (*sad-asad-bhūta*) goer does not perform an act of going [of any] of the three kinds.'[18]

The *Akuto-bhayā*, Buddhapālita and Bhāvaviveka all take 'the three kinds of going' (*tri-prakāraṁ gamanam*) mentioned in Trilemma 6 to refer to the acts of going belonging to the three times, i.e. past, future and present. Candrakīrti

---

[15] MMK 2.18:

*yad eva gamanaṁ gantā sa evêti na yujyate /*
*anya eva punar gantā gater iti na yujyate //*

[16] MMK 2.19–20.

[17] See *Prasanna-padā* (LA VALLÉE POUSSIN (1970: 107.11)): *tatra sad-bhūto gantā sad-bhūtam asad-bhūtaṁ sad-asad-bhūtaṁ tri-prakāraṁ gamanaṁ na gacchati /* . Cf. *Akuto-bhayā* (Peking ed.) 44b7: *rnam gsum du zhes bya ba ni song ba dang ma song ba dang bgom pa zhes bya ba'i tha tshig go //* ; Buddhapālita's *Vṛtti* (Peking ed.) 196b7: *rnam gsum du zhes bya ba ni song ba dang ma song ba dang bgom par ro //* ; *Prajñā-pradīpa* (Peking ed.): *rnam gsum du zhes bya ba ni song ba dang / ma song ba dang / bgom par ro //* .

[18] MMK 2.24–25ab:

*sad-bhūto gamanaṁ gantā tri-prakāraṁ na gacchati /*
*nâsad-bhūto api gamanaṁ tri-prakāraṁ sa gacchati //*
*gamanaṁ sad-asad-bhūtaḥ tri-prakāraṁ na gacchati /*

interprets 'the three kinds' in terms of 'real', 'unreal' and 'both-real-and-unreal'.[19] Although they may be different in their interpretations, I would suggest that they are giving basically the same interpretation. Thus, I think, it is possible that the expressions 'real' (*sad-bhūta*), 'unreal' (*asad-bhūta*) and 'both-real-and-unreal' (*sad-asad-bhūta*) in Trilemma 6 respectively refer to past, future and present.

If we define that the past thing as that which has already come into existence and the future thing as that which has not yet come into existence, the former can be called 'real' in some sense, while the latter is totally 'unreal'. A thing which is presently coming into existence can be regarded as partially real (or past) and partially unreal (or future). In that sense, the present thing can be called 'both-real-and-unreal'. This, I take, seems to be the concepts of the three times held by Nāgārjuna's opponents in MMK chapter 2. Of course, Nāgārjuna does not endorse such a view and points out the contradiction especially in their concept of the present time.

Since each lemma of Trilemma 6 actually consists of a Trilemma, Nāgārjuna seems to presuppose the following nine propositions:

(1) 'A real (i.e. past) goer performs the past act of going' (*sad-bhūto gantā gataṁ gamanaṁ gacchati*).

(2) 'A real goer performs the future act of going' (*sad-bhūto gantā agataṁ gamanaṁ gacchati*).

(3) 'A real goer performs the present act of going' (*sad-bhūto gantā gamyamānaṁ gamanaṁ gacchati*).

(4) 'An unreal (i.e. future) goer performs the past act of going' (*asad-bhūto gantā gataṁ gamanaṁ gacchati*).

(5) 'An unreal goer performs the future act of going' (*asad-bhūto gantā agataṁ gamanaṁ gacchati*).

(6) 'An unreal goer performs the present act of going' (*asad-bhūto gantā gamyamānaṁ gamanaṁ gacchati*).

(7) 'A both-real-and-unreal (present) goer performs the past act of going' (*sad-asad-bhūto gantā gataṁ gamanaṁ gacchati*).

(8) 'A both-real-and-unreal goer performs the future act of going' (*sad-asad-bhūto gantā agataṁ gamanaṁ gacchati*).

(9) 'A both-real-and-unreal goer performs the present act of going' (*sad-asad-bhūto gantā gamyamānaṁ gamanaṁ gacchati*).

Trilemma 6 denies all the nine propositions, which implies that Nāgārjuna denies any possible relation between a goer and an act of going. He concludes that there is

[19] See Note 17 above.

no act of going (*gamana* / *gati*), no goer (*gantṛ*) and no path to be gone over (*gantavya*).[20]

As Candrakīrti notes,[21] Trilemma 6 is applied to the more general case of 'agent' (*kāraka* = *kartṛ*) and 'action' (*karman* = *kriyā*) in MMK chapter 8. As a matter of fact, Nāgārjuna refers back to MMK Chapter 2 at least four times in the rest of the text. Namely,

> 'The example of a fire together with the faculty of seeing (*darśana*) has been refuted by [the arguments of] *gamyamāna*, *gata* and *agata*.[22]
>
> That which is presently arising (*utpadyamāna*), that which has already arisen (*utpanna*), and that which has not yet arisen (*anutpanna*) do not arise in any way at all, which has been explained by [the arguments of] *gamyamāna*, *gata* and *agata*.[23]
>
> The rest [of the arguments] with reference to the fuel [and the fire] has been explained by [the arguments of] *gamyamāna*, *gata* and *agata*.[24]
>
> The rest [of the arguments concerning "binding"] has been explained by [the arguments of] *gamyamāna*, *gata* and *agata*.'[25]

This fact clearly indicates that the argument found in MMK Chapter 2 is one of the standard procedure for Nāgārjuna to refute a set of two or more related concepts, such as 'going', 'goer' and 'the path to be gone over'. That is why, I believe, Nāgārjuna puts the analysis of *gata*, *agata* and *gamyamāna* as the second chapter of MMK before he goes on to scrutinise various philosophical and analytical concepts of both Buddhists and non-Buddhists in the subsequent chapters.

---

[20] MMK 2.25cd quoted in note 2 above.

[21] *Prasanna-padā* (POUSSIN (1970: 107.12)): *etac ca karma-kāraka-parīkṣāyām ākhyāsyate* / .

[22] MMK 3.3cd:

> *sadarśanaḥ sa* [= *agni-dṛṣṭântaḥ*] *pratyukto gamyamāna-gatâgataiḥ* // .

[23] MMK 7.14:

> *nôtpadyamānaṁ nôtpannaṁ nânutpannaṁ kathaṁcana* / .
> *utpadyate tad ākhyātaṁ gamyamāna-gatâgataiḥ* // .

[24] MMK 10.13cd: *atrêndhane śeṣam uktaṁ gamyamāna-gatâgataiḥ* // .

[25] MMK 16.7cd: ... [*ś*]*eṣam uktaṁ gamyamāna-gatâgataiḥ* // .

## 2. The Trilemma Arguments in the *Vigraha-vyāvartanī* and the *Vaidalya-prakaraṇa*: *traikālyâsiddhi*

The Trilemma arguments which are similar to those in MMK Chapter 2 discussed above are found in the *Vigraha-vyāvartanī* (= VVy) and the *Vaidalya-prakaraṇa* (= VPr) commonly attributed to the same Nāgārjuna, author of MMK. That type of argument seems to be called '*gamyamāna-gata-agata*' ('present-past-and-future') in MMK as seen above and '*traikālyâsiddhi*' ('non-establishment in the three times') in the other two texts.

In this connection it is to be noted that Fernando TOLA and Carmen DRAGONETTI denied the authorship of Nāgārjuna regarding VPr and VVy,[26] and that Shiro MATSUMOTO also questioned the authenticity of both texts.[27] The fact that the similar type of Trilemma argument is differently named in MMK and VVy–VPr may give support to the conclusion of TOLA, DRAGONETTI and MATSUMOTO. However, it may be possible that Nāgārjuna changed his terminology over his career. Regarding the authorship of VVy and VPr, I would like to follow David BURTON's attitude in treating them as representing philosophical thought not inconsistent with that presented in MMK.[28] For the sake of convenience, I shall keep the name of Nāgārjuna as the author of both texts.

VVy consists of two sections, viz. Objection (*pūrva-pakṣa*) and Reply (*uttara-pakṣa*). At the end of the Objection section the opponent presents the following Trilemma in order to reject Nāgārjuna's thesis that all things are empty of their intrinsic nature (*niḥsvabhāvāḥ sarva-bhāvāḥ*):

Trilemma 7

'(1) It is not possible (*anupapanna*) to hold that the negation (*pratiṣedha*) comes first and then the thing to be negated (*pratiṣedhya*).

(2) Nor is it possible to hold that the negation comes after [the thing to be negated],

(3) or that they are simultaneous.

— The intrinsic nature [of the things] is, therefore, existent.'[29]

---

[26] TOLA–DRAGONETTI (1995: 7–15), TOLA–DRAGONETTI (1998: 151–166).

[27] MATSUMOTO (1997: 149–154).

[28] BURTON (1999: 13–14).

[29] Translation by K. BHATTACHARYA (1990: 106)—VVy v.20:
*pūrvaṁ cet pratiṣedhaḥ paścāt pratiṣedhyam ity anupapannam /*
*paścāc cânupapanno yugapac ca yataḥ svabhāvaḥ san //*

Here the opponent is pointing out that Nāgārjuna's negation of the intrinsic nature is impossible in the three times (past, future and present) with reference to the thing to be negated, i.e. the intrinsic nature itself. It is to be noted that it is not Nāgārjuna but his opponent who is applying the Trilemma argument from the three times.

Towards the end of VVy Nāgārjuna replies to the above objection as follows:

> 'We have already answered [the question relating to] the reason [for a negation] in the three times (*traikālya*), for the case is the same. And a counter-reason for the three times (*traikālya-pratihetu*) is obtained for the upholders of the doctrine of voidness (Śūnyatā-vādin).'[30]

In the commentary to the above verse, he says that if, as the opponent says, the negation of Śūnyatā-vāda is impossible in the three times, the negation of the opponent is similarly impossible in the three times because they are not different with respect to being 'negation'. Here Nāgārjuna is pointing out that the opponent's argument against the negation of Śūnyatā-vāda commits the fallacy of *sādhya-sama*: 'The reason is of the same nature as the thesis to be established' (*sādhya-samatvāt*)[31]. He declares that that very reason which expresses a negation in the three times (*trikāla-pratiṣedha-vācī hetuḥ*) is possible only for Śūnyatā-vādins because they negate the intrinsic nature of ALL things (*sarva-bhāva-svabhāva-pratiṣedhakatvāt*).

Next in order to reply to the above objection Nāgārjuna refers to VVy v.63, which runs as follows:

---

[30] Translation by K. BHATTACHARYA (1990: 135)—VVy v. 69:
*yas traikālye hetuḥ pratyuktaḥ pūrvam eva sa samatvāt /*
*traikālya-pratihetuś ca śūnyatā-vādināṁ prāptaḥ //*

[31] The name '*sādhya-sama*' is given to the fallacious reason (*hetvâbhāsa* or *ahetu*) by the Naiyāyika and the *Caraka-saṁhitā* (= CS). However, Nāgārjuna's notion of *sādhya-sama* does not seem to be identical with the Naiyāyika definition of *sādhya-sama* or CS's *varṇya-sama*. N.B.: all *hetvâbhāsa*s are included in the category of *nigraha-sthāna* (the point of defeat) in the *Nyāya-sūtra* (= NS) chapter 5.

Cf. NS 1.2.8: *sādhyâviśiṣṭaḥ sādhyatvāt sādhya-samaḥ //* — GANGOPADHYAYA (1982: 59): '(The pseudo-probans called) the unproved (*sādhyasama*) (is the mark which) being yet to be properly established (*sādhyatvāt*) is not different (*a-viśiṣṭa*) from the characteristic sought to be proved (*sādhya* or probandum).'

Cf. CS 3.8.57: *varṇya-samo nāmâhetuḥ—yo hetur varṇyâviśiṣṭaḥ; yathā—kaścid brūyāt—asparśatvād buddhir anityā śabdavad iti; atra varṇyaḥ śabdo buddhir api varṇyā, tad-ubhaya-varṇyâviśiṣṭatvād varṇya-samo 'py ahetuḥ //*.

'I do not negate anything, nor is there anything to be negated. You, therefore, calumniate me when you say: "You negate".'[32]

Finally he assumes that the opponent concedes that the negation is established in all the three times. Then he objects that the opponent faces the same difficulties that are pointed out to Nāgārjuna in VVy v.20 above.

Furthermore, he states: 'You admit (*tvayâbhyupagamyate*) the existence of a negation and abandon your own thesis (*pratijñā-hāni*).' In this way Nāgārjuna points out that the opponent commits two fallacies, viz. *matânujñā* and *pratijñā-hāni*.[33] The early manuals of Indian debate, such as the *Vimāna-sthāna* portion of the *Caraka-saṁhitā* (= CS) and the *Nyāya-sūtra* (= NS) Chapter 5, call those fallacies 'points of defeat' (*nigraha-sthāna*). NS, for instance, lists twenty-two of those points[34]—if someone commits any one of them during a debate, he is immediately declared to have been defeated. In any case Nāgārjuna seems to be well acquainted with the techniques of Indian debate which are later recorded in NS Chapters 1 and 5.

As a conclusion Nāgārjuna seems to want to insist that he can negate anything in the three times because he denies the intrinsic nature of all things, while the opponent cannot do so because he posits the intrinsic nature of those which are to be

---

[32] Translation by K. BHATTACHARYA (1989: 131)—VVy v.63:
*pratiṣedhayāmi nâhaṁ kiṁcit pratiṣedhyam asti na ca kiṁcit /*
*tasmāt pratiṣedhayasîty adhilaya eṣa tvayā kriyate //*

[33] NS 5.2.20: *sva-pakṣe doṣâbhyupagamāt para-pakṣe doṣa-prasaṅgo matânujñā /* —GANGOPADHYAYA (1982: 418): 'The admission of a charge (*matānujñā*) occurs when one admits a fallacy in one's own position and attributes the same fallacy to the other's position.'

Cf. CS 3.8.62: *athâbhyanujñā—abhyanujñā nāma sā ya iṣṭâniṣṭâbhyupagamaḥ //*, and NS 5.2.2: *pratidṛṣṭânta-dharmâbhyanujñā sva-dṛṣṭānte pratijñā-hāniḥ /* —GANGOPADHYAYA (1982: 409): 'The loss of thesis (*pratijñā-hāni*) occurs if one admits in one's own instance the presence of a property belonging to the counter instance.'

Cf. CS 3.8.61: *atha pratijñā-hāniḥ—pratijñā-hānir nāma sā pūrva-parigṛhītāṁ pratijñāṁ paryanuyukto yat parityajati, yathā prāk pratijñāṁ kṛtvā nityaḥ puruṣa iti, paryanuyuktas tv āha—anitya iti //*

At the conference Dr. Prets pointed out to me that Nāgārjuna is following CS's definition of *pratijñā-hāni* rather than that of NS. This may indicate the temporary sequence among CS *Vimāna-sthāna*, Nāgārjuna and NS 5.

[34] NS 5.2.1: *pratijñā-hāniḥ pratijñântaraṁ pratijñā-virodhaḥ pratijñā-sannyāso hetv-antaram arthântaraṁ nirarthakam avijñātârtham apārthakam aprāpta-kālaṁ nyūnam adhikaṁ punar-uktam ananubhāṣaṇam ajñānam apratibhā vikṣepo matânujñā paryanuyojyôpekṣaṇaṁ niranuyojyânuyogo 'pasiddhânto hetvâbhāsāś ca nigraha-sthānāni //*

negated. Therefore, it is only Nāgārjuna who can apply the argument from *traikālyâsiddhi* in order to negate any concept held by their opponents.

VPr is a polemical text which tries to deny the sixteen categories (*padârtha*) of the Naiyāyika one after another. It applies the *traikālyâsiddhi* argument twice in order to reject the categories of *pramāṇa* (a means of valid cognition) and *prameya* (an object to be cognised by *pramāṇa*) (VPr 12–16),[35] and the notion of the whole (*avayavin*) (VPr 36).[36]

In VPr 12 Nāgārjuna rejects the independent reality of *pramāṇa* and *prameya* on the ground that they are not established as existing in any of the three times, viz. past, future, and present. In this connection he seems to be presupposing the following three propositions:

(1) *pramāṇa* exists before *prameya*.
(2) *pramāṇa* exists after *prameya*.
(3) *pramāṇa* and *prameya* exist at the same time.

---

[35] *Vaidalya-sūtra* 12–16 (ed. by TOLA–DRAGONETTI (1995: 26–28): *tshad ma dang gzhal bya dag ni dus gsum du ma grub po* // 12 // *dus gsum du tshad ma dang gzhal bya dag ma grub pas 'gag pa mi 'thad do* // 13 // *dgag pa grub na tshad ma dang gzhal bya yang grub po zer ba ni ma yin te* / *sngar khas blangs pa'i phyir ro* // 14 // *gal te tshad ma dang gzhal bya dag ma grub par khas blangs pa yin na ni khas blangs pa dang dus mnyam pa kho nar rtsod pa rdzogs pa yin no* // 15 // *ma grub pa'i rtog pa spong ba yin no* // 16 //.

Translation by TOLA–DRAGONETTI (1995: 63–66):

> '(12) The means of valid knowledge and the knowable (object) are not established (as existing) in (any of) the three times.
> (13) Because the means of valid knowledge and the knowable (object) are not established (as existing) in (any of) the three times, (its) denial is not logically possible.
> (14) To say that if the negation is established (as existing), the means of valid knowledge and the knowable (object) are also established (as existing)—this is not (possible), because of the previous acceptance.
> (15) If there is acceptance of the non-existence of the means of valid knowledge and the knowable (object), in the very moment of this acceptance, the discussion is over.
> (16) (Because, in the negation, only) the idea of (something) non-established (as existing) is eliminated.'

[36] *Vaidalya-sūtra* 36 (ed. by TOLA–DRAGONETTI (1995: 35): *dus gsum la ma grub pas yan lag med pa nyid do* // Translation by TOLA–DRAGONETTI (1995: 75): 'Because (the whole) is not established (as existing) in any of the three times, the parts (*avayava*) do not exist.'

As before they exhaust all the possible relationships between *pramāṇa* and *prameya*. Then for each proposition he applies *reductio ad absurdum* (*prasaṅga*) in the following manner:

(1) If *pramāṇa* existed before *prameya*, what should be called '*pramāṇa*'? Something obtains the name *pramāṇa* because it cognises *prameya*, but there is no *prameya* at the time of *pramāṇa*; hence, it cannot be called '*pramāṇa*'.

(2) If *pramāṇa* existed after *prameya*, what could be *pramāṇa* for that already existing *prameya*? Because a not yet arisen thing cannot be the *pramāṇa* of something already arisen; otherwise even the hare's horns would become *pramāṇa*.

(3) It is impossible that *pramāṇa* and *prameya* exist at the same time, because there is no causal relationship between them, just as between the two horns on the head of a cow.

In this way Nāgārjuna rejects all three propositions cited above and we can construct the following Trilemma:[37]

Trilemma 8

(1) *pramāṇa* does not exist before *prameya*.

(2) *pramāṇa* does not exist after *prameya*.

(3) *pramāṇa* and *prameya* do not exist at the same time.

As VPr 2 and 3 indicate,[38] Nāgārjuna seems to assume that *pramāṇa* and *prameya* are mutually dependent. Therefore (1) if there is no *prameya*, there is no *pramāṇa* and (2) if there is no *pramāṇa*, there is no *prameya*. Thus the first two lemmas are justified. The third lemma, however, cannot be so easily proved, for, as BURTON says, it appears to be plausible that the *pramāṇa* and *prameya* exist in mutual dependence as well as simultaneously.[39] As a matter of fact, BURTON seems to be the first modern scholar who analysed the *traikālyâsiddhi* argument in any detail.

---

[37] Though Nāgārjuna does not explicitly mention it, we may be able to reconstruct the following Trilemma similar to those found in MMK chapter 2:

(1) *prameya* is not cognised by the already existing (i.e. past) *pramāṇa*;

(2) *prameya* is not cognised by the not yet arisen (i.e. future) *pramāṇa*;

(3) *prameya* is not cognised by the simultaneously existing (i.e. present) *pramāṇa*.

[38] VPr 2 and 3, ed. by TOLA–DRAGONETTI (1995: 21–22); Translation by TOLA–DRAGONETTI (1995: 58).

[39] BURTON (1999: 193).

He is critical of the persuasiveness of Nāgārjuna's argument and supports the Naiyāyika's objection to be discussed below.[40]

BURTON seems to take it that causation in general is here at issue, but I would rather think that the specific causal relation between *prameya* and *pramāṇa* is under discussion. In this connection, some general accounts of Indian *pramāṇa* theories are in order. There are two rival theories concerning the order of *pramāṇa* and its object *prameya*; namely, according to the Naiyāyika (and probably the Buddhist Vaibhāṣika), *pramāṇa* and *prameya* exist simultaneously at least in the case of perception, while according to the Buddhist Sautrāntika, *prameya* must always exist before *pramāṇa*. For the former school admits that a cause can be simultaneous with its effect, while the latter insists that a cause must be prior to its effect. As far as I know no Indian epistemologist claimed that *pramāṇa* exists before and without *prameya*.

Therefore, the first lemma can be regarded as a kind of common-sense criticism supported by both schools of Indian epistemology. The second lemma may be a criticism by the Naiyāyika against the Sautrāntika, while the third lemma may be a criticism by the Sautrāntika against the Naiyāyika. Nāgārjuna seems to be letting his opponents fight each other.

Then what is Nāgārjuna actually trying to achieve by Trilemma 8? I think that he wants to negate the concepts of *pramāṇa* and *prameya* as well as the *pramāṇa* theory in general, by indicating the mutual rejection of alternative hypotheses by the rival schools of epistemology. It is to be noted that Nāgārjuna himself does not make any commitment to any epistemological theory. On the contrary, he seems to have felt the danger of the newly arisen epistemological realism in India, wishing to defeat it in its infancy. Unlike BURTON, I find Nāgārjuna's argument not so unconvincing. Nāgārjuna does not make any commitment; hence, he is ultimately beyond the controversy and contradiction.

VPr 13 records an objection from the Naiyāyika, which essentially amounts to the following Dilemma:

(1) If Nāgārjuna insists that *pramāṇa* and *prameya* are not established (i.e. are negated) in the three times, it will follow that his negation itself is not established in the three times by the same force of argument applied by Nāgārjuna to *pramāṇa* and *prameya*.

(2) If Nāgārjuna insists that his negation is established in the three times, then he should admit that both *pramāṇa* and *prameya* are also established in the three times; otherwise he should explain why they differ.

[40] BURTON (1999: 191–199).

The first lemma seems to correspond to the opponent's argument in VVy v.20 and the second lemma appears to be criticising Nāgārjuna's position in the commentary on VVy v.69, which distinguishes his own negation of all the intrinsic natures from the opponent's negation of Nāgārjuna's negation.

Nāgārjuna answers the above criticism in VPr 14 and 15, by saying that once the Naiyāyika admits Nāgārjuna's negation of *pramāṇa* and *prameya* in the three times even hypothetically, they commit the fallacy of 'previous acceptance' and that the discussion is over in the very moment of their acceptance of Nāgārjuna's negation. Nāgārjuna, by the expression 'previous acceptance', seems to be referring to the same point of defeat called '*matânujñā*', just as in the commentary on VVy v.69 mentioned above.

Although BURTON criticises Nāgārjuna's response as pure sophistry,[41] as a historian of Indian logic, I would like to support Nāgārjuna's move. As I shall discuss later, according to the early manuals of Indian debate, he is quite justified to use any means in order to defeat his opponents. As a matter of fact, the Naiyāyika should accept and obey the rules of Indian debate because they themselves had set them.

So far Nāgārjuna has responded to the objection raised in the first lemma but he still faces the problem hinted at by the second lemma. Namely, why can he justify his own negation, while rejecting the Naiyāyika's? How can he distinguish them? As BURTON rightly points out, the Naiyāyika here is applying a sort of hypothetical argument, called *tarka* in the Nyāya system, which is *reductio ad absurdum*. Nāgārjuna seems to insist that the Naiyāyika is not allowed to apply such an argument, while he himself frequently uses *reductio ad absurdum* (*prasaṅga*) in order to refute the opponents. Is he caught in a contradiction as BURTON suggests?

Nāgārjuna does not answer this objection directly. Instead in VPr 16 he says that his negation does not imply the existence of what is to be negated, just as the statement 'The river is not deep', simply eliminates a fear of the deep water without implying the existence of that deep water. Thus he seems to be suggesting that he can apply hypothetical reasoning without admitting the existence of what is to be negated and that his opponent cannot apply hypothetical reasoning, because once he negates something, he has already admitted the existence of what is to be negated. Nāgārjuna seems to insist that the opponent, being the proponent of Realistic philosophy, cannot posit an 'empty subject', i.e. a subject which has no reference to the real state of affairs. Nāgārjuna, on the other hand, being an advocate of Śūnyatā-vāda, is free to posit an 'empty subject' in his hypothetical argument. In this connection, it is to be noted that in the Nyāya tradition of logic *tarka* did not play so important a role as the five-membered (*pañcâvayava*) direct proof—it was always

[41] BURTON (1999: 195).

regarded as a kind of supplement to the latter— precisely because Indian logicians in general were not favourable towards an 'empty subject'.

This is the way I would reconstruct Nāgārjuna's response to the second objection. There are of course loopholes in Nāgārjuna's argument; some objects of negation are totally fictitious like hare's horns and *gandharva-nagara*, while others are not entirely unreal—deep water exists somewhere in the world. But there is no such apparent contradiction in Nāgārjuna's argument as indicated by BURTON.

### 3. The Trilemma Arguments criticised by the Naiyāyika

It is well known that Nāgārjuna's criticism against Nyāya theory of *pramāṇa* in VVy and VPr is also found in NS Chapters 2 and 5. In NS 2.1.8–11 an opponent attacks the Naiyāyika by claiming that perception (*pratyakṣa*) and others are not *pramāṇa* because they are not established in the three times (*traikālyâsiddhi*). Since he presents an argument which is quite similar to the one we have seen in VPr 12, it seems plausible that the opponent here is Nāgārjuna or some of his followers.

'(Objection) Perception etc. are without validity (*aprāmāṇya*), because of their ineffectiveness in the three times (*traikālya-asiddhi*).

(1) If *pramāṇa* exists prior to its object, then there will be no perception resulting from sense-object contact.

(2) If (*pramāṇa*) exists posterior to (its object) then the objects cannot be determined by the *pramāṇa*-s.

(3) If (*pramāṇa*) exists simultaneously with (its object), then there will be the absence of the succession of one knowledge after the other, because each knowledge is restricted to its specific object.'[42]

In NS 2.1.12–15 the Naiyāyika answers the above objection as follows:

'(Answer) The refutation (i.e. the objection raised against *pramāṇa*) is untenable, because of its (i.e. of the refutation itself) ineffectiveness in the three times.

[42] Translation by GANGOPADHYAYA (1982: 77–78).

NS 2.1.8: *pratyakṣâdīnām aprāmāṇyaṁ traikālyâsiddheḥ //*

NS 2.1.9: *pūrvaṁ hi pramâṇa-siddhau nêndriyârtha-sannikarṣāt pratyakṣôtpattiḥ //*

NS 2.1.10: *paścāt-siddhau na pramāṇebhyaḥ prameya-siddhiḥ //*

NS 2.1.11: *yugapat-siddhau pratyartha-niyatatvāt krama-vṛttitvâbhāvo buddhīnām //*

> The refutation (i.e. the objection raised against *pramāṇa*) is untenable, because of the total negation of *pramāṇa*.
>
> [If it is claimed that] these (i.e. *pramāṇa*-s underlying the inference-components of the opponent himself) are valid, the negation of all *pramāṇa*-s cannot be established.
>
> Further, ineffectiveness in the three times is not established, because it (i.e. *prameya*) is established (by the *pramāṇa* which is posterior), just like proving the musical instrument from its sound (which is produced later).'[43]

First they assert that the negation of *pramāṇas* is impossible because it is not established in the three times either. This reminds us of the Naiyāyika's objection mentioned in VPr 13. Next they present the following Dilemma:

(1) If you negate all *pramāṇas*, your negation itself will be impossible.
(2) If your negation is regarded as *pramāṇa*, then it will follow that you are not negating ALL *pramāṇas*.

This objection seems to have been known to Nāgārjuna, since a similar argument is referred to as *pūrva-pakṣa* at the very beginning of VVy and as a view of Nāgārjuna himself in VPr 5.[44] Finally the Naiyāyika refutes the negation in the three times by presenting a counter-example of the musical instrument and its sound, which may suggest that the prior existence of the means (*pramāṇa*) can be inferred and established by its result. This is the end of the Naiyāyika's critique of *traikālyâsiddhi*.[45]

It is curious that they do not answer to Nāgārjuna's accusation of '*matânujñā*'. Perhaps they have tacitly ignored it. In any case, it is quite natural that the Naiyāyika claims that they won the debate against Nāgārjuna with reference to *traikālyâsiddhi* but I would think that their objections are presupposed or known to and answered by Nāgārjuna in VVy and VPr as we have seen above.

---

[43] Translation by GANGOPADHYAYA (1982: 80–81).

NS 2.1.12: *traikālyâsiddheḥ pratiṣedhânupapattiḥ* //

NS 2.1.13: *sarva-pramāṇa-pratiṣedhāc ca pratiṣedhânupapattiḥ* //

NS 2.1.14: *tat-prāmāṇye vā na sarva-pramāṇa-vipratiṣedhaḥ* //

NS 2.1.15: *traikālyâpratiṣedhaś ca śabdād ātodya-siddhivat tat-siddheḥ* //

[44] BHATTACHARYA (1990: 95–96); TOLA–DRAGONETTI (1995: 59–60).

[45] NS 2.1.16–20 continues the debate with Nāgārjuna or his followers on the topic of *pramāṇa*, which also has parallels in VVy 32–33 and VPr 5–6.

In this connection I would rather go into NS Chapter 5 where *traikālyâsiddhi* is regarded as a false rejoinder or sophistry (*jāti*) called '*ahetu-sama*' (similar to the pseudo-reason).

> '(When the opponent objects by saying that) the ground (of the proponent) is not a proper ground because of its non-establishment in the three times, it would be a case of *ahetu-sama*.
>
> There is no non-establishment in the three times, because the probandum (*sādhya*) is established by the ground.
>
> The opposing ground (offered by the opponent) also cannot be established (in the three times). Hence, it cannot refute what it seeks to refute.'[46]

Just as in NS 2.1.12 here the argument from the three times is rejected because the refutation by the three times itself is not established in the three times. Nāgārjuna is again facing the same charge, one which I believe he has successfully answered in his own way.

Having discovered that several *jāti*s (false rejoinders or sophistries) enumerated in NS Chapter 5 have a close resemblance to the *reductio ad absurdum* (*prasaṅga*) arguments found in VVy and VPr, Yuichi KAJIYAMA once proposed, following Vātsyāyana's (or Pakṣilasvāmin's) definition of *jāti* in the *Nyāya-bhāṣya*,[47] that the expression '*jāti*' might have come from the compound '*prasaṅga-jāti*' (production of *prasaṅga*) and that the category of *jāti* might have been a collection of Nāgārjuna's peculiar uses of *prasaṅga* (i.e. *reductio ad absurdum*) especially aimed against the Naiyāyika.[48] In other words, KAJIYAMA is suggesting that the Naiyāyika

---

[46] Translation by GANGOPADHYAYA (1982: 389–390).

NS 5.1.18: *traikālyâsiddher hetor ahetu-samaḥ* //

NS 5.1.19: *na hetutaḥ sādhya-siddhes traikālyâsiddhiḥ* //

NS 5.1.20: *pratiṣedhânupapatteś ca pratiṣedha-vyāpratiṣedhaḥ* //

[47] NS 1.2.18: *sādharmya-vaidharmyābhyāṁ pratyavasthānaṁ jātiḥ* //.

NBh *ad loc.*: *prayukte hi hetau yaḥ prasaṅgo jāyate sa jātiḥ / sa ca prasaṅgaḥ sādharmya-vaidharmyābhyāṁ pratyavasthānam upālambhaḥ pratiṣedha iti* / Translation by GANGOPADHYAYA (1982: 68): 'Futile rejoinder (*jāti*) is refuting the opponent by (pointing to) superficial similarity and dissimilarity. *Jāti* (literally) means an opportunity (for one of the contestants) born out of the employment of a probans (by the other). This opportunity is nothing but the refutation or rejection or demolition by pointing to superficial similarity or dissimilarity.'

GANGOPADHYAYA translates the word *prasaṅga* by 'opportunity' but I would take it to mean 'undesirable consequence' as in the case of MMK and other texts.

[48] KAJIYAMA (1984: 21–24).

tried to avoid Nāgārjuna's *prasaṅgas* by putting them aside altogether as 'a false rejoinder or sophistry'.

I find his conjectures quite convincing and guess that the Naiyāyika, who is faced with the charge of *matânujñā* from Nāgārjuna in the debate over *traikālyâsiddhi*, might have wanted to avoid such a charge by simply calling it 'a false rejoinder or sophistry'. Unlike BURTON I do not think that the Naiyāyika has given sufficient reason to reject *traikālyâsiddhi*.

## 4. An Appraisal of Nāgārjuna's Method of Arguments

Richard HAYES once caused an outrage among Buddhist scholars when he characterised Nāgārjuna's reasoning 'fallacious or sophistical'.[49] Recently David BURTON also severely criticised Nāgārjuna's reasoning in VVy and VPr and supported the Naiyāyika as we have briefly seen. I am not against their critical reading of Nāgārjuna; I also think that he uses various tricks in his arguments which may be regarded as 'fallacious' or 'sophistry'. Nonetheless, from the point of view of a historian of Indian logic, I do not think that Nāgārjuna is to be blamed for his methodology, since he is simply applying the method of argument recommended and broadly practised by his opponents, i.e. the Naiyāyika and other Indian logicians. I guess he is determined to apply any means to defeat his opponents, even if it is sophistry.

The Naiyāyika holds that there are three forms of debate (*kathā*), viz. 'discussion for the final ascertainment' (*vāda*), 'debating manoeuvre' (*jalpa*) and 'destructive criticism' (*vitaṇḍā*). They define them as follows:

> '*Vāda* is (the form of debate in which the two contestants) uphold the thesis and the anti-thesis (*pakṣapratipakṣaparigraha*) by substantiation (*sādhana*) and refutation (*upālambha*) with the help of *pramāṇa*s and *tarka*, without being contradicted by proved doctrine (*siddhāntāviruddha*) and employing the five inference-components (*pañcāvayavopapanna*).'[50]
>
> '*Jalpa* is (a form of debate) characterised by all the features as previously said (*yathoktopapanna*) (i.e. by all the features mentioned in

[49] HAYES (1994).

[50] Translation by GANGOPADHYAYA (1982: 52)—NS 1.2.1: *pramāṇa-tarka-sādhanôpālambhaḥ siddhântâviruddhaḥ pañcâvayavôpapannaḥ pakṣa-pratipakṣa-parigrahaḥ vādaḥ* // .

> the previous *sūtra* defining *vāda*) where substantiation and refutation are effected through *chala*, *jāti* and (all the forms of) *nigrahasthāna* (*chalajātinigrahasthāna-sādhanopālambha*) (over and above).'[51]
>
> 'This (i.e. *jalpa* mentioned in the previous *sūtra*) becomes *vitaṇḍā* when the opponent has no care for establishing any thesis of his own (*pratipakṣasthāpanahīna*).'[52]

The first type of debate (*vāda*) is a friendly debate between a teacher and a student or between colleagues, while the other two types (*jalpa* and *vitaṇḍā*) represent a hostile debate between the opposing parties. It is most interesting to note that the Naiyāyika admits in a hostile debate even such tricky methods as *chala* (purposive distortion or equivocation), *jāti* (sophistry) and *nigraha-sthāna* (point of defeat). As a matter of fact, they recommend employing *jalpa* and *vitaṇḍā* in a hostile debate for the final aim of protecting the truth. NS 4.2.50–51 says as follows:

> '*Jalpa* and *vitaṇḍā* are (to be employed) for protecting the ascertainment of truth, just as fences with thorny branches are constructed to protect the seedling coming out of the seed.
>
> One may start a debate by attacking (*vigṛhya*) (the opponent) with the help of *jalpa* and *vitaṇḍā*.'[53]

Thus, unlike modern Buddhologists the Naiyāyika and other Indian logicians of Nāgārjuna's time would not object to his method of argument in MMK, VVy and VPr. As I mentioned before, Nāgārjuna seems to be well acquainted with the debate techniques of the early Indian logicians; so, in a debate he points to a *nigraha-sthāna* committed by his opponents to silence them, and at the same time he himself employs *chala*, *jāti* or *nigraha-sthāna* in order to defeat them. I should add that he is taking a risk too because once his trick is discovered and pointed out, he also will lose. He must have been a shrewd debater feared by his contemporaries.

---

[51] Translation by GANGOPADHYAYA (1982: 54)—NS 1.2.2: *yathôktôpapannaḥ chala-jāti-nigraha-sthāna-sādhanôpālambhaḥ jalpaḥ //* For *chala* (purposive distortion), see NS 1.2.10: *vacana-vighāto 'rtha-vikalpôpapattyā chalam //*. Translation by GANGOPADHYAYA (1982: 62): '*Chala* is the rebuttal of the words (or arguments) of the opponent by way of inventing a meaning contradictory to the meaning intended.'

[52] Translation by GANGOPADHYAYA (1982: 55–56); NS 1.2.3: *sa pratipakṣa-sthāpanā-hīnaḥ vitaṇḍā //*

[53] Translation by GANGOPADHYAYA (1982: 373–4); NS 4.2.50–51: *tattvâdhyavasāya-saṁrakṣaṇârthaṁ jalpa-vitaṇḍe bīja-praroha-saṁrakṣaṇârthaṁ kaṇṭaka-śākhâvaraṇavat // tābhyāṁ vigṛhya kathanam //*

After Nāgārjuna's time Indian logicians gradually shifted their interest from the rules of debate, such as *nigraha-sthāna*, to more formal aspects of a logical proof; they started to investigate what makes a correct reason (*hetu*) rather than a pseudo-reason (*hetvâbhāsa*) and some of them discovered 'the three characteristics' (*trairūpya*) of a valid reason.

Later a Buddhist logician, Dignāga, defined *jāti* as a pseudo-disproof (*dūṣaṇâbhāsa*), examined the fourteen kinds of *jāti*, thirteen of which are found in NS Chapter 5, and reassessed them in his new system of logic based on the theory of *trairūpya*; regarding *nigraha-sthāna*, he says that they are not worth discussing because some of them may be regarded as a legitimate disproof, others are too coarse or illogical or sheer sophistry.[54] Another Buddhist logician, Dharmakīrti, wrote *Vāda-nyāya* ('Logic of debate') in which he re-defined *nigraha-sthāna* as *asādhanâṅga-vacana* ('the non-means-of-proof-formulation') and *adoṣôdbhāvana* ('the non-fault-indication'),[55] mentioned two to eleven types of *nigraha-sthāna* constructed in his system of logic based on the theory of three kinds of reason (viz. 'effect' (*kārya*), 'essential property' (*svabhāva*) and 'non-perception' (*anupalabdhi*), and rejected all the twenty-two types of *nigraha-sthāna* mentioned in NS Chapter 5. Thus by the seventh century the roles of old *nigraha-sthāna* and *jāti* seem to have diminished considerably in Indian logic.

Now the most important contribution of Nāgārjuna to the development of Indian logic is that he firmly established the method of argument by means of *reductio ad absurdum* (*prasaṅga* / *prasaṅgâpatti*). First he assumes a certain position of the opponent and then he points out some undesirable consequence from that assumption, so that he can deny the opponent's position. Since he usually does not try to prove his own position in a way the opponents do, by constructing the five-membered proof, his method is generally regarded as a kind of *vitaṇḍā* and he is often called a great Vitaṇḍā-vādin. Nāgārjuna's method of argument, i.e. *prasaṅga*, is adopted not only by his fellow Mādhyamika Buddhists, but also by Jayarāśi, a Lokāyata, and Śrīharṣa, a late Vedāntin.

As a matter of fact, Dharmakīrti adopts *reductio ad absurdum* when he has to prove the universal statement like 'Whatever is existing is momentary', and even the Naiyāyika begins to apply it in order to support their proof of existence of the creator God, etc. It is commonly understood that *reductio ad absurdum* is the most powerful means to defeat the opponents.

[54] See for example *Nyāya-mukha* §§ 9–12; KATSURA (1982: 84, 87).

[55] For the complex meanings of the two compounds, see MUCH (1986: 133–142).

To end my paper, I would like to quote a passage from the *Vimāna-sthāna* of the *Caraka-saṁhitā*. Caraka recommends one who is about to take part in a hostile debate to choose a proper opponent and a proper audience; namely, he should debate with an inferior opponent in front of a favourable audience. Then he gives several advices how to defeat an inferior opponent:

> 'If you think that your opponent is inferior to you, defeat him quickly. There are ways to defeat the inferiors quickly.
>
> Namely, if they are not well learned, overwhelm them by quoting a lengthy *sūtra* passage. If they lack the knowledge, overwhelm them by a sentence full of difficult technical terms. If they are not good at memorising sentences, overwhelm them by the *daṇḍa* of sentences full of long and complex *sūtra* quotations. If they are inferior in the understanding of sentence meanings, overwhelm them by repeating one and the same word with multiple meanings. If they are inferior in linguistic ability, overwhelm them by abusing their half-uttered sentence. If they are not clever, overwhelm them by making them shame-faced. If they are easily angered, overwhelm them by making them fatigued. If they are timid, overwhelm them by making them terrified. If they are careless, overwhelm them by regulating them.
>
> In these ways you should defeat the inferiors quickly.'[56]

Postscript (November 25, 2000): I must confess that I failed to consult the following important monograph on the present topic: Claus Oetke: *Zur Methode der Analyse Philosophischer Sūtratexte, die Pramāṇa Passagen der Nyāyasūtren. Studien Zur Indologie und Iranistik*, Monographie 11, Reinbek 1991.

---

[56] CS *Vimāna-sthāna* 3.8.21: *yatra tv enam avaraṁ manyeta tatrâivâinam āśu nigṛhṇīyāt / tatra khalv ime pratyavarāṇām āśu nigrahe bhavanty upāyāḥ; tad yathā—śruta-hīnaṁ mahatā sūtra-pāṭhenâbhibhavet, vijñāna-hīnaṁ punaḥ kaṣṭa-śabdena vākyena, vākya-dhāraṇā-hīnam āviddha-dīrgha-sūtra-saṁkulair vākya-daṇḍakaiḥ, pratibhā-hīnaṁ punar-vacanenâika-vidhenânekârtha-vācinā, vacana-śakti-hīnam ardhôktasya vākyasyâkṣepeṇa, aviśāradam apatrapaṇena, kopanam āyāsanena, bhīruṁ vitrâsanena, anavahitaṁ niyamanenêti / evam etair upāyaiḥ param avaram abhibhavec chīghram // 21 //*

## BIBLIOGRAPHY


BHATTACHARYA 1990 = Bhattacharya, Kamaleswar: *The Dialectical Method of Nāgārjuna, Vigrahavyāvartanī*. Delhi 1990.

BRONKHORST 1985 = Bronkhorst, Johannes: 'Nāgārjuna and the Naiyāyikas,' *Journal of Indian Philosophy* 13–2 (1985) 107–132.

BURTON 1999 = Burton, David F.: *Emptiness Appraised, A Critical Study of Nāgārjuna's Philosophy*. Curzon Critical Studies in Buddhism, Richmond, Surrey 1999.

CARDONA 1991 = Cardona, George: 'A Path still taken: Some early Indian arguments concerning time.' *Journal of the American Oriental Society* 111/3 (1991) 445–464.

CS = *Caraka-saṁhitā*: ed. by Vaidya Jādavaji Trikamji Āchārya, Nirṇaya Sagar Press, Bombay 1941.

GANGOPADHYAYA 1982 = Gangopadhyaya, Mrinalkanti: *Nyāyasūtra with Vātsyāyana's commentary*. Calcutta 1982.

HAYES 1994 = Hayes, Richard: 'Nāgārjuna's Appeal,' *Journal of Indian Philosophy* 22–4 (1994) 299–378.

DE JONG 1977 = de Jong, J.W.: *Nāgārjuna Mūlamadhyamakakārikāḥ*. The Adyar Library Series 109, Madras 1977.

KAJIYAMA 1965 = Kajiyama, Yuichi: 'The Vaidalyaprakaraṇa of Nāgārjuna,' *Indogaku Shironshū* 6–7 (1965) 129–155.

KAJIYAMA 1974 = Kajiyama, Yuichi: *Ryūju Ronshū*. Tokyo 1974. [Contains Japanese tr. of *Vigraha-vyāvartanī* and *Vaidalya-prakaraṇa*].

KAJIYAMA 1984 = Kajiyama, Yuichi: 'Bukkyo Chishikiron no Keisei (Formation of Buddhist Epistemology),' *Koza Daijo Bukkyo* Vol. 9, Tokyo 1984.

KAJIYAMA 1991 = Kajiyama, Yuichi: 'On the Authorship of the Upāyahṛdaya,' *Studies in the Buddhist Epistemological Tradition*, ed. by Ernst Steinkellner, Wien 1991: 107–117.

KATSURA 1982, 1984, 1987 = Katsura, Shōryū: 'Inmyo-Shorimonron Kenkyu (A Study of the Nyāyamukha)' [5]-[7]. *Hiroshima Daigaku Bungakubu Kiyo* (*Bulletin of Faculty of Letters*) Hiroshima University, Vols. 42, 44, 46, Hiroshima 1982: 82–99, 1984: 43–74, 1987: 46–65.

KATSURA 2000 = Katsura, Shōryū: 'Nāgārjuna and the Tetralemma (*Catuṣkoṭi*),' in *the Festschrift for Prof. Gadjin Nagao*: *Wisdom, Compassion and the Search for Understanding, A Buddhist Studies Legacy*, ed. by Jonathan A. Silk, University of Hawaii Press, 2000.

MATSUMOTO 1997 = Matsumoto, Shiro: *Chibetto Bukkyo Tetsugaku*. Tokyo 1997.

MMK = Nāgārjuna: *Mūla-madhyamaka-kārikā*. See: POUSSIN (1970).

MUCH 1986 = Much, Michael Torsten: 'Dharmakīrti's Definition of "Points of Defeat",' *Buddhist Logic and Epistemology*, ed. by B.K. Matilal and R.D. Evans, Dordrecht 1986: 133–142.

NS & NBh = *Nyāya-sūtra* and *Nyāya-bhāṣya*. In: *Nyāyadarśanam*, ed. by Amarendramohan Tarkatirtha, Calcutta 1936. [Reprinted: Rinsen Book Co., Kyoto 1982].

OGAWA 1991 = Ogawa, Hideyo: '*Gamyate, gamyamāna, gata, agata*—A study of MMK, II. kk.1–6,' [in Japanese] *Indogaku Bukkyōgaku Kenkyū*, 39/2 (1991) 167–172.

POUSSIN 1970 = Poussin, Louis de la Vallée (ed.): *Madhyamakavṛttiḥ Mūlamadhyamaka-kārikās de Nāgarjuna avec la Prasannapadā Commentaire de Candrakīrti. Bibliotheca Buddhica* 4, Pétersbourg 1913. [Reprinted: Osnabrück 1970].

TOLA– DRAGONETTI 1995 = Tola, Fernando; Dragonetti, Carmen: *Nāgārjuna's Refutation of Logic* (*Nyāya*) *Vaidalyaprakaraṇa*. Delhi 1995.

TOLA– DRAGONETTI 1998 = Tola, Fernando; Dragonetti, Carmen: 'Against the Attribution of the *Vigrahavyāvartanī* to Nāgārjuna', *Wiener Zeitschrift für die Kunde Südasiens* 42 (1998) 151–166.

VPr = *Vaidalya-prakaraṇa*. See: TOLA– DRAGONETTI (1995).

VVy = *Vigraha-vyāvartanī*. See: BHATTACHARYA (1990).

# Some Observations on the Date of the *Yukti-dīpikā* (Apropos of the New Edition)*

MAREK MEJOR

## –1–

The *editio princeps* of the *Yukti-dīpikā,* edited by Pulinbe(i)hari Chakravarti, was published in 1938. It was based on a single Ms from Poona [= P]. The same author published in 1951 *Origin and Development of the Sāṁkhya System of Thought,* a study based on his edition of YD.

The second edition of YD was published in 1967 by Ram Chandra Pandeya: *Yuktidīpikā. An Ancient Commentary on the Sāṁkhya Kārikā of Īśvarakṛṣṇa*. Based on two Mss: Poona [P] and Ahmedabad [= A], it meant a further step in the study of *Yukti-dīpikā*.

Wezler's detailed, insightful review article of Pandeya's edition (WEZLER (1974)) marked a new perspective in the study of the *Yukti-dīpikā*. In it WEZLER announced his project of a new critical edition of YD.

The new edition, with a meaningful subtitle, was published jointly by Albrecht WEZLER and Shujun MOTEGI: *Yuktidīpikā. The Most Significant Commentary on the Sāṁkhyakārikā*. Critically edited by Albrecht Wezler and Shujun Motegi. Vol. I. *Alt- und Neu-Indische Studien* 44, Stuttgart 1998.[1] It was based on the following five Mss:

* My thanks are due to Professor Albrecht Wezler for kindly supplying me with the edition of *Yukti-dīpikā*. I am very much indebted to both Editors, Albrecht Wezler and Shujun Motegi, for their critical comments on my paper. I would also like to thank Professor Minoru Hara, Dr. Kodo Yotsuya and Ms. Monika Nowakowska for their kind help in obtaining some materials as well as Ole Holten Pind for his comments. Last but not least, my thanks are due to Dr. Piotr Balcerowicz for his suggestions and improvements.

[1] All quotations are from that edition, unless otherwise stated.

1. P = Poona, Bhandarkar Oriental Research Institute;
2. A = Lalbhai Dalpatbhai Institute of Indology, Ahmedabad, Gujerat;
3. K = Śāradā Ms, University Library of Kashmir, Śrīnagar. The most important MS;
4. D = Devanāgarī Ms, National Archives in New Delhi;
5. B = Fragmentary Ms from the Library of the Benares Hindu University.

K2 = Ms marked as K2 by Murakami is but a modern Devanāgarī transcript of a part of Ms D and therefore it was ignored by the present Editors [p. xvii, n. 28].

A sequel volume, 'containing a word index to the whole of the Yuktidīpikā', was announced by the Editors ('Introduction' § 1 (9), p. xi).

## –2–

The special importance of the *Yukti-dīpikā*, 'an ancient commentary on the *Sāṁkhya-kārikā* of Īśvarakṛṣṇa,' 'the most significant commentary on the Sāṁkhya-kārikā,' as it was labelled by the Editors, has been duly acknowledged since the time of its discovery. P. CHAKRAVARTI published a study of the history of Sāṁkhya on the basis of YD, and E. FRAUWALLNER (1953: 287) valued highly YD in his attempted historical reconstruction of the Sāṁkhya doctrine.

FRAUWALLNER suggested c. 550 C.E. as the probable date of YD. The following observations on the date of YD, which are based on the parallel passages culled mainly from the commentaries on the SK as well as from the other works (e.g. the Buddhist and Jaina texts), are deemed—first of all—to show the potential topics of further investigation. Especially the presence of the *Kāśikā* passage(s) in YD requires such a careful investigation. Now it seems that we possess rather strong arguments for the lower limit of YD, i.e. the period after Dignāga: since it quotes Dignāga's *Pramāṇa-samuccaya*, includes a few verses from Bhartṛhari's *Vākya-padīya*, and is silent about Dharmakīrti, in consequence it must be placed after Dignāga (480–540 C.E.) and before Dharmakīrti (600–600 C.E.) (1953: 287, n. 151). The problem of the upper limit still remains open, although it must be stressed that so far an equally strong argument for the dating of YD after Dharmakīrti is lacking.

### –2.1–

WEZLER and MOTEGI assign the date of YD to the period ca. 680–720 C.E. ('Introduction § 6. Title of the Text, Authorship and Date'), on the testimony of a presumed quotation from the *Kāśikā-vṛtti* (YD p. 11; analysis in WEZLER (1974: 438–440)), which 'can be dated with a high degree of certitude to 680–700 C.E.' (WEZLER–MOTEGI (1998: xxviii)), although they admit that 'this conclusion about the date of the *Yukti-dīpikā* is rather puzzling because most of those who have read this text or part of it will have gathered the impression that it is ca. 100 years younger. The quotation from the *Kāśikā* cannot, however, be simply done away with by assuming that it is but a later addition to the text: it forms an essential part of the paraphrase of a *vārttika*—which is in its turn confirmed by a subsequent passage. It is, hence, necessary to reckon seriously with the possibility that the author, in spite of his dates, did not know the works of Dharmakīrti, for whatever reason, but was aware of the works of Kumārila as cautiously assumed by Halbfass' (WEZLER–MOTEGI (1998: xxviii)).

### –2.2–

Following the latter statement of the Editors, viz. that the Yukti-dīpikā-kāra 'was aware of the works [sic!—MM] of Kumārila,' one should not hastily take for granted what was only a very cautious *suggestion* of HALBFASS. W. HALBFASS (1983: 6) observed that 'the *pūrvapakṣa* presented in the commentary section on verse 2, which deals with Vedic rituals [= YD (ed. Pandeya p. 15 f.) = WEZLER–MOTEGI (1998: 31 ff.)—M.M.], comes surprisingly close to Kumārila's own argumentation [= MŚV 79 ff. (v. 201 ff.)—M.M.].' However, it is not clear whether YD 'is indeed earlier than Kumārila', and 'there is certainly no definitive evidence to exclude the possibility that it [= YD—M.M.] contains reminiscences of the *Ślokavārttika*.' (HALBFASS (1983: 6)) In HALBFASS (1991: 94), which is a revised version of HALBFASS (1983), we read: 'The date of the *Yuktidīpikā* remains uncertain; moreover, the work may comprise different layers. There is no conclusive evidence for FRAUWALLNER's suggestion that the work was composed around C.E. 550. As a matter of fact, the passage just cited and discussed [= YD (ed. Pandeya p. 15) = ed. WEZLER–MOTEGI (1998: 31 ff.)—MM.] seems to be a response to the *Ślokavārttika*.'

It should be noted, however, that HALBFASS did not present a detailed comparative analysis of the long polemics contained in the *Yukti-dīpikā* ad SK 2, which could substantiate his conclusion. He summarised the lengthy, many-layered discussion of YD in a few lines, without pinpointing those passages from

Kumārila's MŚV which—in the opinion of HALBFASS—show dependence of the Yukti-dīpikā-kāra on his arguments. Such an analysis goes far beyond the scope of the present paper too, nevertheless we would like to give here a few observations which may be taken into consideration in future investigations. Although in the course of my perusal of the text of YD I found a few references to Kumārila's MŚV, yet it seems that they do not offer any argument for the dating of YD as post-Kumārila (see below, p. 421 ff., 'Appendix'). To be sure, this problem requires a separate careful investigation. YD contains several long polemical discussions directed against different authors and/or schools; it would be a desideratum to compile a topical outline of YD in order to show the specific subjects of polemics.

First of all, judging from the scriptural references quoted in the existing commentaries on the SK 2, we can admit that the discussion against the Vedic rituals must have taken place in the Sāṁkhya school since long. The commentaries seem to draw scriptural material from the common source of the school.[2] Especially interesting in this context is Vācaspati's *Tattva-kaumudī* which seems to summarise the lengthy discussion of YD (cf. HALBFASS (1991: 117, n. 26); see also the notes by Har Dutt Sharma ad SK 2, pp. 2–4, in TK (ed. Jha–Sharma)).

Below are collected some parallel passages to YD quotations, taken mainly from the commentaries on SK.

(i) YD 30.13–14:

*yasmād āha "apāma somam amṛtā abhūma"* [ṚV 8.48.3a] *iti* /

= TK (Jha–Sharma), p. 4.2:

*tathā hi śrūyate—'apāma somam amṛtā abhūma' iti* / .

See Sharma's Notes, p. 3: 'fully quoted and explained by Gauḍa[pāda], Māṭhara and Jaya[maṅgalā]'. Add now: *Sāṁkhya-saptati-vṛtti* (V1), p. 6; Bhavya's *Tarka-jvālā* (Derge Tanjur 267a) (KAWASAKI (1976: 1123)); SPBh ad 1.6.

(ii) The two stanzas follow each other in both texts:

(a) YD 36.22–37.2 = TK (Jha–Sharma), p. 5.19–22:

**evaṁ hy āha—*
*na karmaṇā na prajayā dhanena tyāgenaikenāmṛtatvam ānaśuḥ* /
*pareṇa nākaṁ nihitaṁ guhāyāṁ vibhrājate yad yatayo viśanti* //

*) TK: *ata eva ca śrutiḥ*.

[2] MAINKAR (1972: 43) expressed the opinion that '[t]he YD reflects the Sāṁkhya view that favours jñāna and sannyāsa and goes to the Upaniṣadic "tapaḥśraddhe ye hy upavasanty araṇye" for support'.

The quotation is from the *Mahā-nārāyaṇôpaniṣad* 10.5 (see also Jha's translation, TK, p. 8). WEZLER–MOTEGI refer to *Kaivalyôpaniṣad* 3. See SPBh ad 1.6 (94.25); DNCV 144.8–9.

(b) YD 37.5–6 = TK 5.22–24:

*tathā—*
*karmaṇā mṛtyum ṛṣayo *niṣedhuḥ prajāvanto draviṇam **īchamānāḥ /*
****athāpara ṛṣayo ****manīṣiṇaḥ paraṁ karmabhyo 'mṛtatvam ānaśuḥ //*

TK: **niṣeduḥ*; ** *īhamānāḥ*; ****tathā pare*, **** ad. *ye*.

Not identified.

(iii) YD 31.14–15:

*yad āha brāhmaṇe "brāhmaṇam ālabheta"* (Tai.Br. 3.4.1*) ityādi /* .

= *Sāṁkhya-saptati-vṛtti* (V1), p. 7 = *Māṭhara-vṛtti*, p. 6:

*yathā 'brahmaṇe brāhmaṇam ālabheta kṣatrāya rājanyaṁ marudbhyo vaiśyaṁ tapase ca *śūdraṁ nāra-kāya vīrahaṇaṁ*['] (*Taittirīya-brāhmaṇa* 3.4.1) ... /

*) *Māṭhara-vṛtti* has: *taskaraṁ*. Reference to *Āpastamba-śrauta-sūtra* 20.24.8. For further references see HALBFASS (1991: 94) (e.g. Bhavya's *Tarka-jvālā*, Derge 272a) and n. 30, where HALBFASS corrects Pandeya's text: '*brahmaṇe* (instead of *brāhmaṇe* in the printed text) ... .' WEZLER–MOTEGI read: *brāhmaṇe*.

(iv) The above quoted passage (iii) is immediately followed by the stanza which is also found in the *Sāṁkhya-saptati-vṛtti* (V1), *Māṭhara-vṛtti*, and *Gauḍapāda*:

YD (15)16–17(18):

*tathā—*
*ṣaṭśatāni niyujyante* paśūnāṁ madhyame 'hani /*
*aśva-medhasya vacanād ūnāni paśubhis tribhiḥ // iti /*

*) In V1 reading not clear: *puṣṭyante* (?), see Solomon, Notes, p. 88.

(v) YD 45.8–9:

*evam ihāpy ucyate "tarati mṛtyum"* (cf. *Muṇḍakôpaniṣad*. 3.2.9*) iti /*

= *Sāṁkhya-saptati-vṛtti* (V1), p. 6.4 = *Māṭhara-vṛtti*, p. 4:

*evaṁ hy āha—'tarati mṛtyuṁ tarati śokaṁ tarati pāpmānaṁ tarati brahma-hatyāṁ yo 'śva-medhena yajate'* (Śa.Br. 13.3.1.1*) iti /* .

This is followed in V1 and *Māṭhara-vṛtti* by the ṚV stanza quoted above (i).

## –3–

YD contains a number of explicit references to the Buddhist views and bears clear evidence to its author's good acquaintance with the Buddhists scriptures. Here is a provisional list of such references:

YD 70.22 f.—*vaiśeṣikabauddhāḥ*;
104.11—*bauddhaṁ prati*;
109.9—*bauddhāḥ*;
125.9—*bauddhapakṣe*;
129.6—*Śākyaputrīyāḥ*;
164.3—*bauddhānām*;
167.5—*Śākyaputrīyāḥ*;
167.11—*bauddhānām*;
266.24—*bauddhaiḥ*.

For other references see also below, p. 421 ff., 'Appendix'.

## –3.1–

Three stanzas from Bhartṛhari's VP have been identified by the scholars—here are the references to the edition of W. Rau:

YD 13.11–14 = VP 2.423–424 (p. 97 f., with some v.l.);
YD 75.12–13 = VP 2.147 (p. 71).

## –4–

It has already been observed by Pandeya in his YD edition—and the number of references has been increased in the WEZLER–MOTEGI's edition (cf. 'Appendix VIII', pp. 344–347)—that Vasubandhu's works, such as AK, *Viṁśatikā*, and *Triṁśikā*, were subject to the criticism of the Yukti-dīpikā-kāra.

## –4.1–

In MEJOR (1999) it has been shown that 'from the textual references in the *Yukti-dīpikā* it clearly follows that its author must have known also the works of Vasubandhu on *viñjaptimātratā*—the *Viṁśatikā* and *Triṁśikā*, and the

*Abhidharmakośa*, especially its ninth chapter, the *Pudgalaviniścaya*.' The Yukti-dīpikā-kāra did not only criticise the opinions which were expressed in the above mentioned works of Vasubandhu, but he also included many quotations from them into YD.

Vasubandhu's refutation of the notion of *ātman*: AKBh ad 3.18–20 (ed. Pradhan, 129.5 ff.; Shastri, 432.8 ff.), AKBh 9 (ed. Pradhan, 461.1–12; Shastri, 1189.1–1191.2), were criticised by the Yukti-dīpikā-kāra in his commentary on SK 17 (= YD 167.2 ff.). YD 167.11–19 contains a quotation of a passage which comes from the Buddhist *Āgama*; the same authority is quoted by Vasubandhu in his *Pudgala-viniścaya* (AKBh 9, Pradhan 466.5–13, Shastri 1202.22–1203.6) (cf. MEJOR (1999: 110 f.)).

### –4.1.1–

A long polemic directed against the *vijñāna-vāda* doctrine is found in YD ad SK 34 (218.22 ff.). A close parallel is Vasubandhu's *Viṁśatikā* (and *Triṁśikā*)[3]:

(i) YD 218.22–30 refers to *Viṁśatikā* 1–2;
(ii) YD 218.31–219.6 refers to *Viṁśatikā* 2–3a;
(iii) YD 219.7–26—cf. Viṁś. 3–4;
(iv) YD 219.26–29—cf. Viṁś. 18.

For further references see below, p. 421 ff., 'Appendix'.

### –4.1.2–

YD possibly contains a reference to Vasubandhu's *Vāda-vidhi*, a lost work on logic. Vasubandhu's definition of thesis: *sādhyâbhidhānaṁ pratijñā* from the *Vāda-vidhi*[4] is apparently referred to by the Yukti-dīpikā-kāra (YD 93.5): *na hi yathâbhidhānaṁ tathā sādhyam ity eka-kriyā yujyata iti* / [underline mine—M.M.].

---

[3] Cf. MAINKAR (1972: 135): 'The YD, taking advantage of the "pañca viśeṣāviśeṣaviṣayāni" in the Kārikā, refutes the Vijñapti-mātratā doctrine of Vasubandhu: it asks kathametat avagamyate viśeṣāviśeṣaviṣayāṇi indriyāṇi, na punarasadviṣayāṇi and goes on to mention and develop the points: (i) viśeṣāṇāmasatva siddheḥ, (ii) Vikalpānupapatteḥ, (iii) viparītadarśanaprasaṁgāt, (iv) arthakriyā ca na syāt, (v) asiddhatvāt, (vi) karmaśaktivaicitryāt, and (vii) dharmādharmānupapattiś ca syāt.'

[4] Quoted in the NV 117.20; PSV fol. 45b5/127b5; see FRAUWALLNER (1933: 303, 482).

### –4.1.3–

Similarly, YD seems to refer also to Dignāga's *Nyāya-mukha* (which is also lost in Sanskrit but preserved in Chinese translation):

YD 95.10 f.: *yathā sādhyatvenêpsitaḥ pakṣa iti pratijñālakṣaṇam ācakṣāṇo bhavān na sādhyalakṣaṇam ācaṣṭe* / [underline mine—M.M.].

*Nyāya-mukha* v. 1 (= NV 116.7,9,17; see FRAUWALLNER (1933: 303, 482)): *svayaṁ sādhyatvenêpsitaḥ pakṣo viruddhârthânirākṛtaḥ* // .

### –4.2–

YD contains a long critical discussion of the Buddhist concept *sarvaṁ kṣaṇikam*. It was shown by A. von ROSPATT that the Yukti-dīpikā-kāra's refutation of the opinions of the Vijñāna-vādins and the Kṣaṇika-vādins at some places comes close to the opinions which were expressed in Vasubandhu's commentary on the *Mahāyāna-sūtrâlaṁkāra*—cf. von ROSPATT (1995: 38, n. 68(a)), remark about the date of YD: 'ca. 700?', and von ROSPATT (1995: 158, n. 354, *354(a); 164 n. 364; 188 n. 410).

### –4.2.1–

Explicit references to the *kṣaṇika-vāda* in YD:

(i) YD 69.15 f. (and n. 4): *na hi kṣaṇabhaṅgasāhasaṁ yuktim antareṇa daṇḍabhayād api pratipadyāmahe* / .

(ii) YD 129.5 f.: *sarvam eva kṣaṇikaṁ buddhibodhyam ākāśanirodhavarjitam iti śākyaputrīyāḥ pratipannāḥ* / .
—Cf. AK I.4b-c (*saṁskṛtā mārga-varjitāḥ sāsravāḥ*) and I.5a-c (*anāsravā mārga-satyaṁ trividhaṁ câpy asaṁskṛtam / ākāśaṁ dvau nirodhau ca*).

(iii) YD 132.14–133.2: *vināśahetvabhāvāt kṣaṇikatvam iti cet / … / tasmān na vināśahetvabhāvāt kṣaṇikaṁ saṁskṛtam iti* / .

(iv) YD 134.8–12: *viśeṣagrahaṇāt kṣaṇikatvasiddhir iti cet / syān matam / yady utpannamātrôparatir nâsti bhāvānāṁ kiṁkṛtaḥ śarīrâdīnāṁ prāṇâpānaśrama-rūpâdikṛto 'bjâśmaprabhṛtīnāṁ ca śītôṣṇasparśakṛto bhedaḥ / ghaṇṭâdīnāṁ câśabdakānāṁ paścāc chabdavatāṁ grahaṇam / tasmād aniṣiddhaḥ kṣaṇabhaṅga iti* / .

(v) YD 163.24 f.: *ucyate kṣaṇabhaṅgapratiṣedhāt / prāg eva kṣaṇabhaṅg<e> nirdiṣṭaṁ* (YD 133.8) *vinaṣṭānāṁ bhāvānāṁ punarutpattau nâsti kāraṇam / tadabhāve côtpattir ayuktêti / .*

(vi) YD 169.10–15: *tathā ca kṣaṇabhaṅgâdhikāre bhavadbhir apy uktaṁ "yasya hi pratikṣaṇam anyathātvaṁ nâsti tasya bāhyapratyayo bhedaḥ / paścād viśeṣagrahaṇe nâsti tadyathā bhūmer apacyamānāyāḥ pākajānām / na ca bhūmeḥ pratikṣaṇam anyathātvaṁ nâsty akṣaṇikatvaprasaṅgāt" <iti> / saukṣmyād duradhigamo bheda iti dṛṣṭântaḥ pratyuktaḥ / tasmāt siddhaṁ saṅghātaparârthatvād asti puruṣaḥ <iti> / .*

(vii) YD 188.20–23: *atra kṣaṇikavādy āha: yady arthagrahaṇaṁ buddhir anityā / kasmāt / hetvapekṣaṇāt / arthagrahaṇaṁ hîndriyâdiviṣayasannidhānam āvaraṇâdyabhāvaṁ câpekṣate na ca nityasya kāraṇâpekṣôpapadyate / tasmād anityā buddhiḥ / .*

(viii) YD 190.18 f.: *kṣaṇabhaṅgapratiṣedhe côktaṁ na pṛthivyādīnām anyathā cânyathā côtpattiḥ / .*

## –4.3–

This 'reliance' of the Yukti-dīpikā-kāra on Vasubandhu's works could suggest not only great influence of the Buddhist master on the Sāṁkhya teacher, but also point to a rather short distance in time between them (Vasubandhu: 400–480 C.E., cf. FRAUWALLNER (1961: 129 ff.)). CHAKRAVARTI (1952: 153) went so far in his opinion as to say that '[i]n short, the *Yukti-dīpikā* may be better called a rejoinder of the *Paramārtha-Saptati*'. Tradition has it that Vasubandhu composed an anti-Sāṁkhya treatise under the title *Paramārtha-saptatikā* in order to reject the opinions of a Sāṁkhya teacher, Vindhyavāsin (cf. Paramārtha's Life of Vasubandhu, FRAUWALLNER (1951); CHAKRAVARTI (1952: 142–155)). In his AK Vasubandhu mentioned only the name of Vārṣagaṇya. A harsh attack on Vindhyavāsin is found in the *Abhidharma-dīpa*, a post-Vasubandhu Sarvāsti-vāda treatise (cf. MEJOR (1999: 112 f.)). References to *Paramârtha-saptatikā* have been collected in MEJOR (1999: 107 ff.) (now one can add also a reference to the *Rāja-vārttika* of Akalaṅka, a Jaina author (see below)).

If we combine the references to Vasubandhu, to Dignāga's definition of *pratyakṣa* (Dignāga: 480–540 C.E., FRAUWALLNER (1961: 137)), and quotations from Bhartṛhari's VP (Bhartṛhari: 450–510 C.E., FRAUWALLNER (1961: 135)), all that gives a solid basis for the lower limit of the *Yukti-dīpikā* at ca. 550 C.E., which is in agreement with the date proposed by FRAUWALLNER. Still the upper limit remains an open question.

## –5–

Now, a serious problem is posed by the alleged *Kāśikā* quotation(s). The passage which comes from the *Kāśikā-vṛtti* ad Pāṇ 2.2.16, as it was pointed out by the present Editors (*vide supra* § 2), deserves a very careful consideration, since its testimony moves the date of YD behind 700 C.E., i.e. after Dharmakīrti.

In the following, I am going to introduce a passage from the *Jaya-maṅgalā* commentary on the SK 1, which may throw a new light on the difficulty. First, the relevant text of the *Yukti-dīpikā*, containing the *Kāśikā* passage, will be given together with Wezler's analytical translation (WEZLER (1974)). In the next paragraph the parallel passage from JM will be analysed.

To make the things even more complicated, there is still another passage from YD which has its parallel in the *Kāśikā* (ad Pāṇ 5.2.93), as it was pointed out by OBERHAMMER (1967–68: 616). This fragment will be analysed below as well.

## –5.1–

The text of YD fragment is reproduced here according to WEZLER–MOTEGI's edition, together with the Editors' references (the *vārttika*s are marked by the Editors with the bold face):

[p. 11.6] *yad uktaṁ*

[7] (10.5) *kasminn arthe bhavatīti tatrāha—*

[8] *TADAPAGHĀTAKE HETAU* / (SK 1b')

[9] *apahantīty apaghātakaḥ, tasyāpaghātakas tadapaghātakaḥ* /

[10] *āha:* ***tadapaghātake iti samāsānupapattiḥ pratiṣedhāt*** / "*kartari**

[11] *yau tṛjakau tābhyāṁ saha ṣaṣṭhī na samasyate*" (Kāśikā 2.2.16, Pāṇ 2.2.15) /

[12] *tasmāt tasyāpaghātaka iti vaktavyam* /

[13] *ucyate:* ***na śāstre darśanāt*** / "*tatprayojako hetuś ca*" (Pāṇ 1.4.55) *iti*

[14] *śāstre dṛṣṭaḥ prayogaḥ* / *padakāraś cāha* "*jātivācakatvāt*" (Vār. 7 on Pāṇ 4.1.14,

[15] MBhāṣya 2.206.23; Vār. 1 on Pāṇ 1.2.10, MBhāṣya I.107.21) / *tathā* "*kadācid*

[16] *guṇo guṇiviśeṣako bhavati kadācit tu guṇinā guṇo viśiṣyate*" (cf. MBhā

[p. 12.1] 2.356.8–9) *iti cūrṇikārasya prayogaḥ* / *tasmād anavadyam etat* / *ayaṁ tu*

[2] *piṇḍārthaḥ* / *trividhena duḥkhenābhihato brāhmaṇas tadapaghātakaṁ hetuṁ*

[3] *jijñāsate* / *ko nāmāsau hetuḥ syād yo duḥkhatrayam abhihanyād iti* /

*) *Kāśikā* ad Pāṇ 2.2.16 (p. 74.17) reads: *kartari ca yau* ... Cf. *Kāśikā* ad 2.2.15 (p. 74.13): *kartari yā ṣaṣṭhī sā tṛcâkena ca saha na samasyate* / . [M.M.].

### –5.1.1–

Below is reproduced Wezler's translation of the above fragment (WEZLER (1974: 439 f.)); some passages left untranslated by WEZLER (as irrelevant for his discussion) were translated here by the present author.

> (YD 11.6–9, transl.—M.M.:) 'It was asked [before:] "What is the purpose [of that desire for enquiry (*jijñāsā*)]?", here he [= the author] says: "[Enquiry] with regard to the warding-off of that [threefold suffering]." [That which is] warding off, i.e. removing; "warding off that," i.e. getting rid of that [triad of suffering].'

WEZLER (1974: 439.2–3):

> (YD 11.10) 'as for *tadapaghātaka-* (or: *-apaghātake*), impropriety of the compound because of the prohibition.'

WEZLER (1974: 439.10–15):

> (YD 11.10–12) 'a sixth [case-ending] (i.e. a noun ending in a genitive) is not compounded with the two [primary suffixes] *tṛc** and *aka*** that are added [to a root] to denote the agent [i.e. with a noun ending in either of these suffixes]; therefore [the compound *tadapaghātaka-* is grammatically incorrect and] it ought to be said *tasyāpaghātake*.'

WEZLER (1974: 439.25–27):

> (YD 11.13) 'no (i.e. the formation of the compound *tadapaghātaka-* is not improper, it is, on the contrary, admitted), since [compounds of this structure] are met with in the *śāstra*.'

WEZLER (1974: 439.32–440.4):

> (YD 11.13–12.1): 'in the *śāstra* (i.e. the *Aṣṭādhyāyī* of Pāṇini) there is seen the usage "*kartṛ* as well as *hetu* is he who instigates him" (i.e. by Pāṇini himself such a compound is used); and Kātyāyana says [*vārttika* 7 on Pāṇ 4.1.14, *Mahābhāṣya* II 206.23, and *vārttika* 1 on Pāṇ 1.2.30, *Mahābhāṣya* I 197.21): 'because it denotes the generic form' (i.e. Kātyāyana, too, employs such a compound); likewise there is the usage of Patañjali (*Mahābhāṣya* II 356.8–9): 'sometimes a quality is found to qualify that which possesses the quality, sometimes

a quality is qualified by that which possesses the quality' (i.e. as Pāṇini and Kātyāyana, just so the third of the munitrayas, Patañjali, does use a genitive tatpuruṣa compound with a nomen agentis forming its posterior member). Therefore this (i.e. *tadapaghātake* in kā 1) is unobjectionable'.

(YD 12.1–3 [translation—M.M.]): 'And this is the summary meaning. A Brahmin affected by the threefold suffering desires to know a cause which could ward it off, [thinking:] "What would be namely that cause which could destroy the triad of suffering?".'

*) *tṛc* = *kṛt* suffix *-tṛ-* (cf. Pāṇ 3.1.133; 2.2.15) [M.M.];
**) *aka* = *kṛt* suffix *-aka-* (cf. Pāṇ 3.1.133; 2.2.15) [M.M.].

**–5.2–**

From among the eight existing commentaries on the SK[5], i.e. *Suvarṇa-saptati* (Paramārtha's Chinese version from 557–569 C.E.), *Sāṁkhya-saptati-vṛtti* (V1), *Sāṁkhya-vṛtti* (V2), *Gauḍapāda*, *Māṭhara-vṛtti*, *Yukti-dīpikā*, *Jaya-maṅgalā*, and *Tattva-kaumudī* (Vācaspatimiśra, ca. 850 C.E.), it is only YD and JM which contain a grammatical comment on the '*Kāśikā*' passage.

It should be noted that JM[6] is exceptional among the other commentaries on the SK (besides, of course, YD itself) as being relatively rich in grammatical comments: it has as many as seven grammatical references to Pāṇini.[7] Grammatical references in the *Jaya-maṅgalā* (ed. Satkāriśarmā Vaṅgīya) are the following:

ad SK 1 (p. 66): Pāṇ 2.2.15; Pāṇ 1.4.55; ad SK 4 (p. 69): *svârthe ṣyañ*;
ad SK 12 (p. 77): Pāṇ 3.3.113; ad SK 13 (p. 79): Pāṇ 3.3.113;
ad SK 32 (p. 94): Pāṇ 3.3.113; ad SK 41 (p. 100): Pāṇ 2.3.32.

[5] Cf. SOLOMON (1974: 111–181: 'Chronological Order of the Commentaries of the Sāṁkhya Kārikā')

[6] See SHARMA (1929); CHAKRAVARTI (1975: 164–168); EIPHIL IV (: 271–287).

[7] Cf. TK ad SK 1 (p. 3): *ṣaṣṭhī-sthāne sārva-vibhaktikas tasiḥ*; ad SK 14 (p. 32): Pāṇ 1.4.22; ad SK 51 (p. 66): Pāṇ 6.4.68; ad SK 64 (p. 77): *yathâhuḥ—'kṛ-bhv-astayaḥ kriyā-sāmānya-vacanāḥ' iti* [*Siddhânta-kaumudī*] [sic!—MM]. Other commentaries do not have such references. The editors of TK identified the quotation in SK (from the seventeenth century), but it must go back to an earlier common source for both TK and SK.

### –5.2.1–

On the basis of the following references it can be admitted that the *Jaya-maṅgalā* refers to YD, and Vācaspatimiśra's TK refers to the *Jaya-maṅgalā*.

(i) YD 2.12 ff.:

= JM ad SK 51, p. 108:

*tathā câha saṅgraha-kāraḥ—*
*astitvam ekatvam athârthavattvaṁ pārārthyam anyatvam *akartṛ-bhāvaḥ /*
*yogo viyogo bahavaḥ pumāṁsaḥ sthitiḥ śarīrasya ca śeṣa-vṛttiḥ // iti //*

*) *atho nivṛttiḥ*; so also *Māṭhara-vṛtti* ad SK 72, p. 63.5; V1, p. 80.

= TK ad SK 72, p. 81:

*tathā ca rāja-vārttikam //*
*pradhānâstitvam ekatvam arthavattvam athânyatā /*
*pārārthyaṁ ca tathânaikyaṁ viyogo yoga eva ca //*
*śeṣa-vṛttir akartṛtvaṁ *maulikârthāḥ smṛtā daśa /*
*viparyayaḥ pañcavidhas tathôktā nava tuṣṭayaḥ //*
*karaṇānām asāmarthyam aṣṭa-viṁśatidhā matam /*
*iti ṣaṣṭiḥ padârthānām aṣṭabhiḥ saha siddhibhiḥ // iti //*

*) YD 2.15: *cūlikârthāḥ*; *daśa maulikāḥ* = *Māṭhara-vṛtti*, p. 63.4; V1, p. 80. Cf. Sharma, TK ('Introduction', p. 29).

Comment: Here are listed the so-called 'ten basic topics' (transl. in WEZLER (1974: 450)). It is evident that the TK quotes directly from YD while JM and the M must have taken their quotation from another (common) source.

(ii) YD 180.1: JM discussion of the seven types of action ad SK 19; cf. Sharma, TK, Notes, p. 28 f. (§ 134).

(iii) JM 84.15–19: *tatra siddhe puṁsi vivādaḥ / …* = YD 173.30 ff.; 174.15 ff., esp. l. 20 ff. Here clearly JM summarises the discussion which is found in YD. This passage is another important evidence that JM in its explanations must have referred also to YD.

(iv) Miscellaneous references:

—Interpretation of *kāraṇa-kārya-vibhāga* ad SK 15:
JM, p. 81.20 f.: *asmin vyākhyāne … anyair vyākhyāyate …*
See Sharma, TK, Notes, p. 24 (§ 112); CHAKRAVARTI (1952: 166 f.; n. 2).

—8 *siddhi* ('attainments')—Vācaspati describes and rejects an interpretation ad SK 51 set forth only in JM, p. 106 f.

—TK, p. 66: *anye vyācakṣate* ...

Cf. SHARMA (1929: 429); Sharma, TK (Notes, p. 44, § 237); CHAKRAVARTI (1952: 166, 167).

—V1 ad SK 17: *saṁghāta-parârthatvāt*; Solomon (Notes, p. 106): 'Compare T which is clearly indebted to J'.

—V2 ad SK 31: *kāryam*; Solomon (Notes, p. 97): 'Y explains .... J has .... This is clearly an exposition of Y here'.

—JM 71.4 f.: *sambandhāś ca sapta*—YD?

—JM 80.15: *tasmād iha loke kāraṇa-guṇakaṁ kāryaṁ dṛṣṭam* / = YD 140.9.

—JM 80.25 f.: *yathā mūla-* = YD 141.18 ff.

—JM 81.2: *mahad-ahaṁ-kāra-* = YD 141.18 ff.

—JM 81.24,25,26 = YD 148.9 f.

—JM 84.9: *yaś ca bhoktā sa eva puruṣaḥ* ... = YD 170.6–7.

—JM 85.22 = YD 180.1.

—JM 85.23 = YD 180.25; 177.1.

—JM 85.25 = cf. YD 180.28.

—JM 85.27 = cf. YD 179.34 f.

—JM 89.18 f. = YD 195.1.

—JM 92.19 f., 21 = YD 206.6 f.

—JM 92.22 = YD 206.35 f.

—JM 95.12 = YD 217.2.

—JM 102.20–21 (stanza) = cf. YD 235.21.

—JM 104.25–28 = YD 243.7–9.

—JM 105.1–2 (stanza) = YD 243.4–5; TK p. 62.

—JM 107.1–12 = TK p. 66–67; SHARMA (1929: 428 f.).

—JM 109.18 ff. = TK p. 69.

—JM 111.1–2 = TK p. 70.

—JM 112.3–4 (stanza) = cf. *Māṭhara-vṛtti*, p. 3.28–29 (*tathā ca laukikānām ābhāṇakaḥ*); YD 51.11–12.

## –5.3–

Now, let us analyse the JM passage commenting on SK 1b in the light of the above given analysis of YD made by Wezler.

*Jaya-maṅgalā* (ed. Satkāriśarmā Vaṅgīya; plain text without editor's comments):

[p. 66.3] *kasmin viṣaya ity āha* / ***tad-avaghātake hetāv*** *iti* / *avaghātayaty apanayatîty*
[4] *avaghātakaḥ* / *tasya duḥkha-trayasyâvaghātakas tad-avaghātakaḥ* / *tṛjakābhyāṁ*
[5] *ṣaṣṭhī-samāsa-pratiṣedhaḥ tat-prayojako hetuś ca*
[6] *iti jñāpanāt na bhavati* / *duḥkhavān aham etat-pratīkāram anveṣayā-*
[7] *mîti prāyo-vādaḥ* / *sa ca pañca-viṁśati-tattvajnānān nânya iti manasi vartate* /

Translation:

'[In answer to the question] "With regard to what?"—[the author] says: "[There arises desire for enquiry] into the means of warding that off." "[That which is] warding off," means "[that which] causes to drive away (to expel, to keep off, to fend off)" (*ava√han*), [i.e.] "takes away, removes" (*apa√nī*). "[That which is] warding that off" [means] warding off/removing that triad of suffering.

[Objection:] [According to the rule of Pāṇ 2.2.15,] "with the primary suffixes *tṛc* and *aka*," [when they denote the agent,] there is a prohibition of a sixth-case-ending compound …

[Answer:] [but] because [the acceptable usage of a similar compound, viz.] "*kartṛ* as well as *hetu* is he who instigates him" was made known [from the rule of Pāṇ. 1.4.55,] there is no [such prohibition, i.e. such a compound like *tad-av(p)aghātaka* is acceptable, one cannot object to its correctness].

"I am suffering, [and] I am seeking a remedy to that [miserable condition]," so says the current saying. "That [remedy can come only] from the knowledge of the twenty five principles, there is no other [than that]," thus it is passing through his [i.e. Īśvarakṛṣṇa's] mind.'

**–5.3.1–**

It follows from the above translation that JM refers to YD discussion: It contains a grammatical explanation of the compound *tad-ap(v)aghātaka*, which is directly based on Pāṇini's rules 2.2.15 and 1.4.55. The former rule is referred to in the objection which has been raised with regard to the correctness of the compound *tad-apaghātaka*, while the latter one forms part of the answer which justifies that compound. YD *vārttika* words: *samāsa* and *pratiṣedha*, together with the conjectured *ṣaṣṭhī*, are present in JM laconic sentence which combines both the objection and the clarifying answer. It seems therefore that the *Jaya-maṅgalā* contains a true parallel to YD, which consists of a brief grammatical comment, including references to the Pāṇini's rules, together with a concluding statement. Its wording fits well into the wording of the *vārttika* pattern of YD and reflects well the polemics with regard to the correctness of the compound *tad-apaghātaka*. Moreover, JM passage continues YD conclusion of the whole paragraph, speaking about the possibility to remove the triad of suffering.

It should be made clear, however, that the present author does not claim that JM passage represents *the* original reading of YD. Perhaps JM has preserved the reading closer to the original reading of YD which was only later replaced by a lucid explanation taken from the *Kāśikā*, maybe by the way of insertion of a marginal note. Consequently, if we agree that the *Kāśikā* passage is a later insertion, then the earlier date for YD, i.e. ca. 550 C.E., is secured. Such a statement is, of course, subject to criticism as a mere guess work. The fact that JM refers to and summarises a grammatical question which was discussed in YD does not explain or rule out the occurrence of the passage from the *Kāśikā*. But, at the same time, we should remember that YD—as it was so keenly observed by WEZLER (1974)—has been modelled on MBhā and right in its very structure it follows its pattern. It is sufficient to look into the index of quotations compiled by the present Editors of YD to see how much MBhā influenced YD. How then to explain the occurrence of the quotation(s) from the *Kāśikā*? Obviously, it is not enough to say simply that it is a later interpolation. Another passage from YD and its relation to the *Kāśikā* deserves more attention of competent scholars.

## –5.4–

G. OBERHAMMER in his analysis of 'the formal elements which gave form to a scientific work' (*tantra-yukti*) in YD, observed strong influence of grammar in the context of the theory of the *tantra-yukti*s, and called attention (OBERHAMMER (1967–68: 614 ff.)) to the passage YD 8.2–3; 6–7.

(i) YD 8.2–3, 6–7 (ed. WEZLER–MOTEGI):

*itikaraṇaṁ** (3.11) *prakārārtham / evamprakārā* (*recte: evaṁ-*) *anye 'pi draṣṭavyaḥ / tadyathotsargo 'pavādo 'tideśa ityādi / ... / ity evam anyā api tantrayuktayaḥ śakyā iha pradarśayitum /*

*) MBhā and *Kāśikā* read: *-karaṇaḥ*.

Translation: 'The word *iti* has the meaning of "type". Other [*tantra-yukti*s] should be explained as of the same type, too. As for example:

> *utsarga* 'general rule', *apavāda* 'special rule, exception', *atideśa* 'extended application', etc. ... Thus, also other *tantra-yukti*s can be indicated here in a similar way.' [M.M.]

OBERHAMMER (1967–68: 615) commented: 'Apart from *atideśaḥ* these terms [i.e. *utsarga*, *apavāda*—M.M.], obviously regarded by the author of the *Yukti-dīpikā* as *tantrayukti-s*, are not to be found in the old tradition of the *tantrayukti-s*. They are, however, to be found in grammar, for instance in Patañjali's *Mahābhāṣya*'. As a parallel to YD expression *iti-karaṇaṁ prakārârtham* OBERHAMMER (1967–68: 616 and n. 2) mentioned the passage from Kātyāyana's *vārttika* on Pāṇ 1.1.44(3), and pointed out—what is most important in our context—that '[t]he definition of the *Yukti-dīpikā* is also found in the *Kāśikā*: *itikaraṇaḥ prakārārthaḥ*' [= *Kāśikā* ad Pāṇ 5.2.93].

(ii) The definition is found in the MBhā *vārttika* 3 ad Pāṇ 1.1.44: (*na vêti vibhāṣā* / ) *iti-karaṇo 'rtha-nirdeśârthaḥ* // 3 //

> Translation of Pāṇ 1.1.44: '(The t[erminus] t[echnicus]) *vibhāṣā* denotes the meaning of the combined particles *na vā* "or not" (literally "not or") and signifies optionality' [KATRE (1989: 18)].

*Kāśikā* p. 12 l. 1 from below–13.1: *iti-karaṇo 'rtha-nirdeśârthaḥ* / .

> Translation: 'The word *iti* has the meaning of 'specification of sense''.

(iii) Pāṇ 5.2.93: *indriyam indra-liṅgam indra-dṛṣṭam indra-sṛṣṭam indra-juṣṭam indra-dattam iti vā* //

> Translation: 'The expression *indr-iyá* is introduced to denote the following senses: (1) means (*liṅga-m*) by which the self is inferred; (2) perceived by the Self; (3) created by the Self; (4) nourished by the Self, or (5) given by the Self.' [KATRE (1989: 572)].

*Kāśikā* ad Pāṇ 5.2.93 [298.3–4]: *iti-karaṇaḥ prakārârthaḥ* / *sati saṁbhave vyutpattir anyathâpi kartavyā, rūḍher aniyamād iti* //

> Translation: 'The word *iti* has the meaning of "type". When possible, also other derivation can be made, because there is no limitation of a [conventional] usage [of the word].'

### –5.4.1–

The Yukti-dīpikā-kāra while commenting on the summary stanza (YD 3.10–11) in which the *tantra-yukti*s are enumerated, explained the meaning of the word *iti* (*iti* *tantra-sampat*) with the definition *iti-karaṇaṁ prakārârtham* which is also found in the *Kāśikā* commentary on Pāṇini's sūtra 5.2.93. This definition differs from the one given in *Vārttika* 3 on Pāṇ 1.1.44: *iti-karaṇo 'rtha-nirdeśârthaḥ*. The *Kāśikā* knows both definitions while commenting on Pāṇ 5.2.93 and Pāṇ 1.1.44, respectively. As far as I can see, YD has only the former one (with the reading °-*karaṇaṁ*). Now it is of crucial importance to decide whether it is YD which borrowed the definition from the *Kāśikā* or vice versa. If the latter is proved by further investigation, herewith we would obtain an argument that the *Kāśikā* is posterior to the *Yukti-dīpikā*. In consequence, we could accept 550 C.E. as a terminus post quem, and 700 C.E. as a terminus ante quem for YD.

## –6.1–

In his paper of 1981, Wezler called attention to Siṁhasūrigaṇi's commentary *Nyāyâgamânusāriṇī* (probably sixth century) on Mallavādin's *Dvādaśâra-naya-cakra* (here abbr. DNCV), since it contains a few interesting passages related to YD. It is difficult to say whether they testify to its author's direct acquaintance with YD, rather they may refer to a common source (Wezler (1981: 174, n. 55)). Here are collected the most distinct fragments, culled from the references which are found in the extensive notes of Śrī Muni Jaṁbūvijaya (underline is mine—M.M.):

(i) YD 89.7 (ed. Wezler–Motegi):

*tatra yadā hetuḥ parapakṣam <an>*apekṣya yathārthena svarūpeṇa **sādhya-siddhāv apadiśyate tadā vītākhyo bhavati* /

= DNCV 313.10–314.1 (cf. p. 313 n. 7):

*yadā hetuḥ para-pakṣam avy*apekṣya svenâiva rūpeṇa **kārya-siddhāv apadiśyate tadā vītâkhyo bhavati* /

*) Wezler–Motegi (1998) observe in n. 6: 'all the Mss read *apekṣya*'.
**) Reading *sādhya-siddhau*(*āv*-°) confirmed in the body of the text of YD, while the DNCV reads consequently: *kārya-siddhāv*-°.

(ii) YD 92.19–21 (ed. Wezler–Motegi):

*yo 'yam ādhyātmikānāṁ bhedānāṁ kāryak<a>*raṇātmakānāṁ caikajātisamanvayo dṛṣṭa ity evamādiḥ sādhanaprapañcaḥ so 'hetur ity uktaṁ bhavati* /

= DNCV 314.7–8 (cf. note 3):

*prayogaś ca—asti pradhānaṁ bhedānām anvaya-darśanāt, ādhyātmikānāṁ bhedānāṁ kārya-kā*raṇâtmakānām eka-jāti-samanvayo dṛṣṭa ity candana-śakalâdi-dṛṣṭântaṁ vakṣyati /*

*) In their note 12 WEZLER–MOTEGI observe that 'all the Mss read *kāryakāraṇātmakānāṁ*'; DNCV reads: °*-kāraṇa-*°.

(iii) YD 261.1 (ed. WEZLER–MOTEGI):

*sukhaṁ ca duḥkhaṁ <cānu>*śayaṁ ca vāreṇāyaṁ sevate tatra tatra //*

= DNC 267.1:

*sukhaṁ ca duḥkhaṁ cânuśayaṁ ca vāreṇâyaṁ sevate tatra tatra //*

*) In their n. 1 WEZLER–MOTEGI observe: 'All the Mss read *ca hi saṁśayaṁ*'; their emendation agrees with the reading of DNC.

### –6.2–

The passages given above may not be of decisive value in our attempt to trace links to other texts which could throw a light on the possible date of YD. There is however one more testimony which is of such a value, viz. the DNCV reproduces two lists of Sāṁkhya terms which exactly correspond to those of YD. To be sure, other commentaries on the SK also reproduce these old lists, apparently quoting from a common older source (see the comparative table in EIPHIL IV (: 632); Solomon, V1, Notes). The point is that it is the DNCV alone which has them exactly in the same form as YD. Therefore it may be surmised that Siṁhasūri might have consulted YD text (or the same source). In this case YD cannot be placed later than 600 C.E. In case of the second possibility—viz. if Siṁhasūri had consulted the same source, but not YD directly—YD could be much later.

### –6.2.1–

List of nine contentments, YD ad SK 50 (244 ff.): … *navavidhā tuṣṭiḥ /*

= (four *ādhyātmika*:) 1. *ambha*, 2. *salila*, 3. *ogha*, 4. *vṛṣṭi*; (five *bāhya*:) 5. *sutāra*, 6. *supāra*, 7. *sunetra*, 8. *sumārīca*, 9. *uttamâbhaya*.

The same list is reproduced in DNCV 316.5–317.3:

*sannihita-viṣaya-santoṣāc cikīrṣitād arthād ūnasya nivṛttir ekâiva tuṣṭir upāyanavattvād nava-vidhā tuṣṭiḥ / prakṛty-upādāna-kāla-bhāgya-kāraṇa-pūrvaka-puruṣânyatvâparijñānād mādhyasthya-lābho 'mbhaḥ salilâugha-vṛṣṭyâkhyāḥ śarīra-śarīri-viśeṣaṇôpāyāś catasra ādhyātmikās tuṣṭayaḥ / bāhyāś ca viṣaya-nirvedajāḥ pañca viṣayeṣv arjana-rakṣaṇa-kṣaya-saṅga-hiṁsā-doṣa-darśanāt sutāra-supāra-sunetra-[su]mārīcôttamâbhayâkhyā iti nava tuṣṭayaḥ /*

–6.2.2–

List of eight accomplishments, YD ad SK 51 (251 ff.): *aṣṭau siddhayaḥ /*

= 1. *tārakam*, 2. *sutāram*, 3. *tārayantam*, 4. *pramodam*, 5. *pramuditam*, 6. *modamānam*, 7. *ramyakam*, 8. *sadā-pramuditam*.

The same list in DNCV 316.1–4:

*siddhir ūhena sādhanaṁ tārakam, śabdena sutāram, adhyayanena tārayantam, vātâdīny ādhyātmikāny abhyatītya kriyayā tāraka-sutāra-tārayantānām anyatamena pramodam, mānuṣyâdy-ādhibhautikâtyayena tat-trayânyatamenâiva pramuditam, śītâdy-ādhidaivikâtyayena tat-trayânyatamenâiva modamānam, yadā kuśala-saṁsṛṣṭa-vyapāśrayāt sandehâtikramāt tad-anyatamena ramyakam, daurbhāgyâtikrameṇa sadā-pramuditam ity aṣṭau siddhayaḥ /*

–6.2.3–

Other passages in common:

Cf. DNCV 144: *na karmaṇā na prajayā dhanena* ... [*Kaivalyôpaniṣad* 3] = = YD 37.1.

Cf. DNCV 267: *sukhaṁ ca duḥkhaṁ cânuśayaṁ ca* ... = YD 261.1.

Cf. DNCV 107.24: *śrotrâdi-vṛttiḥ pratyakṣam* ... = YD 5.11; 76.21 (cf. WEZLER (1981: 368, n. 43)).

Cf. DNCV 107.16: *kalpanâpoḍhaṁ pratyakṣam* ... (YD 76.21).

Cf. DNCV 106.2,15: *tatra katamad vijñāna-mātram idaṁ sarvaṁ traidhātukam*; 105.4: *vijñāna-mātram idaṁ tribhuvanam* (cf. WEZLER (1981: 368, n. 41)).

–6.3–

The *Rāja-vārttika*, a Jaina work composed by Akalaṅka, being a commentary on the *Tattvârthâdhigama-sūtra*, has been compiled on a similar pattern as YD: *vārttika cum* commentary (see BRONKHORST (1990: 123–146)). Moreover, it bears the same title as YD: *Rāja-vārttika*. It contains references to Māṭhara (see below p. 420). It is difficult, however, to say whether there is any direct link connecting the two texts. Nevertheless, I would like to point out that it contains—besides a few quotations in common—the same set of five definitions of *pratyakṣa* which are discussed in YD (76.17–22; 5.11–14). The order of definitions is slightly different from that of YD: 2–3–5–4–1, viz.:

(i) RVār 53.29–30:

*pratyakṣaṁ kalpanâpoḍhaṁ nāma-jātyâdi-yojanā /*
*asādhāraṇa-hetutvād aikṣas tad vyapadiśyate //* [= PS 1.3,4];

(ii) RVār 53.31–32: *indriyârtha-sannikarṣôtpannaṁ jñānam avyapadeśyam avyabhicāri vyavasāyâtmakaṁ pratyakṣam* [= *Nyāya-sūtra* 1.1.4];

(iii) RVār 53.32: *ātmêndriya-mano 'rtha-sannikarṣād yan niṣpadyate tad anyat* [= *Vaiśeṣika-sūtra* 3.1.18];

(iv) RVār 54.1–2: *śrotrâdi-vṛttiḥ pratyakṣam* [= *vārṣagaṇāḥ*, M.M.];

(v) RVār 54.2: *sat-saṁprayoge puruṣasyêndriyāṇāṁ buddhi-janma tat pratyakṣam* [= *Mīmāṁsā-sūtra* 1.1.4] *iti ca sarvair abhyupagamyate /* .

**–6.3.1–**

Other parallel passages include the following:

(i) Quotation of a stanza:
RVār ad 5.22 (483.):

*ārambhāya prasṛtā yasmin kāle bhavanti kartāraḥ /*
*kāryasyâniṣṭhātaḥ tan madhyama-kālam icchanti // iti.*

= YD (118.11–12):

*ārambhāya prasṛtā yasmin kāle bhavanti kartāraḥ /*
*kāryasyā niṣ<ṇ>ātās taṁ madhyamaṁ kālam icchanti //*

(ii) Quotation of a stanza which has been ascribed to Vasubandhu, from his lost work *Paramârtha-saptatikā* (cf. MEJOR (1999: 107 ff.)):
RVār (459.21–22):

*atra kaścid āha—*
*varṣâtapābhyāṁ kiṁ vyomnaś carmaṇy asti tayoḥ phalam /*
*carmôpamaś cet so 'nityaḥ kha-tulyaś ced asat-phalam //*

= YD 182.4 f.

(iii) Quotation from Bhartṛhari's VP 2.235:
RVār ad 1.13 (57.4–5):

*śāstreṣu prakriyā-bhedair avidyâivôpavarṇyate /*
*anāgama-vikalpā hi svayaṁ vidyā pravartate //*

(iv) Cf. also reference to the Buddhist concept of *nirvāṇa*:
RVār ad 1.12 (54.23–55.1):

*'nirvāṇaṁ dvividhaṁ sopadhi-viśeṣaṁ nirupadhi-viśeṣaṁ côti / tatra sopadhi-viśeṣe nirvāṇe boddhâsti' iti /* .

Cf. YD (266.24 f.):

*etac cāvasthānaṁ bauddhair <nirupadhiśeṣanirvāṇam ity ayam> apavargo vyākhyātaḥ / etat paraṁ brahma dhruvam amalam abhayam /* . (Cf. also *Prasanna-padā*, p. 519).

(v) Quotation from the PG 5; see von ROSPATT (1995: 16, n. 14,15):

*kṣaṇikāḥ sarva-saṁskārāḥ, asthirāṇāṁ kutaḥ kriyā /*
*bhūtir yeṣāṁ kriyā sâiva kārakaḥ sâiva côcyate //* .

Cf. YD 129.5: *sarvam eva kṣaṇikaṁ* … . YD quotes the PG 2–4, see notes below.

(vi) RVār mentions Kapila, Gārgya, Māṭhara and others among the followers of the *akriyā-vāda*:

(a) RVār 74.4–5: *marīci-kumāra-kapilôlūka-gārgya-vyāghra-bhūti-vādvali-māṭhara-maudgalyayānâdīnām akriyā-vāda-dṛṣṭīnāṁ catura-śītiḥ /* ;

(b) RVār 562.4–6: *marīci-kumārôlūka-kapila-gārgya-vyāghra-bhūti-vādvali**-māṭhara-maudgalyāyana-prabhṛti-darśana-bhedāt akriyā-(kriyā-)vādā aśīti-śata-saṁkhyāḥ pratyetavyaḥ /* .

*) *-vāddhaliṁka-*.

(vii) Miscellaneous:

(a) *Pratītya-samutpāda*. RVār (12.15–13.22) contains a long quotation from the *Śālistamba-sūtra*.

(b) References to AK:

RVār 55.16–17 = AK I.32:

*savitarka-vicārā hi pañca vijñāna-dhātavaḥ /*
*antyās trayas tri-prakārāḥ śeṣā ubhaya-varjitāḥ //*

RVār 55.26 = AK I.17a-b:

*ṣaṇṇām anantarâtītaṁ vijñānaṁ yad dhi tan manaḥ /*

## APPENDIX

Miscellaneous references to WEZLER–MOTEGI's edition of the *Yukti-dīpikā*:

YD 3.21: *sūcanāt sūtram* /

—*Sgra sbyor bam po gñis pa* (§ 126): *sūtra zhes bya ba artha-sūcanād(t) sūtra zhes bya ste* / .

—AS (p. 78.5–10): *yad abhipretârthaṁ sūcanâkāreṇa gadya-bhāṣitam* / ;

—ASBh (p. 95, § 113): *tatra yad abhipretârtha-sūcanâkāreṇa gadya-bhāṣitam* / ;

—*Sāratamā* (p. 2.4): *yatra [gambhīra-]padair artha-sūcanam*.

YD 16.2–3: *mokṣo hi kāmarūpārūpyadhātutrayād iṣyate* /

—cf. YD 18.2–5.

YD 7.19–20: *tadyathā 'pācako lāvaka' iti* /

= vide YD 206.29: *yathaiko devadatta pācako lāvaka iti kvacit* /

—Cf. ŚBh (p. 20.7): *yathā pācako lāvaka iti* / .

YD 26.7 (stanza): *āhāraś ca vihāraś ca* ... /

= vide infra YD 219.21: ... *karmanimitto vāgbuddhisvabhāvāhāravihāraśakti-bhedabhinno vicitraḥ saṁsāra(ḥ)* ... ; seemingly refers to AKBh 4.1 and 3.38d, see below.

—Cf. WEZLER (1990). See AKBh ad 3.38d (theory of *āhāra*: *āhāra-sthitika jagat*; *vihāra* = ed. Pradhan 224.1, 225.16, 244.15); RVaiBh ad 4.62 (p. 145.24 f.), sixfold *āhāra*; JBP, pp. 7.22, 24 and 8.20.

YD 37.1: *na karmaṇā na prajayā dhanena tyāgenaikenāmṛtatvam ānaśuḥ* // (cf. *Kaivalyôpaniṣad* 3).

= See YD 51.1.

—SPBh (p. 94.25, *pada*s c-d of a stanza): *na karmaṇā na prajayā dhanena, tyāgenâike amṛtatvam ānaśur* / [= Appendix III: *Taittirīyâraṇyaka* 10.10.3].

YD 38.13 f.: *agnihotraṁ juhuyāt svargakāmaḥ* /

= See YD 232.26.

—*Maitry-upaniṣad* 6.36;

—Cf. PV I.318a-b (Gnoli, p. 167):

> *tenâgni-hotraṁ juhuyāt svarga-kāma iti śrutau* /
> *khādec chva-māṁsam ity eṣa nârtha ity atra kā pramā* // .

—PVin. (Teil I, p. 63);

—TSP (p. 535.6 [ad 1501–1502 (*Pramāṇântara-bhāva-parīkṣā*)]; p. 782.22 [ad 2335–2337 (*Śruti-parīkṣā*)];
—MNP (p. 195 n. 6).
—Cf. also DNCV (p. 45, 89).

YD 51.1: *tam eva viditvāmṛtatvam eti nānyaḥ panthāyanāya vidyate* / (cf. *Śvetāśvatarôpaniṣad* 3.8; 6.15).
= See above YD 37.1.
— SPBh (p. 94.24, *padas* a-b of a stanza): *tam eva viditvâti mṛtyum eti nânyaḥ panthā vidyate 'yanāya* / [= Appendix III: *Śvetāśvatarôpaniṣad* 3.8; 6.15]. See OBERLIES (1996: 145, n. 112).

YD 53.5–6: *dadhnā juhoti* /
—MNP (p. 204.21 f.; cf. p. 204 n. 54 for further references).

YD 70.20–21 (stanza):

*tathā ṣaḍ ity anye—*
*pratyakṣam anumānaṁ ca śabda<ś> copamayā saha* /
*arthâpattir abhāvaś ca hetavaḥ sādhyasādhakāḥ* //

—The Tibetan version of Bhavya's *Madhyamaka-hṛdaya-kārikā*, chapter 9 on Mīmāṁsā, contains a supernumerary verse (7'), without any equivalent in the Sanskrit original, which reads:

*mngon sum rjes su dpag pa dang* /
*sgra las byung dang ñer 'jal bcas* /
*don gyis go dang dngos med pa'i* /
*gtan tshigs bsgrub bya sgrub par byed* //

Identified in KAWASAKI (1976: 8–9; n. 4):

'Direct perception, inference, verbal testimony, together with resemblance, presumption, and non-existence—these [six] means of knowledge demonstrate what should be demonstrated' (KAWASAKI (1976: 9)).

—Cf. MMU 1.15 (p. 8):

*pratyakṣam anumānaṁ ca śābdaṁ côpamitis tathā* /
*arthâpattir abhāvaś ca ṣaṭ pramāṇāni mādṛśām* //

YD 71.16: *vītāvītāv api hetū* ... / See also YD 84.19 ff.; 89.1; 92.25; 96.2; 97.5 ff.
—Cf. FRANCO (1999).

YD 86.20: *<vya>bhicārād viśeṣās tu pratītāḥ pratipādakāḥ /*

—In addition to the Editors' references to PS(V) add:

cf. MŚV (*abhāva-pariccheda*) v. 39:

*na câpy abhāva-sāmānye pramāṇam upajāyate /*
*vyabhicārād viśeṣās tu pratīyeran kathaṁ tayā //*

YD 86.23: *... anityaḥ śabdaḥ kṛtakatvād iti /*

Cf. e.g.:

—*Nyāya-sūtra-bhāṣya* ad I.1.35;

—NP § 2.4;

—TSP ad 1437–38 (p. 514.11);

—Cf. also FRAUWALLNER (1957: 753) (Fr. 18a); TŚ (p. 14.3).

YD 88.9 f.: *śayanādīnāṁ ca saṅghātatvāt ... /*

—Add reference to YD 168.5.

YD 89.21: *anupalabhyamānasyobhayathādṛṣṭatvāt /*

—Add reference to YD 167.3.

YD 104 n. (1) (*pramāṇaviṣayatvāt*) [Marginal Notes] stanza:

*yathoktam—*
*janmatulyaṁ hi buddhīnām āptānāptagirāṁ śrutau /*
*janmādikopayogaṁ* ca nānumāne trilakṣaṇaḥ //*

*) Marked by the Editors as uncertain reading.

= MŚV (*vākyâdhikaraṇam*) v. 246:

*janma tulyaṁ hi buddhīnām āptânāpta-girāṁ śrutau /*
*janmâdhikôpayogī ca nânumāyās tri-lakṣaṇaḥ //*

YD 111.15 ff.: *parimāṇo* hi nāmāvasthitasya dravyasya ... /*

*) read: *pariṇāmo.*

—Cf. VāN (I: 13.11–13): *avasthitasya dravyasya dharmântara-nivṛttir dharmântara-pradur-bhāvaś ca pariṇāmaḥ /* ; (cf also 66.3–5).

YD 111.21–22 stanza:

*jahad dharmāntaraṁ pūrvam upādatte yadā param /*
*tattvād apracyuto dharmī pariṇāmaḥ sa ucyate //*

= See also YD 163.12–13.

—Cf. references in VāN (II: 32 n. 155).

YD 118.6–7 stanza:

*asattvān nāsti sambandhaḥ *kārakaiḥ sattvasaṅgibhiḥ* /
*asambandhasya cotpattim icchato na vyavasthitaḥ* //

—Quoted in SDS (p. 636);
*) *kāraṇaiḥ*.

YD 154.24: *jagadvaicitryopalambhāt* /

—Cf. AK 4.1a: *karmaja loka-vaicitryam*.

Cf. also BA 9 (p. 305.18–20; 359.3); *Abhisamayâlaṁkāra* (p. 730.22; 968.6); AVN (p. 87.11); AD v. 154 (118.5–6).

Cf. YD 219.20: *karmaśaktivaicitryāt* / .

Cf. YD 43.2–3: *dṛśyate cāyaṁ vāgbuddhisvabhāvāhāravihārabhedabhinna<ḥ> karma<vipāka>vaicitrya-nimittaḥ saṁsāraḥ* /

—Cf. MŚV (*citrâkṣepa-parihāra*) v. 3:

*karmaṇāṁ câpi vaicitryād deśa-kālâdy-apekṣaṇāt* /
*kasyacic cârddha-bhuktatvāt karmānyat pratibadhyate* //

YD 167.13–14:

*ātmaiva hy ātmano nāsti viparītena kalpyate* /
*naiveha sattvam ātmāsti dharmās tv ete sahetukāḥ* //

= PG 4 (p. 168):

*ātmâiva hy ātmano nâsti viparītena kalpyate* /
*nâiveha sattvam* [MS: *sattvo*] *ātmā vā dharmās tv ete sahetukāḥ* //

'The Self does not belong to the self; it is deludedly imagined. Here there is no being or oneself. These *dharma*s have their causes.'

—Cf. Vasubandhu, *Viṁśatikā-vṛtti* (p. 5.22):

*nâstîha sattva ātmā vā dharmās tv ete sahetukāḥ* /

YD 167.15–16:

*dvādaśaiva <bh>avāṅgāni skandhāyatanadhātavaḥ* /
*vicintya sarvāṇy etāni pudgalo nopalabhyate* //

= PG 2 (p. 168):

*dvādaśâiva bhavâṅgāni skandhâyatana-dhātavaḥ* /
*vicintya sarvāṇy etāni pudgalo nôpalabhyate* //

'The twelve members of phenomenal existence are the *skandhas*, *āyatanas*, and *dhātus*. Pondering all those, a person (pudgala) is not found.'

YD 167.18–19:

*śūnyam ādhyātmikaṁ paśya śūnyaṁ paśya bahirgatam /*
*na dṛśyate so 'pi kaścid yo bhāvayati śūnyatām //*

= PG 3 (p. 168):

*śūnyam ādhyātmikaṁ sarvaṁ śūnyaṁ sarvaṁ bahir-gatam /*
*na vidyate so 'pi kaścid yo bhāvayati śūnyatām //*

'Void is all within; void all without. Nor exists anyone who contemplates the void.'

Further references in: MEJOR (1999: 104; 110–112, nn. 70–74).

YD 167.23: *tasmāt sarvapramāṇānupalabdher nāsty ātmeti /*

— NV ad 3.1.1 (p. 341.6): *nâsty ātmânupalabdher iti cet /*. Cf. OETKE (1988: 374 ff.).

YD 168.5: *iha saṅghātāḥ parārthā dṛṣṭās … /*

—TSP ad v. 307 (p. 149.14): *yac côktam—yat saṅghāta-rūpaṁ tat parârthaṁ dṛṣṭam ity-ādi /* ;

—PV, Manorathanandin ad 4.29 (Svāmī Dvārikādās Śāstri, p. 373.18 ff.): *yathā "ātmâsti na vā" iti vivāde tat-sādhanârthaṁ sāṁkhyena "parârthāś cakṣur-ādayaḥ saṅghātatvāt śayanâsanâdy-aṅgavat"—ity uktasya … /* ;

—*Māṭhara-vṛtti* (p. 22.7): *iha loke ye saṅghātās te parârthā dṛṣṭāḥ paryaṅka-ratha-śaraṇâdayaḥ /*

—*Jaya-maṅgalā* (ed. Śrī Satkāriśarmā Vaṅgīya, p. 83.20–21): *iha loke saṅghāta-bāhyāḥ śayanâsanâdayo ye te parârthā dṛṣṭāḥ /* ;

—SK, Paramārtha's Chinese transl. ad SK 17 (TAKAKUSU (1904: 1002 (1))).

—Cf. also MŚV (*ātma-vāda*) v. 114:

*saṅghāta-sanniveśau ca na staḥ pārārthya-varjitau /*
*bhoktā ca cetanaḥ kaścid astîty atrâviruddhatā //*

YD 170.9: *ucyate: bhoga … /*

—Cf. SPBh ad I.104 (p. 51): *cid-avasāno bhogaḥ / puruṣa-svarūpe caitanye paryavasānaṁ yasyâitādṛśo bhogaḥ siddhir ity arthaḥ /*.

YD 170.14: *cittaṁ mano vijñānam iti* (Viṁś. p. 3.3, AKBh. p. 62.1–2).

—Correct reference:

(a) *cittaṁ mano 'tha vijñānam ekârtham* / = AK 3.34a (ed. Pradhan, p. 61.22; ed. Swami Dwarikadas Shastri, p. 208.2);

(b) *Viṁśatikā-vṛtti* (p. 3.3) [text reconstructed by LÉVI from the Tibetan and Chinese, fully agrees with the Tibetan translation, cf. POUSSIN (1912)]: *cittaṁ mano vijñānaṁ vijñaptiś cêti paryāyāḥ* / .

YD 195.6: *yasya asmipratyayasya viśeṣagrahaṇaṁ bhavati—śabde 'haṁ sparśe 'haṁ rūpe 'haṁ rase 'haṁ gandhe 'ham iti* /

—Reference is to *Krama-dīpikā* (*Tattva-samāsa-sūtra-vṛtti*), App. VII (as a prose passage); EIPHIL IV (: 321 f.):

> *ahaṁ śabde ahaṁ sparśe ahaṁ rūpe ahaṁ rase* /
> *ahaṁ gandhe ahaṁ svāmī dhanavān aham īśvaraḥ* // .

—V1, ed. Solomon, p. 40:

> *ahaṁ śabde, ahaṁ sparśe, ahaṁ rūpe, ahaṁ rase, ahaṁ gandhe, ahaṁ vidvān, ahaṁ spa(da)rśanīyo ya ity evamâdy abhima(mā)na-lakṣaṇasvā(ścā ?)* ...

—Cf. *Māṭhara* ad SK 24, p. 31.1 f.:

> *rūpe aham, rase aham, gandhe aham, ahaṁ vidvān, ahaṁ darśanīya ity evamâdy abhimāno 'haṁkāraḥ* / .

—Cf. also TK, p. 43; JM, p. 89.15 f.

YD 218.30: *jñānamātram idam iti* /

—*Viṁśatikā* 1a: *vijñapti-mātram evâtad* / .

—*Triṁśikā* 17d (p. 35.9): *idaṁ sarvaṁ vijñapti-mātrakam* / ;

—*Triṁśikā* 27a (p. 42.25): *vijñapti-mātram evêdam ity api* ... / ;

—Vinītadeva's *Triṁśikā-ṭīkā* ad 17 (p. 488.3–2 from below): *tasmāt sarvam idaṁ jagad vijñapti-mātrakam* ... / .

—Cf. also DNC (p. 105.4, 106.2): *vijñāna-mātram idaṁ tri-bhuvanam* / ; *tatra katamad vijñāna-mātram idaṁ sarvaṁ traidhātukam* / ; Siṁhasūri's *Vṛtti* (ad loc.). See WEZLER (1981: 368, n. 41).

YD 219.33: *tathā hi gandharvanagarādiṣu* ... /

—Cf. *Triṁśikā-bhāṣya* (p. 35.18 f.): *vijñānaṁ ca māyā-gandharva-nagara-svapna-timirâdāv asaty ālambane jāyate* / .

—*Viṁśatikā-vṛtti* (p. 3.15): *gandharva-nagareṇâsattvān nagara-kriyā na kriyate* ... / .

YD 219.15: *iha pratyakṣaṁ balīya iti* / .

—Cf. *Viṁśatikā-vṛtti* (p. 8.23): *sarveṣāṁ ca pramāṇānāṁ pratyakṣaṁ pramāṇaṁ gariṣṭham ity ... /* .

YD 228.2 ff. ad SK 39a-b, esp. stanza, p. 228.18–19:

> *jarāyujaṁ gavādīnām aṇḍajaṁ caiva pakṣiṇām /*
> *tṛṇādeś codbhijjaṁ kṣudrajantūnāṁ svedajaṁ smṛtam //*

—Cf. *Manu-smṛti* 1.43–46.

—JM 109.10–11: *jarāyujâṇḍajôṣmajôdbhijjâkhyāś catvāro bhedāḥ śāstrântare draṣṭavyāḥ //* .

Also cf. AKBh ad 3.8c-d, 9; POUSSIN (1980: III: 26 f.); *Laṅkâvatāra* 10.845. See GARBE (1917: 306; n. 2). [SK 53; *Sūtra* 5.111, 3.46].

YD 232.19: *ājavañjavībhāva*.

—Cf. MMK 218.4; BHSD s.v. ('state of moving restlessly to and fro'); *Sāṁkhya-ṣaptati-vṛtti* (V1), notes, p. 130.

YD 240.11: *tamo moho mahāmohas tāmisro 'ndhatāmisra iti /*

= *Yoga-sūtra-bhāṣya* ad 1.8;

—Cf. NSaṁ, *Sūtra* 16.4: *ajñānam adarśanam anabhisamayas tama saṁmoho 'vidyânu(śayaḥ)* (recte: *'vidyândhakāram*—M.M.), *ayam* (recte: *iyam*—M.M.) *ucyate 'vidyā*.

YD 243.4–5:

> *bādhiryam andhyam aghratvaṁ mūkatā jaḍatā ca yā /*
> *unmādakauṣṭhyakauṇyāni klaibyodāvartapaṅgutāḥ //*

= JM 105.1–3:

> *bādhiryam āndhyâghrātṛtve mūkatā jaḍatā tathā /*
> *unmāda-kauṇḍya-kuṣṭhāni klaibyôdāvarta-paṅgutāḥ //*
> *iti // eta indriya-vadhā aśaktir ity upadiṣṭāḥ sāṁkhyâcāryaiḥ //*

= TK 62.10–11:

> *bādhiryaṁ kuṣṭhitândhatvaṁ jaḍatâjighratā tathā /*
> *mūkatā-kauṇya-paṅgutva-klaibyôdāvarta-mandatāḥ //*

—Cf. *Laṅkâvatāra* 10.782a: *badhirândha-kāṇa-mūkānāṁ vṛddhānāṁ vaira-vṛttinām /* .

YD 245.25–26: *kālaviśeṣād bījād aṅkuro jāyate ...*

—Cf. e.g. *Śālistamba-sūtra*.

YD 259.1–10 = AK 3.19, see MEJOR (1999).

## BIBLIOGRAPHY

Texts:

*Abhisamayâlaṁkāra* = *Abhisamayâlaṁkārâlokā Prajñā-pāramitā-vyākhyā by Haribhadra*. Ed. by U. Wogihara, Tokyo 1932–35.

AD(V) = *Abhidharmadīpa with Vibhāṣāprabhāvṛtti*. Critical edition with notes and introduction by Padmanabh S. Jaini. Patna 1977.

AK = *Abhidharma-kośa-kārikā*. See: AKBh.

AKBh (Pradhan) = *Abhidharmakośabhāṣyam of Vasubandhu*. Edited by P. Pradhan. Revised second edition with introduction and indices etc. by Aruna Haldar. Patna 1975.

AKBh (Shastri) = *Abhidharmakośa and Bhāṣya of ācārya Vasubandhu with Sphuṭārthā Commentary of ācārya Yaśomitra*. Critically edited by Swami Dwarikadas Shastri. *Bauddha Bharati Series* 5, 6, 7, 9, Varanasi, 1970: Part I (1 and 2 *Kośasthāna*); 1971: Part II (3 and 4 *Kośasthāna*); 1972: Part III (5 and 6 *Kośasthāna*); 1973: Part IV (7 and 8 *Kośasthāna*).

AKVy = *Abhidharma-kośa-vyākhyā*. (1) Wogihara *Sphuṭārthā Abhidharmakośavyākhyā, the work of Yaśomitra*. Edited by U. Wogihara. Tokyo 1989. [First edition: 1936]. (2) Ed. by Shastri. See: AKBh (Shastri).

AS = *Abhidharmasamuccaya of Asaṅga*. Ed. P. Pradhan. Santiniketan 1950.

ASBh = *Abhidharma-samuccaya-bhāṣya*. Deciphered and edited by N. Tatia. Patna 1976.

AVN = *The Artha-viniścaya-sūtra and its commentary* (*nibandhana*). Ed. N.H. Samtani. Patna 1971.

BA = *Bodhicaryâvatāra*: Poussin, Louis de la Vallée: *Bouddhisme. Études et matériaux. Ādikarmapradīpa. Bodhicaryāvatāra-ṭīkā*. London 1898.

DNC = Mallavādin Kṣamāśramaṇa: *Dvādaśâra-naya-cakra. Dvādaśāraṁ Nayacakraṁ of Ācārya Śrī Mallavādī Kṣamāśramaṇa. With the commentary Nyāyāgamānusāriṇī of Ācārya Śrī Siṁhasūri Gaṇi Vādi Kṣamāśramaṇa*. Ed. with critical notes by Muni Jambūvijayajī. Pt. I (1–4 Aras) Bhavnagar 1966; Pt. II (5–8 Aras) Bhavnagar 1976; Pt. III (9–12 Aras) Bhavnagar 1988.

DNCV = Siṁhasūri: *Nyāyâgamânusāriṇī*. See: DNC.

*Gauḍapāda* = *Gauḍapāda-bhāṣya*. See: MAINKAR (1972).

*Jaya-maṅgalā* = Śaṅkara: *Jaya-maṅgalā*. (1) Ed. by Satkāri Śarmā Vaṅgīya. See: *Māṭhara*. (2) *Śrī Śaṅkarâcārya-viracitā Jaya-maṅgalā nāma Sāṁkhya-saptati-ṭīkā*. Ed. by H[aradatta] Śarma, with an Introduction by Gopi Nath Kaviraj. *Calcutta Oriental Series* No. 19, Calcutta 1926.

JBP = *Jñāna-bindu-prakaraṇa*. Ed. by Sukhlāl Saṅghavi. Ahmedabad 1942.

*Kāśikā* = *The Kashika, being a commentary on the sutras of Panini*. Edited with notes by Vyākaranāchārya-Mīmāṁsā Tīrtha Pandit Ananta Sastri Phadake. *The Kashi Sanskrit Series* No. 37, Benares 1931.

*Māṭhara-vṛtti* = Māṭharâcārya: *Māṭhara-vṛtti*. *Sāṁkhyakārikā of Śrīmad Īśvarakṛṣṇa with the Māṭharavṛtti of Māṭharācārya* [ed. by Sāhityāçārya Pt. Viṣṇu Prasād Śarmā] *and the Jayamaṅgalā of Śrī Śaṅkara* [critical edition with an Introduction by Śrī Satkāri Śarmā Vaṅgīya]. 2nd ed. *Chowkhamba Sanskrit Series* 296 (56), Varanasi 1970.

MBhā = Patañjali's *Vyākaraṇa-mahā-bhāṣya*.

MMK = Nāgārjuna: *Mūla-madhyamaka-kārikā*. *Mūlamadhyamakakārikās (Mādhyamikasūtras) de Nāgārjuna, avec la Prasannapadā, commentaire de Candrakīrti*. Publié par L. de la Vallée Poussin. *Bibliotheca Buddhica* 4, St. Pétersbourg 1903–1913.

MMU = Nārāyaṇa: *Māna-meyôdaya*. Ed. Kunhan Raja and Suryanarayana Sastri, Madras 1975.

MNP = *The Mīmāṁsā-nyāya-prakāśa, or Āpadevī: A Treatise on the Mīmāṁsā System by Āpadeva*. Translated into English, with an introduction, transliterated Sanskrit text, and glossarial index, by Franklin Edgerton. New Haven 1929.

MŚV = Kumārila Bhaṭṭa: *Mīmāṁsā-śloka-vārttika*.

NP = Śaṅkarasvāmin: *Nyāya-praveśa*. Balcerowicz, Piotr: 'Śaṅkarasvāmin: *Nyāyapraveśa*—"Wprowadzenie w logikę" Część pierwsza' [Part I: Sanskrit text, Polish translation and annotations], *Studia Indologiczne* 2 (1995) 39–87.

NSaṁ = *Nidāna-saṁyukta*. Tripathi, Ch.: *Fünfundzwanzig Sūtras des Nidāna-saṁyukta*. Berlin 1962.

NV = Uddyotakara: *Nyāya-vārttika*. Ed. by Pt. Vindhyeśvarī Prasāda Dvivedin. Vārāṇasī 1916.

Pāṇ = Pāṇini, *Aṣṭâdhyāyī*.

PG = *Paramârtha-gāthā* (ascribed to Asaṅga). Wayman, Alex: *Analysis of the Śrāvakabhūmi Manuscript*. Berkeley–Los Angeles 1961.

*Prasanna-padā* = See MMK.

PS = Diṅnāga: *Pramāṇa-samuccaya*.

PSV = Diṅnāga: *Pramāṇa-samuccaya-vṛtti*.

PV = Dharmakīrti: *Pramāṇa-vārttika*. (1) Gnoli, Raniero: *The Pramāṇavārttikam of Dharmakīrti. The First Chapter with the Autocommentary*. Text and Critical Notes. *Serie Orientale Roma* 23, Roma 1960. (2) *Pramāṇa-vārttika of Acharya Dharmakīrti with the Commentary 'Vṛtti' of Acharya Manorathanandin*. Ed. Svāmī Dvārikādās Śāstri. *Bauddha Bharati Series* 3, Vārāṇasī 1984.

PVin. = Steinkellner, Ernst: *Dharmakīrti's Pramāṇaviniścayaḥ. Zweites Kapitel: Svārthānumānam*. Teil I: Tibetischer Text und Sanskrittexte. Teil II: Übersetzung und Anmerkungen. Wien 1979.

RVaiBh = *Bhadanta Nāgārjuna's Rasavaiśeṣika-sūtra with Nārasiṁha bhāṣya*. Ed. N.E. Muthuswami. Published by N. Sridharan. *Kerala Government Ayurvedic Publication Series* 2, Trivandrum 1976.

RVār = *Tattvârtha-vārtika* (*Rāja-vārtika*) *of Śrī Akalaṅkadeva*. Edited with Hindi Translation, Introduction, appendices, variant readings, comparative notes etc. by Prof. Mahendra Kumar Jain. Parts I-II. 5th ed., *Jnanpith Moortidevi Jain Granthamala: Sanskrit Grantha* No. 10; 20, Bharatiya Jnanpith, Delhi 1999.

*Sārạtamā* = *Sāratamā*: *A Pañjikā on the Aṣṭasāhasrikā Prajñāpāramitā Sūtra*. Ed. Padmanabh S. Jaini. K.P. Jayaswal Research Institute, Patna 1979.

ŚBh = *Śabara-bhāṣya*. Frauwallner, Erich: *Materialien zur ältesten Erkenntnislehre der Karmamīmāṁsā*. Wien 1968.

SDS = Mādhavācārya: *Sarva-darśana-saṅgraha*. Ed. by Umāśaṅkar Śāstri Śarmā, *Vidyabhawan Sanskrit Granthamala* 113, Chowkhamba Vidyabhawan, Varanasi 1964.

*Sgra sbyor bam po gñis pa* = *Sgra sbyor bam po gñis pa*. A Critical Edition of the *Sgra sbyor bam po gñis pa*, An Old and Basic Commentary on the *Mahāvyutpatti*. Ed. by M. Ishikawa. The Toyo Bunko, Tokyo 1990.

SK = *Sāṁkhya-kārikā*.

SPBh = *The Sāṁkhya-pravacana-bhāṣya, or Commentary on the Exposition of the Sānkhya Philosophy by Vijñānabhikṣu*. Ed. R. Garbe. *Harvard Oriental Series* 2, Cambridge, Mass. 1895.

TK = *The Tattvakaumudī (Vācaspati Miśra's Commentary on the Sāṁkhya-Kārikā)*. Translated into English and containing a synopsis of the cardinal doctrines of the Sāṁkhya philosophy by Mahāmahopādhyāya Ganganatha Jha, and with an historical introduction and critical notes by Vidyāsudhākara Har Dutt Sharma. 2nd. ed. Poona 1934.

*Triṁśikā* = Vasubandhu: *Triṁśikā*. See LÉVI (1925).

*Triṁśikā-bhāṣya* = Sthiramati: *Triṁśikā*. See LÉVI (1925).

*Triṁśikā-ṭīkā* = Jaini, Padmanabh S., 'The Sanskrit fragments of Vinītadeva's *Triṁśikā-ṭīkā*', BSOAS 48 (1985) 470–492.

TŚ = *Tarka-śāstra*. Tucci, Giuseppe: *Pre-Diṅnāga Buddhist Texts on Logic from Chinese Sources*, Baroda 1929.

TSP = *Tattvasaṅgraha of Ācārya Śāntarakṣita with the commentary Panjikā of Śrī Kamalaśīla*. Critically edited by Swami Dwarikadas Shastri. 2 vols. *Baudha Bharati Series* 1, 2, Varanasi 1981–1982.

VāN = Much, Michael Torsten: *Dharmakīrti's Vādanyāyaḥ*. Teil I: Sanskrit-Text. Teil II: Übersetzung und Anmerkungen. *Veröffentlichungen der Kommission für Sprachen und Kulturen Süd- und Ostasiens* 581, Österreichische Akademie der Wissenschaften, Wien 1991.

V1 = *Sāṁkhya-saptati-vṛtti*. Ed. Esther A. Solomon, Gujarat University, Ahmedabad 1973.

V2 = *Sāṁkhya-vṛtti*. Ed. Esther A. Solomon, Gujarat University, Ahmedabad 1973.

V2' = *Sāṁkhya-vṛtti*. Ed. Naomichi Nakada, under the guidance of Prof. Dr. V.V. Gokhale. The Hokuseido Press, Tokyo 1978.

*Viṁśatikā* = see LÉVI (1925).

*Viṁśatikā-vṛtti* = see LÉVI (1925).

VP = *Bhartṛhariṣ Vākyapadīya. Die Mūlakārikās nach den Handschriften herausgegeben und mit einem Pāda-Index versehen* von Walter Rau. Abhandlungen für die Kunde des Morgenlandes XLII, 4. Franz Steiner Verlag, Wiesbaden 1977.

YD = (1) *Yuktidīpikā*. Ed. by Pulinbihari Chakravarti. Calcutta Oriental Series 23. Calcutta 1938. (2) *Yuktidīpikā. An Ancient Commentary on the Sāṁkhya-Kārikā of Īśvarakṛṣṇa*. Ed. by Ram Chandra Pandeya. Delhi-Varanasi-Patna 1967. (3) See: WEZLER–MOTEGI (1998).

Secondary Sources:

BHSD = Edgerton, Franklin: *Buddhist Hybrid Sanskrit Grammar and Dictionary.*—Vol. I: *Grammar.* Vol. II: *Dictionary.* Motilal Banarsidass, Delhi 1993. [First edition: New Haven 1953].

BRONKHORST 1990 = Bronkhorst, Johannes: 'Vārttika', *Wiener Zeischrift für die Kunde Südasiens* 34 (1990) 123–146.

CHAKRAVARTI 1975 = Chakravarti, Pulinbihari: *Origin and Development of the Sāṁkhya System of Thought.* 2nd ed. Oriental Books Reprint Corporation, New Delhi [First edition: Calcutta 1952].

EIPHIL IV = *Encyclopedia of Indian Philosophies.* (General editor: Karl H. Potter.)—Vol. IV: Larson, Gerald J.; Bhattacharya, Ram Shankar: *Sāṁkhya—A Dualist Tradition in Indian Philosophy.* Princeton University Press, Princeton–New Jersey 1987. [Indian edition: Motilal Banarsidass, Delhi 1987].

FRANCO 1999 = Franco, Eli: 'Avīta and āvīta', *Asiatische Studien / Études Asiatiques* 53:3 (1999) 563–577.

FRAUWALLNER 1933 = Frauwallner, Erich: 'Zu den Fragmenten buddhistischer Logiker im Nyāyavārttikam,' WZKM 40 (1933) 281–304 = FRAUWALLNER (1982: 460–483).

FRAUWALLNER 1951 = Frauwallner, Erich: 'Amalavijñānam und ālayavijñānam,' *Festschrift Schubring*, Hamburg 1951: 148–159 = FRAUWALLNER (1982: 637–648).

FRAUWALLNER 1953 = Frauwallner, Erich: *Geschichte der indischen Philosophie*. 1. Band, Otto Müller Verlag, Salzburg 1953.

FRAUWALLNER 1957 = Frauwallner, Erich: 'Vasubandhu's Vādavidhiḥ,' *Wiener Zeitschrift zur Kunde des Süd- und Ostasiens* 1 (1957) 104–146 = FRAUWALLNER (1982: 716–758).

FRAUWALLNER 1961 = Frauwallner, Erich: 'Landmarks in the History of Indian Logic.' *Wiener Zeitschrift für die Kunde Süd- und Ostasiens* 5 (1961) 125–148 = FRAUWALLNER (1982: 847–870).

FRAUWALLNER 1982 = Frauwallner, Erich: *Kleine Schriften*. Ed. by G. Oberhammer and E. Steinkellner. *Glasenapp-Stiftung* Bd. 22, Wiesbaden 1982.

GARBE 1917 = Garbe, Richard: *Die Sāṁkhya-Philosophie, eine Darstellung der indischen Rationalismus nach den Quellen*. 2. umgearb. Aufl. Leipzig 1917.

HALBFASS 1983 = Halbfass, Wilhelm: *Studies in Kumārila and Śaṅkara. Studien zur Indologie und Iranistik, Monographie* 9, Reinbek 1983.

HALBFASS 1991 = Halbfass, Wilhelm: *Tradition and Reflection. Explorations in Indian Thought*. SUNY.Press, Albany 1991.

KATRE 1989 = Katre, Sumitra M.: *Aṣṭādhyāyī of Pāṇini*. Roman Transliteration and English Translation by ..., Delhi 1989.

KAWASAKI 1976 = Kawasaki, Shinjo: 'The Mīmāṁsā Chapter of Bhavya's Madhyamaka-hṛdaya-kārikā. Text and Translation. (I) Pūrva-pakṣa', *Studies* (Institute of Philosophy, University of Tsukuba) (1976) 1–16.

LARSON 1979 = Larson, Gerald J.: *Classical Sāṁkhya – An Interpretation of its History and Meaning with The Sāṁkhya-kārikā of Īśvarakṛṣṇa (romanized text with translation)*. Second revised ed., Motilal Banarsidass, Delhi–Varanasi–Patna 1979.

LÉVI 1925 = Lévi, Sylvain: *Vijñaptimātratāsiddhi: Deux Traités de Vasubandhu; Viṁśatikā (la Vingtaine) accompagnée d'une Explication en Prose et Triṁśikā (la Trentaine) avec la commentaire de Sthiramati*. Bibliothèque de l'École des Hautes Études 245, Paris 1925.

MAINKAR 1972 = Mainkar, T.G.: *Sāṁkhyakārikā of Īśvarakṛṣṇa with the commentary of Gauḍapāda*. Translated into English with Notes by .... 2nd revised and enlarged edition, Oriental Book Agency, Poona 1972. [First edition: 1964].

MEJOR 1999 = Mejor, Marek: '"There is no self" (nātmāsti)—Some observations from Vasubandhu's Abhidharmakośa and the Yuktidīpikā', in: *The Notion of 'Self' in Buddhism*, ed. Bart Dessein. *Communication & Cognition* 32:1–2 (1999) 97–126.

OBERHAMMER 1960 = Oberhammer, Gerhard: 'The authorship of the *Ṣaṣṭitantram*', *Wiener Zeitschrift zur Kunde des Süd- und Ostasiens* 4 (1960) 71–91.

OBERHAMMER 1967–68 = Oberhammer, Gerhard: 'Notes on the *tantrayukti-s*', *Adyar Library Bulletin* 31–32 (1967–68) 600–616.

OBERLIES 1996 = Oberlies, Thomas: 'Die Śvetāśvatara-Upaniṣad. Edition und Übersetzung von Adhyāya II-III. (Studien zu den "mittleren" Upaniṣads II—2. Teil)', *Wiener Zeischrift für die Kunde Südasiens* 40 (1996) 123–160.

OETKE 1988 = Oetke, Claus: *'Ich' und das Ich. Analytische Untersuchungen zur buddhistisch-brahmanischen Ātmankontroverse. Alt- und Neu-Indische Studien* 33, Stuttgart 1988.

POUSSIN 1912 = Poussin, Louis de la Vallée: 'Vasubandhu: *Viṁśakakārikāprakaraṇa*. Traité des Vingt Ślokas, avec le commentaire de l'autor', *Le Muséon N.S.* 13 (1912) 53–90.

POUSSIN 1980 = Poussin, Louis de la Vallée: *L'Abhidharmakośa de Vasubandhu*. Traduction et Annotations. Nouvelle édition anastatique présentée par Étienne Lamotte. 6 vols. *Mélanges Chinois et Bouddhiques* XVI, Bruxelles 1980. [First edition: 1923].

von ROSPATT 1995 = Rospatt, Alexander von: *The Buddhist Doctrine of Momentariness. A Survey of the Origins and early Phase of this Doctrine up to Vasubandhu. Alt- und Neu-Indische Studien* 47, Stuttgart 1995.

SHARMA 1929 = Sharma, Har Dutt: '*Jayamaṅgalā* and the other Commentaries on *Sāṅkhya-Saptati*', *Indian Historical Quarterly* 5 (1929) 417–431.

SOLOMON 1974 = Solomon, Esther A.: *The Commentaries of the Sāṁkhya Kārikā—A Study*. Gujarat University, Ahmedabad 1974.

TAKAKUSU 1904 = Takakusu, J.: 'La *Sāṁkhyakārikā* étudiée à la lumière de sa version chinoise', *Bulletin de l'École Français d'Extrême Orient* 4 (1904) 1–65 (Introduction), 978–1064 (Traduction).

WEZLER 1974 = Wezler, Albrecht: 'Some observations on the Yuktidīpikā', *30. Deutscher Orientalistentag, Wiesbaden 1973*. Suppl. II, xviii, 1974: 434–455. [Review article of YD, ed. Pandeya.]

WEZLER 1981 = Wezler, Albrecht: 'Studien zum Dvādaśanayacakra des Śvetāmbara Mallavādin: I. Der sarvasarvātmakatvavāda', in: *Studien zum Jainismus und Buddhismus. Gedenkschrift für Ludwig Alsdorf.* Ed. by K. Bruhn, A. Wezler. *Alt- und Neu-Indische Studien* 23, Wiesbaden 1981: 359–408.

WEZLER 1990 = Wezler, Albrecht: 'On Two Medical Verses in the Yuktidīpikā', *Journal of the European Āyurvedic Society* 1 (1990) 127–148.

WEZLER–MOTEGI 1998 = Wezler, Albrecht; Motegi, Shujun: *Yuktidīpikā. The Most Significant Commentary on the Sāṁkhyakārikā*. Critically edited by Albrecht Wezler and Shujun Motegi. Vol. I. *Alt- und Neu-Indische Studien* 44, Stuttgart 1998.

# Theories of Debate, Proof and Counter-Proof in the Early Indian Dialectical Tradition

ERNST PRETS

In the *Vimāna-sthāna* of the *Caraka-saṁhitā*[1] we find—in addition to other philosophically interesting passages of this famous medical compendium, which have been dealt with by various scholars[2]—a whole chapter dealing with various modes of learning and teaching. Here we come across a section discussing the method of debate (*saṁbhāṣā-vidhi*) which is well known to historiographers of Indian logic and dialectic.[3]

According to this passage, debates or discussions are divided into friendly and hostile debates.[4] The friendly debate (*saṁdhāya-saṁbhāṣā*, or *anuloma-saṁbhāṣā*)[5] is carried out by learned and eloquent fellow scholars who pleasantly discuss questions or problems of their science in the spirit of co-operation, and who interrogate and answer confidently without fear of being defeated.[6] Standing in contrast to such friendly dialogues, the hostile debate (*vigṛhya-saṁbhāṣā*) is carried out in the spirit of opposition. The obvious aim of such a dispute is to defeat the opponent and to win the day.

The *Caraka-saṁhitā* gives an elaborate description[7] of what a debater must take into consideration before he agrees to enter a hostile debate. Remarkably interesting,

---

[1] CarS vim 8.

[2] Cf. e.g. (in alphabetical order): BEDEKAR (1957), COMBA (1987), FILLIOZAT (1990), FILLIOZAT (1993), KATSURA (1986), MEINDERSMA (1989), MEINDERSMA (1992), MIYASAKA (1963), RAO (1962), SASTRI (1952) and SHARMA (1984).

[3] Cf. e.g. VIDYĀBHŪṢAṆA (1920: 28–31), DASGUPTA (1922: 378 f.), SOLOMON (1976: 74–78), FRAUWALLNER (1984: 67–71), MATILAL (1987: 55 f.) and MATILAL (1998: 38–41).

[4] CarS vim 8.15 f.

[5] Cf. OBERHAMMER–PRETS–PRANDSTETTER (1991: I, 61).

[6] CarS vim 8.17.

[7] Cf. CarS vim 8.18–25. This passage has already been translated as early as 1872 by Rudolf von ROTH, cf. ROTH (1872). Recently this passage has been dealt with carefully according to its importance by KANG (1998).

*Essays in Indian Philosophy, Religion and Literature*, pp. 435–448.

this description is unique in the history of the Indian dialectical tradition, giving a lively picture of various types of debaters (*vādin*) and juries (*pariṣad*), which sounds like a guide to modern public political panel or TV discussions. Accordingly, the debater must examine his opponent, the opponent's personal and intellectual strengths or weaknesses which might be superior, equal or inferior to those of his own, and must also examine the jury's level of knowledge, which is described as either learned (*jñānavat*) or ignorant (*mūḍha*), and which may have a friendly (*suhṛd*), indifferent (*udāsīna*) or hostile (*pratiniviṣṭa*) attitude towards the debater.

According to this passage, a debater should enter a debate only if the opponent is equal or inferior, and only in the presence of a friendly or, at the very least, an ignorant or indifferent jury. No discussions should be carried out in the presence of a hostile jury or with a superior opponent. After having considered the weak points of his enemy in the course of debate, he should overpower him quickly:

> 'Under these circumstances the following [procedures] are ways of quickly defeating inferior [opponents]: He should overpower an unlearned [opponent] by long citations of *sūtra*s; moreover, [he should overpower] an [opponent] who is weak in theoretical knowledge by [the use] of sentences containing troublesome words; an [opponent] who is unable to retain sentences, by a continuous series of sentences composed of long-strung *sūtra*s; an [opponent] devoid of presence of mind, by the repetition of the same [words] with a difference in meaning; an [opponent] devoid of eloquence, by pointing to half-uttered sentences; an [opponent] devoid of self-confidence, by embarrassing [him]; an [opponent] of irritable temper, by putting [him] to exertion; one who is frightened, by terrifying [him]; [and] an inattentive [opponent], by reprehending him. In these ways he should overpower an inferior opponent quickly.'[8]

Over and above that, he should take the jury into his confidence before entering such a debate, influencing it to name that with which he is familiar or that which could present great difficulties to the opponent as the subject of the debate and, at

---

[8] CarS vim 8.21: *tatra khalv ime pratyavarāṇām āśu-nigrahe bhavanty upāyāḥ. tad yathā—śruta-hīnaṁ mahatā sūtra-pāṭhenâbhibhavet, vijñāna-hīnaṁ punaḥ kaṣṭa-śabdena vākyena, vākya-dhāraṇa-hīnam āviddha-dīrgha-sūtra-saṅkulair vākya-daṇḍakaiḥ, pratibhā-hīnaṁ punar-vacanenâika-vidhenânekârtha-vācinā, vacana-śakti-hīnam ardhôktasya vākyasyâkṣepeṇa, aviśāradam apatrapaṇena, kopanam āyāsanena, bhīruṁ vitrâsanena, anavahitaṁ niyamanenêti. evam etair upāyaiḥ param avaram abhibhavec chīghram* <$\text{CarS}_2$ om. *chīghram*>.

the beginning of the debate, he should pretend that the jury will set the subject and the rules of debate independently.

After this literary exposition, the *Caraka-saṁhitā* continues with the enumeration and definition of forty-four topics of the course of debate (*vāda-mārga-pada*)[9] which should be known to debating physicians.[10] It is remarkable that this section, in contrast to the passage previously mentioned, no longer speaks of hostile or friendly discussions, but only of the formal debate (*vāda*) as such. Moreover, it is not a description of situations within a debate, but a compendium of definitions and examples which forms a homogenous whole. It is most likely that it represents the oldest version of a manual on Indian dialectic and logic transmitted to us, comparable to the ancient *vāda*-manual which may be reconstructed out of the first and last chapters of the *Nyāya-sūtras*.[11] Caraka's manual deals with the same topics to a certain extent, but apparently in a less systematic manner than that which is found in the *Nyāya-sūtras*.[12]

---

[9] Cf. CarS vim 8.27: *imāni tu* <CarS$_{1,2}$ om. *tu*> *khalu padāni bhiṣag-vāda-mārga-jñānârtham* <CarS$_{1,2}$ om. *bhiṣag*> *adhigamyāni bhavanti; tad yathā vādaḥ, dravyaṁ, guṇāḥ, karma, sāmānyaṁ, viśeṣaḥ, samavāyaḥ, pratijñā, sthāpanā, pratiṣṭhāpanā, hetuḥ, dṛṣṭântaḥ, upanayaḥ, nigamanam, uttaraṁ, siddhântaḥ, śabdaḥ, pratyakṣam, anumānam, aitihyam, aupamyaṁ, saṁśayaḥ, prayojanaṁ, savyabhicāraṁ, jijñāsā, vyavasāyaḥ, artha-prāptiḥ, saṁbhavaḥ, anuyojyam, ananuyojyam, anuyogaḥ, pratyanuyogaḥ, vākya-doṣaḥ, vākya-praśaṁsā, chalam, ahetuḥ, atīta-kālam, upālambhaḥ, parihāraḥ, pratijñā-hāniḥ, abhyanujñā, hetv-antaram, arthântaraṁ, nigraha-sthānam iti.* It should be mentioned that there exists another version of this list (cf. e.g. CarS$_2$ 357b,3 ff.) which enumerates *dṛṣṭânta* not between *hetu* and *upanaya*, but between *uttara* and *siddhânta*. This reading is also supported by the manuscripts of the *Caraka-saṁhitā* which I have inspected. All the editions and manuscripts with this reading also differ from CarS and CarS$_1$ with regard to the formulation of *dṛṣṭânta* and *upanaya* in the presentation of *sthāpanā* and *pratiṣṭhāpanā* (v. fn. 31 and 34). To decide which reading may be the genuine one, Cakrapāṇidatta's commentary is of no help since he comments only marginally on these passages (cf. ĀDī 266b,25–28, 267a,18–21 and 28–34).

[10] CarS vim 8.27–65.

[11] The idea that these two books as a whole form the basis of the original manual of debate is supported e.g. by RUBEN (1928: 218, fn. 291); TUCCI (1929: xxvii f.); RANDLE (1930: 342 f.); FRAUWALLNER (1956: 321, fn. 78); OBERHAMMER (1963: 70) etc. Recently it has been shown by a text-critical study (cf. MEUTHRATH (1996: 232 ff.)) that it is rather book 1.1 and 1.2 with the addition of book 5.2, which form a reconstructible unit, whereas book 5.1 most probably is a later insertion.

[12] Cf. FRAUWALLNER (1984: 71).

In a cursory glance, the forty-four technical terms of this manual seem to be an arbitrary compilation, but on closer inspection they show a certain structure: The central notion, the debate (*vāda*), is discussed first. It is of two kinds, namely disputation (*jalpa*) and eristic wrangle (*vitaṇḍā*). This is followed by the six Vaiśeṣika categories: substance (*dravya*), attribute (*guṇa*), movement (*karman*), universal (*sāmānya*), particularity (*viśeṣa*) and inherence (*samavāya*). Caraka then proceeds with the proposition (*pratijñā*), the description of proof (*sthāpanā*) and counter-proof (*pratiṣṭhāpanā*) as well as the members of the proof, i.e. reason (*hetu*), example (*dṛṣṭânta*), application (*upanaya*) and conclusion (*nigamana*). The following technical term, the 'rejoinder' (*uttara*),[13] is also related to the proof, since its definition hints at a close similarity to the Nyāya-category *jāti*, the so-called 'unsound rejoinder.'[14]

[13] Cf. CarS vim 8.36: 'A rejoinder (*uttara*) is a statement by means of dissimilarity (*vaidharmya*) when the argument (*hetu*) is brought forward by means of similarity (*sādharmya*), or a statement by means of similarity when the argument is brought forward by means of dissimilarity … . This is a rejoinder with reversal [of arguments].'—*uttaraṁ nāma sādharmyôpadiṣṭe* <CarS$_{1,2}$ *vā*> *hetau vaidharmya-vacanaṁ, vaidharmyôpadiṣṭe vā hetau* < CarS$_2$ om. *hetau*> *sādharmya-vacanam … etat saviparyayam uttaram.*

[14] Cf. NSū 1.2.18: 'An unsound rejoinder (*jāti*) is an objection (*pratyavasthāna*) by means of similarity (*sādharmya*) and dissimilarity (*vaidharmya*).'—*sādharmya-vaidharmyābhyāṁ pratyavasthānaṁ jātiḥ*. I will discuss the question as to whether NSū 1.2.18 understands this kind of rejoinder as being 'unsound' or not, in a forthcoming paper. The explanation of the *Nyāya-bhāṣya*'s commentary on this *Sūtra* supports at least the close similarity of the concept of *jāti* and that of Caraka's *uttara*: 'The directly following consequence (*prasaṅga*), which arises when an argument (*hetu*) has been brought forward [in a debate], that is the *jāti*. And this "directly following consequence" is an objection (*pratyavasthāna*), [i.e.] a rejection (*upālambha*), a refutation (*pratiṣedha*) by means of similarity or dissimilarity. [In the case that according to NSū 1.1.34] the reason (*hetu*) [put forward] is that which proves the [property] to be proven because of its similarity to the example (*udāharaṇa*), [the *jāti*] is the objection to this [reason] by means of its dissimilarity to the exemplification. [In the case that according to NSū 1.1.35] the reason [put forward] is that which proves the [property] to be proven [in the instance to be proven] because of its dissimilarity to the example, [the *jāti*] is the objection to this [reason] by means of its similarity to the exemplification. That [objection] which comes into existence, because it stands in opposition [to the argument], is the *jāti*.'—*prayukte hi hetau yaḥ prasaṅgo jāyate sā* <NBh$_1$; *sa* NBh> *jātiḥ. sa ca prasaṅgaḥ sādharmya-vaidharmyābhyāṁ pratyavasthānam upālambhaḥ pratiṣedha iti. udāharaṇa-sādharmyāt sādhya-sādhanaṁ hetur ity asyôdāharaṇa-vaidharmyeṇa pratyavasthānam, udāharaṇa-vaidharmyāt* <*tathā udā°* NBh$_1$> *sādhya-sādhanaṁ hetur ity asyôdāharaṇa-sādharmyeṇa pratyavasthānam. pratyanīka-bhāvāj jāyamāno 'rtho jātir iti.* (NBh 401,8–402,5).

Subsequently the four kinds of established doctrines (*siddhânta*)[15] are discussed. Then follows a group of items which is introduced with the discussion of the meaning of 'word' (*śabda*), followed by the four accepted means of cognition (*upalabdhi-kāraṇa*)[16], namely perception (*pratyakṣa*), inference (*anumāna*), verbal testimony (*aitihya*) and comparison (*aupamya*), and subsequently deals with terms which are somehow connected with cognition in a broader sense, namely doubt (*saṁśaya*), purpose (*prayojana*), inconclusiveness (*savyabhicāra*), inquiry (*jijñāsā*), ascertainment (*vyavasāya*), implication (*artha-prāpti*), and cause of origination (*saṁbhava*). The remaining sixteen terms are all of a purely dialectic nature, including—apart from general notions of conversation[17]—the defects and excellences of statement (*vākya-doṣa*[18] and *vākya-praśaṁsā*[19]), equivocation (*chala*)[20], fallacious reasons (*ahetu*)[21] and the points of defeat (*nigraha-sthāna*)[22].

---

[15] As in the *Nyāya-sūtras* (cf. NSū 1.1.26–31), Caraka supports four kinds of *siddhânta*, namely *sarva-tantra-siddhânta, pratitantra-siddhânta, adhikaraṇa-siddhânta* and *abhyupagama-siddhânta* (cf. CarS vim 8.37).

[16] Cf. CarS vim 8.33, in which the reason (*hetu*) is defined as the means of cognition: *hetur nāmôpalabdhi-kāraṇam, tat pratyakṣam anumānam aitihyam aupamyam iti. ebhis hetubhir yad upalabhyate, tat tattvam.* In this context it should be mentioned that in the *Sūtra-sthāna* of the *Caraka-saṁhitā* another set of four means of cognition (*pramāṇam*; cf. CarS sū 11.33) are taught as the four means of investigation (*parīkṣā*; cf. CarS sū 11.17: *dvividham eva khalu sarvaṁ sac câsac ca. tasya catur-vidhā parīkṣā—āptôpadeśaḥ pratyakṣam anumānam yuktiś ceti.* Cf. OBERHAMMER–PRETS–PRANDSTETTER (1996: II, 161 f.).

[17] Cf. such notions as *anuyojya* ('That which is to be objected / to be specified'; cf. CarS vim 8.50), *ananuyojya* ('That which is not to be objected'; cf. CarS vim 8.51), *anuyoga* ('Question'; cf. CarS vim 8.52), *pratyanuyoga* ('Counter-question'; cf. CarS vim 8.53), *upālambha* ('Rejection of an argument'; cf. CarS vim 8.59) and *parihāra* ('Confutation of a rejection'; cf. CarS vim 8.60) in OBERHAMMER–PRETS–PRANDSTETTER (1991, 1996: I, II) s.v.

[18] The defects of statement (*vākya-doṣa*; cf. CarS vim 8.54) in a debate, all of which are understood as points of defeat (*nigraha-sthāna*), are the following: an insufficient statement (*nyūna*), a superfluous statement (*adhika*), a senseless statement (*anarthaka*), a meaningless statement (*apārthaka*) and a contradictory statement (*viruddha*). Cf. OBERHAMMER–PRETS–PRANDSTETTER (1991, 1996: I, II) s.v.

[19] The excellences of statement (*vākya-praśaṁsā*; cf. CarS vim 8.55) consist of the negation of the *vākya-doṣas* with the addition of one more excellency: the statements should be sufficient (*anyūna*), not superfluous (*anadhika*), senseful (*arthavat*), meaningful (*anapārthaka*), not contradictory (*aviruddha*) and the statement should be to the point (*adhigata-padârtha*).

This compilation obviously reminds one of the main sixteen categories (*padârtha*) of the *Nyāya-sūtras*,[23] despite some terminological differences and divergent interpretations of the various topics. Both manuals discuss the question of the debate in general (*vāda, jalpa, vitaṇḍā*) with the difference that *vāda* in the *Nyāya-sūtras* is understood as the friendly form of debate,[24] and disputation (*jalpa*) and eristic wrangle (*vitaṇḍā*)[25] are the hostile forms, whereas in the *Caraka-saṁhitā* disputation and eristic wrangle are subdivisions of *vāda*:

---

[20] According to the *Caraka-saṁhitā*, equivocation is of two kinds (cf. CarS vim 8.56): verbal equivocation (*vāk-chala*) and generalising equivocation (*sāmānya-cchala*).

[21] The CarS supports three fallacious reasons (*ahetu*; cf. CarS vim 8.57: *ahetur nāma prakaraṇa-samaḥ, saṁśaya-samaḥ, varṇya-samaś cêti.*), which seem to be understood as fallacious forms of substantiations in a broader sense, not in the strict sense of the fallacies of the logical reason (*hetv-ābhāsa*) which were supported by later logical traditions.

[22] The enumeration of the points of defeat (*nigraha-sthāna*) is somewhat non-homogenous and consists of a literal description of three censurable faults (1. the debater does not comprehend an argument even when it has been stated three times, 2. censuring a statement which is not to be censured, and 3. not censuring a statement which is to be censured), the enumeration of the defects of statement (*vākya-doṣa*), fallacious reasons (*ahetu*, without mentioning its subdivisions) and five faults which were already discussed as individual topics of debate, namely to mistime a statement (*atīta-kāla*; CarS vim 8.58), to abandon the proposition (*pratijñā-hāni*; CarS vim 8.61), concession of something undesired (*abhyanujñā*; CarS vim 8.62), change of reason (*hetv-antara*; CarS vim 8.63) and change of subject (*arthântara*; CarS vim 8.64). Cf. CarS vim 8.65: *nigraha-sthānaṁ nāma parājaya-prāptiḥ. tac ca trir abhihitasya vākyasyâparijñānaṁ* <*vākyasyâvijñānaṁ* $CarS_{1,2}$> *pariṣadi vijñānavatyām, yad vā ananuyojyasyânuyogo 'nuyojyasya cânanuyogaḥ. pratijñā-hāniḥ, abhyanujñā, kālātîtavacanam* (scil. *atīta-kālam*), *ahetuḥ, nyūnam, adhikam* <*atiriktam* $CarS_{1,2}$>, *vyartham* (scil. *apārthakam*), *anarthakam, punar-uktam, viruddham, hetv-antaram, arthântaraṁ ca* <$CarS_2$ om. *ca*> *nigraha-sthānam.*

[23] NSū 1.1.1: *pramāṇa-prameya-saṁśaya-prayojana-dṛṣṭânta-siddhântâvayava-tarka-nirṇaya-vāda-jalpa-vitaṇḍâhetv-ābhāsa-cchala-jāti-nigraha-sthānānāṁ tattva-jñānān niḥśreyasâdhigamaḥ.*

[24] Cf. NSū 1.2.1: 'A [friendly] debate (*vāda*) is [carried out by the opponents] taking up the thesis (*pakṣa*) and the counter-thesis (*pratipakṣa*), [both of] which contain the five members of proof (*avayava*), are not contradictory to the [respective] doctrines (*siddhânta*) and consist of the proving (*sādhana*) [of their respective thesis] and the refuting (*upālambha*) [of the counter-thesis] based upon the means of knowledge (*pramāṇa*) and reasoning (*tarka*).'—*pramāṇa-tarka-sādhanôpālaṁbhaḥ siddhântâviruddhaḥ pañcâvayavôpapannaḥ pakṣa-pratipakṣa-parigraho vādaḥ.*

[25] Cf. NSū 1.2.2 f: 'Disputation (*jalpa*) consists of [the same attributes] as mentioned [in the definition of the friendly debate (*vāda*) and is carried out] by proving and refuting with

> 'A debate (*vāda*) is when one [disputant] discusses with an opponent in a hostile way, with a doctrine presupposed. In short, this is of two kinds: disputation (*jalpa*) and eristic wrangle (*vitaṇḍā*) .... In the following manner: The position of one [disputant] is that rebirth exists, [the position] of the other is that it does not exist. Both disputants substantiate their respective position by reasons [and] present the [respective] opposite position [for discussion]. This is disputation (*jalpa*) .... Eristic wrangle consists exclusively of pointing out the faults with regard to the opposite position'[26]

This means that in the *Caraka-saṁhitā*, *vāda* is only the hostile variety of debate.

Both manuals also list, with one small terminological divergence,[27] the same members of the proof. Nevertheless, one central point of their interpretation is differing, a fact to which historiographers have paid too little attention: Unexpectedly, the *Nyāya-sūtra*s do not have a *terminus technicus* as an independent category for that which one would call 'proof' or 'establishing the thesis'. The five individual members of the proof are merely listed under the topic 'members' (*avayava*)[28] and are defined without any hint of a generic category.

In contrast, the manual of the *Caraka-saṁhitā* shows a different and clearly structured concept. The proposition (*pratijñā*), defined nearly identically in both works, is not a constituent of the proof and is listed as an independent topic of debate (*vāda-mārga-pada*): 'The proposition is the communication of the [object] to be proven. As for example: "The *puruṣa* is eternal".'[29] Apart from the proposition,

---

[the addition] of equivocation (*chala*), unsound rejoinders (*jāti*) and points of defeat (*nigraha-sthāna*). A [disputation] without the establishment (*sthāpanā*) of the counter-thesis is an eristic wrangle (*vitaṇḍā*).'—*yathôktôpapannaś chala-jāti-nigraha-sthāna-sādhanôpālaṁbho jalpaḥ. sa pratipakṣa-sthāpanā-hīno vitaṇḍā.*

[26] CarS vim 8.28: *vādo nāma sa yat pareṇa* <*paraḥ pareṇa* CarS$_{1,2}$> *saha śāstra-pūrvakaṁ vigṛhya kathayati. sa ca* <*vādo* CarS$_{2}$> *dvividhaḥ saṁgraheṇa jalpo vitaṇḍā ca ... yathā—ekasya pakṣaḥ punar-bhāvo 'stîti, nâstîty aparasya. tau ca hetubhiḥ* <CarS$_{2}$; *svasvahetu°* CarS$_{1}$; *svasvapakṣa-hetu°* CarS> *svasvapakṣaṁ sthāpayataḥ para-pakṣam udbhāvayataḥ. eṣa jalpaḥ ... vitaṇḍā nāma para-pakṣe doṣa-vacana-mātram eva.*

[27] In addition to the general example (*dṛṣṭânta*), which is mentioned in the *Caraka-saṁhitā* as the second member of *sthāpanā*, the *Nyāya-sūtra*s have the special term *udāharaṇa*, 'exemplification', as the designation of the third member of proof.

[28] Cf. NSū 1.1.32: *pratijñā-hetûdāharaṇôpanaya-nigamanāny avayavāḥ.*

[29] CarS vim 8.30: *pratijñā nāma sādhya-vacanaṁ. yathā—nityaḥ puruṣa iti.* Cf. NSū 1.1.33: *sādhya-nirdeśaḥ pratijñā.* The term *puruṣa*, literally meaning 'human being',

the dialectic proof or establishment (*sthāpanā*) of the proposition consists of the reason (*hetu*), the example (*dṛṣṭânta*), the application (*upanaya*) and the conclusion (*nigamana*): 'Proof (*sthāpanā*) is the proof (or establishment) of exactly that proposition by means of reason, example, application, and conclusion. First is the proposition and then the proof. For, what can be proven when it has not been proposed?'[30] Subsequently Caraka gives an example of this kind of dialectic proof: 'Proposition: the *puruṣa* is eternal; reason: because it is not produced; example: like the ether; application: and as the ether is unproduced and it is eternal, so is the *puruṣa*; conclusion: therefore it is eternal.'[31]

In accordance with this example, a proof of this kind could possibly represent the following structure: The thesis (*pratijñā*) that the *puruṣa* is eternal is given, followed by three further propositions, namely 1. that the *puruṣa* is not produced (*hetu*), 2. that an example—the ether—exemplifies both attributes, i.e. eternity and non-producedness (*dṛṣṭânta*), and 3. the *puruṣa* is like the example, i.e. non-produced and eternal (*upanaya*). By means of these three propositions one comes to the conclusion (*nigamana*) that the *puruṣa* is eternal. The recent book of Claus OETKE, which is an investigation of the earliest structures of the so-called Indian syllogism, offers possible logical implications and interpretations of such early types of proof.[32]

We are now confronted in the *Caraka-saṁhitā* with a unique phenomenon: The dialectic proof (*sthāpanā*) is contrasted with a counterproposition propounding exactly the opposite of the thesis,[33] which is correctly established by a statement

'man', 'individual soul', 'personal principal', 'supreme being' etc. is left untranslated in this context, because it is not exactly clear which concept is meant in the *Caraka-saṁhitā*. Most probably it is to be understood as the 'individual soul' or the 'personal principal'. But the question is not of real importance for the structure of the proof.

[30] CarS vim 8.31: *tasyā eva pratijñāyā hetu-dṛṣṭântôpanaya-nigamanaiḥ sthāpanā. pūrvaṁ hi pratijñā, paścāt sthāpanā, kiṁ hy apratijñātaṁ sthāpayiṣyati*.

[31] CarS vim 8.31: *nityaḥ puruṣa iti pratijñā, hetuḥ—akṛtakatvād iti, dṛṣṭântaḥ—yathâkāśam iti, upanayaḥ—yathā câkṛtakam ākāśaṁ tac ca nityaṁ tathā puruṣa iti, nigamanam—tasmān nitya iti*. In the editions and manuscripts containing the other version of the list of the *vāda-mārga-padas* (cf. fn. 9), example (*dṛṣṭânta*) and application (*upanaya*) are formulated in the following way: 'example: the ether is unproduced, and it is eternal; application: and as the ether is unproduced, so is the *puruṣa*.'—*dṛṣṭântaḥ—akṛtakam akāśaṁ tac ca nityam, upanayo—yathā câkṛtakam ākāśaṁ tathā puruṣaḥ*. $CarS_2$ 358a,31–33.

[32] OETKE (1994: 12 ff.).

[33] Although proof and counter-proof should be the normal opening of a debate, we do not have any further example in the transmitted texts.

which is called counter-proof (*pratiṣṭhāpanā*) in the *Caraka-saṁhitā*, and which consists of another set of the same proof members:

> 'Counter-proof is the proof (or establishment) of exactly the contrary of the opponent's proposition. For example: proposition: the *puruṣa* is non-eternal; reason: because it is perceptible by the senses; example: as the pot; application: and like the pot is perceptible, and it is non-eternal, so is the [*puruṣa*]; conclusion: therefore it is non-eternal.'[34]

Clearly this is a situation of counterbalancing arguments. But what does it imply for the interpretation of Caraka's proof? Should one suppose that one of these two proofs is logically inconsistent? There is no hint of such an assumption. Both argumentations seem to be at least formally correct. Must we differentiate in this early stage of Indian logic between logically correct argumentations, and argumentations which claim to prove the truth of the proposal? It seems so. Due to the very sparse source material in the earliest development of Indian dialectic, one can only make conjectures. But it is highly probable that, at least for the *Caraka-saṁhitā*, the function of a proof is not to guarantee truth but to justify propositions. The truth of the conclusion and with it, the truth of the thesis, depends on the truth of the propositions, which are exemplified in the first three members of the *sthāpanā*, namely *hetu*, *dṛṣṭânta* and *upanaya*. It therefore reminds one of the European classical formal criterion of correctness, which does not claim the truth of a conclusion but states that if the propositions are true then the conclusion is also true. But it is not my aim to compare Indian and European logic.

Nevertheless, Caraka's presentation of *sthāpanā* and *pratiṣṭhāpanā* seems to indicate that truth is not guaranteed by a logical proof. As for the proof in the *Nyāya-sūtras*, it is difficult to make up one's mind. On one hand, the *Nyāya-sūtras* claim that debates are carried out by the opponents establishing opposite positions (*pakṣa* and *pratipakṣa*) within a debate, on the other hand the concepts of proof (*sthāpanā*) and counter-proof (*pratiṣṭhāpanā*) are lacking in the *Sūtras*, although the term *sthāpanā* is used once to define the eristic wrangle (*vitaṇḍā*). Of course, the

[34] CarS vim 8.32: *pratiṣṭhāpanā nāma yā tasyā eva* <CarS$_2$ om. *tasyā eva*> *para-pratijñāyā viparītârtha-sthāpanā. yathā—anityaḥ puruṣa iti pratijñā* <(*viparītârtha*)*prati*° CarS$_1$>; *hetuḥ—aindriyakatvād iti; dṛṣṭântaḥ—yathā ghaṭa iti; upanayo—yathā ghaṭa aindriyakaḥ sa cânityaḥ, tathā câyam iti; nigamanaṁ—tasmād anitya iti*. The other transmitted version (cf. fn. 31) of the example (*dṛṣṭânta*) and the application (*upanaya*) in the *pratiṣṭhāpanā* is formulated in the following way: 'example: the pot is perceptible by the senses, and it is non-eternal; application: and as the pot, so is the *puruṣa*.' *dṛṣṭântaḥ—ghaṭa aindriyakaḥ sa cânityaḥ; upanayo—yathā ghaṭas tathā puruṣaḥ*. CarS$_2$ 358b,1 f.

definitions of debate (*vāda*) and disputation (*jalpa*)[35] in the *Nyāya-sūtra*s taken literally, according to their requirement of proving the respective thesis, must presuppose a comprehension of some kind of counter-proof as indicated in the *Caraka-saṁhitā*. But what could have been the reason not to treat the counter-proof as an independent topic of debate? Is the situation of debate so clear that there is no need to mention the counter-proof, since it consists of the same proof members anyway? Or do we have to presuppose already in the *Nyāya-sūtra*s the claim that only one of the proofs of the two disputants ensures the truth of his proposition? At least in first book of the *Nyāya-sūtra*s there seems to be no hint of a solution for these questions.

The fact that, at least in Caraka's presentation, truth is not guaranteed by one of the contradictory proofs, may have been the starting point of early speculations on solutions to these kinds of problems. One finds rudiments of such discussions in the chapter on unsound rejoinders (*jāti*) in the fifth book of the *Nyāya-sūtra*s,[36] in which at least some rejoinders remind one of the situation of proof and counter-proof in the *Caraka-saṁhitā*. In the examples of the two basic kinds of rejoinders[37] given by the *Nyāya-bhāṣya*,[38] namely the 'equally [possible rejoinder] by means of similarity' (*sādharmya-sama*) and 'equally [possible rejoinder] by means of dissimilarity' (*vaidharmya-sama*), the general question is raised as to whether the reason, the example, and the application prove the object to be proven or, whether—when another set of arguments are employed—it can also prove the exact contrary.[39] The opponent in this discussion argues that there is no decisive reason (*viśeṣa-hetu*) for the correctness of the first argumentation as opposed to his argumentation, which

---

[35] Cf. fn. 24 and 25.

[36] Cf. NSū 5.1.

[37] Cf. the general definition of *jāti* (NSū 1.2.18) in fn. 14; cf. also TUCCI's retranslation of the Chinese translation (cf. $UH_c$) of the lost **Upāya-hṛdaya* in which these kinds of rejoinders are understood as valid refutations of syllogistic arguments (cf. KAJIYAMA (1991)): *eṣāṁ viṁśati-vidhānāṁ sāro dvividhaḥ. vaidharmyaṁ sādharmyañ ca. sajātīyatvāt sādharmyaṁ vijātīyatvād vaidharmyam. arthasya hi tat samāśrayatvāt te viṁśati-dharmān vyāpnuvataḥ* (UH 26,7–9).

[38] It is remarkable that exactly in the context of these rejoinders, Pakṣilasvāmin uses the term *sthāpanā* when he states in the introduction to the *Sūtra*s on *sādharmya-sama* and *vaidharmya-sama* (cf. NSū 5.1.2): 'An objection by means of similarity, which differs [basically] not from the reason of the [objected] proof (*sthāpanā*), is the [unsound rejoinder called] *sādharmya-sama*.'—*sādharmyeṇa pratyavasthānam aviśiṣyamāṇaṁ sthāpanā-hetutaḥ sādharmya-samaḥ*. NBh 2002,2 f.

[39] Cf. NBh 2005,6–2007,4.

would correctly prove the contrary of the former proposition.[40] Without going into the problem of unsound rejoinders here in detail, the question of the proponent of the *jāti* would indicate that his rejoinder is in no way unsound but hits the nail on the head. The notion of the correctness of proof and the justification of a thesis has shifted to the question as to whether the assumed propositions are capable of proving the object to be proven. In other words, the problem has shifted to the question of a logical relation between the proving attribute and the attribute to be proven and its applicability to the object of proof, i.e. the general justification of the three propositions *hetu*, *dṛṣṭânta* and *upanaya*.

[40] Another kind of *jāti* should be mentioned here because its contents concern a problem which reoccurs in Dignāga's system of logic, the *prakaraṇa-sama*. Corresponding to the example of the *Nyāya-bhāṣya*, it is the following situation in a debate: 'One [disputant] propounds [for example] as [his] thesis: "Sound is non-eternal because it [originates] directly preceded by an effort, like a pot." And the second [disputant] propounds the counterthesis on the basis of similarity to eternal [things]: "Sound is eternal because it is audible, like soundness".'—*anityaḥ śabdaḥ prayatnânantarīyakatvād ghaṭavad ity ekaḥ pakṣaṁ pravarttayati. dvitīyaś ca nitya-sādharmyāt pratipakṣaṁ pravarttayati—nityaḥ śabdaḥ śrāvaṇatvāt, śabdatvavad iti.* (NBh 2027,3–5). This example is nothing but that which is called the 'contradictory non-deviating' (*viruddhâvyabhicārin*) as a special variety of an inconclusive (*anaikāntika*) reason in Buddhist logical tradition. This fallacy is expounded by Śaṅkarasvāmin in the following way: 'A *viruddhâvyabhicārin* is for instance: Sound is non-eternal, because it is produced, like a pot; sound is eternal, because it is audible, like soundness. As the two [reasons] are occasions for doubt, although they are two, they are taken together as one inconclusive [reason] (*anaikāntika*).'—*viruddhâvyabhicārī, yathā anityaḥ śabdaḥ kṛtakatvād ghaṭavad. nityaḥ śabdaḥ śrāvaṇatvāt śabdatvavad iti. ubhayoḥ saṁśaya-hetutvād dvāv apy etāv eko 'naikāntikaḥ samuditāv eva.* (NPr 4.21–5.2). Neither of the reasons applied for proving contradictory results, taken individually, violate any of the required three conditions (*trairūpya*) of a valid reason for their respective propositions.

## BIBLIOGRAPHY


Texts:

ĀDī = *Āyur-veda-dīpikā*. See: CarS.

CarS = *Caraka-saṁhitā. The Charakasaṁhitā of Agniveśa*. Revised by Charaka and Dṛidhabala. With the Āyurveda-Dīpikā Commentary of Chakrapāṇidatta. Ed. by V.J. Trikamji. Bombay [4]1981.

$CarS_1$ = *Caraka-saṁhitā. Maharṣinā Agniveśena praṇītā Caraka-dṛḍhabalābhyāṁ pratisaṁskṛtā Caraka-saṁhitā. Y. Śarmaṇā saṁśodhitā*. Bombay 1933.

$CarS_2$ = *Caraka-saṁhitā. Caraka-saṁhitā mahiṣiṇā bhagavad-agniveśena praṇītā mahā-muninā carakeṇa pratisaṁskṛtā, āyur-vedâcārya-śrī-jayadeva-vidyâlaṅkāreṇa praṇītayā tattvârtha-dīpikâkhyayā hindī-vyākhyayā ṭippaṇyā ca samanvitā*. Vārāṇasī, Dilli, Patanā [8]1970. [1[st] ed.: Lahore 1934–1936].

NBh = *Nyāya-bhāṣya. Nyāyadarśanam. With Vātsyāyana's Bhāṣya, Uddyotakara's Vārttika, Vācaspati Miśra's Tātparyaṭīkā and Viśvanātha's Vṛtti* (Chapter I, Section I). Crit. Ed. with Notes by Taranatha Nyaya-Tarkatirtha and (Chapters I.ii–V) by Amarendramohan Tarkatirtha. Vol. II, Crit. Ed. with Notes by Amarendramohan Tarkatirtha and Hemantakumar Tarkatirtha. *Calcutta Sanskrit Series* 18, 29, Calcutta 1936, 1944.

$NBh_1$ = *Nyāya-bhāṣya. Nyāyadarśana of Gautama*. With the Bhāṣya of Vātsyāyana, the Vārttika of Uddyotakara, the Tātparyaṭīkā of Vācaspati & the Pariśuddhi of Udayana [Volume 1, Chapter 1]. Ed. by Anantalal Thakur. Darbhanga 1967.

NPr = Śaṅkarasvāmin: *Nyāya-praveśa. Nyāyapraveśa of Diṅnāga*. With Commentaries of Haribhadrasuri & Parsavadeva. Ed. by A.B. Dhruva, *Gaekwad's Oriental Series* 38, Delhi [2]1987. [First edition: 1930].

NSū = *Nyāya-sūtra*. See: RUBEN 1928.

sū = *Sūtra-sthāna*. In CarS.

UH = **Upāya-hṛdaya*. See: TUCCI (1929).

$UH_c$ = **Upāya-hṛdaya*: *fang-pien hsin-lun*, Taishō 1632, Vol. 32, 23b–28c.

vim = *Vimāna-sthāna*. In CarS.

Secondary Sources:

BEDEKAR 1957 = Bedekar, V.M.: 'Studies in Sāṁkhya: Pañcaśikha and Caraka,' *Annals of the Bhandarkar Oriental Research Institute* 38 (1957) 140–147.

COMBA 1987 = Comba, Antonella: '*Caraka-saṁhitā*, Śārīrasthāna I and Vaiśeṣika philosophy,' in: *Studies on Indian Medical History. Papers presented at the International Workshop on the Study of Indian Medicine held at the Wellcome Institute for the History of Medicine 2–4 September 1985*. Ed. by G. Jan Meulenbeld and Dominik Wujastyk. Groningen 1987: 43–61.

DASGUPTA 1922 = Dasgupta, Surendranath: *A History of Indian Philosophy*. Vol. II. Cambridge 1922. [Reprinted: Delhi 1991].

FILLIOZAT 1990 = Filliozat, Pierre-Sylvain: '*Yukti*, le quatrième *pramāṇa* des medecins (*Caraka-saṁhitā*, Sūtrasthāna XI. 25),' *Journal of the European Āyurvedic Society* 1 (1990) 33–46.

FILLIOZAT 1993 = Filliozat, Pierre-Sylvain: 'Caraka's Proof of Rebirth,' *Journal of the European Āyurvedic Society* 3 (1993) 94–111.

FRAUWALLNER 1956 = Frauwallner, Erich: *Geschichte der indischen Philosophie*. 2. Band, Salzburg 1956.

FRAUWALLNER 1984 = Frauwallner, Erich: *Nachgelassene Werke I. Aufsätze, Beiträge, Skizzen*. Hrsg. Ernst Steinkellner. Wien 1984.

KAJIYAMA 1991 = Kajiyama, Yūichi: 'On the Authorship of the Upāyahṛdaya,' in: *Studies in the Buddhist Epistemological Tradition. Proceedings of the Second International Dharmakīrti Conference. Vienna, June 11–16, 1989*. Ed. by E. Steinkellner. Wien 1991: 107–117.

KANG 1998 = Kang, Sung Yong: *Zur altindischen Tradition der Debatte gemäß der medizinischen Überlieferung. Übersetzung und ideengeschichtliche Untersuchung von Caraka-saṁhitā Vi.8.15–28*. Wissenschaftliche Hausarbeit zur Erlangung des akademischen Grades eines Magister Artium der Universität Hamburg. Hamburg 1998.

KATSURA 1986 = Katsura, Shōryū: 'Indo-ronrigaku ni okeru henjyū gainen no seisei to hatten—*Caraka-saṁhitā* kara Dharmakīrti made' ['The Origin and Development of *vyāpti* in Indian Logic—from the *Caraka-saṁhitā* to Dharmakīrti'], *Hiroshima Daigaku Bungakubu Kiyō* 45/1 (1986) 1–122.

MATILAL 1987 = Matilal, Bimal Krishna: 'Debate and Dialectic in Ancient India,' in: *Philosophical Essays. Professor Anantalal Thakur Felicitation Volume*. Calcutta 1987.

MATILAL 1998 = Matilal, Bimal Krishna: *The Character of Logic in India*. Ed. by Jonardon Ganeri and Heeraman Tiwari. New York 1998.

MEINDERSMA 1989 = Meindersma, Tabe E.: '*paralokasiddhi* in the *Caraka-saṁhitā*,' *Indologica Taurinensia* 15/16 (1989/90) 265–273.

MEINDERSMA 1992 = Meindersma, Tabe E.: 'Caraka and the Materialists,' *Proceedings of the VIIIth World Sanskrit Conference Vienna 1990. Wiener Zeitschrift für die Kunde Südasiens* 36, Suppl. (1992) 299–306.

MEUTHRATH 1996 = Meuthrath, Annette: *Untersuchungen zur Kompositionsgeschichte der Nyāya-sūtras*. Würzburg 1996.

MIYASAKA 1963 = Miyasaka, Y.: 'The philosophical View of the Vaiśeṣika found in the *Caraka-saṁhitā*, an Indian medical Text' [in Japanese], *The Mikkyo Bunka* 64/65 (1963) 50–67.

OBERHAMMER 1963 = Oberhammer, Gerhard: 'Ein Beitrag zu den Vāda-Traditionen Indiens,' *Wiener Zeitschrift für die Kunde Süd- und Ostasiens* 7 (1963), 63–103.

OBERHAMMER–PRETS–PRANDSTETTER 1991, 1996 = Oberhammer, Gerhard; Prets, Ernst; Prandstetter, Joachim: *Terminologie der frühen philosophischen Scholastik in Indien. Ein Begriffswörterbuch zur altindischen Dialektik, Erkenntnislehre und Methodologie.* Herausgegeben von Gerhard Oberhammer. Österreichische Akademie der Wissenschaften, Philosophisch-Historische Klasse, Denkschriften, 248. *Beiträge zur Kultur- und Geistesgeschichte* 17. Band 1: A-I (1991), Band 2: U-Pū (1996), Wien.

OETKE 1994 = Oetke, Claus: *Vier Studien zum Altindischen Syllogismus*. Reinbek 1994.

RANDLE 1930 = Randle, H.N.: *Indian Logic in the Early Schools*. Oxford 1930.

RAO 1962 = Rao, K.B. Ramakrishna: 'The *Sāṁkhya* Philosophy in the *Caraka-saṁhitā*,' *The Adyar Library Bulletin* 26/3–4 (1962) 193–205.

ROTH 1872 = Roth, Rudolf von: 'Indische Medicin,' *Zeitschrift der Deutschen Morgenländischen Gesellschft* 26 (1872) 441–452.

RUBEN 1928 = Ruben, Walter: *Die Nyāyasūtra's*. Text, Übersetzung, Erläuterung und Glossar. Leipzig 1928.

SASTRI 1952 = Sastri, N. Aiyaswami: 'Comparative Study of the Sankhya Tenets Found in the Buddhacarita and the Carakasamhita,' *Bhāratīya Vidyā* 13 (1952) 102–114.

SHARMA 1984 = Sharma, Priya Vrat: 'La notion de *vedanā* dans la *Caraka-saṁhitā*,' *Indologica Taurinensia* 12 (1984) 415–418.

SOLOMON 1976 = Solomon, Esther A.: *Indian Dialectics. Methods of Philosophical Discussion*. 2 Vols. Ahmedabad 1976, 1978.

TUCCI 1929 = Tucci, Giuseppe: *Pre-Diṅnāga Buddhist Texts on Logic from Chinese Sources*. Baroda 1929.

VIDYĀBHŪṢAṆA 1920 = Vidyābhūṣaṇa, Satis Chandra: *A History of Indian Logic (Ancient, Mediaeval and Modern Schools)*. Delhi [3]1978. [First edition: Calcutta 1920].

# SANSKRIT MANUSCRIPTS

# Sanskrit Manuscripts and Photos of Sanskrit Manuscripts in Giuseppe Tucci's Collection. A Preliminary Report[1]

FRANCESCO SFERRA

## –1–

During his scientific expeditions to India, Nepal and Tibet in the thirties and forties (1933, 1935, 1939, 1949), Giuseppe TUCCI (1894–1984) had an opportunity to photograph, and in some cases to ask someone to copy, many important Buddhist works. Subsequently, some of the manuscripts that he had photographed became part of the collections in Indian and Nepalese libraries, but others were lost. TUCCI's photos of several of these manuscripts are the only documentation at our disposal. The study and the cataloguing of the photos and manuscripts (now held at the Oriental Department of the Library of the Istituto Italiano per l'Africa e l'Oriente [IsIAO, formerly IsMEO] in Rome) was begun about three years ago by Claudio CICUZZA and myself. This paper consists in a brief presentation of the first results of our work.

Regarding the photographic reproduction and the acquisition of manuscript material, the most important missions were those TUCCI carried out in 1939 and 1949. He concludes the brief report on his expedition to Tibet in 1939 with the following:

> 'The journey lasted ... seven months. My researches ... had specific archaeological and historical aims. The photographic documentation and the collection of scientific material are such as to permit a complete and definitive study of the political, artistic and religious history not merely of the regions crossed, but of most of Tibet in general. The hundreds of Sanskrit manuscripts discovered and photographed in the libraries of the explored monasteries will make a

[1] Special thanks are due to the authorities of the IsIAO for their financial support and permission to publish the photographs. I would also like to thank Mauro MAGGI for having read this paper and made some useful suggestions.

*Essays in Indian Philosophy, Religion and Literature*, pp. 451–501.

great contribution to the study of Indian civilisation itself, which has been a source of continuous inspiration to Tibet'.[2]

In his summing up, he laconically states:

> 'More than 1,500 pages of Indian palm-leaf manuscripts from X$^{th}$ to XIV$^{th}$ centuries, discovered in various monasteries, were photographed'.[3]

The first task we carried out, with the approval of the authorities of the Institute and with the collaboration of the former librarian, Mauro MAGGI, was to once again assemble the collection that was located in drawers and filing cabinets in various parts of the library, and kept in various folders and boxes, according to the criteria of TUCCI's study.

The collection actually consists in (A) four palm-leaf manuscripts[4] written in Sinhalese characters (which most probably were not acquired on TUCCI's missions) and in (B) forty-one manuscripts written on Nepalese paper and in Devanāgarī script.

The forty-one manuscripts are modern copies of ancient manuscripts commissioned by TUCCI himself, the originals of which have remained in the East. The manuscripts are of considerable scientific importance, because sometimes they are modern copies of otherwise unknown ancient manuscripts; for instance, we have a copy of the *Vimala-prabhā*, which at first glance does not seem to correspond to any of the manuscripts used by the editors; apart from some significant variants, not

---

[2] TUCCI (1996c: 151–152): 'Il viaggio è durato [...] sette mesi. Le mie ricerche [...] hanno avuto scopi specialmente archeologici e storici. La documentazione fotografica e la raccolta del materiale scientifico è tale da permettere uno studio completo e definitivo sulla storia politica e artistica e religiosa non solo delle contrade attraversate, ma in generale di gran parte del Tibet. Allo stesso studio della civiltà indiana, che è stata l'ispiratrice continua del Tibet, grande contributo porteranno le centinaia di manoscritti in sanscrito scoperti e fotografati nelle biblioteche dei conventi esplorati.'

[3] TUCCI (1996c: 153): 'Fotografate oltre 1500 pagine di manoscritti indiani su foglie di palma dal X al XIV sec. scoperti nei vari monasteri.' In 1956, in the 'Preface' to the first part of *Minor Buddhist Texts*, he wrote: 'During my travels in Tibet and Nepal I came across many manuscripts of Sanskrit works which are, to my knowledge, so far unedited. I could acquire the originals of some of them; of others I took photos, of some I had copies made. The works which I so collected are chiefly Buddhist. It is my purpose to edit them in this series or to have them edited by my pupils. Though the works are not all of equal importance they will certainly contribute to a better knowledge of Buddhist thought' (1986: xi).

[4] There is also a tiny fragment of a manuscript written on birch bark.

even the numbering of the verses of the *Laghu-kāla-cakra-tantra* corresponds to that so far established for the text.

Even more important are the photographic copies (negatives and prints) of ancient Indian manuscripts that TUCCI had made during his expeditions. In reorganising the collection we have therefore given precedence to this material.

Thus we have: (C) seven microfilms (including part of the manuscripts discovered in Gilgit); (D) fifty rolls of film (35 mm) containing on average twenty-four exposures, each of which reproduces a recto and a verso (among these manuscripts there are, for example, the Nepalese chronicles in Sanskrit); (E) circa four hundred negatives measuring 7 × 11 cm and containing on average the rectos or the versos of 15 palm-leaf folios, written in Newari script; and (F) approximately 650 photographic prints of various sizes also containing on average about a dozen folios, none of which corresponds either to the negatives or to the rolls of film (some prints contain only two folios, others as many as thirty). Some of these prints are on photographic paper, while others are on book paper—as if they had been prepared for publication. Half the texts had already been divided up and filed in grey folders bearing the title of the work.

Thus we have a total of about one-hundred and fifty codices and a slightly higher number of actual works. Obviously, we shall only be able to calculate the exact number of manuscripts and works when our task is completed.

## –2–

Some examples will suffice to give an idea of the value of the material that we are now studying. In 1996 David Pingree pointed out that among the photographic prints there are two of a Nepalese manuscript of the *Yavana-jātaka* by Sphujidhvaja, now kept in Kathmandu with some folios missing and in a worse state of conservation than it was when photographed by TUCCI during his expeditions to Nepal (cf. *Bollettino*). The National Archives of Kathmandu also hold the originals of other works photographed by TUCCI, such as one of the manuscripts of the *Amṛta-kaṇikā* by Raviśrījñāna; the manuscript of Vimuktisena's *Abhisamayâlaṁkāra-vṛtti* that belonged to Gurujī Hemraj Sharma;[5] and, as was most kindly pointed out to me by Harunaga Isaacson, also a copy of the *Muktâvalī* by Ratnākaraśānti.

In other cases, the photos reproduce manuscripts that have either been completely lost or of which, as far as we know, the originals are not to be found in other

[5] The first part of this work has been edited by Corrado PENSA (1967). The second part will be published by Claudio CICUZZA.

European and Asiatic libraries. Regarding this, the negatives containing a manuscript of the *Laghu-tantra-ṭīkā* by Vajrapāṇi and a very important copy of the *Laghu-kāla-cakra-vimala-prabhā-ṭīkā* by Puṇḍarīka in Bhujimol script are noteworthy. We have given a photograph of the latter to S.S. Bahulkar who is preparing a new edition of the text. There is no trace of the original manuscript brought to Rome by TUCCI (cf. SFERRA (1995)). Neither do we know the exact location of a very important manuscript of the *Prasanna-padā* by Candrakīrti, known as the 'manuscript of Rome', which is a part of this collection.[6]

The photographs of other manuscripts belong to the above group. Two at least are worth mentioning: a manuscript entitled *Yukti-pradīpa*, which contains a brief Buddhist work that attempts to justify Tantric practices (the work is being studied by Harunaga Isaacson), and another manuscript entitled *Sarva-śuddhi-viśuddhi-krama*[*], which corresponds to the second chapter of the *Pañca-krama* by Nāgārjuna in the edition by MIMAKI–TOMABECHI (1994). This manuscript has not been used in their recent edition of the text.[7]

Lastly, we are justified in saying, at least in one case, that TUCCI's photos are more useful to scholars than the original manuscript. I am referring specifically to a photograph and a microfilm of a portion (about 200 folios) of a manuscript from Gilgit (Pakistan) written on birch bark leaves and containing unique Buddhist texts (sections of the Vinaya of the Mūlasarvāstivādins: *Śayanâsana-vastu, Adhikaraṇa-vastu* and the *Saṅgha-bheda-vastu*). TUCCI acquired this manuscript in Rawalpindi (Swāt) in 1956, gave it to the Pakistani Government, brought it to Italy for restoration by the Istituto centrale per la patologia del libro (Italian Office for the Restoration of Books) and for publication, and then returned it to the Museum of Karachi (cf. GNOLI (1977: xiv)).

The latter manuscript was laminated, a technique that subsequently proved inadequate. The disastrous effects of lamination can be seen, for instance, in the edition of the Khotanese *Karma-vibhaṅga* by Mauro MAGGI and, more specifically, within the facsimiles of fragments of a manuscript, some folios of which are divided in two parts and kept respectively in London and Munich. The part held in London is laminated and hardly legible; the part in Munich, which was not treated in any way, is perfectly legible and well conserved (cf. MAGGI (1995: plates 4–7, 9)).

---

[6] See *Bollettino*. In a well-known paper, J.W. DE JONG (1978) uses the *sigla* R (= Rome) when he quotes Tucci's photographs of this manuscript.

[*] See the facsimile in the present volume on pp. 469–475 (eds.).

[7] On the authorship of the *Sarva-śuddhi-viśuddhi-krama* (*alias Anuttara-sandhi*)—which Samayavajra, Abhayākaragupta and Parahitarakṣita consider to be a later interpolation—see MIMAKI–TOMABECHI (1994: x and note 12).

It is worth noting that in some instances TUCCI photographed the same works as RĀHULA SĀṄKṚTYĀYANA[8] (e.g. the commentary by Karṇakagomin on the *Svārthânumāna* chapter of the *Pramāṇa-vārttika* by Dharmakīrti, the *Abhidharma-kośa* by Vasubandhu, the *Sahôpalambha-prakaraṇa* by Jitāri[*]). Due to the undeveloped photographic techniques of the period and the often unfavourable conditions in which the photographers had to work, which resulted in the photographs being blurred at the edges, it is not unusual to find that the photos taken by TUCCI and SĀṄKṚTYĀYANA are of poor quality and that shadows, over-exposure and out of focus images, prevent a correct reading of the text. In many cases, a clear reading is made possible by comparing the two photographic reproductions, as I was personally able to verify when working on my critical edition of the *Hevajra-tantra-piṇḍârtha-ṭīkā* by Vajragarbha, which will soon be published in the Rome Oriental Series. For this work I benefited from both the photos taken by SĀṄKṚTYĀYANA (which I obtained thanks to Gustav Roth and Raffaele Torella) and those taken by TUCCI. As luck would have it, the parts of the manuscript that were illegible in SĀṄKṚTYĀYANA's photos were readable in TUCCI's, and vice versa.

It is well-known that SĀṄKṚTYĀYANA's photos have been used for the critical editions of many works, especially of Buddhist *pramāṇa* tradition (Dharmakīrti, Ratnakīrti, Karṇakagomin, Paṇḍitāśoka). In his introduction to the *Dharmottara-pradīpa* by Durvekamiśra, Dalsukhbhai MALVANIA (1955: iii) writes: 'The original copy covers 84 leaves. It is written in Newari script. When the photo-copy was made, the 60th leaf was not reversed. Consequently, 60a has been photographed twice, whereas there is no photo of the reverse, i.e. 60b. The manuscript is correct, but here and there it is indistinct.' I have verified that folio 60b is actually present in TUCCI's photos, though unfortunately a shadow obscures the extreme left of the folio. Also regarding this text, TUCCI's photos permit the reading of other parts that the editor was obliged to indicate with ellipses.[9]

In some cases, TUCCI's photos contain more leaves than SĀṄKṚTYĀYANA's: this happens with the *Sāratamā*, the commentary by Ratnākaraśānti on the *Aṣṭa-sāhasrikā-prajñā-pāramitā-sūtra*. It must be said, however, that the editor of this text was able to consult the manuscript as it was seen and documented by TUCCI (cf. JAINI (1979: 2)).

[8] See SĀṄKṚTYĀYANA (1935) and SĀṄKṚTYĀYANA (1937).

[*] See the facsimile in the present volume on pp. 477–501 (eds.).

[9] The manuscript photographs of the *Dharmottara-pradīpa* are presently on loan to Birgit Kellner, who will publish a study on this work.

## –3–

While we were cataloguing the negatives, we found that often the contents of the envelopes did not correspond to what was indicated on the outside. For example, the important commentary by Vajrapāṇi on the first chapter of the *Cakra-saṁvara-tantra*—soon to be published by Claudio CICUZZA (forthcoming)—, which was not photographed by SĀṄKṚTYĀYANA, was discovered in an envelope on which was written 'Commentary on the *Evaṁ-tantra*', while the *Guhya-samāja-tantra-pradīpôddyotana* by Candrakīrti was in an envelope on which 'Commentary on the *Hevajra-tantra*' was indicated. The unfamiliarity with Sanskrit suggests that the person who wrote the indications on the envelopes and the notes contained in them, was not TUCCI.[10] There is also a mystery surrounding the envelopes. These are numbered from one to forty-one, but there are nine envelopes missing (8, 9, 13, 14, 24, 26, 28, 29, 39). They were already missing on 9th June 1960, as can be seen from the essential list made by Lionello Lanciotti.[11] Each envelope usually contains twelve photographic plates; therefore about one-hundred and eight prints, and hence possibly over one thousand folios, are missing. Neither are we certain if there were more envelopes after no. 41. We can, nevertheless, suppose that there were, due to the fact that a number of the photographic prints without corresponding negatives are filed in grey folders marked with a number: numbers that correspond to some of the missing envelopes or envelopes that would have come after number forty-one; as in the case of the *Hevajra-ḍākinī-jālā-saṁvara-pañjikā* (= *Tri-vajra-ratnâvalī-mūlikā*) by Kelikuliśa that consists of 120 palm-leaves, documented with 7 photos and filed in folder 43; the *Saṁpuṭa-nāma-mahā-tantra-rāja* (folder 42); and the *Pārājikā* that consists of 77 palm-leaves (documented with 6 photos; folder 39). It is worth mentioning that the latter manuscript was not photographed by SĀṄKṚTYĀYANA and also differs from the two manuscripts written on Nepalese paper, kept in the National Archives of Kathmandu. In any event, as we have mentioned, there are many photographs without negatives, files and reference numbers; for instance the *Cittânanda-paṭī*, a short treatise on alchemy divided into fourteen chapters and attributed to Nāgārjuna. Among these photos, there are also some that reproduce folios belonging to an important Buddhist Tantra, the *Advaya-*

[10] The notes—when present—concern the title of the work, the number of negatives and, sometimes, the numbers of the folios, the name of the monastery where the manuscripts were kept and the date of reproduction.

[11] Envelope 22 does not appear on the list compiled by Lionello Lanciotti, but it is part of the material we have recovered.

*samatā-vijaya*, quoted by Indrabhūti in his *Jñāna-siddhi* (chap. 15) and identified by Harunaga Isaacson during a visit to Rome in March 2000 (folder 42).

Unfortunately, I do not think that it will ever be possible to recover all the material that has gone astray; material that appears to have been badly conserved and that TUCCI himself generously lent to anyone who requested it. As he himself wrote, 'there is nothing less scientific than jealously exercising a monopoly on the discovered material'.[12] Nevertheless, as we shall see, it is still possible to find more material that was considered lost.

During his 1949 mission, TUCCI found two very important manuscripts in Kongkar. In the diary he kept on that journey we read:

> 'In Kongkar there is a reincarnation of not much more than twenty. He was born in Lhasa; after he had received religious instruction, they took him to this place far away from all main roads. He lives with a small community of monks who are all older than him. He perhaps longs for the life in Lhasa, the friends from his childhood and the diversions that the Holy City also offers to reincarnations. ... But this poor young man finds himself cloistered in an isolated monastery, far from the caravan routes, with a desire in his heart, which all young people experience, to see new things, to travel through the regions whose wonders have been described to him by the merchants who sometimes go to visit him. He also desires in his spirit to go on a pilgrimage to India, but the monastery is too poor to allow him to realize his aim. ... When he hears that I am arriving, he runs to meet me: finally something new is happening in his uneventful life! He hangs on to me as if I were an old friend, he invites me to eat with him, he himself shows me round the monastery, he asks me a thousand questions: he wants to know what my country is like and how long it takes to get there; what a steamboat and an aeroplane are, and how cars work; he is filled with wonderment like a child listening to a fairy-tale read by his nanny, and does not want to be parted from me .... When time mercilessly demands that I take my leave of him I see that he is deeply moved. Friendship has blossomed in a few hours from the depths of harsh solitude. But the friendship of the young reincarnation was precious to me. While we were sitting discussing various matters, and I was speaking to him of the great masters of India, he took out from a chest some Indian manuscripts, written on palm-

[12] TUCCI (1996d: 12): 'non vi è nulla di meno scientifico che arrogarsi un geloso monopolio del materiale scoperto.'

leaves, from the IX[th] or X[th] century: as pristine as if they had been made by the copyist yesterday. I examined them with great trepidation: they were poetic works by two authors who had been unknown until that moment. One is a summary in metre of Buddhist dogmatics and the other is a poem on one of the previous lives of the Buddha (*Abhidharma-samuccaya-kārikā* by Saṅghatrāta and *Maṇi-cūḍa-jātaka* by Sarvarakṣita respectively). The history of Indian literature has thus been unexpectedly enriched by two new authors and two new works'.[13]

These two valuable works photographed by TUCCI were subsequently lost again. However, on Friday 2[nd] October 1999, while I was idly searching through a cupboard in the library, I found a roll of film with twenty-four exposures that reproduced a Sanskrit manuscript. It was in fact the *Maṇi-cūḍa-jātaka* by Sarvarakṣita. The negative of this manuscript was hidden in a small container in a

[13] TUCCI (1996a: 169–170): 'A Kongkar c'è un incarnato che ha poco più di vent'anni. E' nato a Lhasa; dopo compiuta la istruzione religiosa l'hanno condotto in questo luogo lontano da tutte le strade. Vive con una piccola comunità di monaci di lui tutti più anziani, forse sospiroso della società di Lhasa, delle amicizie dei suoi primi anni e degli svaghi che la Città Santa offre anche ai rincarnati. [...] Ma questo povero giovane si trova rinchiuso in un monastero fuori mano, lontano dalle carovaniere battute, con un desiderio in cuore, che tutti i giovani hanno, di vedere cose nuove, di viaggiare per le contrade di cui i mercanti, che qualche volta lo vanno a trovare, gli descrivono le meraviglie. Ha in animo di andare anche lui in pellegrinaggio in India, ma il convento è troppo povero perché egli possa condurre a compimento il suo proposito. [...] Quando sa del mio arrivo mi corre incontro: finalmente c'è un avvenimento nuovo nella sua vita sempre uguale! Egli si attacca a me come ad un vecchio amico, mi invita a pranzo, mi conduce egli stesso per il monastero, mi pone mille domande: vuol sapere come è fatto il mio paese quanto ci vuole per arrivarci, che cosa sono il piroscafo e l'aereoplano, come funzionano le macchine; si riempie di meraviglia ingenua come un bimbo cui la fantesca racconti le fiabe e non si vuole separare da me [...]. Quando la tirannia del tempo mi costringe a prendere commiato da lui lo vedo sinceramente commosso. Amicizia sbocciata in poche ore dal fondo di una solitudine acerba. Ma l'amicizia del giovane incarnato mi è stata preziosa. Mentre sedevamo a parlare di vari argomenti, discutendo io dei grandi maestri dell'India, egli ha tratto fuori da uno scrigno alcuni manoscritti indiani su fogli di palma del IX o del X secolo: freschi come se fossero usciti ieri dalle mani del copista. Li esamino con grande trepidazione: si tratta di opere poetiche di due autori fino ad oggi sconosciuti. Uno è un riassunto metrico della dommatica buddhista e l'altro un poema su una delle vite anteriori del Buddha (*Abhidharma-samuccaya-kārikā* di Saṅghatrāta e *Maṇi-cūḍa-jātaka* di Sarvarakṣita). La storia della letteratura indiana si trova così arricchita improvvisamente di due nuovi nomi e di due nuove opere.'

drawer that was thought to hold only microfilms of Chinese texts. The work will be edited and translated by Michael Hahn and Kiyoshi Okano. To date, we have not been able to find any trace of the *Abhidharma-samuccaya-kārikā* by the Vātsīputrīya Saṅghatrāta. A critical edition of the work was announced by the late Antonio Gargano and Giuseppe TUCCI, and at the beginning of the sixties it still appeared in the list of works being prepared for the *Rome Oriental Series*. It seems also that the manuscript was seen by Edward CONZE—in a note he quotes the numbers of two folios of the manuscript (CONZE (1962: chap. 2.2.1, note 7)). Kazunobu Matsuda kindly informed me in a letter of 6$^{th}$ June 2000 that some years ago, after Giuseppe TUCCI's death, Professor Namikawa had tried to contact Antonio Gargano through Namikawa's Italian friend at the University of Rome, and that Gargano told his friend that he himself was not involved in the *Abhidharma-samuccaya-kārikā* project and he had never seen the photos of the manuscript; furthermore, he suggested that TUCCI had added his name only as a collaborator.

Nor have we been able to locate the manuscript of Gopadatta's *Jātaka-mālā* in which Michael Hahn expressed an interest, or the manuscript of the *Abhisamayâlaṁkāra-śāstra-vivṛti* of which TUCCI himself spoke during a lecture given in 1955 and published in Japanese the following year (TUCCI (1956a)) and a copy of which was recently requested by Koei H. Amano. As I mentioned at the beginning, the collection was neither catalogued nor kept in one place in the library of the Institute. This explains why it was difficult both to assemble it and to meet the requests of Italian and foreign scholars who wished to obtain copies of specific manuscripts. Regarding the modern manuscripts on Nepalese paper, the situation is, naturally, more simple. We can easily verify their existence and, furthermore, we have benefited from a preliminary list of the titles of some of these manuscripts, compiled by Ernst Steinkellner some years ago. In some cases we were able to locate the original held in the National Archives of Kathmandu or in other libraries (e.g. *Abhisamayâlaṁkāra-vṛtti* by Vimuktisena, *Laghu-tantra-ṭīkā*, *Kapphinâbhyudaya-kāvya*, *Ḍākinī-vajra-pañjara-tantra-ṭippaṇī*).

## –4–

We are in the process of reorganising the photographic material, which has not been given due attention up till now. This reorganisation will be divided into various phases: completion of the printing of the negatives; restoration and conservation of the negatives and prints; completion of the identification of the works represented and cataloguing of same. The first phase, the printing of the negatives and the compilation of a provisional list, is currently underway. The task is not easy; often the works are not even complete in the original version and are difficult to read, and therefore it is not always possible to identify or read the colophons. Nevertheless, we foresee completing the work and publishing a catalogue of the entire collection in a relatively short time. We have seen that it is possible to scan and transfer the negatives and the photographs to a CD-ROM.[14] After carrying out some tests we decided to entrust the work to a company in Rome concerned with the preservation of archives (GAP S.r.l.), which already works with the Istituto Centrale per la Patologia del Libro as well as with prestigious libraries, like the Casanatense. The work is still in progress. Recently, Akira YUYAMA (1992: vii) wrote:

> 'One must lament the fact that there are still a number of important collections, even in the West, about which we know very little. ... There are frustrating examples. Certain institutions hold extremely important collections of rare materials. Every scholar knows about them. But nobody knows their exact nature and content. The Istituto Italiano per il Medio ed Estremo Oriente in Rome seems to be one such institution. Giuseppe Tucci (1894–1984) made immeasurably significant contributions to Indo-Tibetan Buddhist studies as a result of his expeditions to Himalayan and Tibetan regions. In his monumental works one finds information about a good many important manuscript materials. Alas! They are practically inaccessible to serious scholars in related fields of study.'

We trust that this will be the last negative observation concerning the TUCCI collection at the IsIAO, which in the near future will be readily accessible to scholars throughout the world; something that most certainly would also have gratified such an extraordinary master as Giuseppe Tucci.

---

[14] A similar project, which focuses more on art history, is underway in Holland (Kern Institute Leiden) (DE BOER (1999: column 5)).

## BIBLIOGRAPHY


*Bollettino* = 'Riorganizzazione, catalogazione e restauro del fondo fotografico di manoscritti indiani nella Biblioteca dell'IsIAO'. *Il lettore ben informato: Bollettino delle biblioteche del polo SBN IEI / Istituti culturali* 2/2 (1998) 5.

BÜHNEMANN 1985 = Bühnemann, Gudrun: *Jitāri: Kleine Texte. Beschrieben und ediert vom* .... Zweite, ergänzte Auflage, *Wiener Studien zur Tibetologie und Buddhismuskunde* 8, Wien 1985.

CICUZZA (forthcoming) = Cicuzza, Claudio: 'A commentary by Vajrapāṇi on the first chapter of the *Cakra-saṁvara-tantra*.' *Rome Oriental Series* 86, forthcoming.

CONZE 1962 = Conze, Edward: *Buddhist Thought in India*, London 1962.

DE BOER 1999 = de Boer, Gerda Theuns: 'Photographic Prints at the Kern Institute Leiden'. *IIAS Newsletter* 19 (1999) 19.

DE JONG 1978 = de Jong, J.W.: 'Textcritical Notes on the Prasannapadā'. *Indo-Iranian Journal* 20/1–2 (1978) 25–59.

EIPHIL I = Potter, Karl H.: *Encyclopedia of Indian Philosophies.*—Vol. I: *Bibliography*. Compiled by .... Third Revised Edition. Princeton University Press, Princeton–New Jersey 1995. [Indian edition: Motilal Banarsidass, Delhi 1995].

GNOLI 1977 = Gnoli, Raniero: *The Gilgit Manuscript of the Saṅghabhedavastu. Being the 17th and Last Section of the Vinaya of the Mūlasarvāstivādin*. Part I. Edited by ..., Foreword by G. Tucci. *Serie Orientale Roma* 49.1, IsMEO, Roma 1977.

JAINI 1979 = Jaini, Padmanabh S.: *Sāratamā. A Pañjikā on the Aṣṭasāhasrikā Prajñāpāramitā Sūtra by Ācārya Ratnākaraśānti*. Edited by ... Kashi Prasad Jayaswal Research Institute, Patna 1979.

MAGGI 1995 = Maggi, Mauro: *The Khotanese Karmavibhaṅga. Serie Orientale Roma* 74, IsMEO, Rome 1995.

MALVANIA 1955 = Malvania, Dalsukhbhai: *Paṇḍita Durveka Miśra's Dharmottarapradīpa. Being a sub-commentary on Dharmottara's Nyāyabinduṭīkā, a commentary on Dharmakīrti's Nyāyabindu*, Edited by ..., Kashi Prasad Jayaswal Research Institute, Patna 1955.

MIMAKI–TOMABECHI 1994 = Mimaki, Katsumi; Tomabechi, Tōru: *Pañcakrama. Sanskrit and Tibetan Texts Critically Edited with Verse Index and Facsimile Edition of the Sanskrit Manuscripts. Bibliotheca Codicum Asiaticorum* 8, The Centre for East Asian Cultural Studies for UNESCO, The Toyo Bunko, Tokyo 1994.

PENSA 1967 = Pensa, Corrado: *L'Abhisamayālamkāravṛtti di Ārya-Vimuktisena. Primo Abhisamaya*, Testo e note critiche. Serie Orientale Roma 37, IsMEO, Roma 1967.

SĀṄKṚTYĀYANA 1935 = Sāṅkṛtyāyana, Rāhula: 'Sanskrit Palm-Leaf MSS. in Tibet'. *Journal of the Bihar and Orissa Research Society* 21 (1935) 21–43.

SĀṄKṚTYĀYANA 1937 = Sāṅkṛtyāyana, Rāhula: 'Second Search of Sanskrit Palm-Leaf MSS. in Tibet [with plates]'. *Journal of the Bihar and Orissa Research Society* 23 (1937) 1–57.

SFERRA 1995 = Sferra, Francesco: 'Textual Criticism Notes on the *Vimalaprabhā* by Puṇḍarīka'. *East and West* 45 (1995) 359–64.

THAKUR 1975 = Thakur, Anantalal: *Ratnakīrti-nibandhāvalī* (*Buddhist Nyāya Works of Ratnakīrti*). *Tibetan Sanskrit Works Series* 3; K.P. Jayasal Research Institute, Patna 1975.

TUCCI 1956a = Tucci, Giuseppe: 'Chibetto oyobi Nepōru-ni oite Aratani Hakkenserareta Bukkyō Tenseki-ni tsuite' ['On Newly Discovered Buddhist Texts in Tibet and Nepal']. *Ōtani Gakuhō (The Journal of Buddhology and Cultural Science)* 36.1 (June 1956) 1–16.

TUCCI 1956b = Tucci, Giuseppe: *Preliminary Report on Two Scientific Expeditions in Nepal*. *Serie Orientale Roma* 10.1, IsMEO, Roma 1956.

TUCCI 1986 = Tucci, Giuseppe: *Minor Buddhist Texts. Parts I & II*, Delhi 1986. [First edition: *Serie Orientale Roma* 9.1, 9.2. IsMEO, Rome 1956, 1958].

TUCCI 1996a = Tucci, Giuseppe: *A Lhasa e oltre*. 3rd ed., Roma 1996. [First edition: 1950].

TUCCI 1996b = Tucci, Giuseppe: *Nepal. Alla scoperta del regno dei Malla*. 3rd ed., Roma 1996. [First edition: 1960].

TUCCI 1996c = Tucci, Giuseppe: *Tibet ignoto*. 3rd ed., Roma 1996. [First edition: 1937].

TUCCI 1996d = Tucci, Giuseppe: *Tra giungle e pagode*. 3rd ed.. Roma 1996. [First edition: 1953].

YUYAMA 1992 = Yuyama, Akira: *Buddhist Sanskrit Manuscript Collections (Bauddha-saṁskṛtabhāṣāhastalikhita-pustakālayāḥ). A Bibliographical Guide for the Use of Students in Buddhist Philology*. *Bibliographia Indica et Buddhica* 2, The Library of The International Institute for Buddhist Studies, Tokyo 1992.

WARDER 1980 = Warder, A.K.: *Indian Buddhism*. Second Revised Edition. Motilal Banarsidass, Delhi 1980. [First edition: 1970].

## APPENDIX I

# Giuseppe Tucci's Collection: Index of Works

The following list is provisional. The titles of works have been taken from the texts, where possible, and/or from the brief notes written on the envelopes (transcribed *verbatim*), which in many cases have proved to be inaccurate. A correct and more detailed list will be published with the catalogue and the CD-ROMs.

### 1. Negatives – 7 × 11 cm

| Title | Author | Envelope | Negatives | Monastery |
|---|---|---|---|---|
| *Pramāṇa-vārttika* | Dharmakīrti | 1–5/A | 51[1] | Sa-skya |
| *Daśa-bhūmika-sūtra* | — | 5–6/B | 21 | Sa-skya |
| *Dāsarasāyana-ṭīkā* | Nāgārjuna | 7/Ca | | Sa-skya |
| *Tri-skandha-deśanā* | — | 7/Cb | } 2 | Sa-skya |
| *Yukti-pradīpa* | — | 7/Cc | | Sa-skya |
| *Adhyardha-śataka* | Mātṛceṭa | 7/D | 2 | Sa-skya |
| *Artha-viniścaya-sūtra* | — | 7/E | 8 | Sa-skya |
| *Pramāṇa-vārttika* | Dharmakīrti | 10–12/F | 25[2] | Sa-skya |
| *Sāratamā* | Ratnākaraśānti | 12/G | 8 | Sa-skya |
| *Hetu-bindu-ṭīkâloka* | Durvekamiśra | 15/H (I) | 11 | Ngor |
| *Dharmottara-pradīpa* | Durvekamiśra | 16/H (II) | 11 | Ngor |
| *Artha-viniścaya-sūtra* | — | 17/I | 3 | Ngor |
| *Abhidharma-kośa* | Vasubandhu | 17/L | 1 | Ngor |
| *Abhidharma-kośa-bhāṣya* | Vasubandhu | 18–19/M | 19 | Ngor |
| *Abhidharma-samuccaya* | Asaṅga | 19/N | 5 | Ngor |
| *Pratimokṣa* | — | 21/O | 4 | Ngor |
| *Dharma-kārikā* | — | 21/P | 2 | Ngor |
| *Sarva-śuddhi-viśuddhi-krama* | (see above, n. 7) | 21/Q | 2 | Ngor |
| *Dharma-vibhaṅga* | — | 21/R | 4 | Ngor |
| *Hevajra-tantra-piṇḍârtha-ṭīkā* | Vajragarbha | 22/S | 2 | Ngor |
| *Chaṁdo-ratnâkara* | Ratnākaraśānti | 22/T | 2 | Ngor |
| *Sarvajña-siddhi-saṁkṣepa* | Śaṅkaranandana | 22/U | 2 | Ngor |

[1] Negative No. 29 is missing and negative No. 6 is completely indecipherable.

[2] Negative No. 14 is missing.

| | | | | |
|---|---|---|---|---|
| *Sahôpalambha-prakaraṇa* | Jitāri | 22/V | 2 | Ngor |
| *Tarka-rahasya* | — | 22/Z | 4 | Ngor |
| *Vāda-rahasya* | — | 23/AA | 4 | Ngor |
| *Guhya-samāja-pradīpôddyotana* | Candrakīrti | 23/BB | 8 | Ngor |
| Comm. on *Guhya-samāja* | — | 25/CC | 6 | Ngor |
| *Subhāṣita-ratna-kośa* | Bhīmārjunasoma | 25/DD | 6 | Ngor |
| *Catur-aṅga-sūtra* | — | 27/EE | 8 | Zha-lu |
| *Laghu-tantra-ṭīkā* | Vajrapāṇi | 27/FF | 4 | Zha-lu |
| *Bodhisattva-bhūmi* | Asaṅga | 30/GG | 8 | Zha-lu |
| *Bodhisattva-bhūmi* | Asaṅga | 31/HH | 3 | Zha-lu |
| *Artha-viniścaya* | — | 31/II | | Zha-lu |
| *Abhidharma-koṣa* | Vasubandhu | 31/II | 6 | Zha-lu |
| *Bhāvanā-krama* | Kamalaśīla | 32/LL | 1 | Zha-lu |
| (*Vinaya*) | — | 32/MM | 11[3] | Zha-lu |
| (*Vinaya*) | — | 33/NN | 12 | Zha-lu |
| *Pramāṇa-vārttika* | Dharmakīrti | 34/OO | 2 | Zha-lu |
| *Tarka-jvālā* | Bhavya | 34/PP | 10 | Zha-lu |
| (*Vinaya*) | — | 35/QQ | 2 | Zha-lu |
| *Abhisamācārikā* | — | 35/RR | 10 | Zha-lu |
| (*Vinaya*) | — | 36/SS | 2 | Zha-lu |
| *Bodhisattva-bhūmi* | Asaṅga | 36/TT | 10 | Zha-lu |
| *Abhidharma-pradīpa* | — | 37–38/UU | 7 | Zha-lu |
| *Ratna-gotra-vibhāga* | — | ?/VV | 3 | Zha-lu |
| *Abhidharma-pradīpa* | — | 37/ZZ | 2 | Zha-lu |
| *Abhidharma-pradīpa* | — | 39/AAA | 6 | Zha-lu |
| — | — | 40/BBB | 12 | Piocan Gompa |
| *Daśa-bhūmika-sūtra* | — | 41/CCC | 5[4] | Piocan Gompa |
| — | — | ?/DDD | 15 | (?) |

2. Microfilms and Negatives – 35 mm

| **Title** | **Author** | **Folios** |
|---|---|---|
| Nepalese Cronicles | — | — |
| *Maṇicūḍa-jātaka* | Sarvarakṣita | 12 |
| *Vimalaprabhā* | Puṇḍarīka | 367 |
| Gilgit MS of the *Saṅgha-bheda-vastu* | | fols. 323–512[5] |

[3] Negative No. 12 is missing.

[4] A negative has been cut in half.

[5] Fols. 398–405, 428, 432, 478–79 are missing; fol. 468r is blank.

## 3. Photographs

### Group I (photographic paper)

| Title | Author | Folder No. | Photos |
|---|---|---|---|
| *Avayavi-nirākaraṇa* | Paṇḍitāśoka | 1 | |
| *Sthira-siddhi-dūṣaṇa* | Ratnakīrti | 1 | } 13 |
| *Kṣaṇa-bhaṅga-siddhi* | Ratnakīrti | 1 | |
| — | — | 2 | 4 |
| — | — | 3 | 11 |
| — | — | 4 | 2 |
| — | — | 5 | 3 |
| — | — | 5bis | 9 |
| — | — | 6 | 2 |
| — | — | 7 | 1 |
| — | — | 8 | 2 |
| — | — | 9 | 5 |
| — | — | 10 | 12 |
| *Pramāṇa-vārttika-vṛtti* | Karṇakagomin | 11 | 23 |
| — | — | 12 | 13 |
| — | — | 29 | 8 |
| *Abhisamācārikā* | — | 34 | 10 |
| *Pramāṇa-vārttika-vṛtti* | Manorathanandin | 35 | 11 |
| *Daśa-bhūmika-sūtra* | — | 40 (= env. 5) | 10 |
| *Daśa-bhūmika-sūtra* | — | 41 (= env. 6) | — |
| *Advaya-samatā-vijaya-tantra* | — | 42 | 3 |
| *Saṁpuṭa-tantra* | — | 42 | 2 |
| *Tri-vajra-ratnâvalī-mūlikā* | Kelikuliśa | 43 | 11 |
| *Guhya-samāja-pradīpôddyotana* | Candrakīrti | 44 | 4 |
| *Artha-viniścaya-sūtra* | — | 45 (= env. 7) | — |
| *Abhisamayâlaṁkāra-vṛtti* | Vimuktisena | — | 53 |
| *Muktâvalī* | Ratnākaraśānti | — | 117 |
| *Cittânanda-paṭī* | Nāgārjuna | — | 10 |
| *Apoha-prakaraṇa* | Ratnakīrti | — | 10 |
| *Bhāvanā-krama* | Kamalaśīla | — | 10 |
| *Tattva-jvālā-nāma-sūtra* | — | — | 5 |
| *Uttara-tantra-ṭippaṇī* | Vairocaṇarakṣita | — | 8 |
| *Praṃāṇa-vārttika-kārikā* | Dharmakīrti | — | 41 |
| *Ratnâvalī* | Nāgārjuna | — | 23 |
| — | — | — | 27 |

Group II (book paper)

| Title | Folder No. | Photos | Folios |
|---|---|---|---|
| *Ḍākârṇava-tantra-ṭīkā* | 1 | 2 | 6 |
| *Ḍākinī-vajra-pañjara-ṭippaṇī* | 2 | 4 | 16 |
| *Nirvikalpa-stuti* | 3 | 2 | 5 |
| *Maṇicūdâbadān* | 4 | 16 | 87 |
| *Paśupati-purāṇa* | 5 | 23 | 86 |
| *Hevajra-tantra-piṇḍârtha-ṭīkā* | 6 | 14 | 67 |
| *Amṛta-kaṇikā* | 7 | 18 | 200 |
| *Tāttva-jñāna-saṁsiddhi* | 8 | 2 | 12 |
| History of the Kings of Nepal | 9 | 10 | 25 |
| History of Nepal | 10 | 4 | 14 |
| *Nāgārjuna-pāda* | 11 | 2 | 14 |
| (*Folios of Tantric Buddhist texts*) | 12 | 2 | 15 |
| *Yavana-jātaka* | 13 | 18 | 144 |
| *Skanda-purāṇa* | 14 | 86 | 258 |
| *Svayambhu-caitya-bhattarakôddeśa* | 15 | 15 | 56 |
| *Mahā-vāni-bansâbali* | 16 | 9 | 16 |
| *Saṁpuṭa-tantra-ṭīkā* | 17 | 4 | 21 |
| Raṇa Bāhādur Sāh Barṇanam | 18 | 4 | 20 |
| *Kīrti-patākā* | 19 | 8 | 33 |
| *Catuṣpīṭha-nibandha* | 20 | 6 | 35 |
| *Herukâbhyudaya-mahā-yoginī-tantra* | 21 | 4 | 21 |
| *Āsir-bādâbali* | 22 | 6 | 34 |
| *Khasama-tantra-ṭīkā* | 23 | 4 | 22 |
| *Āsir-bādâbali* | 24 | 2 | 5 |
| *Vaṁsābali* (History of Nepal) | 25 | 24 | 103 |
| *Madhyamaka-vṛtti* (*Prasanna-padā*) | 26 | 173 | — |
| *Herukâbhidhāna* | 27 | 14 | — |
| *Tri-daṇḍa-mālā* | 28 | 17 | 341 |
| *Padmavatī-pañjikā* | 29 | 9 | 75 |
| *Abhidharma-kośa* | 30 | 6 | 180 |
| *Dāsarasāyana-ṭīkā* | 31 | 2 | 8 |
| *Tri-skandha-deśanā* | 32 | 2 | 6 |
| *Yukti-pradīpa* | 33 | 1 | 2 |
| *Yavana-jātaka* | 34 | 9 | 68 |
| *Pārājikā* | 35 | 6 | 77 |
| *Prajñâlaṁkāra-kārikā* | 36 | — | — |
| *Sarvajña-siddhi-kārikā* | 36bis | — | — |
| *Rūpa-stava* | 37 | 1 | 5 |
| *Tattva-jñāna-saṁsiddhi-ṭīkā* | 38 | — | — |
| Rules of the Svayaṁbhūnāth | 39 | 13 | — |

## 4. Nepalese Paper MSS

The MSS kept in the Library contain the following texts:

1) *Abhisamayâlaṁkara,*
2) *Abhisamayâlaṁkara-vṛtti* by Vimuktisena,
3) *Ārya-mahā-sahasra-pramardanī,*
4) *Cakra-saṁvara-pañjikā,*
5) *Catuṣ-pīṭha-ṭīkā,*
6) *Daśa-bhūmîśvara,*
7) *Ekallavīra,*
8) *Ekallavīra-tantra-pañjikā,*
9) *Ḍākârṇava,*
10) *Ḍākinī-guhya-samama-sādhana,*
11) *Ḍakinī-vajra-pañjara-ṭippaṇī,*
12) *Guṇa-karaṇḍa-vyūha,*
13) *Herukâbhyudaya-pañjikā,*
14) *Hevajra-sādhana-pradīpa,*
15) *Hevajra-tantra,*
16) *Kṛṣṇayamāri-pañjikā,*
17) *Kalpa-rāja-tantra,*
18) *Kapphinâbhyudaya-kāvya,*
19) *Khasama-tantra-ṭīkā,*
20) *Laghu-kāla-cakra-tantra,*
21) *Laghu-tantra-ṭīkā,*
22) *Laghv-abhidhāna,*
23) *Mahā-samaya-kalpa-rāja,*
24) *Marma-karṇikā* (= *Tattva-jñāna-saṁsiddhi-pañcikā*),
25) *Padminī* (Comm. on the *Saṁvarôdaya-tantra*),
26) *Pañca-rakṣā,*[6]
27) *Pāramitā-samāsa,*
28) *Rājapraśrī,*
29) *Sūtra-vṛtti,*
30) *Rāma-vinoda,*
31) *Rāyaparasaraṇī,*
32) *Saṁvarôdaya-tantra-ṭippaṇī,*
33) *Vasanta-tilaka,*
34) *Vimalaprabhā.*

[6] This MS is illustrated.

## APPENDIX II

# Facsimile of Śakyaśrīmitra's *Sarva-śuddhi-viśuddhi*

Here are reproduced two manuscripts photographed by Giuseppe Tucci during his research missions to Tibet. Both manuscripts are reproduced following the original order of the folios, i.e. *as* they appear in Tucci's photographic prints. The photographic prints available to us do not reproduce the manuscripts in their original size.

The first of them are the photographs of the *Sarva-śuddhi-viśuddhi-krama* [= Chapter II of the *Pañca-krama*], recto and verso, contained in envelope 21/Q.

The original MS was photographed on 20 July 1939 at the Ngor Monastery (Tibet). The manuscript is complete and consists of seven folios (seven versos and six rectos), each of five lines, except the last one (folio 7v), which has 7 + 2 lines. The size of each folio *as* it is reproduced in Tucci's original photographic print is on average 28.2 × 5 cm. The MS is written in Nevārī script. It begins with: *oṁ namo buddhāya / namas te <'>stu namas te <'>stu namas te <'>stu namo namaḥ*. The colophon of the manuscript is hardly legible, but it allows the identification of the name of the author and the title of the work: *sarva-śuddhi-viśuddhi-kramaḥ samāptaḥ // // kṛtir iyaṁ śākyamitra-pādānām*, which is also transcribed below in the Tibetan script. The name of the author is likewise written in Tibetan: Śā kya bśen (abbreviated from Śā kya bśes gñen; *bśes gñen = mitra*).

This manuscript was inaccessible to K. MIMAKI and T. TOMABECHI, the editors of the *Pañca-krama*. It is complete and shows several variant readings. There are some variants between this MS and the edition of MIMAKI–TOMABECHI to be noticed. For instance, on fol. 1v, line 3 of the MS we read *ca cātiśūnyañ ca* instead of *ca atiśūnyaṁ ca* of the edition (p. 15) and on fol. 1v, line 4 of the MS we find the word °*viśuddhis* but °*viśuddhaṁ* in the edition.

[Francesco Sferra, Piotr Balcerowicz, Marek Mejor]

S1

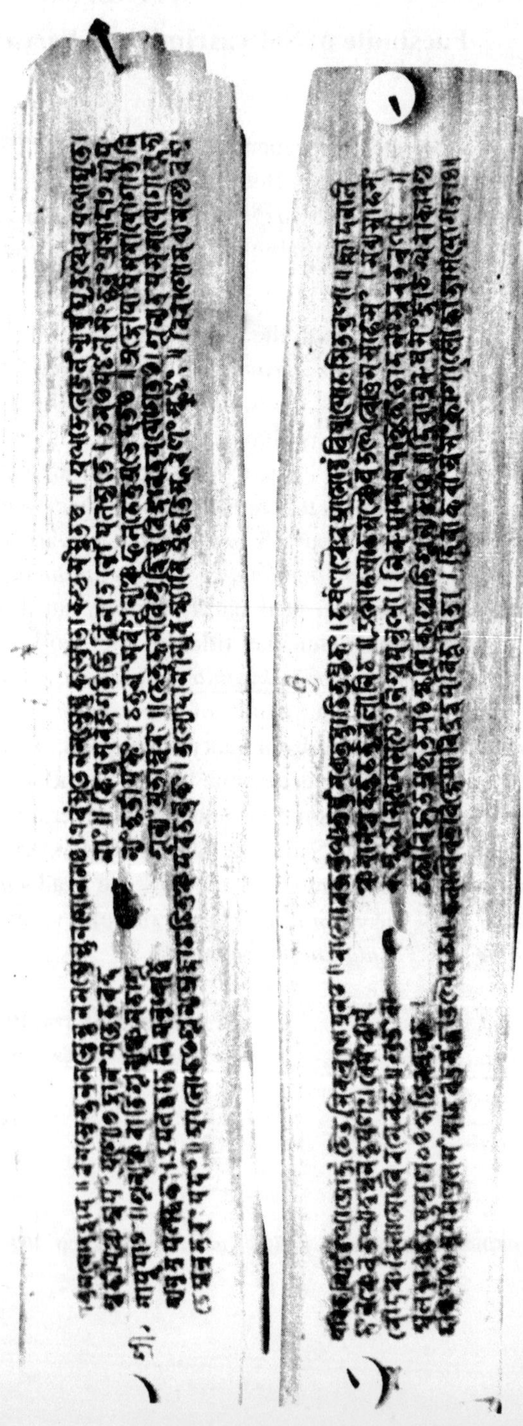

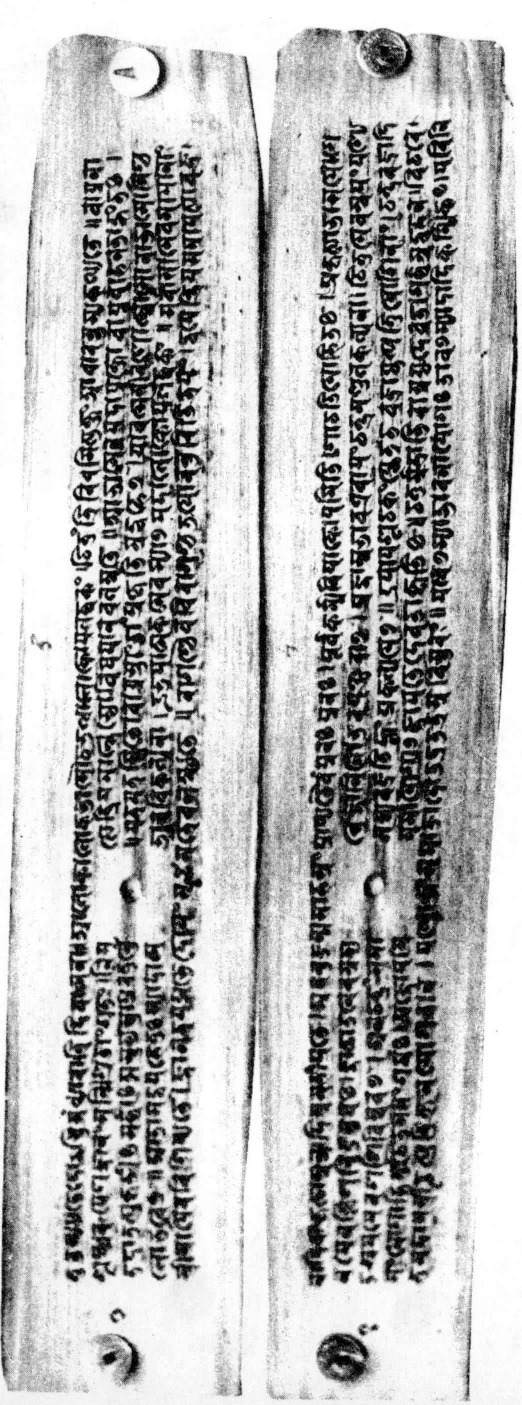

S2

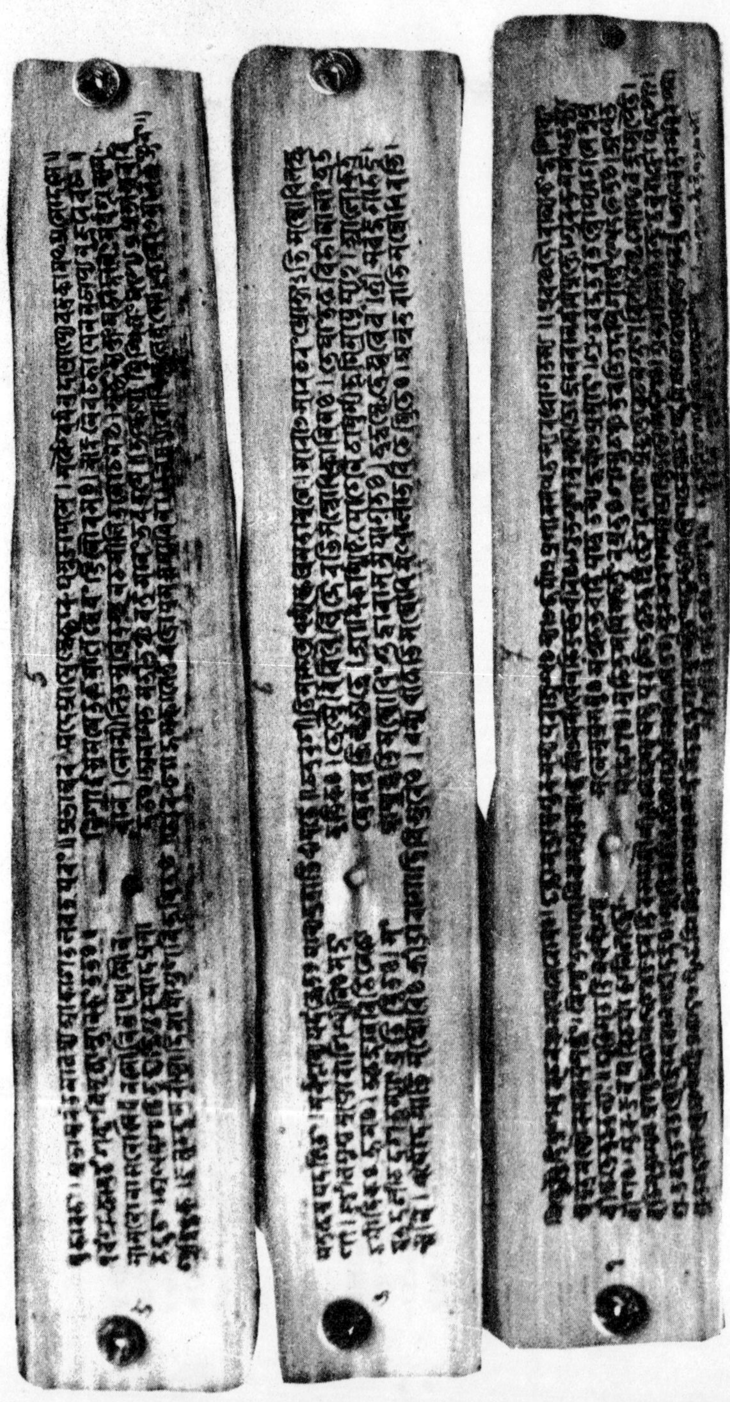

S3

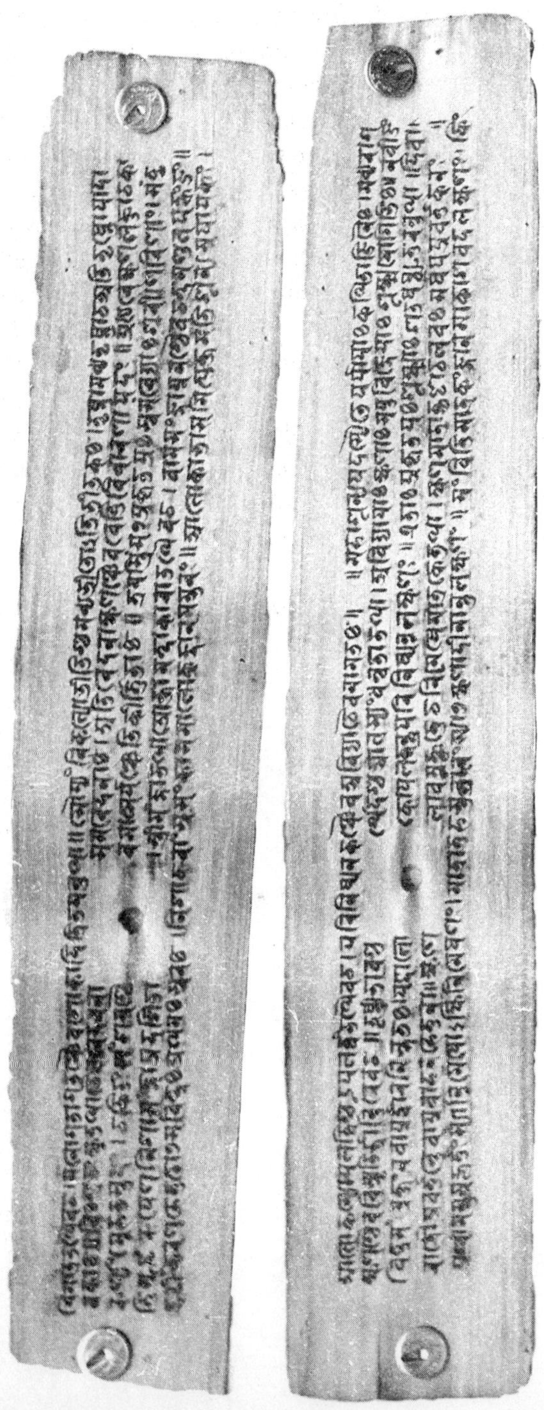

S4

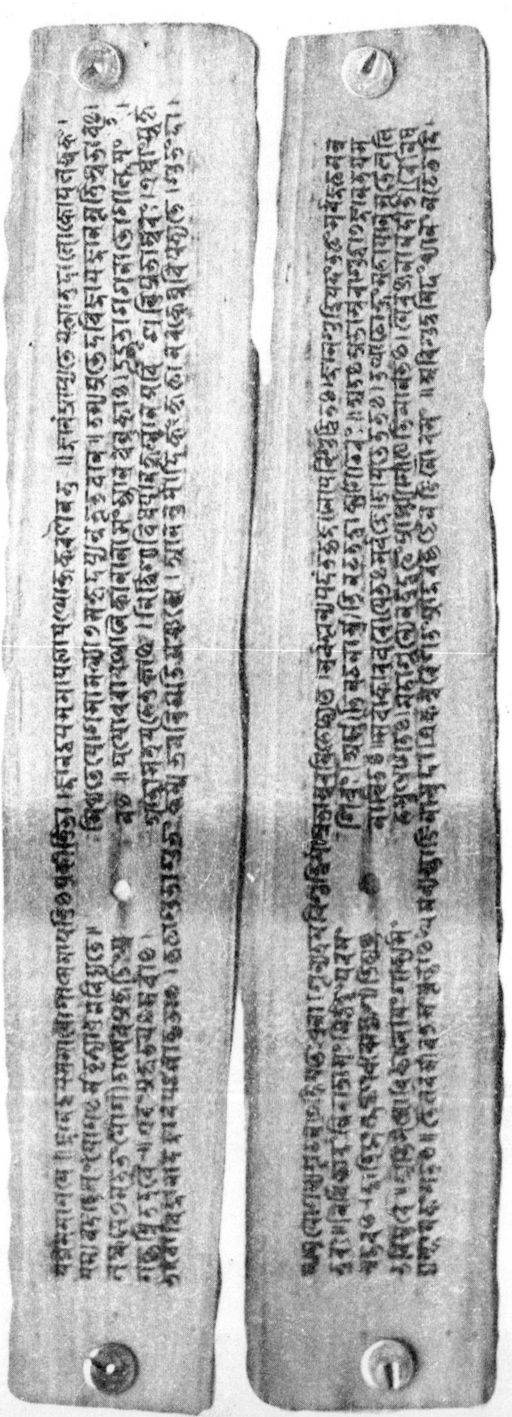

S5

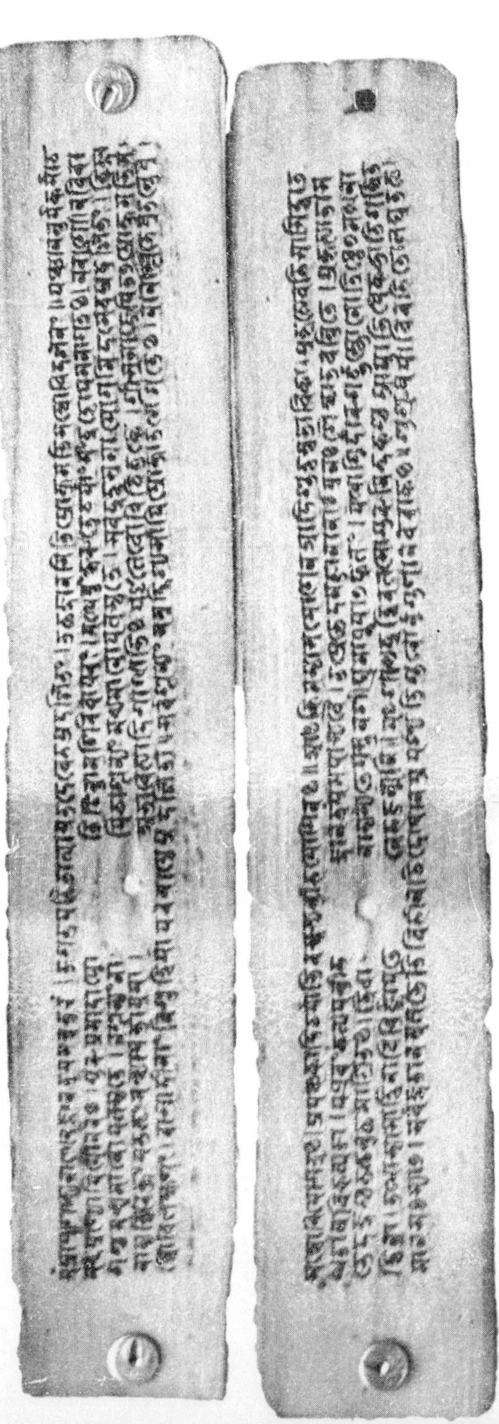

S6

## APPENDIX III

# Facsimile of Jitāri's *Sahôpalambha-prakaraṇa*

The following facsimile is the photograph of the twenty-three leaves of the *Sahôpalambha-prakaraṇa* by Jitāri, contained in envelope 22/V.

This MS was photographed on 21 July 1939 at the Ngor Monastery (Tibet). It is incomplete and first four folios on the photographs are partly damaged. We have 23 rectos and 22 versos, put side by side, in two columns on each photograph. Several folios are missing (apparently the first fourteen folios, viz. approx. one-third of the whole text). All the leaves are pinpointed onto a board. Each folio has seven lines, whereas the last verso with the colophon has five lines. The leaves are differently numbered on the right margin (top—middle—bottom). The size of the whole photographs at our disposal is 7.5 × 24 cm. The size of each folio as it is reproduced on Tucci's original print is on average 8.6 × 1.7 cm.

The MS is written in the Nevārī script. The title of the work is found on folio 36v, lines 4–5 (= 10th folio at the bottom of the right column of the first photograph), where we read in its colophon: *sahôpalambha-prakaraṇaṁ nāma samāptam iti. kṛtir iyaṁ mahā-paṇḍita-cakra-cūḍāmaṇi-jitāri-pādānām*.

The text is only briefly mentioned by Gudrun BÜHNEMANN (1985: 7, n. 4). It is also referred to by WARDER (1980: 541), who is followed by Karl Potter in EIPHIL I (: 378, ad 564. Jitāri, no. 9): '*Sahopalambhaprakaraṇa* (Skt. manuscript in Ngor; copy in Patna, acc. to Warder),' as well as by Anantalal THAKUR (1975: 11).

This MS was also photographed by Rāhula Sāṅkṛtyāyana during his journey to Tibet in 1936 (cf. SĀṄKṚTYĀYANA (1937: 56)). The negatives of his photographs are held at the Kashi Prasad Jayaswal Research Institute, Museum Buildings, Patna, and a copy of the negatives by the Niedersächsische Staats- und Universitätsbibliothek in Göttingen.

[Francesco Sferra, Piotr Balcerowicz, Marek Mejor]

*Essays in Indian Philosophy, Religion and Literature*, pp. 477–501.

1–J1L

1–J2L

1–J3L

1–J4L

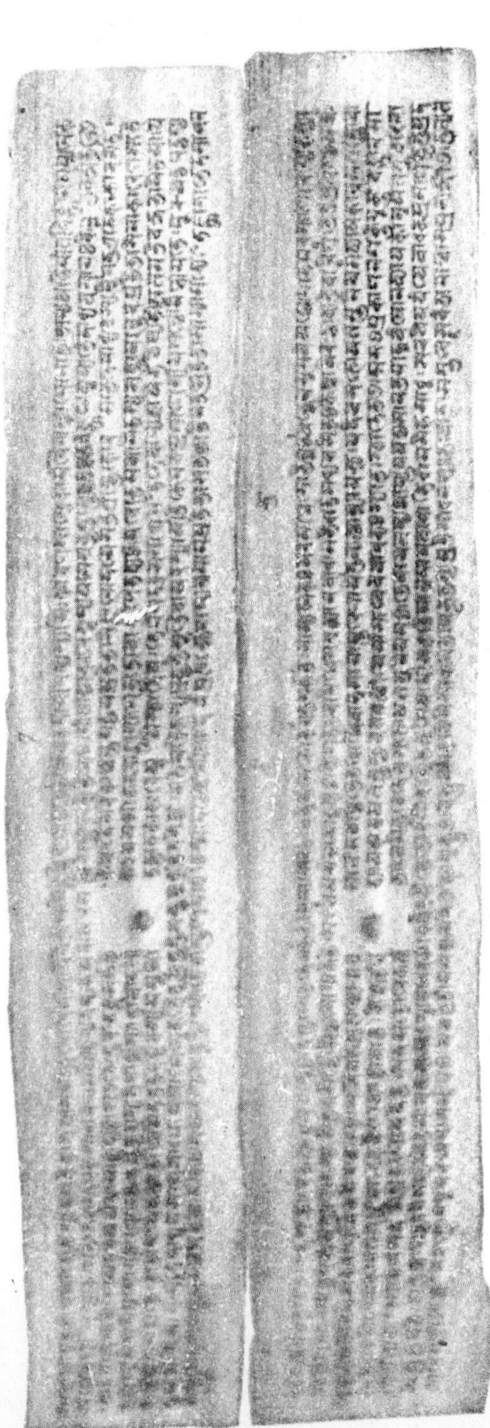

1–J5L

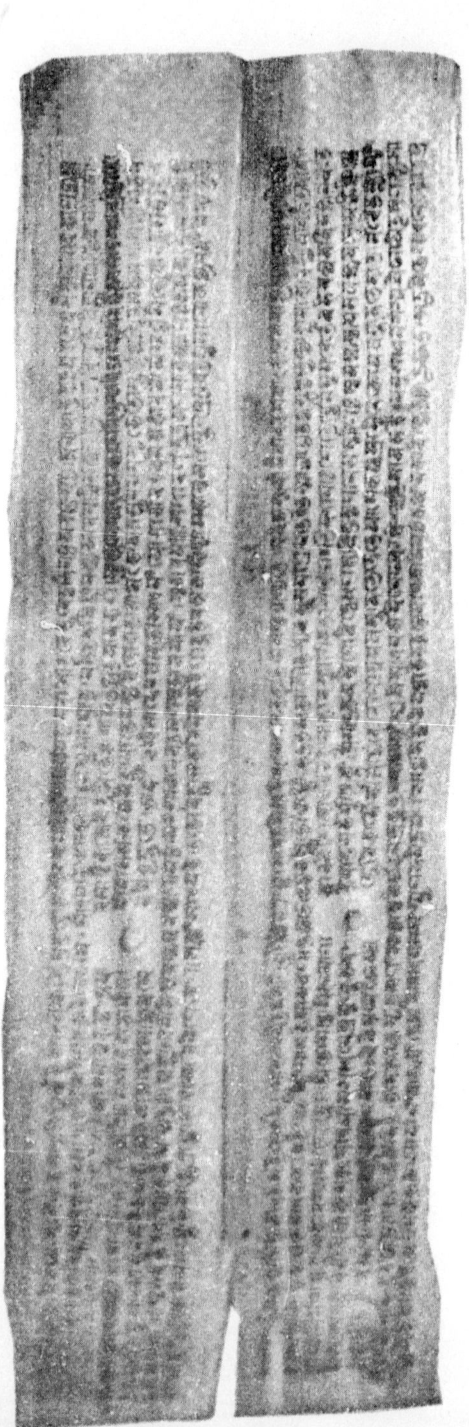

1–J6L

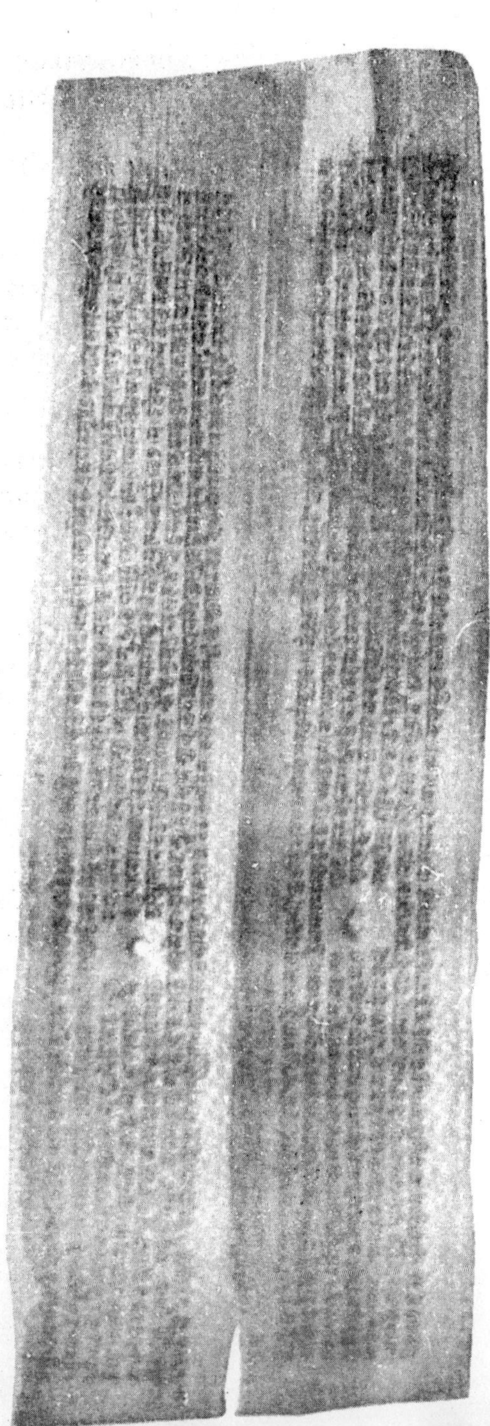

1–J7R

1–J8R

1–J9R

1–J10R

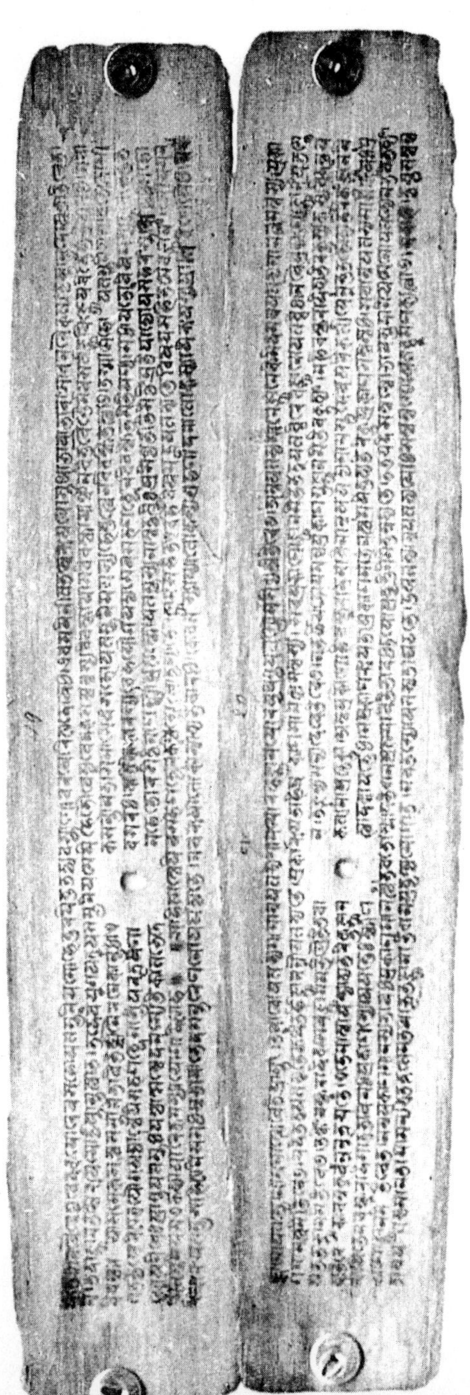

1–J11R

J1L

J2L

J3L

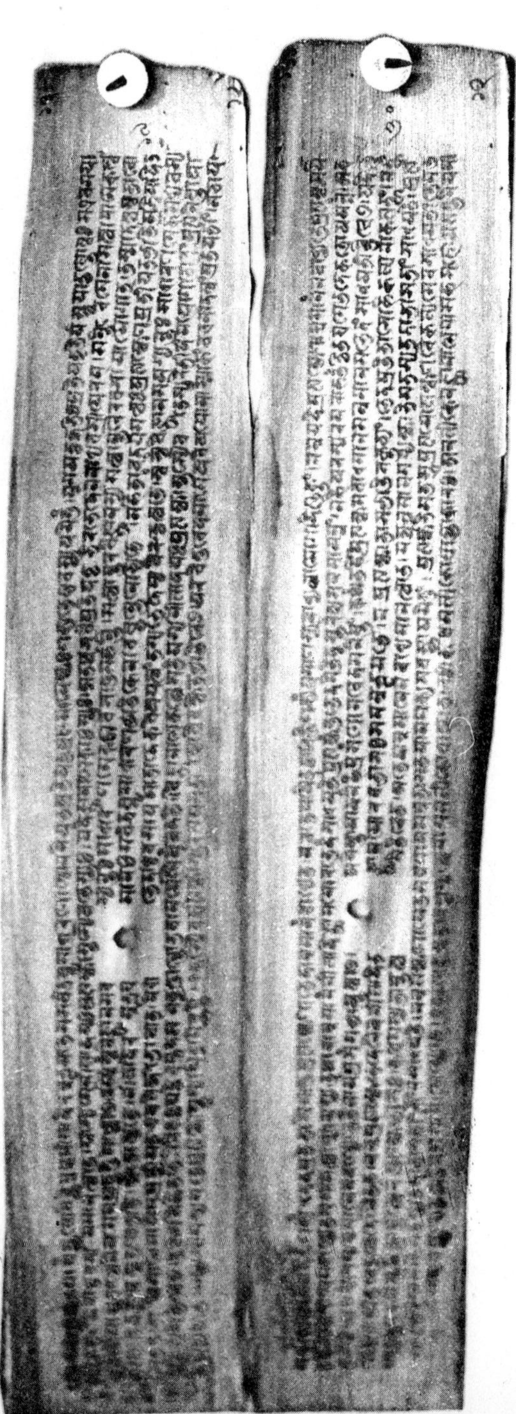

J4L

J5L

J6L

J7R

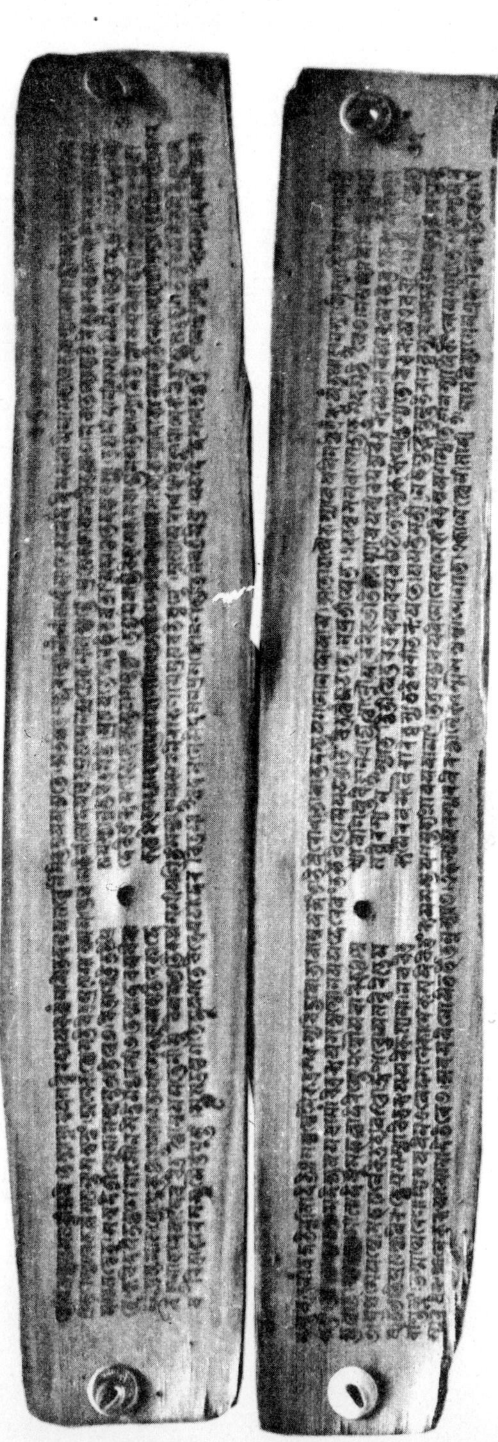

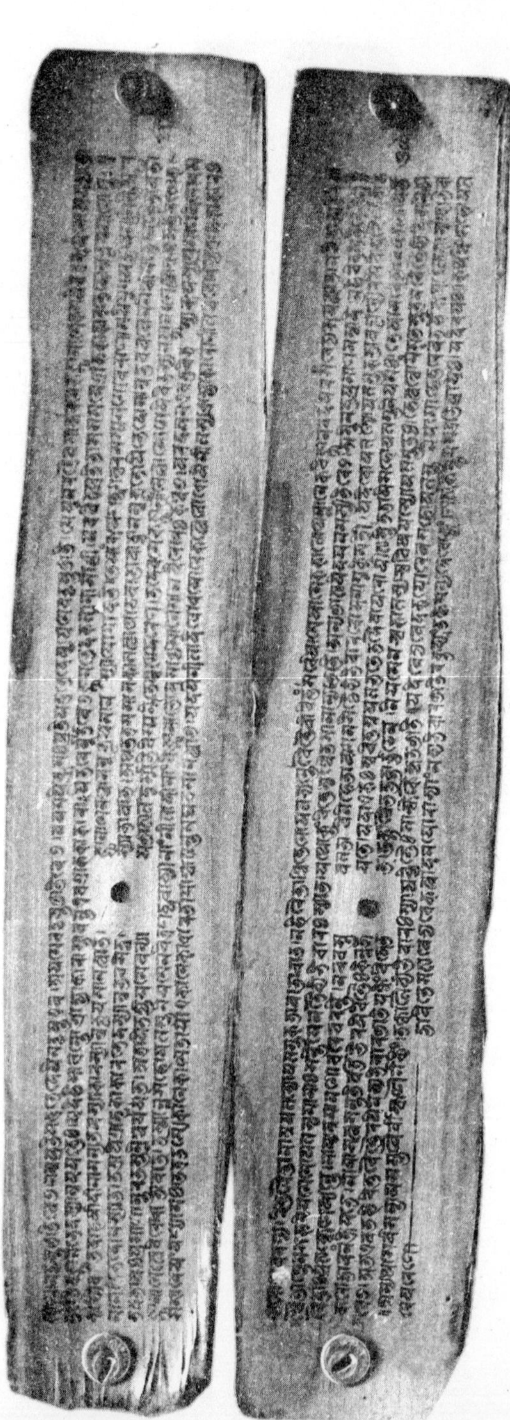

J8R

J9R

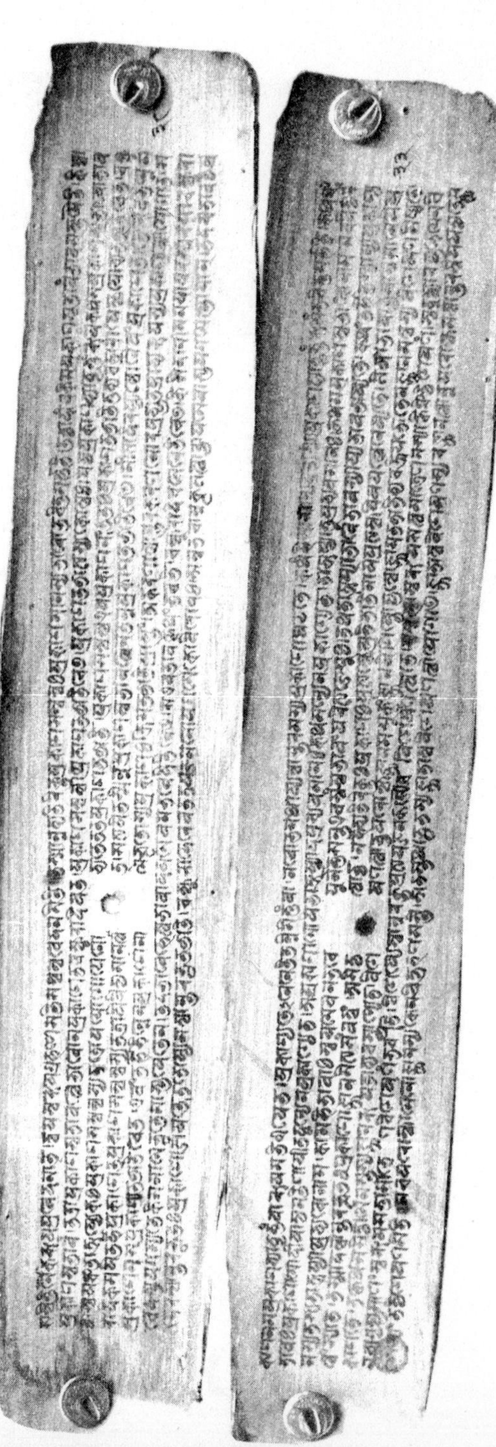

J10R

J11R

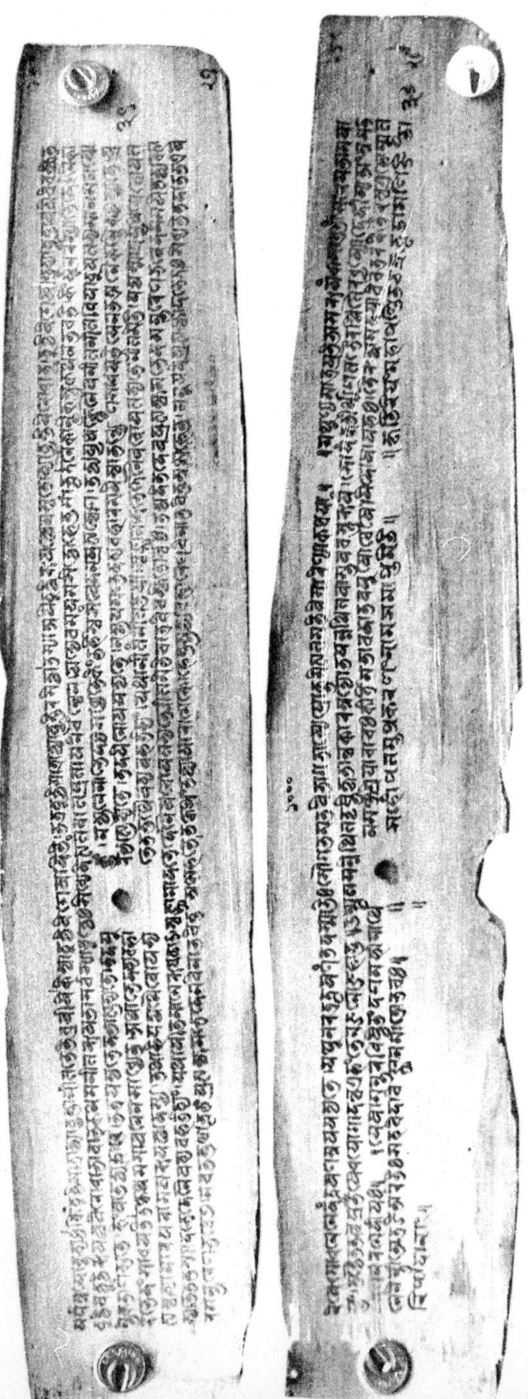